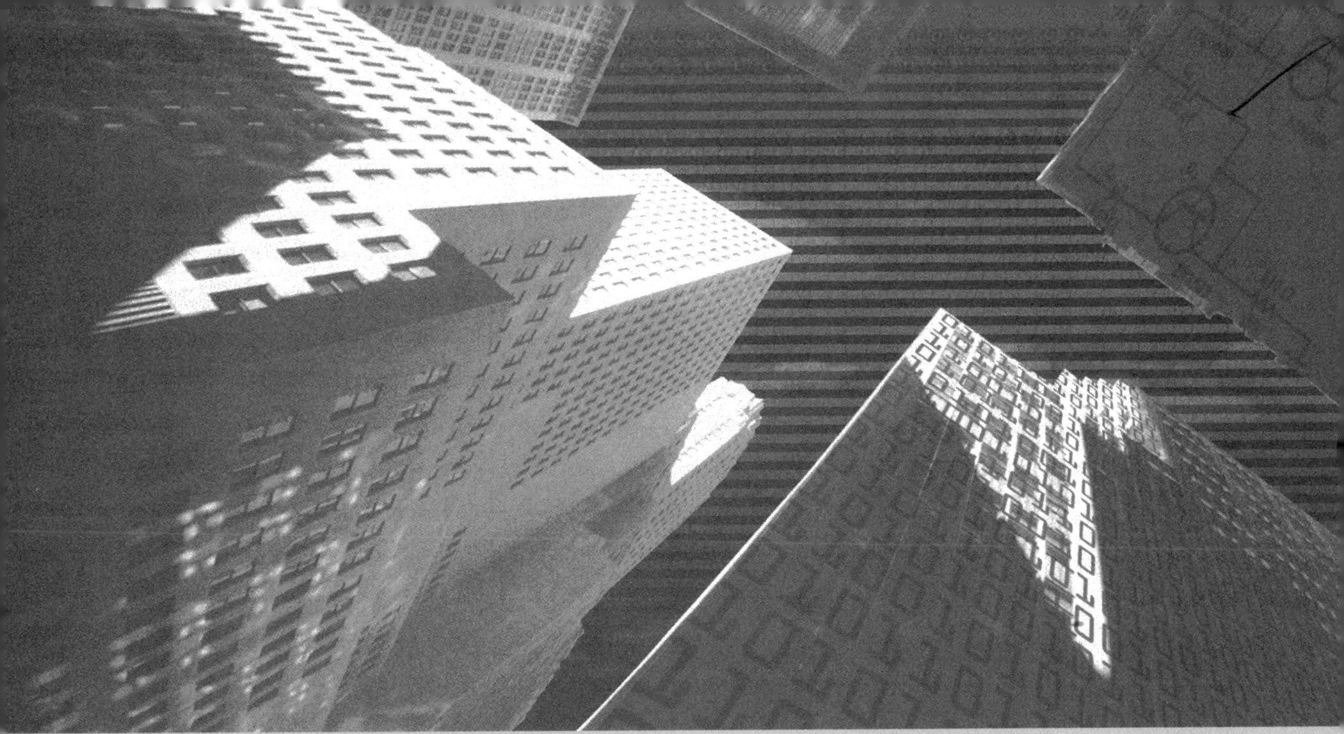

Crystal Reports® 9 Essentials

Jill K. Howe

WITH

William H. McRae
and
Scott M. Spanbauer
The BridgeBuilder
Company

Publisher:
Stacy L. Hiquet

Marketing Manager:
Heather Hurley

Acquisitions Editor:
Todd Jensen

Book Production Services:
Argosy

Technical Reviewer:
Summer Pearson

Cover Design:
Mike Tanamachi

With love to my mother, Judy Ann Listowich –jkh

With love to my family: Wendy, Ty, Meg, and Sandy –sms

Acknowledgments

There are many people to thank for their contributions, both direct and indirect. I'd like to thank Will McRae for taking the Web and Crystal Enterprise chapters and running with them, start to finish; Matt Hager and Scott Spanbauer for their contributions to the text; my friend and once coworker Rick Kaminski for his contributions to the text and for helping me unravel the functionality of the repository and custom functions; and my other coworkers at The BridgeBuilder Company for providing me the time to complete this project.

Thanks also to the editors at Premier Press and Argosy Publishing for their assistance and patience, particularly Todd Jensen, Bill McManus, and Adriana Lavergne. I am indebted to Summer Pearson at Crystal Decisions for excellent technical editing and information. Lastly, I'd like to thank my coworkers, family, and friends for having the patience to watch me do this again.

About The BridgeBuilder Company

BridgeBuilder helps companies by transforming everyday data into meaningful managerial information using a number of technology tools and techniques. We offer both Business Intelligence (BI) and Customer Relationship Management (CRM) services.

The BridgeBuilder Company is a veteran Crystal Decisions technology partner and has trained and consulted on Crystal Reports since 1995. BridgeBuilder is a Crystal Decisions Partner-of-the-Year award winner and is recognized as a leader in the Crystal Reports industry. All three authors are Crystal certified trainers and consultants. They are experienced and professional instructors who have trained thousands of users, built hundreds of reports, and implemented Enterprise level data reporting systems for corporations nationwide.

CRM solutions are designed to help companies gain access to information that drives revenue, enhances client retention, and maximizes the effectiveness of sales and marketing processes. BridgeBuilder is a multiple award winning consulting firm in CRM and has developed a strong and repeatable process for implementing CRM systems. Our best practices include analysis and focus on: 1) people, 2) process, and 3) technology. By partnering with the leading software companies in each industry, BridgeBuilder is uniquely qualified to leverage the best in CRM and BI solutions.

About the Authors

The BridgeBuilder Company is a Certified Crystal Decisions Partner that has been providing Certified Training and Consulting for clients throughout North America for over 7 years. With offices in Charlotte, Cincinnati, and Chicago, BridgeBuilder trainers and consultants have provided Crystal Reports training to over 25,000 students and completed over 600 consulting projects. BridgeBuilder's Certified professionals provide training, report development, and implementation services and create custom training materials. BridgeBuilder's Jill Howe was the main contributing author of both *Prima's Official Guide to Crystal Reports 7* and *Prima's Guide to Crystal Reports 8*, and has expanded on all topics in this new book.

Jill Howe is a Crystal Decisions Certified Trainer and Consultant in Crystal Reports, Seagate Info, and Crystal Enterprise. Jill writes custom courseware and teaches regular and custom courses around the country, along with working on large and small report development and custom implementation projects on many database systems. She has extensive experience writing reports for clients in most all business areas. Jill enjoys working with clients to build an overall reporting strategy and then helping them implement it. She likes building reports, solving problems, and sharing knowledge.

William McRae is a Crystal Decisions Certified Trainer and Consultant in Crystal Reports and Crystal Enterprise as well as being a Microsoft Certified Professional (MCP). Will has extensive experience with many other MS products, with multiple database platforms, Data Junction and SalesLogix making him "an answer man" around BridgeBuilder and extremely popular with clients.

Scott Spanbauer is the founder and CEO of BridgeBuilder. He is a Crystal Decisions Certified Trainer and Consultant (since 1995). He is also a certified consultant with SalesForce.com and SalesLogix (both CRM products). Scott is currently the Chairman of Crystal Decisions worldwide Partner Advisory Council and has been a speaker at the CDUGNA (Crystal Decisions User Group North America) for the past two years. Scott enjoys working with people to help them achieve their desired results and building relationships.

Mon

	1	2	3	4
4pr	10	15	11	11
A2	15	11	12	10
pam	2	3	4	5
BIN				

Contents at a Glance

Contents

Chapter 5   Sorting, Grouping, and Totaling Data on Your Report 119

Chapter 18   Web Reporting Using Crystal Enterprise 9 . . 565

Chapter 19   Tips for Report Development Projects 593

Introduction

Is This Book for You?

This book is instructive for a large array of business report designers and users. Rather than focus on a group of users, this book focuses on the tool itself. All functionality of Crystal Reports 9 is covered. This book will get you started if you are completely new to Crystal Reports, as well as take you through complex report design and the advanced features and components of the product. This book is a comprehensive guide to using all the functionality Crystal Reports has to offer, so you will not outgrow it. This book gets new users started with basic concepts and examples, then continues to be useful catering to experienced report writers looking for a complete guide to existing and new Crystal functionality. This book explains functionality in a straightforward fashion, then takes concepts further explaining the interplay between basic functionality concepts to create exceptional reports. You will find this book to be a useful learning and reference tool, supplementing training and serving as a comprehensive reference for all Crystal Reports functionality.

How This Book Is Organized

By following the chapters of this book in order you'll learn to design reports step-by-step. Each part contains chapters that build on the previous part to help you learn the process of designing reports one step at a time. The topics do get more and more advanced as you move through the book, but once you have the basics of the first two sections, the rest builds on that foundation. You can decide which of the advanced topics serve your needs and skip any that do not apply.

We've also included tips and notes throughout the book, providing extra insight, information not documented elsewhere, and tips from our own experience using Crystal Reports.

What's in This Book

We've organized the book into five parts, with each part containing chapters covering specific topics. Read through the following outline to learn more about what this book covers or to help you locate a particular discussion.

Part I—Introduction to Crystal Reports

This first part covers how to begin using Crystal Reports. The section covers basic concepts with lots of instruction to help the beginner become comfortable writing basic reports and the intermediate user to pick up on the easiest way to create reports.

- ◆ Chapter 1—Overview and New Features in Crystal Reports 9
- ◆ Chapter 2—Creating Your First Crystal Report

Part II—Adding to Your Crystal Report

This part covers several of the topics touched on in Chapter 2 in much more detail. Chapter 2 got you through designing a report, but did not provide much information or explanation of how something works or why it is important for your report. Part II explains topics in more detail, gives step-by-step instructions, and provides extra information and hints as to how to use the functionality in Crystal Reports to meet your specific needs.

Though this group of chapters may seem like a tremendous amount of material to master, once you get a feel for how Crystal Reports functions with the easy-to-use menus and commands, you will see how much flexibility all these functions give your reports.

- ◆ Chapter 3—Connecting to Your Database and Linking Data
- ◆ Chapter 4—Selecting Records
- ◆ Chapter 5—Sorting, Grouping, and Totaling Data on Your Report
- ◆ Chapter 6—Formatting Your Report

Part III—Advanced Reporting Topics

Advanced reporting may be intimidating at first, but do not let it be! Once you have a feel for designing basic reports, the sections in this chapter introduce you to advanced features and functions. They all use now familiar methods—Experts and dialog boxes. The functionality in this part really lets you use the tool to its potential to create reports that look and function exactly the way you want.

- ◆ Chapter 7—Formula Workshop
- ◆ Chapter 8—Crystal Repository
- ◆ Chapter 9—Custom Functions

- Chapter 10—Working with Subreports
- Chapter 11—Cross-Tab Reports
- Chapter 12—Using Parameters Creatively
- Chapter 13—Adding Charts and Maps for Better Data Analysis
- Chapter 14—Leveraging SQL Commands for Efficient Reporting
- Chapter 15—OLAP Reporting

Part IV—Managing Your Data and Reports

This part covers some basic interactions between Crystal Reports—a popular and versatile product within the Windows environment—and other tools and software programs. Report distribution using exporting, the Web Application Server, or Crystal Enterprise are all discussed.

- Chapter 16—Distribution Considerations and Add-In Tools
- Chapter 17—Publishing Crystal Reports to the Web: Report Application Server vs. Crystal Enterprise
- Chapter 18—Web Reporting Using Crystal Enterprise 9
- Chapter 19—Tips for Report Development Projects

Part V—Appendixes

This last part contains additional useful information for making the most of Crystal Reports. Data quality is so integral for accurate reports the topic could have its own book! Use this section to supplement your report development.

- Appendix A—Data Quality Management and Integration
- Appendix B—Setting Up an ODBC Data Source
- Appendix C—How to Get Help
- Appendix D—Top Tech Support Issues Answered

Conventions Used in This Book

This text assumes that you are knowledgeable in a Windows environment. As is standard in Windows, you will find that most dialog boxes or commands can be reached any of three ways: a main menu command, a toolbar button, or a shortcut menu command. We usually just point out the menu command and the toolbar in this text, but if you like shortcut menus please take advantage of them.

Also note that you can rest the pointer over almost any object in the Crystal Report Designer and a bubble appears with a text description of that object. This goes for the toolbar buttons as well. Just be patient—it sometimes takes a moment for the text to appear.

Each chapter walks you through completing tasks while explaining why you do certain things, giving you hints and tips along the way. We have kept the instructions as generic as possible, so that you can follow the steps as many times as you need, just filling in your own data.

Many times we reference exact search words for the online Help files in places where the online Help augments the discussion. The online Help is quite good with Crystal Reports, and scrolling through topics will help you become aware of all it can do. Our goal with this book is to pack as much in as possible, and then point you in an exact direction to find additional helpful information. We hope that we can encourage you to be creative and try things once you have the basics and some ideas as to Crystal Reports' potential.

We hope that you find this book useful if you're a brand new user and valuable as a reference and great source of extra information if you're a more experienced report writer. We hope that if you are a beginner now, by about the time you get half way through you will consider yourself comfortable with reporting and be ready to use the more advanced functionality. Good luck using one of the best report writer programs available!

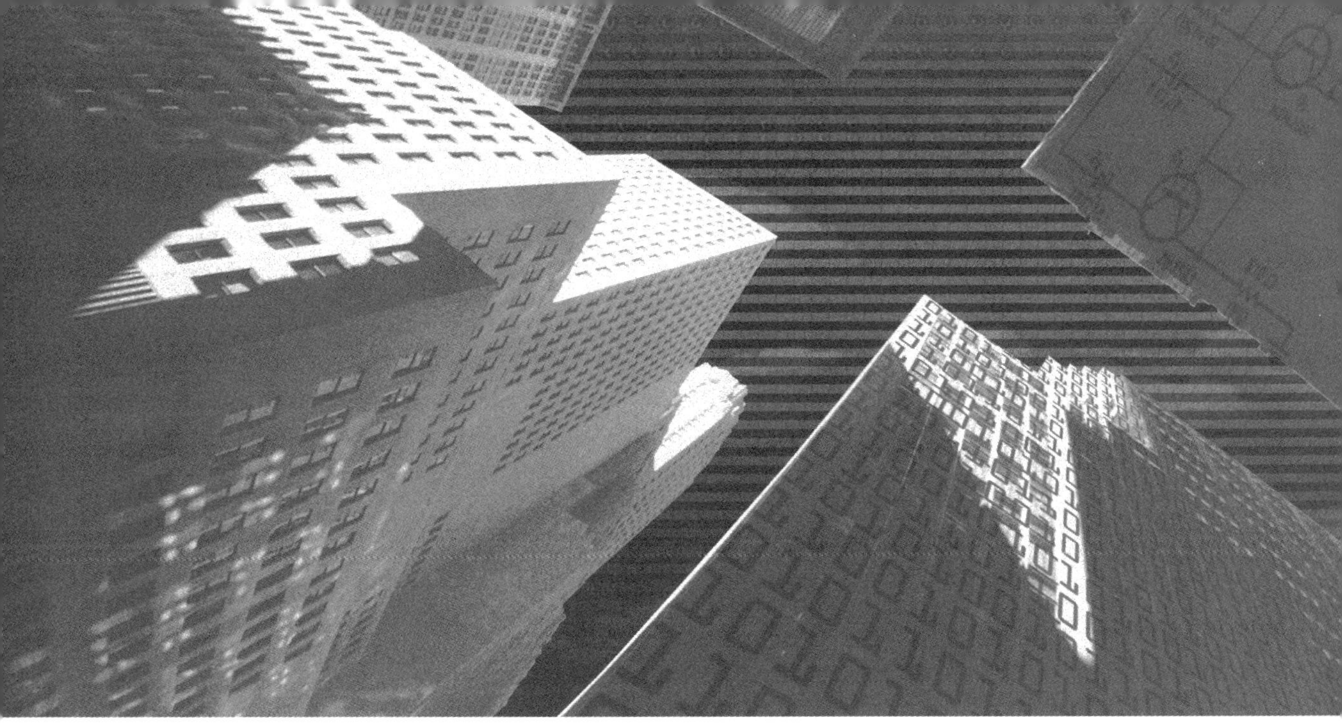

PART I

Introduction to Crystal Reports

Chapter 1

**Overview and
New Features in
Crystal Reports 9**

This first chapter introduces you to some of the basics of Crystal Reports (also referred to in this book as Crystal or CR). You'll learn the basic layout of Crystal Reports, how to navigate through it, and how to find what you need. This chapter outlines the new features found in Crystal Reports 9, which are sure to impress you.

Getting Started

You first need to install Crystal Reports on your computer. The software includes installation instructions and requirements. Though this book does not cover installation, this section emphasizes a few details that will help you understand that there are several different components to Crystal Reports, and that the installation has changed slightly from previous versions.

The typical installation includes the Crystal Report Designer with basic database connectivity and report design functionality. There are many options that you may want to take advantage of that are not installed by default, such as specific database DLLs, charting and mapping features, exporting options, and development tools (see Figure 1-1).

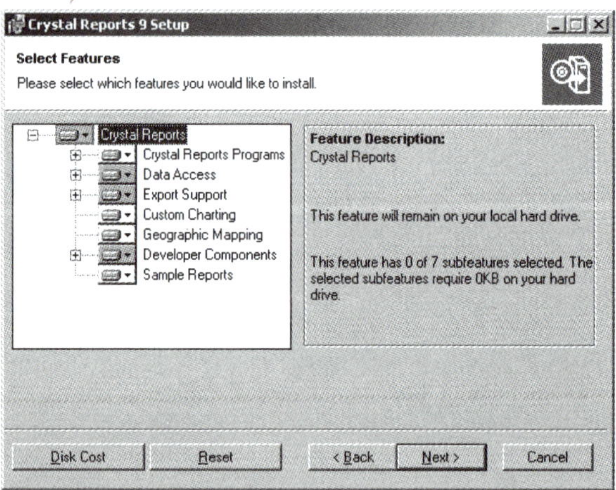

FIGURE 1-1 *Some installation options are not included in a typical install that you may need for full functionality of the product.*

Crystal Dictionaries and the Crystal SQL Designer are no longer included with this product. They can be downloaded and installed from the Crystal Decisions Web site, specifically **http://support.crystaldecisions.com/communityCS/FilesAndUpdates/cr9_data_tools.zip.asp**. Crystal Queries are covered in Chapter 14. For most of this book, we focus on the Crystal Report Designer.

Launching the Crystal Report Designer

Open the Crystal Report Designer by selecting Start, Programs, Crystal Reports 9. When you first open Crystal Reports, one of several dialog boxes may open. If you have not yet registered your software, a Registration dialog box appears. It is highly recommended that you register your software. (Registration of the product is free and can quickly be accomplished online.) This gives you access to free technical support for a limited time, among other benefits.

NOTE

You receive 60 days of free technical support from the date you register your product, so do not register when you install if you are not planning to start your first reporting project for a few weeks to make the most of this free support.

You can click Register Later to move on, but this dialog box will come up every few times you open your software until you register. After the registration dialog box, or if you have already registered your software, the Welcome dialog box opens, offering three options for starting a report (see Figure 1-2).

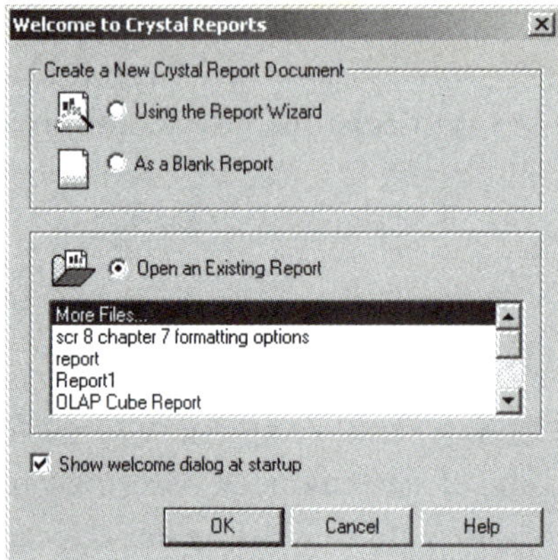

FIGURE 1-2 *The Welcome dialog box offers three options to get you started designing a report.*

◆ Using the Report Wizard

◆ As a Blank Report (custom)

◆ Open an Existing Report

NOTE

If the Crystal Report Designer is already open, and you select File, New or click the New button, the only two choices are Using the Report Wizard and As a Blank Report.

TIP

Figure 1-2 shows several reports listed in the Open an Existing Report list box. If you have just installed your software you will not have any reports listed.

Chapter 2 provides detailed instructions that walk you through designing two reports, one using a Report Wizard and the other using the blank, or custom, report option. You can modify an existing report by selecting the Open an Existing Report option when you launch the Crystal Report Designer.

If the Welcome dialog box did not appear, then it has been turned off. You can turn it back on so that it shows up every time you open the Crystal Report Designer by choosing Help, Welcome Dialog and then selecting the Show Welcome Dialog at Startup check box. Of course, you can also start a new report by clicking File, New and selecting either the Using the Report Wizard or As a Blank Report option.

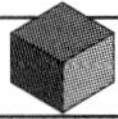 **NOTE**

You can get to the registration screens via Help in the main menu toolbar. This Help option also lists other resource links like tech support and the Crystal Decisions Web site.

Using the Report Wizards

Report Wizards are instructional tutors that you can use to assist you, step by step, in designing a report (see Figure 1-3). Report Wizards come in four flavors, each containing a series of steps to follow that build a report. Each screen contains prompting text and dialog box functionality that help you build a report. Keep in mind that some options only appear in certain wizards.

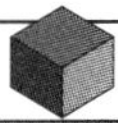 **NOTE**

The four Report Wizards are Standard, Cross-Tab, Mail Label, and OLAP. Chapter 2 covers each of these in detail. The Report Wizards and their functionality have changed in this version of Crystal Reports.

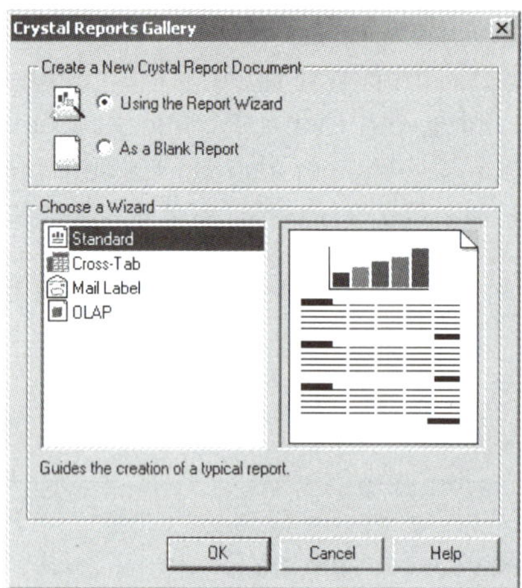

FIGURE 1-3 *Report Wizards walk you through basic report design one step at a time.*

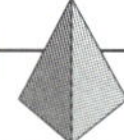

TIP

Many new users find the Report Wizards to be a great way to start a report. A wizard walks you through report design and prompts you for the most important elements of a report.

Using Blank Reports

You do not have to use a Report Wizard when you create a new report. Crystal Reports also gives you the ability to design reports through the As a Blank Report option. Using this option, you have the functionality of all the wizards combined, plus countless formatting and functional options. Using the As a Blank Report option, you design and format a report using the main menu and toolbar commands, instead of being prompted for information for your report by the wizards.

A new feature in Crystal Reports 9 is the ability to build your own report templates. A report template can be applied to an existing or new report to add formatting attributes, header and footer information, company logos or pictures, hyperlinks, and so forth.

Starting with a Wizard, and Then Customizing

Once you have designed a report using a wizard, you can make further modifications using any of the toolbars or menus. When you use a wizard, you can pick from one of 11 style formats in the Template Expert in order to format the report, and then you can customize. If you do not select a style the report opens in the preview window in a generic format. Once you click Finish to exit the wizard and build a report, you cannot go back into the wizard—if you want to make any further changes to the report, you must use the menu and toolbars. When you design a report using the As a Blank Report option, you have complete freedom and control over all functionality and formatting from the start.

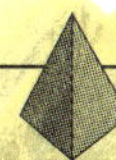

TIP

As you go through each screen within the Wizard, there is an image in the top right-hand corner. This image is the same shortcut icon you will find for that function in the Crystal Report Designer. This is to help users make the connection between the action they can perform in the Wizard and where to find that same action in the Designer.

NOTE

All of the formatting styles referred to above for the wizards are available by selecting the menu option Report, Template Expert or by selecting the Template Expert toolbar button.

Connecting a Report to a Data Source

Throughout this book, the information included in reports is referred to as *data*. Typically, this data resides in a database or data warehouse of some sort. Crystal Reports provides several options for connecting to your data, all organized in the Database Expert. There are many options to ensure that Crystal can connect to your specific data. The Database Expert is an organized place where you create and store all of your data connections (see Figure 1-4).

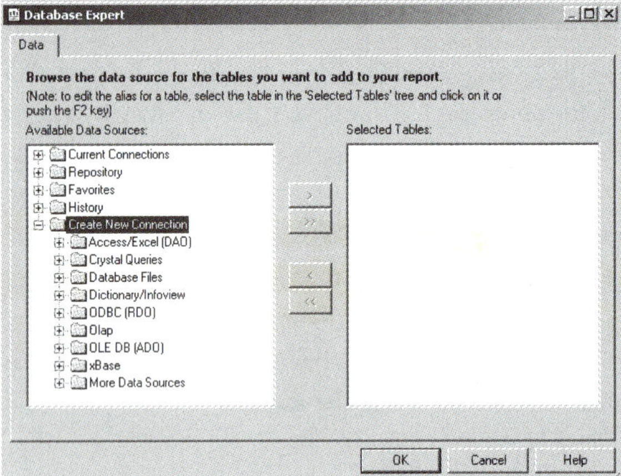

FIGURE 1-4 *The Database Expert is where you create and store database connections.*

Your database itself determines which option is best to use for connecting to that database. The Database Expert provides folders where you can store connections for easy future use. Using the Database Expert is covered in detail in Chapter 3.

The type of data source you use for reporting determines the type of connection to use. The flexible nature of Crystal Reports provides compatibility with almost any data source. Chapter 2 introduces the Database Expert and describes how to use an ODBC connection to an MS Access database. More information follows in Chapter 3 about this database connection, as well as general database connectivity information. Chapter 3 will help you decide which connection works best with your database, and explains the other options in the Database Expert.

Finding Functionality with Menus and Toolbars

By default, Crystal displays a menu bar and four toolbars across the top of the Designer (refer to Figure 1-4). To hide any of these toolbars, or view them if they are not currently available, choose View, Toolbars and select which toolbar you want to hide or add from the four listed in the Toolbars dialog box.

Clicking any of the menus opens lists containing the actions and functions you use when designing and running reports. The toolbars contain buttons that duplicate some of the menu commands. The toolbar buttons offer a quicker way to open a dialog box or apply an option. Each button and menu command will be introduced as that functionality is covered in the text.

TIP

Crystal places toolbars in the locations shown in Figure 1-4 by default. By dragging the toolbars, you can move them wherever you prefer in the application window. If you "lose" a toolbar or want to turn one off temporarily, use the View, Toolbars option to turn the toolbars on and off. You can also right-click on a toolbar and use the quick-select menu that appears.

Throughout this book, both menu commands and the related toolbar buttons are pointed out. You can choose which method to use. You will notice that for almost every tool, Crystal provides two or three different ways to invoke the function or open the dialog box. You can use the main menu, the toolbar, the Report Explorer, keyboard shortcuts or, in many situations, shortcut menus that open when you right-click in the proper area. For example, if you want to format a field on your report, you can click a toolbar button, choose Format, Format Field, or right-click the field you want to format and choose Format Field from the shortcut menu. You could also open the Report Explorer, select the field you want to format, right-click, and select Format Field from the shortcut menu. Crystal gives you complete functionality using whichever method you like best.

Designing Reports: Where Do I Start?

Before you start clicking away, it is best to consider what data you need on your report, and get a conceptual idea of how you want your report to look. This just might be the most important and most overlooked part of successful report design. A few basic questions to ask yourself include:

- What data will be on my report? Can I currently connect to that data source? Do I have/need a password?

- Once I connect to my data, what database fields do I need for the report? In which tables are they located?

- Will the data need to be sorted or grouped? Do I want summaries?

- Who or what is the report for? This question will help you determine formatting and how many of the more advanced functions you will need or want to play a part in your design.

When you design a report, you have to think about many issues. After you read Chapter 2, you will realize that you need to have a good idea about what you want and need on your report before you start. Each chapter will help you become more comfortable with what Crystal Reports can do, and lend insight into what questions you might ask when planning a report project. At any time, refer to Chapter 19 for information, ideas, and hints to help you understand the design process and come up with an appropriate strategy to meet your reporting needs.

New Features in Version 9

Crystal Reports 9 includes so many new features, from entire new tools full of new functionality to the simplest formatting enhancements, that this section lists only the advertised biggies, and some others that are just fun and exciting for long-time Crystal users. Other new features not listed here are described throughout the book.

New Features

Crystal Reports 9 is rich with new features, from the smallest formatting enhancement to completely new tools and ground breaking functionality. This section is a quick list of the most flashy features. You'll find information on each in context within the chapters.

Report Explorer

This tool allows you to see all sections of a report in a dockable Explorer environment, which enables you to format sections, and select and format objects within sections.

Crystal Repository

Report objects such as SQL Commands, custom functions, text objects, and bitmaps can all be stored in the Crystal Repository and shared across several reports. When an object is updated in the Repository, reports that reference the object can be updated selectively or automatically.

SQL Commands

Finally! This is the SQL functionality we have all been waiting for! CR 9 supports extended SQL commands and provides SQL support for any read functionality that your database supports. This functionality includes unions, subselects, functions, and parameters. These SQL Command objects can be stored in the Crystal Repository and shared among reports.

Unicode Support

Full support for Unicode fields is available in CR 9. This allows multiple languages to be displayed in the same report, including double-byte characters.

Custom Functions

Using either Crystal or Basic syntax, you can write and save custom functions into the Crystal Repository for use in all reports. You can write custom functions "from scratch" or convert existing formulas into reusable functions using the Custom Function Extractor.

Custom Report Templates

You can create and use custom report templates to apply standardized formatting to corporate reports, ensuring a consistent look and faster, easier formatting.

Formula Workshop

This new, centralized workshop provides the tools to develop formulas and custom functions, along with introducing a new codeless wizard for formula building.. You can also edit all formulas from this one interface, including record selection, group selection and conditional formatting formulas.

Updated Developer Tools

Crystal Reports 9 introduces new application development tools, including a 100 percent Java SDK, an updated MS Visual Studio .Net SDK, and an enhanced COM SDK. Using these tools to develop custom software applications is not covered in this book.

ePortfolio ZeroClient Viewer

A new zeroclient viewer using the Report Application Server (RAS) is available with CR 9, providing improved user interactivity with reports. Enhanced functionality includes the ability to perform advanced searches on report data and the ability to export search result grids to MS Word, MS Excel, and HTML.

Report Parts

You can identify and view specified parts of existing reports via a special Report Part Viewer, or integrate them using the SDK into your own portal or wireless applications. Designating objects on a report as a report part is as easy as formatting. This functionality allows you to route certain specified data from a report to a Web viewer, where application developers can build wrap-around applications to send the report part to a wireless device without sending the entire report.

Guided Navigation

You can set up seamless navigation paths within one report or between reports or report parts. This simplifies the development process of delivering information to portals and wireless devices.

Support for MS Office Smart Tags

You can integrate key report objects like charts or tables into MS Outlook, Word, or Excel documents.

Small but Awesome Formatting Enhancements

The following is a sample of some of the formatting enhancements in Crystal Reports 9. Many more enhancements are described throughout the text, but here is a partial list of features to get excited about.

- Outside Borders icon—this feature allows you to insert a border to all sides of an object with one click
- Lock Format and Lock Size & Position—allows you to make certain objects or sections on the report read-only
- Top N now called Sort Group Expert—much more intuitive name
- Docked Field, Repository, and Report Explorers—gives you more flexibility over the real estate in the application

- View Rulers, Guidelines, Grid, and Tooltips options from the main menu—the ability to quickly turn these options on or off

- Insert Summary dialog box fixed so that the Field to Summarize is listed first

- Show SQL Query dialog box is completely uneditable—all editing of the SQL query is done in the Database Expert through the SQL command functionality

- Delete a field from the Details section and its column heading is automatically deleted as well

- Guidelines are attached to the right side of number and currency fields

- Equal joins are finally called Inner joins, which is a more common name with other tools

- Font color menu shortcut—format the font color of a selected field by clicking the font color palate drop down arrow to display a palate of font colors

Other Key Enhancements

This section lists features that are more enhancements to the existing tool rather than completely new, though no less powerful.

Side-by-Side Installation

Crystal Reports 9 can be installed on the same machine as previous versions of Crystal Reports without problems.

New User Interface Explorers and Wizards

New 'Explorer' dialog boxes allow for easier navigation, viewing of available objects, and editing. All Explorers are dockable for better design environment control.

Enhanced Database Query Engine

Crystal Reports 9 includes new database drivers for Oracle 8 and SQL-based DAO, along with better support for multiple databases in one report and improved client-side linking.

Updated and Improved Exporting Functionality in Several Formats

This version includes extensive enhancements to Excel and Acrobat exporting functionality, including the option to export the full format or data only. Also, Crystal supports vector-based images and new HTML export enhancements with support for cascading style sheets.

Enhanced Formatting Options and New Functionality for Cross-Tabs and OLAP Grids

Summaries on running total fields, vertical or horizontal summary display, editable summary labels, percent of summary calculations, and support for relative positioning within a section are all new features of cross-tabs and OLAP grids.

New Charting Functionality

New chart types and formatting improvements have been made, including support for date-time, numeric x-axis, in-place formatting, and enhanced conditional formatting functionality. The Analyzer is gone, with all chart and mapping functions built into the Designer.

New Function for Drill-Down Summary Reports

A new function built just for formatting drill-down reports, DrillDownGroup-Level allows you to specify exactly which drill-down level you want a particular section to show. This is critical for controlling when certain sections are viewed.

Suppress Blank Subreports Option

A formatting option specifically for subreports provides the opportunity to suppress blank subreports so other formulas are no longer needed to suppress the subreport or section if no data is collected.

Report Bursting

This new functionality allows you to index fields within a report to be used for faster processing within Crystal on the client side (within Crystal Reports). This does not replace taking advantage of indexed fields in your database for processing speed, but provides an option within Crystal for further improving report performance.

Performance Information for Each Report

Performance Information provides a dialog box with performance statistics for the open report, including a report definition, saved data information, processing, latest report changes, and performance timing data.

Making Reports Available on the Web

Publishing a Crystal Report on the Web is not a new feature, but technology changes and enhancements in version 9 make the reports more functional and gives users and designers more options. A new Report Application Server (RAS) used with ePortfolio Lite provides sophisticated Web-enabled reporting. Using and configuring these components is covered in Chapter 17.

Summary

The Crystal Report Designer is a powerful tool for designing reports, with several methods for starting a new report using the Data Explorer. Chapter 2 discusses these methods in detail, and walks you through designing two reports step by step.

With an updated user interface and so many new features in Crystal Reports 9, sophisticated functionality is at your fingertips. This tool is capable of doing things that no other tool on the market can match. I am so much more excited about the tool after using all of these great enhancements than when I first learned about them—this is great stuff! Enjoy!

Chapter 2

Crystal Reports provides extensive dynamic report development capabilities. To build useful reports, you must start with the basics and build upon them. This chapter introduces you to the Crystal Reports Designer and how to build a basic report in a variety of ways. Crystal Reports offers two methods to start a new report:

◆ Report Wizards
◆ A Blank Report (custom)

NOTE

You can edit an existing report by opening the RPT file in the Crystal Reports Designer. Use the Open an Existing Report option on the Welcome to Crystal Reports dialog box, or select File, Open, or click the Open button on the standard toolbar. The option to edit an existing report is discussed at the end of this chapter.

Both methods are explained in this chapter. First, the Standard Report Wizard is explained, followed by sections briefly explaining each of the other Report Wizards and the different functionality of those wizards. Then, you'll walk through the steps to design a report using the Blank Report option. Lastly, I will explain how to edit an existing report.

Creating a Report Using the Standard Report Wizard

As mentioned in Chapter 1, Crystal Reports has four Report Wizards to assist you in designing reports. In this chapter, two reports are designed step by step, one using the Standard Report Wizard, and another using the Blank Report option. You can design your reports either way. If you start a report using a Report Wizard, you can most certainly add to it or change it using the custom options.

Opening the Crystal Reports Designer and Starting a Report

First, you need to open the Crystal Reports Designer and start a new report in order to use a wizard.

1. Select Start, Programs, Crystal Reports 9. The Crystal Reports Designer application window opens with the Welcome to Crystal Reports dialog box open.

2. Select Using the Report Wizard on the Welcome to Crystal Reports dialog box, and then click OK (see Figure 2-1).

3. The Crystal Report Gallery dialog box opens. If you cancelled the Welcome dialog box in the previous step, select File, New or the New toolbar button ▯. The Crystal Reports Gallery dialog box opens (see Figure 2-2).

4. In the Choose a Wizard list, click Standard. The Standard Report Wizard template appears on the right side. Click OK to launch the wizard.

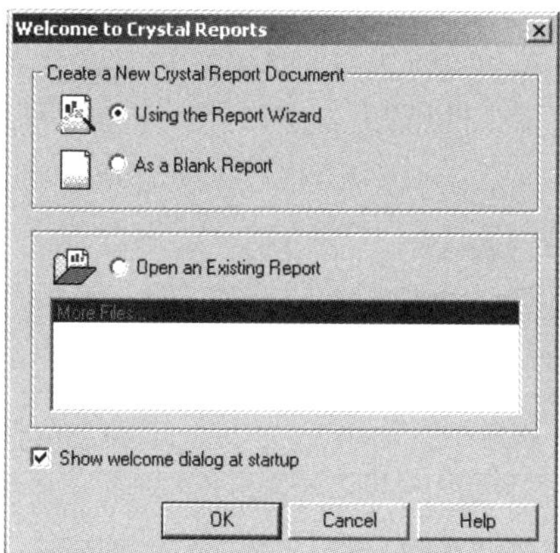

FIGURE 2-1 *The Welcome dialog box greets you upon opening Crystal Reports. Choose an option for starting your report.*

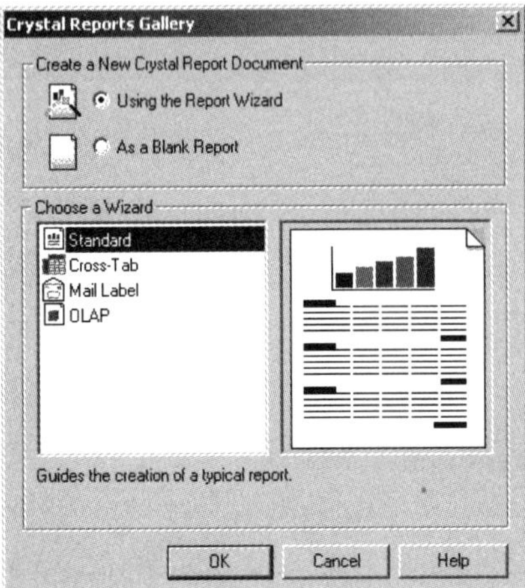

FIGURE 2-2 *Open the Standard Report Wizard from either the Welcome dialog box or the Reports Gallery dialog box.*

Report Wizards walk you through the main elements involved in designing reports. Once you start a wizard, you navigate from page to page, responding to the prompts. The information you provide creates the basis of your report. Which Report Wizard you use dictates which pages appear.

Choosing the Source of Report Data

Each page in the Standard Report Creation Wizard prompts you to take a particular action. First, the Data page asks what data you want to use for your report.

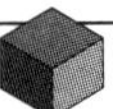

NOTE

You can use data from most any source on your reports. The Data page allows you to organize your data sources in folders. The examples in this chapter and much of this book are all based on the Xtreme Sample Database 9, which is shipped and installed with your software automatically.

Choose a data source for your report by following these steps:

1. Begin the Standard Report Wizard. The Data page opens, providing a list of Available Data Sources (see Figure 2-3).

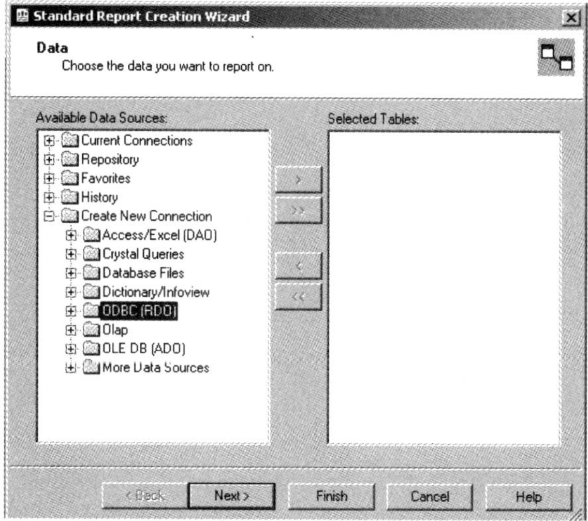

FIGURE 2-3 *Choose the data source you need for your report by navigating through the folders beneath the Create New Connection folder.*

2. Select the Create New Connection option in the Available Data Sources list to expand the list of data source types. Double-click the ODBC (RDO) option to launch the Data Source Selection page of the ODBC (RDO) dialog box. This dialog box lists all ODBC data sources configured on the machine.

3. For the examples in this chapter, I select the Xtreme Sample Database 9. Click the name of your database in this dialog box (see Figure 2-4).

4. Click Next. If your database has security, enter your password on the Connection Information page. If there is no security on your database, leave the password blank and click Finish (see Figure 2-5).

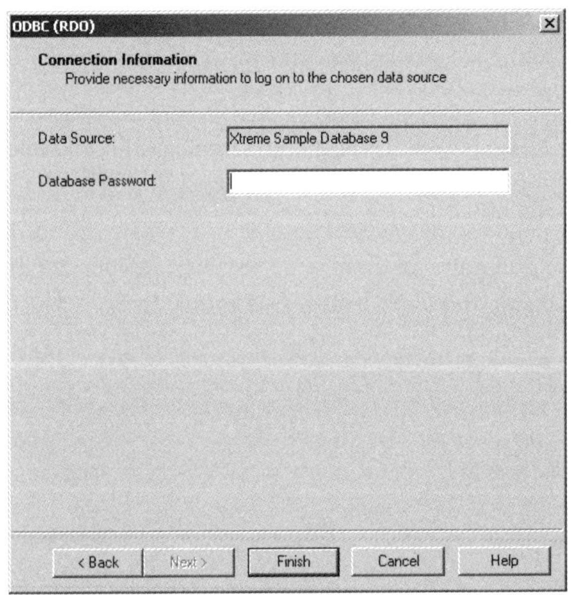

FIGURE 2-4 *Select the data source for your report using the Data Source Selection page.*

FIGURE 2-5 *Provide a password if your database requires one.*

5. The database you chose to connect to is listed under the ODBC (RDO) option in the Available Data Sources list of the wizard's Data page. Different database element folders are listed including Tables, Views and Stored Procedures. Expand each folder to see a list of elements.

6. Select individual database elements from the list for reporting and move them to the Selected Tables list on the right by clicking the forward arrow (>) button (see Figure 2-6).

7. Click the Next button to move to the wizard's Link page (see Figure 2-7). If you have only one table chosen for a report, the Link page is not necessary and thus does not appear. If you choose two or more tables for your report, you need to link the tables together to use information from both tables on your report. Crystal Reports automatically displays the Link page, and completes the linking using Auto Link. (You'll learn about linking in detail in Chapter 3.)

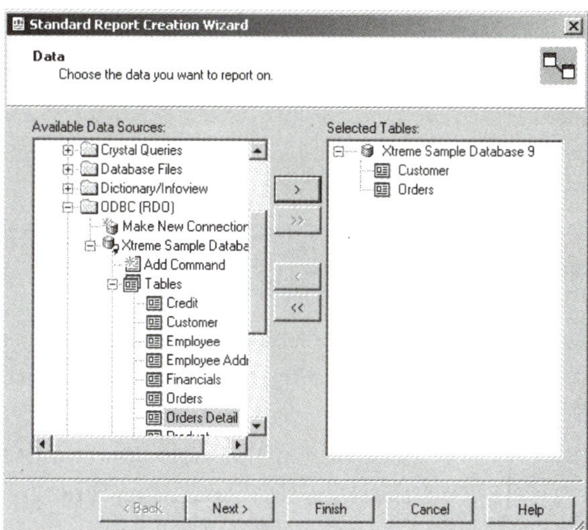

FIGURE 2-6 *Move tables for reporting to the Selected Tables list.*

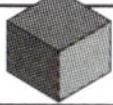

NOTE

Many of the examples in this book use the Xtreme Sample Database 9 that ships with Crystal Reports. Crystal Decisions, the company that manufactures and sells Crystal Reports, provides this MS Access database as a sample to be used for report design practice.

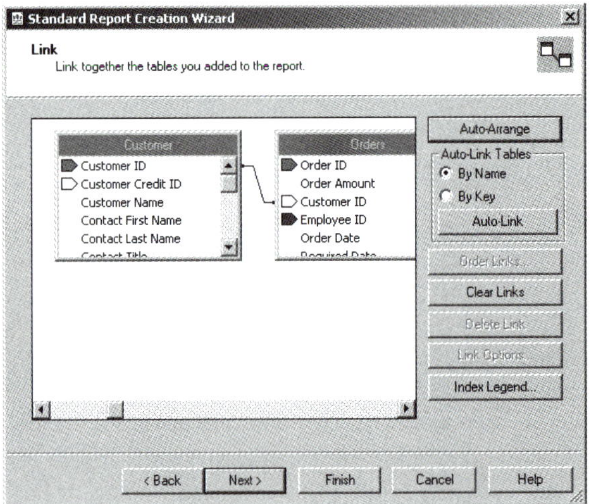

FIGURE 2-7 *The Link page appears only if you have chosen more than one table for your report.*

You now have chosen the source of your report data. Next, you need to select fields to display on the report. Click Next on the Link page to go to the wizard's Fields page.

FIELDS PAGE FUNCTIONALITY

The Fields page offers several options to help you select database fields:

◆ **Browse Data.** With a field selected in the Available Fields list, click this button to browse a sample of the data found in this field in your database.

◆ **Find Field.** Click this button to open a dialog box in which you enter the name of the field you want to find. When you click OK, the dialog box closes and the selection box jumps to the desired field.

◆ **Up and down arrow buttons.** Use the arrows in the upper-right corner to adjust the left-to-right display order of the database fields on your report.

Selecting Fields to Display on the Report

You specify which fields to display on your report by using the Standard Report Wizard's Fields page. You can choose from any of the fields in the tables that you selected on the wizard's Data page. The Available Fields list shows a tree, with all the field names listed below the table names. By default, the tree has the first table expanded, listing the fields within that table. You can expand the second table by clicking the plus sign next to its name in the tree.

The plus and minus signs make navigating through your available database tables and fields easier. To add fields to your report:

1. In the Available Fields list, either double-click the field you want to add to your report or select the field and click the forward arrow button (>). The field shows up in the Fields to Display list. Add fields to your report in the order in which you want them to display across your page from left to right (see Figure 2-8).

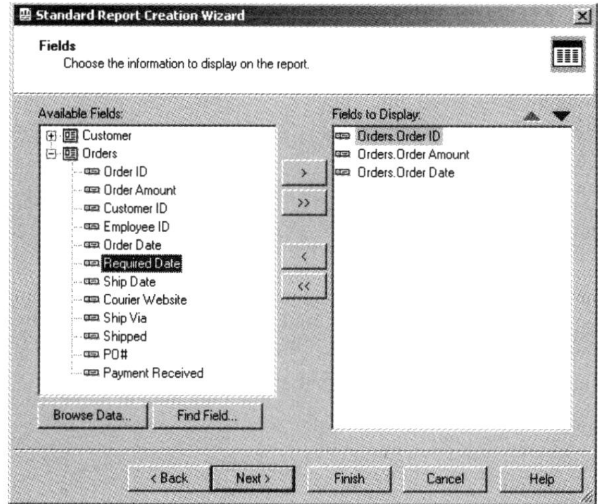

FIGURE 2-8 *Add fields to your report by moving them from the Available Fields list to the Fields to Display list.*

2. Once you have all the fields you want on your report listed in the Fields to Display list, click Next to go to the Grouping page.

Adding Groups to a Report

Crystal Reports helps you to organize your report by grouping records. You can use any field available to your report for grouping. To add a group to your report:

1. In the Available Fields list, click the field on which you want to base your group. Click the forward arrow button (>) to move the field to the Group By list (see Figure 2-9).

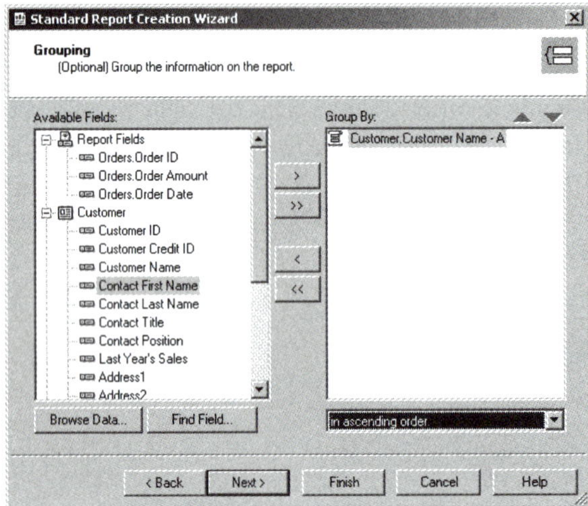

FIGURE 2-9 *Click the field you want to base your group on from the Available Fields list and add it to the Group By list.*

2. With a field chosen in the Group By list, select the order of your group from the Sort Order drop-down list (under the Group By list).

3. Click Next to go to the Summaries page.

NOTE

Chapter 5 provides more information on grouping and group sort orders. You must select a field to group by in order to use the Totals page.

Adding Summaries

On the Summaries page, you can specify whether you want to add any summaries or subtotals to the report. Crystal calculates summaries and subtotals; all you need to do is specify which field you want the function to act upon and which summary function you want to use. To add a summary to a report:

1. Click the field you want to summarize in the Available Fields list. Click the forward arrow button (>) to add the field to the Summarized Fields list.

2. Notice that the wizard has already selected the Order ID and Order Amount fields (see Figure 2-10). You can add and remove fields if Crystal does not add the correct fields that you want to summarize.

TIP

The wizard automatically adds any number type fields to the Summaries page, assuming that you want to sum up any and every number field on the report. This is not true in some cases, so you need to remove any fields that you do not want to summarize, and add any other fields (such as counting a string type field) to the list.

NOTE

Chapter 5 includes detailed information regarding summarizing your data.

3. Select which summary or subtotal function you want to perform from the Summary Type drop-down list below the Summarized Fields list. For Order Amount, I have left Sum. For Order ID, I summarize by counting the number of orders placed. With Order ID selected, change the Summary Type field to Count (see Figure 2-10).

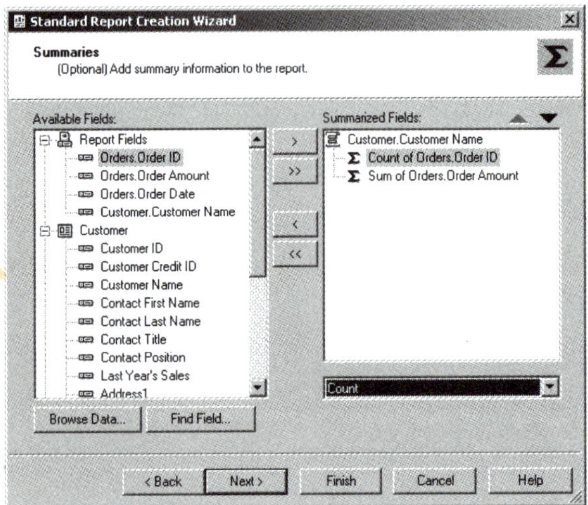

FIGURE 2-10 *The Order ID field will be counted per customer.*

4. Be sure to check any fields that Crystal Reports selects for totaling. Sometimes the program may add a field that you do not want to total. To remove fields you do not want to total, select the field and click the backward arrow button (<).

After you have finished configuring the Summaries page, click Next to move to the Group Sorting page.

Group Sorting

The Group Sorting page provides options for you to sort your groups based on the summaries calculated for each group. (If you're familiar with previous versions of Crystal, you'll recognize this as the Top N functionality.)

Figure 2-11 demonstrates how you would list only the top five customers (groups) on the report, based on each group's sum of order amount. Chapter 5 covers this functionality and demonstrates the increased functionality beyond what the wizard allows. If you do not wish to employ group sorting, leave None selected and click Next to move to the Chart page.

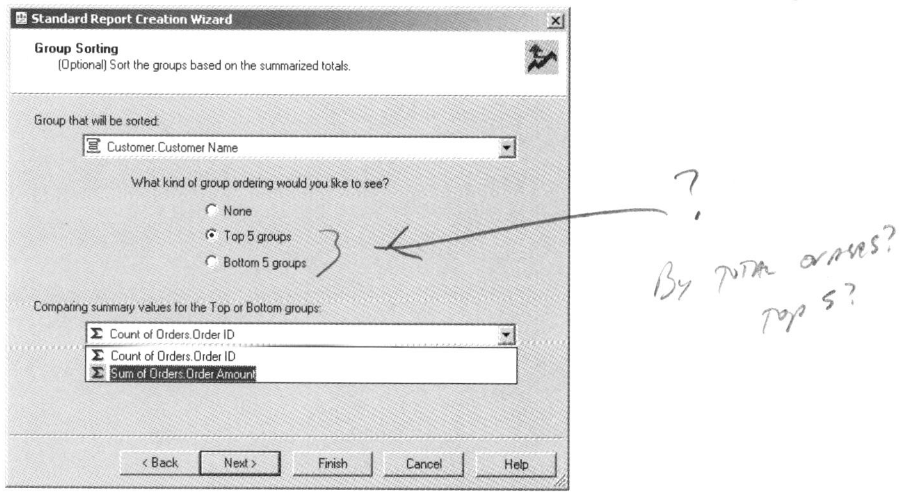

FIGURE 2-11 *Sort your groups based on summary values for the groups.*

Adding a Chart or Graph with the Chart Page

Use the Chart page (see Figure 2-12) to add a basic chart to your report. You have three types of charts to choose from. This is an extremely watered-down version of the full Chart Expert tool within Crystal.

1. Select the type of chart you would like to insert from the chart types.

2. Edit the system generated title for your chart in the Chart Title area.

3. Select a field from the On change of drop-down list. This is a group on the report that will represent each bar, line, or slice of pie.

4. Select a field from the Show summary drop-down list. This determines the size of the bar, location of the line, or size of each slice of pie.

5. Click Next to go to the Record Selection page.

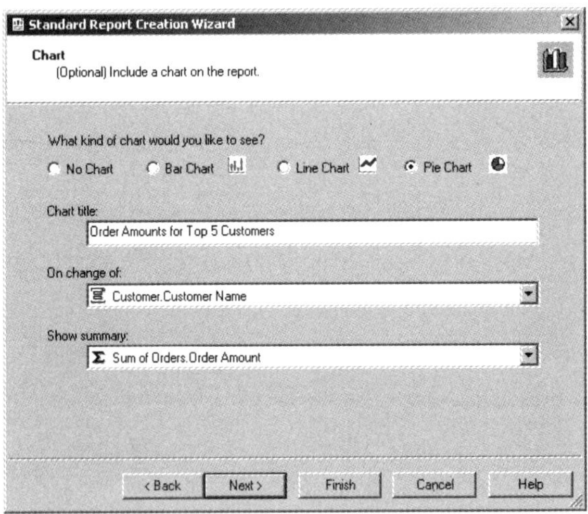

FIGURE 2-12 *Set options in the Chart page to add a chart to your finished report.*

NOTE

Chapter 13 covers charting in detail. Crystal offers much more sophisticated charting and formatting options in the full Crystal Reports Designer.

Selecting Records to Include

You specify which records from your database to display on a report using the wizard's Record Selection page. This page allows you to select which records you want to display on the report. For example, you may want to run a report for only one month, not for every month. Or, you may need to run a report for only one region or state, not every state. There is no limit to the number of selection criteria you can set. To define selection criteria:

1. From the Available Fields list, select the field on which you want to base your selection criteria.

2. Click the forward arrow button (>) to move the field to the Filter Fields list. Below the Filter Fields list, a drop-down list appears, giving you conditions for setting selection criteria, as shown in Figure 2-13.

3. Once you select a condition (I have chosen "is equal to"), a second drop-down list appears. This second list contains actual values from your database, pulled from the field on which you are basing the selection criteria.

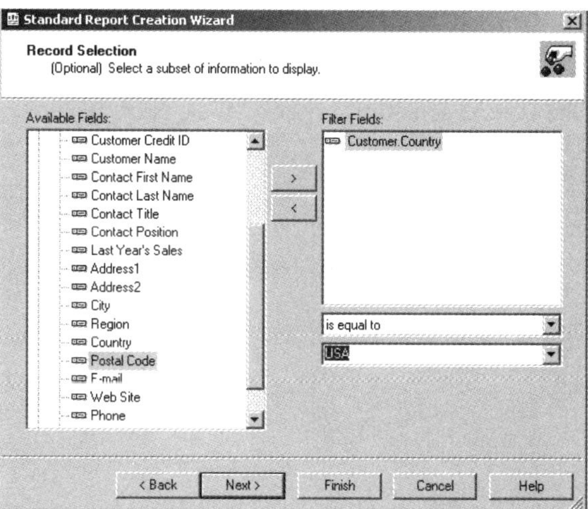

FIGURE 2-13 *Use the drop-down lists to define your selection criteria.*

4. From the second drop-down list, select the value that completes the selection.

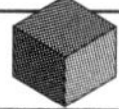

NOTE

Figure 2-13 illustrates how to select only records that equal USA for the example report. The report will not include any customers from other countries. Chapter 4 goes into detail about the many options available to you when setting record selection criteria.

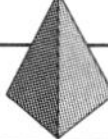

TIP

When you use the second drop-down list on the Record Selection page, every value in your database may not show up. You can also type the value that you want to use. The browsed data that appears in the drop down list is sample data pulled in from your database. Seeing this data helps you with the format and case of your actual data.

5. Add a second selection criteria to this report by selecting the Order Date field from the Available Fields list. Use the "is between" condition from the first list, and browse the two subsequent lists to set criteria between January 1, 2001 and March 31, 2002 (see Figure 2-14).

6. Once you have set the record selection criteria, click Next to move to the last wizard page, Template.

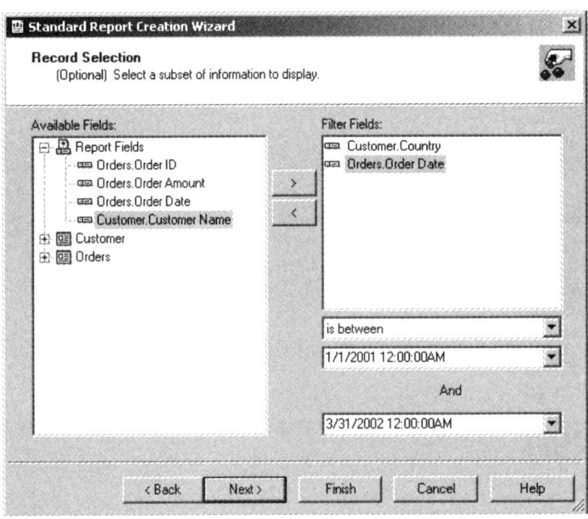

FIGURE 2-14 *The "is between" condition allows you to select a date range for records to be included on this report.*

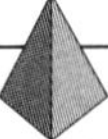

TIP

Notice that the format you see when browsing data in the Order Date field is in date/time format. If you need to type data, you must enter your selection criteria in the format that Crystal recognizes, which is the format shown in the list of browsed data. I find that the easiest way to deal with date formatting is to select a browsed field—even if it is not the date I want—and then just replace the date numbers with the actual date that I want. This lets Crystal tell me the format, and I just replace the listed numbers with the actual date I want.

Applying a Report Template

You can select a template for the formatting of your report from the Template page. There are ten templates to choose from and a No Template option.

1. Select a template from the Available Templates list. A sample of the formatting displays to the right of the list, in the Preview box (see Figure 2-15).

2. Select a custom template by clicking the Browse button in the lower-left corner. You or someone at your company must have created a custom template in order for you to select it for your report.

3. Click Finish. Once you click Finish, you can never return to the wizard, so be sure you have set up the report the way you want it!

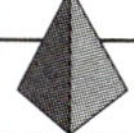

TIP

Details and instructions for creating your own template and adding graphics to reports can be found in Chapter 6.

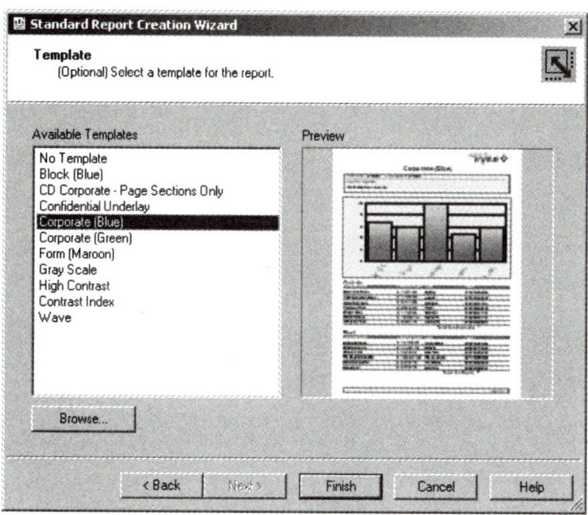

FIGURE 2-15 *Use the Template page to select a template for your report.*

Now that you have gone through all the pages of the Standard Report Wizard, you are ready to preview the report you designed. Keep in mind that any further changes you wish to make to the report need to be made through the designer. You cannot go back into the wizard.

> **NOTE**
>
> It is not necessary to complete all the wizard pages to create a report using a Report Wizard. At a minimum, you need to select one table and one field.

CUSTOMIZE A REPORT STARTED WITH A REPORT WIZARD

Once you preview a report built with any of the Report Wizards, you will see that you also have access to the Design tab (see Figure 2-17). Click this tab to see what the wizard designed "for you" with the instructions you gave Crystal through the wizard. Any changes you need or want to make to this report must be done using the menus and toolbar buttons. Most of this book is dedicated to your understanding of how to build and edit reports using the toolbar and menu functions, not the wizards.

Finish Your Report

Next, you want to run your report with real data. Click Finish on the Template page, and your report will collect data from the database and display the Preview tab in Crystal Reports, shown in Figure 2-16.

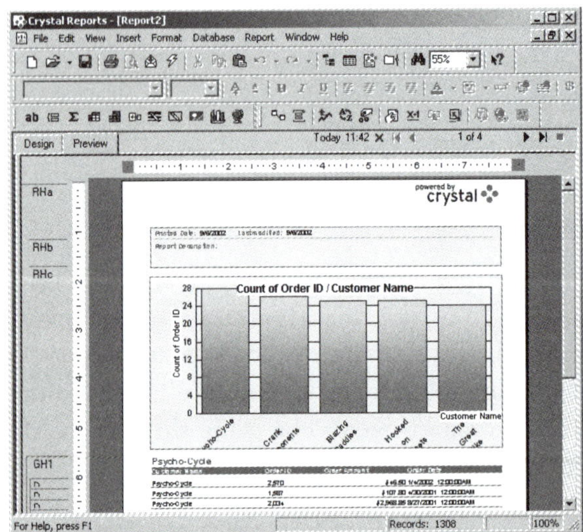

FIGURE 2-16 *The Preview tab of this sample report shows the actual report with data.*

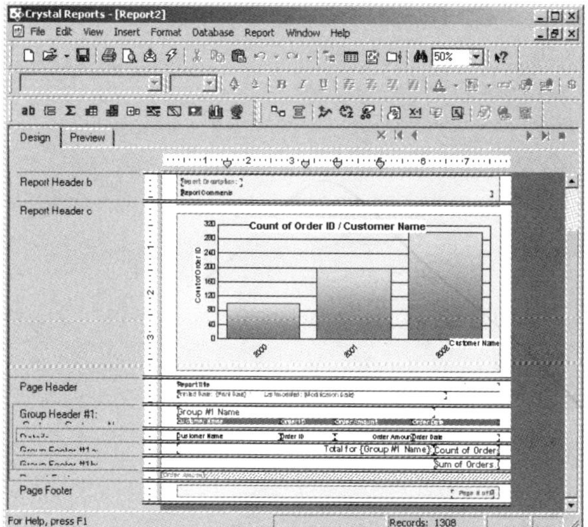

FIGURE 2-17 *Use the Design tab to customize a report originally designed with a Report Wizard.*

The Other Wizards: Creating Specific Report Types

Report Wizards come in many flavors, each of which helps you design a certain type of report. Though you can create any type of report using the Blank Report option, the Report Wizards help you design by giving you instructions to follow.

NOTE

You will find sample reports built using these wizards on Bridgebuilder's Web site, **www.bridgebuilder.com**.

Cross-Tab Report Wizard: Analyzing Data in a Spreadsheet

The Cross-Tab Report Wizard provides the instructions to create a basic cross-tab report (see Figure 2-18). The Cross-Tab Report Wizard contains the same basic options as the stand-alone Cross-Tab dialog box explained in Chapter 11.

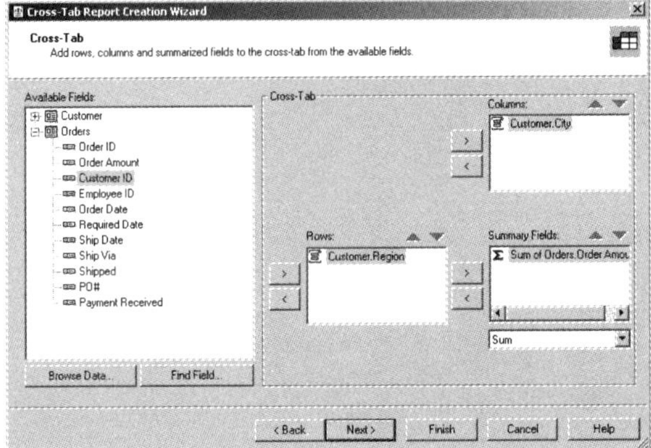

FIGURE 2-18 *The Cross-Tab Report Expert helps you create Cross-Tab reports.*

Mailing Labels Report Wizard: Printing Data on Standard or Custom Labels

The Mailing Labels Report Wizard makes creating mailing labels from your database easy. You select the fields you want on your labels using the Fields page. Using the Label page (see Figure 2-19), you select what type of labels you want to print. The Mailing Label Type drop-down list contains Avery label numbers. Or, you can set the label dimensions yourself.

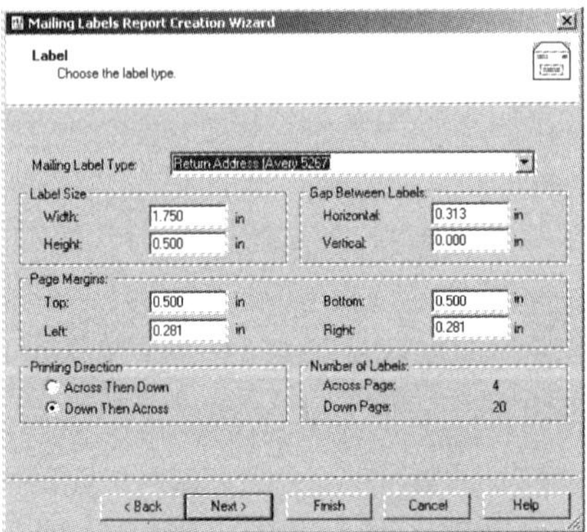

FIGURE 2-19 *Use the Label page to choose your label style.*

TIP

If you want to print multiple database fields on one line, such as City, State, and Postal Code, you can use a formula to pull the fields together into one field. Such a formula might look like:

```
{tablename.City} + ", " + {tablename.Region} + "   "+ {tablename.Postal Code}
```

This formula is written using Crystal syntax in the Formula Editor. You do not have access to the Formula Editor from the wizards, so you must make this customization after. See Chapter 7 for information on how to write formulas.

OLAP Report Wizard

To design a report using an OLAP cube as a data source, choose the OLAP Report Wizard. OLAP, Online Analytical Processing, is a technology used to create multidimensional data structures, sometimes called cubes. Crystal has a Report Expert to help you design reports from these structures, which Chapter 15 thoroughly covers. Please see that chapter for full instructions and more information about OLAP.

Designing from a Blank Report

Designing a custom report gives you freedom to use all the functionality of the full Crystal Reports design environment from the beginning. By building a report using the As a Blank Report option, you have control over everything from the start. The Report Wizards walk you through a series of windows that assist you in creating a report, but they are extremely limited. The custom Design tab provides the necessary functionality to build real-world functional reports. You can customize a report built with a wizard, but I find it much easier to start from scratch and build a report the way I want from the start.

When you start a report using the As a Blank Report option, you design your report from a blank Design tab. You must use commands found on menus and toolbars to create your entire report.

Some people like this Blank Report option because they have complete flexibility and control from the start over what goes where. Others find it more difficult to start from a blank Design tab because Crystal does not prompt for the basic elements of a report, and the designer has to remember to add them. In the next section, you will become familiar with how to design a report using the Blank Report option, and then you can decide which way you like best.

NOTE

Keep in mind that if you design a report using one of the Report Wizards, you can change or add anything to the report on the Design tab using the toolbars. You are able to start the report using a wizard and then customize it using the toolbars. My personal preference is to use a Blank Report, but the decision is yours to make.

In the next section, I will begin designing the same report that was created using the Standard Report Wizard, except this time it will be created step by step from a Blank Report. This way, you can see how the two methods differ in process, yet result in the same data on the final report. The goal for this section, like the steps using the Standard Report Wizard, is to get you familiar with the Crystal Reports Designer and the basic elements of reports. Chapters 4, 5, 6, and 7 add elements to the report, such as record selection criteria, grouping, summarizing, formatting, and formulas. These chapters cover basic functionality and more thoroughly discuss the various features and functions.

Connecting to Data

After you tell Crystal that you want to start a report As a Blank Report, you then select the database containing the information on which you want to report.

Begin Designing a Custom Report

Beginning a report using the As a Blank Report option starts in the Crystal Report Gallery just as when using a wizard. The following steps walk you through starting a new report.

1. Click New on the toolbar or choose File, New. The Crystal Reports Gallery opens.

2. Click As a Blank Report and then click OK. The Database Expert dialog box opens.

3. Click Create New Connection, click ODBC (RDO), and select the sample database, Xtreme Sample Database 9.

4. If under ODBC (RDO) the only option listed is Create a New Connection, then double-click the ODBC (RDO) option to launch the Data Source Selection page (see Figure 2-20).

5. Select the data source for your report from the Data Source Name list.

6. Click Next and provide a password on the Connection Information page if your database requires one (see Figure 2-21). The sample database does not require a password, so it is left blank. Click Finish.

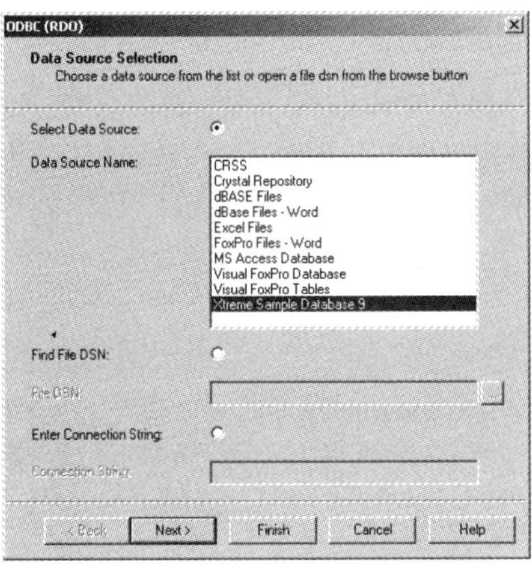

FIGURE 2-20 *Select the data source you want to use for the report.*

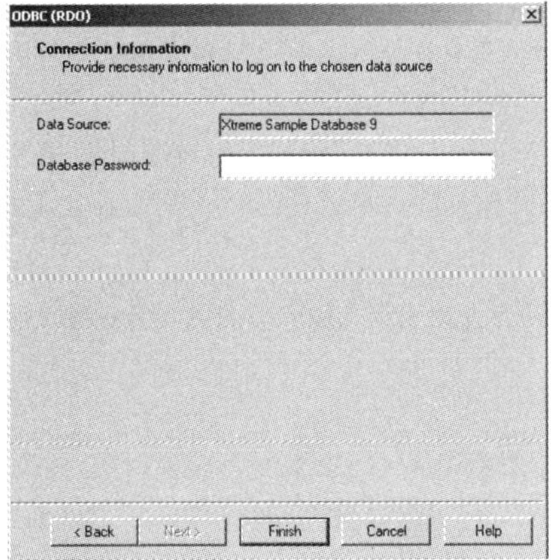

FIGURE 2-21 *Enter a password for your database on the Connection Information page.*

The Database Expert is still open with the database listed that you chose to report from. If there are objects other than tables available for reporting in your database, such as views and stored procedures, they will be listed here just like for Xtreme Sample Database 9. Reporting from views and stored procedures is as easy as reporting from tables and will be covered in detail in Chapter 14.

Add and Link Tables for Your Report

Once a data source is selected you must choose the table(s) you want to report from and link them if you choose more than one.

1. In the Database Expert click the plus sign (+) next to your data source name to expand the list of available database elements.

2. Select the elements you wish to report from and move them to the Selected Tables list by clicking the forward arrow button (>). The Customer and Orders tables were selected in the report used for the figures.

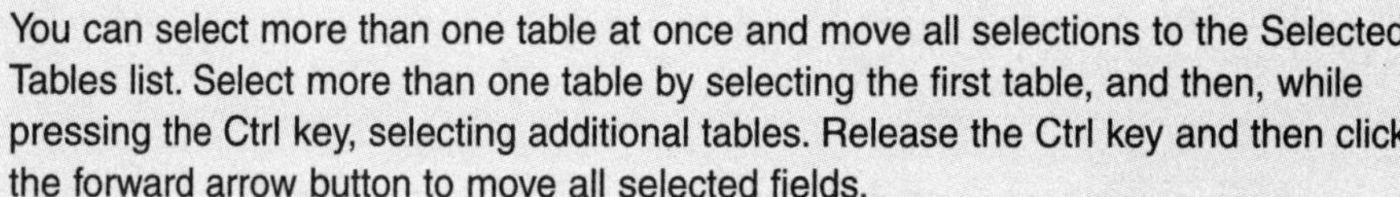

TIP

You can select more than one table at once and move all selections to the Selected Tables list. Select more than one table by selecting the first table, and then, while pressing the Ctrl key, selecting additional tables. Release the Ctrl key and then click the forward arrow button to move all selected fields.

3. As soon as you add more than one table to the Selected Tables list, a Links tab appears behind the Data tab in the Database Expert. Click this Links tab to link your tables together.

4. Since Auto-Link is turned on, Crystal links the tables together for you (see Figure 2-22). This is fine for the sample database, which links perfectly.

5. Click OK to close the Database Expert and open the Design tab.

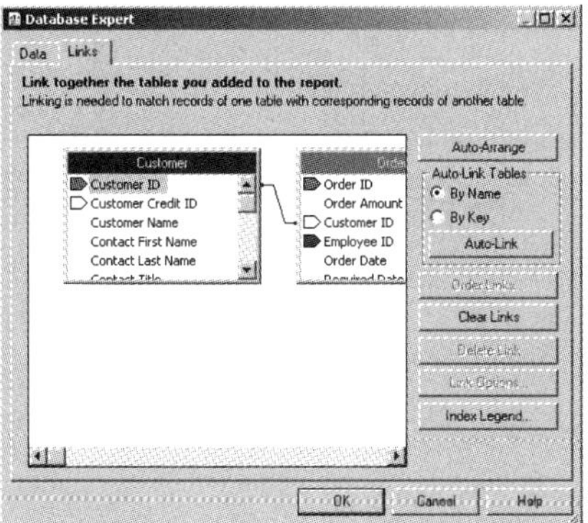

FIGURE 2-22 *Use the Links tab to link tables together and manage table relationships.*

NOTE

Chapter 3 covers the Database Expert in detail, along with many other database-related topics, including linking and join types.

Basic Design Tab Sections

A basic report consists of five sections, as shown in Figure 2-23 and described in the following list. You cannot delete or change the order of these sections, though you can manipulate their size. You also can hide or suppress and format these sections to meet your needs. You can add more sections to the basic five, as needed. Which section you insert a field or object into determines where and how many times that field or object prints on your report. Chapter 6 discusses sections in detail.

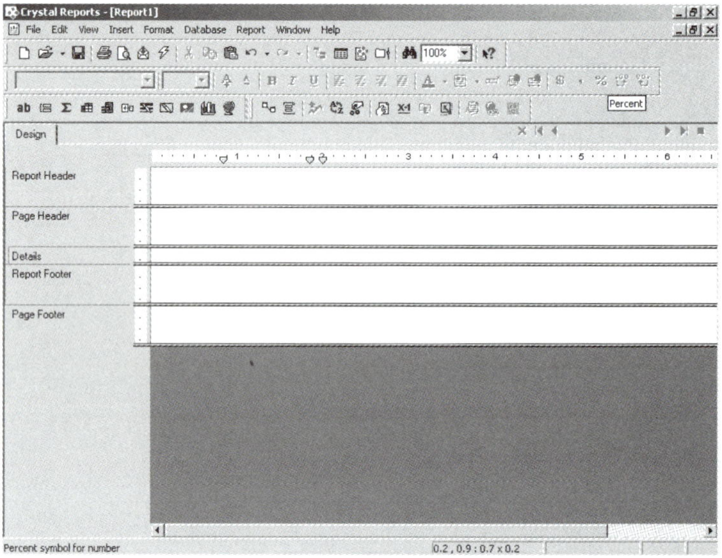

FIGURE 2-23 *The Design tab consists of five basic sections.*

◆ **Report Header.** The Report Header prints once per report, at the top of the first page. In this section, you can place a report title, date, or any other information you want to print first on your report. You can even put a graph in the Report Header section, and size it to use the whole first page of your report, if you like.

◆ **Page Header.** The Page Header section prints once at the top of every page of your report. You can place page numbers in this section, or any other information that you want to print at the top of every page. For some reports, you may want the title to print in the page header, or maybe a company logo or company confidential message.

◆ **Details.** In the Details section, you insert most of the database fields to print on the report. This section repeats once for every record the report pulls from the database.

◆ **Report Footer.** The Report Footer area prints once per report at the end of the report. This section is a good place for notes about the report and grand totals. The last page footer follows this section.

◆ **Page Footer.** The Page Footer area prints at the bottom of every page of your report. You might insert page numbers, comments, or any other information you want to repeat at the bottom of every page.

Depending on which section an object is inserted into determines how it will behave—when and where it prints. For example, a field object in a Report Header section prints once on the report, where that same object in the Page Header prints once on every page of the report.

Inserting Fields into Your Report

The next step in creating a report from scratch involves placing database fields onto the report. To insert fields on your report, open the Field Explorer. You can either click the Field Explorer toolbar button ▦ or select View, Field Explorer.

Click the plus sign next to the table name (see Figure 2-24). This expands the list, showing the fields in the table available for your report.

Add Fields to Your Report

1. Select the field you want to insert onto your report. Click the Insert button (at the top left of the Field Explorer) or double-click the field name. The field *attaches* to the pointer.

2. Drag the field from the Field Explorer and drop it in the Details section of your report (see Figure 2-24). Once you insert a field into the Details section, a column heading is automatically inserted into the Page Header section.

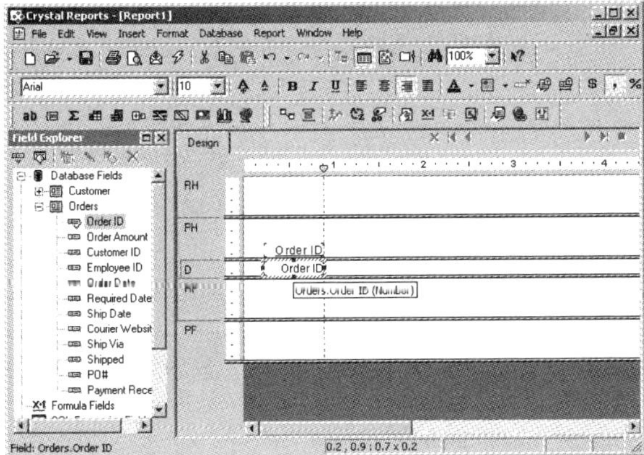

FIGURE 2-24 *Drop a field onto the Details section of the Design tab.*

3. Repeat the preceding steps to place as many fields as desired from any of the tables listed on your report.

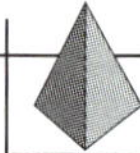

TIP

There are several different methods to insert fields. You can click the Insert button, double-click the field to attach it to the pointer, right-click and select Insert to Report, select the field and press Enter, or just drag and drop the field. With the field attached to your pointer, click anywhere on the report to place the field. Remember that what section you place fields in determines where and how many times the field prints on the actual report.

Crystal gives you the ability to sort your tables and fields in alphabetical order instead of the order they occur in your database. You can also sort your tables by name or description or both. Select File, Options to open the Options dialog box. On the Database tab, select the appropriate options in the List Tables and Fields By area and the Sorting area. More information on these options can be found in the Online Help files using the keyword "options."

RESIZING AND ORGANIZING FIELDS

There are several ways to move and resize fields on a report. As explained in the text, if you select a field by clicking it once, you will see four resizing handles on the four sides of the field. Hover your mouse over a resizing handle and you will see a double-sided arrow. Hold down the regular mouse button and drag the arrow to resize the field.

If you resize a field, the column heading for that field will mirror the database field and resize automatically.

To just outright move a field, there are two ways. One is to select the field by clicking it once, and hover the cursor over the middle of the field. This will produce a

(continues)

Resize a Field

You will notice that sometimes a field is quite large on your report. All objects on a report, including fields, can be resized.

1. Select the field you want to resize by clicking it once with your mouse.

2. Move the pointer over one of the resizing handles. The pointer changes to a double-headed arrow (see Figure 2-25).

3. Drag the resizing handle to adjust the size of the field.

4. Click off the field to deactivate the resizing handles.

You'll notice that when you resize a database field, the column heading for that field resizes with the field. The same is true if you delete a field off your report—the column heading automatically deletes as well.

Typical Crystal Reports functionality is to provide more than one way to do everything. An example of this is that you can also move and resize fields using the keyboard. To move an object with the keyboard, simply use the arrow keys and the object will move. To resize an object with the keyboard, hold down the Shift key and the arrow keys, and the object will resize accordingly.

RESIZING AND ORGANIZING FIELDS (CONTINUED)

four-headed arrow cursor. Hold down the regular mouse button and drag the field wherever you want on the report.

The second way to move fields is to use guidelines. When you insert a field into the Details section of your report from the insert fields dialog box, a guideline will be added to the horizontal ruler. Hold this arrowhead with your mouse and drag it in the ruler to slide fields horizontally. This keeps the field and its column heading together and lined up perfectly, so it is a good way to move fields around on a report. Look for more information on guidelines in Chapter 6.

To select more than one field at a time, select one field and then press either the Ctrl or Shift key and select other fields. You can also draw a marquis around the fields you want to select by dragging your mouse diagonally from the upper-left corner to the lower-right corner.

Unlike resizing or deleting fields, to move a field and its column heading, you must either use the guidelines or select both the field and the heading using the Ctrl or Shift key.

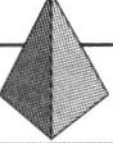

TIP

If you resize a database field, the column heading resizes automatically at the same time. However, if you grab a column heading to resize, the field does not follow.

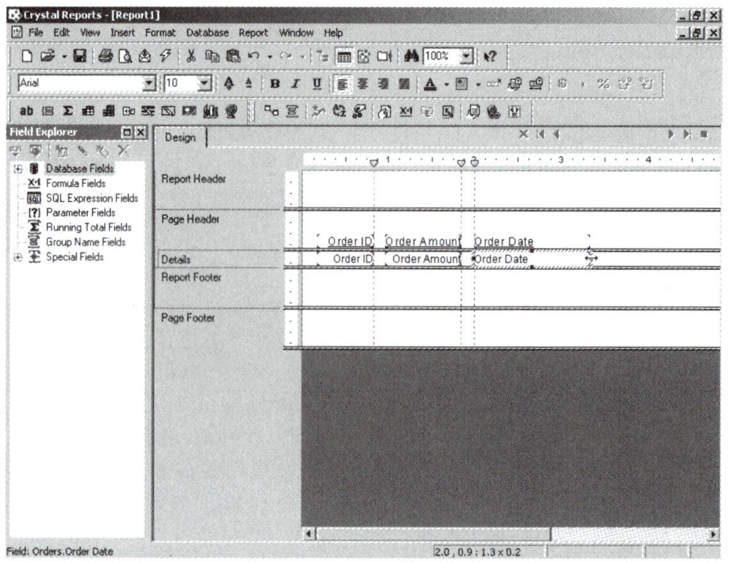

FIGURE 2-25 *Use the resizing handles to change the size of any field.*

Browsing Field Data

Many places in Crystal Reports afford you the luxury of the Browse function. Browse allows you to browse a field of data from your database and see the actual data in that field. This is extremely useful to assist you in choosing fields from your database for a report. If you are not sure if a certain field is the one you want, for example the field name is paymentcode1 and there is also a paymentcode2, you can browse the data and hopefully this will help distinguish which field you need to use. You can access this Browse function through an icon button or by right-clicking in many areas of Crystal Reports. Look for the Browse button on experts and dialog boxes, and when right-clicking.

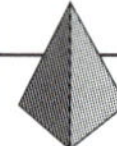

TIP

If you select File, Options, the Database tab enables you to choose to browse only unique values. Select the Select Only Distinct Values for Browsing check box (which is selected by default). You may browse saved data if not connected to the data source for the report, and you can browse formula and SQL expression fields. This added functionality greatly slows the Browse function. If browsing only unique values is not necessary for your reporting, I suggest that you uncheck the option, for better performance.

Grouping Data on Your Report

You may want to group the data on your report to make it easier to read and more meaningful. If you do not group or sort your data, it appears on your report in the same order as it was entered into your database.

Create a Group

1. Click the Insert Group toolbar button, or select Insert, Group. The Insert Group dialog box opens (see Figure 2-26).

2. The first drop-down list allows you to select which field you want to base your group on. The field name you select is then listed in the text at the bottom of the dialog box.

3. Use the second drop-down list to select a sort order for the group. Use the Options tab to specify your groups, create custom groups, create custom names for your groups, and select other formatting options. Chapter 5 covers all of these features.

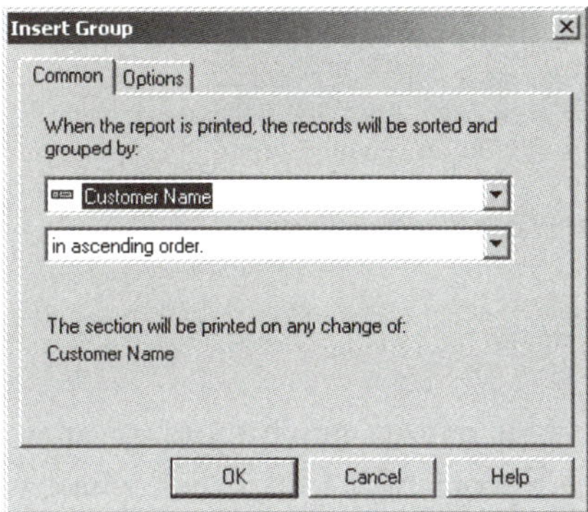

FIGURE 2-26 *Use the Common tab on the Insert Group dialog box to set group criteria.*

4. The Options tab has group options that are discussed in Chapter 5. Click OK to close the dialog box.

Notice that Crystal added Group Header and Group Footer sections on either side of the Details section, as well as a Group Name field (see Figure 2-27). Using these sections, you can print a name at the start of each new group, and insert summary information after each group.

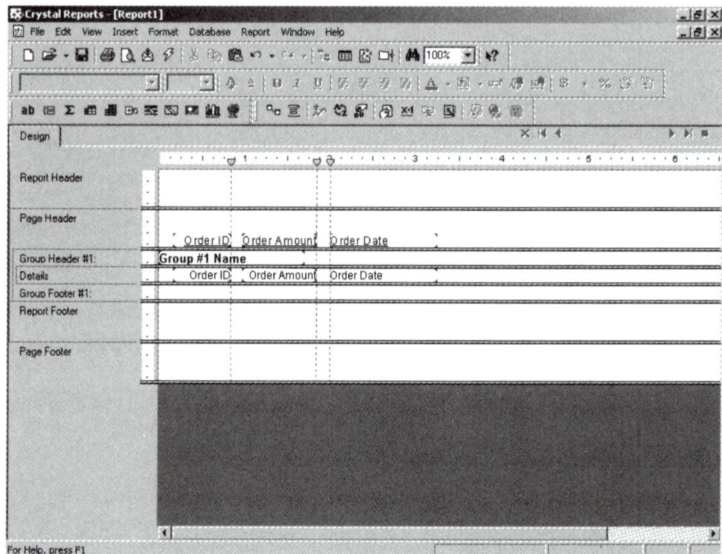

FIGURE 2-27 *Adding a group to a report results in additional sections.*

Sorting Records

Having the ability to sort records makes your reports much more useful and easy to read. By sorting your records using the Record Sort Order dialog box, you can easily set the sort order for the fields on your report.

Define a Record Sort Order

1. Open the Record Sort Order dialog box by either clicking the Record Sort Expert toolbar button or selecting Report, Record Sort Expert.

2. The Record Sort Order dialog box lists all the Available Fields on the left and the Sort Fields on the right (see Figure 2-28). The group you created in the last section appears here because grouping is a type of sorting.

3. Add a sort field by selecting a field in the Available Fields list and clicking the forward arrow button (>) to add the field to the Sort Fields list.

4. Once you have a field in the Sort Fields list, you can set the Sort Direction by clicking Ascending or Descending.

5. Click OK to save your sort settings and exit the dialog box.

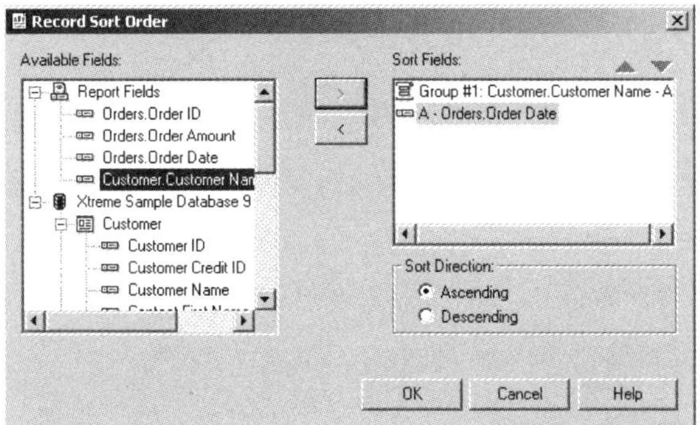

FIGURE 2-28 *Use the Record Sort Order dialog box to sort the records on your report.*

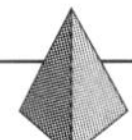

TIP

You can have as many levels of sorting as you like on a report.

Totaling and Subtotaling

Adding totals to your reports can be as easy as a few clicks with your mouse. Totals add value to reports and give you information that may not be in your database.

Insert a Summary

1. Select Insert, Summary or click the Summary button **Σ** from the toolbar to open the Insert Summary dialog box (see Figure 2-29).

2. Select the field you want to summarize from the drop-down list. If you had a field selected before launching the Insert Summary dialog box, Crystal Reports assumes that you want to summarize that field.

3. Select the function you want performed from the second drop-down list.

4. Select a summary location. If your report has no groups, Grand Total (Report Footer) is listed. This option inserts a grand total for the whole report. Select a group from the drop-down list to create subtotals for the selected group level.

5. Click OK to close the dialog box. Crystal inserts the summary fields on the report in the Group Footer section, right below the fields being summarized.

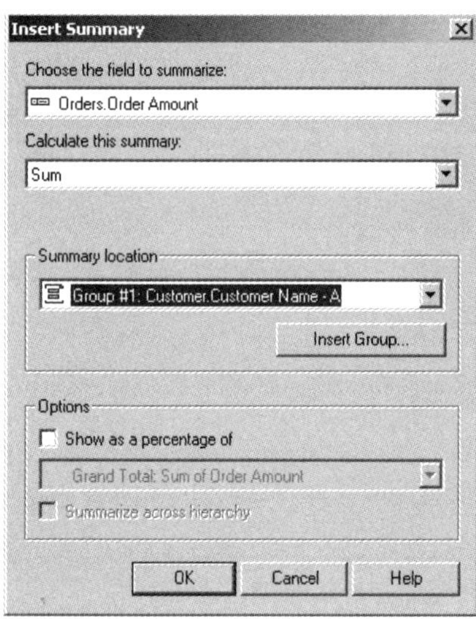

FIGURE 2-29 *Use the Insert Summary dialog box to add totals or summaries to your groups.*

 **NOTE**

Chapter 5 discusses other options included in this dialog box.

Adding Titles and Special Fields to the Report

Using the previous steps, you have created the body of a report, but it would not be complete without a title, page numbers, and a date. Crystal makes it easy to add this information to your report.

Adding Text Objects

Text objects serve as miniature word processors. A text object can be placed any-where on your report—in any section, any size you want. You can then type text into the object, such as a report title, a label for a summary field, or any other information you want to print on your report.

Add Text to a Report

1. Click the Text Object toolbar button **ab** or select Insert, Text Object.

2. The text object attaches to the pointer, acting just like it does when inserting a database field. Move the pointer over the report and click once where you want to place the text object.

3. Once you place the text object, it appears with a shaded border and blinking insertion point, indicating the object is in Edit mode. You can now enter the text (see Figure 2-30).

4. Once you have added text or edited the text object, click outside the text object to take the object out of edit mode.

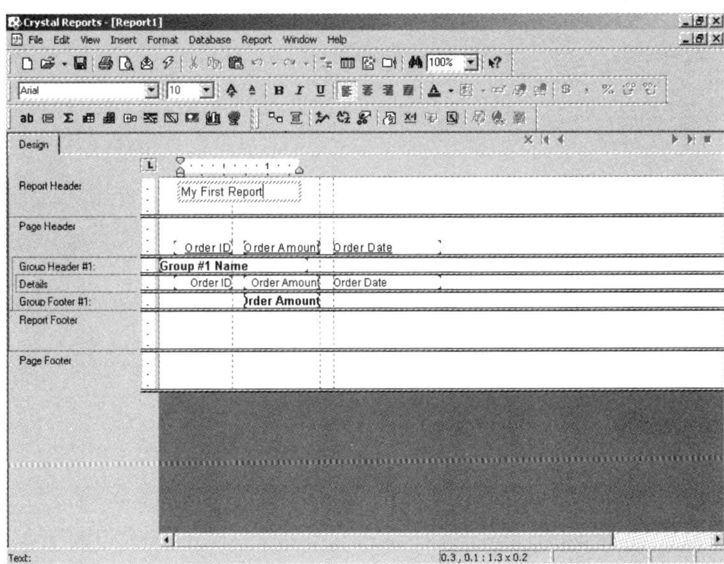

FIGURE 2-30 *Use a text object to add a title to your report.*

You can move this text object anywhere you want on your report and make it as big as you want by using the resizing handles. Keep in mind that the section in which you place the text object determines how many times and where it prints. You'll learn about formatting text objects in Chapter 6.

Adding Special Fields

Crystal Reports contains in the Field Explorer a selection of Special Fields that you can add to your report, such as Page Number and Print Date. These fields act like database fields and are based on your computer's settings.

1. Open the Field Explorer and expand the Special Fields section (see Figure 2-31).

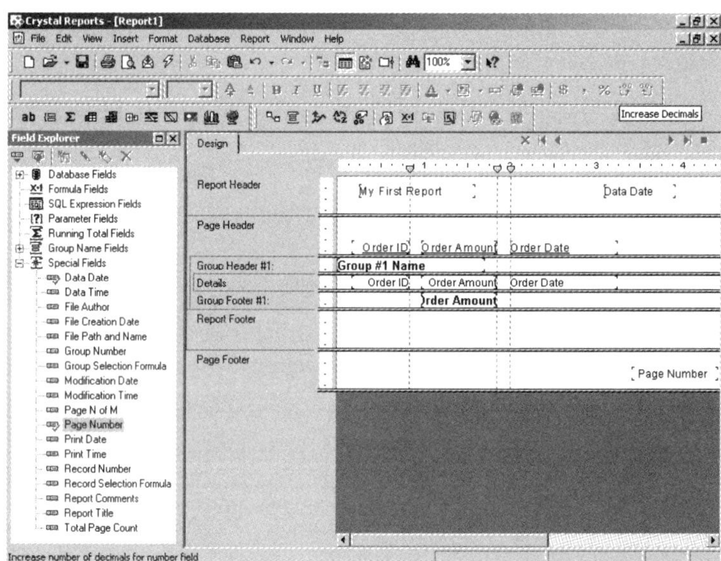

FIGURE 2-31 *The Field Explorer contains Special Fields for your reports.*

2. Add Special Fields as you add any other field: Click the field you want to add and drag it to your report, or click the Insert button. Remember that different sections print at different points in the report, so place your Special Fields accordingly. For this exercise, place the Page Number field on the right side of the Page Footer section.

TIP

If you want to use the Report Title, Report Comments, or File Author fields, you need to enter information in the Document Properties dialog box (select File, Summary Info). If you enter or change data in this dialog box after you place the Special Fields on your report, refresh your report (Select Report, Refresh Report Data, or click F5) and the new information displays.

Saving Your Report

Just like in many other software programs, you can locate the directory and folder where you would like to save your report by using the Save or Save As dialog boxes (see Figure 2-32). Your Crystal Reports have the extension .rpt. It is a good idea *not* to save your reports in the same directory as your program files. Instead, create a separate directory for all of your reports. This way, if for some reason you reinstall your software (an upgrade for example), you will not accidentally overwrite your reports.

BETTER TO SAVE WITH OR WITHOUT DATA?

You can save your report with or without data. Select File, Save Data with Report to turn the option on or off. A check mark appears next to the command when the option is on. By selecting File, Options, you can also change the global option on the Reporting tab.

There are several reasons why you may want to save a report with or without data. You might want to save data with the report if you want to send it to someone without database access, or if you are saving the report for later analysis.

Other times, you might want to turn this option off and not save the data. If you e-mail the report to someone who has database access, the RPT file will be smaller without the data.

When you finish designing a report and save it for the last time before deploying it, you might want to check the option Discard Saved Data when Loading Reports. This is found on the Reporting tab after selecting File, Options. This way, when a user opens the report, the Preview tab won't be full of old data. The report user will be forced to refresh the report to see any data, and thus is sure to collect the most current data from the database.

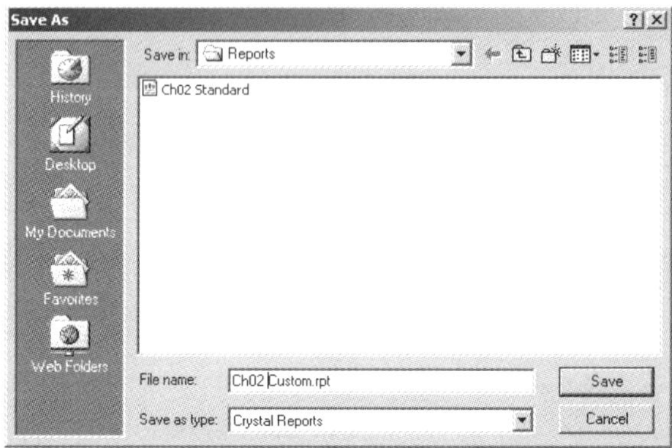

FIGURE 2-32 *Save your reports on your network, not within the Program Files directory.*

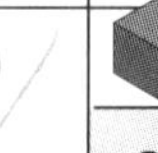

NOTE

Crystal Reports gives you the ability to autosave reports. To turn this option on, go to File, Options. On the Reporting tab, select the Autosave Reports After *n* Minutes check box, where *n* is a number of minutes you can specify.

Previewing Your Report

To collect data from your database and preview your report, you have several options:

- Click the Preview toolbar button to preview all records in the report.
- Select File, Print Preview to preview all records in the report.
- Select File, Preview Sample, which opens the Preview Sample dialog box, in which you can specify how many records you want to collect to preview.

All of these actions open the Preview tab in the Crystal Reports Designer. The Preview tab collects data from your database for your report and formats it according to the instructions you have given on the Design tab.

Crystal holds the data collected for the Preview tab in memory while you work on your report, even if you have not saved the report yet. This way, if you toggle between the Design and Preview tabs many times, the report doesn't have to refresh data from the database every time you preview; instead, the report just works with the data it has already collected. To refresh the report, which forces the report to collect all data that meets the criteria set in the Design tab, click the Refresh button in the standard toolbar or select Report, Refresh report data. When you save the report, you have the option to save the data with the report or to save the Design tab instructions only.

Figures 2-33 and 2-34 show the Design tab and Preview tab for the same report. Take a look to see how the elements in the Design tab translate to the various fields, objects, and other report components you see on the Preview tab.

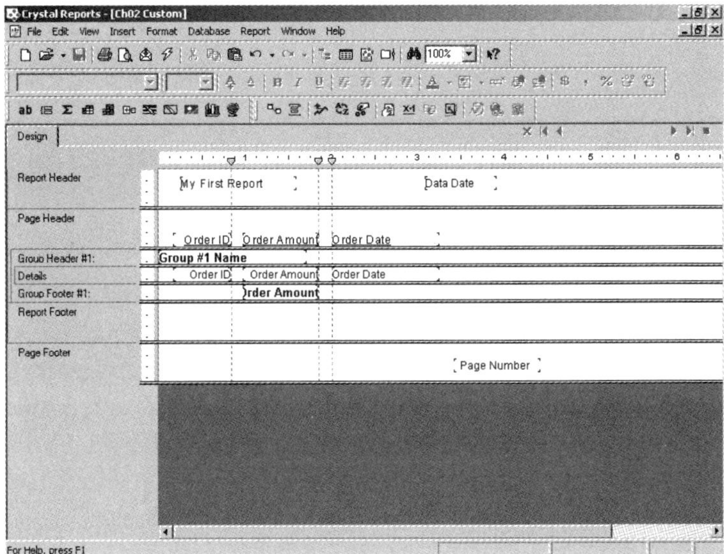

FIGURE 2-33 *The Design tab contains the instructions for building your report.*

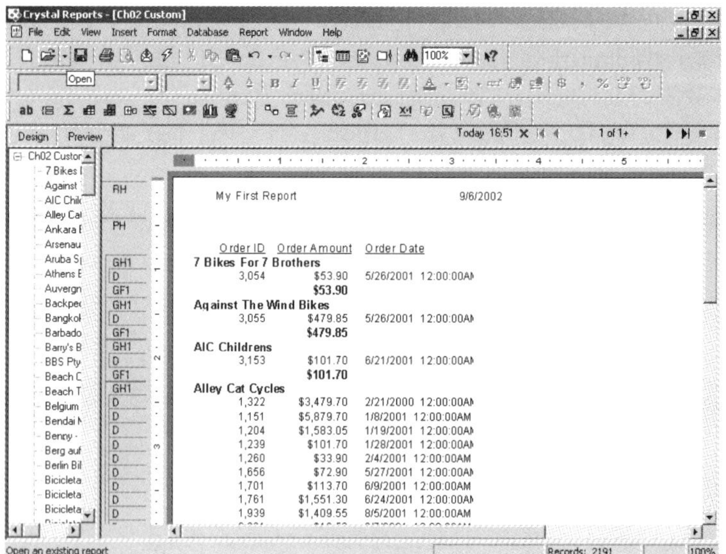

FIGURE 2-34 *The Preview tab collects data from your data source and shows you how your report will print.*

Select Criteria

Under normal circumstances, you always want to set your record selection criteria before you preview a report. This way, you narrow down the records included on your report; otherwise, you pull every record in the whole database! Our sample database is small, so in this example, I did not yet set selection criteria, and will do so in the next chapter in great detail.

Starting from an Existing Report

Once you have a few reports designed, it may be easier to use them as a starting point rather than beginning from scratch with a Blank Report. Sometimes, you need to start off fresh, but other times you can save time and energy by using past work.

In the Welcome to Crystal Reports dialog box, you can select Open an Existing Report, and choose from the list of reports recently designed or select the More Files option if you do not see the report you want. After opening the report you want to use, be sure to immediately rename the report by selecting File, Save As and entering a new name for the report. This way, you won't inadvertently make and save changes to the original report. After renaming the report, start making any changes you want.

The Open dialog box has toolbar buttons in the upper-right corner that allow you to see the first page preview of the report and to view the document properties of that report. In order for either of these features to work, you *must* have entered document properties under File, Summary Info when designing the report, and also selected the Save Preview Picture check box at the bottom of the Document Properties dialog box (see Figure 2-35). The report preview is small (see Figure 2-36), but the document properties (see Figure 2-37) can be useful to help you decipher what each particular report is about.

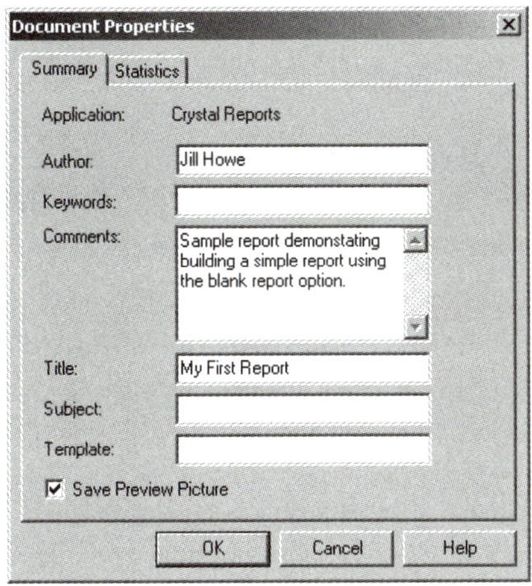

FIGURE 2-35 *Check the Save Preview Picture option at the bottom of the Document Properties dialog box to save the preview picture for viewing in the Open dialog box.*

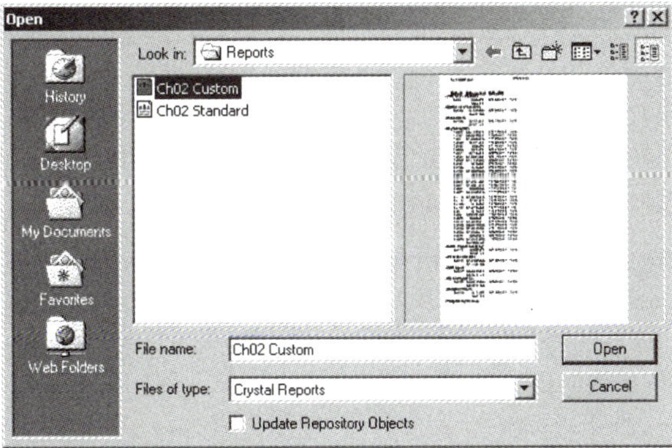

FIGURE 2-36 *Click the rightmost icon in the Open dialog box to view the preview picture of the first page of the selected report.*

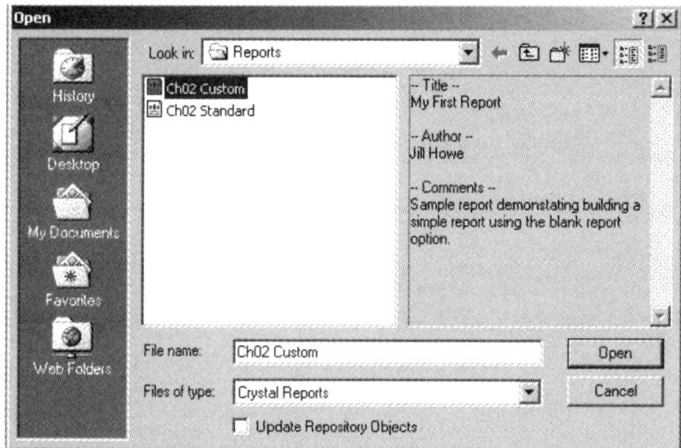

FIGURE 2-37 *Click the Properties button to view the properties of the selected report file. Information added to File/Summary Info is displayed as the properties of the file.*

Summary

This chapter has led you through designing a basic report with the Standard Report Wizard and the Blank Report option. You have connected to a data source and chosen tables and fields for a report. Basic grouping, sorting, and totaling were also covered. Hopefully, you now feel comfortable with the design interface and are excited to learn more about how you can use Crystal Reports to design reports specific to your needs.

The rest of the chapters in this book cover specific tasks and topics of report design in more detail, with explanations of all options, simple and complex examples, and hints. The following chapters start with the basics of each feature, and move into advanced application of each tool. On first glance, you may not understand the application of all the examples, but hopefully you will use the more advanced topics and examples as reference during your report writing experience.

This chapter conquered the tip of the iceberg. In the next chapters, you'll look at what is beneath the water! Crystal contains tons of functionality and options to help make your reports meet your specific expectations.

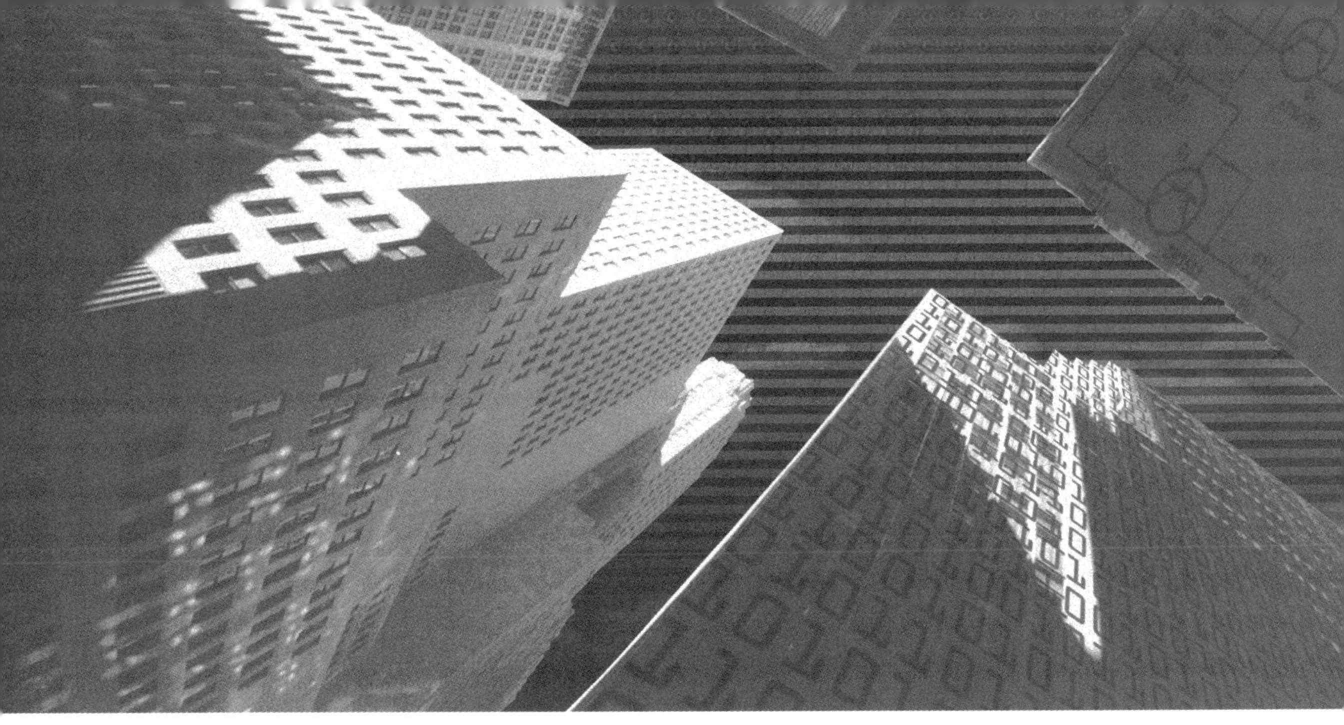

PART II

Adding to Your Crystal Report

Chapter 3

Connecting to Your Database and Linking Data

This chapter formally introduces you to the procedure for connecting a report to a database. The first section, "Databases 101," answers the question, "What *is* a database?" The purpose of this section is to help new users of databases get up to speed quickly, which it does by describing database terms and basic functionality. If you have worked with databases in the past, you may want to skip this section and move right ahead to "Using the Database Expert," later in the chapter, which describes how to use the Database Expert interface to connect to your database.

Once you have some background information about databases, this chapter introduces you to the numerous ways to connect Crystal Reports to your data. Most of these options have to do with what type of database (which vendor) you are reporting from, but there are alternative objects that are usable as data sources that can enhance reporting efficiency. The following are the types of connections:

- A direct access connection
- An Open Database Connectivity (ODBC) connection
- A Crystal Dictionary file
- A Crystal Query file
- A Command object built on the fly or from within the Crystal Repository

Both the Dictionary and Query options are downplayed in Crystal Reports 9 due to new functionality built into Crystal Reports; so much so that the tools to create these files are not even included in your software anymore. These tools are downloadable from the Crystal Decisions Web site.

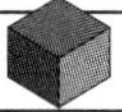

NOTE

Chapter 14 covers using SQL with Crystal Reports and the Crystal SQL Designer for queries, along with other SQL database-related information.

In this chapter, you will learn step by step how to connect reports directly to your database. There are many options in the Database Expert. To help you understand your connectivity options, here are some terms that will be used throughout this chapter:

- **Open Data Base Connectivity (ODBC).** This is basically a translation layer that is able to translate the structure and data in your database into a form that Crystal Reports can interpret and use.

- **Data source name (DSN).** A DSN alone is a neat package of instructions and files that provides an ODBC connection to your database.

- **Data source.** The term used to describe a DSN that has a specific database attached to it, meaning that it is ready to actively create a connection between a particular database and Crystal Reports. A Data source can also refer to any source of data that Crystal Reports is or will report from.

You will learn how to connect to your data using various connection methods. This chapter also covers how to use a Command object found in the Crystal Repository. Managing your database connections in the Database Expert is covered, along with how to add and remove database tables from reports, and how to link tables together.

Databases 101

The intent of this section is to provide some basic background information on databases. If you are knowledgeable with your databases and the concepts in general, skip this section. The intent of this book is to help report designers at all levels, so this section is for the newbies or anyone wanting a little refresher.

What Is a Database Anyway?

A database is any repository of information. There are many types of databases and many vendors that provide software and servers to hold information, but the basic terminology and concepts are all the same.

You can compare a database to a Rolodex. Way back when, before we were all totally computerized, many people had a Rolodex on their desk where they kept track of people who were pertinent to their job. If the person were in sales, their

Rolodex would have their customers' names and addresses. If the person were in purchasing, their Rolodex would have vendors' names and addresses. If the person were in charge of human resources for the company, their Rolodex would have the information for yet another set of people, employees, such as emergency contact information, insurance and benefit contacts, etc. Information would be filled out for each contact, with the name, office address, shipping address, phone number, main contact name, and whatever other information was important. This information would be in each employee's Rolodex, sorted alphabetically, on the appropriate employee's desk.

Now, with computers, this same information is stored in an electronic database. This database is much larger and holds much more information than a Rolodex file, because it is managed electronically rather than on paper. Instead of a separate Rolodex on each employee's desk, each "Rolodex" is a *table* in one database.

Tables, Records, and Fields

Think of a table as one person's Rolodex with a template index card. On that card, or *record*, you may have standard information that is written down for each contact, such as their name, address, shipping address, phone, fax, and so on. Each of these entries is called a *field*. Thus, each individual record in the table contains several fields of information. All the tables are stored in one database.

File Database or Relational Database?

There are countless types of databases that you might encounter, but they will most likely be either a file database or a relational database. The following sections describe each type.

Relational Databases

A relational database has many tables that can be related to one another. Some examples of relational databases with many tables are MS Access, SQL Server, Oracle, and Informix. A relational database contains tables that can be *linked* together based on the relationship between the records in two tables.

To pull information from two tables, such as Orders and Accounting, the report needs to link the Orders table to the Accounting table. This way, information for one customer from the Orders table will pull that same customer's information from the Accounting table.

Suppose you work in shipping and need to keep track of what was sent to whom and when. When you send an order to a customer, you get the order details (which products to send) from the Orders table and then match that customer's order with their name in the Customer table to get the address. This way, the person taking the order does not need to enter the shipping address every time the customer places an order. Likewise, shipping does not have to enter the shipping address into a shipping table every time they send something to the same customer; rather, they just get that address from the Customer table. This saves data entry time and helps reduce mistakes in data entry, because the address doesn't have to be entered over and over. Also, if the customer calls and wants to update their address, the update needs to be entered in only one place.

So, now you have a database, and that database contains tables. Each table contains records, and those records contain fields of data. You can reference several tables on one report by linking the tables together.

File Databases

Sometimes called "PC" type data, a file database is a file that resides either locally on your machine or on a network drive. Examples of file databases include dBase, FoxPro, Clipper, Btrieve, and Paradox databases, among others. Crystal Reports provides direct database drivers for these types of file databases. In the Database Expert, the Database Files folder allows you to navigate to your file database. Once the database is selected, Crystal Reports will use the appropriate database driver.

If you are not sure how Crystal Reports supports your database, go to the Crystal Decisions Web site and search Product Information for supported databases. You can also find various database descriptions and connection information in the online help files by searching with the keyword "database."

What Is a Link?

When you link tables, you want to use a field that uniquely identifies each subject— be it a person or customer, a product, a service, a supplier, etc. Good examples of the type of field that is effective for linking tables together include a customer ID number, social security number, or credit card number. The reason to use this type of field rather than a name field is that two customers might have the same name (such as a chain of stores with the same name that all purchase products from your company but are in different locations and are invoiced individually). The concepts of linking are discussed in detail later in this chapter, but for now, the goal is for you to understand that by linking tables together using a common field, you can extract information for one customer from several tables.

Indexes and Foreign Keys

Index and *foreign key* are terms that you will likely run into (if you have not already) in your database experience. Both are explained in the following section.

Consider the Rolodex analogy one last time. Suppose you need to find John Smith's phone number right away, but while looking it up in your Rolodex, you drop the Rolodex on the floor and the cards scatter everywhere. You have no choice but to start randomly sorting through cards as fast as you can. You may find the number quickly, or you may search through most of the cards before you come across it. This is how a table without an index searches for records. Sometimes it works okay, but sometimes it takes a long time to find the record you are looking for.

To be more efficient at finding John Smith's phone number, you could have disregarded the cards scattered on the floor and instead picked up the phone book, which is indexed. You would go right to *S*, then to Smith, then to first names beginning with *J*, and finally locate John. This is an efficient search for his phone number.

Tables in databases are indexed, similar to a phone book, which makes looking up information in the database efficient. Imagine trying to find a phone number for John Smith if the phone book were random. This is the task your computer is confronted with if your table is not indexed or you do not take advantage of this index when building a report. The index would start the lookup at *S* for Smith.

Foreign keys, which are also used in tables, are used to define the relationship between tables. For example, Customer ID is the primary key in the Customer table. Order ID is the primary key in the Orders table. Customer ID would be the foreign key in the Orders table, for it creates the relationship between the Customer and Orders tables and provides a way to link the Customer and Orders tables together.

It is efficient for your report if you can link to an indexed field, because it makes the lookup of information much more efficient.

With the forgoing background information and clarification of some basic database terms, you are ready to learn how to connect Crystal Reports to a database.

Determining Your Data Source Type

Before designing a report, you first need to know what type of data you will be working with. Business and technology use countless different names to refer to databases. Throughout this book, however, I will stick to the term "database" to refer to a generic source of data from which a report pulls information. "Database" always refers to whatever specific pool of data you pull from to generate a report. Crystal Reports supports reporting through several types of connections:

- **Database connection.** Databases, of which there are countless vendors, hold data either in files or tables, on your client workstation or a large server somewhere on your network. Crystal is able to connect to these databases through the use of various drivers listed in the Database Expert.

- **SQL Command.** A command is a SQL query that can be created on the fly or stored in the Crystal Repository. Its instructions are passed from Crystal to the database, returning only values from the database that meet the specifications and limitations of the statement. This technology allows people who know the database well to create a "pair of glasses" for other people to use when accessing the database. This metaphorical pair of glasses makes the database look much simpler to users who are not as familiar with the setup and structure of the database. People writing reports use SQL commands to access the database and make their job simpler.

- **Crystal Dictionaries.** The ability to connect to Crystal Dictionaries as a data source is for backwards compatibility purposes only.

- **Query.** The ability to connect to Crystal Queries as a data source is for backwards compatibility purposes only.

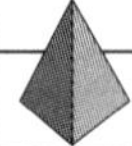

TIP

Stored procedures and views can be used as data sources by Crystal Reports. You use them just like you would use a table for a report. Chapter 14 covers reporting from stored procedures and views.

Starting a New Report

When starting a new report, you have the option to use a Report Wizard or a Blank Report. Basic design choices for both options are covered in detail in Chapter 2. The focus of this chapter is on understanding the actual connection and the relationship between Crystal and your database.

When starting a new report using either a Report Wizard or a Blank Report, you use the Database Expert to select a data source for your report, select tables, link those tables, and manipulate join and/or link relationships. This chapter focuses on the ODBC connection option, because you can apply the concepts learned here to the other connection types.

Using the Database Expert

Whether using a Report Wizard or starting with a Blank Report, the Database Expert is where you select a data source. If using a Report Wizard, the Data page has all the functionality of the Database Expert just a different name. If using the A Blank Report option, the Database Expert opens for selecting a data source for the report. Both the Data page and the Database Expert function exactly the same. Throughout this chapter Database Expert is referred to but the concepts are the same for the Data page of a wizard. The Database Expert (see Figure 3-1) offers several folders where you find available data sources listed, and other folders you can use to store and organize the connections you have set up.

The Database Expert has several options available for connecting to data and managing those connections (see Figure 3-1):

♦ **Current Connections.** Lists all current connections for all open reports. Also lists all connections to any reports opened during this session of using Crystal.

◆ **Repository.** A central location for storing report-related objects, including SQL Commands that can be used as data sources for the report.

◆ **Favorites.** You add data connections to this list to make them easy to find later. To add an item to the Favorites list (an ODBC connection, for example), select the connection you created and then right-click and choose Add to Favorites from the shortcut menu. Crystal copies the connection into the Favorites folder. Now, each time you open Crystal, that connection is all ready for you to use, so you don't have to create it or find it again.

◆ **History.** Lists a history of your last five connections. You can search and quickly find, for example, a certain connection that you used yesterday but did not add to Favorites.

◆ **Create New Connection.** Lists all the connection options available for Crystal Reports. Use the ODBC (RDO) option to select an ODBC data source already configured in the Windows ODBC Administrator.

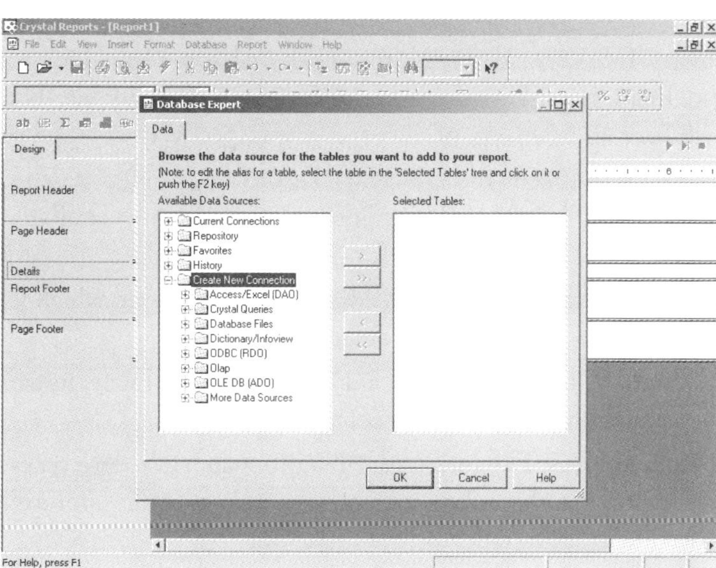

FIGURE 3-1 *Connect to any database and manage your connections from the Database Expert.*

Each of these folders can store data sources for easy reference and use while building reports. The Database Expert acts as an organized place from which you can connect to any database available to you for reporting. The Database Expert lists current connections and saves past connections, giving you easy return access in either the Favorites folder or the History folder.

To start, we will talk about the many options under Create New Connection.

Using Create New Connection

The Create New Connection node contains all of your data source options. Select one of the following options depending on what type of database you are trying to connect to:

- ◆ **Access/Excel (DAO).** Opens the Access/Excel (DAO) dialog box, in which you can make a direct connection to a Microsoft Access database or Microsoft Excel spreadsheet.

- ◆ **Crystal Queries.** Launches the Open dialog box, in which you can navigate to a Crystal Query file. This type of file will have a .qry extension.

- ◆ **Database Files.** Launches the Open dialog box, in which you can make a direct connection to a database.

- ◆ **Dictionary/InfoView.** Launches the Open dialog box, in which you can navigate to a Crystal Dictionary file or Seagate Info View file. These files will have an extension of .dc5 and .civ, respectively.

- ◆ **ODBC (RDO).** Opens the ODBC (RDO) dialog box, in which you can select an ODBC DSN. This folder will list all DSNs configured on the machine.

- ◆ **Olap.** Launches the Crystal OLAP Connection Browser, which you can use to connect to an OLAP data source.

- ◆ **OLE DB (ADO).** Opens the OLE DB (ADO) dialog box, in which you can specify an OLE DB connection.

- ◆ **More Data Sources.** Expands a list of additional data source types. In order to connect to these data sources, you must have the appropriate database client files installed on your machine.

Using ODBC Data Sources

ODBC is a standard language developed by Microsoft Corporation that allows software programs, like Crystal Reports, to communicate with a variety of databases. ODBC opens the door for Crystal to communicate and retrieve data from SQL and non-SQL databases. SQL stands for Structured Query Language, which is the standard language used to create, modify, maintain, and query relational databases. The term *ODBC data source* describes a database connection that has been configured in the Windows ODBC Administrator. The ODBC folder in the Database Expert lists any data sources that are already configured on your PC.

How Does the Translator Work?

Suppose Crystal speaks only English, and your database speaks only Spanish. In order for the two to communicate, both the English and Spanish need to be translated into a common language. This common language is the ODBC layer.

By default, Crystal Reports installs an ODBC driver that is used to communicate to the ODBC layer. This allows Crystal Reports to communicate with any database that can also speak to this ODBC layer. Most databases provide an ODBC driver that can make the connection from the database to the ODBC layer.

Selecting a Data Source

When you open the ODBC node under Create New Connection, DSNs are listed on the Data Source Selection page (see Figure 3-2). The items in this list are the exact DSNs listed in the User DSN, System DSN, and File DSN tabs of your computer's ODBC Administrator. If you do not see a data source for your particular database listed in this ODBC node, then a new data source must be created in the ODBC Administrator.

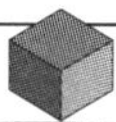 **NOTE**

The ODBC Administrator is a Windows tool for managing ODBC connections. The utility is in the Control Panel of Windows 9x operating systems, and in Administrative Tools of Windows 2000 and higher operating systems.

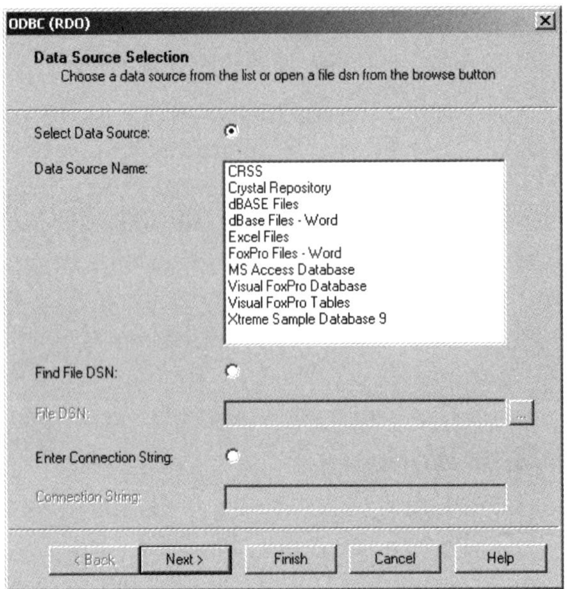

FIGURE 3-2 *Only ODBC DSNs configured on your machine will be listed in the Database Expert.*

You have several choices in the Data Source Name list, including generic DSNs that do not point to a particular MS Access database, like "MS Access Database," and DSNs that point to a particular database, like the Xtreme Sample Database 9.

NOTE

Your computer likely has different DSNs listed since the list of DSNs is machine specific.

After you select a data source from the list, click Next. If your database has any security, you must enter a valid user ID and password on the Connection Information page. Click Finish to connect to your data source. The data source name you connected to is listed under the node in which you found it. If there are tables, views, or stored procedures available for reporting in that database, these categories of objects will be listed (see Figure 3-3).

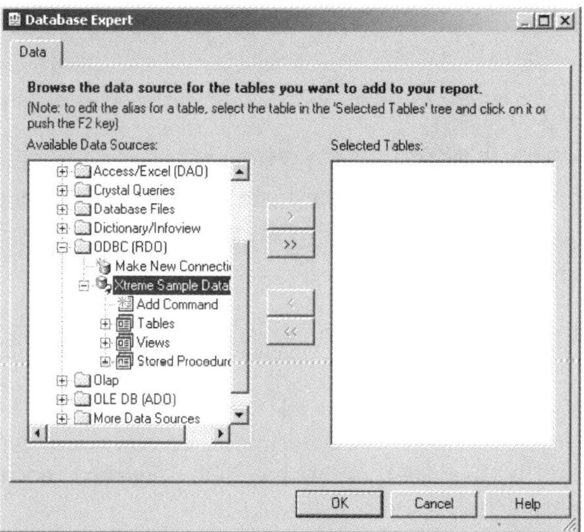

FIGURE 3-3 *The Xtreme Sample Database 9 contains tables, stored procedures, and views available for reporting.*

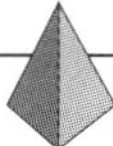

TIP

Many businesses strive to keep all their data sources standardized so that reports can be shared among all users and PCs in an organization. Because of this, check with your network, database, or ODBC administrator before creating your own data source if you do not see what you need in the ODBC node.

You will most likely be able to select your data source from this ODBC list, log on, and be on your way.

Using a SQL Command

Once connected, all SQL type data sources (refer to Figure 3-2), have an option to create a SQL Command, however these data source connection do not store the commands. Commands are stored in the Crystal Repository. To use one of these commands, follow these steps:

1. Open the Database Expert.

2. Select the Crystal Repository node (under the Repository node) from the Available Data Sources list.

3. Locate the command to use by navigating to the Commands folder (see Figure 3-4).

4. Select the command you want to use, and move it to the Selected Tables list by clicking the forward arrow button (>).

5. If the command employs a parameter, the Enter Parameter Values dialog box prompts you to select a value that will be used by the command for collecting data (see Figure 3-5).

NOTE

Where you find commands within the Repository is dependent on how you or your company set up the structure. The Crystal Repository and SQL Commands each have their own chapter later in this book.

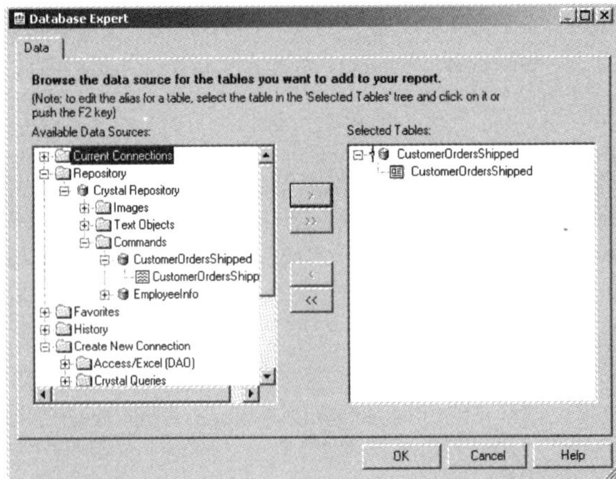

FIGURE 3-4 *Navigate the Repository node to find stored commands.*

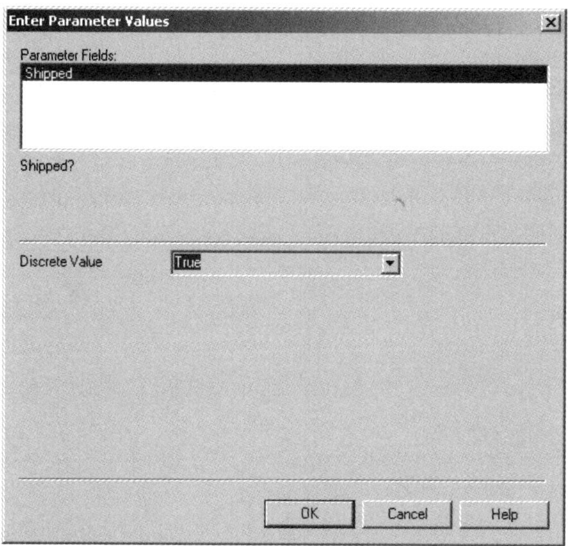

FIGURE 3-5 *If a command employs a parameter, you must answer the prompt before the command is listed in the Selected Tables list.*

More Data Sources

The More Data Sources node under Create New Connection in the Database Expert provides connectivity to various data sources.

Selecting any of the options in the More Data Sources node (see Figure 3-6) launches a connection window or an installer dialog box.

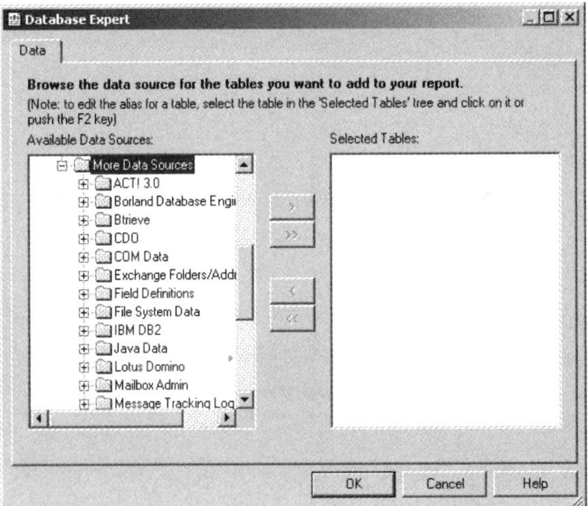

FIGURE 3-6 *There are many data sources available under More Data Sources folder.*

Each database has a slightly different connection window. You will be asked to select the actual database, provide password information if applicable, and sometimes select other options. If the option you selected is not installed, you will be asked to insert your Crystal Reports 9 CD into your CD-ROM drive. A typical install does not install the database driver for every option listed under More Data Sources.

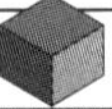

NOTE

Once you work through the connection window(s) for your particular database, that data source is listed under the appropriate folder. You can copy the connection information to the Favorites folder for future use by right-clicking and choosing "Add to Favorites." By default, the connection information will not be saved once you close Crystal Reports, except in the History folder (which only saves the last five connections).

Regardless of how you connect to your data source, you now have tables listed in the Database Expert. Select the tables you want for the report by double-clicking them or selecting them and clicking the forward arrow button (>) (see Figure 3-7). When you have selected all the tables you need, click OK or click the Links tab, both of which will open the tab.

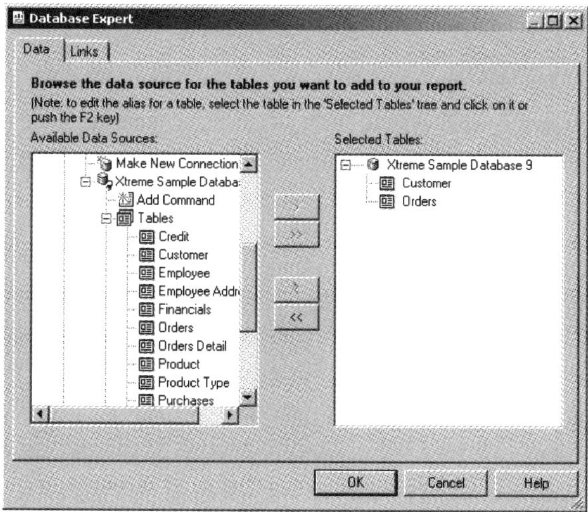

FIGURE 3-7 *Move tables to the Selected Tables list to be available for reporting.*

NOTE

From the Database Expert, right-click on your database connection and choose Options. This opens the Options dialog box containing numerous database options. For example, select the Views or Stored Procedures check boxes if you want to be able to see and use views or stored procedures in your reports (these options are checked on by default). Options in this dialog box also let you manipulate how your tables are listed—by name, description, or both—and sort the tables and/or fields alphabetically, which sometimes makes it easier to find tables and fields. Some of the Advanced Options will be noted where appropriate later in this book, and you can always search Crystal's Help files for more information, using the keyword phrase "database tab."

Linking Tables Together

The Links tab opens automatically when you click OK in the Database Expert if you selected more than one table for your report. Using the Links tab, link your tables together and manipulate the join type. Before we jump right into a discussion of linking tables and join types, let's look at *why* you need to link tables.

Why You Need to Link Tables

When designing reports for your business, you most likely need to link two or more tables together in order to have all the information you need available. Most databases have many tables, each table containing a certain type of information.

Figure 3-8 shows two tables from the Free Credit Bank database, a fictitious credit card company. The company's database contains information needed for reports. To have information on your report from both tables, you need to link the tables together. In addition, the fields used for linking must contain matching values. Linking works best when fields are properly indexed, as in this example (how do you know if your fields are indexed? We should probably include a section which explains the coloured tabs). In order for Auto Link to work properly, the fields must also have matching names and data types, and for string fields, the field length must also match.

It is important to carefully choose the fields to use for linking. An easy way to choose a field, if two tables share several common fields, is to choose the field that uniquely identifies each record—like a social security number, bank account number, or credit card number.

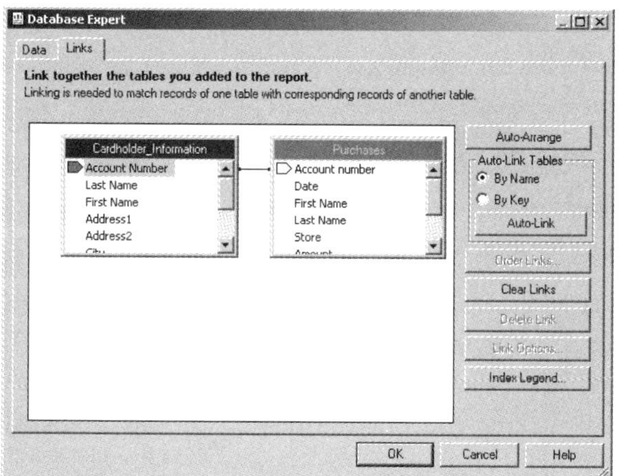

FIGURE 3-8 *Two tables from Free Credit Bank's database.*

When you link two tables together, you need the information from one table to match the corresponding information from the other table. Suppose you work for Free Credit Bank and need to design a report to run monthly invoices. The company has two tables that you have decided to use for your report, Cardholder_Information and Purchases.

To design and run a report to process each cardholder's monthly bill, you might want the cardholder name and address, account number, date of purchase, store/vendor, and amount of each purchase. To design this information into a report, you need several fields from both the Cardholder_Information and Purchases tables, shown in Figure 3-8.

Correct linking ensures that the information the report pulls from the Cardholder Information table matches the information pulled from the Purchases table. This way, the cardholder's name printed on each bill matches the purchases listed on the bill.

Account Number is the best field to link in this example. Every cardholder has a unique account number, so even if two or more cardholders have the same name (the reason the Cardholder Name field is not the best choice), they will each get their correct bill.

Using the Links Tab

The Database Expert is Crystal Reports' tool for linking tables. The Links tab of the Database Expert shows the tables that you added to your report and either links them for you by using Auto Link or allows you to manually link them. The Database Expert gives you several linking options, including adding and removing tables and databases, and manipulating the link direction and join type.

The Links tab opens automatically when you click OK after selecting tables in the Database Expert if you have selected more than one table for your report. You can open the Expert at any time by selecting Database, Database Expert and selecting the Link tab or by or by clicking the Link button ▫▫ on the toolbar to open the link tab directly.

Letting Crystal Perform Auto Linking

The Crystal Reports Auto Link feature links tables together automatically. Crystal looks at the tables you have chosen for your report, evaluates the fields in them, and links the tables together by name or by key, depending on which of the following radio buttons you select on the Links tab:

- ◆ **By Name.** The fields used for linking must have a matching field name and data type. For string type fields field length must also match.
- ◆ **By Key.** Fields are used for linking based on primary key and foreign key relationships.

Whenever you select multiple tables for a report or add a new table to an existing report, Auto Link links the tables together and shows you the links in the Links tab of the Database Expert.

Auto Link can be a great tool—use it to have Crystal figure out which fields to link so you don't have to worry about it! Unfortunately, the success of Auto Link is dependent on how your database was set up, and how well it was structured. Crystal's Auto Link cannot always distinguish between two or more sets of linkable fields if the By Name option is used. If you select the By Key option, there is a much better chance that linking will be correct dependent on the relationships set up within your database.

lt into tables in a database by the database designer. Database
be added by Crystal Reports.

n to the Free Credit Bank example, Crystal has no way to know that
older Name to Cardholder Name is not as good as linking Account
ccount Number. Selecting the Auto-Link Tables By Name option
elds that meet the criteria listed earlier. Auto-Link Tables By Key
y, because the relationships were defined in the database. If too
e created, you will need to delete the unnecessary links.

o links as many fields as it can between two tables, sometimes draw-
s between them. Most of the time, only one link between two tables
ost efficient; more links are effective if multifield indexes are in use.
king creates too many links, you can click Clear Links to get rid of
en manually draw only the links you want.

es

e that Auto Link won't work efficiently for your tables, you need to
le links manually, as follows:

to make the Database Expert as large as possible (maximized) so that you
e the tables easily. Sometimes, all of your tables won't show in the window.
imize the window, then you'll have less scrolling to do.

ick the field in the table you want to link from and drag the pointer
er to the field in the table you want to link to.

2. Once both fields are highlighted and the pointer has changed to include
a small arrow icon, let go of the mouse button (see Figure 3-9). Crystal
shows the link that you drew as a line between the two fields.

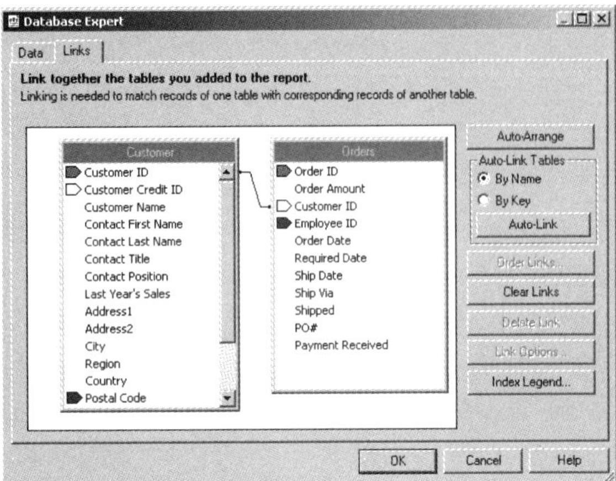

FIGURE 3-9 *Highlight the field you are linking from and drag the pointer to the field you are linking to.*

You can link many tables together, like running a string from one to the next to the next. You can also link one table to two other tables. Rules and options apply to the type of link that you use, which the following section covers.

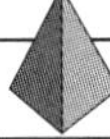

TIP

You might want to work with your database administrator (DBA) to find out how to link your tables and in which order they need to be linked. Generally, you place your main table on the left-hand side of the Links tab and link from left to right. You can also clean up the window from time to time by clicking the Auto-Arrange button to automatically align the tables.

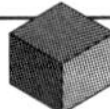

NOTE

For more information, search the online help files using the keyword "link" to locate many subcategories of extra information.

Using Key or Indexed Fields for Linking

An indexed or key field is a field used by the database to organize and sort records in order to quickly retrieve data. This is the type of indexing that works like a phone book (as covered earlier in the section "Databases 101"). The database designer indexed specific fields, which are usually fields that will best assist with looking up data in that table. Database designers use multifield indexes when records require more than one field to be uniquely identified.

In Figure 3-9, the Links tab marks the indexed fields with colored icons to the left of the field. This makes linking easier, but more importantly indexes help your report process faster.

Join Types and Other Link Options

After applying Auto Link or manually drawing links between tables, you may want to alter some of the default settings that Crystal assigns to each link.

Linking Database Objects

Returning again to the Free Credit Bank example, if you connect to your database using an ODBC connection and use the default Inner join type, you would only print statements for cardholders with purchases. The report would not include statements for cardholders without any purchases during the statement period, as there would be no matches in the Purchases table.

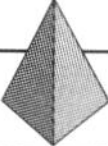

TIP

When linking tables, you will produce the fastest process time for the report by using the "main" table for your report as the first "from" table. This has to do with selection criteria (covered in Chapter 4). If your Select statement applies to a field (preferably an indexed field) used from the first table, fewer records are brought into the Crystal print engine for processing. See the online help topic "SQL database considerations" by searching with the keyword "link."

Join Types

When joining tables, you can change the join type.

By default, the join will be an Inner join. Crystal gives you the ability to change this to one of several different join types:

- **Inner.** Includes all records that have a match between the tables.
- **Left Outer.** Includes all records that have a match between the tables, and all records that have a value in the left table but no value in the right table.
- **Right Outer.** Includes all records that have a match between the tables, and all records that have a value in the right table but no value in the left table.
- **Full Outer.** Includes all records in the linked tables whether there are matching values or not.

Back to Free Credit Bank. If you link the Cardholder Information table to the Purchases table using a Right Outer join, your report would have every purchase made from the Purchases table, and a matching Cardholder Information record. If a cardholder did not have any purchases, that Cardholder Information record would not print. However, if for some reason a record existed in the Purchases table without a related Cardholder Information record, that Purchases record would still print on the report.

Link Types

Link types can be used in addition to join types to help control what records are returned from the database. Link type indicates how the fields being linked (between two tables) are compared. The following are the link types:

- **Equal.** The result set includes all the records where the linked field value in both tables is an exact match.
- **Greater than.** The result set includes all records where the linked field value from the primary table is greater than the linked field value in the lookup table.
- **Less than.** The result set includes all records where the linked field value in the primary table is less than the linked field value in the lookup table.

◆ **Greater or Equal.** The result set includes all records where the linked field value in the primary table is greater than or equal to the linked field value in the lookup table.

◆ **Less or Equal.** The result set includes all records where the linked field value in the primary table is less than or equal to the linked field value in the lookup table.

◆ **Not Equal.** The result set includes all records where the linked field value in the primary table is not equal to the linked field value in the lookup table.

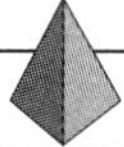

TIP

Search Crystal Reports' online help using the keyword phrase "join types" for more information on each of these join and link types. There is also a sizable section in the user's guide.

Change the Join Type of an Existing Link

The Options dialog box is available to help you change join and link types, as follows:

1. On the Links tab of the Database Expert, select the link you want to change. Click the Link Options button, or right-click the link and choose Link Options. The Link Options dialog box opens (see Figure 3-10).

2. In the Join Type area, select a different join type.

3. In the Link Type area, change the link type if desired and then click OK.

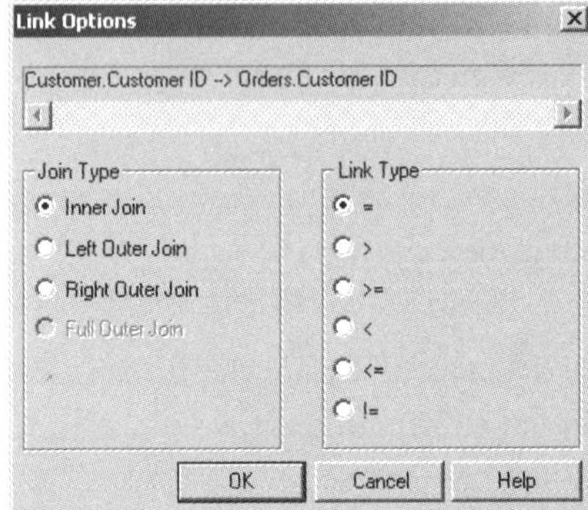

FIGURE 3-10 *Change the join type of your link using the Link Options dialog box.*

You can also manipulate the arrangement of tables in the Links tab to manipulate the join types. The important thing to remember is which table you linked from and which you linked to so that it is easier if you start changing the join types.

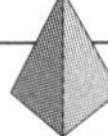

TIP

You can change the link direction if you want, which is different from changing the join type. Select the link, right-click, and choose Reverse Link from the shortcut menu. This reverses which table is the "from" table and which is the "to" table. After reversing a link direction, I suggest that you move your tables so that your link lines flow left to right (or simply click Arrange Tables). Since culturally we usually read English from left to right, it might be easier for you to keep track of tables when arranged left to right.

Adding and Removing Databases and Tables

Once you have a report design started, you can add and delete databases and tables at any time using the Database Expert.

Adding Databases and Tables

You can add tables to your report either from a data source the report already connects to or from a different data source. Use the Database Expert to select more tables from the currently used data source, or select another data source from the list, log on, and add tables to the Selected Tables list.

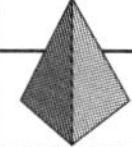

TIP

When linking tables from different database types, you must use fields of the same data type. If linking tables from two databases of the same type, any field type is okay (such as an Oracle table from database A to an Oracle table in database B).

Removing Databases and Tables

To remove a table from your report, first be sure that your report doesn't use that table in any way and that you do not need the table to link through to another table. If you remove a table still in use, you may get an error message that prevents you from removing the table. Or, you may not get an error message until you try to run or preview the report.

Similar to adding a table to a report, simply select the table in the Selected Tables list and click the backward arrow button (<) to remove the table from the list. This removes the table from the report as well.

Verifying Your Database and Changing Its Location

You may find at some point that you want to verify the connection to your database, or need to point an existing report to a new database server. Several options for managing your database connection are found on the Database menu:

◆ **Verify Database.** If the structure of the database has changed in any way since you designed the report, you can check for any changes by selecting Database, Verify Database. If the database is up to date, the message shown in Figure 3-11 appears. If any changes are detected, Crystal opens a Map Fields dialog box that allows you to map old field names to the new field names. Fields that no longer exist in the database will be removed from the report.

◆ **Set Datasource Location.** If the database location or name has changed since you created the report, use this option (Database, Set Datasource Location) to set the new location or name (see Figure 3-12). This command automatically converts the database driver to the data source chosen.

◆ **Log On/Off Server.** This command opens the Data Explorer, in which you can select a data source to log on to or off of.

FIGURE 3-11 *Make sure there have been no changes to the database since the report was built.*

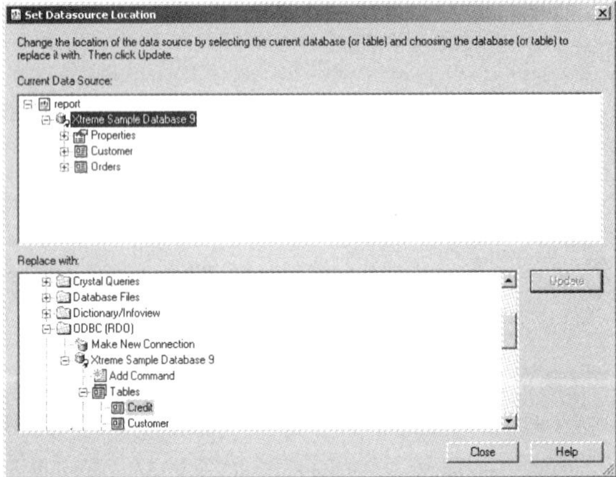

FIGURE 3-12 *Point your report to a new or different data source.*

More information on each of these options is available in the online help files. Search using the name of the option, such as "verify database."

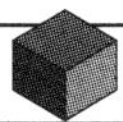

NOTE

More information on the preceding three options can be found in Chapter 14.

Summary

The type of data source you use for reporting determines which connection type you need. You can set up favorites that you use often, and see the history of the last five sources you have used as well as which data sources you are currently connected to. Once you connect to your data source, you must link tables together so that the data within those tables is available for your report.

You have link options that allow you to manipulate the link direction and join type. This affords you more control over what information to actually include on any given report. Two common realizations when people first preview their reports are that data seems to be missing or data seems to be repeating itself. Both of these problems often turn out to be solvable by fine-tuning the linking for that report. As a reminder, Appendix A offers more information pertaining to setting up ODBC data sources, and Chapter 14 covers SQL database concepts and other general database information that may enhance your knowledge.

Chapter 4

This chapter explains the ins and outs of record selection. Chapter 1 introduced record selection, and in Chapter 2, you performed record selection using the Standard Report Expert. In this chapter, you will learn in more detail how to set selection criteria using the Select Expert, as well as how to create more advanced selection criteria using formulas. Though the Select Expert is an excellent tool, you may find that formulas enhance your ability to retrieve the exact data you desire on a report. We have not covered formulas yet (we will in Chapter 7), but you will find formula examples in this chapter that you can come back to once you have worked through Chapter 7.

Using the Select Expert

The Select Expert is the tool to use to set selection criteria for your report. As explained in previous chapters, you need to select which records from your database you want to print on a report. Often, you neither want nor need every record from certain tables. Rather, you want to filter out records not applicable to the purpose of your report. By selecting only the records that you need, your report avoids unnecessary information.

For example, if you run a report to print invoices, you might want to limit the records on your report to only charges incurred during a set date range. You would therefore set up record selection criteria to include only records that fall within the date range that you specify, using a monthly billing cycle function or specific begin and end dates.

Another example might be a human resources report, where you need to include only records of employees who are taking part in a certain benefit plan. In this case, you would define selection criteria to filter out any employees not participating in the particular benefit plan.

Crystal Reports places no limit on the number of selection criteria you can set up for one report. You can use any field available within your report as the basis for selection criteria. The fields you use for selection criteria need not be on the report itself, just in a table properly linked for use by the report.

Setting Selection Criteria

Setting selection criteria involves the Select Expert, which makes setting criteria straightforward, using drop-down lists. Selection criteria can be added to a report at any time, though it is suggested that you set selection criteria before previewing or refreshing any report for the first time.

Add Selection Criteria to a Report

The following steps demonstrate how to add selection criteria to the sample report you created in Chapter 2:

1. Click the Select Expert toolbar button ![] on the Advanced toolbar, or select Report, Select Expert. The Choose Field dialog box opens (see Figure 4-1).

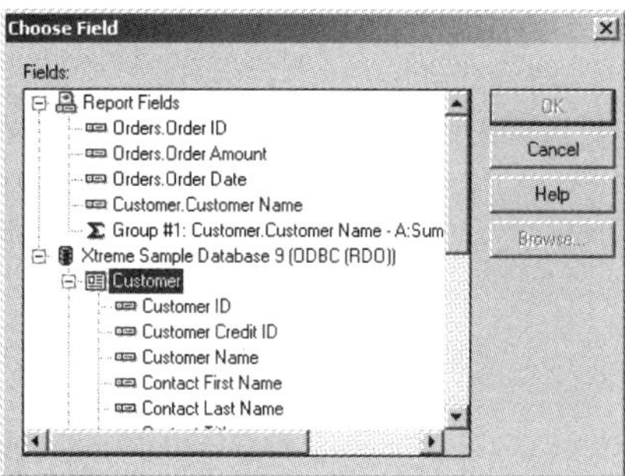

FIGURE 4-1 *Select a field in the Choose Field dialog box.*

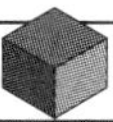

NOTE

If you have a field selected on your report when you open the Select Expert, that field appears as a tab in the Select Expert, bypassing the Choose Field dialog box. If you do not want to use that particular field for your selection criteria, click Delete to delete the tab and then click New to open the Choose Field dialog box.

2. Scrolling if necessary, click the field on which to base your selection criteria. For this report, the Country field is selected within the Customers table. Click OK.

3. The Select Expert opens with the name of the field you chose listed as a tab. One drop-down list appears that, by default, displays the option *is any value* (see Figure 4-2).

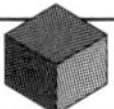

NOTE

If you leave the selection criteria with the default values, no selection will take place. Think of setting criteria as an English statement, such as "select all records where department 'is equal to' sales."

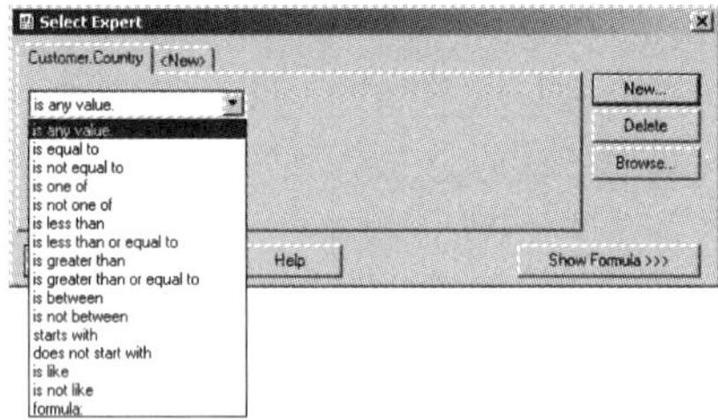

FIGURE 4-2 *The Select Expert opens and supplies a drop-down list to help you set selection criteria.*

4. Select a condition from the drop-down list to narrow the selection criteria. (I selected the *is equal to* condition.) Table 4-1 lists and describes the various conditions available in the drop-down list. Once you select anything other than *is any value* from the list, at least one more drop-down list becomes available (see Figure 4-3).

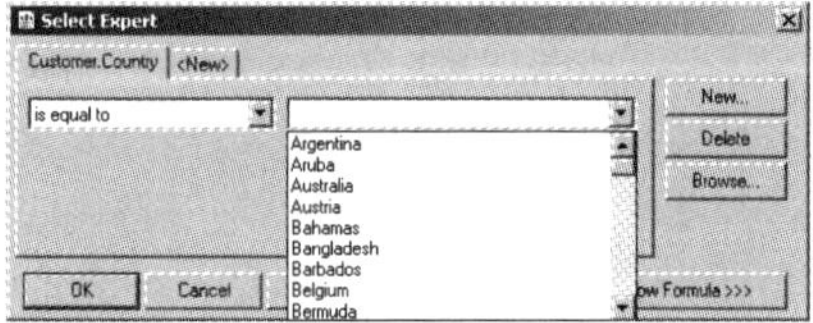

FIGURE 4-3 *Use the additional drop-down lists to continue setting up your criteria statement.*

Table 4-1 Selection Criteria Conditions

Condition	Includes records with a value that . . .
is any value	Equals any value. This condition includes all records.
is equal to	Equals the single value you specify.
is not equal to	Equals anything *except* the single value you specify.
is one of	Equals one of the values you specify.
is not one of	Equals anything *except* one of the values you specify.
is less than	Is less than the value you specify.
is less than or equal to	Is less than or equal to the value you specify.
is greater than	Is greater than the value you specify.
is greater than or equal to	Is greater than or equal to the value you specify.
is between	Falls between the two values you specify.
is not between	Falls outside of the range you specify.
starts with	Starts with character you specify.
does not start with	Does not start with character you specify.
is like	Use a wildcard characters to test for values containing characters you specify.
is not like	Use wildcard characters to test for values without the characters you specify.
is in the period	Falls within the period defined by the built-in CR function you select, such as lastfullweek or over90days.
is not in the period	Falls outside of the period you select.
formula	Returns *true* when evaluated in a formula you write.
* or ?	Matches the value with wildcards you enter. An asterisk replaces any number of characters. A question mark replaces one character.

NOTE

Certain conditions in the table are available only for specific field types. For example, *is in the period* is only available if basing selection criteria on a date field.

BROWSING FIELDS AND CHECKING FOR CASE SENSITIVITY

Opening the second drop-down list in the Select Expert browses your database field for values. If the browse does not show the value you want to use, just type the value in the box. However, note the format of the browsed field values that do appear in the list, making certain the value you type uses the correct format and case.

The option to browse distinct values is turned on by default. This means that when you browse a field, Crystal will return the first 500 unique values that it finds in the database. I suggest that you change this, by going to File, Options, clicking the Database tab, and clearing the Select Distinct Data for Browsing check box. The reason I suggest not using this option is speed—it takes much longer to browse through enough database data to get 500 distinct values that it does to just collect 500 values. Collecting the distinct values is not usually critical to choosing a selection criteria value.

A combination of your database and database driver indicates whether or not your database is case sensitive. If your data is case sensitive, you must match the case (and format) of how the data exists in your database when entering your selection criteria.

When using the Database File connection, your data may or may not be case sensitive. Microsoft Access was designed to allow case insensitivity. Many others in the DB2 family of databases are case sensitive. The same applies if you use a SQL or ODBC connection: Case sensitivity

(continues)

5. The second drop-down list contains actual field data from your data source. Type or select a value to complete the selection criteria (sometimes not every value from the field appears in the list). For this example, USA is selected from the list of data.

6. Click the New tab or New button to add more selection criteria to your report. I am going to set a second selection criteria for this report by choosing the Order Date field from the Orders table. Select the *is between* condition from the leftmost drop-down list. Then, select the January 1, 2001 date from the top drop-down list and December 31, 2001 from the bottom drop-down list (see Figure 4-4).

7. Once you have set up a tab for each criterion, click OK to close the Select Expert.

Your selection criteria is now set. You can go back to the Select Expert at any time to add to or change criteria. The next time you preview your report, a dialog opens asking if you want to Refresh report data or Use saved data. If you have narrowed the selection criteria—meaning you want to have fewer records on the report—you can select Use saved data. If you have changed the selection criteria to include different records, or intend to add more records to the report, you need to Refresh report data. Previewing does not necessarily refresh the report, it just shows the Preview tab with the records that already exist with the report.

BROWSING FIELDS AND CHECKING FOR CASE SENSITIVITY (CONTINUED)

depends on the database itself and the options set up for that database.

Ask your database administrator whether or not you need to go into File, Options and select the Case-Insensitive SQL Data check box on the Database tab.

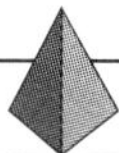

TIP

Which option you select in the first drop-down list affects the choices available. Choosing *is between* displays two drop-down lists with the word "and" in between. Choosing *is one of* displays a list plus Add and Delete buttons.

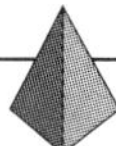

TIP

You may find it easiest to select a date from the drop down list and then just modify it to the date you want. The date must be in the Crystal data function format.

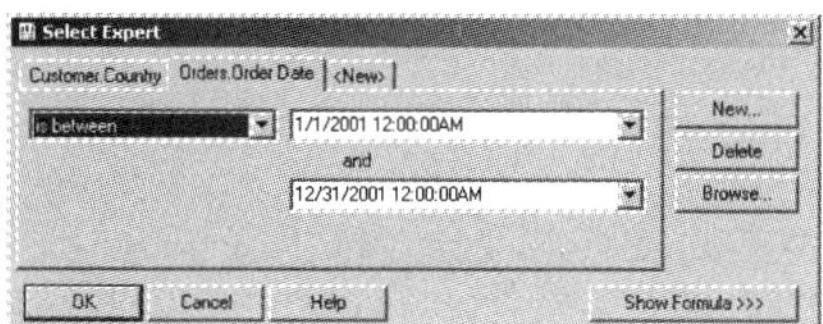

FIGURE 4-4 *Set selection criteria with a start and stop date using the* is between *condition.*

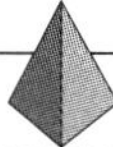

TIP

You can have the selection criteria formula print on a report by inserting the Special Field named Selection Formula. This option is available whether you customized the formula yourself or you let Crystal build the formula for you with the Select Expert. This field is limited to 256 characters, so if your selection formula is longer than that, it will be cut off and not complete.

Beyond the Select Expert: Writing Selection Formulas

As you develop a report, you often have very specific selection criteria in mind. But sometimes you may find that when you try to set up the selection criteria with the Select Expert, you can't quite make it work using the options provided. You might find that the Select Expert does not offer the comparison options you need, or that the way the Select Expert links multiple selection criteria does not work the way you need for a certain report. If you do encounter this problem, don't worry. You can either edit the selection criteria formula created by the Select Expert or enter your own selection formula from scratch. With this feature, you have the power to manipulate selection criteria to meet your exact needs.

Using the Formula Editor for Selection Formulas

Crystal offers several ways for you to create or modify selection formulas—all of which are basically the same, but some are much easier to use than others.

Formula Option in the Conditions List

In the Select Expert, the conditions list contains a *formula* option (refer to Figure 4-2). I suggest not using this option, because Crystal just gives you a blank space, leaving you completely on your own to write the formula with no assistance. Sure, many of you are certainly capable of writing formulas from scratch (at least, you will be after Chapter 7!), but there is an easier way.

Expand the Formula within the Select Expert

Instead of selecting the *formula* option from the drop-down list of conditions, use these simple steps to start with the Select Expert and then customize with the Formula Editor:

1. Build a Select statement as close to what you need as possible with the drop-down menus.

2. Expand the Select Expert by clicking the Show Formula button in the lower-right corner. This displays the selection formula created by the Expert in a text box (see Figure 4-5).

3. Make changes or additions in the text box or, better yet, open the full Formula Editor, which has various tools to assist you in writing the formula, by clicking the Formula Editor button on the Select Expert (see Figure 4-6).

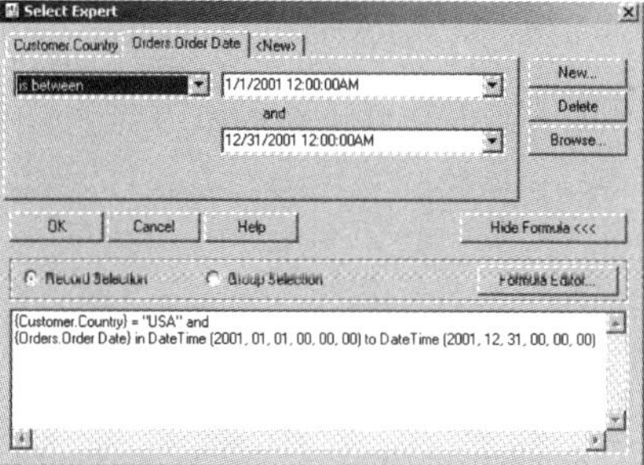

FIGURE 4-5 *Click Show Formula to expand the Select Expert to show the current selection formula.*

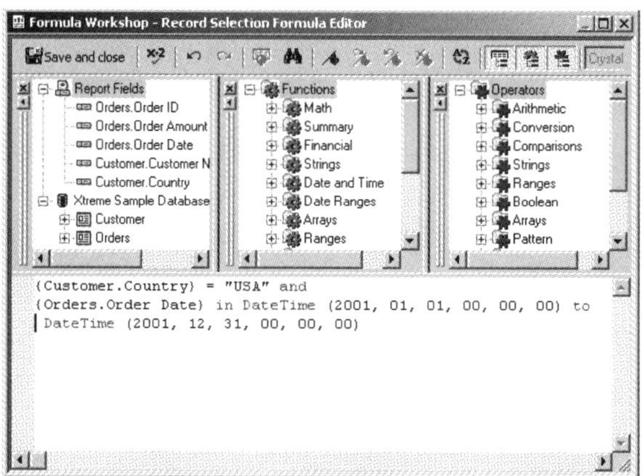

FIGURE 4-6 *Click Formula Editor in the Select Expert to launch the Formula Editor with the current selection formula ready for editing.*

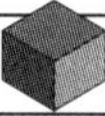 **NOTE**

You must click Show Formula before the Formula Editor button appears. Also, you'll notice that the button name is Formula Editor, yet this launches a dialog box named Formula Workshop. The Formula Editor is the traditional formula editor in Crystal Reports. It now lives within a larger tool named the Formula Workshop, which contains the Formula Editor and other formula writing tools. Chapter 7 covers writing formulas with the Formula Editor, and Chapter 9 covers the new functionality of the Formula Workshop.

With the full Formula Editor available, you have all the tools at your fingertips to help you write your formula. The Formula Editor has some great features, like double-clicking fields, functions, and operators into your formula with the correct syntax rather than typing them out, and having Crystal check your formula for any inadvertent errors. So, why try to write the formula on your own when you can take advantage of the Formula Editor with two more clicks?

Though Chapter 7 covers formulas in detail, the following section suggests a few ways to use formulas to set up and modify your selection criteria. Formulas may seem complicated, but once you go through Chapter 7, you will have a new perspective. Use this section later as a reference to get ideas for selection formulas that you may need to use in your reports. As you read on, focus more on the possibilities that formulas offer than on the actual formula language itself.

Selection Formula Examples

You may need to write formulas for your selection criteria if the options available in the Select Expert do not meet your needs. You may also want to write formulas to compensate for inconsistencies in your data or other special circumstances. This section contains some examples of when and how you might edit a selection formula.

Compensate for Inconsistent Case

Many times, data entry inconsistencies plague data. A basic example of this is how state or region data might be entered into your database.

The value entered for Massachusetts might be Mass. or MA, depending on the age of the data. Writing a formula in the Select Expert allows you to collect all data for this state, regardless of whether it is entered as Mass. or MA (see Figure 4-7).

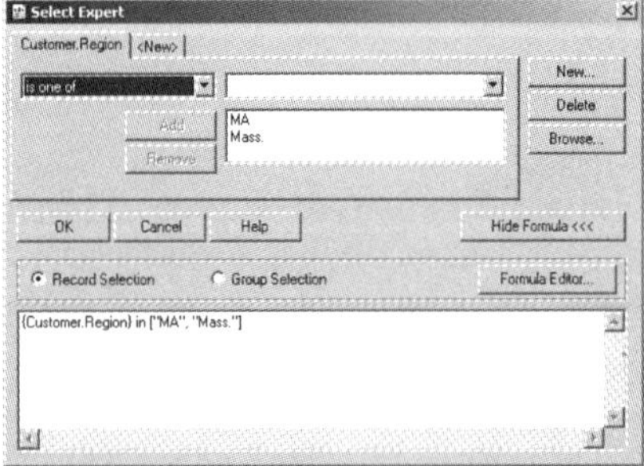

FIGURE 4-7 *Use the is one of option to accommodate different possible values for Massachusetts.*

Sometimes adding several criteria to the formula may not be enough, though. What if some data is entered as Mass without the period, or some data is entered as Ma or Ma. with a period? These options can all cause problems collecting the proper data from your database for your report.

One solution is to add all the potential options to your selection criteria. This will work but can become complicated and overwhelming with so many options. Another solution may be to use a wildcard with the Uppercase() function, to force the value of the field into uppercase and then evaluate it for a match.

Set selection criteria the best you can by using the Select Expert (see Figure 4-8).

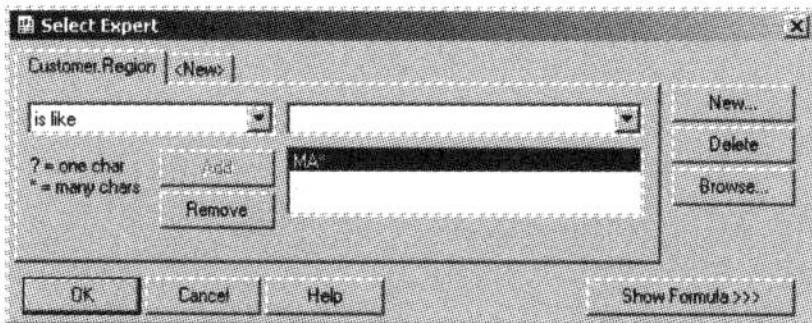

FIGURE 4-8 *Set as much of the desired criteria as possible using the Select Expert drop-down lists.*

Click the Show Formula button, and then the Formula Editor button to launch the Formula Workshop (Formula Editor). Add the Uppercase() function to the selection formula (see Figure 4-9). This function forces the argument (the field within the brackets) into uppercase before it is evaluated by the rest of the formula that contains the selection condition.

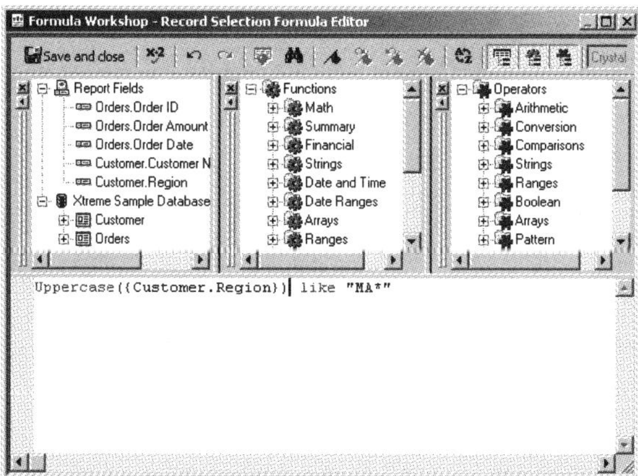

FIGURE 4-9 *Edit the formula by adding the Uppercase() function.*

AND vs. OR

When the Select Expert creates a selection criteria statement, it connects individual statements from each tab with an AND clause (see Figure 4-10). This means that for any record to print on your report, it must match all individual criteria in the statement.

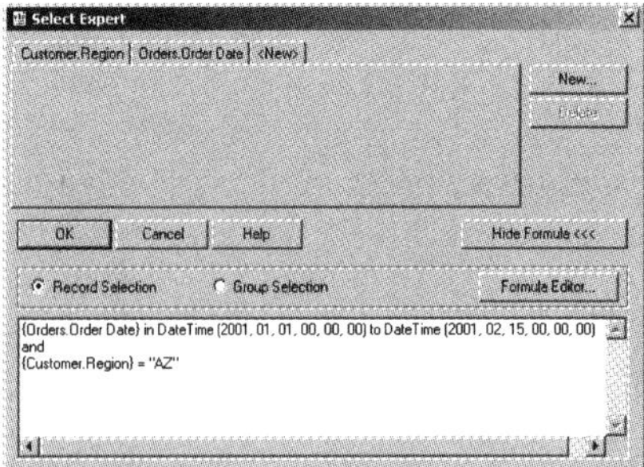

FIGURE 4-10 *The record selection formula that the Select Expert creates connects each statement with an AND clause.*

For some reports, the AND criteria doesn't select the data you want, and you may need to change the AND to an OR.

Changing AND to OR

Imagine that you are looking for a particular order. You believe that the order was placed within a certain date range, or went to a particular state, but are not sure which.

If you click Show Formula in the Select Expert, the dialog box expands to display the complete selection formula. In the formula text box, you can change the AND to an OR, thereby creating the selection criteria formula that will collect all data for each criteria individually, not only data that meets both criteria (see Figure 4-11).

This report now includes records that meet either criteria—state is equal to Arizona *or* the order date was within the range specified.

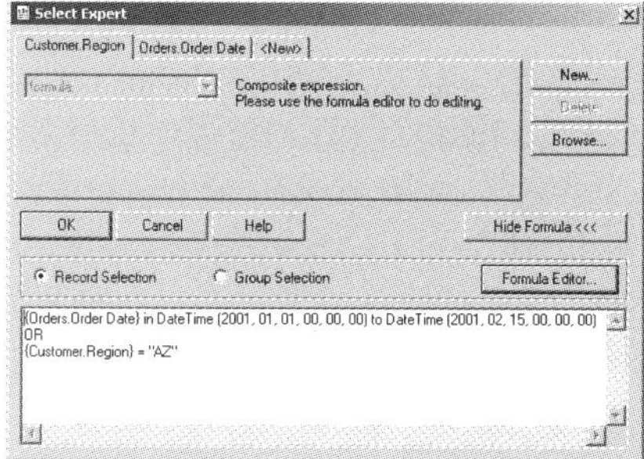

FIGURE 4-11 *Change the AND to an OR and copy the formula once to achieve the selection criteria that you need for a report.*

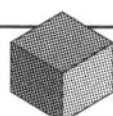

NOTE

The composite expression message in Figure 4-11 means that you can no longer use the tabs of the Select Expert to change the selection formula. However, you can still use the Select Expert to add new tabs and manipulate criteria not affected by the change in your formula.

Handling Null Values

Null values can be useful in selection criteria. If a field in your database has nothing entered in it, Crystal considers this a null value. A null value in a field on your report prints nothing.

You can use null values to your advantage in selection criteria. If you need to include records with null values on your report, you can use the IsNull() function in the Select Expert to collect only the fields that have a null value to print on your report. This selection criteria statement would include all records where the specified field contains a null value.

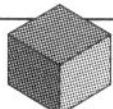

NOTE

You must *not* have Convert Database NULL Value to Default turned on for the IsNull() function to work properly.

When would you use this sort of selection criteria? Think of a financial report where you need to list all orders that have been fulfilled but not paid. You could set up selection criteria based on the Date Paid field in your database. If this field is null for a particular order, you could assume that the payment has not yet been received. Therefore, you can use the Date Paid field in your record selection criteria to select only the unpaid records for your report (see Figure 4-12).

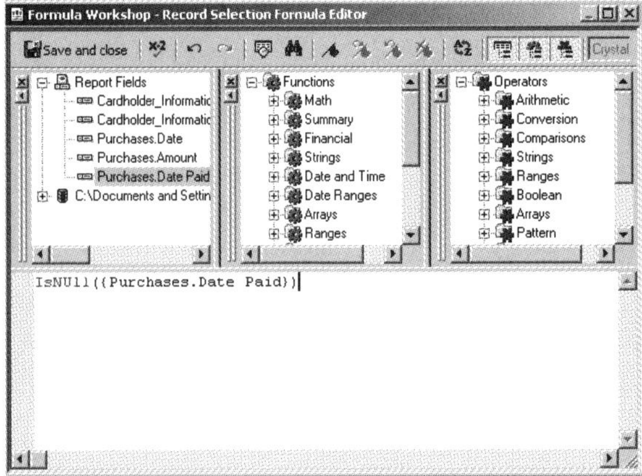

FIGURE 4-12 *You must use the IsNull() function to set selection criteria equal to a null value.*

Converting Null Values to a Default

Crystal gives you the option to keep null values or convert them to the Crystal Reports default. If you keep the null values, you can use the IsNull() function in your record selection criteria. If you do not need to use null values in selection criteria, you might want to convert them to the Crystal default: $0.00 for currency fields, 0.00 for number fields, 00/00/00 for date fields, and a blank for strings.

Why would you want to change null values to the default?

Formatting Consistencies

If you have applied formatting to a field, you might want to change the null value to the default, because Crystal can format the default, but it cannot format a null value.

For example, your report may contain an Amount Paid field. If this field has a null value that you have not converted to the default, the field prints blank on your report. However, if you set this same report to convert null values to the Crystal defaults, that same field would print 0.00. Many databases are designed with default values built in, particularly for number fields, so that they do not have any null values when data is pulled for reporting.

Another example of when you would want to convert a null to the default would be when using conditional formatting. If you've conditionally formatted a background color, but the field is null, the formatting does not apply properly and the blank field may print with a black background color. By changing the null to the default, the proper formatting occurs.

> ### SETTING REPORT OPTIONS FOR NULL VALUES
>
> You can set up individual reports to convert null values to the defaults. Or, you can set a global option to change null values to the defaults for every new report you design.
>
> For a single report, convert null values to the defaults by selecting File, Report Options, and selecting the Convert Database NULL Values to Default check box. This makes the change for the current open report only.
>
> To change this option globally, select File, Options. On the Reporting tab, select the Convert Datbase NULL Values to Default check box. This converts null values to the defaults in any new reports you design.

Of course, if you were using null values in the reports' selection formula, as the previous section demonstrates, converting nulls to defaults would not work.

Converting Null to Default for Selection

If you indeed want or need to convert null values to default values to accommodate the formatting you desire on a report, you can adjust the selection formula in the previous section to achieve the same ends without using the IsNull() function.

Rather than use IsNull({table.fieldname}), convert nulls to default values and use the Crystal default value in your selection formula (see Figure 4-13):

```
{Purchases.Date Paid} = ""
```

In the previous example, the date field is blank, thus using " " tests the field for a blank value. The default value for a text or string type field or a date field is blank, where the default value for a number type field is 0.

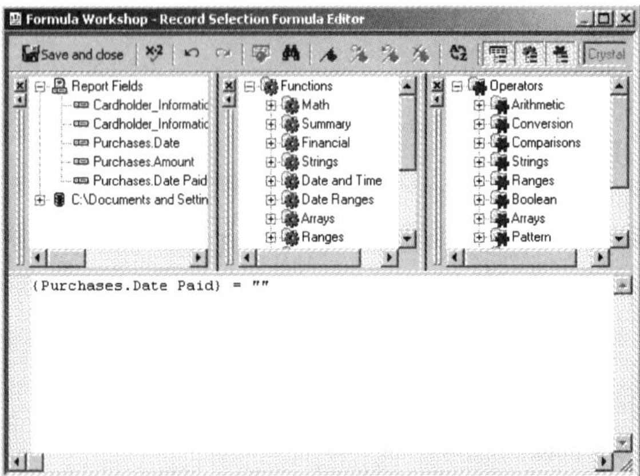

FIGURE 4-13 *Write a selection formula that accommodates a blank space rather than a null value.*

Selecting a Specific Range in a Value

Let's say you want to select part numbers for accessories manufactured in Atlanta. All items manufactured there have a part number beginning with 201. An appropriate selection formula would read:

```
"201" in {PRODUCT.PRODUCT_ID}[1 to 3]
```

This generic formula selects those records in which the first through third digits of the {PRODUCT.PRODUCT_ID} field equal "201", like 20111, 20112, and 20131. This formula would exclude part numbers like 99901 and 23390.

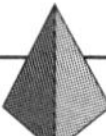

TIP

Search Crystal's help files using the keyword phrase "selection formula templates" to locate many examples that you can cut and paste into your own formulas.

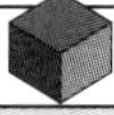

NOTE

Very few selection formulas can be passed to the database server. Check the SQL query through the Show SQL Query dialog box (covered in a later section of this chapter); if the formula appears in the WHERE clause of your Select statement, then the formula is being passed to the database server. If not, then the calculation is being processed in Crystal on your client machine.

Selection Using Boolean Fields

Using a Boolean field in your selection criteria is simple. Boolean values are true/false, or yes/no values that evaluate the field in question to see if it meets a condition or not. The condition drop-down list in the Select Expert includes only conditions appropriate for a Boolean value (see Figure 4-14).

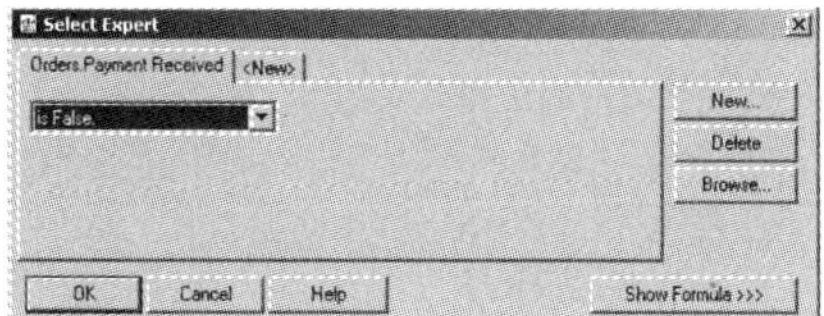

FIGURE 4-14 *Boolean fields in selection criteria have appropriate condition options so you do not have to type a custom formula.*

Group Selection Formulas

Using the Select Expert to filter the groups on your report, as well as the records, can be useful. For example, in the sample report from Chapter 2, each group of the report sums the order amount per customer. If you want this report to include only customers that have ordered more than $20,000 worth of products, you would set up a *group* selection formula. Note that since group selection formulas must involve a summary field (discussed more in Chapter 5), you'll want to work on the main body of your report first, and then return to the Select Expert to add the group selection formula.

Setting Up a Group Selection Formula

The report must already have at least one group and one summary field in order to create a group selection formula. Open the Select Expert, and click the Show Formula button to expand the dialog box. Click the Group Selection radio button. There is no expert for building a group selection formula, so you are completely on your own with the Formula Editor. With the Group Selection radio button selected, click the Show Formula button to open the Formula Workshop, Group Selection Formula Editor (see Figure 4-15).

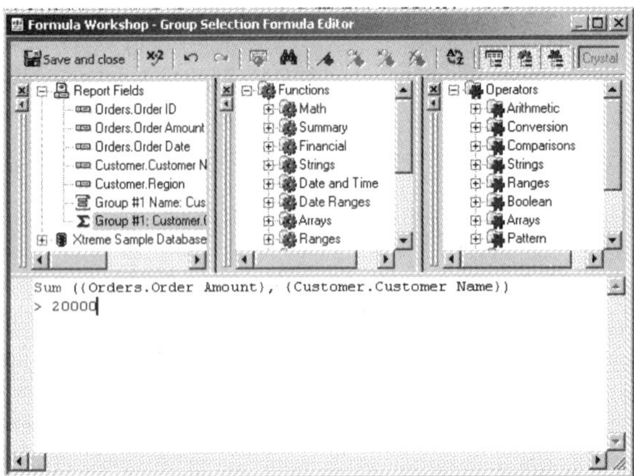

FIGURE 4-15 *Write a Boolean formula, explained in Chapter 7, to select only the groups whose order amount sum exceeds $20,000.*

The group selection formula processes after the grouping and summing functions during the processing cycle of your report. Crystal Reports has a specific evaluation time that it follows when processing all reports, meaning that it always processes each part or function in a report in a specific order.

◆ Crystal applies your record selection criteria.

◆ Crystal groups your records and calculates the sum of the order amount (or any summary fields).

◆ Crystal uses the result of the sum formula in the group selection formula.

Chapter 7 covers formulas, and explains evaluation time in detail, which is the order in which functions are processed when a report is refreshed. In Figure 4-15 only groups (Customer Name) whose order amount exceeds $20,000 will be printed on the report.

Group Formula Gotcha's

Note that a group selection formula may cause your report to look incorrect in some aspects:

◆ The group tree area may show groups that have been filtered out with the group formula, because the group tree is processed before the group selection formula.

◆ Grand totals are incorrect, both because they take all sums into account, not only those that meet the group selection criteria, and because the grand total summary calculation is processed before the group selection is applied. This totaling problem can be overcome by using a running total instead of a grand total, which is discussed more in Chapter 5.

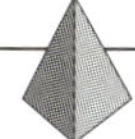

TIP

To use a selection formula for a group, either open the Select Expert as explained above, or just select Report, Edit Selection Formula, Group. This opens the Formula Workshop directly. Different formula types are listed on the left side in the Formula Workshop Explorer.

Using Parameter Fields in Record Selection

Parameter fields allow you—and subsequent report users—to be prompted for selection criteria. You can create a parameter field, and then use it in the Select Expert. (Chapter 13 covers creating and using parameter fields.) Basically, when you refresh a report with a parameter field in use, a prompting dialog box appears. The prompt asks the user for selection criteria values. The value the user picks or enters becomes the value the report uses in selection criteria.

Sales Report Example

A basic sales report might need to be run for each state the company does business in. The exact same report is desired, one for each state. Instead of creating multiple copies of the same report with slightly different selection criteria and a different title, you would use a parameter field.

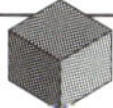

NOTE

Parameter fields are built outside the Select Expert. Chapter 13 covers creating and using parameter fields in detail, and this is just an extra reference to using the parameter field in the selection criteria.

A parameter field in the selection criteria prompts users of the report to select the state to run the report for (see Figure 4-16). Users would type the value or select it from a drop-down list. The Select Expert uses the value entered to determine which records to print on the report. This parameter field can also be used in the title of the report to print the name of the selected state.

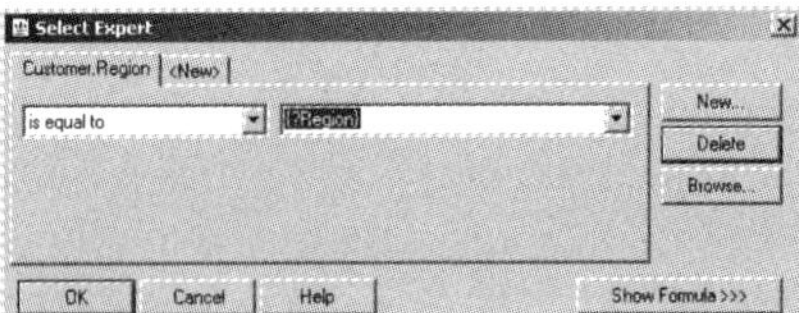

FIGURE 4-16 *Use parameter fields in the Select Expert so that the value entered at the prompt is used to select records for the report.*

CRM Opportunity Report

This sample involves several steps that all use more advanced features of Crystal Reports—taking each function one step further. The report is included in this section because its selection criteria is edited in several ways to accommodate the functional needs of this report.

This report is a listing of opportunities, grouped by what stage the opportunity is currently in. The group is a formula named {@Stage}, which is built to accommodate opportunities whose stage is null in the database.

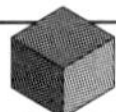

NOTE

Grouping by a formula is covered in Chapter 5.

The user of this report wants a parameter built in, so that they can enter the name of the stage they want to run the report for. This would work fine except that the database field does not accommodate for the null stage. The following selection formula takes care of this problem by evaluating the {@Stage} group for a null value and for other values (see Figure 4-17):

```
if {?Stage} = "No Stage" then isnull({OPPORTUNITY.STAGE}) else

if {?Stage} = "All Stages" then true else

{OPPORTUNITY.STAGE} = {?Stage}
```

Chapter 13 includes advanced examples like this in even more detail. Using parameters often requires editing of the selection formula to get all the options you want at the prompt. Fortunately, the Select Expert is versatile and allows for creative formulas.

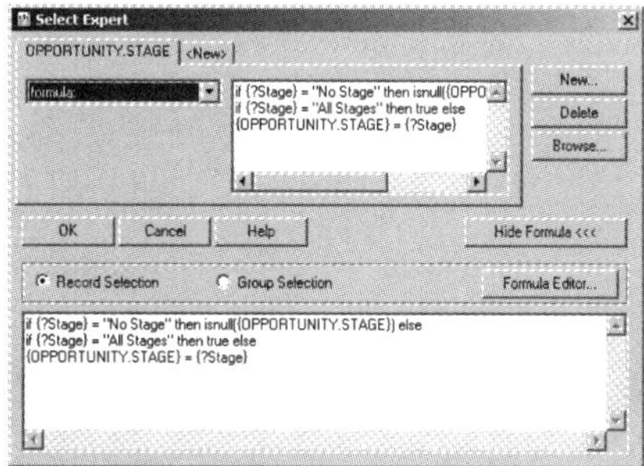

FIGURE 4-17 *Editing the selection formula more extensively allows you to compensate for data issues.*

Performance Considerations with the Select Expert

Selection criteria greatly affects the processing of a report. Not only does it exclude records that you do not need so that they do not print on your report, but it also filters out the records that are pulled from your database so that only what you need is pulled from your database into a report. For example, there may be five million records in your database, but you may need only 2500 for a particular report.

How you create your selection criteria impacts whether Crystal evaluates it on the client machine (your workstation) or on the database server machine. Because the server is usually a larger, more powerful machine, and because it's best to send the smallest amount of data as possible over the network between the database server and your PC, you typically want your server rather than your workstation to process the selection criteria formula.

Selection Criteria and the SQL Statement

When using an ODBC connection for a report, Crystal generates a SQL query. It does this all by itself, using the information you entered in the design of the report. This Select statement can be viewed by selecting Database, Show SQL Query. This is a traditional Select statement, built by Crystal Reports for you, based on the instructions in the Design tab (see Figure 4-18).

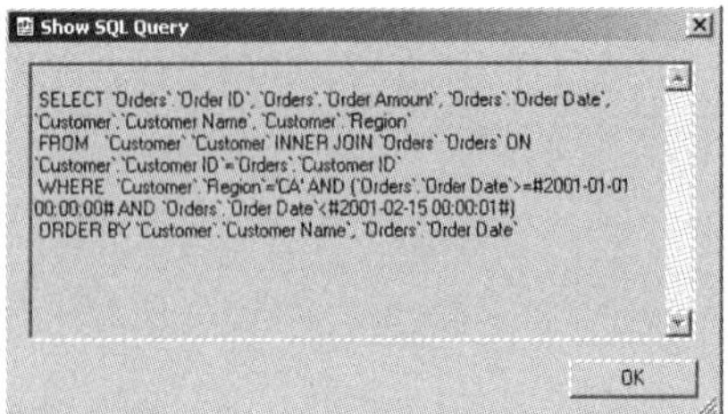

FIGURE 4-18 *Open the Show SQL Query dialog box to see the SQL statement Crystal generates for a particular report.*

When you preview or run the report, Crystal sends this statement to your database server, which uses the statement instructions to collect data for the report. The WHERE clause contains the restrictive conditions to put on the data returned. If your selection criteria is listed in the WHERE clause of this SQL statement, then the server processes it—which is exactly what you want for fast report processing. If you use the basic options provided in the Select Expert, using the drop-down lists, then Crystal includes the selection criteria in the WHERE clause of the SQL statement. This is good.

However, if you customize your selection criteria by manipulating the existing formula or writing a new one, Crystal might be forced to process the selection criteria on your client machine. When you deviate from the standard options of the Select Expert (drop-down lists and basic functions), Crystal does not know how to translate your instructions in the Crystal formula language into SQL that your database understands.

If the SQL statement doesn't include a WHERE clause, or contains only part of your selection criteria, it is likely because the formula contains functions that Crystal cannot translate into SQL. In this case, Crystal applies what selection it can, and then copies all remaining relevant records from the database to the client machine (your PC). Then, Crystal applies the rest of the selection criteria against that set of data on the client machine to filter out the unwanted records.

Customizing your selection criteria will many times be unavoidable, and truly lends necessary power to Crystal Reports. Just be aware that your custom formulas sometimes force part or all of your selection criteria to be processed on the client machine, which typically results in slower report processing. Sometimes this makes no difference, for your report will process fairly quickly without issues. Other times, it makes a report process unbearably slow, forcing you to consider further action.

Forcing Selection Criteria Server Side

There are several ways to force your selection criteria to process on the database server rather than on your PC. These topics are covered in depth later in this book.

If your selection criteria do not all show up in the WHERE clause of the Show SQL Query dialog box, then there are a few things you can do:

- ◆ Build a SQL Command ("Command" for short) and add it to the Database Expert. Commands can also be added to the Crystal Repository. A Command is a custom Select statement that the report will use to collect records from the database, rather than using the Select statement created automatically for you and listed in the Show SQL Query dialog box.

- ◆ Build a stored procedure or database view to use as the data source for your report. The nature of these objects lends them full SQL functionality, to preselect data for your report.

Writing SQL Commands for Faster Report Processing

Crystal Reports 9 has finally answered years of requests for better SQL functionality from within Crystal Reports itself. The previous discussion mentioned that you must use the Select Expert options in order to have your selection criteria show up in the WHERE clause of the Select statement that is sent to your database for processing. This is still true. But we finally have a few better options:

- ◆ The Select Expert is able to translate more functions into the WHERE clause itself, such as IsNull() and the OR operator.

◆ You can build a SQL Command within the Database Expert, which is essentially writing our own Select statement.

If you are an accomplished SQL user, this is music to your ears. For everyone else, this is also music to your ears! Crystal has a new functionality called Commands. These "Commands" are actually SQL Select statements that you can write and edit yourself—thus giving you full control over their content. No longer are you stuck with all the problems experienced with earlier versions of Crystal Reports, with the ins and outs of tiptoeing around editing the Show SQL Query . . . now we have a real tool!

SQL Commands are essentially SQL Select statements that Crystal Reports will use instead of the Crystal self-generated Select statement for collecting records from your database.

With SQL Commands, you are no longer limited by Crystal "getting in the way" of the SQL you could write to pull exactly what you want from your database. You need to understand SQL to be able to write these commands, which use SQL functions that are compatible with your particular database. Or, you can use SQL commands that are stored in the Crystal Repository. The Crystal Repository is a place where objects used in reporting can be stored centrally, for any and all reports in your organization to reference. This way, if a DBA writes a SQL Command that helps you extract the exact data you need for a report, the DBA can save the Command in the Crystal Repository, after which you can just go use it when you start to build a report.

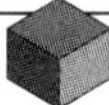

NOTE

Chapter 14 covers SQL Commands and the SQL Query Designer in detail.

Creating Indexes to Force Report Bursting

Crystal has a new feature that allows you to index fields within saved data on a report. This is useful for reports that are for one reason or another forced to apply some selection criteria client side, or within the report itself. By indexing fields, you are telling the report which fields to look at when applying selection criteria. This can help a report to process faster.

Adding Indexes to Saved Data

To add indexes to report fields, follow these steps:

1. Select Report, Report Bursting Indexes to open the Saved Data Indexes dialog box (see Figure 4-19).

2. Select the fields you want indexed within your report's saved data by selecting a field and clicking the forward arrow button (>) to move the field to the Indexed for Bursting list.

3. Click OK to close the dialog box.

4. Refresh and save your report to save the indexes just set.

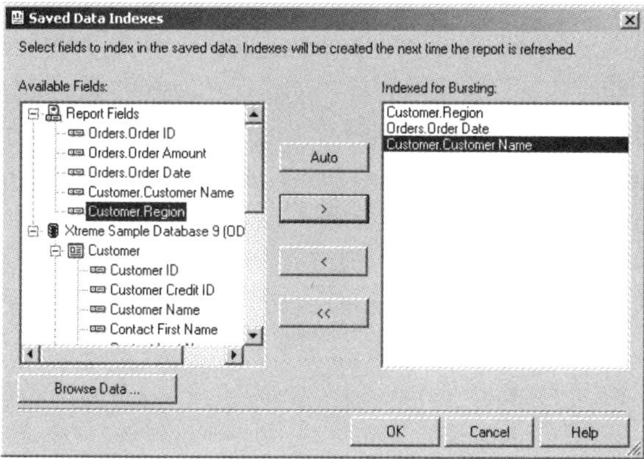

FIGURE 4-19 *Move fields to the Indexed for Bursting list to index saved data for faster report refreshing.*

What Fields Are Best for Indexing?

It is best not to index all fields on a report. Use these basic guidelines to help you select which fields to index:

◆ Index fields that are used in the record selection formula.

◆ Index fields that are referred to by the report's record selection formula, or could be referred to. For example, index the customer name field if selection is sometimes narrowed to look for data for just certain customers.

◆ Do not index all the fields in the report, because this can slow processing time and is unnecessary.

◆ Do not index fields that contain unique values, because this creates a separate index for each value of the field.

Setting report indexes is an additional way to help larger reports process more efficiently and is by no means necessary on all reports.

Summary

This chapter covered setting basic selection criteria, and then explained in more detail when and why you might need to edit the formula created by the Select Expert. Hopefully, with the ideas presented here, you have a solid understanding of how you can use the Select Expert as a tool to help you create the exact filter you need so that your report shows only the records you want. If the formula or criteria you write does not return the records you want, you can always change the criteria back to the way the Select Expert started. Click Undo several times, or simply delete all the selection criteria and start over. You may need to experiment to find the right combination of criteria statements, formulas, and parameters to meet your needs.

Chapter 5

Useful elements of report design include sorting, grouping, and totaling your data. These basic elements of reports have experts and functional dialog boxes to assist you—like the Select Expert you learned about in Chapter 4. In the previous chapters, you learned how to put basic information on your report. Now you will learn how to sort, group, and summarize that information.

Sorting Detail Records

Sorting records on a report makes the report easier to read and understand. Crystal Reports provides the Record Sort Order dialog box to help you sort the detail records on a report. You can have more than one level of sorting on any report. Without a sort order, the records on your report print in their original order, which is the order in which they appear in your database.

Use the Record Sort Order dialog box to set the sort order of the detail records on your report.

1. Open the Record Sort Order dialog box by clicking the Record Sort Expert toolbar button ![button] or by selecting Report, Record Sort Expert.

2. To designate a field to sort records by, click that field in the Available Fields list and then click the forward arrow button (>) to move the field over to the Sort Fields list. You can also double-click a field to move it over to the opposite list. In the example shown in Figure 5-1, the report will be sorted by city.

3. You can adjust the sort direction by selecting Ascending or Descending in the Sort Direction area.

4. Add as many sort fields as you want by moving fields to the Sort Fields list. To remove fields from the Sort Fields list, select the field and click the backward arrow button (<).

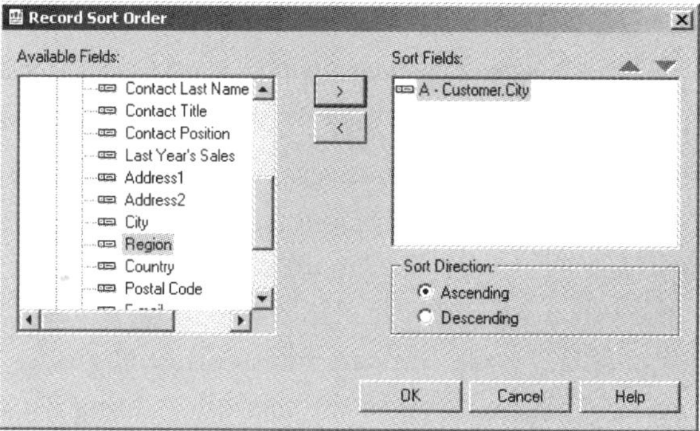

FIGURE 5-1 *Use the Record Sort Order dialog box to set a sort order for the records on your report.*

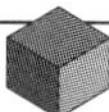

NOTE

If you already have a group on your report, Crystal shows the group in the Sort Fields list of the Record Sort Order dialog box. To remove or change this group, you must use the Change Group Expert, discussed later in this chapter in the sections "Changing the Field You Grouped By" and "Deleting a Group from Your Report."

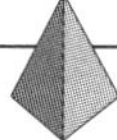

TIP

You can sort records using any field available to the report—the field does not need to print on the report in order to sort by it.

Creating Groups

Creating groups organizes the information on your report and allows you to calculate subtotals for each group. For example, you could group by region and then city to organize the information on your report geographically. Or you could group by sales representative and then opportunity type. Crystal does not limit the number of groups you can have on a report and offers many options for manipulating groups. When you insert a group on a report, Crystal adds Group Header and Group Footer sections, one set for each group created. These sections allow space for the group name and subtotal fields.

Inserting One or More Groups

When inserting groups on your report, you might find it helpful to do so from the Design tab so that you can see how Crystal adds the Group Header and Group Footer sections to your report. There are actually several different ways to insert a group onto a report, and also several places to manipulate that group once it is on the report. The next section demonstrates the "main" function for inserting a group onto a report: using the Group Expert. It also shows how to change that group if need be. (You can repeat the same steps to add additional groups at any time while designing a report, as explained later in the section "Adding More than One Group to a Report.") Then, the section "Additional Ways to Add a Group" describes the other places within Crystal Reports where you can access functionality to change or format groups. The Group Expert is new, but the old functionality still exists (at least for now), providing many ways to do the same thing.

Inserting a Group onto a Report

You can insert and manipulate as many groups on a report as you need using the Group Expert. Several levels of grouping can organize vast amounts of information into more manageable pieces. Groups can help organize summary or drill-down reports, or allow you to insert a graph or cross-tab for each group. To insert a group onto a report, follow these steps:

1. Click the Group Expert toolbar button 📇 on the Expert Tools toolbar or select Report, Group Expert to open the Group Expert dialog box (see Figure 5-2).

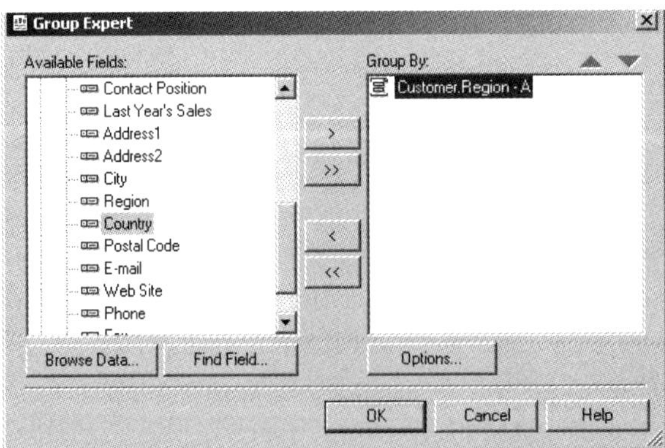

FIGURE 5-2 *Select a field to base your group on using the Group Expert dialog box.*

2. Select a field from the Available Fields list that you want to base your grouping on.

3. Click the single forward arrow button (>) to move the field to the Group By list.

4. Select the field you are grouping by in the Group By list, which causes the Options button to become active. Click the Options button to open the Change Group Options dialog box (see Figure 5-3).

5. On the Common tab, the field you are basing the group on is listed in the first drop-down list. Use the second drop-down list to select one of four options for group order: ascending, descending, specified, or original. Ascending and descending refer to alphanumeric order. The section "Specified Order Grouping: Much More than Ordering Groups," later in this chapter, covers specified order options in detail. Original order is the order in which the records appear in your database, and usually is the order in which the data was entered.

WRITING A FORMULA FOR CUSTOMIZING A GROUP NAME

You have always been able to write a separate formula using the Formula Editor to customize a group name. You also have this option right in the Insert Group dialog box. Perhaps you added a group to your report using a code or ID field, but would rather have the group name reflect the description of that code. In this case, customize the group name field with a field other than the one you grouped by, as described in a tip earlier in this chapter.

Using a formula, you can rename groups that have less than optimal group names in your database but do not have a name field available. Maybe R&D, PM, and HR are field values that you have grouped by, but you would rather your report read Research and Development, Product Management, and Human Resources. You can write an If-Then-Else formula to set common names for all of the abbreviated names in your database field. The If-Then-Else formula might look like this:

```
If {table.field}= "R&D" then
"Research and Development" else
If {table.field}= "PM" then
"Product Management" else . . .
```

(continues)

WRITING A FORMULA FOR CUSTOMIZING A GROUP NAME (CONTINUED)

And so on for all the different departments. You could also write a Select Case formula with exactly the same result:

```
Select [table.field]
Case "R&D" : "Research and Devel."
Case "HR" : "Human Resources"
Default : "No Department Listed"
```

(You could write the formula either way; these are simply examples.) Then, you would base your group name on this formula. Chapter 7 covers formulas in detail.

6. Click the Options tab to customize the group name if need be (see Figure 5-4). Select the Customize Group Name Field check box and then either select an existing field to be the group name or write a formula by clicking the X+2 formula button.

7. Still on the Options tab, select the Keep Group Together check box to prevent groups from being split over two pages. Select the Repeat Group Header On Each Page check box to repeat the Group Header section on as many additional pages as the group extends.

8. Click OK to close the Change Group Options dialog box. Click OK to close the Group Expert dialog box. The Group Header and Group Footer sections appear on your report, with the Group Name field in the Group Header area.

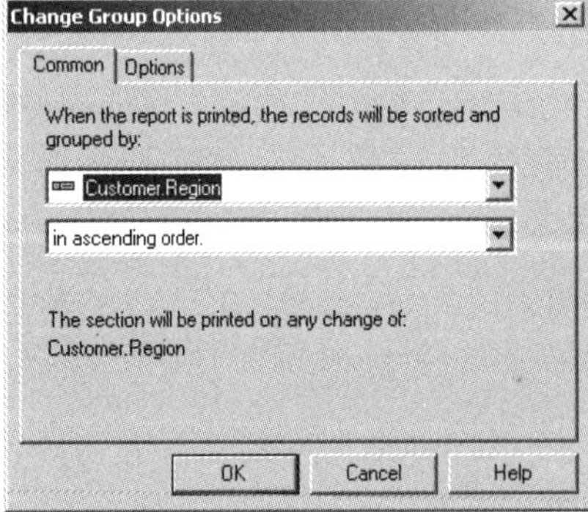

FIGURE 5-3 *Set the order of your group on the Common tab of the Change Group Options dialog box.*

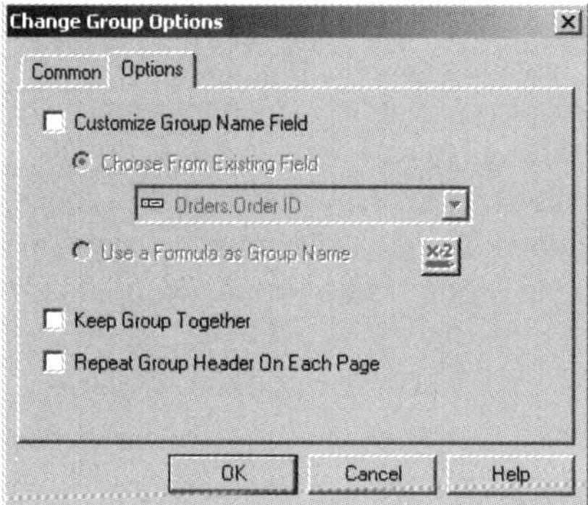

FIGURE 5-4 *Set group name options using the Options tab of the Change Group Options dialog box.*

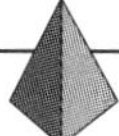

TIP

When would you customize the group name field? Suppose you want to group by supervisor ID number, but you want the group name that prints on the report to be the supervisor name. You might not want to group by the supervisor name, because two supervisors in your company have the same name. But, you really want the name to show up as the group name because people reading the report will recognize the name, not the number. Create your group using the supervisor ID field, and then select the supervisor name field as the group name field. See the sidebar "Using Summaries to Solve Group Sorting Problems," at the end of this chapter, to learn how to sort groups by the name field rather than the ID field.

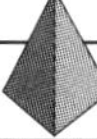

TIP

If you check Keep Group Together and your first group does not fit on the first page of your report, the group skips page one and starts printing on page two, leaving the first page blank after the Page Header. There are several ways to get around this blank first page. You can uncheck Keep Group Together, suppress the Report Header, or format the Report Header section to New Page After. This last option is covered in Chapter 6.

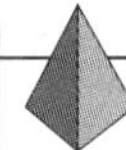

> **TIP**
>
> You can turn off the option that inserts the Group Name field into the Group Header section. Select File, Options and clear the Insert Group Name with Group check box on the Layout tab. If you have deleted the Group Name field from your report, you can add it again from the Field Explorer under Group Name Fields. Drag and drop the field onto your report like you would any other field.

Additional Ways to Add a Group

There are "leftover" tools from previous versions of Crystal Reports for adding and manipulating groups. You also gain functionality to manipulate existing groups from within the new Report Explorer. These are all *in addition* to using the Group Expert to add and manipulate groups.

Using the Insert Group dialog box

The Insert Group dialog box works similarly to the Group Expert, accomplishing the same end result just using a different dialog box. The steps below explain how to add a group to a report using the Insert Group dialog box.

1. Select Insert, Group to open the Insert Group dialog box (see Figure 5-5).

2. Use the first drop-down list to select a field to base the group on.

3. Select a group order from the second drop-down list.

4. Click the Options tab to set group options. You'll notice that this is the same dialog box is the same as the Change Group Options dialog opened by clicking the Options button on the Group Expert.

5. Click OK to insert the group onto the report.

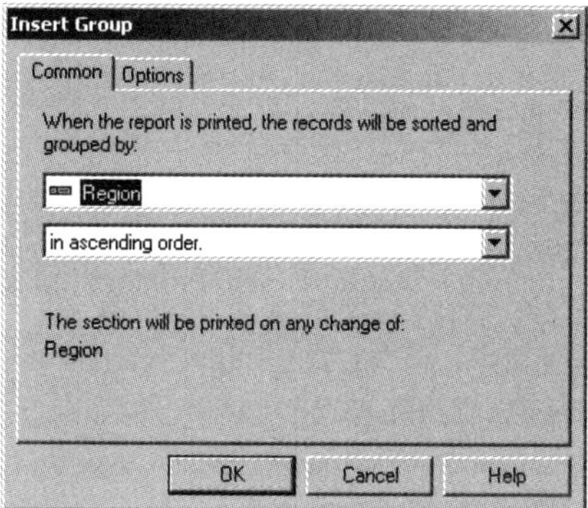

FIGURE 5-5 *Set a field to group by and options using the Insert Group dialog box.*

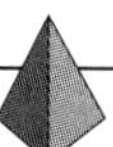

TIP

You can also change group options by right-clicking the Group Header or Group Footer name in the section area on the left side of the Design or Preview tab. This opens a shortcut menu with a Change Group option. This option opens the Change Group dialog box.

Manipulating a group using the Report Explorer

The Report Explorer lists all the sections of a report and provides right-click shortcut menus full of functions for manipulating the field or section selected. The options in these menus are the same as those that are available if you select a group in the section area of the Design tab or select the field on the report. Thus, working with a group using the Report Explorer is just another place to use the same functionality found elsewhere.

To edit a group from the Report Explorer:

1. Open the Report Explorer by clicking the Report Explorer toolbar button or selecting View, Report Explorer. The Report Explorer opens docked on the left side of the design window by default (see Figure 5-6).

2. Select the name of the group you wish to manipulate or change, and right-click to see a large shortcut menu of options for manipulating the group section.

3. If you select the group name field, which is listed below the actual group with a flat-looking node marker, right-clicking opens a shortcut menu with options for formatting or manipulating the group field.

4. If you have many levels of grouping on a report, using the Report Explorer might be easier than working in the section area on the left side of the Design or Preview tab. The Report Explorer spells out all the group names, which when changing the order of groups is reason enough for me to use the new Report Explorer!

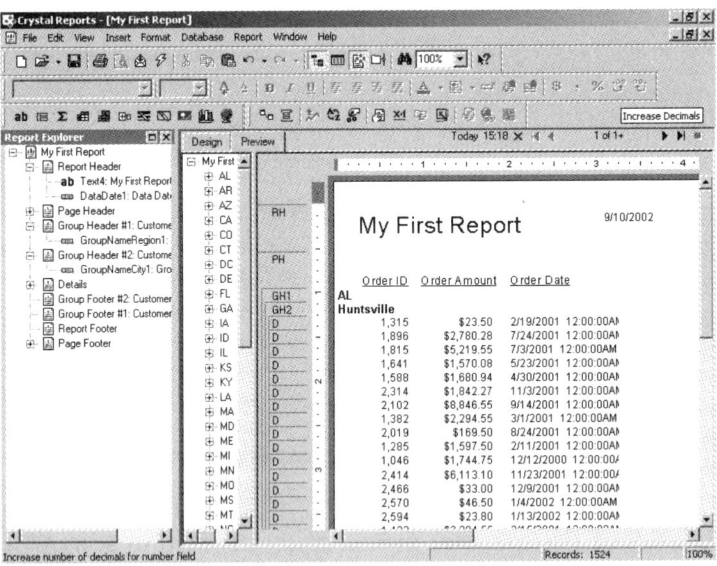

FIGURE 5-6 *Use the Report Explorer to work with groups on a report.*

Using the Group Tree

Use the group tree as a navigation tool for quickly jumping to a particular section of a report. The group tree appears on the left side of the Preview tab as soon as you add a group to a report, and is enabled by default (refer to Figure 5-6). In Figure 5-6 the group tree is positioned between the Preview tab and the Report Explorer.

The group tree lists each group on your report. If you have more than one level of grouping on a report, each group has a plus sign next to it. Click the plus sign to expand the next level of grouping in the tree.

You can turn the group tree display on and off with a toolbar button 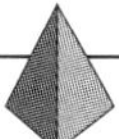, so that you view it on the Preview tab only when you need it to maximize the usable real estate on your desktop. Toggling the group tree off doesn't actually disable it, rather it only hides the group tree from view.

> **TIP**
>
> Disabling the group tree may improve the speed with which you can preview a large report. Each time you preview a report, Crystal Reports creates the group tree. This means that Crystal Reports must read all the groups and then display them in the group tree area. You can disable it if you select File, Options, go to the Layout tab of the Options dialog box, and clear the Display Group Tree check box.

The group tree is an excellent navigation tool for moving through your report. Since it lists all the groups on your report, you can check that the groups you expect are present without having to go page by page through a report. Also, you can navigate to the beginning of a certain group by clicking that group's name in the group tree, instead of scrolling page by page.

Adding More than One Group to a Report

To add any number of additional groups to a report, repeat the steps described in the section "Inserting a Group onto a Report." Use either the Group Expert or select Insert, Group to open the Insert Group dialog box. Once you've added multiple groups to your report, you can change group order. When you add a group, Crystal Reports always adds it as the lowest-level group. If you want to move a group to a higher level, you have two choices:

◆ Open the Report Explorer, and select one group with your mouse. Holding the mouse button down, drag your mouse over the group you want to switch with. Release the mouse, and the groups are switched.

◆ On the Design tab, select the group to be moved in the section area on the left side of the window. Then, holding the mouse button down, drag the group to where you want it.

Changing the Field You Grouped By

If you have a group on your report and you want to change it, you do not need to delete it and insert another. Instead, you can change everything about a group from either the Group Expert or the Change Group Options dialog box.

Change a Group Field or Options Using the Group Expert

1. Open the Group Expert and select the group you want to change from the Group By list.

2. Click the Options button to open the Change Group Options dialog box. Make any changes to your group here, including even changing the field the group is based on.

3. Click OK to close the Change Group Options dialog box, and OK to close the Group Expert.

Change a Group Using the Report Explorer

Another way to change group options is by using the Report Explorer. You cannot add new groups from within the Report Explorer, but it is a nice interface to change or manipulate groups.

1. Open the Report Explorer.

2. Right-click the group you want to change and select Change Group (see Figure 5-7). This opens the Change Group Options dialog box, where you can change any group attribute, including the field the group is based on.

3. Click OK to close the dialog box, and your group will be changed in both the Report Explorer and the report itself.

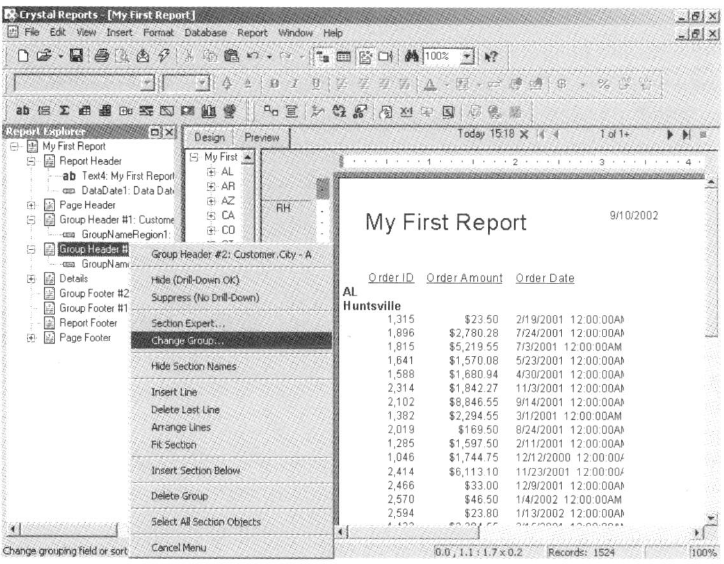

FIGURE 5-7 *Select Change Group from the shortcut menu to open the Change Group Options dialog box.*

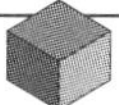

NOTE

Another option for changing a group is by right-clicking on the Group Header or Group Footer section areas in the Design or Preview tabs (that gray area on the left side of the Design or Preview windows) and selecting Change Group from the shortcut menu.

Deleting a Group from Your Report

You have two ways to delete a group from your report:

◆ Select Delete Group from the shortcut menu opened by right-clicking a Group Header/Footer section on the left side of the Design or Preview tab.

◆ Open the Group Expert, select the group you want to remove in the Group By list, and click the backward arrow button (<).

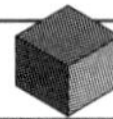

NOTE

If you select a group name field on your report and either click the delete button on your keyboard or right click on the field and select delete from the shortcut menu, you will only be deleting the group name field not the actual group. You will see the Group Header and Group Footer sections still on the report, just without a group name field.

Specified Order Grouping: Much More than Ordering Groups

Crystal Reports provides many options for creating custom groups. The specified order grouping option gives you the ability to customize groups in several different ways:

◆ Change the order of existing groups

◆ Rename existing groups (and change their order if you want)

◆ Create all new groups based on a field in your database

You can select the *in specified order* Grouping option in either the Insert Group dialog box or the Change Group Options dialog box.

Putting Existing Groups into a Specified Order

If you've added a group to your report and the ascending/descending options don't meet your needs, you can use the *in specified order* option. To change the order of existing groups, follow these steps:

1. With either the Insert Group dialog box or the Change Group Options dialog box open, select *in specified order* from the group order list (see Figure 5-8). This adds a Specified Order tab and opens it.

2. Select a group from the Named Group list by clicking the down arrow and selecting a group from the list (see Figure 5-9). The value for the group moves to the group list in the middle of the dialog box.

3. Repeat Step 2 for all the groups you want to specify the order for. Use the up and down arrows to the right of the group list to change the order of the groups (see Figure 5-10).

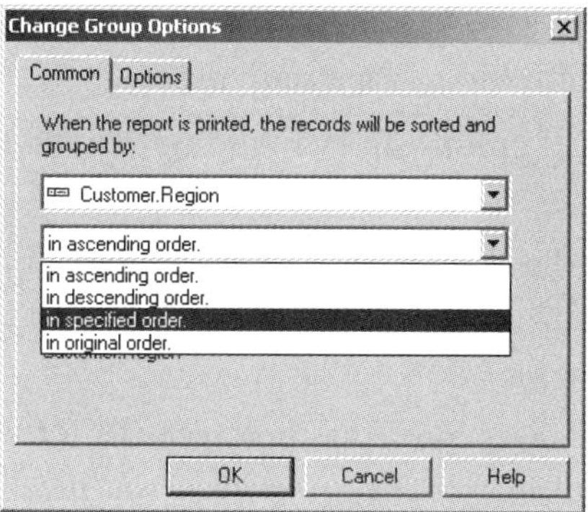

FIGURE 5-8 *Select* in specified order *as the sort order option for the group.*

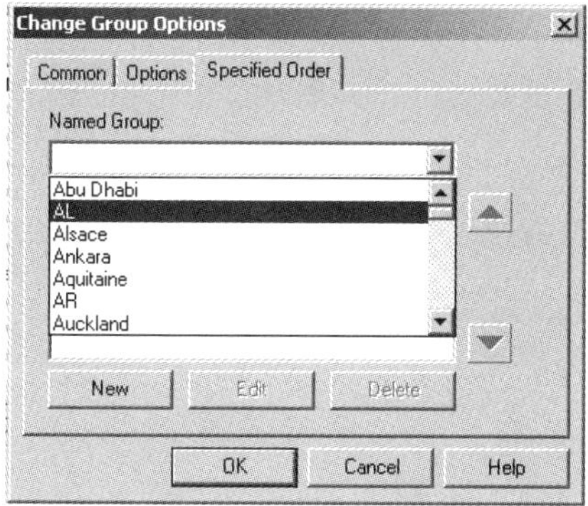

FIGURE 5-9 *Select the groups that you want to reorder one at a time.*

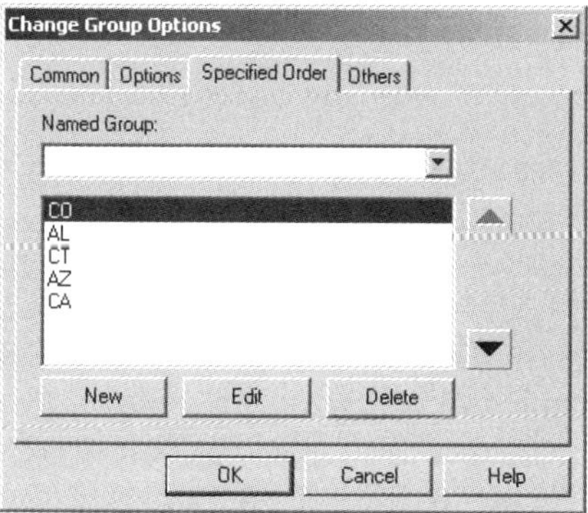

FIGURE 5-10 *Use the up and down arrows on the right side of the dialog box to adjust the order of the groups.*

4. Use the options on the Others tab (see Figure 5-11) to deal with any groups that you did not specifically add to the group order:

◆ **Discard all others.** Discards all groups that you did not specifically include.

◆ **Put all others together, with the name: _____.** Puts all remaining groups into one group with the name "Others" or with whatever name you specify in the text box.

◆ **Leave in their own groups.** Leaves the remaining records in their own groups and lists the groups, after the groups you specifically ordered, in original order.

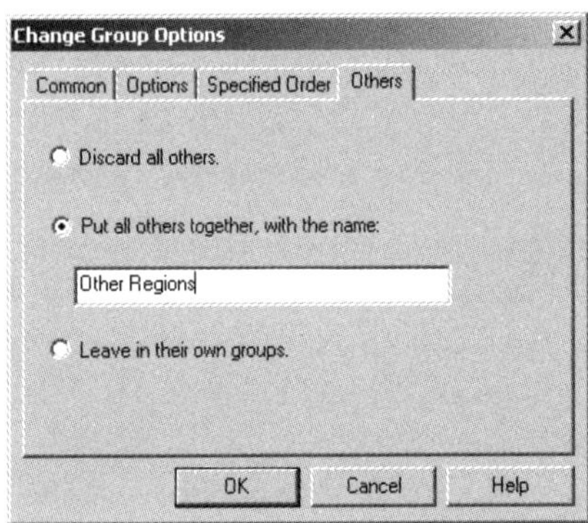

FIGURE 5-11 *Select what to do with any groups not included in your named groups by using the Others tab.*

5. Click OK to close the Change Group Options dialog box. Click OK again to exit the Group Expert, if you used it.

6. Preview your report to see the groups now in the order that you specified.

Creating Custom Groups

You may want or need to customize your groups. Using the *in specified order* option, you can manipulate the actual name and contents of a group.

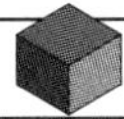

NOTE

Crystal allows you to base a group on a first pass formula as well as using the *in specified order* Grouping option to completely change groups.

In the previous section, we only re-ordered existing groups. Using the *in specified order* option, you can also define new groups. When you define a new group, you can use an existing name or create a new name. You can then add any of the existing groups to the new group to make one big group, or you can use selection tabs and drop down lists in the Define Named Group dialog box to select the groups you want to include in the new group.

Combine Existing Groups into New Groups

For an example of a group using the *in specified order* sort option, think about the database field Region that contains the states of the United States. You want to create four large groups based on the geographic location of the states—such as Northwest, Southwest, Northeast, and Southeast. First, base the group on the Region field, and then select the *in specified order* option. Name the first new group Northwest, and then, using the tabs, select which states you want to include in that group. Then add a second group, Southwest, and add the appropriate states, and so on.

For any records not specifically assigned to a group you create, select one of the three options on the Others tab, as described in Step 4 in the last series of steps:

1. Open the Specified Order tab in the Change Group Options dialog box.
2. Click New to open the Define Named Group dialog box (see Figure 5-12).

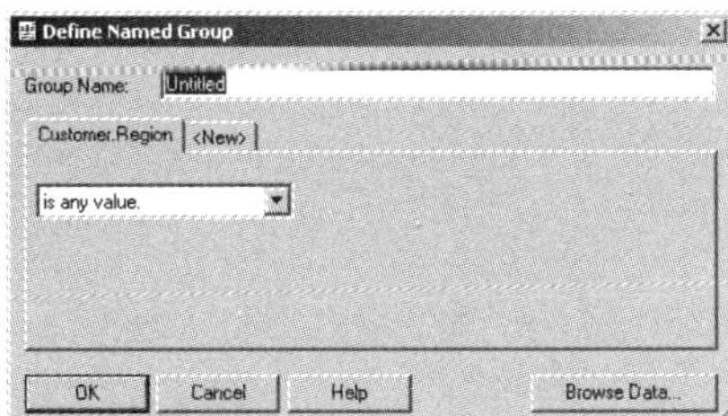

FIGURE 5-12 *Type a name for your new group in the Group Name area, and define the group using the drop-down lists.*

3. Replace the word Untitled with a name for your custom group.

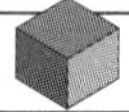

NOTE

You could also type the new name in the empty Named Group box on the Specified Order tab before clicking New.

4. Use the tabs to select the field values you want to include in the specified group (see Figure 5-13). You can only select values from the field you selected earlier to base the group on. Note, however, that when you click the <New> tab, it actually adds an OR and another condition to your selection criteria. So, for example, on the first tab, you might set up the criteria where SalesAmount < 100. On a second tab, you could add another criteria, such as OR SalesAmount > 10000. Your specified group will then include records that match either criteria.

5. Click OK to close the Define Named Group dialog box and save the custom group that you just defined. Crystal adds this group to the list on the Specified Order tab, as shown in Figure 5-14.

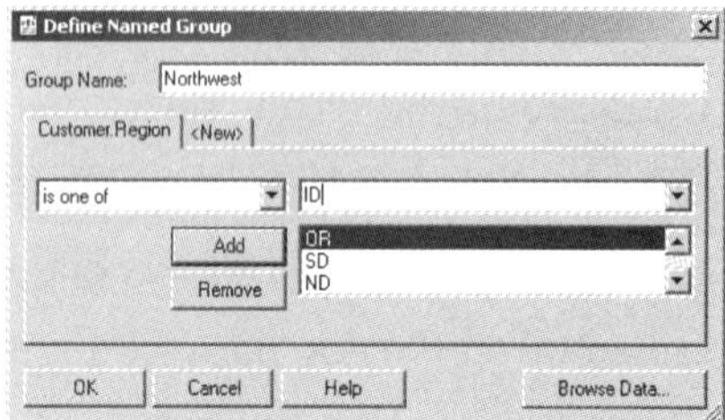

FIGURE 5-13 *Create custom groups using the conditions in the drop-down lists.*

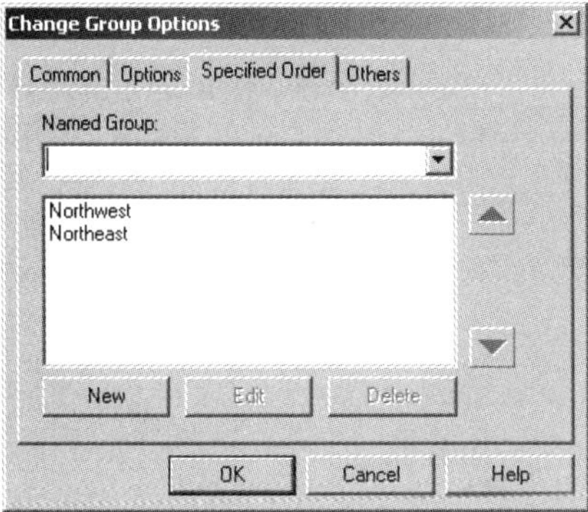

FIGURE 5-14 *All custom groups appear on the Specified Order tab. You can add as many as you want—only two are listed here.*

6. Repeat Steps 2 through 5 for each group you want to add or customize.

7. On the Others tab, select an option to handle any records not included in the groups you specified.

8. Click OK to close the dialog box. Preview your report to see the results of your custom grouping (see Figure 5-15).

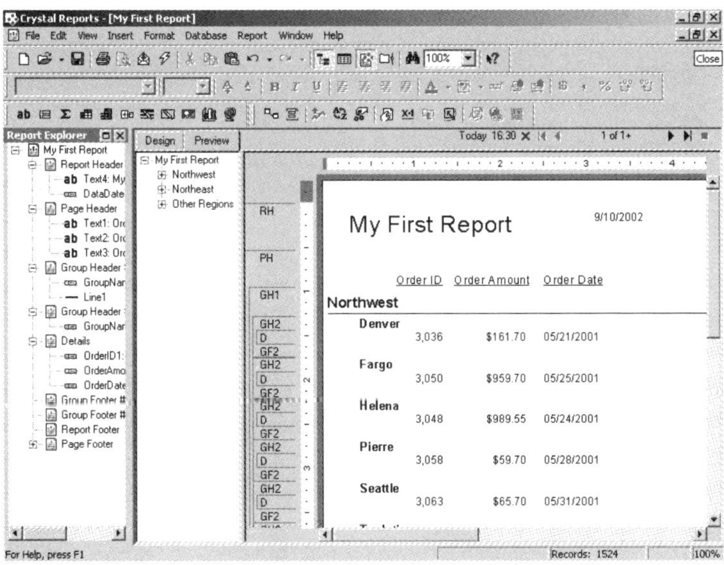

FIGURE 5-15 *Preview the report with the specified order grouping and see that whatever group you listed first on the Specified Order tab appears first on your report.*

Basing a Group on a Formula Field

Sometimes the field you want to base a group on needs to be manipulated before you base the group on it. In this case, you could write the formula in the Formula Editor and then base the group on the formula field.

Creating a Ranged Group

In this example, the report needs to be grouped based on a sales range. The report needs to be grouped by order amount ranges, listing the employees and their sales numbers in the group that their customers fall into. Here, a formula calculates the sales ranges that become the groups. The detail records are then sorted into the proper groups based on the order amounts. I name the formula SalesRange.

```
if {Orders.Order Amount} > 10000 then "Large Account Sales" else
if {Orders.Order Amount} > 5000 then "Mid Level Accounts" else
"Small Accounts"
```

Basing a group on this formula field sorts the orders by their amount (see Figure 5-16).

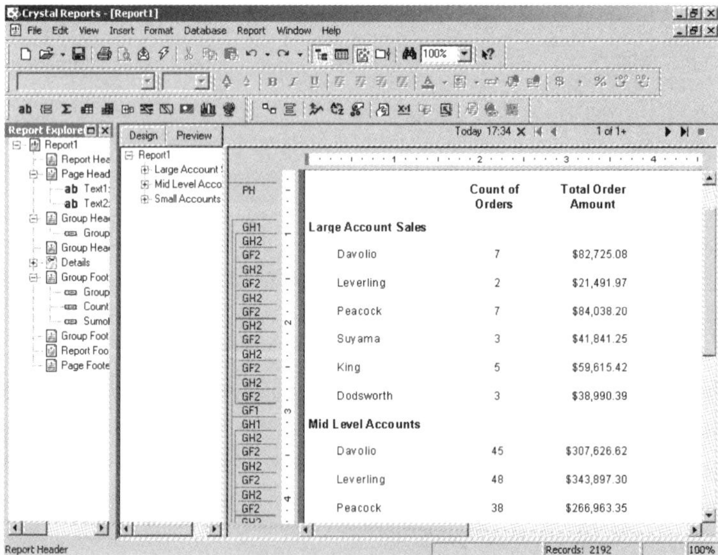

FIGURE 5-16 *Insert a group based on a range formula field.*

NOTE

To insert a group based on a formula field, select the formula field from the field drop down list rather than a database field. This will build the group based on the result of that formula. See Chapter 7 for anther example of a group based on a formula field.

Accommodating a Null Value in a Group Formula

Sometimes database fields contain null values, meaning that the value of the field is unknown. This null value is different than a zero or a blank.

In the next example, a field that I want to group by contains null values. I wrote a formula to accommodate that null value and assigned it a generic name, "No Stage," so that on the report I do not end up with a blank group name for my "null" opportunities that are not designated into a stage at this time.

```
if isnull({opportunity.stage}) then "No Stage" else {opportunity.stage}
```

The group is based on this formula. The group prints all the stage names correctly, and rather than printing a blank group name for the nulls, the group name prints "No Stage."

Adding Totals to Reports

Creating summaries in Crystal Reports can be as easy as clicking your mouse or as complex as writing your own formulas. This section covers inserting the various summary functions that Crystal makes directly available. Keep in mind, however, that if Crystal doesn't offer the specific summary function you need, or you need to do some fancy mathematical footwork, you can always write a formula to do the summarization you want.

Calculating Summaries

Crystal Reports provides the Insert Summary dialog box for inserting group summaries and grand totals on a report. This one tool is used for inserting all types of summaries at any group and/or the full report level. To insert a summary on your report:

1. Select Insert, Summary, or click the Insert Summary toolbar button Σ to open the Insert Summary dialog box (see Figure 5-17).

2. Select the field you want to summarize from the first drop-down list.

3. Select the summary function you want performed from the second drop-down list (see Figure 5-18).

4. Select the level (group or report) you want to summarize from the Summary location list.

5. Click OK to close the dialog box. The summary field appears directly below the field it totals in the Group Footer section.

NOTE

Crystal Reports does not insert a label for any summary fields. Use a text object next to the summary field to add a label. In Chapter 6, which describes formatting reports, you will learn how to use text objects to add labels to fields and even how to insert fields directly into text objects to have them trim automatically.

FIGURE 5-17 *Use the Insert Summary dialog box to sum the selected field for a particular group.*

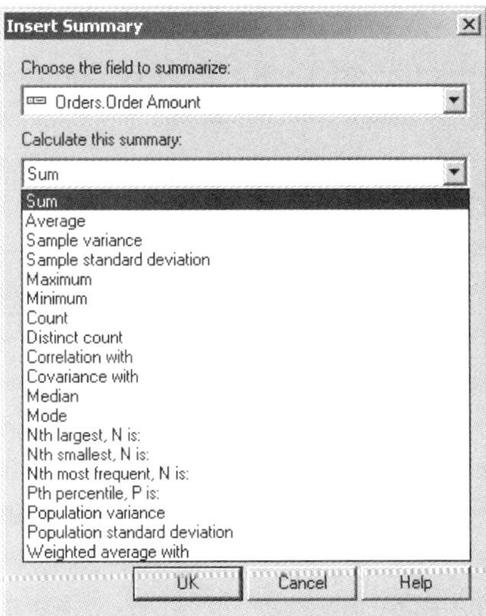

FIGURE 5-18 *Select from many available summary functions. The functions available are dependent on the type of field being summarized.*

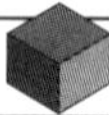

NOTE

The Insert Summary dialog box offers many summary functions. You can find excellent information in the online help file that describes each of these functions in the Functions Index. Some of these functions are only available for number fields.

Creating Grand Totals

Grand totals are totals for an entire report. All the functions available for summarizing groups are also available for creating grand totals. Inserting a grand total is exactly the same as inserting a summary: you choose Grand Total (it is the default) in the Summary location list, as follows:

1. Select Insert, Summary. You can also use the toolbar button. The Insert Summary dialog box opens.

2. Select the field you want to summarize from the first drop-down list.

3. Select the summary function you want to calculate from the second drop-down list.

4. Leave the Summary location on the Grand Total (Report Footer) option. Click OK to close the dialog box.

5. The Grand Total field appears in the Report Footer section of your report, directly below the field that it summarizes.

Percentage Calculations

Crystal gives you the option to calculate percentages as your summary:

1. Open the Insert Summary dialog box.

2. Select the Show as a percentage of check box to calculate a percentage.

3. The default calculation displays the group total as a percent of the report's grand total for the selected field. If there are other available higher-level summaries, you may select them from the list.

For example, say your report shows invoices grouped by customer. If you summarize the invoice total field for each customer and check Show as a percentage of, then the report prints each customer's percentage of total invoice sales.

Editing the Summary

If you have added a summary field to your report, you can easily change the type of summary it performs. The Edit Summary dialog box allows you to change the field you are summarizing as well as change the summary operation. To edit a summary:

1. With the summary field selected, right-click it and select Edit Summary from the shortcut menu.

2. The Edit Summary dialog box opens (see Figure 5-19), in which you can select a different field to summarize and/or select a different summary function to be performed.

3. Click OK to close the dialog box.

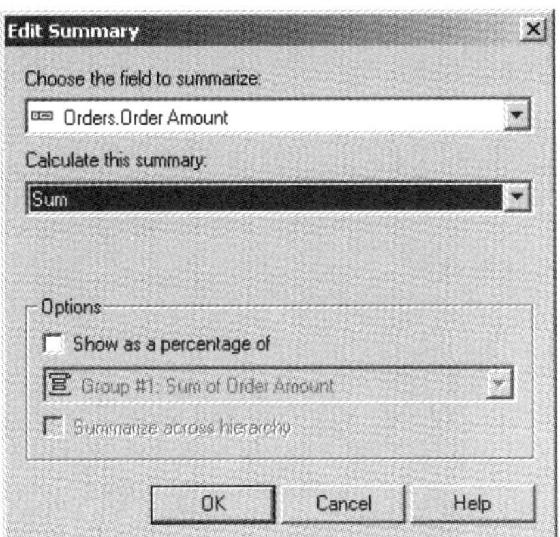

FIGURE 5-19 *Use the Edit Summary dialog box to change the summary field or operation.*

Basing Selection Criteria on a Summary Field

Though Chapter 4 covered the Select Expert, now that we have covered summaries, it's time to mention again that you can select records based on summary and percentage fields. Maybe you only want customers on your report if their order amount total exceeded $25,000; or possibly you only want the sales people on your report who had at least 10 percent of the company's sales for the quarter. You would base your record selection on that summary or percentage field.

The following steps describe how to add a group selection formula to the report:

1. Open the Formula Workshop by selecting Report, Formula Workshop or clicking the Formula Workshop toolbar button.

2. Click the Selection Formulas node, and then the Group Selection option.

3. The Formula Editor opens, ready for you to write the group selection formula (see Figure 5-20). Type the following formula into the Formula Editor so that only customers whose sum of {Orders.Order Amount} is greater than 40000 will print on the report.

```
Sum ({Orders.Order Amount}, {Customer.Customer Name}) > 40000
```

4. Click the Save button to save the formula, and then click the Close button to close the Formula Workshop.

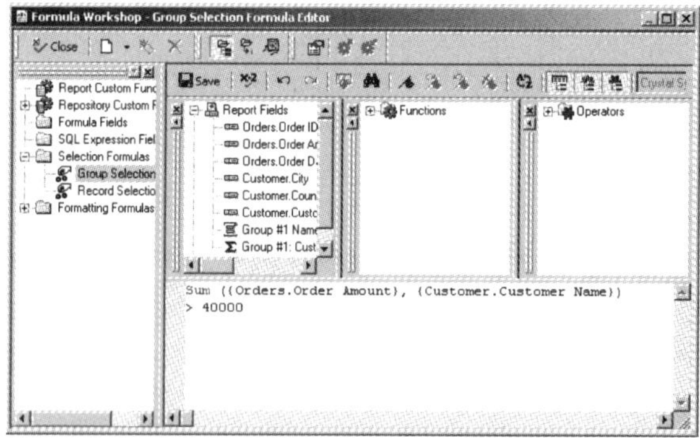

FIGURE 5-20 *Write a group selection formula in the Formula Workshop.*

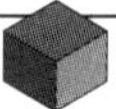

NOTE

You can also use the Select Expert to perform this group selection. Simply right-click on the summary field (or click the toolbar button) and choose Select Expert. Find the summary field you want to base the criteria on, apply the condition and click OK.

Keep in mind that if you base your selection criteria on a summary field, Crystal evaluates that portion of the selection formula on the client workstation running the report and not on the database server (assuming you are using a SQL or ODBC data source).

Creating Running Totals

Running totals are similar to subtotals and summaries in the totaling operation used. They differ in that they calculate the accumulating total record by record or group by group, so you can see the total growing by each record and/or group.

You create Running Total fields with the Create Running Total Field dialog box or by writing a combination of formulas, taking advantage of variables and evaluation time functions. There may be times when you want to write out the formulas, and this is discussed in Chapter 7. However, the Create Running Total Field dialog box makes the process much easier for simple applications.

Using the Create Running Total Field Dialog Box

Running totals require several steps, or parts, to work properly. First, like you do with a basic summary field, you choose the field on which to base the running total, such as a Sales Amount field or Employee Count field.

After determining which field you want to total, you need to consider how the running total should accumulate. The following are your options:

◆ Accumulate the total for each and every record on the report.

◆ Accumulate the total conditionally for each record based on the change of a specified field in the record. For example, if each record on your report corresponds to an invoice, you can accumulate the running total of the invoice amount each time the invoice date changes.

◆ Accumulate the running total for a specified group.

◆ Write a formula that determines how to accumulate the running total.

Finally, you instruct the running total if and when to reset back to zero. By default, the running total always starts from zero at the beginning of the report. If you want, you can reset the total in midreport; for example, you could reset it for each group.

The Create Running Total Field dialog box allows you to set all the running total options in one place:

1. Open the Field Explorer and select the Running Total Fields option.
2. Click the New icon in the Field Explorer toolbar, or right-click the Running Total Fields option and select New from the shortcut menu.

This opens the Create Running Total Field dialog box, shown in Figure 5-21.

3. Type a name for the running total in the Running Total Name box.

4. Select the field for which you want to calculate a running total from the Available Tables and Fields list. Click the forward arrow button (>) to move the field to the Field to summarize box.

5. Next, select a summary function from the Type of Summary list.

6. Specify when and how often you want the running total to calculate in the Evaluate area. I have selected For each record in this example, because I want the running total to add each record to the running total. The following are your options:

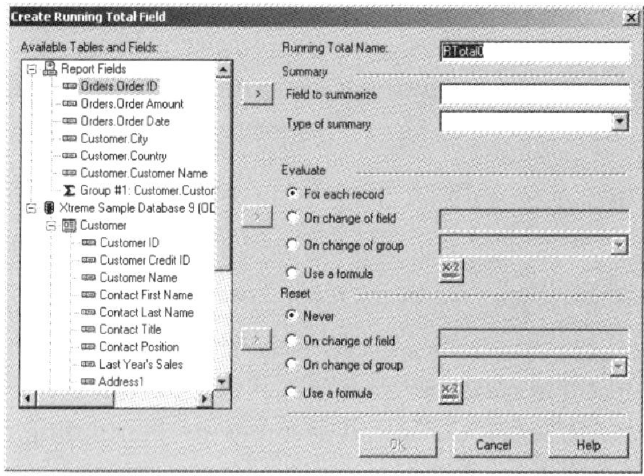

FIGURE 5-21 *Use the Create Running Total Field dialog box to build running total fields.*

◆ **For each record.** The running total evaluates for each record and adds the value (or whatever function chosen) to the total as it comes to it in the report.

◆ **On change of field.** The running total evaluates each time it encounters a certain specified field from the drop-down list on the right.

◆ **On change of group.** The running total evaluates each time there is a change of group (once for each group). Again, use the drop-down list to select a group.

◆ **Use a formula.** The running total is evaluated each time the condition of the formula is true.

7. Select if and when you want the running total to reset in the Reset area. To set your running total to calculate per group, you need to reset it per group here (see Figure 5-22). The following are your options:

    ◆ **Never.** The running total is not reset and calculates continuously for the entire report.

    ◆ **On change of field.** The running total resets each time it encounters a different field value.

    ◆ **On change of group.** The running total resets each time it encounters a new group, as specified in the drop-down list on the right.

    ◆ **Use a formula.** The running total resets when the value of the formula is true.

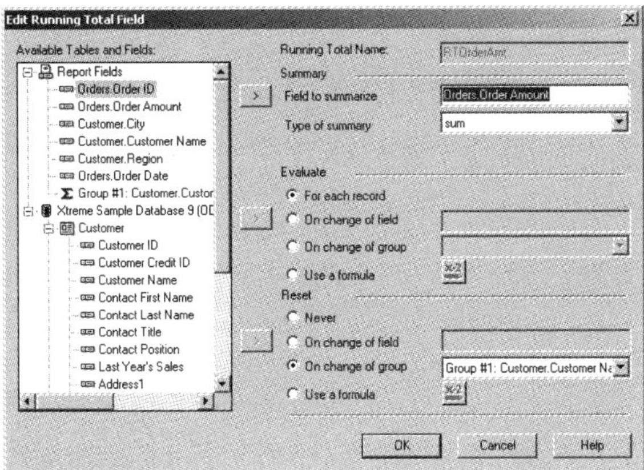

FIGURE 5-22 *Use the Create Running Total Field dialog box to create a running total for a report. This running total calculates the running total of the Order Amount for each group, starting over at zero at the beginning of each new group.*

8. Click OK to close the Create Running Total Field dialog box. Select the name of the running total you just created from the Running Total Fields list in the Field Explorer, and place the field in the Details section of your report. Or, place the running total field in the Group Footer section to have the report print the running total for the group, without accumulating values listed on each detail line.

9. Preview your report to see the running total and verify that it works as you intended (see Figure 5-23).

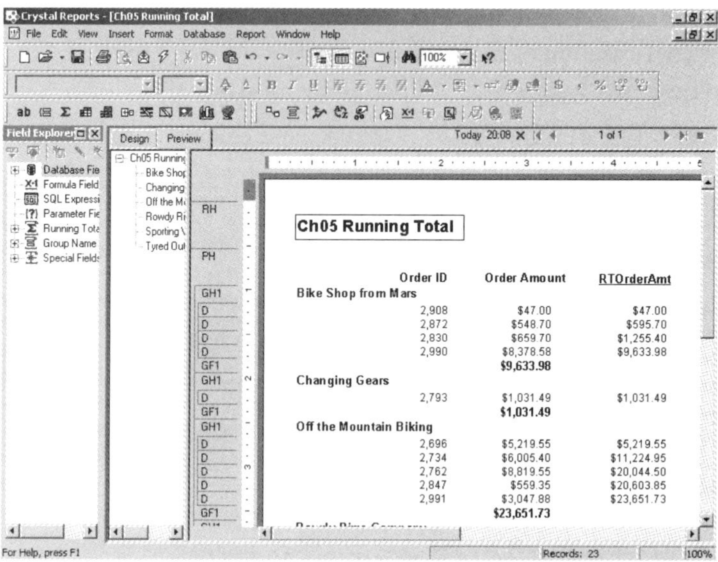

FIGURE 5-23 *Preview your report to see the running total for Order Amount. The running total resets to zero at the beginning of each new group.*

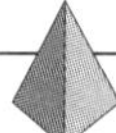

TIP

Change any aspect of your running total by right-clicking on the field and choosing Edit Running Total or clicking the Edit button on the Field Explorer with the running total field selected. The running total field on your report automatically updates with any changes you make.

Limiting/Sorting Groups with the Group Sort Expert

Once you have groups on your report, you may want to sort those groups based on a summary field. You learned earlier how to use the *in specified order* grouping option to customize and combine groups, and set specific orders. Using the Group Sort Expert, you can sort your groups based on a summary field for that group, and you can have the report print only the groups with the highest or lowest values in the summary field.

To begin, you must have a summary field on your report in order to use the Group Sort Expert. Then, to sort and limit groups based on summary fields, follow these steps:

1. Select Report, Group Sort Expert or click the Group Sort Expert toolbar button ☒ on the Expert Tools toolbar. The Group Sort Expert opens.

2. In the Group Sort Expert, a tab represents each group on your report. Select the tab for the group you want to sort.

3. From the For this group sort drop-down list on the left, select the option that describes how you want to sort the group:

   ◆ **No Sort.** No sorting will occur.

   ◆ **All.** Sort all groups on your report. Select a field from the based on drop-down list of summaries on the report.

   ◆ **Top N.** If you want to order your groups starting with the largest summary value for a specific number of groups (not all groups; you set the number of groups you want to see by supplying a value for N).

   ◆ **Bottom N.** If you want to include only a specific number of groups with the lowest values (see Figure 5-24).

USING SUMMARIES TO SOLVE GROUP SORTING PROBLEMS

As described earlier in this chapter, to ensure that your report doesn't merge information from two groups into one, you may need to group your records on a unique ID field. For example, say your report has a group for each manager, and your company has two managers named John Smith. You would need to group by a unique field like ManagerID—rather than by Manager Name—to ensure separate group sections for each of the two John Smiths. But, you do not want the groups sorted by that ID field, you want them sorted by last name.

Based on ManagerID, the groups would be in the numerical order of the ID numbers, and there's no direct way to tell the report to sort the groups based on a different field. However, you can use summaries to change the sort order of a group. Continuing the example, here's how you would make your report sort the manager groups by the managers' last names:

1. Drop the ManagerLastName field into the Details section of your report. From the field's right-click shortcut menu, click Format Field. In the Format Editor, select the Suppress check box on the Common tab.

2. Select Insert, Summary to open the Insert Summary dialog box. Select the ManagerLastName field to summarize. Select the maximum function from the functions list, and select the ManagerID group from the Summary location list. Crystal inserts the maximum summary field in the Group Footer section.

(continues)

◆ **Top Percentage.** Order groups based on the value of the summary field selected being in the top N percentage of the total.

◆ **Bottom Percentage.** Order groups on being members of the bottom percentage set.

4. Set the based on drop-down list box to the field you want the sort based on. This list includes each summary field on your report for the group listed on the tab.

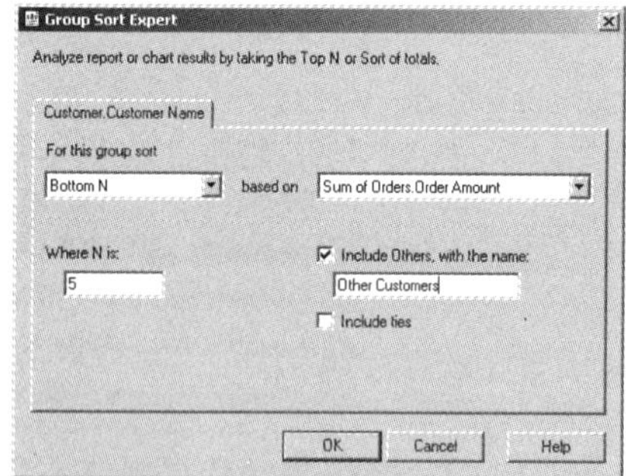

FIGURE 5-24 *Use the Group Sort Expert to sort the groups on your report based on summary information for each group. You can sort all of your groups, or the top or bottom groups.*

5. If you selected All, click either Ascending or Descending for each summary field you want to sort.

6. If you selected Top N or Bottom N, enter how many groups you want to include on your report by entering a number in the Where N is box (refer to Figure 5-24). If you want to include any remaining records in another group, select the Include Others check box and enter a name for the group (Crystal supplies the name "Others" by default, but you can change it).

7. Click OK to close the Group Sort Expert. Preview your report to see the effect of sorting your groups. Go back to the Group Sort Expert at any time to change or remove the sort.

To remove any group sorting you have on your report, open the Group Sort Expert and select No Sort from the first list.

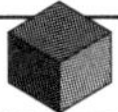 **NOTE**

When using the Group Sort Expert, your grand total fields remain the same regardless of how many groups you print on your report. Thus, if you include only the Top 5 groups, but have 20 groups on the report, the grand total will include all 20 groups. To include only the printed groups in a grand total, create a running total that evaluates only the records that print on the report.

Summary

This chapter covered Crystal Reports features commonly thought of as basic elements of report design. Sorting and grouping records serve to organize information, making the report easier to read and interpret. Summarizing information by group and for the entire report also serves an important role in managing the information on a report and getting more from it.

The different grouping options help you organize your report in a meaningful way, regardless of how information was originally entered and organized in your database. As you become experienced in more advanced features of Crystal Reports, you will begin to use several features simultaneously to create reports that collect and format data exactly the way you want. Creativity working with sorts, groups, summaries, formulas, and group sorting functionality gives you many options beyond the "basics."

Chapter 6

Crystal Reports provides many formatting options to assist you in building a report that looks and functions exactly the way you want. Formatting options range from simple field attributes such as font size and decimal places to more sophisticated underlaying and suppression options. Crystal Reports supports extensive conditional formatting options and allows you to format field and section attributes conditionally depending on a report's actual data.

Three main types of formatting are listed here:

◆ You are able to manipulate the formatting of all objects inserted onto a report.

◆ By formatting section attributes you can control the processing behavior and how the printed copy of a report looks.

◆ Conditional formatting is available for both individual objects and section attributes.

Formatting in Crystal Reports covers the spectrum from simple to complex, where formatting attributes used creatively can help control the overall processing and outcome of a report. There are many special functions built into the Formula Editor that are meant for use in specific conditional formatting situations. Both this chapter and Chapter 7 explore many of these functions.

Formatting Fields

When inserting fields on a report, you may find that the fields do not always have the exact format you need. Crystal Reports uses the default format specified on the Fields and Fonts tabs in the Options dialog box (accessed via File, Options and covered later in this chapter). You can, however, format any field right on your report, which many times is more desirable. You can format one or many fields at a time, by selecting the field(s) in the design or preview tabs or in the Report Explorer.

 **NOTE**

You can set and change the default formatting options. The section "Setting Default Formatting Properties," later in this chapter, covers setting defaults. If you always want certain field types in a particular format, you can change the global default to save yourself from needing to format that field type every time you add them to a report. On the other hand, more specific formatting needs are usually better served by formatting unique situations individually.

Formatting Options for Every Field Type

There are two different ways to open the Format Editor for any field on a report. One method is to select the field on the report (Design or Preview tab, it does not matter), and select Format, Format Field or right-click the field and select Format Field from the shortcut menu. The other method is to select the field you plan to format in the Report Explorer, right-click and select Format Field from the shortcut menu. Either way opens the same Format Editor dialog box where the field attributes are edited.

The options available to format a field depend on the type of field you want to format. By selecting the field you plan to format then opening the Format Editor, Crystal Reports provides the correct formatting options based on the field's data type. Remember, you can select more than one field to format at a time. If the fields have different data types—for example, one is a string and one is a number—Crystal makes available only the common formatting options for the group.

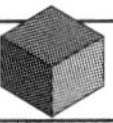 **NOTE**

Formatting options for all fields and sections are accessible either via the design environment itself or via the Report Explorer. Use whichever method you prefer.

Change a Field's Format

The instructions in this section first describe selecting fields for formatting from the Design tab or Preview tab, then another set of steps outlines using the Report Explorer:

1. With one or more fields selected, select Format, Format Field. The Format Editor opens, as shown in Figure 6-1. You can also right-click the field you want to format and select Format Field from the shortcut menu. The type of field selected determines which tabs you'll see in the Format Editor.

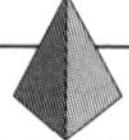

TIP

If you have selected more than one field to format, the menu command reads Format Objects instead of Format Field. If these fields are of different field types, then Crystal makes only the tabs that are common for all selected fields available.

2. The Format Editor has four tabs available for all fields: Common, Border, Font, and Hyperlink. Other tabs are available depending on the type of field selected, such as a number tab for number type fields or a date tab for date type fields. Click from tab to tab to set formatting options for the field selected. As you select formatting options, the Sample area at the bottom of the Format Editor shows you the formatting options in use.

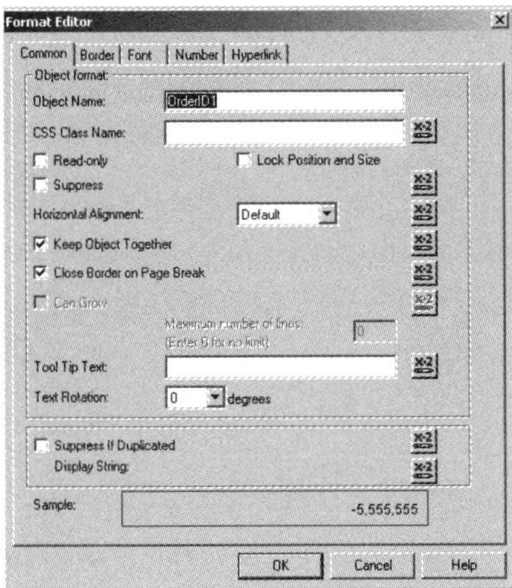

FIGURE 6-1 *Use the Format Editor to change the format of any field.*

NOTE

Next to most options throughout the Format Editor, the Conditional Formula button labeled X+2 indicates that you can control the formatting option based on the value of the field or other conditions in the report. For more information on conditional formatting, see "Absolute vs. Conditional Formatting" later in this chapter. Chapter 7 covers formulas.

3. Click OK at any time to apply the formatting options you selected and close the Format Editor.

You can also format report objects using the Report Explorer. The Format Editor is exactly the same, only the method of opening it is different:

1. Open the Report Explorer by selecting View, Report Explorer or clicking the Report Explorer toolbar button.

2. Expand the section containing the field you want to format, then select the field you want to format.

3. Right click and select Format Field from the shortcut menu to open the Format Editor dialog box.

General Field Attributes: The Common Tab

The Common tab of the Format Editor provides basic formatting options for any field (see Figure 6-1):

- ◆ **Object Name.** Leave the default name or edit it. Naming objects on a report allows you to save and refer to items in the Crystal Repository, Report Explorer, and when defining Report Part hyperlinks.

- ◆ **CSS Class Name.** Use CSS (cascading style sheets) names for Web report formatting.

- ◆ **Read-only.** Locks the formatting of an object. Makes all formatting attributes unavailable.

- ◆ **Lock Position and Size.** Locks the position and size of an object so that it cannot be moved or resized.

- ◆ **Suppress.** Use this option to suppress a field from printing on a report. In formulas, you may need a field for part of a variable, but you do not want that value to print on your report. You may also want to use a formula to suppress a field if some condition is met.

- ◆ **Horizontal Alignment.** Open the drop-down list next to this option to view the alignment choices. Horizontal Alignment aligns the data within an object.

- ◆ **Keep Object Together.** When selected (the default), this option prevents any page breaks within the object. For example, if an object covers two lines, a page break will not be allowed between the two lines of the one object.

- ◆ **Close Border on Page Break.** Exactly as its name implies, this option closes any border on the bottom of a page and reopens it at the top of the next page. Of course, it applies only when you have added a border to the object on the Border tab.

- ◆ **Can Grow.** Similar to text wrapping. By default, no database fields automatically wrap or grow; this way, you can be assured of the formatting and placement of fields on a report. Select the Can Grow check box to allow a field to grow vertically if needed. Use this option for fields in your database where comments or text may have been entered and you need to accommodate various field lengths. The field grows down vertically only; it does not grow horizontally. You need to manually size your field horizontally. The Maximum number of lines setting allows you to set a limit to the number of lines of field growth.

◆ **Tool Tip Text.** Type the text you would like to appear in a text bubble when users rest their mouse pointer over a particular field or click the Conditional Formula button to open the Formula Editor and write a conditional formula. View the tool tip on the Preview tab by resting the pointer over the field with the Tool Tip Text formula. If you do not see the tool tip text, choose View, Tooltips and select the appropriate option.

◆ **Text Rotation.** Allows you to rotate the field 90 or 270 degrees. You must use a TrueType font or printer font. Rotated fields no longer have the Can Grow option available.

◆ **Suppress If Duplicated.** Suppresses a field if it contains the same value more than once consecutively. For example, you might have a report that prints a record for each order a customer placed in the past month. If the customer placed more than one order, you don't want to repeat the customer name on each record. Using this option, the customer name would be listed only once, on the line with the first order.

◆ **Display String.** Click the Conditional Formula button to open the Formula Editor and enter a formula to change the value being displayed on the report. This is useful if you have an order amount field that you would like to display with a "K" if it is over $1 thousand or an "M" if it is over $1 million.

Borders and Background: The Border Tab

The Border tab provides options for adding and formatting a border and the background for a field (see Figure 6-2).

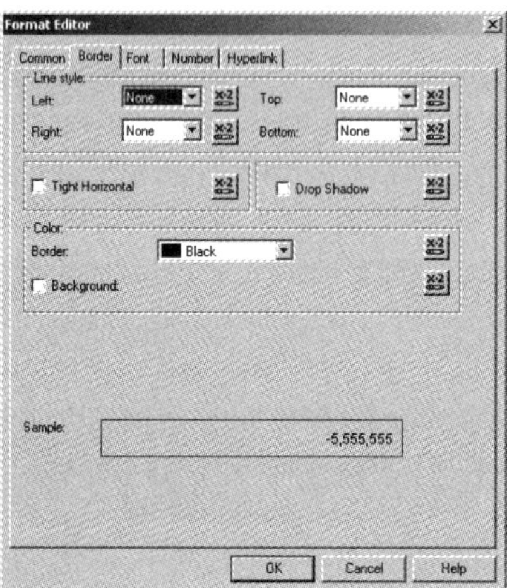

FIGURE 6-2 *Use the Border tab to create a border, drop shadow, or background shading for a field.*

◆ **Line style.** Select the line style to create a border on just one side or all sides of a field. Choose from the drop-down list options Single, Double, Dashed, or Dotted.

◆ **Tight Horizontal.** If you want to have a border around just the data in a field, not the entire field, select this check box. It narrows the border to accommodate just the width of the data within the field for each individual record.

◆ **Drop Shadow.** Select this check box to create a drop shadow around the selected field.

◆ **Border.** From the Border drop-down list, select the color for a border or drop shadow.

◆ **Background.** If you want the field to have a background color, select the Background check box and select a background color. The background color covers the entire field area, as shown in the sample at the bottom of the Format Editor.

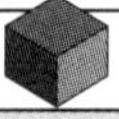

NOTE

The Formatting toolbar contains an Outside Borders button for formatting the selected field with all four border lines at once, creating a square-box border around the field.

Setting Font Style and Color: The Font Tab

The Font tab provides options for formatting the text style of the selected field. Font, Style, Size, and Color are the main options available (see Figure 6-3). The Character Spacing Exactly option is useful for formatting reports in foreign language characters, to accommodate the larger characters. Crystal also offers a Formatting toolbar that contains the font formatting options. If it's not available in your application window, you can turn it on using View, Toolbars.

THE ARGUMENT FOR USING STANDARD FONTS

The Font drop-down list presents a comprehensive list of all the fonts available on your computer; however, not all fonts are necessarily available for use on your reports. If you select a non-Windows standard font, your printer driver may not support it. When you preview the report, Crystal reverts to the default font selected for the field type on the Fonts tab of the Options dialog box. Most printer drivers support standard, fancy, and symbol fonts. Test the font you select by previewing your report. Fonts that change the basic spacing of letters or fields are sometimes not available, but I do suggest giving yours a try.

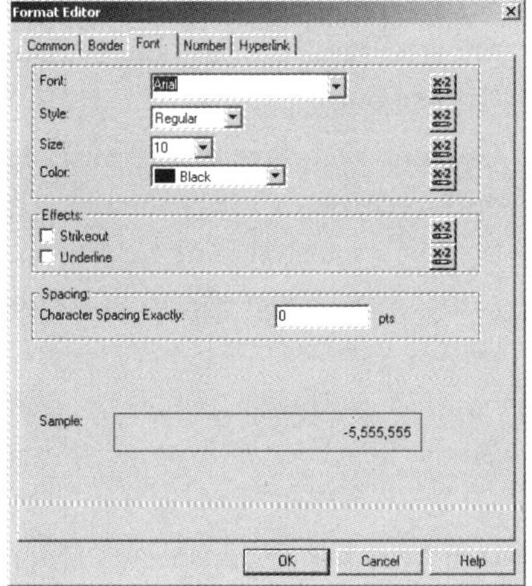

FIGURE 6-3 *Use the Font tab of the Format Editor to set the font for the field selected.*

Linking Your Report to Other Information: The Hyperlink Tab

You can add any of several types of hyperlinks to a report. Not all hyperlink types are available at all times—it depends on the object you select to serve as the link.

The Hyperlink tab contains prompting text to help you enter the correct information for the type of hyperlink you are creating (see Figure 6-4). The following options appear on the Hyperlink tab:

◆ **A Web Site on the Internet.** Create a link to a Web site by typing the name of the Web site; Crystal fills in the http:// for you.

◆ **An E-mail Address.** Add a link with your e-mail address so people can e-mail you if they have questions about the report you designed. Just type your e-mail address in the box.

◆ **A File.** Browse to the location of the file you want to link to by clicking the Browse button.

◆ **Current Web Site Field Value.** This option creates a hyperlink out of the field you selected. The field must be stored as a proper Web site address in your data source.

◆ **Current E-mail Field Value.** This option creates an e-mail hyperlink out of the field you selected. The field must be stored as a proper e-mail address in your data source.

◆ **Report Part Drilldown.** Use this option to hyperlink specific report parts to create objects for the Report Part Viewer.

◆ **Another Report Object.** If you create a hyperlink to another Crystal Report file, you are really creating an on-demand subreport (covered in Chapter 10). For example, if you have a worldwide sales report, you may want to link it to other country-specific reports, which would function as on-demand subreports.

ADDING CUSTOM BUBBLE TEXT TO HYPERLINKS

I like to add customized bubble text to my hyperlinks, so that the reader of my report can hover their mouse cursor over a field and be instructed to "click here to link to whatever." To add this text, you use a tooltip:

1. Select the field with the hyperlink, and select Format, Field.

2. On the Common tab, type the message you would like displayed in the Tool Tip Text area.

3. You can also use the conditional formatting button to add a conditional message.

4. Click OK to close the Format Editor. Now when you hover your mouse cursor over the object on the Preview tab, the text appears.

When you preview a report and click a field that contains a hyperlink, the appropriate application to view the information is launched. Thus, for a Web site, your Web browser is launched, and if you link to a Word document, Word is opened, and so forth. One of the sample reports for this chapter contains several hyperlinks, to another report, an e-mail address, and a Web site.

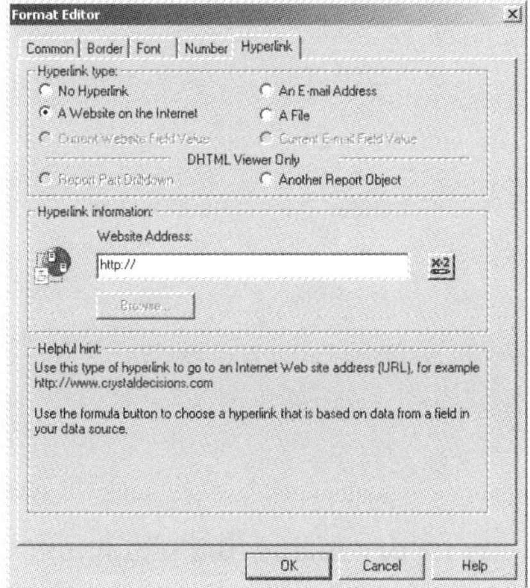

FIGURE 6-4 *Use the Hyperlink tab to link your report data to a variety of objects and places.*

Formatting String and Text Fields: The Paragraph Tab

Use the Paragraph tab to set formatting options for paragraphs in string fields and text objects. You can set the exact spacing and indentations of the paragraphs, as well as the reading order and alignment (see Figure 6-5). You may find the Line Spacing option useful for formatting foreign language characters.

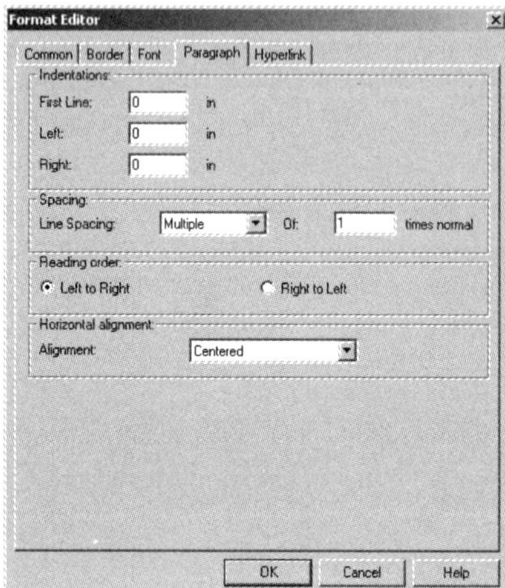

FIGURE 6-5 *Use the Paragraph tab to format text in string fields or text objects.*

Specific Formatting Options

The Format Editor, when opened from any field, contains the Common, Border, Font, and Hyperlink tabs. String fields have an additional Paragraph tab. Other field types have additional tabs that provide formatting options for the particular field type. When you open the Format Editor, the dialog box includes all tabs related to the data type of the field you have selected.

Date, Time, and Date/Time Fields

When formatting a date, time, or date/time field on a report, the Date and Time tab becomes available in the Format Editor (see Figure 6-6). This tab contains many options for formatting date, time, and date/time fields.

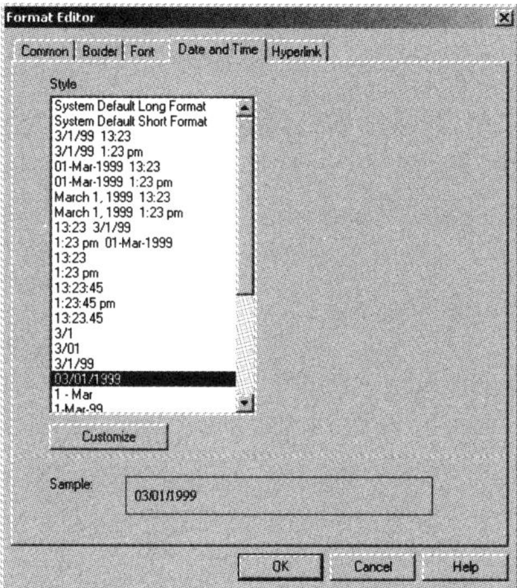

FIGURE 6-6 *The Date and Time tab provides many options for formatting a date field.*

Click the Customize button to customize your date and/or time field format. This opens the Custom Style dialog box, which has one or three tabs that provide more formatting options (see Figure 6-7):

◆ **Date and Time tab.** Select what data to print from the date/time field, such as just Date, Time, Date/Time, or Time/Date.

◆ **Date tab.** Set options for Format, Order, Day of week, and Separators. These areas of the dialog box allow you to format the date to read exactly as you want. Any options you set are displayed in the Sample box at the bottom of the dialog box.

◆ **Time tab.** Set time formatting here for a 12- or 24-hour clock, along with number and separator options.

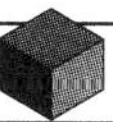 **NOTE**

Several options on the Date tab apply to date formats used in non-Western cultures, namely Japanese. Options such as Calendar Type, Era/period Type, and Encl don't pertain to standard American and European dates but are very useful to people in those cultures that need them.

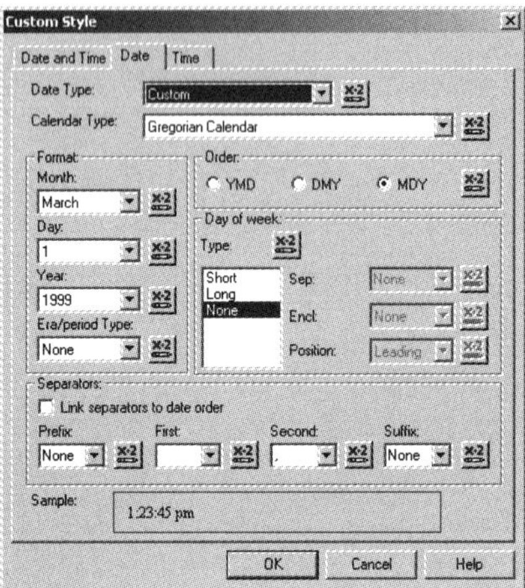

FIGURE 6-7 *Customize the formatting of a date or time field manually.*

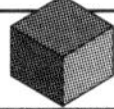

NOTE

Crystal Reports uses a standard date, time, or date/time format for all dates. Whether your dates are in date or date/time, for example, depends on the database from which they come. You can format your dates and times to look just the way you want using the Date and Time tab in the Format Editor dialog box. To change the date format of dates read into each report, go to File, Report Options, and select the format from the drop-down list.

Currency and Number Fields

The Number tab appears in the Format Editor when you select a number field or a currency field to format. The Number tab gives you a list of common options for formatting numbers on a report (see Figure 6-8). Select the Display Currency Symbol check box to display the system default currency symbol (this comes from the Windows regional setting). To customize the number format or currency symbol, click the Customize button to access many options available to specifically format the way numbers look on a report, regardless of how they exist in your database. When you click the Customize button, the Custom Style dialog box opens with Number and Currency Symbol tabs.

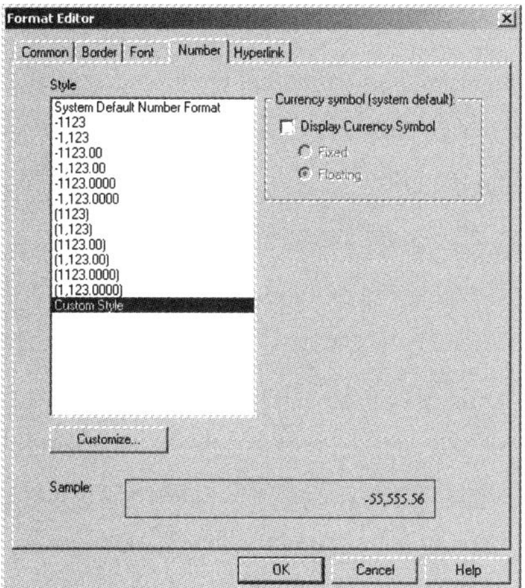

FIGURE 6-8 *Many number formats are available on the Number tab.*

The following options are available in the Custom Style dialog box on the Number tab (see Figure 6-9) to format number fields:

◆ **Suppress if Zero.** Select this check box to suppress the field if it equals zero. The field still exists on the report and figures into any calculations, but it does not print a zero.

◆ **Decimals, Rounding, and Negatives.** These options allow you to format numbers according to your needs. You can set the global default under File, Options, Fields, but you might find that your number formatting needs differ from report to report.

◆ **Allow Field Clipping.** When selected, Crystal cuts off extra digits of numbers too long to print within the width of the field. When cleared, Crystal prints a string of number signs (#) to let you know that the number does not fit within the size of the field.

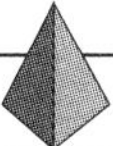

TIP

I highly recommend that you make certain the default setting is a clear Allow Field Clipping check box. Do so by choosing File, Options, Fields, clicking Number, selecting the Number tab, clicking Customize, and then clearing the Allow Field Clipping check box. Repeat for currency field types, subtotals and summaries. This way, you know that numbers in your field, by default, will not be clipped off.

◆ **Decimal and Thousands Separators.** Both of these separators can be set to whatever character you want, including a blank space.

◆ **Leading Zero.** Selecting this option prints a leading zero for any values under 1, such as 0.45 instead of .45.

◆ **Reverse Sign for Display.** Reverse the sign for debit and credit amounts in financial reports with this option.

◆ **Show Zero Values as.** Select from options for how zero values print on the report: the default, found under File, Options, is – or 0.

◆ **Use Accounting Format.** This option, at the top of the Number tab, applies a default general accounting format. The Windows regional settings determine the character to use as a negative sign. Zero values display as a dash, and the currency symbol is fixed on the left side.

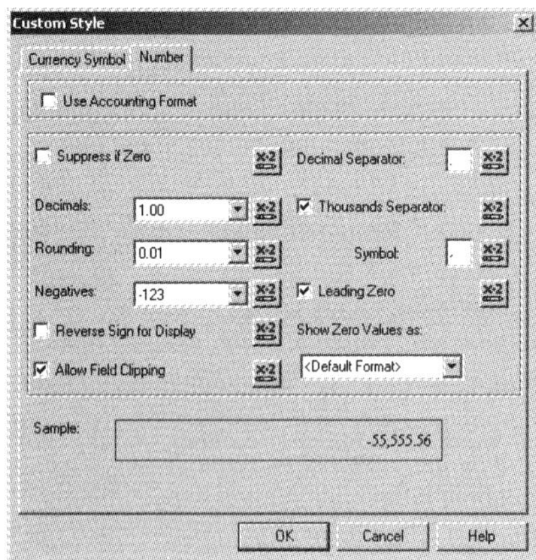

FIGURE 6-9 *Use the Custom Style dialog box to set more specific formatting options.*

The following options are available in the Custom Style dialog box on the Currency Symbol tab to format currency fields:

◆ **Enable Currency Symbol.** If you select this check box, a currency symbol prints on your report. You can specify exactly where to print the symbol by selecting either the Fixed or Floating radio button, or by writing a conditional formula.

◆ **One Symbol Per Page.** After enabling the currency symbol, this check box option is available if you only want one symbol per page of the report.

◆ **Position and Currency Symbol.** These two options allow you to set the position and type of symbol you want to use. Change the options and watch the sample to see exactly how the symbol will print on a report.

NOTE

The Fields tab of the Options dialog box (opened by selecting File, Options) allows you to set default formatting options for all field types. If you always want every number field in a certain format, you can set it here and then not have to format field by field on your reports.

Boolean Fields

The Boolean tab of the Format Editor dialog box gives you formatting options for Boolean fields (see Figure 6-10). Crystal makes the Boolean tab available for both Boolean fields from your database and Boolean formulas that you write using the Formula Editor.

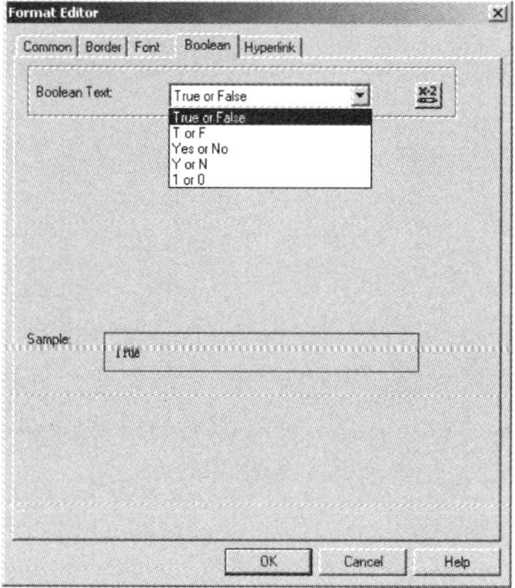

FIGURE 6-10 *On the Boolean tab, set formatting options for a Boolean field used on a report.*

Change Field Type to Accommodate Formatting

Sometimes, in our less than perfect world of databases, a field that you really need to format as a number is actually a string or text field in your database. This means that when formatting the field, you have the options for string type fields but not number fields, because Crystal Reports reads the field type from your database and then gives you the appropriate options. To get around this problem, you can change the field type by using the Formula Workshop.

Convert a String Field into a Number Field

Take a string field that you want to format as a number. Using the function ToNumber() in the Formula Editor, you can write a formula to change the string field to a number field, and then you can format the field as a number. The formula for this example would read:

```
//Convert string field into number type field for formatting
ToNumber({table.field})
```

You would then put this formula field on the report, rather than the database field. This formula field changes the data type to number, so Crystal Reports makes the number formatting options available for the field.

Convert a String Field into a Date Field

Use a formula to convert a string field into a date field by using the DateValue() function:

```
//Convert string or number field into a date type field for formatting
DateValue({table.field})
```

This function works differently depending on the type of field used (number or string) and whether the format of the data fits any of two formats. Sometimes this function does not work based on the field data you are trying to convert, but there are other options. If you had data for a date that looked like 771019, you could pull out the parts of the date, namely the year, month, and day, and save each part as a variable. Then, use the Date() function to build a date type field:

```
//convert string field into date type field for formatting
local stringvar yy := left({table.field},2);
local stringvar mm := mid({table.field}, 3 to 4);
local stringvar dd := mid({table.field}, 5 to 6);
Date(yy,mm,dd)
```

Insert this formula into the Details section. The field will return a date that can be used to compare with other dates and be formatted using the date formatting options.

NOTE

This formula uses variables, which are covered in Chapter 7.

Setting Default Formatting Properties

Crystal Reports lets you set the system defaults for all the formatting options we've discussed so far. Crystal installs with defaults already set, but you can change the defaults to suit your needs at any time. To change the default formatting options:

1. Select File, Options and go to the Fields tab. This tab has buttons for each field type (see Figure 6-11).

SPECIAL FORMATTING OPTIONS FOR FOREIGN CHARACTERS

Crystal Reports has many formatting options especially useful for text in other langugages.

On the Font tab, use the Character spacing and Fractional font size options to help ensure that characters don't overlap or get cut off.

On the Paragraph tab, use the Line Spacing and Indentations options to also adjust printing of character sets.

Crystal Reports also makes special formatting options available to accommodate foreign date formats. In the Custom Style dialog box, click on the Date tab and use the Encl option, which allows for round or square brackets to enclose the day of the week. Also, if running Crystal Reports on a foreign language platform using a specific calendar, you can choose to display the long or short format Era/Period Type.

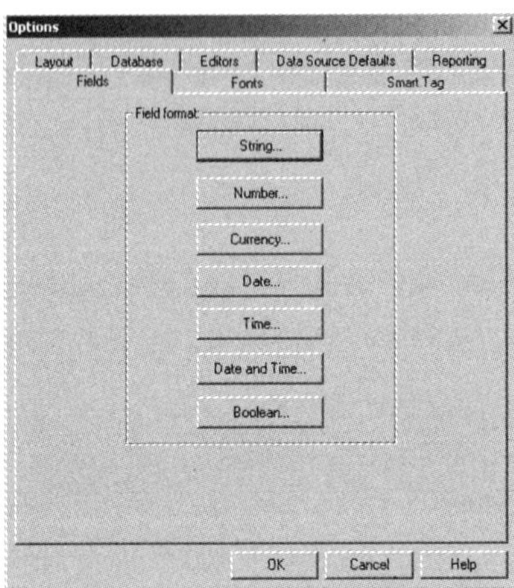

FIGURE 6-11 *Click the button for each field type to set default formatting options.*

2. Click the button of the field type you want to format, and then set the default formatting options. The field type determines the available tabs. The String, Number, Currency, Date, Time, Date/Time, and Boolean fields all use the tabs described in the previous section, "Specific Formatting Options."

3. Click the Fonts tab in the Options dialog box and set default font settings for the different field types.

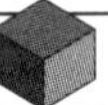

NOTE

When you change the default formatting settings, they apply to any new fields you add to the report, but do not retroactively reformat fields that already appear on the report. This way, any new report you start will have the new default options you set.

Absolute vs. Conditional Formatting

Absolute formatting refers to formatting that applies to a field or object each and every time it prints. So far, this chapter has discussed setting absolute formatting, such as making a font Arial, adding a border around a field, or formatting a number or date to print the exact way you want. *Conditional formatting* applies only if a condition is met. In Crystal Reports, conditional formatting takes precedence over absolute formatting. You can apply conditional formatting to various report objects. The following sections explain how to format conditionally using the Highlighting Expert or conditional formulas.

Conditional Formatting with the Highlighting Expert

The Highlighting Expert is a handy tool that gives you the means to conditionally format font style, font color, border, and background color for all field types without writing any formulas. You may find that using the Highlighting Expert is easier than writing out the formulas, because you can create simple or complex conditional formatting, and you can see all font, border, and background conditions at once.

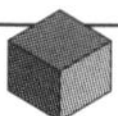

NOTE

The Highlighting Expert is available with all field types. You can use the Highlighting Expert for fields in cross-tabs, as well as individual fields within a report.

The Highlighting Expert lays out all of your formatting choices in front of you. The information and criteria you set in the Item editor side of the Highlighting Expert dialog box show in the Item list (see Figure 6-12). The formatting options you set in the Item editor also show in the Sample box at the bottom of the Item editor. To use the Highlighting Expert:

1. Select the field to which you want to apply conditional formatting. You can select the field either on the report Design or Preview tabs, or select the field in the Report Explorer. Select Format, Highlighting Expert or right-click the field and click Highlighting Expert from the shortcut menu. The Highlighting Expert opens.

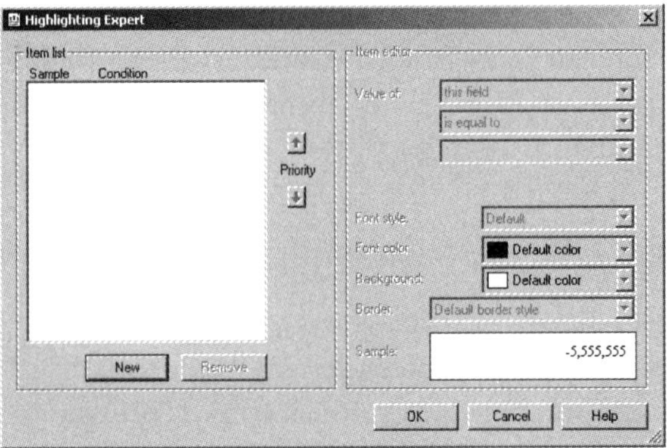

FIGURE 6-12 *Use the Highlighting Expert to conditionally format fields.*

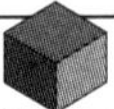

NOTE

You also can use the Report Explorer to open the Highlighting Expert. Just like formatting fields, select the field you want to format, right-click, and select Highlighting Expert from the shortcut menu.

2. In the Item editor area, select a condition from the Value of list. Type or select a value from the other drop-down lists to complete a criteria statement. Note that you can select "this field" or select another field in the report on which to base the condition.

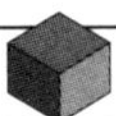

NOTE

Once you set criteria for formatting in the Value of box, that value appears in the Item list as a condition. This way, you can see all conditions you have set for the selected field.

3. Select the formatting options you want to use: Font Style, Color, Background, and Border. These formatting options apply when the condition you entered has been met. For example, you might select Font color and

change it to red. You can set more than one formatting option for one field, so you could also set a condition on the same field for background color yellow if the same or a different condition is met.

4. Click the New button to start a new formatting condition for the same field. If your first criteria worked with the font color, you can set a second criteria for the font style or color, background color, or border style (see Figure 6-13).

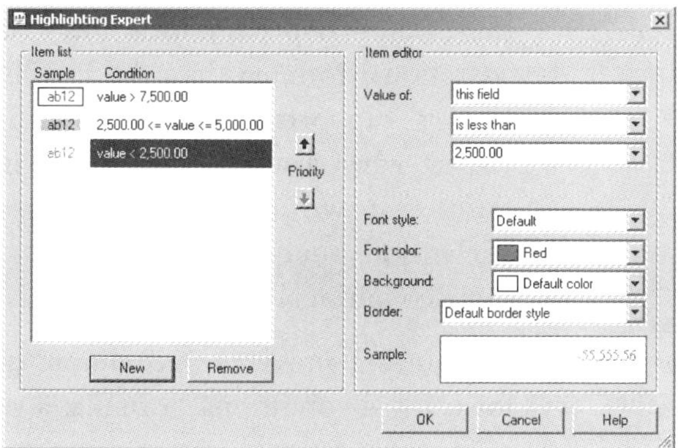

FIGURE 6-13 *Set as many conditions as you want for a field. The Highlighting Expert lists each condition in the Item list.*

5. Click OK to close the Highlighting Expert and save the conditions you set. Go back to the Highlighting Expert at any time to add or delete conditional formatting.

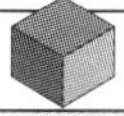

NOTE

When setting several conditions for one formatting attribute, be sure that they follow in order from largest to smallest. For example, if you want the font color to be green if the value is greater than 1000 and blue if the value is greater than 1500, you would need to list the test for greater than 1500 at the top of the Highlighting Expert Item list. Otherwise, the font will be green for all values over 1000 and the blue will be ignored.

Conditional Formatting Using Formulas

There are many instances in which you will not be able to use the Highlighting Expert to conditionally format fields. Many conditional formatting options found in the Format Editor are not available in the Highlighting Expert, such as conditional suppression or field specific formatting attributes such as date order (such as day, month, year or month, day, year). And, third, you may need to use a more complex conditional formula than the Highlighting Expert supports. Use the Highlighting Expert when you can, because using it is easier than writing formulas; but you will likely find yourself writing formulas for some conditional formatting needs.

Accounting provides a common example for using a conditional formula: a value in a currency field is less than or equal to zero, and you want the amount printed in red. You would probably open the Highlighting Expert to conditionally format a number field with font color. But how about if you wanted the number to be suppressed if the condition was met? You would do the following:

1. Select the field you want to format, and select Format, Format Field or right-click the field and select Format Field.

2. With the Format Editor open, click the Conditional Formula (X+2) button next to the formatting option you wish to use, in this case the Suppress option. This opens the Formula Editor.

CONDITIONAL FORMATTING FORMULAS USING THE FORMULA WORKSHOP

This chapter describes conditionally formatting fields using the Highlighting Expert and formulas by selecting the field or section you want to format from the report itself or from the Report Explorer. This opens the Format Editor dialog box, in which you select formatting options to conditionally format.

The Formula Workshop also provides an interface for adding conditional formulas to the fields and sections of a report. The Workshop contains a Formatting Formulas folder, which lists all sections and fields of the report. To add a conditional formula to one of these sections or fields, right-click the field or section and select New Formatting Formula from the shortcut menu. This opens a dialog box with formatting attributes listed. Select an option from the list, and then click the Formula Editor button to open the Formula Editor and write a formula.

The Formula Workshop is covered in detail in Chapter 7, including a specific section on conditional formatting formulas.

3. Write the formula. The top of the Functions list displays options specific to the formatting operation that you are manipulating. If formatting suppression, you have no special options. If writing a formula for font style, you have a list of Font Style Constants available (see Figure 6-14).

4. Once you complete and check your formula, click the Save and close button to close the Formula Editor. The Conditional Formula button becomes a red or maroon color (depending on your system defaults and color settings) and the pencil on the button turns on a diagonal angle, indicating a conditional formula is assigned to the format setting.

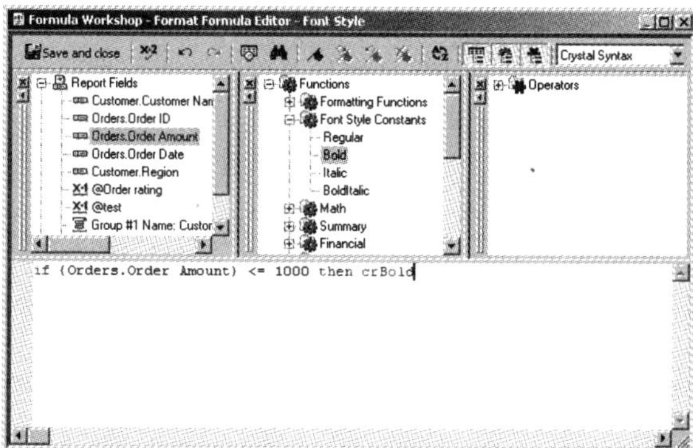

FIGURE 6-14 *Special functions are available for writing conditional formulas depending on which formatting option you use.*

There are countless examples of situations in which conditional formulas could be useful in your reporting. Chapter 7 covers formulas and describes the steps for creating If-Then-Else and Boolean formulas. To help you start thinking creatively about what you could do with conditional formulas, see Table 6-1 for a few examples.

Table 6-1 Examples of Formatting with Conditional Formulas

Goal	Format Attribute	Formula
Change the background color of any field whose payment has not been made and is 45 or more days past due.	Format Editor, Border tab, Background Color	if CurrentDate − {Orders.Ship Date} > 45 and {Orders.Payment Received} = False then crYellow else crNoColor
Display field in red if less than average. The formula calculates the average of a group then compares the value of the field to the calculated average.	Format Editor, Font tab, Color	if {table.field1} < Average ({table,field1}, {table.field3}) then crRed else crBlack
Underline the subtotal if more than five orders.	Format Editor, Font tab, Underline	DistinctCount ({Orders.Order ID}, {Customer.Customer Name})> 5

Formatting Sections

Just as Crystal Reports gives you many ways to format fields, you can also format entire sections of a report. By formatting sections, you can force a page break after each group or hide the Details section of a report to create a summary report. Due to the nature of sections, formatting them differs from formatting fields. You do not set the font or style of a section; rather, you control how the sections act within your report. You will find that being able to manipulate and format sections greatly enhances your ability to create presentation quality reports.

The Section Expert provides many absolute formatting options along with buttons for writing conditional formulas.

Using the Section Expert

This section describes the steps to open and use the Section Expert. The following sections describe using the options available to you with the Section Expert. To open and use the Section Expert:

1. Open the Section Expert either by clicking the Section Expert toolbar button 📳 or, if using the Report Explorer, by right-clicking a section and selecting Section Expert from the shortcut menu. The Section Expert can also be opened by right-clicking on any of the section areas and choosing the Section Expert shortcut.

2. From the Sections list, select the section you want to format (see Figure 6-15).

3. Use any formatting options from either the Common tab or Color tab. Note that along with check boxes to turn options on or off, you can write conditional formulas using the Conditional Formula buttons.

4. Use the Insert, Delete, and Merge buttons to insert additional sections on your report, delete sections you added, or merge sections together.

5. Click OK to close the Section Expert and save any changes or formatting that you set.

CURRENTFIELDVALUE AND DEFAULTATTRIBUTE FUNCTIONS

Two functions in Crystal are available only with conditional formulas. They allow you to easily reuse formula logic within the same report and from report to report. You can find them at the very top of the Functions list in the Formula Editor only when conditionally formatting a field.

Use the CurrentFieldValue function in place of a database field name, variable name, or calculation in a formula. The conditional formula then applies to the current value of the field without having to recalculate the value or specify the field name. This function can be used in most any conditional formula.

For example, to conditionally format a subtotal, you might use the following formula: if CurrentFieldValue < 1000 then crRed, instead of the formula: if @Sum({amount}, {customer}) < 1000 then crRed. This function just simplifies the formula, and makes it easy to copy and paste. CurrentFieldValue is particularly useful when conditionally formatting values in cross-tabs.

The DefaultAttribute function allows you to set an absolute formatting option and then use that default in the conditional formula. For example, you may want to format a field to have a green font color if a condition is met and a blue font color otherwise. Change the font Color setting on the Font tab of the Format Editor to blue, and then enter this conditional formula: if {table.field} > 20000 then crGreen else DefaultAttribute. This function overrides the Windows default of black and uses whatever value has been set in the drop-down list.

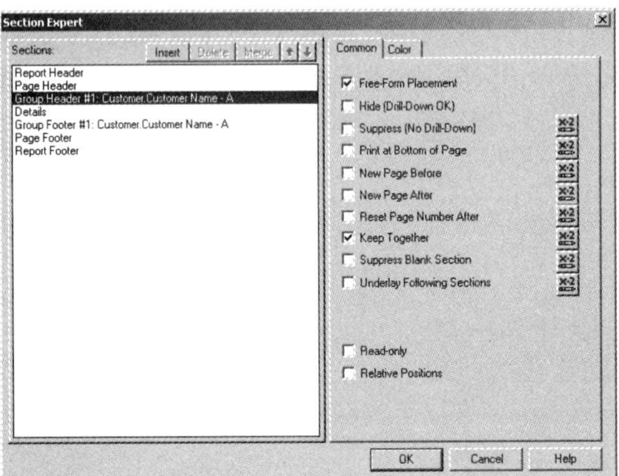

FIGURE 6-15 *Use the many options available in the Section Expert to format the sections of your report.*

Page Setup and Formatting

You have many options when formatting the pages of a report. First, you may want to control the page layout options for a report by using the Printer Setup command. To toggle between portrait and landscape orientation, select File, Printer Setup. From the Print Setup dialog box, you can also select a different size of paper such as legal, assuming your printer has the ability to print that size.

TIP

If you share a report with others or use it on a computer not connected to a printer capable of any expanded size, letter size is the best choice.

Choose File, Page Setup to open a dialog box in which you can specify margins. Selecting the Use Default Margins check box allows the report to print correctly on any machine, because it automatically uses that machine's system default.

The Section Expert dialog box offers many options for formatting the sections on your reports. Table 6-2 provides a brief description of each option.

Table 6-2 Section Formatting Options

Option	Description
Free Form Placement	Allows fields to be placed anywhere on the Design tab (selected by default) as opposed to being restricted by a grid.
Hide (Drill-Down OK)	Hides section in the Preview tab, but allows drill down to see details in a new tab.
Suppress (No Drill-Down)	Suppresses section in Preview. No drill down available.
Print at Bottom of Page	Prints section at the bottom of the page.
New Page Before	Inserts a page break before the section.
New Page After	Inserts a page break after the section.
Reset Page Number After	Resets the page numbering after the section with this option marked.
Keep Together	Prevents a page break in the middle of a section (selected by default).
Suppress Blank Section	Suppresses the section if all fields in that section are blank or null.
Underlay Following Sections	Underlays this section under all sections up to this section's sister section (Group Header to Group Footer, Page Header to Page Footer, etc.).
Format with Multiple Columns	This option allows you to format a multi-column report.
Read-only	Makes the entire section read-only; objects cannot be moved or edited.
Relative Positions	Locks the relative position of a report object next to a grid object within the selected section. For example, if you insert a text object one inch to the right of a cross-tab object, during report generation, the cross-tab will grow based on the data contained within it. Setting a relative position will push the text object to the right, so that the one-inch space is maintained regardless of the width of the cross-tab.
Reserve Minimum Page Footer	This option is only available for the Page Footer section, and it allows you to minimize the amount of reserved space at the bottom of each page for the page footer area.

Setting Page Breaks

Due to the sectional nature of Crystal Reports, you can set page breaks between sections. Select the New Page Before check box or New Page After check box on the Section Expert to set page breaks. For example, if you wanted the grand totals for the report on their own last page, you would select the Report Footer section and select the New Page Before check box. On the other hand, if you wanted to have each group start on a new page, open the Section Expert for the Group Footer and select the New Page After check box. If you had grand totals for the entire report in the Report Footer section, that section would print alone on the last page of a report, because you selected New Page After for the Group Footer section. If you want to keep grand totals in the Report Footer from being stranded on the last page of a report, click the Conditional Formula button beside the New Page After attribute and write the following formula:

```
"OnLastRecord = false"
```

This creates a page break for every group that does *not* contain the last record. If the OnLastRecord function is true, Crystal Reports ignores the New Page After command.

ADDING, MERGING, AND DELETING SECTIONS

The Section Expert includes functionality to add, merge, and delete sections on a report. You can only delete sections you have added. The five main sections cannot be removed, as explained in Chapter 2. You can add and delete sections to meet formatting needs, some of which this chapter describes.

When you delete a section from a report, all the information within that section is also deleted. By merging two sections, Crystal adds the fields in the lower section to the section above, and only the section itself is deleted, not the information within.

NOTE

You could also use the formula

```
not onlastrecord
```

to accomplish the same result as the previous formula.

Underlaying Sections

Crystal Reports gives you the ability to underlay sections of a report. Underlaying a section under another allows you to have information in the background of your report, such as a watermark, shaded company logo, or even the word DRAFT or CONFIDENTIAL in shaded gray letters. You can also use this underlay functionality to underlay charts or maps so that they print beside details they describe, rather than before or after. You can underlay existing sections, or extra sections can be added to facilitate underlaying while maintaining organization and space for information you do not want to underlay.

Underlay a Chart next to Detail Data

It looks great to have a Group Header section containing a graph underlay the Details section so that the detail values being graphed print next to the graph. To make one section underlay following sections:

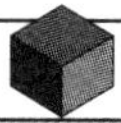

NOTE

You will learn about inserting a graph in Chapter 13.

1. Using the Section Expert, add a second Group Header section by clicking the Insert button with the current Group Header section selected. You now have a Group Header #1a and #1b (see Figure 6-16), and the new Group Header #1b section appears in the Design tab.

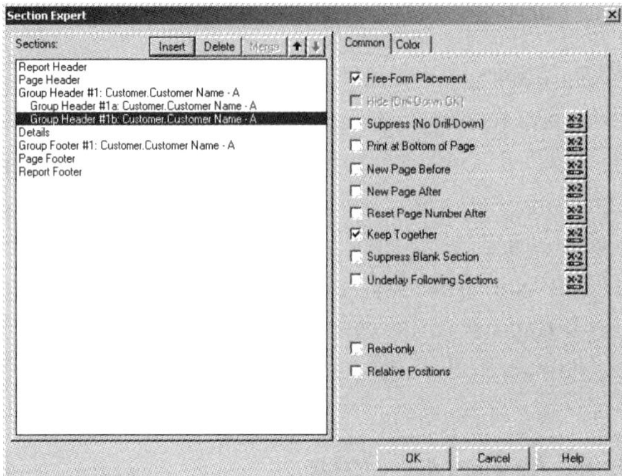

FIGURE 6-16 *Create additional sections on a report using the Section Expert.*

2. Add the information you want to underlay to the Group Header #1a area in the Design tab, and move any group headings to Group Header #1b (see Figure 6-17).

3. Use the Section Expert to underlay Group Header #1a by selecting the section and then selecting the Underlay Following Sections check box. Click OK to close the Section Expert.

4. Preview your report. Both sections display in the Design tab, but in the Preview tab, Group Header #1a underlays Group Header #1b (see Figure 6-18).

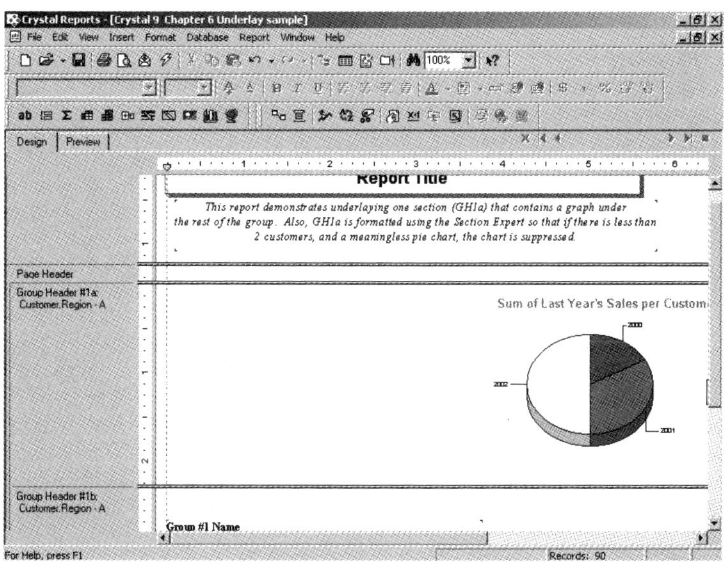

FIGURE 6-17 *Move the group name to the Group Header #1b section, insert a chart into Group Header #1a, and underlay Group Header #1a.*

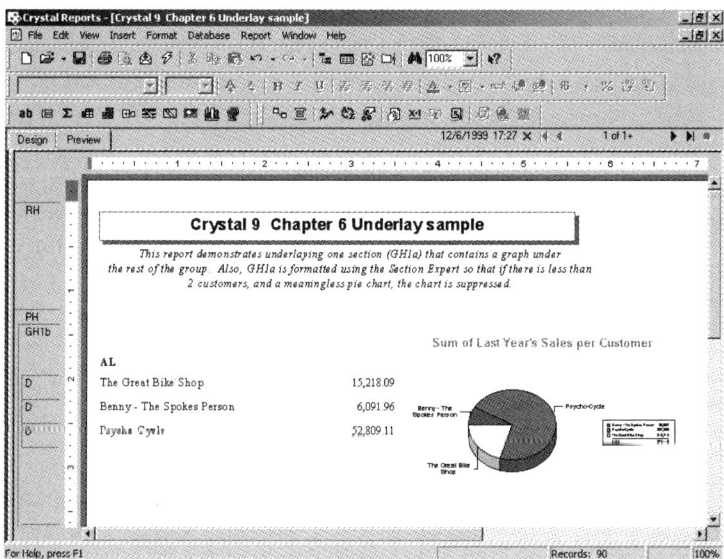

FIGURE 6-18 *Group Header #1a underlays in back of Group Header #1b, up until the Group Footer section prints.*

Underlay the Word DRAFT in the Background of Each Page of a Report

1. Using the Section Expert, add a second Page Header section by clicking the Insert button with the Page Header section selected. You now have a Page Header a and b, and the new Page Header b section appears in the Design tab.

2. Add a text object into Page Header b, type the word DRAFT, and format it big by changing the font size so the object spans the width of the page (about 180 font size).

3. Use the Section Expert to underlay Page Header b by highlighting the section and then selecting the Underlay Following Sections check box. Click OK to close the Section Expert.

4. Preview your report. Both sections display in the Design tab, but in the Preview tab, Page Header b underlays the rest of the page.

Suppressing Blank Sections

There are several different options for suppressing sections. One option is to check Suppress Blank Section in the Section Expert dialog box, which allows you to use Crystal to run perfectly formatted invoices and letters, and any other type of report for which you may have information missing but do not want blank spaces.

The following steps walk you through adding sections to a report. Though there are many uses for additional sections, these steps show how to add sections for use with an invoice or letter type report to accommodate different addresses.

1. Open the Section Expert by clicking the toolbar button.

2. Using the Section Expert, add three Group Header sections by selecting the Group Header section and clicking the Insert button three times. Click OK to close the Section Expert.

3. Go to the Design tab of your report and insert the name and address fields as shown in Figure 6-19. I added Customer Name to Group Header #1a; Address1 to Group Header #1b; Address2 to Group Header #1c; and City, Region, and Postal Code to Group Header #1d.

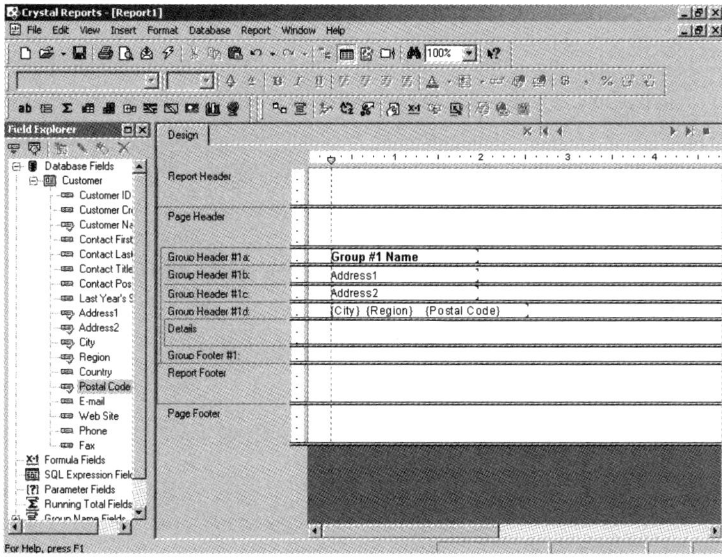

FIGURE 6-19 *Add extra sections to give you individual formatting options for each section.*

4. Using the Section Expert, click the Suppress Blank Section check box for the Group Header #1b and Group Header #1c sections.

5. Click OK to close the Section Expert. Now when you preview your report, both one-line and two-line addresses print with no inconsistencies in spacing.

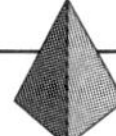

TIP

You can accomplish the same end result as just described when formatting a text object. Insert the fields into a text object, and then check the Suppress Embedded Field Blank Lines option on the Common tab of the Format Editor for the object.

Hiding Sections to Make Drill-Down Reports

Hiding sections on a report creates a drill-down report, also called a summary report. You can hide the Details section of a report so that it does not print in Preview—only the Group Header and Group Footer sections print, showing just the summary information for the report. To hide the Details section of a report:

1. Open the Section Expert. Select the Details section, and check the Hide (Drill-Down OK) option. Click OK to close the Expert.

2. Preview your report. You will see the Details section shaded in the Design tab, and hidden in the Preview tab.

3. Double-click a Group Name or Summary value on the Preview tab to open a drill-down tab containing the detail information for that group.

There is no limit to the number of groups you can hide and then drill down to see. You will want to work with the formatting on a drill-down report so that the summary report and drill-down tabs look professional.

The Suppress (No Drill-Down) option is just like Hide (Drill-Down OK), only it doesn't print the details when you drill down. To suppress an entire section, select the Suppress (No Drill-Down) check box in the Section Expert. This suppresses the section so that it doesn't print on your report. You can set a conditional formula here as well so that your section only suppresses if a certain condition is met.

Formatting a Drill-Down Report

When creating drill-down reports, you will want to do some section formatting to make both the main report and the drill-down tabs look good. Move the column headings off the main report and onto the drill-down tab so that when you view the main report, you see just summary data for each group, and when you view drill-down tabs, you see the column headings for the data displayed.

Format with just one drill-down level

Depending on how much data you want to drill down into determines how you set up a drill down report. If your report has just one drill-down level, follow these steps:

1. Add a horizontal guideline in the Page Header section and attach all column headings to that guideline.

2. Make the Group Header section larger by dragging the bottom section border down using the section resizing cursor.

3. Drag the guideline with the column headings into the Group Header section below the Group Name Field.

4. Insert a second Group Name Field into the Group Footer section. Open the Field Expert, select the Group Name Field node, select Group #1 Name, and insert it into the Group Footer.

5. Open the Section Expert and check Hide (Drill-Down OK) for the Group Header section. Click OK to close the Section Expert and preview the report.

Format with more than one drill-down level

Formatting is tricky when you have more than one drill-down level and you need to manage headings and labels. Crystal 9 has a fantastic new function specifically for this purpose.

The sample report I use in this section is grouped by region and then by customer. The detail information is about specific orders. I want a multilevel summary report where I see just regions and order amounts on the main report. I want the ability to drill down to see a summary of each customer within a region, and then drill down again to see the order details for one customer.

Hide data for drill-down tabs

When drilling down into multiple levels of data you can use conditional section formatting to control what prints with which drill down action. Start by hiding all the data you do not want to see on the main Preview tab:

1. With the report open, hide the Details, Group Header #2 and Group Footer #2 sections.

2. Copy the Group #1 Name and paste another copy into the Group Footer #1 section.

3. Hide Group Header #1.

4. Add a new section below Group Header #2. Open the Section Expert, select Group Header #2, and click the Insert button. Click OK.

5. Move the column headings from the Page Header section into the new Group Header #2b section you just created.

The only nonhidden section at this point is Group Footer #1, and it contains a group name field and summary fields.

Use DrillDownGroupLevel function

Next you need to conditionally suppress group headers to only print for their respective drill-down level. If you preview the report at this point, Group Header #2 prints on the drill-down tab, listing customers, and you only want Group Footer #2 printing on this first drill-down level.

1. Open the Section Expert. Select the Group Header #2a section.
2. Click the X+2 button across from the Suppress (No Drill-Down) option, to open the Formula Workshop for the suppress attribute.
3. Write the following Boolean formula in the Formula Editor:

```
DrillDownGroupLevel = 1
```

4. Click Save and close to save the formula and close the Formula Editor for the suppress attribute.
5. While in the Section Expert still, click the Group Header #2b section.
6. Write the exact same formula as listed in Step 3 for the suppress X+2 icon for this Group Header #2b section.
7. Click OK to exit the Section Expert.
8. Preview the report.

Use formulas to print either the group name or a summary label depending on the drill-down level

The preview of the report is okay at this point, but we can take the report one step further and write formulas for the group names in the footers. A formula can test for different conditions, and depending on which condition is met, carry out a certain action. In this example, rather than list the Group Name Field in both the Group Header and Group Footer sections for the second level drill down, a formula is written to print the Group Name Field if the drill down level is 1 and a label for the summary if the drill-down level is 2.

1. Open the Formula Workshop.
2. Click New to write a new formula, and name it Group1Name.

3. Type the following formula text (see Figure 6-20). Note that I added several tabs to the beginning of the second statement (in quotes) so that the label would print tabbed to the right on the report.

```
if DrillDownGroupLevel = 0 then {Customer.Region} else
"               Totals for "& {Customer.Region}
```

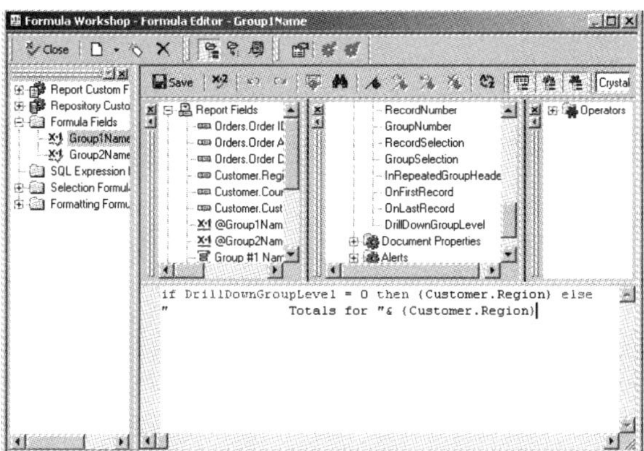

FIGURE 6-20 *Write a formula for Group1Name so it prints different titles for different sections.*

4. Click Save and then click Close to save the formula and close the Formula Workshop.

5. Delete the Group #1 Name field from Group Footer #1, and replace it by inserting the formula you just wrote. Format the field bold.

6. Preview the report.

Follow the steps above to write a formula for Group2Name, replacing {Customer.Region} with {Customer.CustomerName}:

```
if DrillDownGroupLevel = 1 then {Customer.Customer Name} else
if DrillDownGroupLevel = 2 then
"Totals for "&{Customer.Customer Name}
```

Preview the report (see Figure 6-21). Only the highest-level data prints for each group.

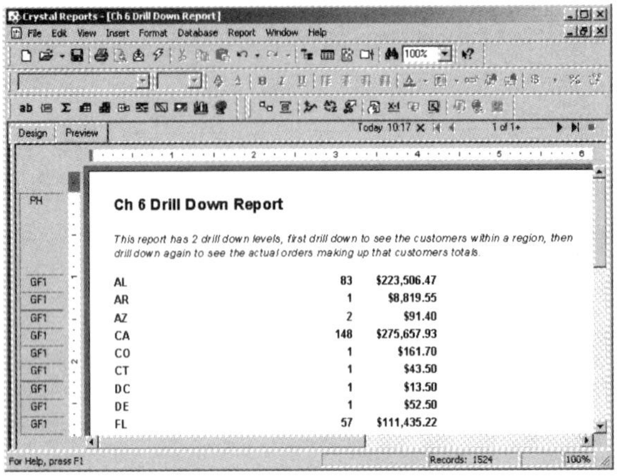

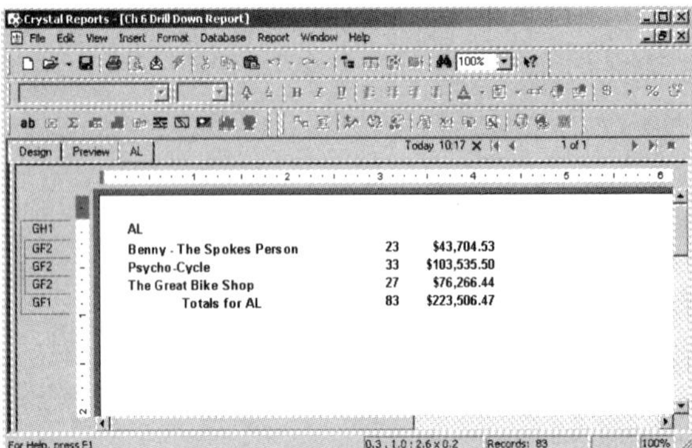

FIGURE 6-21 *The Preview tab displays the highest-level data only.*

Double-click any group name or summary name in the Preview tab to launch a drill-down tab into the details for that group (see Figure 6-22). In this case, I drilled down into a region to see the customers within that region.

FIGURE 6-22 *The AL preview tab displays the second-level data for just one region.*

One more time! Drill down again on a customer name to get all the details for that customer's orders (see Figure 6-23).

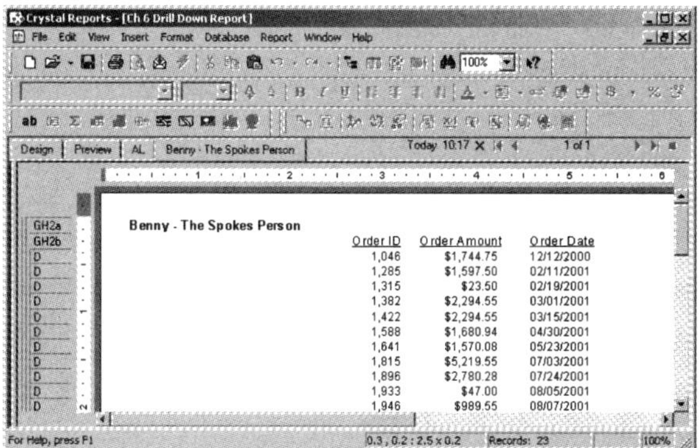

FIGURE 6-23 *The preview tab displays the detail data for one customer only.*

Print Page Headers and Footers in Drill-Down Pages

Normally, drill-down pages do not have Page Header or Page Footer sections, and thus have none of the information that is contained within those sections, like page numbers, dates, or titles.

There is a special option addressing just this issue found in the Report Options dialog. Select File, Report Options, and check the Show All Headers on Drill Down option. Now, the report header and the page header print on drill-down pages as well as main report pages. This option can be set globally by choosing File, Options, Reporting, Show All Headers on Drill Down.

Adding Graphics to Your Report

Adding graphics to a report enhances a report visually. Many times a company logo is added to a header or each page of a report, or a trademark or watermark seal can be added to the background. Inserting graphics is straightforward. You can add any BMP, JPG, TIF, or PNG graphic file to a report.

Insert a Graphic from Your Network or PC

Crystal allows you to insert graphic files directly onto your reports, with basic formatting options:

1. Click the Insert Picture toolbar button ■ on the Insert Tools toolbar or select Insert, Picture to open the Open dialog box. Find the graphic file you would like to add on your computer or the network. Either double-click the picture you want to insert or select it and click Open. The Open dialog box closes and "attaches" the picture to your mouse pointer.

2. Drop the picture on your report by clicking where you want to place it. The section in which the top left-hand corner of the image is the placed will be resized to fit the inserted picture. Resize the picture using the resizing handles.

3. To format the graphic, right-click to open a shortcut menu. Options in the shortcut menu allow you to resize, add a border, and manipulate that border. You can also move the graphic anywhere you want on your report.

Insert an Object from the Crystal Repository

Objects stored in the Crystal Repository can be inserted onto reports as well, as follows:

1. Open the Repository Explorer by clicking the toolbar button or by selecting View, Repository Explorer.

2. Expand the Images node to see any pictures stored in the sample Repository (see Figure 6-24).

3. Select the object you wish to insert onto your report and simply drag it from the Repository and drop it on your report where you want it to print.

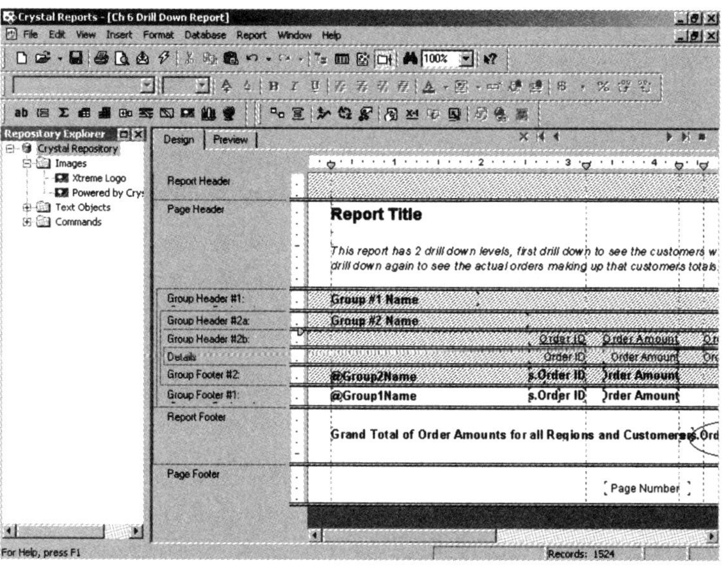

FIGURE 6-24 *Add image files stored in the Repository.*

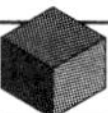

NOTE

If you are not using the sample Crystal Repository but your own corporate repository, you may need to look in a node other than the "Images" node depending on what structure your repository holds and where image files are located.

Adding Lines, Boxes, and Shapes to Reports

You might find lines, boxes, or shapes appealing for organizing and formatting your reports or for drawing attention to a certain area, field, or figure. You insert lines and boxes directly onto a report. For shapes, you format a box to have rounded corners and adjust the size so that you get the custom shape you want.

NOTE

You will format a box to become a shape by rounding the corners and adjusting the size. Thus, all shapes are derived from a simple box, so triangles or irregular shapes are not possible using this option.

To insert a line or box from either the main menu or toolbar buttons:

1. Select Insert, Line or Insert, Box. Or, use the toolbar buttons ⬛ ⬛. This turns your mouse pointer into a pencil icon.

2. Draw a line by dragging the mouse the length of the line. For boxes, start the box in the upper-left corner and drag the mouse diagonally down and to the right. In either case, let go of the mouse where you want the line or box to end.

3. With the line or box selected, you have resizing handles just like with fields to resize the line or box.

4. With your pointer on the border of the line or box, right-click to open a shortcut menu with formatting options.

5. To round the corners of a box to create a shape, select Format Box from the shortcut menu. On the Rounding tab, use the scroll bar across the bottom of the tab to round the box off to create the shape you need.

Using Custom Report Templates

Crystal Reports 9 provides functionality to create custom report templates. Using templates to format reports cuts down on the time needed to format each report with basic features such as corporate logos, titles, page numbers, and other Report or Page Header and Footer information.

There are eleven existing templates in the Template Expert available to apply to any report. These existing templates cannot be edited, though these existing templates can be applied to a report, and then the report itself can be changed to undo or add to the formatting in the template. You cannot change the existing template to accommodate your changes, but you can save a modified report as a new custom template. Creating custom templates is a huge time saver for consistent report formatting.

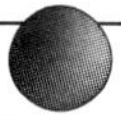

CAUTION

When using any of the existing templates be aware that some of them have formatting that is hard to notice that affect how the report prints. For example, the Block(Blue) template suppresses the totals so they do not print on the report—when you view the report it looks incorrect, when in reality the template suppresses the totals.

Creating a Report Template

Creating a report template is as easy as saving a report. Report templates have the same .rpt extension as any Crystal Report. You could use an existing report as a template for a new report, or you can build reports to be used specifically as templates for other reports by including standard elements that you want included on every report.

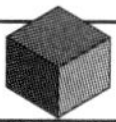

NOTE

You may want to edit a few specific reports to use as report templates and name them accordingly. Report templates cannot be stored in the repository at this time, so you will need to save them somewhere on a network drive for all report designers to use. Crafty names for your templates helps all users find and use custom templates. You could use t, temp or template in the name, and/or save them to a Custom Templates folder on your network.

When applying a report template to a new report, the layout of all objects on the template and all formatting attributes of those objects is applied. For example, if the report template has just 5 fields evenly spaced horizontally across the Details section, then the report that has the template applied to it will have its first 5 fields evenly spaced across the Details section. If that report has more than 5 fields in the Details section, the additional fields will be properly formatted and listed in a Details line.

To apply a custom template to a report:

1. Open the report in which you want to apply a custom template.

2. Select Report, Template Expert to open the Template Expert dialog box (see Figure 6-25).

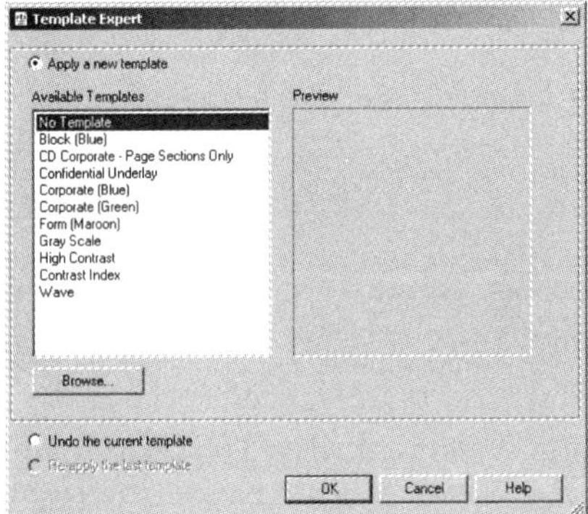

FIGURE 6-25 *Open the Template Expert to select an existing or custom template.*

3. The Apply a new template radio button is selected by default at the top of the dialog box. You can select from the existing templates, or click the Browse button to select a custom template.

4. The Open dialog opens (see Figure 6-26), allowing you to navigate your network to find the report you want to use as a template. Select a report file and click the Open button. The open dialog box closes, and the name of the report chosen as a template is listed in the Available Templates list in the Template Expert (see Figure 6-27).

5. Click OK to close the Template Expert and apply the template to the report.

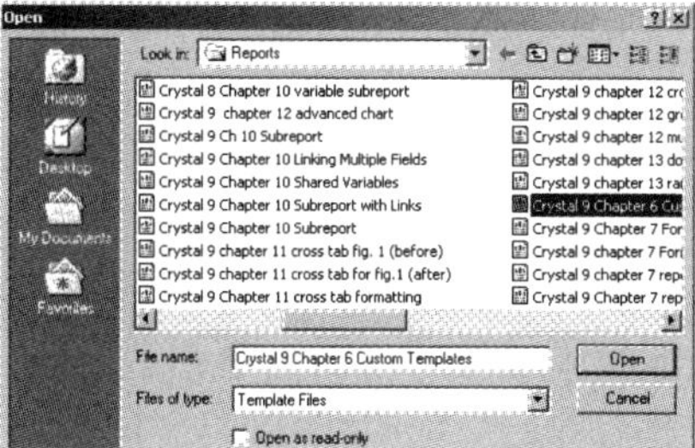

FIGURE 6-26 *Select the report you wish to use as a template in the Open dialog box.*

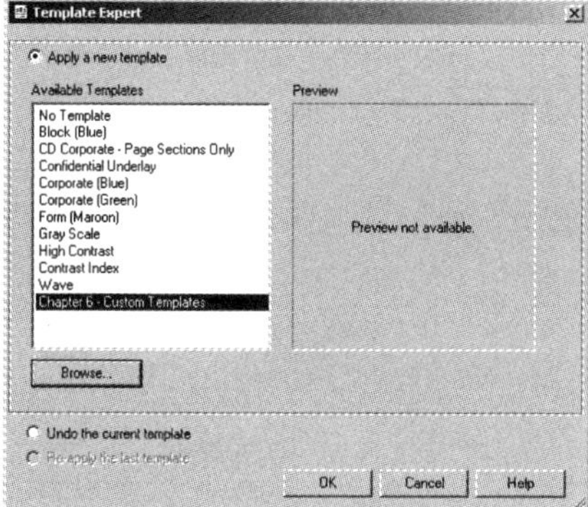

FIGURE 6-27 *Once you have selected a custom template report, that report name is listed and selected in the Template Expert.*

There are two other options on the Template Expert dialog box available when applying templates to reports.

◆ Undo the current template. This option removes the current template if one has been applied to the report.

◆ Re-apply the last template. This option re-applies the last template used.

When applying a custom report template (I will refer to this as just "the template") to a new report, the layout of objects on the template is applied to the report. Imagine the first field in the template on the far left side of the Details section is a number field and formatted to have no decimal places or commas. The second field is a date field formatted like "01/01/2001" (see Figure 6-28).

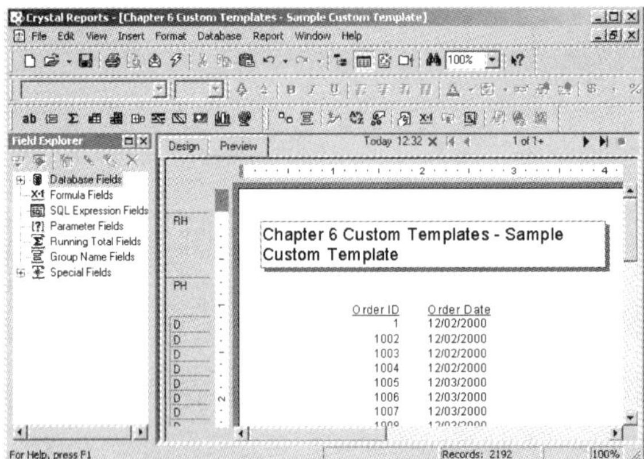

FIGURE 6-28 *This simple report with 2 fields is saved to be used as a custom template.*

A new report has a date field first on the far left side of the Details section, followed by a number field. This is the opposite field placement of the template in Figure 6-28. When the template is applied to the new report, neither the date field nor number field is formatted like the template (see Figure 6-29). The reason is that the order of the objects on the template determines the formatting applied. With templates, the objects contain formatting instructions without paying attention to field type. Thus, if object 1 on the Details line is formatted without decimal places, then object 1 on the new report is formatted the same way. Because object 1 on the template is formatted without decimal places, this is the only formatting applied to object 1 on the new report. Because object 1 on the new report is a date field, it looks like no formatting took place.

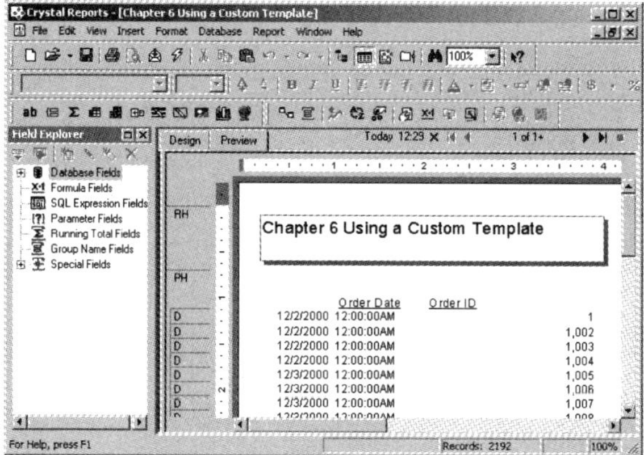

FIGURE 6-29 *The template report in Figure 6-28 applied to a new report.*

Another important consideration of using custom templates is that if you use text objects, for example a text object for the title of the report, the text object is applied when the template is applied to the new report. Thus, the text in the text object in the template report will overwrite the text of the text object in the new report. You can overcome this by using the Report Title special field. Special fields were covered earlier in this chapter, but as a refresher, open the Field Explorer and expand the Special Fields node. Near the bottom of the list is Report Title. Insert this object where you want the title to print. Then, you must enter a title for the report into the Document Properties dialog box, opened by selecting File, Summary Info. Enter a title for the report in the Title area of the dialog (see Figure 6-30).

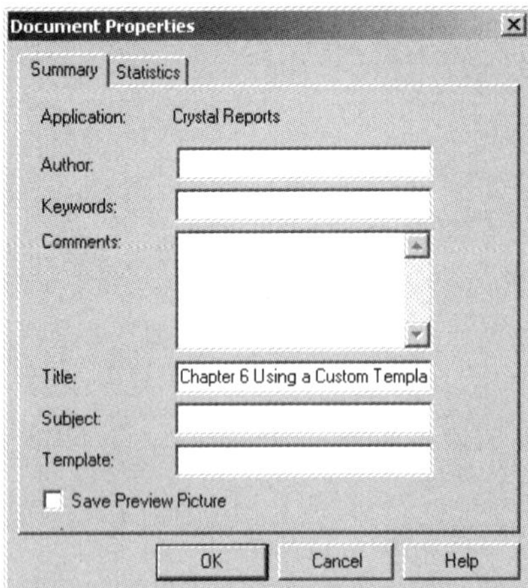

FIGURE 6-30 *The title entered in the Document Properties dialog box will print as the Report Title special field.*

Suggested Objects to Include in Report Templates

Report templates can be simple or complex, depending on their purpose. Since you can apply more than one template to any report, it is possible to build several templates, applying the appropriate templates to specific reports. For example, you may want to build a basic page layout template which includes page and report header and footer information. This basic information could be applied to every report for consistency. There could be another template including different formatting options, such as detail field layout, custom functions, repository objects, and template field objects. The formatting attributes for more specific field objects could be an optional second template applied in addition to the page formatting template. By applying several templates to one report, you can use templates to do more or less of the necessary formatting depending on how you want the report to look.

Templates can be used to format many objects on a report. The following is a list of items Crystal Decisions suggests that you can add to a report template:

◆ Conditional Formatting or field formatting with the Highlighting Expert.

◆ Page Header and Footer information such as page numbers, dates, file names and paths, lines and boxes.

- ◆ Standard charting elements and format including chart types, data, and formatting.

- ◆ Logos and images, text objects, and hyperlinks.

- ◆ Standard custom functions and other repository objects.

- ◆ Field size and position, field locking, color attributes and other field formatting attributes.

There are many options listed here that could work well in specific report templates. Since the basis of applying the report template depends completely on layout and placement of objects on both the template and the new report, it is difficult to create more complex templates if there is any variation in the objects on the new report. To use custom templates realistically, you may choose to keep custom templates fairly simple to take care of basic page formatting, while relying on fine tuning and custom formatting for each report's more specific individual needs.

Using Template Field Objects

Template Field Objects are a special type of formula object you can add to a template report that will format fields with the same field type (date for example) as that Template Field Object. A Template Field Object does not refer to a specific database field; rather its formatting attributes apply to the properly positioned result field of that same type on the report.

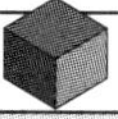

NOTE

Database fields, parameter fields, SQL statements and formulas are all considered result fields. Special fields like data date and page number are not considered result fields and are not formatted using Template Field Objects.

Template Field Objects are generic placeholder fields that you can add to a custom template report (again I will refer to this as "the template"). For example, remember the template referred to in the previous section (refer back to Figure 6-28). It has 2 database fields in the details section of the template, and the second field is a date field, formatted to look like "01/01/2001." Rather than insert an actual date field into the template and format it, you can build a Template Field

Object with the date formatting attributes you want the object in that particular position on the report to have. Thus, using a Template Field Object allows you to use a generic object to specific formatting attributes rather than using a specific database field.

You can add and format Template Field Objects to a report following these steps:

1. Open the template report. Select Insert, Template Field Object.

2. A field object frame will attach to your cursor, like a text object. Place this object on the template report by positioning your cursor and clicking the mouse button. Remember that position is everything in custom templates, so position the Template Field Object where the object to be formatted will be located on the new report (see Figure 6-31).

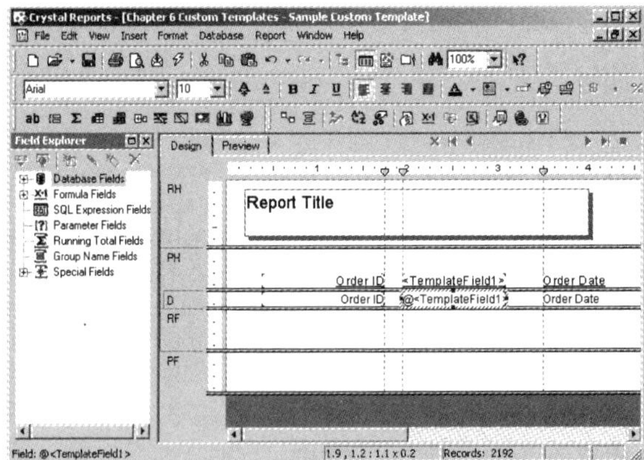

FIGURE 6-31 *Insert the Template Field Object where you want the formatting to take place. In this figure, the second detail object is where the formatting will be applied.*

3. Right-click the object and select Format Template Field from the shortcut menu. Set the formatting options desired using the tabs on the Format Editor for the Template Field Object (see Figure 6-32). Click OK to close the Format Editor.

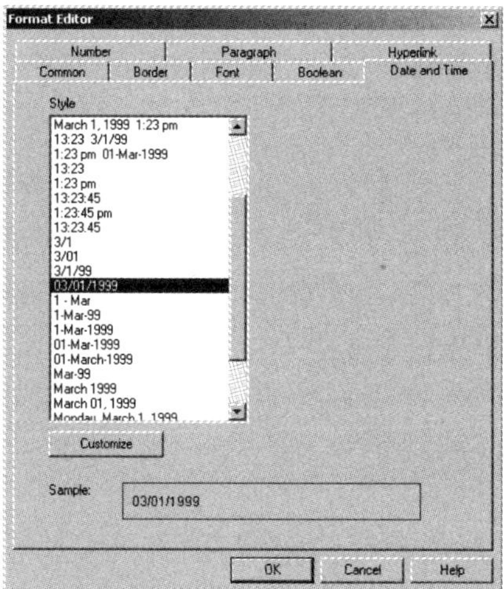

FIGURE 6-32 *Set formatting options for the Template Field Object using the Format Editor.*

4. Save the template report.

5. Open the new report and apply the custom template again. You cannot just refresh the report, you must re-apply the custom template.

6. Select Report, Template Expert. Click Browse, and select the custom template from the Open dialog. Click the Open button, then click OK on the Template Expert dialog box.

7. The template is re-applied to the report. The Template Field Object formats the object positioned second on the Details line of the new report. (See Figure 6-33.)

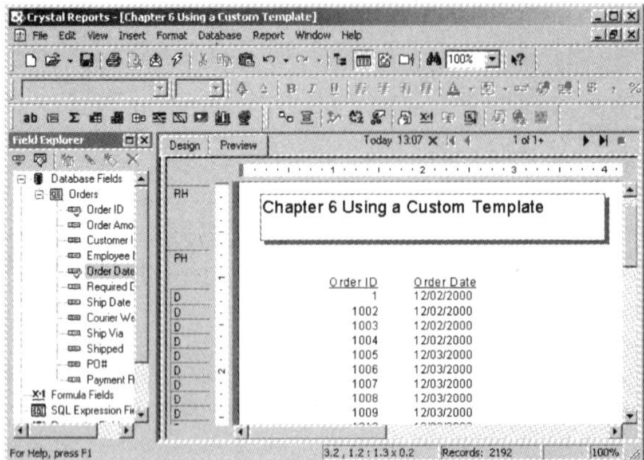

FIGURE 6-33 *The Template Field Object formats the object positioned second in the Details section.*

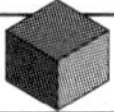

NOTE

You can add sample data to a Template Field Object. Open the object in the Formula Workshop and replace the portion of the formula text that reads "Space(10)" with the database field you want to use as sample data.

Template Field Objects provide an option for adding objects to a custom report template without using actual database fields. This creates a more generic template. Layout is the tricky issue with this tool, because layout and field type must match between the template report and the new report in order for the application of the template to format all objects correctly.

Summary

This chapter covered the basics of formatting fields on a report using the Format Editor. You learned how to look at the default settings and how to reset them to meet your exact needs. Though you may be tempted to change the default settings, sometimes it is easier to adjust each report if you will be creating several different types of reports.

You also found out how the Highlighting Expert and conditional formatting provide options for customizing reports and making information stand out. Conditional formulas can be used in many ways and places in Crystal Reports—many more than the few examples given here. Be creative!

You discovered how to format sections and add more sections using the Section Expert. Conditional formulas were used to control formatting options that apply to entire sections. You also learned how to format sections to create drill-down summary reports, and how to format those reports.

Adding graphics, lines, boxes, and shapes was covered to provide yet another way to specialize formatting so that your reports are presentable and easy to read. There are several reports demonstrating the concepts covered in this chapter on the BridgeBuilder Web site (**www.bridgebuilder.com**), all containing Chapter 6 in their titles.

Last, you learned how to build Report Templates which employ template objects with formatting options so that you can keep a consistent look and feel across all corporate reports.

PART III

Advanced Reporting Topics

Chapter 7

The Formula Workshop is a new tool within Crystal Reports that consolidates into one interface all the different types of formulas that can be used. Formulas of all types are written in the workshop, including selection formulas, conditional formulas, and calculation formulas. The Formula Workshop provides an interface for building and using Custom Functions and the Formula Expert. The Formula Workshop provides access and editing capability for all formulas on a report in one place.

What Is a Formula?

Crystal Reports has far-reaching formula capabilities. This chapter explains what formulas are and how to write many types of formulas using Crystal syntax. Formulas are used in many ways and places on reports, from calculations to formatting.

Crystal Reports 9 has a fantastic new tool wrapped around the good old Formula Editor, called the Formula Workshop. The Formula Editor is still the backbone of Crystal Reports formulas, and the bulk of this chapter covers writing different types of formulas for a variety of uses on reports using this editor. The Workshop provides an entirely new user interface for interacting with all the formulas on a report in one place. It also contains a completely new tool, the Formula Expert, which takes advantage of another new capability in Crystal Reports 9, Custom Functions.

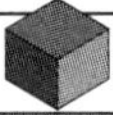 **NOTE**

Custom Functions are covered in detail in Chapter 9. They are covered briefly at the end of this chapter as well to provide a complete understanding of the Formula Workshop.

This chapter covers the basics for people new to Crystal Reports, starting with how to open the Workshop, syntax rules, and an orientation to the Formula Editor functionality. This chapter starts simple, with basic formula examples and step-by-step instructions for building formulas. This chapter then moves right into advanced concepts and examples, discussing examples of different function types, solutions for data type consistency, arrays, multi-pass reporting, conditional variables, shared variables, using control structures, and other hints and tricks. A comparison of Crystal syntax to Basic syntax is also included to help bridge the gap for those interested in learning Basic syntax.

Lastly, this chapter briefly discusses using custom functions within the Formula Expert. This new tool is covered in detail in Chapter 9 but is covered here as well in reference to how great it works with the other available formula tools.

What Can Formulas Do for Me?

Formulas can do many things on your reports. Using formula functions, you can provide additional information on your reports by performing calculations and analysis of existing data. They can be used to manipulate data in your report, such as changing the data type or the way a certain field looks or prints. Formulas provide a means to combine data and create dynamic conditional functionality for both fields and formatting options.

Formulas can also be transformed into functions within a report using Custom Functions. A function can then be saved to the Repository and used throughout your organization's reports and shared by other users via the Repository. Building custom functions from formulas is covered in Chapter 9.

Where Do I Use Formulas?

Formulas can be used in countless different places on reports depending on what you want them to do. Formulas are written using the Formula Editor or can be written using the Formula Expert. The Expert uses custom functions to build formulas, so you must have a custom function in your Repository available for the work you want the formula to perform. This chapter introduces you to the Formula Editor, different types of formulas, functions, examples, and basic information that you will use in all the formulas you write. Chapter 9 covers writing custom functions from scratch, and converting formulas written in the Editor into Custom Functions.

Formulas, regardless of which tool is used to write them, can be used in numerous ways and places on a report; for example:

- Formulas can perform calculations or manipulate data and then print on a report just like a database field.
- Formulas can be used in conditional field and section formatting.
- Formulas are used in selection criteria.
- Formulas pass data between a main report and a subreport.
- Parameter fields can be used within formulas for extended functionality.

Again, this chapter focuses mainly on the process of writing formulas using the Formula Editor. It is up to you where and when you want to use them. There are lots of examples and ideas, because formulas have limitless potential. You will find uses specific to your business's reports.

What Is the Formula Workshop?

The Formula Workshop is a new tool that has been added in Crystal Reports 9. It is used as a central location from which you can create, modify, and delete most types of formulas. The Workshop consists of a toolbar and a tree that contains a node for each formula type and Crystal Repository custom functions. Formulas are listed under their respective node. Depending on the type of formula you are working with, the work area on the right side changes between the Formula Editor and Formula Expert.

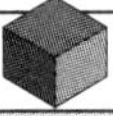

NOTE

Running Total condition formulas within the Running Total Expert are not included in the Formula Workshop. Use the Create (or Edit) Running Total Field dialog box for these formulas. Chapter 6 covers using the Running Total Expert.

Accessing the Formula Workshop

Some version of the Workshop opens whenever you work with any type of formula—be it starting a new formula from the Field Explorer, editing a selection formula, or adding a conditional formatting formula to a report.

Opening the Formula Workshop, as follows, provides access to almost any type of formula for any field object on the report:

1. Click the Formula Workshop button 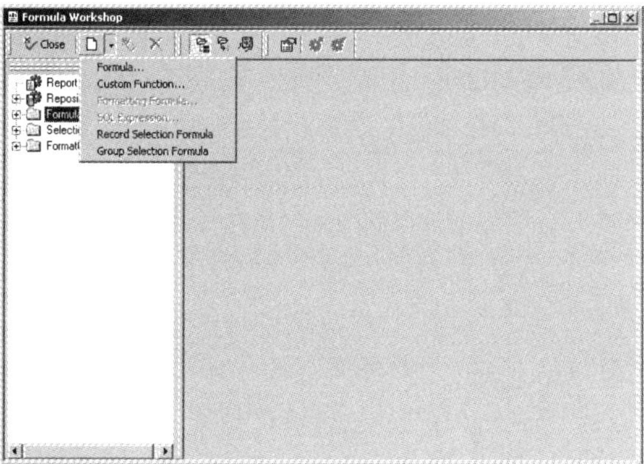 on the Expert toolbar, or select Report, Formula Workshop to open the Formula Workshop.

2. Click the down arrow next to the New button and select the kind of formula you want to create from the list (see Figure 7-1). The appropriate editor or dialog box opens.

3. Or, select the appropriate folder in the Workshop Tree and click the New button.

FIGURE 7-1 *Select the type of new formula you wish to write.*

Workshop Toolbar and Tree

The Workshop toolbar contains the following buttons for navigating the Formula Workshop. These controls are for the Workshop only; the editors that open in the work area may have their own toolbar.

- ◆ **Close.** Close the Formula Workshop.

- ◆ **New.** Begin a new formula. Use the drop-down arrow to the right to select the type of formula to build.

- ◆ **Rename.** Rename an existing formula.

- ◆ **Delete.** Delete a formula.

- ◆ **Hide/Show Workshop Tree.** Toggle on or off to hide or show the Workshop Tree.

- ◆ **Expand/Collapse Node.** Toggle to expand or collapse the selected node.

- ◆ **Show Formatting Formula Nodes Only.** Show only formatting nodes in the tree.

- ◆ **Toggle Properties Display.** Toggle between the Custom Function Editor and the Custom Functions Properties dialog boxes in the work area.

- ◆ **Add to Repository.** Add the selected report object to the Repository.

- ◆ **Add to Report.** Add the selected repository object to the report.

The Workshop Tree is displayed when you first open the Formula Workshop, and contains folders for each type of formula:

- ◆ Report Custom Functions

- ◆ Repository Custom Functions

- ◆ Formula Fields

- ◆ Selection Formulas

- ◆ Formatting Formulas

If the Workshop appears as the result of using a specific command, such as clicking a conditional formatting icon, the Formula Workshop opens in the appropriate mode to work on that particular type of formula. For example, if you select Report, Selection Formula, Record, the Selection Formulas node is expanded, with the Record Selection folder highlighted, and the Formula Editor opens ready to add or modify the selection formula.

When you expand a folder node on the Workshop Tree, all existing formulas within that folder are displayed. New formulas can be added, and existing formulas can be edited or deleted.

The Workshop Tree is a free-floating window that can be docked on either side of the Design tab.

Formula Editor vs. Formula Expert

Crystal Reports has two formula writing tools, the Formula Editor and the Formula Expert. Both exist within the Formula Workshop. Both are used to build formulas for use on a report, but they are different in several critical ways.

The Formula Editor is a straightforward, code-based tool (see Figure 7-2). Crystal and Basic syntaxes can be used in the Editor, where formulas of all types can be written for use on a report. The bulk of this chapter demonstrates using this tool to create functional formulas for data and report manipulation.

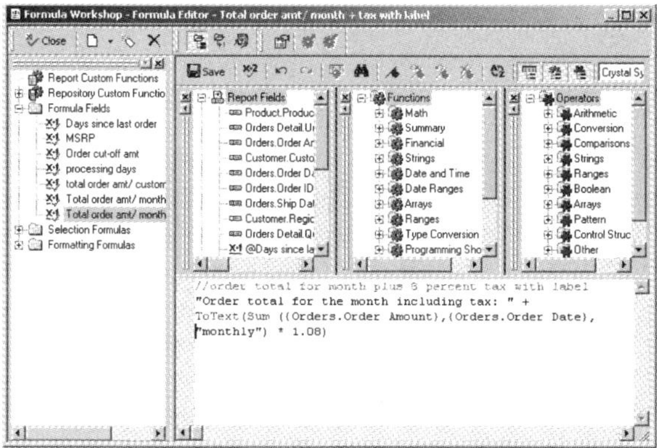

FIGURE 7-2 *Use the Formula Editor to write formulas using Crystal or Basic syntax.*

The Formula Expert is a new tool that uses prebuilt Custom Functions for building formulas. This tool requires that you use a Custom Function and just select fields to plug into the function arguments (see Figure 7-3). This tool does not require the writing of any actual formula text; rather, you just plug in values where prompted to do so.

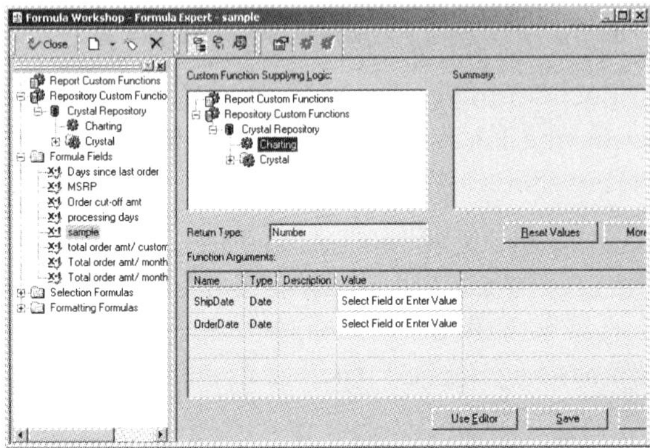

FIGURE 7-3 *Select fields to fill in the arguments in the Formula Expert.*

Some formulas built in the Formula Editor can be extracted into Custom Functions. Once saved as a Custom Function, the object can be saved in the Repository and becomes available for other reports and report designers at your organization to use by plugging in data fields. This provides an easier way to share formulas (as custom functions) with other reports and report designers, and provides a means for more consistent use across reports in an organization. Also, one formula guru can create Custom Functions from appropriate formulas and add them to the Repository, and then other report designers can easily take advantage of the custom functions.

Using the Formula Editor

When writing formulas using the Formula Editor, Crystal does most of the work for you. All of your fields, functions, and operators are available for you in navigable lists; you just double-click to move them into the formula text area. An excellent feature of the Crystal Editors is the Check button that checks your formula and tells you if it finds any errors before you use it on a report.

In the following sections, you will walk through the basic steps of opening and using the Formula Editor to write formulas. The different buttons and additional functionality of this Editor also are discussed.

Opening the Formula Editor

There are several ways to open the Formula Editor, depending on what type of formula you plan to write or edit. To build a new formula field, you have two options from the Design tab:

◆ Click the Formula Workshop button or select Report, Formula Workshop. Select the Formula Fields folder, and then click the New button.

◆ Open the Field Explorer, select the Formula Fields node, and then click the New button on the Field Explorer toolbar.

Either of these options opens the Formula Name dialog box, where you can type a name for the formula you are about to write (see Figure 7-4). Once a name is entered, the Formula Expert and Formula Editor buttons are available. Choose Formula Editor to open that tool (see Figure 7-5).

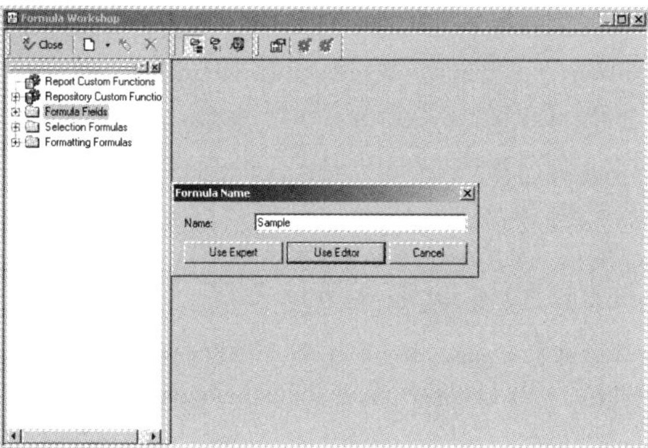

FIGURE 7-4 *Type a name for the new formula, after which the Editor buttons become active.*

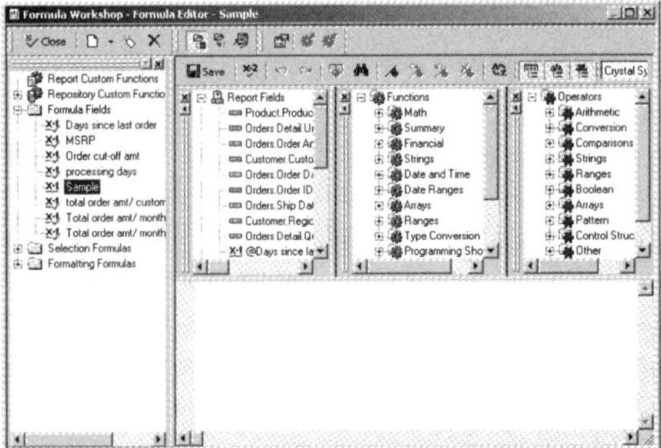

FIGURE 7-5 *Select Formula Editor to open that tool.*

Looking at the Formula Editor you can see the new formula you just named in the Fields pane. Note the following about the editor:

◆ Any formulas already written for the report appear under Report Fields in the Fields pane of the Formula Editor. Formulas are also listed in both the Field Explorer under the Formula Fields node, and in the Formula Workshop in the Formula Fields folder.

◆ Each formula has an X+1 icon before it (in the Editor and the Workshop) so that you know it is a formula field.

◆ Even though the formula you are currently working on or editing is listed in the Fields pane, you cannot use a formula within itself.

Selecting Items from Trees

The Formula Editor contains five windows or panes: the Workshop Tree, Report Fields, Functions, Operators, and Formula Text (refer to Figure 7-5). You "write" a formula by moving items from the three Editor panes (Report Fields, Functions, and Operators) into the Formula Text pane by double-clicking an item or by selecting the desired item and dragging it into the Formula Text pane. When you add items to the Formula Text pane in this way, Crystal Reports takes care of the formula syntax for you; thus, you do not have to memorize complicated rules to write formulas. Of course, once you use this tool for a while, you will become familiar with the syntax and can start writing your own formulas from scratch. But rest assured that you do not need to memorize the syntax rules in order to use the Formula Editor tools.

Formulas can be composed of many components. Double-click to move any item from the four data panes of the Formula Editor to the Formula Text pane, or type directly in the Formula Text pane. The different possible components of a formula are listed and described below:

- **Database fields.** Any field available to your report can be used in a formula.

- **Numbers.** Any number you can type using your keyboard can be used in a formula.

- **Functions.** A comprehensive list of over 260 action instructions, such as manipulating strings, type conversions, evaluation times, and more, that can be used within formulas to carry out some action.

- **Operators.** Operators include add, subtract, percent, and control structures such as If-Then-Else that tell other parts of a formula what to do to compare one value to another.

- **Text.** Type any text from your keyboard for evaluation within the formula. (Remember text must be enclosed in either single or double quotes.)

- **Other formulas.** You can use one formula within another formula for further comparison or analysis.

- **Parameter fields.** Use parameter fields in selection criteria formulas, regular formulas, and other places on a report such as text objects.

- **Summary fields.** Many summary functions are available for use in formulas, including financial, mathematical, and sum functions.

- **SQL expressions.** SQL expressions can be built using the SQL Expression Editor and are available to use in formulas just like other field types.

If you type directly into the Formula Text pane, remember that you need to use the proper syntax. If you double-click, the Formula Editor takes care of the syntax for you. You may find that some of the operators are easier to just type in, whereas fields and functions are much easier to add by double-clicking them in the Fields and Functions panes.

Features of the Formula Editor

The Formula Editor has many features to make your formula writing as simple as possible. Once you open the Editor and write a formula, several functions are available for working with your formulas.

The formulas you write are listed in both the Formula Workshop in the Formula Fields folder, and in the Formula Fields node of the Field Explorer. Add them to your report from the Field Explorer just like database fields. The following list briefly describes some of the functions accessible from the Formula Editor toolbar, from left to right:

NOTE

If you forget to check a formula with the Check button, Crystal Reports checks it for you anyway when you save the formula, and provides a message to let you know if your formula has any errors. If you have an error, the Formula Editor will place your cursor as close to the error as possible in the Formula Text pane. No message appears if the formula is correct.

- ◆ **Save.** This action saves the formula currently open in the Editor.
- ◆ **Check.** Crystal checks the formula for syntax errors. If errors are detected, a dialog box provides text as to why the formula might be failing, and highlights the piece of the formula where it thinks the error is located.
- ◆ **Undo or Redo.** Click Undo or Redo to alter previous actions.
- ◆ **Browse.** Select a database field and then click the Browse button to browse the database for sample field values for the selected field.
- ◆ **Search (Find/Replace).** Use this to search for a database field to replace with a different field. This tool is great if you are cutting and pasting formulas from one area or report to another and want the bulk of the formula but need to change any database fields.
- ◆ **Bookmarks.** Create bookmarks in long formulas so that you can easily jump from bookmark to bookmark to view the formula or make changes.

◆ **Sort.** Click this button to sort the database Fields, Functions, and Operators panes into alphabetical order, which you may prefer for locating items from the lists.

◆ **Pane docking.** Customize the locations and sizes of the four panes of the Formula Editor; hide a pane by clicking that pane's button.

◆ **Syntax choice.** Select which syntax you want to use for each formula you write, Crystal or Basic.

Rules of the Road

You can write many types of formulas to manipulate your data and report. A few generic notes, which apply to all formulas, to keep in mind include:

◆ Crystal calculates all formulas on your PC workstation.

◆ Crystal reads your database but in no way ever writes to your database.

◆ All of your formulas are saved in the report in which they were written.

Crystal saves formulas only in the report in which you wrote them. Many people find it helpful to create a separate document in a word processor program, like Word, to store formulas. Copy your formula text out of Crystal and paste it into a text document. This way, you have all of your formulas in one place, and you can copy and paste them from this document into other reports as needed. Crystal supports the copy and paste functions of Ctrl+C and Ctrl+V. When you copy a formula to a separate document, you'll find it especially useful to add comments for future reference, documenting the purpose of and processing within the formula.

If you have commonly used formulas that you need in several reports, it might be more worthwhile for you to consider creating a Custom Function for the calculation or operation. Chapter 9 discusses building Custom Functions in detail.

Preparing to Experiment with Formulas

Crystal Reports includes excellent help files that you can search to learn about all the different functions that Crystal Reports has to offer. In the Design window, simply press F1 to open the help file. If you prefer, you can also click Help in the main menu, and select Crystal Reports Help Files. I prefer to use the Index tab, and type in a search keyword. Type "Functions" to get to the full Functions list, or type the name of the function you are interested in to get the rundown on just that function. Each function is described with examples in the help file.

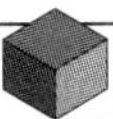

> **NOTE**
>
> The sample reports used in the figures throughout this chapter (and the whole book) can be found online at **www.bridgebuilder.com**.

The following section demonstrates several functions using Crystal syntax. It walks you step-by-step through creating the first formula. Then, it just gives you the formula text and an explanation for the other examples.

Basic Calculations

The Formula Editor can be used to perform simple and complex mathematical calculations. Arithmetic functions are available to work with your data. Building this type of formula works like standard mathematics, using parentheses and the MDAS strategy of multiply, divide, add, subtract, and do what is in brackets first.

MSRP Calculation

A sample report lists products with their unit price. Assume that this is the price that the bike shop (Customer Name) pays Xtreme for the merchandise. You want to calculate what the MSRP (manufacturer's suggested retail price) of the different products would be if you were to mark up the price 35 percent. Yes, for a moment fantasize about only a 35 percent markup in cycling gear.

To write this formula, start by opening the Formula Workshop:

1. Use the toolbar button or select Report, Formula Workshop.

2. Select the Formula Fields folder and then click the New button to open the Formula Name dialog box. Enter the name MSRP for the formula. Click OK and the Formula Editor opens in the work area.

3. Double-click the Orders Detail.Unit Price field located in the Fields pane. This copies the field into the Formula Text pane, with the proper syntax (French braces, {}, around the field).

4. Click the Arithmetic list in the Operators pane to expand and see your choices. Double-click the Multiply sign to copy it to the Formula Text pane.

5. Type the numbers 1.35 from your keyboard after the multiply sign. Your formula should now look like the one pictured in Figure 7-6.

6. Click the Check button. Hopefully, you will get the message "No Errors Found." You just wrote your first formula!

7. Click the Save button to save the formula. The formula is listed in the Workshop Tree in the Formula Fields folder.

8. Click the Close button on the Formula Workshop toolbar to close the Workshop.

9. Open the Field Explorer and expand the Formula Fields node. Select the MSRP formula and insert it into the Details section of your report, to the right of the Unit Price field. Insert formula fields the same way you insert database fields. The formula name you entered appears as the column heading.

10. Preview your report (as shown in Figure 7-7). Notice that the MSRP formula now looks and acts like any other field on your report—and it has calculated the MSRP for each product ordered.

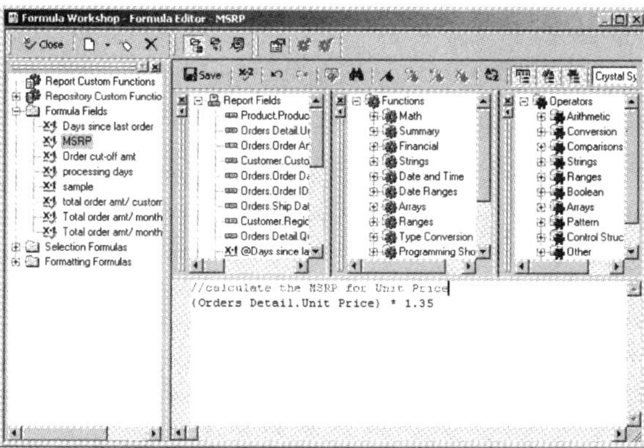

FIGURE 7-6 *Formula text to calculate MSRP for each product's unit price.*

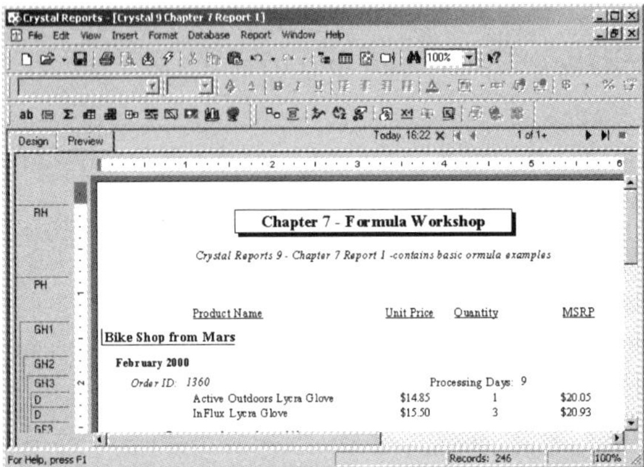

FIGURE 7-7 *Preview the report to see the formula performing calculation of MSRP.*

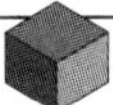

NOTE

While in the Formula Editor, if you use the key combination Ctrl+Space, a list of the functions you are most likely to use appear in as drop-down list where you can select one to use.

Weighted Sales Potential Formula

This next example is from a CRM database, where the sales potential is multiplied by the close probability for an opportunity, and then divided by 100 to calculate a percent. The brackets force the multiplication function to process first.

```
({OPPORTUNITY.SALESPOTENTIAL}*{OPPORTUNITY.CLOSEPROBABILITY})/100
```

Calculations with Dates

Many functions are available to use with date fields. You can compare date fields to each other, compare dates in your database to system dates, or use date functions for more complex calculations and use in selection criteria and grouping.

Compare Date Fields

In a report, you want to calculate the number of days it took for each order to be processed. Write a formula named Processing Days to subtract the Ship Date from the Order Date and insert the formula field into Group Header #3 (refer to Figure 7-7):

```
//calculate processing days
{Orders.Ship Date} - {Orders.Order Date}
```

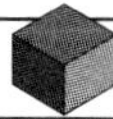 **NOTE**

It is possible to insert this formula into either the Group Header #3 or Group Footer #3 section, because it is calculating the processing days for each Order ID. If you place the field in the Details area, it will just list the same number for each detail line. The calculation will still be correct, but the value will be repetitive and possibly confusing on the report.

You can label this field in several ways. Add a text object next to the field in the Group Header section and type a label, or add a label as a column heading in the Page Header section. You could also add a label to the formula text, which is covered later in this chapter.

This formula returns the difference in days between the two dates, such as 1.00 for one day, 2.00 for two days, and so on. When Crystal pulls date fields from your database, it converts them to its own format so that dates can be easily compared with one another and used with the date functions Crystal provides. This formula returns a number, and so it (by default) has two decimal places (1.00, 2.00, and so on). You may want to format the field to remove the decimals using the Format Editor or the Remove Decimal button on the Formatting toolbar.

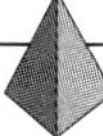 **TIP**

This formula starts with double slashes to indicate a note explaining what the formula does. This is not necessary, but helpful for more complex formulas. Since I have a carriage return (manual line break) after my comment, Crystal Reports ignores the first line and just interprets the formula text on the second line.

CurrentDate() Function

Another example involving dates uses the CurrentDate() function. Let's say you want your report to calculate how many days ago orders were placed. Create a new formula and name it "Days Since Last Order." You can insert this formula into either Group Header or Footer #3.

```
//Number of days since order was placed based on current date
CurrentDate - {Orders.Order Date}
```

This formula subtracts the Order Date from the CurrentDate and returns a number of days. TheCurrentDate() function returns the value set under Report, Set Print Date and Time. By default, it will be the system clock time for your pc but if the date under Report, Set Print Date and Time has been changed, the CurrentDate() function will also change. You could use this type of formula within an If-Then-Else statement, so that, depending on the outcome of the formula, something would occur or print on the report. The formula "Payment Flag" in the If-Then-Else section later in this chapter will do just that.

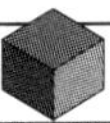

NOTE

This formula will have a different outcome every time you run this report, because every day that goes by means more days since the last order was placed. You will get a different number result than shown in the figures if you practice with this formula.

Formula fields always have an at sign (@) in front of the name in the Report Fields pane and on the actual report. This way, you can easily distinguish the formula fields from other report fields. Do not type the @ sign; Crystal Reports adds it to whatever name you use automatically.

Calculating Summaries with Formulas

To add a summary to a report, you can use the menu-driven functionality described in Chapter 5 or you can write a formula. One way is no better than the other, so use your preference.

Summary Calculations

The following formula calculates the total Unit Price ordered per customer and returns a number value. This formula is named Total Order Amount per Customer.

```
//calculate total Order Amount per customer name, which is grouping field
Sum ({Orders.Order Amount },{Customer.Customer Name})
```

This formula calculates the sum of the {Order Amount} field per Customer Name group. The second argument (Customer Name) indicates the group for which you want to sum the Order Amount. To create a summary for a group from within the Formula Editor, the group must already exist on the report. This formula is added to the Group Footer #1 section, because it is calculating the total order amount for the group based on the Customer Name field.

In the Functions pane of the Formula Editor, click the plus sign (+) next to Summary and then click the plus sign (+) next to a summary function. A list of all the options for that summary function appears. For help, search the online help files using the keyword "Functions" or the exact function name in which you are interested. The help files provide a written explanation of the function, options available for it (such as what arguments are needed and what they mean), and samples using the function.

Using Summary Fields in a Formula

You may want to use a summary field that you added to your report on the Design tab as part of a formula. If you inserted a summary of any type with the Insert, Summary command, that summary field is contained in the Fields pane of the Formula Editor with the sum sign in front of it (Σ).

Double-click this field to copy it into your formula, the same as any other field. In this example, let's imagine that the customers are invoiced just once per month, with all orders from that month totaled and then the tax applied. Here, a new formula is created called "Total Order Amount per Month Plus Tax." When complete, this formula is inserted into the Group Footer #2 section, to the right of the other fields.

```
//total Order Amount per month plus tax of 8 percent
Sum ({Orders.Order Amount}, {Orders.Order Date}, "monthly") * 1.08
```

This formula takes advantage of built-in date functions. Crystal Reports recognizes "monthly" as a set of specific instructions. Daily, weekly, monthly, and yearly are all possibilities depending on what choice you made when you created the group on your report.

Functions to Convert Data Type

Sometimes your database will not use the data type you need to properly work with a field in Crystal Reports. For example, your database may store a date in a field with a string data type, which prevents you from formatting the field using the date formatting features. This also might happen with a number field (though less likely), preventing you from applying numeric summary calculations to the field. To work around this potential problem, Crystal Reports has functions to assist you with converting data types:

- **ToText().** Converts argument to a text (string) type field.
- **ToNumber().** Converts argument to a number type field.
- **Date().** Converts argument into a date type field. Field must be (YYYY,MM,DD).
- **DateTime().** Converts argument into DateTime field. Field must be (YYYY,MM,DD,HH,MM,SS).
- **DateValue().** Converts argument to a date type field.
- **TimeValue().** Converts argument to a time type field.
- **DateTimeValue().** Converts argument to a date/time type field.
- **ToWords().** Converts the number or currency argument into words (for example, "1000" becomes "one thousand"). This is useful for creating number amounts on checks.

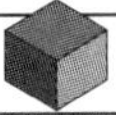

NOTE

DateValue(), TimeValue(), and DateTimeValue() functions do not work for all fields. You may want to test the field you are attempting to manipulate with the IsDate() function first. This function tests the field to see if it is actually a date capable of being used in the DateValue() function. I have found that dates from the Crystal SQL Designer that are strings are able to use this function, but dates from many production databases are not.

There are also many type conversion functions listed in the Functions pane of the
Formula Editor (see Figure 7-8). Search the help files using the name of the particular function you are interested in for an example of each.

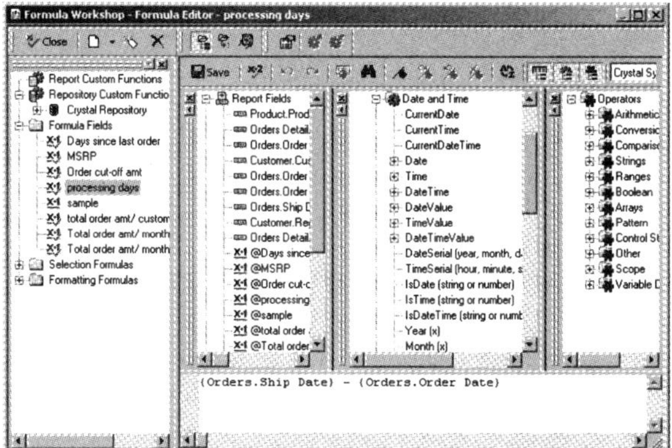

FIGURE 7-8 *There are many type conversion functions to choose from that function the same as
the functions in the Strings and Date/Time lists, but are derived from Basic syntax.*

Use these data type conversion functions alone—to convert a field to another data
type for formatting benefits—or as part of a larger formula where you convert the
field into another type and then perform a calculation.

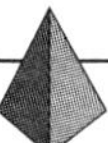

TIP

Use the ToNumber() function when a formula produces a string or currency result but
is needed to compare to another number. If, when checking a formula, you encounter
the error message "A number is required here," or something similar, you might need
to convert a result in your formula to a number type in order to compare it with
another number type field.

Adding Labels with the ToText Function

Chapter 2 describes how to add labels using text objects. Text objects work really
well, but it is sometimes hard to create uniform spacing. This next example shows
how to add the label within the formula.

The type of field that a formula yields determines what steps to take to add a text label to the formula within the formula text itself. If the result of a formula is a string, then it is possible to concatenate text to the formula.

```
//concatenate customer first and last name and add label
"Customer Name: " & {Customer.CustomerFirstName} & " " &
{Customer.CustomerLastName}
```

In Crystal Reports, the Total Order Amt per Month Plus Tax formula is selected. Choose the Edit Formula option from the shortcut menu or select Edit, Formula from the main menu. Edit the formula to match the changes shown next:

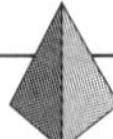

TIP

You can also edit a formula by selecting the formula field you want to edit from within the Field Explorer and then clicking the Edit button. The graphic on this button looks like a pencil.

```
//Order total for month plus 8% tax with label
"Order Total for the month including tax: " & Sum
({Orders.Order Amount}, {Orders.Order Date}, "monthly") * 1.08
```

I edited the formula field to read as the preceding formula. You could also have created an entire new formula, as shown in Figure 7-9.

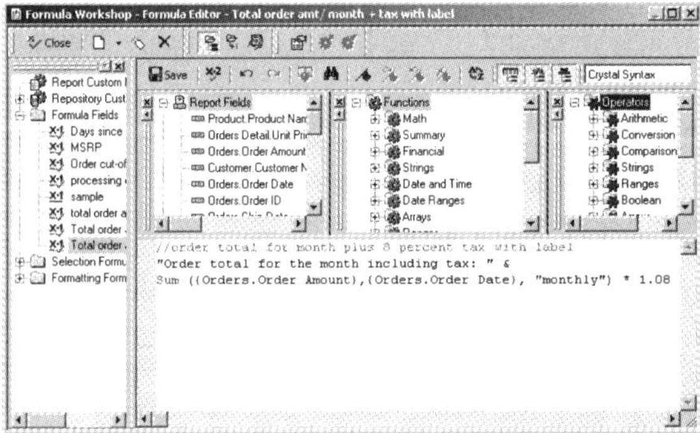

FIGURE 7-9 *Formula text with label built into the formula.*

Adding text labels to formulas is helpful because formulas process efficiently and sometimes faster than text objects containing formulas. There are really three options when labeling a formula field:

- Have two fields, the text field and the formula field, right next to each other.
- Drop the formula (or data) field into the text field.
- Add the text into the formula as the last example describes.

Combining the text in the formula is neat and sometimes easier to maneuver than fields combined in text objects, but the formatting can be a little tricky because you must include formatting that is specific for the formula field in the formula (such as removing decimals). Also, if you convert a number field to text using the ToText() function, you cannot use the formula in other calculations (just as you couldn't include a text object in a calculation).

Total Sales Potential Per Stage Formula

```
"Sales Potential Total for " & {@Stage} & " is " &
sum({OPPORTUNITY.SALESPOTENTIAL},{@Stage})
```

Using & works fine if you do not need to format the number value, sum({OPPORTUNITY.SALESPOTENTIAL},{@Stage}). In the case of this formula, I want to remove the decimal places. To do so, I must use the ToText() function (as in Figure 7-10) to take advantage of the formatting options available for ToText():

```
"Sales Potential Total for " & {@Stage} & " is " + ToText(
sum({OPPORTUNITY.SALESPOTENTIAL},{@Stage}),0)
```

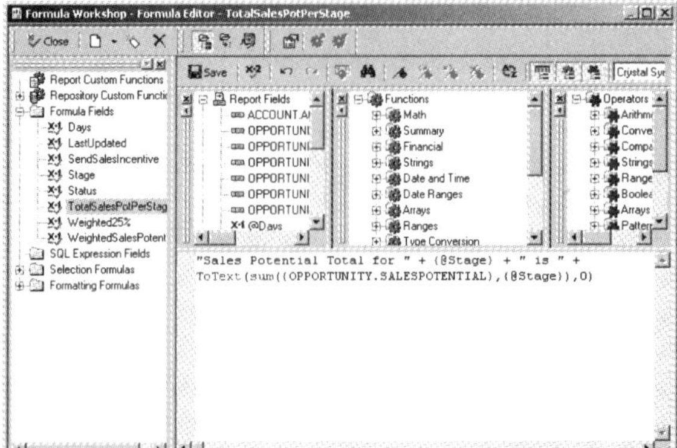

FIGURE 7-10 *Sales Potential formula in editor taking advantage of the ToText() function formatting options.*

Note the ,0 at the end of the formula, indicating no decimal places for the field that was converted to text. The ToText() and CStr() functions have several options to assist with formatting:

- **ToText(x).** x = number or currency value to be converted
- **ToText(x,y).** y = whole number indicating decimal places
- **ToText(x,y,z).** z = single character text string indicating thousands separator
- **ToText(x,y,z,w).** w = single character text string indicating decimal separator
- **ToText(x,y,z,w,q).** q = w, and y = text string indicating field format such as "xxx.xx"

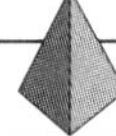

TIP

The Cstr() function works the same way as ToText().

Boolean Formulas

Boolean formulas return a true or false answer. You can format these formula fields to return the words you prefer, such as yes/no, Y/N, T/F, or true/false. Select the Boolean field and then select Format, Format Field. The Format Editor dialog box contains a Boolean tab for formatting the field. You can also set default formatting options for Boolean fields by selecting File, Options, and then using the Fields tab.

Your database may include some Boolean fields, which have values such as true/false or yes/no. These fields have a Boolean tab available on the Format Editor so you can set how you want the result to print on your report. In the Xtreme sample database, {Orders.Payment Received} is a Boolean field, which I will use in a sample formula ("Payment Flag") in a later section, "Flag overdue payments," which discusses using the If-Then-Else structure in formulas.

Boolean Sample

Suppose you want the word "yes" to print on a report if the order amount exceeds a certain value, and "no" if it does not. You could write the following Boolean formula, titled "Order Cut-off Amt." Some people think of this Boolean type formula as a test. A Boolean formula tests itself against a field value and returns a true/false answer. In this case, you would format it so that the formula returns a yes/no answer.

```
//Boolean order cut off yes over 500
{Orders.Order Amount } > 500
```

When placed in the Group Footer #3 section, this formula prints "true" if the order amount exceeded 500 and "false" if the order amount was less than 500. Format the field by changing the Boolean text on the Boolean tab to Yes or No.

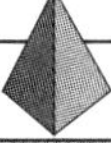

TIP

When adding fields like this last Boolean formula, you can insert the field into the Details section so that the column heading prints in the page header, and then move the field down into the proper Group Footer section. The label will stay in the page header. Only when inserting fields into the Details area do the column headings get inserted.

Boolean Formulas for Conditional Formatting

Conditional formatting allows you to turn on a formatting option if the condition of the formula is met. For example, you could use conditional formatting to specify that if an order amount is less than 500, the field is underlined. You would use the exact same formula as above, only you would not create the formula as a stand-alone formula field. Instead, you would attach the formula to the underline formatting option.

1. Open the Format Editor for the field you want to conditionally format.

2. Click the X+2 button across from the formatting attribute you want to control. This launches the Formula Workshop and Formula Editor for that option in one window.

3. Write a Boolean formula to turn on the formatting attribute if the result of the formula is true, in this example:

```
{Orders.Order Amount } < 500
```

4. Click the Close and Save button to close the Formula Editor. Notice that the X+2 button is red. When you preview the report, the field will be formatted if the value is less than 500.

Chapter 6 covered conditional formatting in detail, including step-by-step instructions and examples. Boolean formulas are great for testing whether or not a condition is true, and then turning on a formatting option. Section formatting, described in Chapter 6, uses many Boolean formulas to help control the way a report looks and prints.

Conditional Formatting Formulas within the Formula Workshop

The exact same formula above could be added to the report using just the Formula Workshop. This is just a different way to achieve the exact same result:

1. Open the Workshop and select the Formatting Formulas folder.

2. Expand the section the field you want to format resides in, and select the actual field you want to format.

3. Right-click and select New Formatting Formula from the shortcut menu to open the New Formatting Formula dialog box (see Figure 7-11).

4. Scroll through the available formatting options to apply a conditional formula to, and select the option you want to format.

5. This opens the Formula Editor for that particular formatting attribute in the work area. Write a formula to format the field, and then click Save.

6. Select another field to format, or another attribute for the same field, or close the Workshop.

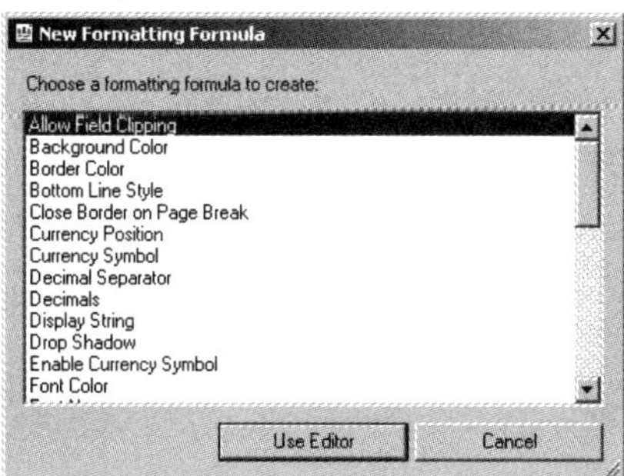

FIGURE 7-11 *Select the formatting attribute in which to apply a conditional formula.*

Once you have a conditional formula formatting a field attribute, that attribute is no longer listed in the New Formatting Formula dialog box. Setting conditional formatting attributes using the Workshop is interchangeable with setting formatting options on a field-by-field basis using the Format Editor and X+2 buttons. Use whichever method you prefer.

The If-Then-Else Statement

If-Then-Else formulas (sometimes called "If statements") allow you to set conditions within formulas. In the Formula Editor, you can find the If-Then-Else statement in the Operators pane under Control Structures, but you may find it easier to simply type the words yourself.

The basic rationale behind If-Then-Else statements is that:

```
If the condition is met then do this,
if the condition is not met then do that,
or do nothing.
```

Conditional Incentive Example

If-Then-Else statements can be applied many ways in Crystal Reports. Continuing to work with the sample report used throughout this chapter, the following section presents some conditional problems with the formulas to resolve them. These formulas are found in the sample reports for Chapter 7 on BridgeBuilder's Web site (**www.bridgebuilder.com**).

Suppose you have been directed to create a report that calculates a conditional incentive structure. The rule is, if the total order amount for any given month exceeds a certain value, then print the words "Send Sales Incentive." The following formula is named Sales Incentive:

```
//print 'send incentive' if monthly Order Amt over 1500
if Sum ({Orders.Order Amount }, {Orders.Order Date}, "monthly")
> 1500 then "Send Sales Incentive" else ""
```

To create this formula:

1. Type the word if in the Formula Text pane of the Formula Editor. Or, expand the Control Structures group in the Operators pane, selecting the 'if x then y else z' option.

2. Go to the Fields pane and double-click the summary field listed with the name Group 2 Orders.Order Date – A:Sum of Orders.Order Amount. This copies the entire Sum function into the formula so it does not have to be created again.

3. Complete the formula by typing > 1500, and then typing (including quotes) "Send Sales Incentive" after the Then clause.

4. After "Send Sales Incentive" you can include the Else portion of the statement. The Else is not required, but some prefer to use it to complete the clause. In this formula add Else "" after the "Send Sales Incentive" to mean that if the condition is met, print Send Sales Incentive else print "" or nothing.

5. When you're finished entering the formula, save it and drop it into the Group Footer #2 area of the report, where it now returns the words "Send Sales Incentive" next to any month's total order amount that is over $1500 (see Figure 7-12).

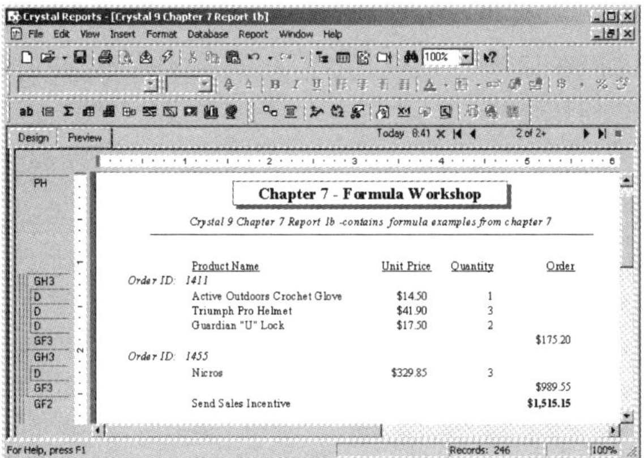

FIGURE 7-12 *A conditional If-Then-Else formula prints text only if the condition is met.*

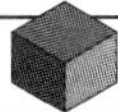

NOTE

If you do not have the summary you want to include in an If-Then-Else formula already on your report, create that part of the formula just as in the previous examples in this chapter. Start by typing **if**, and then select the Sum function and fill in the arguments.

Flag Overdue Payments

You can create a formula to flag customers whose payment is overdue. Insert this formula right into your report, and the words print if the formula returns true or yes. You could also use this formula to conditionally format some attribute, like a yellow background color, to flag customers rather than have text print on the report. The following formula, called "Payment Flag," includes text to print on the report if the formula returns true:

```
if CurrentDate - {Orders.Order Date} > 60 and
IsNull ({Orders.Payment Received}) = true then
"Call to collect payment"
Else ""
```

Use this same formula to conditionally format the background color of the customer name field. There are two options as to where to insert the conditional formula, though the formula is the same:

◆ Open the Formula Workshop and select the Formatting Formulas folder. Select the section the field is located in that you want to format, and then select the field to format. Right-click and select New Formatting Formula from the shortcut menu, select a formatting option, and then click Formula Editor to launch the Editor and write the formula.

◆ Select the field you want to format on the Design tab right on the report. Right-click and select Format Field from the shortcut menu. Click the X+2 button across from the attribute you want to conditionally format to open the Formula Editor (see Figure 7-13).

```
if CurrentDate - {Orders.Order Date} > 60 and
IsNull ({Orders.Payment Received}) = true then
CrYellow else crNoColor
```

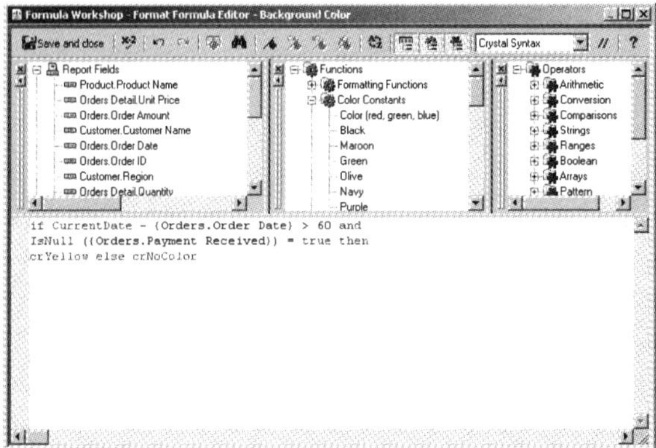

FIGURE 7-13 _Add conditional formatting formulas using the Formula Workshop or the Format Editor._

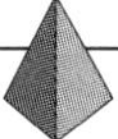

TIP

The default color for any formatting option in Crystal Reports, determined by your Windows default color, is usually black. This includes the background color, so be sure that when formatting background colors, you include an Else clause with a specific color or crNoColor (transparent). Otherwise, Crystal Reports applies a black background when the condition is not met, which does not work very well most of the time.

Conditional Sum Calculation

You can write a similar formula to assess a sum conditionally. For example, you could write a formula that determines whether the total amount ordered over the course of the year is greater than $20,000 and, if so, calculates a 5 percent bonus. You would insert this formula, called "Bonus Calc," into the Group Footer #1 section for the Customer Name group.

Any summary fields in the Fields pane of the Formula Editor are noted with a sum sign (Σ) so that you can distinguish them from group name and other fields available for your report.

```
//calculate bonus amount if order amt total was
//over 20000 for customer with label
if Sum ({Orders.Order Amount}, {Customer.Customer Name}) > 20000
then {Customer.Customer Name} +" has earned a 5% cash bonus,
based on your year's purchases, of $" + ToText (Sum
({Orders.Order Amount}, {Customer.Customer Name})* .05)
Else ""
```

If-Then-Else and Conditional Formatting

Another common use for If-Then-Else formulas is in conditional formatting. Options such as font color, currency symbol, background or border style, and many other formatting options found in the Format Editor can be conditionally applied. A basic If-Then-Else formula applied to the font color format attribute might read as follows:

```
If {Orders.Order Amount} <= 0 then crRed else crBlack
```

With this conditional formula, the number field prints in red font color if the actual value of the field is less than or equal to zero. If the condition is not met, then the field prints in black font color. Look for more information on conditional formatting in Chapter 6.

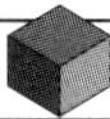

NOTE

Crystal Reports puts cr in front of many attribute names, like crRed and crBlack used above. If you type your formula and type just Red, the formula will work. If you double-click the color Red from the Functions pane of the Formula Editor, Crystal Reports adds the cr. Both ways are correct.

Nesting If-Then-Else Statements

With seemingly never-ending possibilities, you can nest If-Then-Else statements to set several conditions with appropriate actions. Take the following formula as an example. I have changed the previous Sales Incentive formula to have several conditions, each with its own Then action to be taken. When nesting If-Then-Else statements, the result of each If statement must be the same data type throughout the formula. Thus, you could not write a formula that would type words if one condition were true, and figure a calculation if another condition were true.

```
if Sum ({Orders.Orders Amount }, {Orders.Order Date}, "monthly")
> 3000 then "Send Sales Incentive sunglasses" else
if Sum ({Orders.Order Amount}, {Orders.Order Date}, "monthly")
> 2000 then "Send Sales Incentive duffle bag" else
if Sum ({Orders.Order Amount }, {Orders.Order Date}, "monthly")
> 1000 then "Send Sales Incentive t-shirt"
Else ""
```

With so many types of formulas, the uses are virtually limitless. Many times, several options will accomplish the same ends, including more than one way to write a formula correctly.

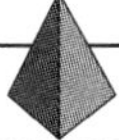

> **TIP**
>
> You could insert a group based on the formula above that would group orders based on what incentive the customer was to receive. The customers who do not meet a condition to qualify for an incentive would be put together in a "no-name" group. Change Else "" to Else "No incentive" in the last line of the formula so that all groups are named.

Select Case Formulas

You can write long nested If-Then-Else statements to set and give instructions for many conditions. You could also write a Select Case formula to accomplish the same ends without having to repeat as much. A Select Case formula to replace the previous If-Then-Else formula would read as follows:

```
select month({Orders.Order Date})
case 7 to 9 : "Quarter 1   Jul - Sept"
case 10 to 12 : "Quarter 2  Oct - Dec"
case 1 to 3 : "Quarter 3  Jan - Mar"
default: "Quarter 4  Apr - Jun"
```

This is just a taste of what is to come later in the chapter, in the section "Control Structures in Crystal Syntax," and is provided to demonstrate that there are usually several ways to accomplish the same ends using formulas.

You could also use a variable to replace a long If-Then-Else statement, and you will soon see that variables can cut down on the length of some formulas as well as provide the additional functionality of being able to share values from one formula to another.

Print State Functions

Crystal Reports supports a long list of Print State functions. Print State functions return a value based on where the report is in the process of printing, such as a page number. You'll find some Print State functions under Special Fields in the

Field Explorer. The following list summarizes the set of Print State functions in the Formula Editor:

- Previous (fld)
- PreviousValue (fld)
- Next (fld)
- NextValue (fld)
- IsNull (fld)
- PreviousIsNull (fld)
- NextIsNull (fld)
- PageNumber
- TotalPageCount
- PageNofM
- RecordNumber
- GroupNumber
- RecordSelection
- GroupSelection
- InRepeatedGroupHeader
- OnFirstRecord
- OnLastRecord
- DrillDownGroupLevel

Though you can use Print State functions in countless ways, I offer a few explanations to help stimulate your own creativity. For more ideas, search Crystal Reports online help files with the phrase "print state functions."

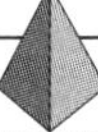

TIP

The online help files are an excellent resource! You'll find an explanation for each function as well as examples of the functions in action. Do not let this great resource pass you by.

IsNull()

The IsNull() function evaluates the specified field and returns true if the field contains a null value. A null value is equal to nothing. Nothing is different than zero. You might use this function in record selection to limit the report to records that have something other than a null value in the field. Or use IsNull() to search out records and take some action whenever the report encounters a null value. The IsNull() function behaves differently depending on how your database is built and configured, as suggested below:

- Some databases support null data values and others do not. The IsNull() function will not work if the active database does not support null values.

- If the database supports null values, you can use the IsNull() function to find the null values that get created as the result of a failed lookup while joining.

- The IsNull() function can be passed to the server in the SQL statement as part of the record selection formula or used in SQL commands if your database supports nulls. Check with your database administrator to determine the exact function used with your database.

Evaluate database field for null value

The following formula uses the IsNull() function to evaluate whether the value of a field is null and, if it is, prints the words "No Contact Named." If the value of the field is not null, then print the value of the field.

```
if  IsNull({Customer.ContactName}) then "No Contact Named" else
{Customer.ContactName}
```

IsNull() in selection criteria

An example of using the IsNull() function in a selection formula is a formula that selects a record for the report only if the {Payment Received} field is null. You can insert this formula in either of two places:

- Open the Select Expert, click the Show Formula button, and then click the Formula Editor button (see Figure 7-14). This opens the Formula Editor, in which you can edit the existing formula.

◆ Open the Formula Workshop, and expand the Selection Formulas folder. Select Record Selection, which opens the current record selection formula in the Formula Editor in the work area of the Formula Workshop, as shown in Figure 7-15.

```
IsNull({Orders.Payment Received})
```

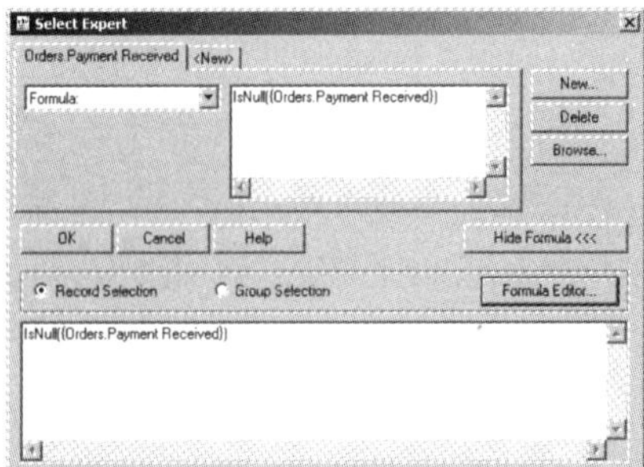

FIGURE 7-14 *Use the IsNull() function in the Select Expert to select only records with a null value in the Payment Received field.*

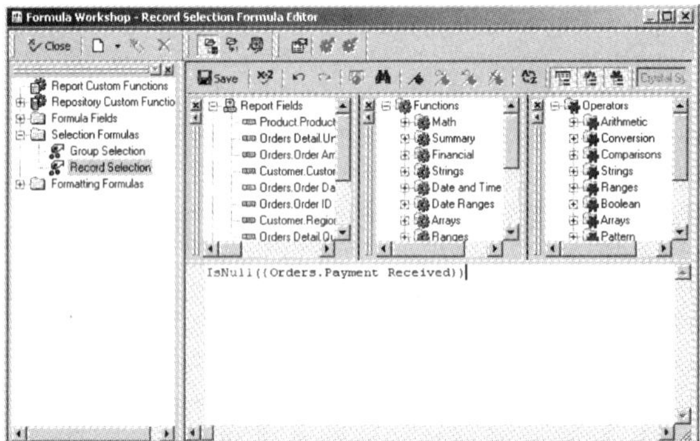

FIGURE 7-15 *Edit the selection formula from within the Formula Workshop.*

OnLastRecord

This function returns true for the last record of the report. Use the following Boolean formula to conditionally format the New Page After option for the Group Footer section.

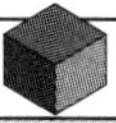

NOTE

Enter the conditional formula for the Group Footer section New Page After option using either the Section Expert or from within the Formula Workshop in the Formatting Formulas folder by selecting the section and then right-clicking and choosing New Formatting Formula.

```
OnLastRecord = false
```

For example, if I formatted a group on a report to start a new page after each Group Footer, the Report Footer gets stranded on the last page of the report, possibly with summary or grand total information. To have the Report Footer print right after the last Group Footer, I insert the formula above as a conditional formula for the New Page After option in the Section Expert. Now the report ignores the New page After direction when it encounters the last record of the report.

The next formula could be used to test if the record is indeed the last record on the report. The formula is named RecordCheck and is dropped into the Details section of a report. It will only print once on the last detail line of the report. If your report were to stop processing midstream for some reason, such a severed database connection, then you would not see this note at the bottom of the report, tipping you off that maybe something happened that caused the report to not complete its processing.

```
If OnLastRecord = True then "Last record"
```

Previous

The Previous() function allows you to check for repeated values, as in the following example:

```
if Previous ({Order.Order Amount}) = {Order.Order Amount} then
"Check for Repeated Value" else ""
```

This formula flags repeated values in the {Order.Order Amount} field with the words Check for Repeated Value. You could change the action of this formula to do something other than print words if the condition is met, depending on where you use the formula.

Use the Previous() Function to Suppress Duplicate Records

The Previous() function can be used to overcome duplicate records in a report. There are many ways to remove duplicate records, such as adjusting your linking, manipulating data with grouping, or writing a better selection formula to eliminate duplicates. But sometimes these options just don't work for a particular circumstance.

Use the previous function to flag detail line records if their value matches the value of the previous record. Then, write a conditional formula in the Section Expert to suppress all detail line records that have the flag.

1. Write a formula in the Formula Workshop that flags records if a certain criteria is met. Name the formula OrderFlag.

   ```
   if Previous ({Order.OrderID}) = {Order.OrderID} then
   "Flag"
   Else ""
   ```

2. Insert this formula into the Details section of the report and suppress the field so that if the value is Flag it prints nothing. You don't want the word flag printing and seen by people reading the report.

3. Within the Formula Workshop, select the Formatting Formulas folder, select the Details section, and then right-click and choose the New Formatting Formula option. Select Suppress and click the Formula Editor button.

4. Or, open the Section Expert (Format, Section), select the Details section on the left side, and click the X+2 icon next to Suppress.

5. In the Formula Editor behind the Suppress option, type the following formula:

   ```
   if  {@OrderFlag} = "Flag"  then true
   ```

6. Save and close the Formula Editor and then preview the report.

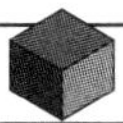

> **NOTE**
>
> A different formula, with the same result as the previous formula example, would be entered in the same place to conditionally suppress the section.
>
> ```
> Previous ({Order.OrderID}) = {Order.OrderID}
> ```

There are countless other ways to use these Print State functions, so search those help files for ideas. The more you know what is available, the easier your report designing will be.

Multi-Pass Reporting

When Crystal Reports processes a report, you see the results in the Preview tab. But in the background, Crystal Reports performs many actions in order to collect the records, format them, perform any calculations, and get the report ready for viewing. Crystal Reports actually "passes over" the report several times before you see the results in the Preview tab. This concept is, sensibly, called multi-pass reporting. The ability to pass over the report data multiple times makes Crystal Reports a powerful reporting tool.

The Design tab for a report contains many instructions, and some of them must occur after others. For example, if you want to calculate a running total, you must sort the records before calculating the running total. Or, to calculate the percent of a subtotal compared to the grand total, the grand total must be calculated first. Then, on its second pass, the report can return to calculate the subtotal percentage.

There are several passes each time data is read and manipulated:

◆ Pre-pass #1, or BeforeReadingRecords

◆ Pass #1, or WhileReadingRecords

◆ Pre-pass #2

◆ Pass #2, or WhilePrintingRecords

◆ Pass #3

BeforeReadingRecords

During pre-pass #1, or BeforeReadingRecords, Crystal Reports evaluates the objects and formulas in the report design and performs any functions or calculations possible before reading any records from the database. For example, a simple formula like 10*2 would be evaluated during this pre-pass.

WhileReadingRecords

During pass #1, or WhileReadingRecords, Crystal Reports performs the following actions:

- Reads and collects database records
- Evaluates and applies record selection criteria
- Performs sorts, groups, and totaling
- Evaluates recurring formulas
- Creates cross-tabs
- Saves work done so far

During pre-pass #2, Crystal Reports applies any group sorting or Top N sorting, and hierarchical grouping if this functionality exists in the report design.

WhilePrintingRecords

During pass #2, or WhilePrintingRecords, Crystal Reports takes one more look to see if anything still remains to be done. Based on the saved results of pass #1, Crystal Reports performs the following actions:

- Calculates totals, like percentage of sum totals or running totals that must be calculated after pass #1
- Applies the group selection formula, if applicable
- Evaluates any print-time formulas, such as formulas using RecordNumber, GroupNumber, Previous, or Next functions, or that explicitly use the WhilePrintingRecords function
- Creates charts and maps
- Creates subreports
- Creates OLAP grids and cross-tabs
- Generates pages on demand

You may notice that cross-tabs were also listed as a function carried out during the While Reading Records pass. A cross-tab may process in either pass depending on what type of formulas the cross-tab contains.

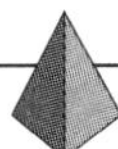

TIP

It is recommended that you do not combine the use of a group selection formula with grand totals, because Crystal Reports processes the grand total in pass #1, based on all groups, and then processes the group selection formula in pass #2. This may remove some groups from the report, but doesn't update the grand totals. You can use a running total to calculate grand totals when you are using either Top N/Bottom N or group selection criteria. The running total will accurately reflect the records displayed on the report.

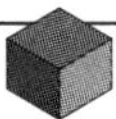

NOTE

During the final pass, pass #3, the total page count is determined if the Total page count field, the Page N of M field, or a special variable field is used on the report to determine total page counts.

So, why do you need to know about multi-pass reporting? You may have formulas that you want to force to process during a certain pass of the report. Four functions are available for this use in the Formula Editor:

- **BeforeReadingRecords.** Forces formula to be performed during pre-pass #1.

- **WhileReadingRecords.** Forces formula to be processed during pass #1.

- **WhilePrintingRecords.** Forces formula to be processed during pass #2.

- **EvaluateAfter().** Forces formula to be processed after another formula that processes earlier during the same pass.

Many functions in Crystal Reports have these evaluation time functions built into them, so that the formula using that function evaluates at the proper time. However, to use these functions independently, you'll find them in the Functions pane under the Evaluation Time node. To use one of these evaluation time functions, enter the function at the top of your formula, followed by a semicolon (Crystal syntax) to separate it from the next statement.

Evaluation time functions are commonly used in formulas with variables, or in formulas where one formula is referring to another formula in the same report.

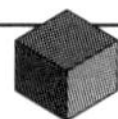

> **NOTE**
>
> Custom Functions can be extracted from many formulas, but not all formulas. Extracting Custom Functions from formulas is covered in Chapter 9, and you will see reference to limitations in Custom Functions due to evaluation time and variable usage.

EvaluateAfter

This function forces an order to formulas that might be processing at the same time or during the same pass of the report. For example, if you use one formula within another formula, then you want formula A to process before you try to use it in Formula B:

```
EvaluateAfter({@formulaA});
({table.field} * {@formulaA}) / 100
```

Using Variables

Think of a variable as a container that you can place values into and retrieve values from. The container stays the same, but what is in it can change. Variables provide expansive flexibility to formulas and can be used in many ways.

Variables can shorten lengthy If-Then-Else formulas by storing a value and referring to it later. To use a variable, follow three basic steps:

1. Declare the variable, including the variable scope and name.

2. Assign a value to the variable.

3. Use the variable in a formula.

Variable Scope

When using variables, you must identify the variable scope, which describes where the variable is available. If you do not specify a variable scope, Crystal Reports assumes it's Global. The following are the variable scopes:

- ◆ **Global**. Can be used and referenced in any formula in one report. Declare a global variable and any number of other formulas in the same report can use that variable.

- ◆ **Shared**. Can be used to share variables between a main report and a subreport, and can be used any number of times by different subreports of the main report.

- ◆ **Local**. Can be referenced and used only in the formula in which it is declared.

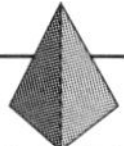

TIP

Variable names cannot exceed 254 characters and cannot have the same name as any Crystal Reports function, operator, or keyword.

Variable Declarations

Before you can use a variable, you must first tell Crystal Reports the name of the variable and what type of data the variable will contain. The data type of the variable you wish to declare determines which variable declaration you use. You can find all of these in the Operators pane of the Formula Editor, under the Variable Declarations heading.

This chapter focuses on the most common use of a variable at first—to store a single value. Variables can also be used to store multiple values, as in an array or a range. Keep in mind that Range and Array variables use the same basic rules as single-value variables.

Components of a Variable

It is best to first declare the scope of the variable you are about to create. The default scope is Global if one is not declared. It is good to be in the habit of declaring variable scope, because there is no reason to store a global variable in memory if you are never going to refer to it somewhere else.

After scope, a variable declaration contains two basic components: the variable data type and the variable name. Then, assign an initial value to the variable in the same statement by adding the assignment operator and a value. The following is a dissection of a variable declaration with each part explained:

- **Scope.** Declares the variable scope: Global, Shared, or Local.

- **<Datatype>Var.** Declares the type of variable, such as NumberVar, StringVar, DateVar, etc., depending on the data type.

- **x.** Name of the variable, such as WeeklyTotal or First3Letters.

- **:=.** The assignment operator (colon and equal sign), which translates to "is assigned a value of" in English.

- **y.** The value being initially assigned to the variable, such as 2000 or "Smith" (you can change the value of the variable later in your formula).

- **;.** The statement separator (semicolon), which keeps each variable declaration separate from the others, as well as from the rest of the formula.

To write a formula using a variable, open the Formula Workshop. Select New, Formula, and name the formula. Then, do the following:

1. Go to the Variable Declarations folder in the Operators pane (see Figure 7-16). Double-click the variable declaration you want to use, based on the data type you want the variable to store.

2. Once you have a declaration in the Formula Text pane of the Formula Editor, you can "fill in" the x by typing a variable name.

3. After the assignment operator, enter the value you want to initially assign to the variable. After the semicolon, press Enter to begin a new line. The semicolon signals to Crystal Reports that you are now starting a new expression in this formula—in other words, what comes before the semicolon is separate functionally from what comes after.

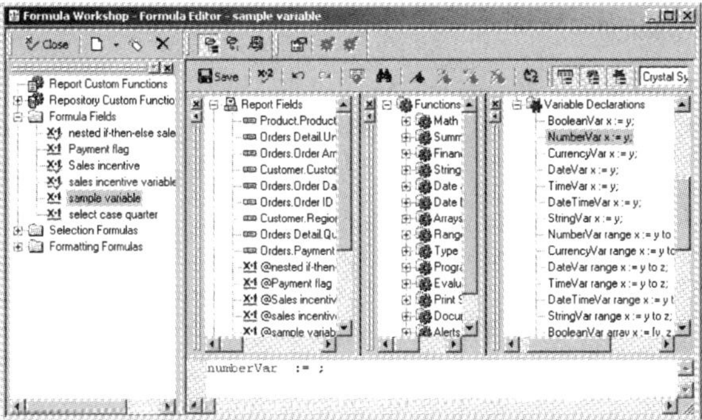

FIGURE 7-16 *Formula Editor with the Variable Declarations list available.*

Using a Variable Instead of a Nested If-Then-Else Statement

Previously, the following formula example was used to illustrate nested If-Then-Else statements. In that formula, the nested If-Then-Else statements designate different incentive products that would be sent out to Xtreme's customers depending on each customer's total order amount.

```
if Sum ({Orders.Order Amount}, {Orders.Order Date}, "monthly")
> 3000 then "Send Sales Incentive sunglasses" else
if Sum ({Orders.Order Amount}, {Orders.Order Date}, "monthly")
> 2000 then "Send Sales Incentive duffle bag" else
if Sum ({Orders.Order Amount}, {Orders.Order Date}, "monthly")
> 1000 then "Send Sales Incentive t-shirt"
```

Instead, let's use a variable to accomplish the exact same result. This formula is named Var Incentive:

```
Local CurrencyVar incentive := Sum ({Orders.Order Amount},
{Orders.Order Date}, "monthly");
if incentive > 3000 then "Send Sales Incentive sunglasses" else
if incentive > 2000 then "Send Sales Incentive duffle bag" else
if incentive > 1000 then "Send Sales Incentive t-shirt"
```

This second formula declares the variable name, incentive, and then assigns a value. A semicolon separates the variable declaration from the If-Then-Else statement that follows. Using a variable in this way can shorten long If-Then-Else statements, especially if you have a long list of conditions.

Product Code Example

Your database may have products or services, and those products or services may have numbers associated with them rather than names. When you print a report, grouping by the product category number is not an option for the readers of the report who do not know what all the numbers mean. You need the name of the category to print.

You could write a long, nested If-Then-Else statement that prints a particular name according to the product category number, or you could declare a variable and write a much shorter If-Then-Else formula (this one is called Product Type):

```
LocalNumberVar idname := {Product.Product Type ID};
if idname = 1 then "Competition Bicycles" else
if idname = 2 then "Hybrid Bicycles" else
if idname = 3 then "Mountain Bikes" else
if idname = 4 then "Kids Bicycles" else
if idname = 5 then "Gloves" else
if idname = 6 then "Helmets" else
if idname = 7 then "Locks" else
if idname = 8 then "Saddles"
else "Unknown product"
```

Manipulate Non-Y2K Number Field into Usable Date Field

A call center database uses a number type field for its date fields, as a three-character year followed by month and date. This format is unusable for normal date parameters or scheduling, or comparing one date to another. Use variables to pull out each part of the date, and manipulate the parts using the Truncate() and Remainder() functions. Convert the field to a Crystal Reports date format.

```
//all dates are number type fields. This formula converts the
//orig_date field (which is a number field in the db) into a date field
Local NumberVar DateNumber := {CALLDETAIL.ORIG_DATE};
Local NumberVar YearNumber := Truncate(DateNumber / 10000);
Local NumberVar MonthNumber := Truncate((DateNumber-(YearNumber * 10000))/100);
Local NumberVar DayNumber := Remainder(DateNumber, 100);
Date(YearNumber + 1900, MonthNumber, DayNumber)
```

Running Total Using Variables

Calculating a running total using variables is sometimes preferable to using the Running Total Expert (covered in Chapter 5). The Expert is easier to use, but limited in the number of conditions or counts you can do at once.

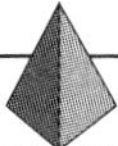

TIP

Large reports with over 300,000 records or so did not accommodate running totals using the Running Total Expert in Crystal Reports versions 8 or 8.5. The report just stops processing, seeming to get "stuck," and never finishes. I usually used variables for any running totals that encounter more than 100,000 records. If you experience similar issues you may choose to use variables rather than the running total expert.

Running totals are extremely useful in reports in which you want to conditionally accumulate a field or value. For example, if you want to count the number of customers who ordered this month, but you also want another count of the number of customers who ordered more than a certain dollar amount that same month, you could use a running total.

You can easily generate the first summary, the number of customers placing an order last month, by inserting a count of customer ID on the report.

The second summary is actually a running total, where you want to count the number of customers whose order amount was greater than some cut-off value you set.

You must create three separate formulas to generate a running total using variables. The following points explain the purpose of each formula:

◆ Set the value of the variable equal to zero.

◆ Perform a calculation or accumulation of the variable.

◆ Print the value of the variable on a report or use it in another formula.

Set the variable equal to zero

You must use the evaluation time function WhilePrintingRecords before each step of any running total formulas. This way, all the sorting and grouping is performed *before* the formula is processed. This is imperative for the count to be correct.

```
//reset variable count500 to zero
WhilePrintingRecords;
global numbervar count500 := 0;
```

Insert this formula into whatever section you want the running total to reset. If once per report, then put this formula in the Report Header. If once per group, insert this formula into the Group Header section. This formula *must* be in a section above the next formula, which performs the actual accumulation calculation.

Declare the variable

Declare the type of variable, the variable name, and what the variable is equal to:

```
//calculate running total of count of customers with over 500 order amount
WhilePrintingRecords;
if {Orders.Order Amount} > 500 then global numbervar count500 := count500 +1;
```

 **NOTE**

You may want to declare your variable separately from the formula statement if this is easier for you to understand and keep the parts of the formula straight. The following formula has the exact same result as the formula above, but declares the global numbervar count500 in a separate statement.

```
//calculate running total of count of customers with over 500 order amount
WhilePrintingRecords;
global numbervar count500;
if {Orders.Order Amount} > 500 then count500 := count500 +1;
```

Print result on the report

The last step once the calculation is performed is to refer to the variable and print it on the report. Insert this field where you want the running total to print on the report, which is in the Group Footer for this example:

```
WhilePrintingRecords;
Global numbervar count500;
count500
```

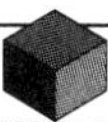

NOTE

In the formula above the last line is not necessary but sometimes included (especially in text meant to help people learn).

Use Running Total Value in a Formula

The next example takes using variables one small step forward—using the variable in a simple formula. This example accumulates the order amount for all orders over 500.

Set variable equal to zero

This formula sets the sumAmt variable equal to zero:

```
//reset sumAmt variable to zero
WhilePrintingRecords;
Global numbervar sumAmt := 0;
```

Declare the variable

Declare the type of variable, the variable name, and what the variable is equal to:

```
//sum up order amount for all customers with > 500 order amount
WhilePrintingRecords;
Global Numbervar sumAmt;
if {Orders.Order Amount} > 500 then sumAmt := sumAmt + {Orders.Order Amount};
```

NOTE

The formula above does not need the global numbervar sumAmt; declared separately if you do not want. The formula is also correct as stated in the code below:

```
WhilePrintingRecords;
if {Orders.Order Amount} > 500 then Global Numbervar sumAmt :=
sumAmt + {Orders.Order Amount};
```

Print result on the report

The last step once the calculation is performed is to refer to the variable and print it on the report. If you do not care to see the variable accumulate, but want it to print, you can suppress the variable calculation in the Details section and it will just print the accumulation total in the Group Footer with the following formula:

```
//print value for sumAmt variable on report
WhilePrintingRecords;
numbervar sumAmt;
sumAmt
```

NOTE

The last line of the previous formula is not necessary, just used to help spell out what is going on a little more for new users. Feel free to omit it, I often do when developing production reports.

Control Structures in Crystal Syntax

The If-Then-Else statement has been around forever, but other control structure functions greatly enhance Crystal syntax. Their application is fairly specific and very powerful.

Control structures enable a formula to evaluate expressions repeatedly or to skip some expressions altogether, depending on the conditions. You access Crystal syntax control structures in the Formula Editor, in the Operators pane under the category Control Structures (see Figure 7-17).

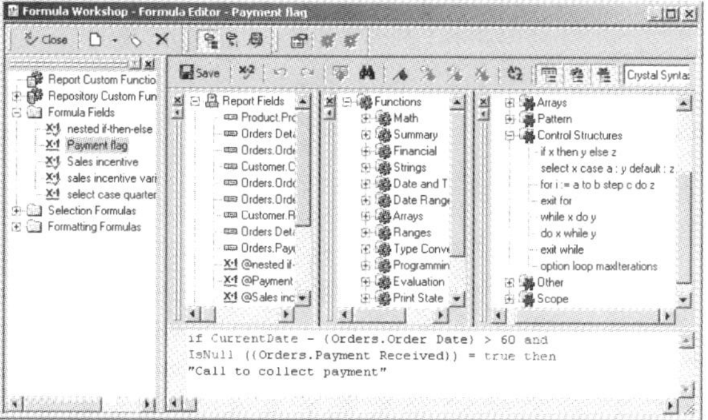

FIGURE 7-17 *Crystal syntax control structures are located in the Formula Editor's Operators pane.*

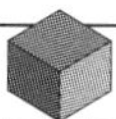

NOTE

This section contains a few formulas in Crystal syntax. The control structures work essentially the same way in either syntax, following that syntax's specific guidelines. See the section "Introducing Basic Syntax," later in the chapter, for examples in that syntax.

If Expressions: The Good, the Bad, and the Ugly

To ease you into what these structures can do, start with the good old If-Then-Else statement. To be proper, and to talk like a real know-it-all, we can call the If-Then-Else statement an If expression. Consider an example. In simple terms, an If expression states:

If condition then instructions

Crystal syntax displays the If expression in the Formula Editor as follows:

If x then y else z

The following is a sample formula:

```
//sample if expression 1
if {Orders.Order Amount} > 5000 then "Apply Discount" else ""
```

Multistatement If-Then-Else formulas accommodate many conditions and instructions:

If condition1 then instructions1 else
  If condition2 then instructions2 else
    If condition3 then instructions3 else
      condition 4

An example multistatement If formula looks like this:

```
//if statement
if {department.departmentname} = "R&D" then "Research and Development" else
    if {department.departmentname} = "Mfg" then "Manufacturing" else
        if {department.departmentname} = "HR" then "Human Resources" else
            "Marketing"
```

This example formula could go on and on for all the possible departments. Long formulas like this could get on your nerves. You can shorten the statement slightly by declaring the department as a variable:

```
//variable to shorten the if formula
Local stringvar Dept := {department.departmentname};
If Dept = "R&D" then "Research and Development" else
    If Dept = "Mfg" then "Manufacturing" else
        If Dept = "HR" then "Human Resources" else
            "Marketing"
```

Using the variable shortens the formula just a little bit by replacing the full field name {department.departmentname} with a shorter variable name, but we can still do better.

Creating Efficiencies with the Select Expression

Another control structure is called a Select expression, or Select Case statement. The Select expression is similar to an If expression, but it sometimes creates clearer formulas. When looking for the Select expression in the Formula Editor, you'll find it as:

select x case a : y default : z

You can read this generic expression of the Select Case statement as:

select {field}
case condition1 : instruction1
case condition2 : instruction2
default : instruction3

An even more English-sounding version of the statement might read:

Regarding this {field}
When a test registers true<condition1>, do <instruction1>
When a test registers true <condition2>, do <instruction2>
Otherwise, when a test doesn't register any of these conditions, do <instruction3>

Select Case is a more efficient way of restating a long If-Then-Else statement. This involves replacing the If expression with a Select expression, as shown in the following example:

NOTE

Select Case statements are good for replacing nested If statements that repeatedly test the same thing for different values.

```
//select case formula
Select {Department}
Case "R&D" : "Research and Development"
Case "Mfg" : "Manufacturing"
Case "HR" : "Human Resources"
Case "Mkg" : "Marketing"
Default : "No Named Department Specified"
```

You may find this Select Case statement much easier to follow and shorter than the traditional If-Then-Else statement. If an expression does not meet any of the cases, then the instruction assigned to Default applies.

Repeating an Action with Loops

Crystal Reports offers several types of loops, as well as methods for exiting the loop when the time is right.

A basic For loop lets you evaluate a sequence of expressions a multiple number of times. The If and Select statements evaluate an expression once against the conditions, and then the next expression is evaluated against the conditions, and the next expression, and so on. Loops evaluate one expression over and over until meeting the condition for exiting the loop.

Think of this like one of those computer programs that bank robbers use in movies to find a safe's combination. The robber hooks a laptop up to the safe's keypad, and the program begins trying every number until verifying the first digit. Then the program goes to the next digit and loops through all the possible numbers, and so on. I am not sure if you could use Crystal for this purpose, and I don't recommend that you try! But the concept of evaluating an expression until meeting some condition is right on.

You'll find many functions available for loops under the Control Structures group in the Operators pane:

- for i := a to b step c do z
- exit for
- while x do y
- do x while y
- exit while

Crystal syntax has three types of loops: the For loop and two types of While loops. For loops cycle through the expression a known number of times, which you determine at the beginning of the formula. While loops continue indefinitely until a specific condition is met. Following are examples of each.

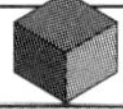

NOTE

Basic syntax has the same loops as Crystal syntax, and several other types as well that lend even more flexibility and options.

Repeating a Set Number of Times with the For Loop

A For loop evaluates an expression a known number of times. Consider the following example of a For loop in Crystal syntax. This formula prints multiple parameter values for the parameter {?Region}.

> **NOTE**
>
> Chapter 12 covers parameters in detail. A parameter is a user-created field (like a formula field) that accepts values via a prompt to the user. Often, parameters are used in selection criteria so that users can enter a value at a prompt and have that value passed to the selection criteria for processing. In the examples in this chapter, I use a loop formula to evaluate each value entered for the parameter {?Region}. This formula addresses a problem that users have when they create a multivalue parameter and then try to display the multiple values on their report. In this case, simply placing the parameter field on the report only prints the first value. The reason for this is that the multivalue parameter is really an array of values, and to show all the values in the array, you have to make Crystal loop through the array and pull out each value and place each value into a string.

```
//each line of comment is meant to help explain the next line of the formula.
//declare a string variable named temp and make it equal to nothing
        Local stringVar temp := "";
//declare a numbervar i
        Local numberVar i;
//the for determines how many items are in the array. This would be
//how many regions were entered into the parameter in this example.
//use the count function to count the number of regions entered.
        for i := 1 to Count({?Region}) do
//the next section of the formula in the parentheses create the variable
//that will increment for each run through the loop and compare itself
//to the counter. Each time the incremented variable goes through
//the loop, its value increases by one. That variable is used as a
//subscript to pull each value in the parameter array out and place it
//in a string to then print on the report.
```

```
(
    if i = 1 then temp := temp & {?Region} [i];
    if i > 1 then temp := temp & ", " & {?Region} [i];
);
//temp is the string that will print all the values taken from the array
    temp
```

The preceeding loop formula is necessary if you want multiple numbers to print on a report that are entered at a prompt. Another example formula to accomplish the same result is listed below. The Join() function works only for string type fields, not number, so you will still need to power through the loop for number fields.

```
Join({?Region}, ", ")
```

The variables used must be declared, accomplished by the first two lines of the formula. The variable i is the counter variable; its value changes with each iteration of the loop. The parentheses (round braces) enclose the instructions to be executed with each iteration of the loop. The value returned by the formula always equals the last evaluated expression in the formula. In this example, the variable temp, which contains the string constructed by the For loop, is the last expression evaluated.

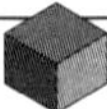

NOTE

The step value in a For loop can be a negative number. For example, in the following expression, the value of i is equal to 25 during the first iteration of the For loop and decreases to 1 during successive loops at intervals of negative 1. The step variable is 1 by default and can be specified as some other value if needed.

```
For i := 25 to 1 step -1
```

The Exit For statement allows you to designate a condition under which to exit the loop. This statement is found within the instructions portion of the formula. The following formula uses the Exit For statement to stop executing the For loop if the number of regions in the field {?Region} equals zero:

```
Local stringVar temp := "";

Local numberVar i;

for i := 1 to Count({?Region}) do

(

if Count({?Region}) = 0 then Exit For;

if i = 1 then temp := temp & {?Region} [i];

if i > 1 then temp := temp & ", " & {?Region} [i];

);

temp
```

Repeating Conditionally with While Loops

Another type of loop is the While loop. Crystal syntax supports two different types of While loops:

- ◆ **While ... Do**. This loop evaluates the condition and, if true, it evaluates the expression following the do keyword. Then it repeats the process until the evaluation of the condition is false. You can think of this as *while condition (is true) do expression.*

- ◆ **Do ... While**. This loop evaluates the expression once, then it evaluates the condition. If the condition is true, then the expression is evaluated again until the condition is false. Think of this one as *do expression while condition (is true)*. See Figure 7-18 for an example of a Do ... While formula in Basic syntax.

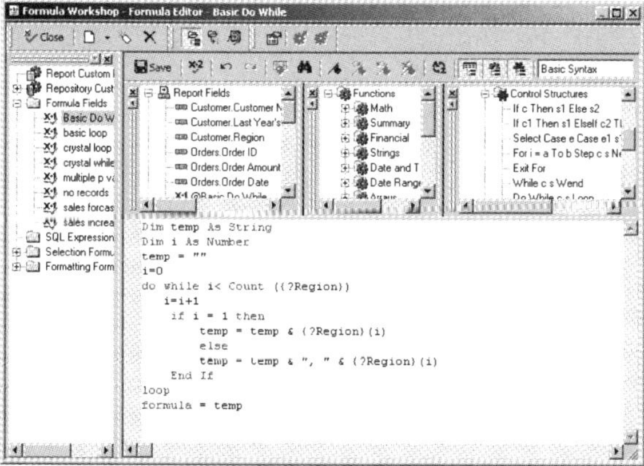

FIGURE 7-18 *This Do ... While formula evaluates the formula while a condition is being met and prints the value entered for {?Region}.*

NOTE

Exit While is supported by these While loops to jump out of the loop. If the Exit While condition evaluates to true, the loop is exited.

The While loop, when considered an expression, always returns the Boolean value true.

Preventing a Never-Ending Loop

To prevent the possibility of an endless loop, any one evaluation of a formula can have no more than 100,000 loop evaluations. In the event that a formula goes through more than 100,000 loop evaluations, Crystal presents an error message. If a single formula contains multiple loops, this safety mechanism applies to the entire formula and not to each individual loop.

Loop Formula Limitations

As you develop formulas, you'll want to be aware of certain size limitations. Since the limitations are quite generous, you may never encounter them. Just in case, though, the following list recaps formula limitations:

◆ The maximum number of loop condition evaluations per evaluation of a formula is 100,000.

◆ The maximum length of a string (constant, value held by a sting variable, value returned by a function, or string element of a string array) is 65,534 characters.

◆ The maximum size of an array is 1000 elements.

◆ The maximum number of arguments to a function is 1000 (applied to functions that can have an indefinite number of arguments, like Choose).

◆ Datetime functions modeled on Visual Basic accept dates from year 100 to year 9999. Traditional Crystal Reports functions accept dates from year 1 to year 9999.

Programming Shortcuts

Crystal now has several programming shortcut functions that act like control structures. They are different from control structures in that they can be used in selection formulas and pushed down to the server for processing.

Using the IIF Function in Place of If-Then-Else

The IIF function can replace an If-Then-Else statement in some cases. This function needs a true part and a false part, and must have an Else statement. This function gets unwieldy for nested If statements. IIF is a VB function that is now included in both Crystal and Basic syntax.

An IIF function takes three arguments:

- **expression.** Contains the condition that will evaluate to either true or false. It corresponds to the if clause of an If expression.
- **truePart.** The action to be executed when the expression evaluates to true. It corresponds to the then clause of an If expression. In this argument, you can include single or range values, but no arrays.
- **falsePart.** The action to be executed when the expression evaluates to false. It corresponds to the else clause of an If expression. It must be of the same type as truePart.

The following example illustrates usage of the IIF function:

```
IIF ({Orders.Order Amount} > 20000, "Apply Discount", "Standard Price")
```

This formula returns the words Apply Discount if the order amount is greater than 20,000 and returns the words Standard Price for all other orders (that do not meet the greater than 20,000 condition).

Specify an Array with the Choose Function

Use the Choose function to specify an array of values and select from it all at once in one statement. The function Choose(index, choice1, choice2, . . . choiceN) is listed in the Functions pane of the Formula Editor under Programming Shortcuts.

This function uses the index value to choose from the values.

◆ The range of index values (choice1, choice2, choice3, etc.) depends on the number of choices. (You could not have 20 as the index value with only 10 choices.)

◆ All choices must be of one of the simple data types (Number, Currency, String, Boolean, Date, Time, or DateTime) or a range type (Number Range, Currency Range, String Range, Date Range, Time Range, or DateTime Range).

◆ The choice field cannot be an array.

For example, the following formulas demonstrate the Choose function. The first formula is "choosing" the third value (or choice) from the three choices available.

The second formula is "choosing" the first value from the available choices, which is 12.

```
Choose (3, "good", "better", "best") //returns best
Choose (1, 12, 24, 36, 48) //returns 12
```

Replacing a Select Case Statement with the Switch Function

The Switch function evaluates the expressions from left to right, and returns the value associated with the first expression to evaluate to true.

The function Switch(Expr1, value1, expr2, value2, . . . exprN, valueN) is found in the Functions pane of the Formula Editor under Programming Shortcuts.

Switch consists of pairs of expressions and values—Expr1, value1, expr2, value2, etc. For example:

◆ If expr1 is true, value1 is returned.

◆ If expr1 is false and expr2 is true, then value2 is returned.

◆ If expr1 and expr2 are false and expr3 is true, then value3 is returned.

◆ If all the expressions are false, then a default value is returned. (The default value returned depends on the type of the values in the value list. For example, if the values are of Number type, the default value is 0 and if the values are of String type, the default value is the empty string ("").)

For example, the following formula evaluates if expr1 is true; if yes, then value1 is returned. If no, then expr2 is evaluated. If expr2 is true, then value2 is returned, and so on.

```
Switch ({Orders.Order Amount} > 10000, "Excellent Sales",
{Orders.Order Amount} > 5000, "Good Sales",
True, "Below Goal Sales")
```

Introducing Basic Syntax

For people already familiar with Visual Basic or other versions of Basic, this alternate formula syntax uses Visual Basic Script with specific extensions for reporting. This means you do not need to learn Crystal syntax; you can use the formula language that you already know.

What Is Basic Syntax?

Basic syntax is similar to Visual Basic Script and can be used as an alternative formula language in Crystal. You have the choice of using either Crystal syntax or Basic syntax to write formulas and Custom Functions. If you are already familiar with VB or Basic script, you can use Basic syntax instead of Crystal syntax. Also, many VB-like functions included in Basic syntax have been added to Crystal syntax in order to make formulas more powerful and versatile than ever in either syntax. Both Crystal syntax and Basic syntax formulas can coexist in the same report. Basic syntax causes no degradation in compiling or processing time and does not require any additional libraries.

 **NOTE**

A note for those already familiar with the current formula language, referred to as Crystal syntax: There are many VB Script-based functions available in Crystal syntax, including control structures derived from Visual Basic. You can continue using the formula language you already know.

In the Formula Editor, a drop-down list in the upper-right corner lets you select which syntax you want to use for each individual formula. You can also set a default formula language to use under File, Options, on the Reporting tab.

Why Learn Basic Syntax?

Basic syntax enhances the power of Crystal Reports. The Crystal syntax language for writing formulas works well and lends a great deal of flexibility and power to your formulas. Basic syntax is based on the Visual Basic programming language, which in some cases might be more efficient than Crystal syntax or contain functions that lend different functionality or flexibility to formulas.

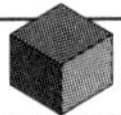

NOTE

Basic syntax is a specific formula syntax in Crystal Reports that is based on VB Script. This basic syntax is different than the Basic programming language.

Do not mistakenly think that you have to learn Basic syntax. Crystal syntax has lists of functions that mimic VB Script and offer more options, flexibility, and power. But if you already know VB Script, you do not have to learn Crystal syntax to write formulas in Crystal Reports.

Differences Between Crystal Syntax and Basic Syntax

Basic syntax differs from Crystal syntax in several ways. The differences are minor, but knowing them is important to writing successful formulas using Basic syntax. The following sections outline the differences between Crystal syntax and Basic syntax.

Comments

Crystal Syntax. Comments begin with double slashes (//). Comments may begin anywhere in a line, before, after, or in the middle of the actual formula. Each new line of comments must begin with a repeated set of double slashes.

```
2+2 //This comment is fine
//This comment is also fine
2+2 This comment will cause an error
```

Basic Syntax. Comments begin with Rem (for remark) or an apostrophe (').
Because Rem is a statement, it must start a new line or be separated from the previous statement with a colon (:). Comments starting with an apostrophe can begin
anywhere in a line.

```
X=2:Rem This comment is fine.
X=2 Rem This comment will generate an error.
X=2 'This comment is fine.
```

Line Continuation

Crystal Syntax. A statement may continue on to the next line (such as an If-
Then-Else statement). Separating consecutive statements requires a semicolon (;).
The first example does *not* require a semicolon because the two lines belong to a
single If-Then-Else statement:

```
If {Orders.Order.Amount} > 500
Then "Apply Discount"
Else ""
```

The next example requires a semicolon to separate two independent statements
within a single formula:

```
Local StringVar Dept := {Department Code};
If Dept = 01 then "HR" else
If Dept = 02 then "Marketing"
```

Basic Syntax. To continue a statement onto the next line, a line continuation
character—an underscore (_)—must be used. To separate consecutive statements, use a colon (:) or a line break (paragraph return). The first example shows
the use of the underscore (at the end of the first line) to indicate that the two
lines belong to a single statement:

```
If {Orders.Order Amount} > 500 _
Then Formula = "Apply Discount"
```

The second example shows two separate statements on one line, separated by a colon:

```
X = 2 : Rem this is a sample for colon use
```

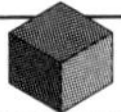 **NOTE**

Multiline If-Then-Else statements do not need the line continuation character. Use the End If statement to create a multiline If statement in Basic syntax.

Value Returned from a Formula

Crystal Syntax. A formula returns the result of the final statement. The following formula returns either "Good Sales" or "Bad Sales" as its result:

```
if {Customer.Last Year's Sales} > 5000 then "Good Sales" else "Bad Sales"
```

Basic Syntax. Returns the value of the special variable, formula. You can set the value of this variable once or many times in a single formula. You don't need to declare this variable.

The following is the same formula as the preceding formula, but written in Basic syntax. The result of the formula is the final value assigned to the variable named formula.

```
if {Customer.Last Year's Sales} > 5000 then
formula ="Good Sales"
else formula = "Bad Sales"
End if
```

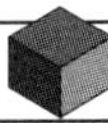 **NOTE**

You must use the formula variable in Basic syntax formulas. You may have legitimate circumstances where the formula variable is equal to zero. For example, the formula may assign a value to another user-declared variable, which then gets used by a second formula.

Constants

A variety of constants have been added to both Crystal and Basic syntax. All of these constants start with the prefix cr. The following list gives you a flavor of the kinds of constants available. These constants are listed in the Functions pane of the Formula Editor only when they can be used—which is usually only when writing conditional formulas.

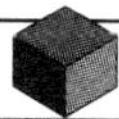

NOTE

Search the online help files for any of these constants by typing in the constant as the keyword. This is only a partial list of the functions available.

◆ **Paragraph formatting:** crUniterpretedText, crRTFText, crHTMLText

◆ **Dates:** crUseSystem, crSunday, crMonday, etc.

◆ **Date formatting:** crDayOfWeekInParenthesis, crDayOfWeekInSquare-Brackets

◆ **Font formatting:** crRegular, crBold, crItalic, crBorderline; you can also use the font names available in the Functions pane, such as Arial and Courier

◆ **Mathematical value:** crPi

Fields

Treat database fields the same for both Basic and Crystal syntax. Enclose fields in curly, or French, braces ({}). Follow the table name by a period and then the field name, as in *{tablename.fieldname}*.

Simple Data Types

The following sections contain some simple data type notes that will help you learn Basic syntax, especially if you're already familiar with Crystal syntax. Refer to these sections as a summary, comparing the two syntaxes.

Numbers

Do not use commas or currency symbols in either syntax; for example, 20000, -400, and 73.35.

Currency

Crystal Syntax. Add the dollar sign ($) or use the CCur() function to convert numbers to currency:

```
$20000, $-400.00, $73.35 or
CCur(20000), CCur(-400), CCur(73.35)
```

Basic Syntax. Use the CCur() function only.

Strings

Crystal Syntax. Enclose strings in either double quotes ("   ") or single quotes ('   '):

```
"This is a string"
'This is a string'
"123"
'The word "hello" is quoted'
"This is not valid'
```

Basic Syntax. You must use double quotes.

Extracting characters from strings

Crystal Syntax. Use square braces ([]):

```
"Hello" [2] //returns e, the second character in the string
"Hello" [-5] //returns H, the fifth character from the end of the string
```

Basic Syntax. Use parentheses:

```
formula = "Hello" (2)
'returns e, the second character in the string
formula = "Hello" (3 to 5)
'returns llo, the third through fifth characters in the string
```

Boolean values

Both Crystal and Basic syntaxes return true or false. You can use yes and no as substitutes in either syntax.

Date, time, and datetime

Both Crystal and Basic syntaxes hold date, time, and datetime types of field data. Though the datetime type is most versatile, the date type and time type are more efficient. Datetime literals cannot be split between lines in either syntax. Create a datetime literal in either syntax by surrounding the date with pound signs (# #):

```
#1/3/00 2:00 pm#
#September 17, 1992#
#23 Aug 1976#
#23 Aug 1976 12:44 pm#
#9:30 am#
```

Range data types

Both syntaxes accept ranges for all simple data types except Boolean. There are a few differences between the syntaxes when it comes to including the value in the range.

Crystal Syntax. There are several options when defining a range. Use any of the following options, depending on what values you want returned:

- **to.** Includes low and high ends and all values in between
- **_to.** Includes high end only and values in between
- **to_.** Includes low end only and values in between
- **_to_.** Includes only values in between
- **Upto.** Includes all values less than or equal to the value

```
2 to 5 //returns 2,3,4,5
2 _to 5 //returns 3,4,5
2 to_ 5 //returns 2,3,4
2 _to_ 5 //returns 3,4
UpTo 5 //returns all numbers less than or equal to 5
UpTo_ 5 //returns all numbers less than 5
UpFrom 5 //returns all numbers 5 and greater
#July 1, 1985# to #July 1, 1995#
UpFrom #April 1, 1999#
```

Basic Syntax. Basic syntax ranges are the same as Crystal syntax. Use to, _to, to_, and _to_, as follows:

```
Is <= 5 'all numbers less than or equal to 5
Is < 5 'all numbers less than 5
#July 1, 1985# to #July 1, 1995#
Is >= #April 1, 1999#
```

Variables

Fundamentally, variables work the same way in Basic syntax as they do in Crystal (which was described earlier in this chapter). Though the functionality is basically the same, the syntax involving variables differs somewhat.

A variable declaration in Crystal syntax looks different than in Basic. To declare a variable in Crystal syntax, you might write a statement such as:

```
Local StringVar x := y;
```

To make this same declaration using Basic syntax, you would write:

```
Dim x As String
```

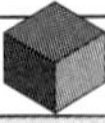

NOTE

In Basic syntax, Dim is the same as Local variable scope.

Table 7-1 outlines other subtle differences between the two syntaxes with regard to variables.

Table 7-1 Handling Variables Differently in Crystal and Basic Syntaxes

Crystal Syntax	Basic Syntax
Variables must be declared before use, and the declaration must include the data type.	Variables must be declared before use, but the data type does not have to be specified at declaration.
Variable data types are indicated by keywords such as BooleanVar, NumberVar, CurrencyVar, and DateVar.	Variable data types are indicated by VB keywords such as Boolean, Number (or Double), Currency, and Date.
Variable scopes include Local, Global, and Shared. If no scope is specified, Global is assumed.	Variable scopes include Local (Dim), Global, and Shared.

Declaring a variable follows this format:

Local numbervar x;	Global stringvar y;

Declaring a variable follows this format:

Dim x As Number	Global y As String
Variables can be initialized at declaration.	Variables cannot be initialized at declaration.
Use colon-equals (:=) to assign a value to a variable.	Use just an equal sign (=) to assign a value to a variable.
Do not use the keyword Let.	Optionally use the keyword Let, as in Let x=10.
Use square braces when declaring an array: Numbervar array x := [1,2,3];	Use round braces (parentheses) when declaring an array: Dimx X=Array(1,2,3) 'create x by calling array Dim y () as Number 'create y without specifying size
A range can be used as an element or part of an element in an array.	A range can be an element in an array.

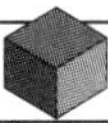

NOTE

The default scope in Crystal syntax is Global. The default scope in Basic syntax is Local. Local scope is more efficient because memory space is not held after the formula has been processed. If you don't need the variable to be used in multiple formulas, it is best to make it Local. Because variables in formulas from version 6 and earlier reports did not have scopes, Seagate makes Crystal syntax default to Global so that reports can be brought into later versions. You should always declare scopes (and data types) when you declare variables. This not only helps you to make your reports as efficient as possible, but also helps you to document your formula when you do a full declaration.

Arrays

Arrays function basically the same for both Crystal and Basic syntaxes, the main difference being that Crystal uses square braces ([]) where Basic uses round braces, ().

Crystal Syntax. Use square braces to enclose an array:

```
[10, 20, 30]
["Sun","Mon","Tues","Wed","Thurs","Fri","Sat"]
[10, 20, 30]  //returns 20, the second value in the array
```

Basic Syntax. Use the Array() function to enclose an array:

```
(10, 20, 30)
Array("Sun","Mon","Tues","Wed","Thurs","Fri","Sat") (3):Rem returns Tues
Array(10, 20, 30) (2) 'returns 20, the second value in the array
```

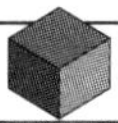

NOTE

You can pull more than one value from an array by using a subscript operator, as in [10, 20, 30] [2 to 3], which returns the smaller array [20, 30].

Table 7-2 outlines other differences between Crystal and Basic syntaxes, related to arrays.

Table 7-2 Handling Arrays Differently in Crystal and Basic Syntaxes

Crystal Syntax	Basic Syntax
Arrays are indexed from 1 (not 0).	Arrays are indexed from 1 (not 0).
When declaring an array variable, type must be specified, and the array must be either initialized or the size must be specified.	When declaring an array variable, type and size are not necessary. If size is given at declaration, type must be given also.
Supports only one-dimensional arrays.	Unlike VB, Basic syntax only supports one-dimensional arrays.

Examples of Crystal Syntax vs. Basic Syntax

So, enough of the guidelines! Let's look at a simple If-Then-Else formula and see how it looks in Crystal syntax and in Basic syntax. Many new functions in Crystal syntax, including control structures, improve functionality in that syntax. Other functions and control structures are exclusive to Basic syntax. Many of these control structures, in conjunction with variables, can shorten and simplify formulas.

Writing an If-Then-Else statement in Crystal syntax is almost the same as writing it in Basic syntax. Considering an example I used earlier, a formula in Crystal syntax reads:

```
//example of if statement in Crystal syntax
if {order.order amount} > 10000 then
{order.order amount} * 0.10
else 0
```

In Basic syntax, this same formula reads:

```
Rem example of if statement in Basic syntax
if {order.order amount} > 10000 then
formula = {order.order amount} * 0.10
else formula = 0
End if
```

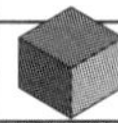

NOTE

In Basic syntax, a single-line If statement needs a line continuation character, whereas a multiline If statement using the End If statement does not need a line continuation character. When using the multiline If statement, you must have a line break after the Then and Else, and before the End If.

The only differences between the syntaxes include replacing the double slashes (//) in Crystal syntax with Rem in Basic, assigning values to the formula variable in Basic syntax, and using the End If command to complete the If-Then-Else statement in Basic syntax.

Basic syntax formulas use the special variable called Formula to return the value of the formula. The Basic syntax example shows how this special variable is one of the main differences between the two syntaxes. In Basic syntax, you must also declare the end of the If-Then-Else statement with the End If statement clause. But, this rule applies only when you break the If-Then-Else statement onto more than one line.

Of course, the formula could have more than one instruction. For both the Crystal and Basic syntax versions of the formula, let's add a 2-percent bonus to the total amount if the order amount doesn't exceed 10000. First, let's make the change to the Crystal syntax version of the formula:

```
// if statement example 2 in Crystal syntax
if {order.order amount} > 10000 then
{order.order amount} * 0.10 else
{order.order amount} * 0.02
```

The same change to the Basic syntax formula looks like this:

```
Rem if statement example 2 in Basic syntax
if {order.order amount} > 10000 then
formula = {order.order amount} * 0.10 else
formula = {order.order amount} * 0.02
End if
```

Formula Expert

The Formula Expert is a component of the Formula Workshop that can be used to build formulas for a report. All formulas built with the Formula Expert must use a Custom Function, not the traditional Formula Editor. Thus, there must be a Custom Function available to the report to perform the function desired in order to build a formula using the Formula Expert.

Some Custom Functions are shipped with Crystal Reports in the Sample Crystal Repository. You can build your own Custom Function "from scratch," or you can extract Custom Functions from existing formulas. Chapter 9 covers building and using Custom Functions in detail, but this chapter also covers building a few formulas using the Formula Expert.

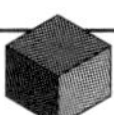

NOTE

See Chapter 9 to learn more about the Formula Expert's user interface.

Create a Formula Using the Formula Expert

The Formula Expert uses Custom Functions to build formulas. Thus, you must have a Custom Function available to the report to perform the desired function. To create a formula using the Formula Expert:

1. Open the Formula Workshop.

2. Click the down arrow on the New button and select Formula from the list that appears. Enter a name for the formula in the Formula Name dialog box that opens (see Figure 7-19).

3. Click the Use Expert button, and the Formula Expert opens in the work area to the right of the Workshop Tree.

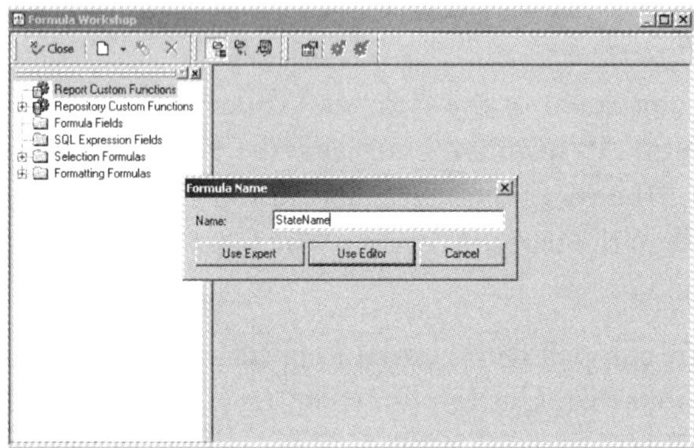

FIGURE 7-19 *Use the Formula Expert to build formulas using Custom Functions.*

4. In the Custom Function Supplying Logic area, choose the custom function on which to base your formula. Expand your Repository to see all the available functions. The Sample Repository shown in Figure 7-20 has many custom functions available for use on reports.

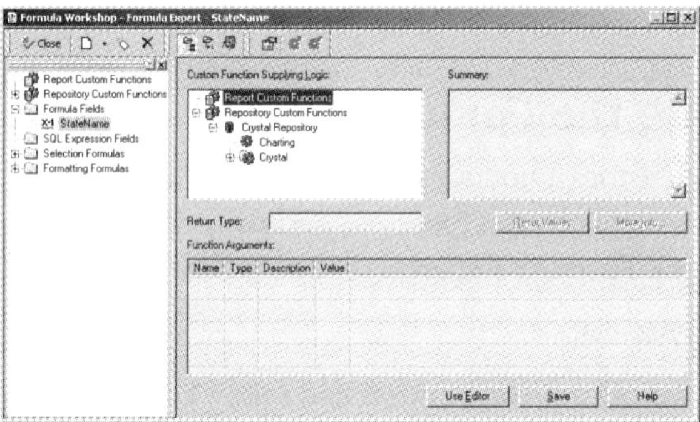

FIGURE 7-20 *You must select a Custom Function from either the Report Custom Functions node or the Repository Custom Functions node.*

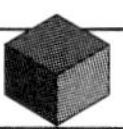

NOTE

You can choose a Report Custom Function (a custom function that exists in the current report) or a Repository Custom Function (a custom function that is stored in the Repository). If you select a Repository Custom Function, that custom function is added to the current report. If that custom function requires other custom functions from the Repository, it will be added automatically.

5. In the Function Arguments area, specify a value for each argument in the appropriate Value field (see Figure 7-21). You can enter constant values, or use the drop-down list to select predefined values or report fields. Click the area labeled Select Field or Enter Value and a pick list arrow appears.

6. Once you have selected a value, click the Save button to save the formula to the Formula Fields folder of the Formula Workshop.

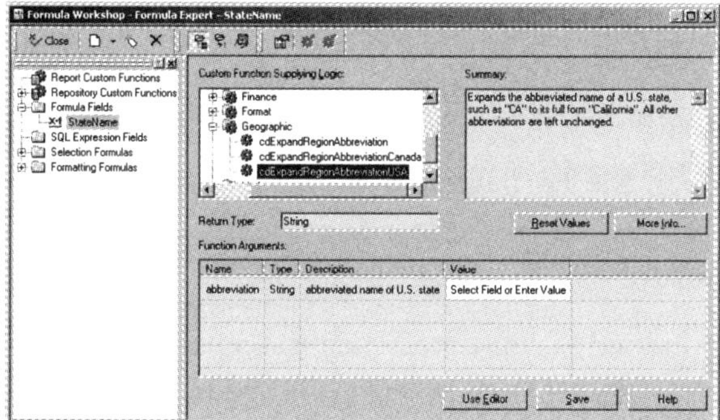

FIGURE 7-21 *Select a field value as the Value Function Argument.*

You can now use this formula in your report just as you would use a formula you created in the Formula Editor.

Extracting Custom Functions from Formulas

Crystal Reports provides an Extract Custom Function dialog box to extract a Custom Function out of formula text. To use the tool, you must have a functional formula from which to have Crystal extract the logic and build a Custom Function.

The Extract Custom Function from Formula dialog box does most of the work for you; all you need to do is name and describe the Custom Function, and set the variable arguments.

This custom function can then be saved in the Repository, making it available for use in any report, and in a variety of situations by entering different values as the arguments.

Custom Functions can also be built from scratch without extracting from an existing formula. Chapter 9 covers both extracting Custom Functions from formulas and instructions for building your own.

Debugging Evaluation Time Errors

When you check a formula in the Formula Editor and it reports that no errors were found, you believe that you are home free and the formula will definitely work in the report. Alas, this is not always the case.

Sometimes an error is encountered at run time, when the report refreshes. This is called an *evaluation time error*. When such an error is encountered, the Formula Workshop opens with a call stack in the Workshop Tree that shows the current values of all variables used in the formula. An error message appears, and the cursor is placed in your formula where the error occurred (see Figure 7-22).

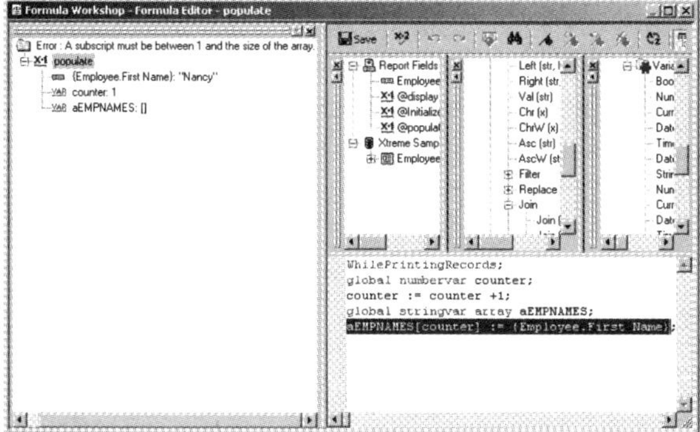

FIGURE 7-22 *A call stack is listed in the Workshop Tree area (expanded here to show the entire error message).*

Use the call stack to help troubleshoot what might have caused the error:

◆ The root of the tree provides a description of the error that occurred.

◆ The nodes in the tree provide the names of the custom functions and/or formulas that were being evaluated when the error occurred.

◆ The custom function/formula at the top of the call stack is where the error was detected.

◆ The custom function/formula next in the stack has invoked the custom function/formula above it in the stack.

If you select a custom function/formula node in the tree, the text of the custom function/formula is displayed in the Editor window, and the text of the expression being evaluated when the error occurred is highlighted, as shown in Figure 7-22. If you expand a custom function/formula node in the tree, the variables being used in the custom function/formula are shown along with the value they had at the time the error occurred.

Examples of Evaluation Time Errors

An evaluation time error occurs when a formula's parts are all correct, but one of the formulas is not inserted into the correct section of the report for processing. The evaluation time error that results lets you know that there is an error, but it is not always exactly where the error lies. In the example shown in Figure 7-22, the formula is actually fine but the initialize formula is in the wrong section, causing this formula to error out.

Another, simpler, sample evaluation time error occurs when a formula tries to divide a value by zero. For example, the following formula is correct, but when the report runs, it produces an evaluation time error because the value is not divisible by zero (see Figure 7-23):

```
1/{@Calendar Days Between}
```

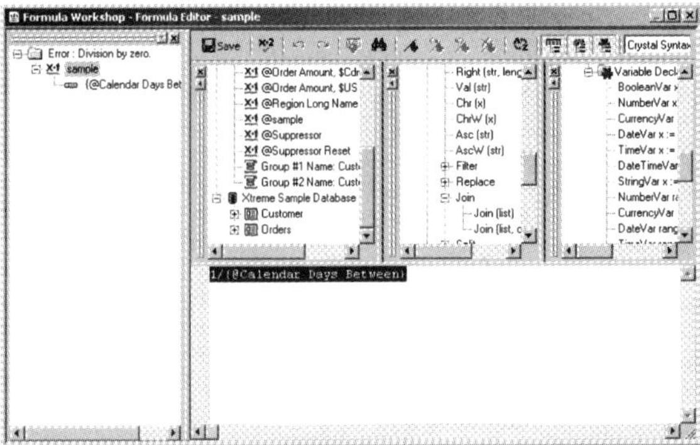

FIGURE 7-23 *A call stack lists the error in the Workshop Tree at evaluation time.*

Troubleshooting formula errors in general, and evaluation time errors in particular, can be tricky because the error is not always in the formula text; rather, it is sometimes in how the formula is used or the results of a portion of the formula. Be patient and creative while trying to figure out why a formula is not working properly.

Summary

Formulas have seemingly limitless potential to give you the tools to make any report perform the way you want. Formulas are used not just in calculations, but also to manipulate object formatting and section printing. Formulas are used all over the design palate in Crystal Reports. Many chapters in this book refer to formulas with examples demonstrating how and where they can be used.

Chapter 8

The Crystal Repository is a new tool in Crystal Reports 9. The Repository is a central locale for storing and managing objects that can be shared among reports. Repository objects are stored in a database that is accessible via the Repository Explorer, Formula Workshop, and the Database Expert within Crystal Reports. Having a central location for report objects helps you to manage your reports, because when you modify a single report object in the Repository, all reports containing that object will be updated when they are opened for use.

Where Is the Crystal Repository Database?

The default Repository shipped with Crystal Reports is an MS Access database. This sample Repository database is installed at the following default location when you install Crystal Reports 9: Program Files\Common Files\Crystal Decisions\2.0\bin\Repository_en.mdb.

Once your product is installed, you can migrate the Repository database from MS Access to a database type of your choice and then point Crystal Reports to the new Repository database location.

Using Your Own Database for the Crystal Repository

You may want to use something other than MS Access in order to apply security or maintain a more robust database. If you wish to use a different database as your Repository, you must take the following steps:

- Create a new database to serve as your Repository.
- Configure an Open Database Connectivity (ODBC) data source (DSN) for the new Repository database.
- Edit the orMap.ini file (found in the same folder) to point the Crystal Repository to the new database DSN rather than the default Repository DSN.

◆ Most database types can be used for the Repository as long as you have a valid ODBC DSN set up for the type you choose and it supports the following object types: text objects, bitmaps, custom functions, and commands (queries).

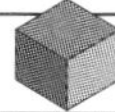

NOTE

Custom functions and commands are stored in the repository as simple text fields, which most database types will support.

By configuring a new Repository database, you are replacing the sample Access database shipped with Crystal Reports.

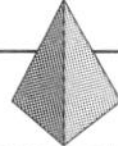

TIP

Use an ODBC database as your Repository and set security at the database level.

Configuring a New Repository Database

You may want to use a database other than MS Access to store your Crystal Repository. MS Access may not have all the security features you would like to implement, and might not be as robust a database as other systems designed to hold more data and handle more users and complex transactions. The following steps outline the process for setting up the Repository on another database system.

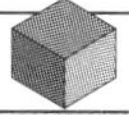

NOTE

Crystal Reports can point to only one Repository database at a time.

Configure a New Repository

You may want or need to configure a new database to serve as the Crystal Repository. To do so, follow these steps:

1. Create and save a new blank database of the type and on the server of your choice.

2. Open the ODBC Data Source Administrator, which is usually found in the Windows Control Panel (in Windows 2000, it is in Administrative Tools).

3. Click the System DSN tab, and then click Add to create a new ODBC data source.

4. In the Create New Data Source dialog box, choose the ODBC driver appropriate for your data source type from the list and click Finish.

5. Configure your ODBC connection as appropriate to the driver you chose (you may need to consult with your DBA for the proper configuration settings).

6. Click OK when finished.

Next, Crystal Reports needs to be told where to find the new Repository database. Edit the orMap.ini file, installed by default at Program Files\Common Files\Crystal Decisions\2.0\bin\orMap.ini.

1. Open the orMap.ini file in a text editing program such as Notepad, WordPad, or MS Word.

2. Change the existing data source mapping as follows:

   ```
   <the name of your new repository database>=<the name of the ODBC DSN you
   created>
   ```

3. Save the changes you made to the orMap.ini file.

The following is the contents of the default orMap.ini file (see Figure 8-1):

```
# Syntax:
#
# <repository name>=<real data source name>
#
# Please note that <repository name> cannot contain these special
# characters - " { } ; /
# Any entry that contains such will be ignored.
```

```
# Also, this file is saved with UTF8 encoding. This allows

# <repository name> to be of unicode characters.

#

Crystal Repository=Crystal Repository
```

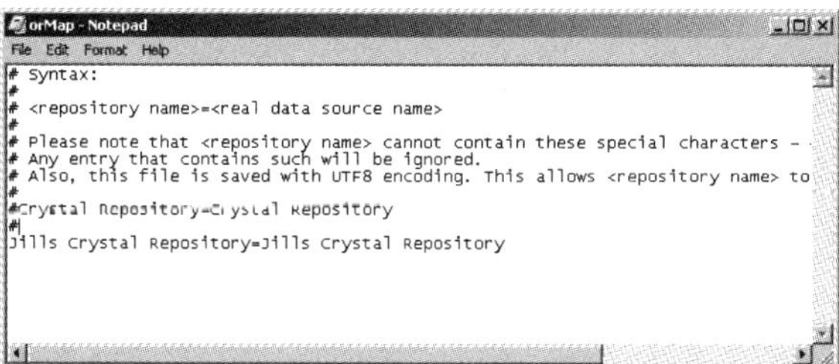

FIGURE 8-1 *Edit the orMap.ini file to point to the new Repository database, in this figure the new Repository is named Jill's Crystal Repository and the DSN is named Jill's Crystal Repository.*

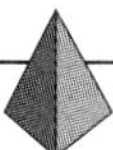

TIP

If you wish to save the original configuration of the orMap.ini file, simply place a # in front of the last line in the file and add your new data source mapping on the next line.

Your new Repository location is now configured. If your new database is secure, you'll be prompted to log on the next time you open the Repository Explorer in Crystal Reports. Otherwise, no logon is required for the MS Access default Crystal Repository.

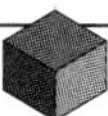

NOTE

You may need to close and then reopen Crystal Reports to see the new Repository database. All PCs in your office need to have their orMap.ini file edited to reflect the new Repository location.

Using the New Repository

The new database you create as the Repository is blank. To create the Repository structure within the database, simply add an object to the new Repository. There are no folders by default, so you can create any folders you need to organize your Repository objects. Once you add one object of each type to the new Repository, six tables will be created.

To migrate all the data in one Repository to a new Repository database, you would use whatever tools that database includes or suggests for importing data from another source. There are other third-party data migration tools that could do the job as well.

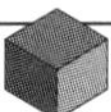 **NOTE**

Once you migrate the Repository database to a new data source, the old MS Access Repository database is not accessible. You can only have one Repository database connected to Crystal at a time.

Using the Crystal Repository

The Crystal Repository is accessible from within Crystal Reports. With the Design tab open, click the Repository Explorer button on the main toolbar or select View, Repository Explorer (see Figure 8-2). From within the Formula Workshop, only Custom Function objects are available in the Repository. In the Database Explorer, only Command objects are available. All objects are saved to the Repository from within Crystal Reports.

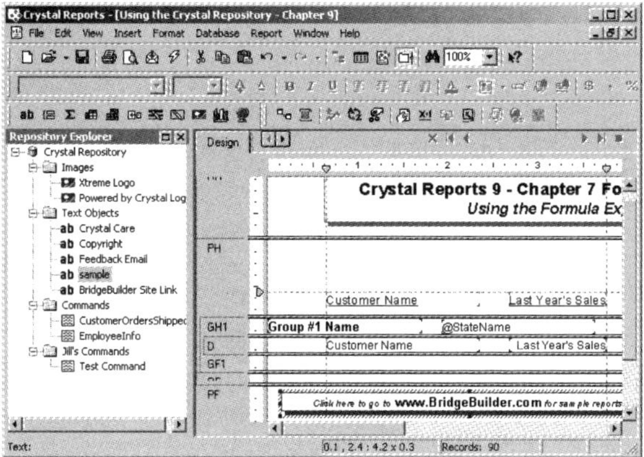

FIGURE 8-2 *The Repository is docked on the left side of the Design tab by default.*

Objects added to a report from the Repository cannot be edited. To edit the object, it must be disconnected from the Repository. If an object is deleted from the Repository, it is not deleted from the reports that use that object. Find details in the following sections on each type of Repository object, and how to add, edit, and delete objects.

Check Out the Sample Crystal Repository

To open the Crystal Repository, you must have the Crystal report designer open. The Repository Explorer is the tool used to work with all Repository objects. The sample Repository supplied by Crystal Reports has an ODBC System DSN called Crystal Repository. This Repository is configured by default when you install Crystal, so it is ready to use immediately without any configuration.

To open the sample Crystal Repository:

1. Click the Repository Explorer button on the standard toolbar or select View, Repository Explorer.

2. Expand the node called Crystal Repository to see the sample Repository folders.

3. Expand the folders to see sample Repository objects available to reports.

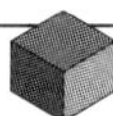

NOTE

The Repository Explorer is a free-floating window that can be docked on either side or the bottom of the design window.

All objects in the Repository are available to you to use in a report. When beginning a new report, all Command objects in the Repository are available for use from within the Database Expert under the Repository node (see Figure 8-3).

NOTE

The folders not containing Commands show ". . . no items found . . .," because those other object types are not useful in the Database Expert.

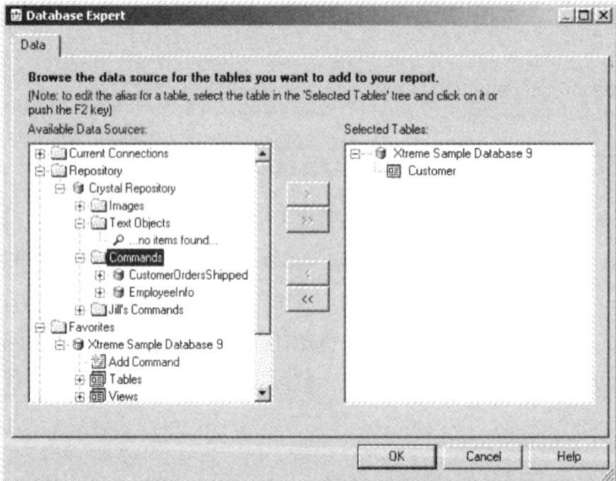

FIGURE 8-3 *Commands are accessible from the Repository node of the Database Expert.*

Creating Your Own Repository

You can organize the contents of the Repository by creating a folder structure that makes sense for your business and the types of objects you'll be storing. Create folders for the types of objects on the first level, and then add subfolders as necessary.

Adding Folders to the Repository

Add folders to the Repository to organize the objects you plan to store. You can add folders at any time, but if you consider a scalable organizational structure now, managing sharable objects will be easier later.

1. In the Repository Explorer, right-click the Crystal Repository node and click New Folder on the shortcut menu (a new folder is added to the bottom of the Repository tree, as shown in Figure 8-4).

2. Name the new folder and press Enter. The new named folder appears in the tree.

3. To add a subfolder, right-click an existing folder and click New Folder on the shortcut menu.

4. Name the new subfolder and press Enter.

5. To delete a folder, right-click the folder and click Delete from the shortcut menu.

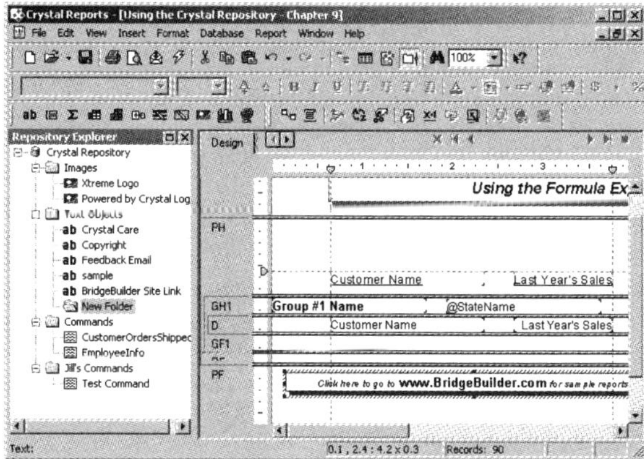

FIGURE 8-4 *Add as many folders as necessary to organize your objects.*

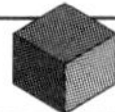

NOTE

Deleting a folder deletes all objects within that folder.

Adding Objects to the Repository

There are several types of objects that can be stored in the Repository. The type of object determines how it is added to the Repository.

Text Objects and Bitmap Images

You can add text objects and bitmap images to the Repository by dragging them from your report to the appropriate Repository folder. A dialog box appears so that you can add identify information about the object.

1. With the report design window open, open the Repository Explorer.

2. Select a text object or bitmap image in your report and drag it to the appropriate folder in the Repository Explorer. This opens the Object Information dialog box (see Figure 8-5).

3. In the Name field, create a name for your text object or bitmap image.

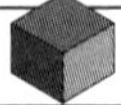

NOTE

You cannot use the following characters in the object's name: # " {} ; /.

4. Enter an author or description, if desired, and click OK.

5. The text object or bitmap image is added to the appropriate folder. If you don't see the new object, right-click the Repository node and click Refresh on the shortcut menu.

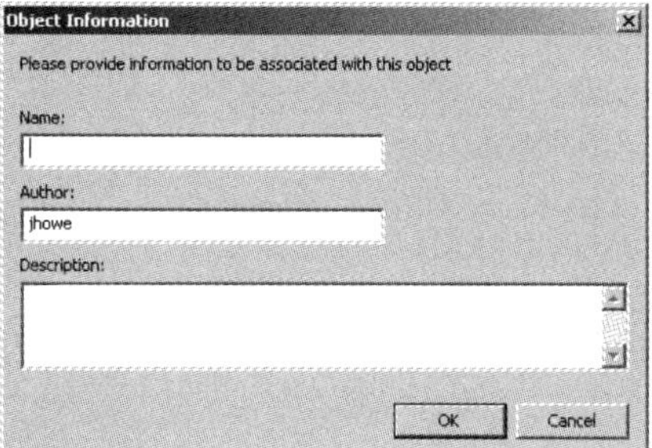

FIGURE 8-5 *Complete the Object Information dialog box when adding an object to the Repository.*

You can also add a text object or bitmap image without dragging and dropping it by using the following steps:

1. Right-click a text object or bitmap image in your report and click Add to Repository from the shortcut menu. The Add Item dialog box opens (see Figure 8-6).

2. In the Name field, create a name for your text object or bitmap image. Add author and description information if desired.

3. In the Location area, select the folder you want to add the object to, and then click OK.

4. The text object or bitmap image is added to the appropriate folder. If you don't see the new object, right-click the Repository node and click Refresh on the shortcut menu, and the new object should show up in the list.

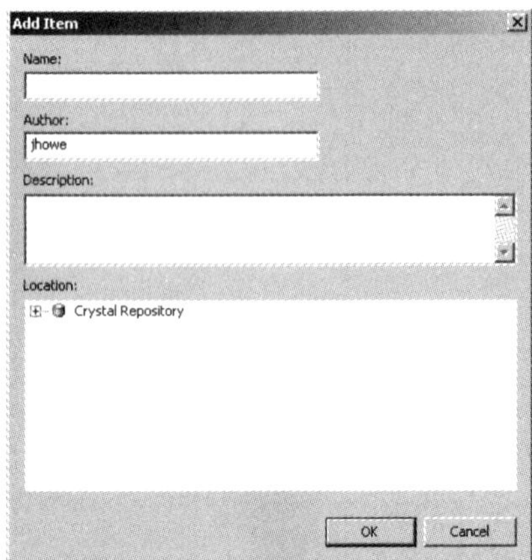

FIGURE 8-6 *Complete the Add Item dialog box when adding an object to the Repository.*

Adding Custom Functions to the Repository

You add custom functions to the Repository through the Formula Workshop. With the Formula Workshop open, there are many custom functions built into the sample Repository database that are available for use in reports. Build your own custom functions (see Chapter 9) and save them in the Repository using the following steps:

1. In the Formula Workshop, expand the Report Custom Functions node and select the custom function you want to add to the Repository.

2. Click the Add to Repository button. The Add Custom Functions to Repository dialog box appears (see Figure 8-7).

3. Select the Repository to which the custom function is to be added.

4. Click the OK button.

5. The custom function is added to the Report Custom Functions node. If you don't see the new object, right-click the Repository node and click Refresh on the shortcut menu.

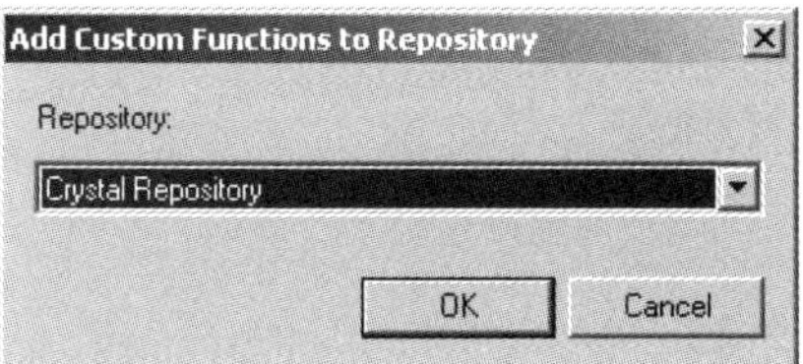

FIGURE 8-7 *Select the Repository in which you want to add the selected Custom Function.*

TIP

A custom function can also be added to the Repository by simply dragging its node from Report Custom Functions, in the Workshop Tree, to the Repository Custom Functions node.

Adding Commands to the Repository

Commands are added to the Repository via the Database Expert. You type commands right into the Add Command to Report dialog box. See Chapter 14 for instructions on how to build commands and the different tools to use for assistance.

When you build a command, you have the option to add it to the Repository when you save it by checking the Add to Repository check box in the Add Command to Report dialog box (see Figure 8-8). If you have an existing command that you want to add to the Repository, follow these steps:

1. In the Selected Tables area of the Database Expert, right-click the command you want to add to the Repository and select Edit Command from the shortcut menu.

2. In the Modify Command dialog box, select Add to Repository and click OK.

3. In the Add Item dialog box, specify a name and Repository location for the command. Click OK.

4. The command now appears in the Repository node of the Database Expert.

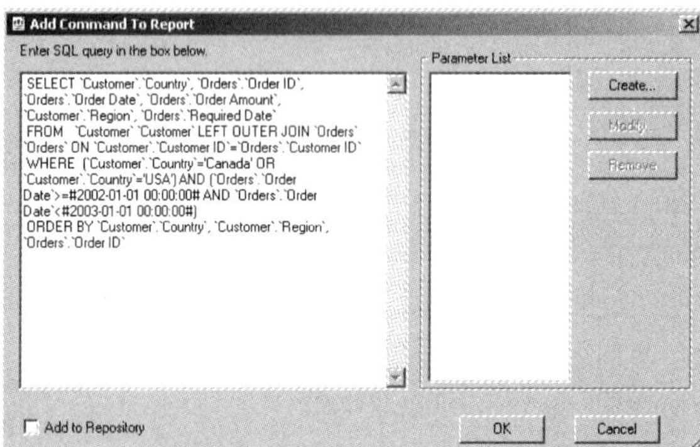

FIGURE 8-8 *Type a command or cut and paste one from another tool.*

Editing Objects in the Repository

Any object stored in the Repository cannot be altered; all objects are in read-only mode. This is true of any object that has been placed into a report—as long as the object is connected to the Repository, it cannot be changed in either the report or the Repository.

If you right-click the object in the report and choose Disconnect from Repository from the shortcut menu, the report object is disconnected from the Repository and can now be edited or changed. If you want other reports to be updated with the changed report object, you must right-click the object and choose Add to Repository, and overwrite the existing report object.

Using Repository Objects on Reports

Once you have objects in the Repository, you can start using them in your Crystal reports. Each type of object is added through its own user interface. In the case of text objects and bitmap images, simply drag them from the Repository Explorer onto a report. You select custom functions when you work in the Formula Workshop, and select commands in the Database Expert.

When you add a Repository object to a report, it remains connected to the Repository and is in read-only mode. To edit the object, you must disconnect it from the Repository and unlock its formatting.

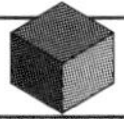

NOTE

To reconnect a report object that has been disconnected from the Repository, re-add the object or update the Repository copy. Objects that remain disconnected from the Repository cannot be automatically updated when the report is next opened.

Adding a Text Object or Bitmap Image to a Report from the Repository

Adding a text object or image from the Repository is as simple as dragging and dropping it:

1. Click the Repository Explorer button on the standard toolbar or click View, Repository Explorer.

2. Expand the Text Objects or Images folder of the Repository and drag a text object or bitmap image onto your report.

Adding a Custom Function to a Report (from the Repository)

Custom functions are added from the Formula Workshop:

1. Click the Formula Workshop button on the Expert Tools toolbar or click View, Formula Workshop.

2. In the Formula Workshop, expand the Repository Custom Functions node until you find the custom function you want to add.

3. Right-click the custom function and click Add to Report from its shortcut menu. If the custom function you are adding requires other custom functions from the Repository, you can add them at the same time.

4. The custom function is added to the Report Custom Functions node in the Formula Workshop.

NOTE

You can also add custom functions to a report while creating formulas in the Formula Workshop.

Using a Command in a Report from the Repository

Reports can be based on commands rather than directly connecting to a database:

1. Click the Database Expert button 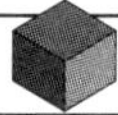 on the Expert Tools toolbar or click View, Database Expert.

2. In the Database Expert, expand the Repository folder until you find the command you want to add.

3. Right-click the command and click Add to Report from its shortcut menu.

4. The command is added to the Selected Tables area of the Database Expert.

NOTE

If the command contains parameters, you need to answer the prompts before the command will be added to the report. Also, in order to use a command a DSN to the appropriate database must be configured on your machine. For example, if the command was built using an ODBC connection to an Oracle database, that DSN must exist on the machine using the command.

Updating Objects

You can modify Repository objects by changing them in a report and adding them back to the Repository under the same name (this updates the object) or under a different name (this creates a new object). Rename an object by right-clicking the object and selecting Rename from the shortcut menu. Objects can also be moved within the Repository by dragging the object and dropping it into a different folder.

When you modify an object and add it back to the Repository, reports that contain the modified object may be updated when they are opened in Report Designer. A renamed object will affect all other users who use the same Repository. To other users of the Repository, a commonly used object will seem to have disappeared if it has been renamed.

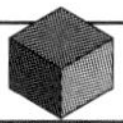 **NOTE**

You cannot use Undo on any action that updates the Repository. However, you can undo actions that affect only the report and not the Repository. For example, you can undo the disconnect activity.

Updating an Object in the Repository

This procedure shows how to modify and update a text object in the Repository. Custom functions and commands are modified and updated in their respective user interfaces.

1. Right-click the object and select Disconnect from Repository (see Figure 8-9).

2. Edit the object on the report.

3. Save the object back to the Repository by right-clicking the object and choosing Add to Repository.

4. If you want to save the object back to the Repository with the same name, to replace the old copy, choose the same object's name from the Workshop Tree in the Location area of the Add Item dialog box.

5. A dialog box opens, confirming you want to replace the older copy of the object. Click OK.

6. The object on the report is again connected to the Repository and has updated the previous version of that object.

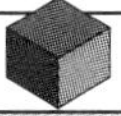 **NOTE**

You can also drag the modified text object from the report back to its original location in the Repository Explorer. When you drop the text object, the Add or Update Object dialog box appears.

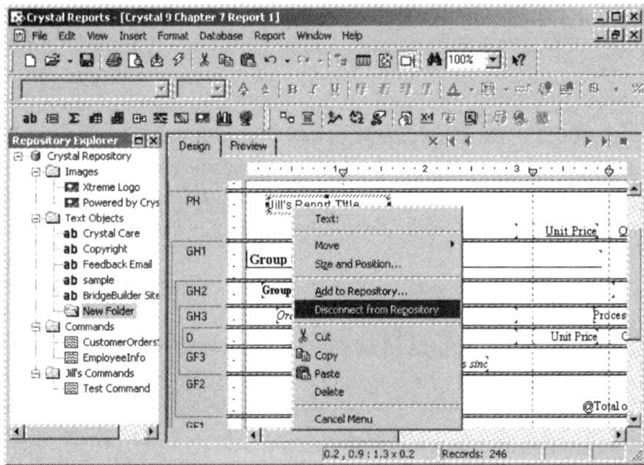

FIGURE 8-9 *You must disconnect an object from the Repository to edit that object.*

Each time an object is edited, the version number increases by one in that object's Properties dialog box. Right-click an object in the Repository and select Properties to view this information.

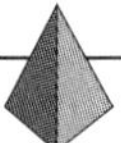

TIP

If you save a new version of an object back into the Repository, with the *same name,* reports are then updated with the new object. If you delete an object from the Repository, you can always copy a report version of the object back into the Repository.

Updating an Object across All Reports Referencing that Object

Repository objects used in a report that are connected to the Repository can be updated automatically when the report is opened in Crystal Reports. Automatic updating is an Options setting and can be set globally for all reports.

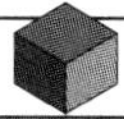

NOTE

Objects contained in a report that are disconnected from the Repository are not updated when the report is opened.

To set all objects to update each time a report is opened:

1. Click File, Options. The Options dialog box opens.
2. Click the Reporting tab.
3. Select the Update Connected Repository Objects When Loading Report check box.
4. Click OK.

You can also choose to update repository objects on a report by report basis. When opening a report, check the "Update Repository Objects" checkbox in the Open dialog box.

Deleting Objects from the Repository

Any object stored in the Repository can be deleted from the Repository without removing the object from reports that contain the object.

Once you remove an object from the Repository, it is no longer accessible by any user. It is not, however, deleted from reports that were pointing to the object. You may encounter the following situations and messages when an object is deleted or you try to delete an object from the Repository:

◆ When an object is deleted from the Repository, it appears to remain connected in the reports that contain the object. When you try to update the Repository object in a report (when the report is opened), a warning message appears indicating an object could not be found in the Repository, and that it may have been deleted.

◆ The ability to delete Repository objects is controlled by the permissions of the database. Once you accept the warning message in Crystal Reports, you will get an error message if you do not have adequate permission to delete the object from the Repository. The object is actually flagged for deletion, which is considered an update to the database. You must have database update privileges before you can delete an object from the Repository.

To delete an object from the Repository:

1. Open the Repository.

2. In the appropriate folder, select the object you want to remove and click Delete on your keyboard, or right-click the object you want to delete and select Delete from the shortcut menu.

3. You need to confirm the deletion, so click the Yes button. The object is removed from the Repository.

NOTE

When deleting a command, the shortcut option is called Remove from Repository.

Summary

The Crystal Repository is an easy-to-use storage area for many types of reusable report objects. Take advantage of this new tool for storing frequently added objects to reports. Making commonly used objects easily available to all report developers brings more consistency to reports across your business. The Repository provides a common area for database developers to store commands for report developers, and experienced formula writers to build Custom Functions for commonly used formulas.

Chapter 9

Custom functions are procedures you can create in Crystal Reports to evaluate, calculate, or transform data. When you use a custom function in a formula, all the operations within the function are executed without needing you to specifically enter all the function's logic. Using custom functions provides a way for you to share and reuse formula logic, providing consistency and making it easier and less time consuming for you and other users to create reports.

When Would I Use a Custom Function?

For example, suppose your database stores dates as numbers. In other words, January 1, 2002, looks like 20,020,101 in your database. Unfortunately, every time you need to place these date fields on a report or use a date in a calculation, you must convert the numeric date into a proper date format. Creating a formula to convert the date will work, but you have to copy the formula from report to report. It is much easier if you extract the logic that does the conversion and save it as a custom function. Then you can use the custom function in the Formula Expert in each new report without having to reenter the formula text.

NOTE

A custom function cannot be placed directly into a report; it must be used as the basis for a formula built using the Formula Expert.

Consider the following advantages to using custom functions:

- ◆ Custom functions reuse formula logic for formulas common to many reports; they can be stored in the Repository and used in reports as needed.
- ◆ Existing formulas can be converted to custom functions using the Custom Function Extractor.

◆ Custom functions reduce the need for report designers to write or understand formulas themselves. The Formula Expert guides the designer through building a formula without having to write any code.

◆ When you modify or update a custom function, you can update the Repository copy, then refresh each report without having to find and open the formulas that use that particular function.

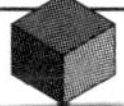

NOTE

Custom functions, unlike User Function Libraries (UFLs), are saved as part of the report file (RPT) and don't have external dependencies.

There are many custom functions in the sample Repository shipped with Crystal Reports. You can add to the custom functions residing in the Repository by creating your own. This can be accomplished either by using the Custom Function Editor to create a custom function from scratch or by using the Extractor to pull the logic from an existing report formula.

Using Custom Functions in Reports

Custom functions are used in the Formula Expert within the Formula Workshop. There are many custom functions included in the sample Crystal Repository. You can use custom functions in your company's Repository if any have been added, or you can build your own custom functions using either the Custom Function Extractor or the Custom Function Editor.

This section covers using an existing custom function in the Formula Expert to build a formula. When you select a custom function to use from the Repository, that custom function will be automatically added to the Report Custom Functions node in the Formula Expert.

Using the Formula Expert

Use the Formula Expert to build formulas using the available custom functions. The Formula Expert provides both an easy interface for less seasoned report designers and an easy way for anyone to use shared custom functions across many reports, ensuring that calculations are consistent.

1. Open the Formula Workshop. Click the New icon down arrow and select Formula from the list.

2. Enter a name for the formula in the Formula Name dialog box (see Figure 9-1). Select the Formula Expert button to open the Formula Expert dialog box.

3. Select a Custom Function to use from the Custom Function Supplying Logic list (see Figure 9-2). If you select a function in the Repository, that function will be added to the Report Custom Functions node at this time.

4. Click the Value box for each argument (v1 and v2). A drop-down arrow appears, with the first default value printed in the box (see Figure 9-3). Select a value or type a value for each argument.

5. Click Save to save the formula. Click Close to exit the Expert and the Formula Workshop.

6. Add the formula to your report as you would any other object.

FIGURE 9-1 *Name your new formula and click the Use Expert button.*

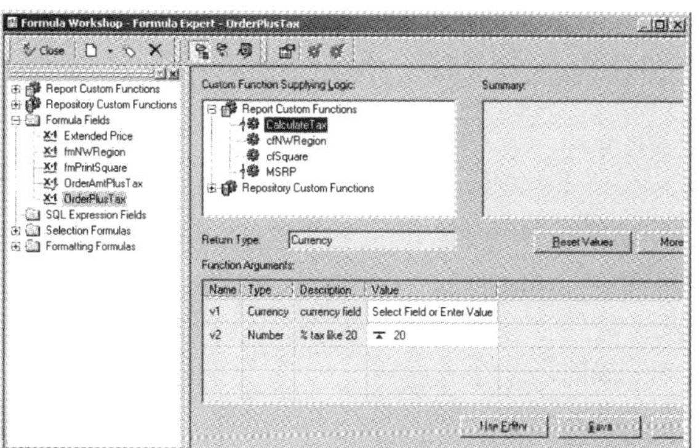

FIGURE 9-2 *Select a custom function to use as the logic for your formula.*

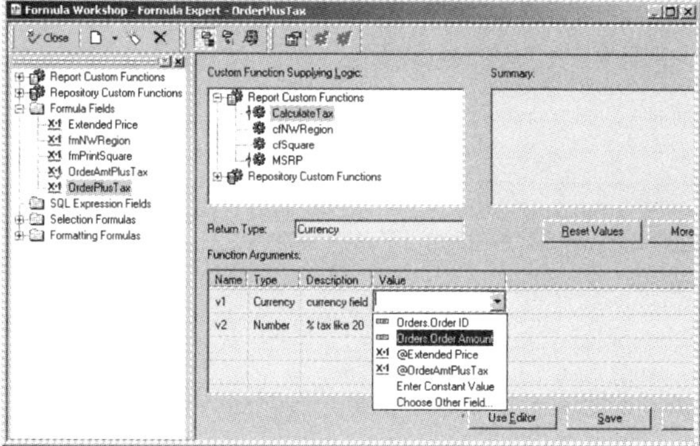

FIGURE 9-3 *Select a value for each argument in the function.*

Using a Custom Function in the Formula Editor

Custom functions can be used in formulas just as you would any other function. Once a custom function has been placed in the Report Custom Functions node, it becomes available for selection. This is true for custom functions that you create, as well as for Repository custom functions that have been placed into the Report Custom Functions node. For example, let's use the same custom function as in the example above but use it in the Formula Editor rather than the Formula Expert.

1. In the Formula Workshop, click the down arrow on the New button and select Formula from the list.

2. Enter a name for your new formula in the Formula Name dialog box.

3. Click the Use Editor button to open the Formula Editor.

4. From the Functions pane in the Formula Editor (not the Workshop Tree), expand the Custom Functions folder and double-click the custom function you want to use in the formula (see Figure 9-4). Specify any required argument values.

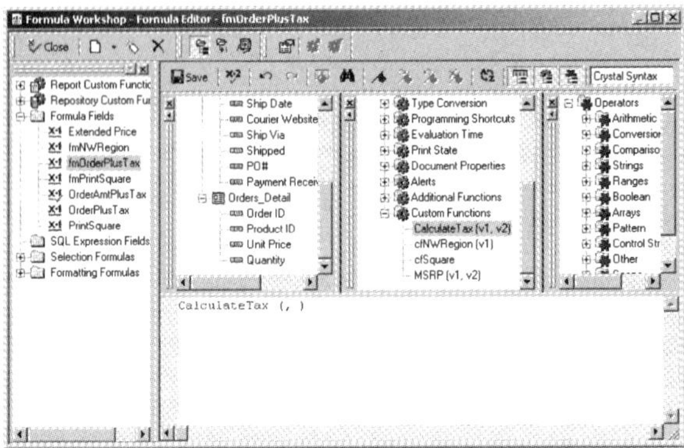

FIGURE 9-4 *Select a custom function from the Custom Functions folder in the Functions pane of the Formula Editor.*

5. You can now enter any additional logic that may be needed to complete the formula.

6. Once the formula is complete, be sure to save it. The formula can now be used in your report.

When custom functions are built, you have the option to supply names for the arguments replacing the v1, v2, and so on. It might be helpful to take the time to change these values when building the function, so that the function can be easily used in the Formula Editor as well as in the Expert. The example above would be hard to use if you did not know what the arguments were.

Replace the argument values v1 and v2 by editing the custom function. You will need to disconnect the function from the Repository, then open it in the Formula Editor. Select the custom function you want to edit then toggle the Properties button to open the Custom Function Editor, as in Figure 9-5.

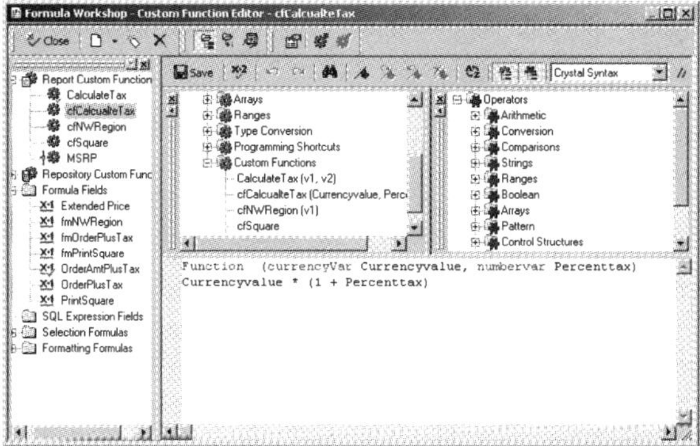

FIGURE 9-5 *Use the Custom Function Editor to replace argument values.*

Extracting a Custom Function from an Existing Formula

Extracting a custom function from an existing formula is accomplished using the Custom Function Extractor. This tool within the Formula Workshop takes an existing formula that you specify and builds an appropriate custom function for you, with some direction by means of drop-down lists, prompts, and dialog boxes. When you extract a custom function from an existing formula, the Extractor copies the formula and replaces its fields with arguments.

NOTE

A custom function created using the Extractor can only return simple types, like strings and integers. To create custom functions for complex types, like arrays, you must use the Custom Function Editor.

Using the Custom Function Extractor

The Custom Function Extractor is found in the Formula Workshop. This tool extracts a custom function from the formula you select. The custom function can then be saved in the Report Custom Functions folder for use on the open report, or in the Crystal Repository folder for use in other reports. To extract a custom function from a formula:

1. In the Formula Workshop, click the down arrow on the New button and select Custom Function from the list.

2. Enter a name for your custom function in the Custom Function Name dialog box. A custom function name cannot contain spaces.

3. Click the Use Extractor button (see Figure 9-6).

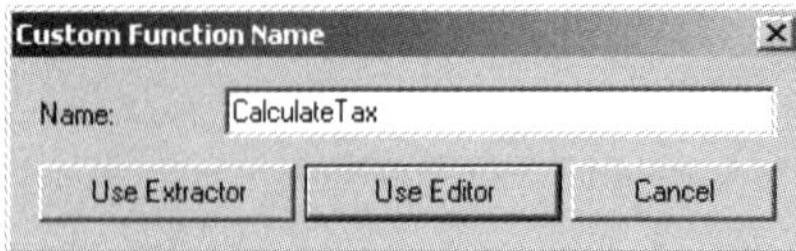

FIGURE 9-6 *Type a name for the Custom Function, then click the Use Extractor button to open the Extract Custom Function from Formula dialog box.*

4. In the Formula list, select the report formula whose logic you want to use in your custom function. When the formula is selected, the Return Type, Arguments, and Formula Text fields are completed with information that relates to that formula. These fields cannot be changed without selecting a different formula (the remaining fields are optional).

5. You can rename the arguments in the custom function. The Extractor assigns generic names (v1, v2, v3, and so on) by default (see Figure 9-7).

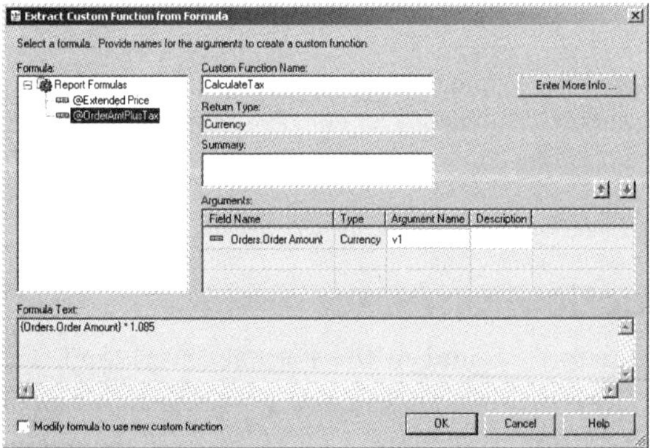

FIGURE 9-7 *Use the Extract Custom Function from Formula dialog box to build a custom function from an existing formula.*

6. To edit the function—in this case, to add another argument so that the user of the function could enter the tax rate as well as the currency value—click in the Formula Text area of the Extract Custom Function from Formula dialog box and click Enter to launch the Custom Function Editor (see Figure 9-8).

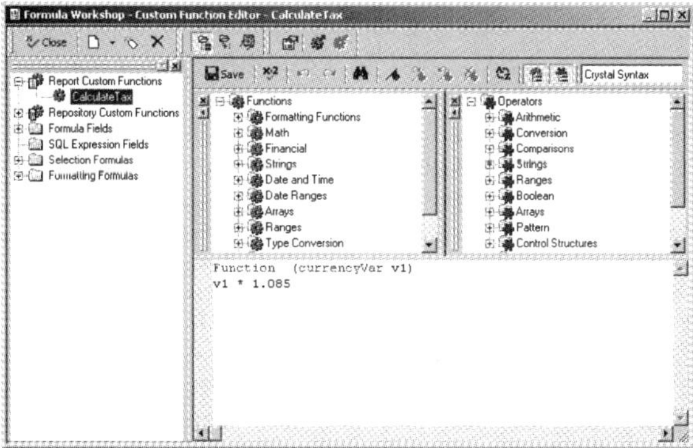

FIGURE 9-8 *Custom function syntax is extracted from the formula text.*

7. Edit the formula to accommodate another variable for the desired tax rate (see Figure 9-9).

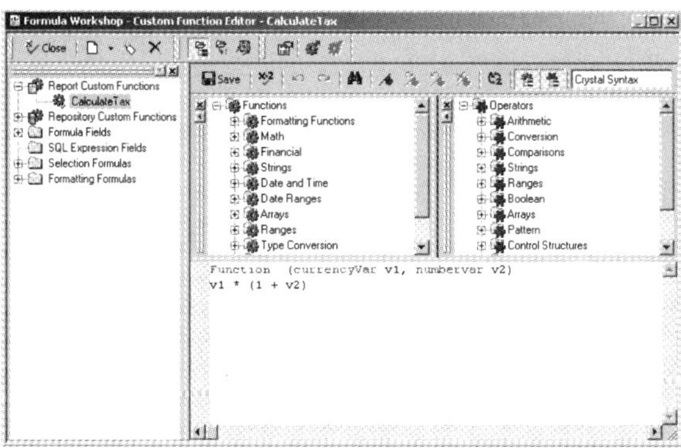

FIGURE 9-9 *Edit the formula to accommodate the desired calculation and argument options.*

8. Once the formula is edited, click Save to save the new function, then click the Properties toggle button in the toolbar to view the properties for the new function (see Figure 9-10).

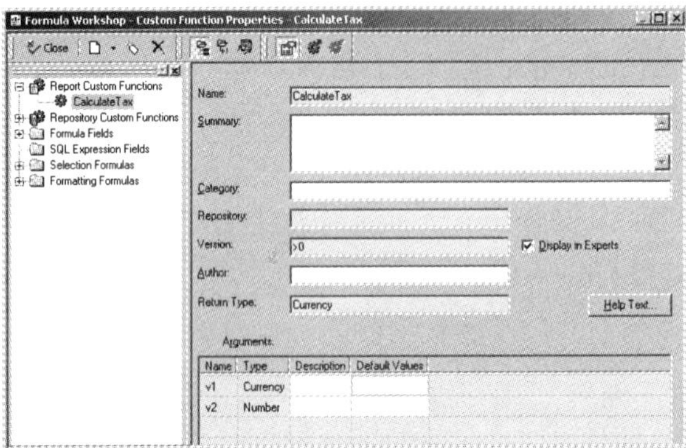

FIGURE 9-10 *Toggle the Properties button to view and add to the custom function properties.*

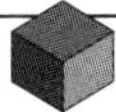

NOTE

Editing these options is covered later in this chapter.

9. Click Close. The custom function is saved in the Report Custom Functions node of the Formula Workshop tree. Once the custom function is saved, you can modify it or use it in report formulas as needed.

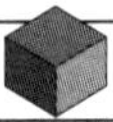

NOTE

You cannot add new arguments to your custom function while you are creating it in the Extract Custom Function from Formula dialog box. To add new arguments, save the custom function and modify it in the Custom Function Editor. Open the Editor as explained in Step 6 above.

TIP

Select Modify formula to edit the original formula to use the new custom function.

You can add more descriptive details to any custom function. Add details such as author information, which subfolder to save the custom function into within the Report Custom Functions folder, and custom help text by selecting the Enter More Info button on the Extract Custom Function from Formula dialog box.

Custom Function Example

The following section demonstrates an example of extracting a custom function from a formula field. Below is an example of a formula before it is extracted into a custom function:

```
//Formula fmNWRegion - determines region based on area code
Select Left({Customer.Phone},3)
    Case "206" : "Washington"
    Case "253" : "Washington"
    Case "360" : "Washington"
    Case "425" : "Washington"
    Case "509" : "Washington"
    Case "564" : "Washington"
    Case "503" : "Oregon"
    Case "541" : "Oregon"
    Case "971" : "Oregon"
    Case "406" : "Montana"
    Case "208" : "Idaho"
    Case "307" : "Wyoming"
    Default : "Other Region"
```

Use the Extractor to extract the formula above into a Custom Function. Start by opening the Extract Custom Function from Formula dialog box from within the Formula Workshop, then select the fmNWRegion formula. The following is the result of using the Extractor option to create the custom function (see Figure 9-11):

```
//Custom function cfNWRegion - determines region based on area code
Function  (stringVar v1)
Select Left(v1,3)
    Case "206" : "Washington"
    Case "253" : "Washington"
    Case "360" : "Washington"
    Case "425" : "Washington"
```

```
Case "509" : "Washington"
Case "564" : "Washington"
Case "503" : "Oregon"
Case "541" : "Oregon"
Case "971" : "Oregon"
Case "406" : "Montana"
Case "208" : "Idaho"
Case "307" : "Wyoming"
Default : "Other Region"
```

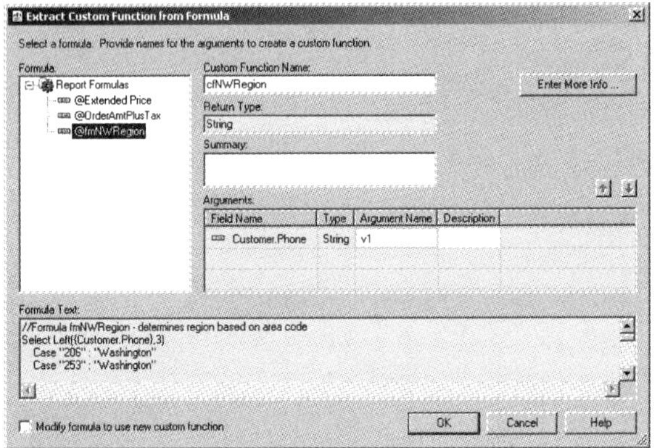

FIGURE 9-11 *Crystal extracts a custom function from a formula for you.*

Save the custom function by clicking the OK button on the Extract Custom Function from Formula dialog box. The function can be saved to the Crystal Repository by right-clicking it in the Report Custom Functions folder and selecting Add to Repository.

Viewing and Modifying Custom Functions

Once you've created a custom function, you can view or modify it at any time by using the Custom Function Editor. When you view a custom function stored in the Repository, the Custom Function Editor and the Custom Function Properties dialog box appear in read-only mode. Remember, you cannot modify a Repository custom function without first adding it to your report and disconnecting it from the Repository.

The following steps walk you through the process of modifying a custom function.

1. In the Formula Workshop, expand the Report Custom Functions node of the Workshop Tree and select the custom function you want to modify.

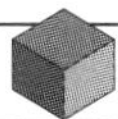

NOTE

If the custom function appears in read-only mode, it may still be connected to the Repository. Check the Workshop Tree for the Connected to Repository icon. If necessary, disconnect the custom function from the Repository by selecting the function and selecting Disconnect from Repository from its right-click shortcut menu.

2. Modify the text of the custom function by using the Custom Function Editor (see Figure 9-12).

3. Modify the custom function's properties by using the Custom Function Properties dialog box (instructions in the next section). Switch between the two interfaces by clicking the Toggle properties display button in the Formula Workshop toolbar.

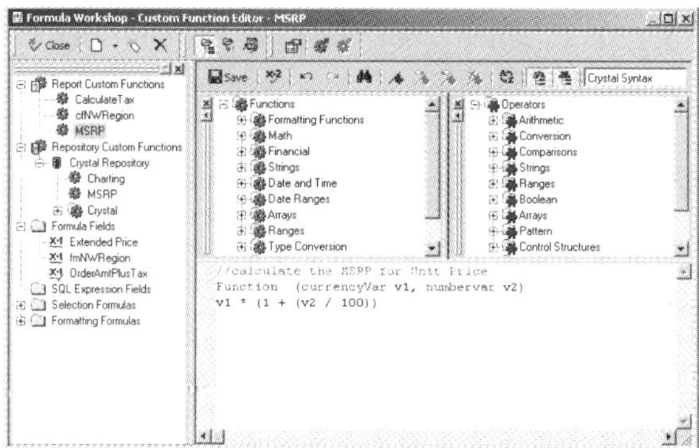

FIGURE 9-12 *Use the Custom Function Editor to make changes to a custom function.*

4. Check and save your changes.

5. If the custom function you are modifying has been added to the Repository, be sure to update the Repository copy when you are done. Click the Add to Repository toolbar button, which will prompt you to add the new version to the Repository (see Figure 9-13).

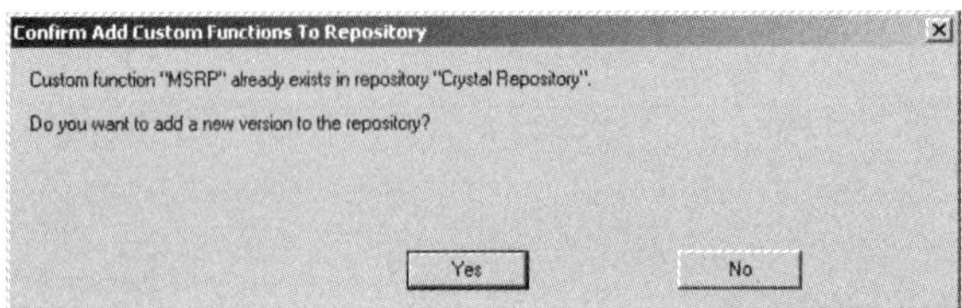

FIGURE 9-13 *Confirm that you want to update the Repository with the new edited version of the custom function.*

Changing Argument Values for Custom Functions

Instead of using the existing default argument values, you can define your own values in the Custom Function Properties dialog box. You can choose from the default values in the Function Arguments area of the Formula Expert. Optional values can also be specified for an argument, but must be created using the Custom Function Editor.

Define Default Argument Values

In order to define default argument values, you need to open the custom function you wish to edit in the Formula Workshop:

1. Open the Formula Workshop and make sure the Toggle properties display button on the toolbar is clicked. This brings up the Custom Function Properties dialog box instead of the Custom Function Editor.

2. Next, expand the Report Custom Functions node of the Workshop Tree and select the custom function for which you want to define default argument values.

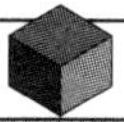

NOTE

The custom function must be a report custom function and have defined arguments. Otherwise, the Default Values field will not be accessible. Remember, if you have placed a Repository custom function in your report or added your Report Custom Function to the Repository, the function must be disconnected from the Repository before you can do any editing.

3. If you have not already done so, add a description for each argument by clicking your cursor and typing a brief description in the description field for each argument (see Figure 9-14).

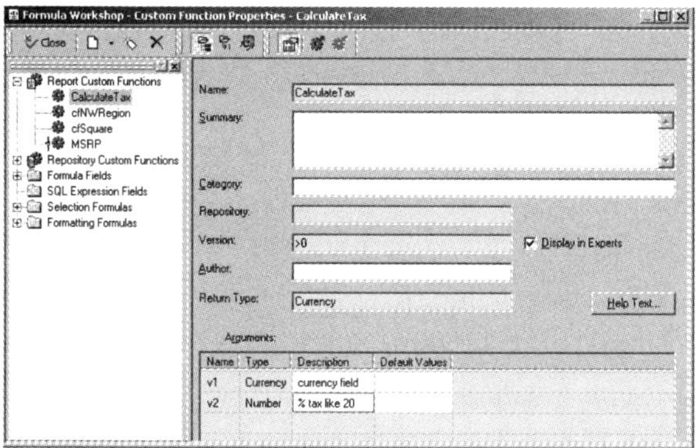

FIGURE 9-14 *Use the Custom Function Properties dialog to set description and default values.*

4. Click the Default Values field for an argument, and the Default Values for dialog box opens (see Figure 9-15). The name and type of dialog box that appears depends on the argument field you have selected.

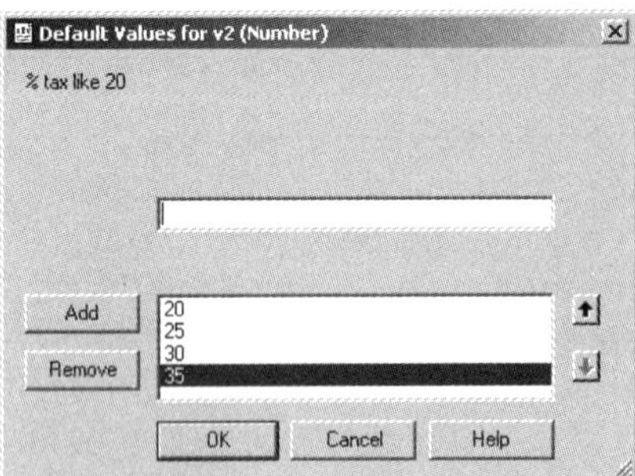

FIGURE 9-15 *Add as many default values to the list as you want. You can also type a value so you do not have to include all possible choices.*

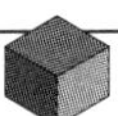

NOTE

You cannot create default values for range, array, or range array argument types (including case statements).

5. Alter the default values by the following methods:

 ◆ Click Add to include a new value that you type in the box above (the dialog box won't let you add the same value twice).

 ◆ Click Remove to delete a value.

 ◆ If you have multiple default values for the argument, click the arrow buttons to change the order in which the values are listed.

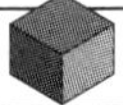

NOTE

The value in the first position becomes the default value for the argument. For arguments that are not optional, this value is used by the Formula Expert if no value is entered for the custom function or if the Reset Values button is clicked.

6. Click OK when you are done editing the default values. Multiple default values for the same argument are displayed separated by blanks in the Default Values field of the Custom Function Properties dialog box. In the Formula Expert, if an argument has multiple default values, the first

default value is shown with the other values appearing in a drop-down list.

7. When you click Close or take any action to move to another dialog box, you will be prompted to save the changes you just made. Click OK to save the changes.

Adding Optional Values to Custom Functions

An alternative to the default value for an argument is using an optional value. An optional value has its advantages in that its value is not determined until the custom function is executed. Since the value is determined by the custom function, a change made to the value in the custom function will be reflected in any formulas based on that custom function.

NOTE

Optional values must be created in the Custom Function Editor, not the Custom Function Properties dialog box.

The first line of the custom function, cdFirstDayOfMonth, is an example of using the current date as an optional value for the variable dayInMonth:

```
Function cdFirstDayOfMonth (Optional dayInMonth As DateTime = CurrentDate) As Date
```

When you look at a custom function in the Formula Expert, optional values are displayed with their current value. In the cdFirstDayOfMonth custom function, the current date (with a time of 12:00 AM) will be shown. The Formula Expert will use the optional value in an optional argument if no value is entered or if the Reset Values button is clicked.

Note that when you look at the cdFirstDayOfMonth custom function in the Formula Editor, no value is shown between the parentheses (as you would see with a default value) because the value is optional.

Adding Custom Functions to the Repository

Since reusability is one of the main virtues of custom functions, it makes since to store your report custom functions in the Repository. Once a custom function is in the Repository, it becomes available to all Crystal Reports users who have access to the Repository. When custom functions are updated in the Repository, the reports that use them can be refreshed with the latest version.

1. Open the Formula Workshop and expand the Report Custom Functions node of the Workshop Tree. Select the Custom Function you want to add to the Repository.

2. Right-click the custom function, and select Add to Repository from the shortcut menu. Or, with the function selected, click the Add to Repository button 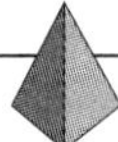.

3. In the Add Custom Function to Repository dialog box, select the Repository to which you want to add the custom function (see Figure 9-16). Since you can have only one Repository connected to Crystal Reports at any one time, you must select the only Repository in the list. Maybe this is a hint of future functionality? Click OK.

4. If the selected custom function already exists in the Repository, you are prompted to add a new version. The version number is increased in the Custom Function Properties dialog box.

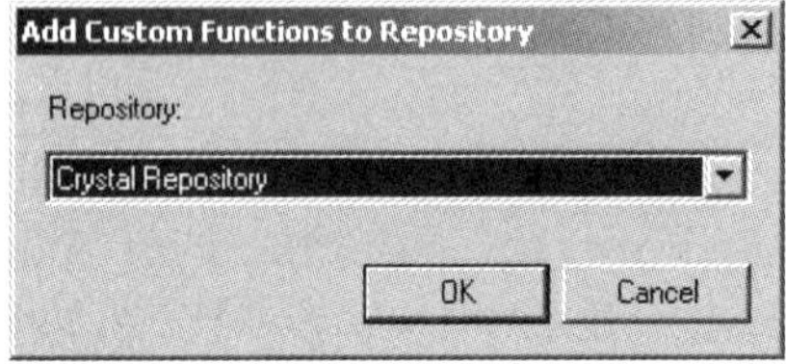

FIGURE 9-16 *Select the Repository in which to add the custom function.*

TIP

Typical Crystal Reports drag-and-drop functionality exists here. You can add a custom function to the Repository by dragging its Report Custom Function node (in the Workshop Tree) and dropping it on the Repository Custom Function node.

Adding Repository Custom Functions to Reports

Before you can use a Repository Custom Function in your report, it must be copied to the Report Custom Function node. This can be done while using the function to build a formula in the Formula Expert so it is not necessary to add it beforehand in a separate step.

1. Open the Formula Workshop and expand the Repository Custom Functions node of the Workshop Tree. Select the custom function you want to use in the report.

2. Click the Add to Report button to add a copy of the Custom Function to the Report Custom Functions node.

3. If the selected custom function already exists in your report, you are prompted to replace it with a new version. If you choose Yes, the existing version of the function is overwritten. If the custom function selected requires other custom functions from the Repository, they are added at the same time.

4. You can also add a Repository custom function to a report by dragging its Repository Custom Function node (in the Workshop Tree) and dropping it on a Report Custom Function node.

Refreshing Repository Custom Functions in Reports

Once a custom function has been modified and the Repository version updated, you can update any report that uses the custom function by simply opening the report in Crystal Reports.

There are two options for when and how Repository objects are updated. A global option can be set so that every time any report is opened, all Repository objects will be updated. There is also an option to update Repository objects report by report when a report is opened in Crystal Reports.

Setting the Global Update Option

Set a global Repository update option, and every report will be automatically updated each time it is opened.

1. With Crystal Reports open, click File, Options to open the Options dialog box.

2. Click the Reporting tab, and check the Update Connected Repository Objects When Loading Reports option (see Figure 9-17).

3. Click OK to close the Options dialog box. All reports built from this moment forward will have this option enforced.

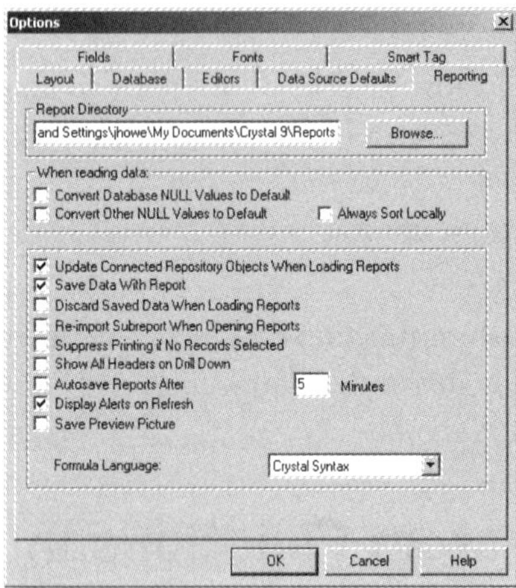

FIGURE 9-17   *Select the Update Connected Repository Objects When Loading Reports option to have all report Repository objects updated any time any report is opened.*

Update Each Report Individually on Demand

Control if and when a report's Repository objects are updated when each report is opened in Crystal Reports.

1. With Crystal Reports open, click File, Open or click the Open button. Select the report whose custom functions need to be updated.

2. Select the Update Repository Objects check box on the bottom of the Open dialog.

3. Click the Open button to open the selected report. The report's custom functions (and all other updateable Repository objects) within the report are refreshed when the report loads.

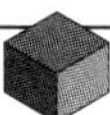

> **NOTE**
>
> If you have some Repository objects in reports that you do not want updated, you may not want to set the global option in order to retain updating control on a report-by-report basis.

Creating a Custom Function Using the Custom Function Editor

Custom functions can be built in a way similar to how formulas are written in the Formula Editor, using Crystal or Basic syntax in an editor interface.

1. Open the Formula Workshop, click the down arrow on the New button, and select Custom Function from the list.

2. Enter a name for your custom function in the Custom Function Name dialog box. Note that the custom function name cannot contain spaces.

3. Click the Use Editor button to open the Custom Function Editor.

4. Define your custom function in the Custom Function Editor (see Figure 9-18).

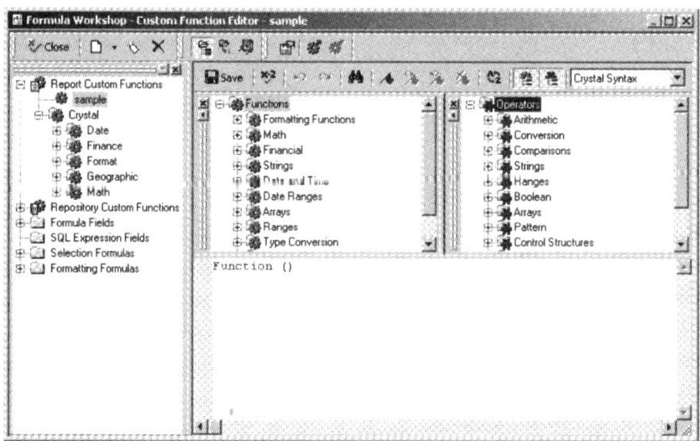

FIGURE 9-18 *Use the Custom Function Editor within the Formula Workshop to build new custom functions.*

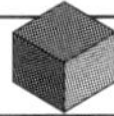

> **NOTE**
>
> Using the Custom Function Editor is similar to using the Formula Editor to create a report formula.

5. Check and save your custom function. Once the custom function is saved, you can modify it or use it in report formulas as needed.

Once a custom function is built, it is saved to the Report Custom Functions folder in the Formula Workshop tree. This makes the custom function only available to the report in which it was built. To add the custom function to the Repository so other reports can reference the function, you must save the function to the Repository.

Custom Function Syntax

As with formulas, custom functions can be written in either Basic or Crystal syntax. Contained in the following sections are syntax rules and guidelines, as well as a discussion of *evaluation time*, one of the most important characteristics of custom functions.

Crystal Syntax for Custom Functions

Crystal syntax custom functions are expression oriented, like the syntax of Crystal formulas. You can use either of the syntax formats listed below:

```
Function ([argList])
Expressions

Function ([argList])
(
expressions
)
```

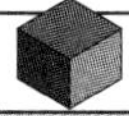

NOTE

Any syntax enclosed in square brackets ([]) is optional.

The following is a breakdown and explanation of Crystal syntax. The existing custom function, cdIncreaseNumberByAPercentage, from the Crystal Repository (shown below) is used as an example.

```
//cdIncreaseNumberByAPercentage
Function (NumberVar valueToIncrease, NumberVar percentIncrease)
 valueToIncrease + valueToIncrease * percentIncrease / 100;
```

◆ **Function.** This "reserved" word is required; it indicates the beginning of a function.

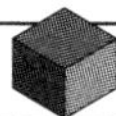

NOTE

The only statements you can place before the start of the function or at the end of the function declaration are comments. In this case, the name of the custom function is listed first as a comment (as denoted by "//" preceding the line).

◆ **NumberVar valueToIncrease, NumberVar percentIncrease.** These values are optional. This represents the type of data value accepted by the function. It can be any of the simple Crystal Reports data types (Number, Currency, String, Boolean, Date, Time, DateTime) or range types (Number Range, Currency Range, String Range, Date Range, Time Range, DateTime Range).

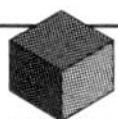

NOTE

Search using the keywords custom functions in the help files for more information regarding specific details about using the Custom Function Editor.

♦ **valueToIncrease + valueToIncrease * percentIncrease / 100;.** This statement is required. The value returned by the Crystal syntax custom function is the value of the last expression evaluated in the expression
sequence. The syntax is the same as that in Crystal syntax formulas.

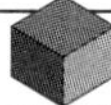

> **NOTE**
>
> Variable declarations within a custom function are local in scope by default. This con-
> trasts with variable declarations in Crystal syntax formulas, where global scope is the
> default.

Basic Syntax for Custom Functions

The syntax for custom functions in Basic syntax is very similar to the syntax for
functions in Visual Basic:

```
Function name [(argList)] [As type]
[statements]
[name=expression]
[Exit Function]
...
End Function
```

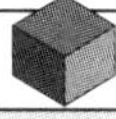

> **NOTE**
>
> Any syntax enclosed in square brackets ([]) is optional.

The following is a breakdown and explanation of Basic syntax. The existing custom function, cdFirstDayOfMonth, from the Crystal Repository (shown below)
is used as an example.

```
Function cdFirstDayOfMonth (Optional dayInMonth As DateTime = CurrentDate) As Date
    cdFirstDayOfMonth = CDate (Year (dayInMonth), Month (dayInMonth), 1)
End Function
```

◆ **Function, End Function.** Both are required. These two "reserved" words indicate the beginning and end of a function. Note: The only statements you can place before the start of the function or at the end of the function declaration are comments (either with apostrophes or Rem statements).

◆ **cdFirstDayOfMonth.** This function is required. This is the name of the function, and it must be the same name given to the function when it was created. The name cannot begin with a number and cannot contain any spaces or punctuation marks other than the underscore. Also, it cannot be the same as a keyword in either Basic or Crystal syntax (for example, DateTime).

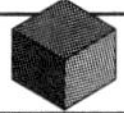 **NOTE**

The names of all functions created by Crystal Decisions begin with "cd". This prefix is not required when you name your custom functions.

◆ **Optional dayInMonth As DateTime = CurrentDate.** This statement, like in Crystal syntax, has expansive syntax.

 **NOTE**

Unlike Visual Basic, if an argument is optional, a default value must be supplied.

◆ **As Date.** This statement is optional and represents the type of data value returned by the function. It can be any of the simple Crystal Reports data types (Number, Currency, String, Boolean, Date, Time, DateTime) or range types (Number Range, Currency Range, String Range, Date Range, Time Range, DateTime Range).

As Type is optional: If type is present, it explicitly specifies the data type to be returned by the function. Otherwise, the return type is implicitly given the data type from the expression where a value is first

assigned to name. In other words, in the custom function cdFirstDayOf-
Month, the explicit data type is Date (As Date). The implicit data type
is also Date, because cdFirstDayOfMonth is assigned (=) the results of
another function CDate (Year (dayInMonth), Month (dayInMonth), 1)
(the ConvertDate function), whose return type is the Date data type.

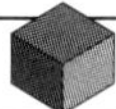

NOTE

If an array return type is desired, you must explicitly declare this since there is no
implicit notation for it.

◆ **cdFirstDayOfMonth = CDate (Year (dayInMonth), Month (dayIn-
Month), 1).** This expression is optional if (as noted above) the data type
returned by the function is explicitly stated. Otherwise, expression is
required in order for the type of data value to be returned by the function to be implicitly determined.

◆ **Exit Function.** This statement is optional; it causes Crystal Reports to
immediately exit from the function. You can use this statement any
number of times, anywhere in the body of the function. It is most often
used to exit the function if an error occurs.

NOTE

All arguments are passed to and from a custom function by value. In Visual Basic,
arguments can be passed either by value or by reference and are passed by reference by default. However, custom functions do not support reference arguments.

Custom Function Syntax Rules

In order for custom functions to be independent of the report in which they are being used, there are certain restrictions on how custom functions can be created.

- ◆ Report or database fields, including summary fields, cannot be used within a custom function, but they can be used as arguments.
- ◆ Shared or global variables cannot be used within a custom function, but you can pass in a global or shared variable as an argument when calling a custom function from within a formula.
- ◆ A custom function cannot call itself (known as *recursion*), either directly or indirectly.
- ◆ You cannot directly use UFLs in a custom function.
- ◆ You cannot call Evaluation Time, Print State, or Document Properties functions.
- ◆ You cannot use the functions Rnd, CurrentFieldValue, DefaultAttribute, and GridRowColumnValue.

You can use local variables and argument variables within custom functions. If you need to use a shared or global variable in your custom function, it can be passed in as an argument.

Evaluation Time

One important difference between custom functions and formulas is that custom functions are evaluated on demand, or called. In other words, a custom function can call another custom function to do some processing exactly when it needs the value. Formulas cannot call another formula on demand, even through the use of global variables.

The following is an example (in Crystal syntax) of one formula processing its results using the value of a second formula to do its calculation:

```
//Formula 1 fmPrintSquare
NumberVar x := 5;
"The square of "+ToText(x,0)+" is "+ToText({@fmSquare},0)+"."

//Formula 2 fmSquare
NumberVar x;
x ^ 2
```

The result of using the formula fmPrintSquare in a report can be either:

The square of 5 is 0.

—or—

The square of 5 is 25.

In the example above, formula fmPrintSquare uses formula fmSquare. Crystal Reports sets the order of their processing; one formula is always processed before the other. If fmSquare is evaluated first and then fmPrintSquare is evaluated, the correct result occurs. When fmPrintSquare is evaluated first, the value of the global variable x in the fmSquare formula is 0, since that is the value of an uninitialized Number variable.

This can be fixed by using an evaluation time function within the fmPrintSquare formula.

```
//Formula 1 fmPrintSquare
EvaluateAfter(fmSquare);
NumberVar x := 5;
"The square of "+ToText(x,0)+" is "+ToText({@fmSquare},0)+"."
```

In contrast, custom functions are evaluated on demand, or called. The following example replaces the formula fmSquare with a custom function:

```
//Formula fmPrintSquare
NumberVar x := 5;
"The square of "+ToText(x,0)+" is "+ToText(cfSquare(x),0)+"."

//Custom function cfSquare
Local NumberVar x ^ 2
```

Now if you use formula fmPrintSquare in your report, you'll get:

The square of 5 is 25.

This is because the custom function, cfSquare, is called to process within the formula fmPrintSquare exactly when the formula asks for the value. Because of this difference in evaluation time between formulas and custom functions, using custom functions may help eliminate the need for some complicated evaluation time scenarios.

Summary

Custom functions provide an entire new world of possibilities for sharing formula functionality among reports in an organization. Using custom functions in reports provides a new and possibly easier way for less experienced users to take advantage of simplified formula logic. They also provide a means for more consistent data if all reports use the same function to perform the same calculation.

Chapter 10

A *subreport* is a report that exists inside another report. Subreports lend your reports increased diversity of information in what looks to the reader like one report. Subreports can be used for several different purposes.

Use a subreport to present a different view of your data within the same report, such as a graph, chart, or summary listing, so that you can view data from two perspectives in the same report.

Use a subreport to pull in values from another data source without needing to link tables. For example, although Crystal Reports allows you to link together tables from different data sources, sometimes the ODBC is not compatible or just dreadfully slow. A subreport provides an alternative to increase processing speed or combine "unlinkable" data.

Sometimes a report processes faster or more efficiently if a calculation is performed in a subreport with the necessary data, and only the summary value is passed to the main report to interact with values there.

All of these are potential uses for subreports beyond the obvious and are covered in this chapter. Be creative with subreports and you'll be surprised at what you can do.

Inserting a Subreport

You can add a subreport to a main report in either of two ways. Both start by designating a report as the main report. To add a subreport, you can either insert a report that you already designed and saved somewhere on your network or PC, or create a brand new report on-the-fly for the sole purpose of being a subreport.

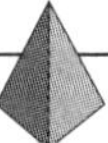

TIP

A subreport is an independent object within a report. For clarification, the term *subreport* is used in this chapter to refer to the subreport object within a main report; it does not refer to a report that happens to contain a subreport.

There are some basic guidelines to follow when using subreports:

◆ You insert a subreport as an object inside a main report.

◆ You can place subreports in any report section, and the entire subreport prints in that section.

◆ You can add any number of subreports to a main report.

◆ You cannot add subreports to other subreports.

◆ You can use an existing report as a subreport, or build a new report on-the-fly.

◆ You can build subreports either off the same data source as the main report or off a completely different data source.

◆ The subreports that you add can have data that is related in some way to a main report, or data that is completely unrelated.

Using Existing Reports as Subreports

You can insert a prebuilt report into a main report to function as a subreport. Depending on the purpose of the report, the subreport can be unrelated, related, linked, or unlinked to the main report.

Insert an Existing Report into a Main Report

1. Open the main report in the Design tab.

2. Select Insert, Subreport, or click the Subreport 🔳 button found on the Insert Tools toolbar.

3. In the Insert Subreport dialog box, click the Subreport tab and select Choose a report (see Figure 10-1).

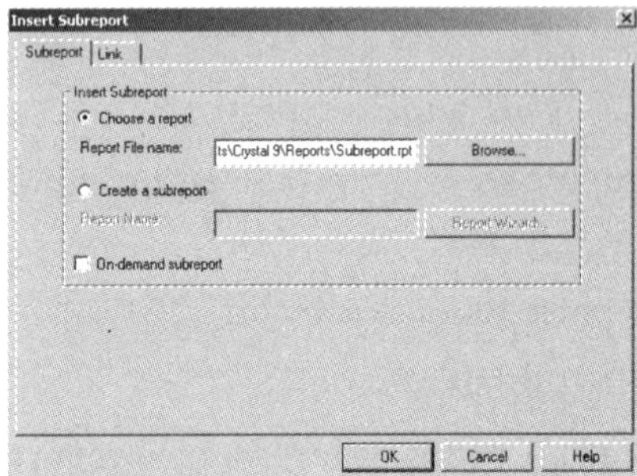

FIGURE 10-1 *Use the Insert Subreport dialog box to add an existing report as a subreport.*

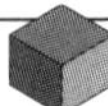

NOTE

The On-demand subreport check box on this tab is covered later in the chapter, in "How Do I Format a Subreport to Process On-Demand?"

4. After you select Choose a report, the Browse button becomes available. Browse your computer or network to locate the report you want to use as the subreport.

5. When you select a report to become the subreport, its path appears in the Report File name box. Click OK. The subreport object attaches to your mouse pointer.

6. Place the subreport where you want it to print by clicking in that section (see Figure 10-2).

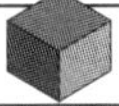

NOTE

The subreport is a sizable, movable, editable object in the section in which you placed it. Depending on the data in the subreport, you might need to resize and/or hide sections so that only the part you want prints.

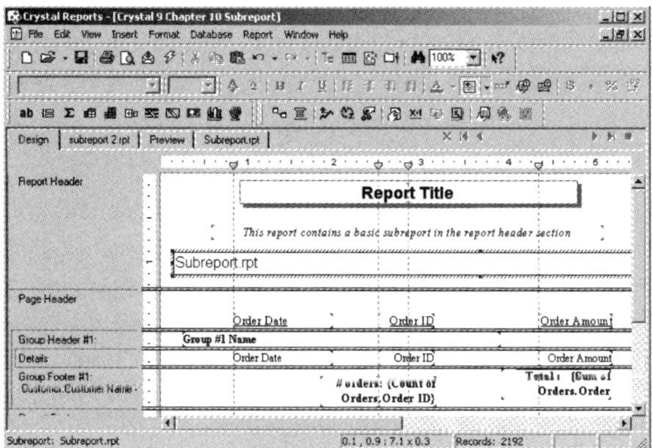

FIGURE 10-2 *Insert the subreport into the main report in the section in which you want the subreport to print. In this case, the subreport will print in the Report Header.*

7. Open the Preview tab to view the main report and the subreport you just added (see Figure 10-3). You may need to resize or reposition the subreport, or manipulate some formatting so that it looks good in the main report.

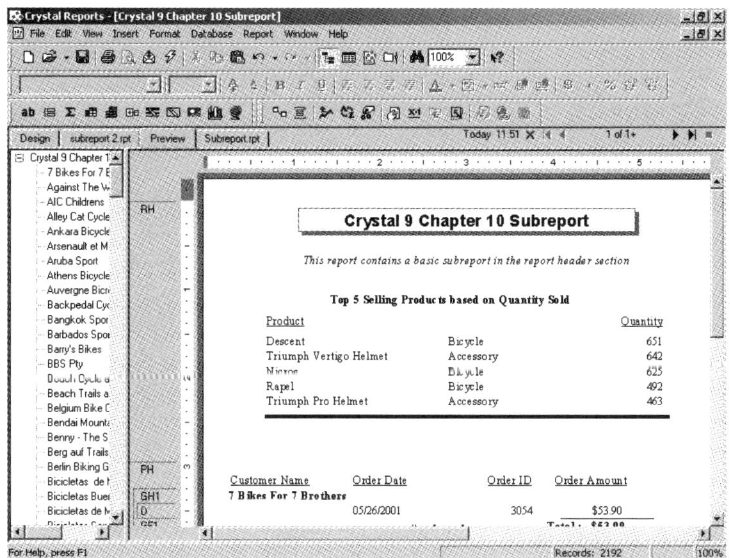

FIGURE 10-3 *Preview the main report to see the main report and the subreport.*

After you've added the subreport to the main report, notice the subreport Design tab next to the Preview tab of the main report. This tab allows you to edit the subreport at any time. To edit the subreport from within the main report, double-click the subreport object or select the subreport and select Edit, Subreport. And, of course, there is yet another way to edit the subreport. Select the subreport, right-click, and choose Edit Subreport from the shortcut menu.

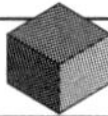

NOTE

When a subreport is inserted onto a report, the subreport object has a border around it. Remove the border easily if you want by selecting the subreport object then clicking the border icon in the Formatting toolbar.

It is important to note that any editing you do to the subreport in this way *does not* save back to the original report (on your network or PC) that you added to the main report. The subreport is part of the main report at this point, not a separate entity. The changes you make on the subreport Design tab save only in the main report. When you click Save, you are saving the main report and the subreport within it as one RPT file.

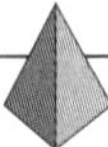

TIP

If you want to save the subreport as a separate report, independent from the main report, open the subreport Design tab. With this tab open, select File, Save Subreport As, and then name the subreport. Or, you could right-click on the subreport object and choose Save Subreport As from the short-cut menu. This saves the subreport as a separate file wherever you designate on your PC or the network, with the name you have given it.

Reimporting a Subreport

The Reimport Subreport option, found on the shortcut menu for the subreport, offers the opportunity to reimport the subreport. Clicking this option prompts you that the action will close all open Preview tabs and cannot be undone.

Why would you want to reimport the subreport? Maybe you edited the subreport outside the main report, and want those changes to take effect in the subreport object. Or, after importing the subreport, perhaps you changed the report in a way you dislike (or made a big mistake) and starting over would be easier than undoing unwanted changes.

Another, similar option allows you to reimport a subreport from its original standalone report object every time a report is opened. This option is found in the Options dialog box (choose File, Options), on the Reporting tab. Make sure that if you select this option for one report, you save and close that report but reset your global option (under File, Options) back to the way you want it for most reports.

Creating a New Subreport from within the Main Report

If you have not already designed the subreport that you want to insert into a main report, you can design that report at any time during your development of the main report.

Building a Subreport On-the-Fly

Once you have started designing the main report, you can insert a subreport, as described in the following steps:

1. Select Insert, Subreport from the menu or click the Subreport button on the Insert Tools toolbar. This opens the Insert Subreport dialog box, with the Subreport tab in front. This is exactly the same tab as shown earlier in Figure 10-1, but this time click Create a subreport and give the subreport a name (see Figure 10-4). Once named, the Report Wizard button becomes available.

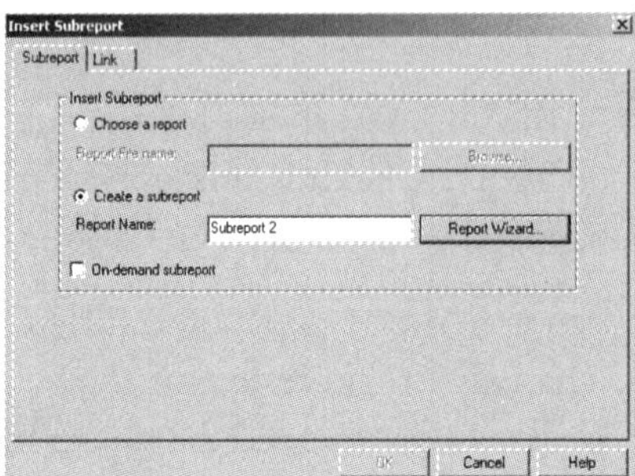

FIGURE 10-4 *Name your new subreport and then click the Report Wizard button to design the subreport.*

2. Click the Report Wizard button to open the Data page of the Standard Report Creation Wizard (see Figure 10-5). Use the wizard to design a subreport, referring to Chapter 2 for any assistance you might need.

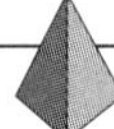

TIP

If you are planning to link the subreport to the main report, you might not need to set any selection criteria or "filters" in the wizard. The link between the main report and the subreport serves as selection criteria.

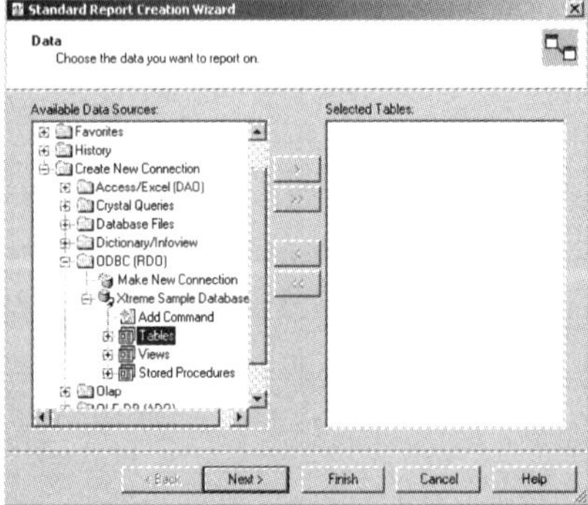

FIGURE 10-5 *Use the Standard Report Creation Wizard to design a report that will become the subreport.*

3. When you have finished designing your subreport, click Finish to return to the Insert Subreport dialog box.

4. If you want to link the subreport to the main report, click the Link tab. Linking a subreport to the main report is covered in the next section of this chapter. For now, click OK to close the Insert Subreport dialog box and attach the subreport object to your mouse pointer.

5. Drop the subreport into the main report in the section where you want the subreport to print. You may need to adjust the size or formatting attributes so that it looks just the way you want.

Fine-Tuning a Subreport

Often times, if the purpose of a subreport is to pull in data, the Report Header, Page Header, and Page Footer sections are better off hidden. Left to print, they just take up space unnecessarily.

If you're trying to match up the main report and subreport so that they look like one report, you may find it easier to format both reports at the same time. If you want a subreport to "match" the main report, wait until you've inserted the subreport and then toggle between the two Design tabs to complete any format fine-tuning. Use the guidelines and the rulers in both Design tabs to line up columns and rows.

When you preview or refresh the main report, you refresh both the main report and subreport data. If you click Preview from within the subreport's Design tab, you get a Preview tab for just the subreport (see Figure 10-6).

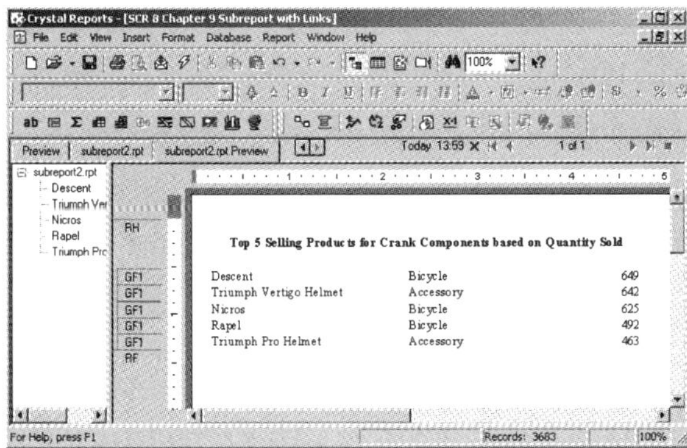

FIGURE 10-6 *Preview the subreport from the subreport's Design tab the same way you preview any other report.*

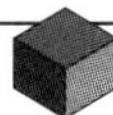

NOTE

If the subreport is linked to the main report, you'll be prompted for the link value in the form of a parameter field. This will make sense once you work through the next section on linking subreports.

Linking the Subreport to the Main Report

After you have designed the main report and subreport, you may want to select a field or several fields to link together. This enables the report to show specific data in the subreport as it corresponds to data in the main report.

Linking a subreport to a main report can be done at any time. When you link a subreport to a main report, Crystal Reports actually creates a parameter field in the subreport and uses it in the subreport selection criteria. When you refresh the main report, the main report answers the prompt asked by the subreport for what data is needed. The subreport then sends the main report the data that meets the specification of the prompt.

How Does Subreport Linking Work?

Crystal Reports processes each section of a report as it comes to it. For example, sections process in order down the page, starting with the Report Header, followed in order by the Page Header, Group Header, Details, and Group Footer sections. The report cycles through the Group Header, Details, and Group Footer, repeating for all groups. The Page Header and Page Footer print on each page regardless of other sections, and the Report Footer and a Page Footer print on the last page. Thus, the subreport processes when the section it sits in processes.

When it becomes time to process the subreport, the following scenarios occur:

◆ If the subreport is not linked to the main report, then subreport just processes, returning a result that prints on the main report when the section it lives in processes.

◆ If the subreport is linked to the main report, when it comes time to process the subreport, the subreport asks the main report via the parameter what value(s) to refresh the subreport for. This parameter is added to the selection criteria of the subreport automatically.

◆ If the subreport is linked and located in a Group Header or Group
Footer, then each time that section is processed, the group value (or
linked field) is passed via the parameter from the main report to the subreport.

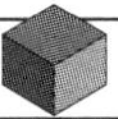

NOTE

Chapter 12 covers parameter fields in detail. Basically, a parameter is a prompt.
When a report refreshes, a prompt dialog box opens asking the user to enter a value
or the answer to a question. The report uses the answer to the prompt in its selection
criteria (among other places described in Chapter 12), affecting which records print
on the report. For the current sample report, the prompt asks: "What customer do you
want to run this subreport for?" The main report responds with the group field, Customer ID. The subreport passes this value to its selection criteria, which causes the
subreport to print only the specific customer's records.

You will not see any of this parameter action. Crystal Reports does it all for you
automatically. Only if you preview just the subreport portion of a linked subreport
will you be prompted for a value for the subreport parameter.

This will make more sense when you see it in action, so the next section shows
you how to link the main report and subreport together.

Filtering Data in a Subreport by Linking to a Main Report

What if you want a subreport to print the top five products sold based on quantity for each customer, rather than for the entire report? You then need to move
the subreport so that it prints once for every group, and also link the subreport to
the main report so that the subreport prints the appropriate records associated
with the group it describes. There are several steps to accomplish this by simply
editing the main report and subreport already used in this chapter:

1. Add another Group Header section to the report using the shortcut
menu or the Section Expert.

2. Move the subreport into the Group Header #1b section. In the sample
report, this is the Customer group.

3. While in the Design tab, select Edit, Subreport Links to open the Subreport Links dialog box (see Figure 10-7).

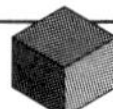

NOTE

When you initially insert the subreport into a main report, the Links tab is available in the Insert Subreport dialog box. You can link the subreport to the main report at this time, or you can come back later to open the Subreport Links dialog box, as done in these steps.

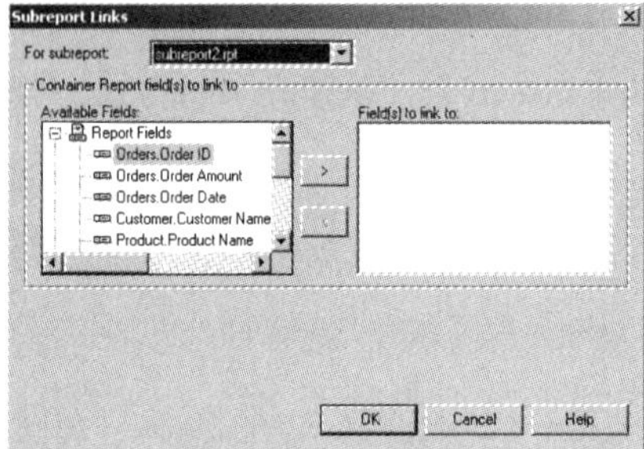

FIGURE 10-7 *Use the Subreport Links dialog box to link a field in the main report to a field in the subreport.*

4. Select a field from the Available Fields list (the main report) and click the right arrow button to move the field to the Field(s) to link to list.

5. With this complete, two list boxes appear at the bottom of the dialog box, showing that Crystal Reports has created a parameter field for you based on the field you chose to link the two reports together. From the list below the Select data in subreport based on field check box, select the field in the subreport to which you want to link. Crystal Reports seems rather smart and has already chosen the correct field for me, as shown in Figure 10-8.

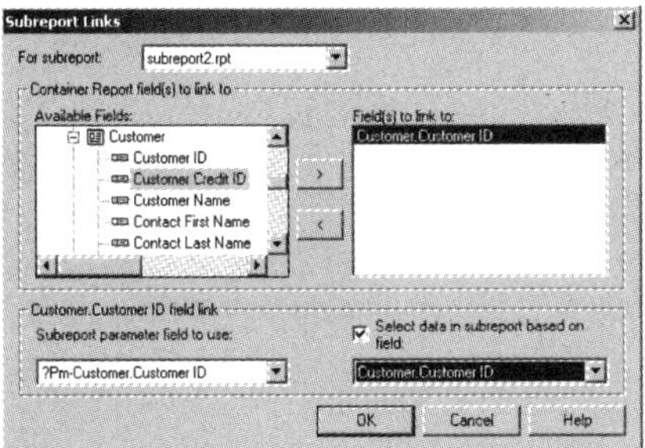

FIGURE 10-8 *Be sure that Crystal Reports has chosen the correct field to link to in the subreport.*

6. Click OK to close the Subreport Links dialog box. Preview your report (as shown in Figure 10-9). You may need to move the subreport around or fine-tune your formatting so that the subreport lines up and looks the way you want in relation to the main report.

 **NOTE**

The Select data in subreport based on field check box activates the field list below it. Select the field from the list that you want to have passed into the selection criteria for the subreport—select the field you are using to link the subreport to the main report.

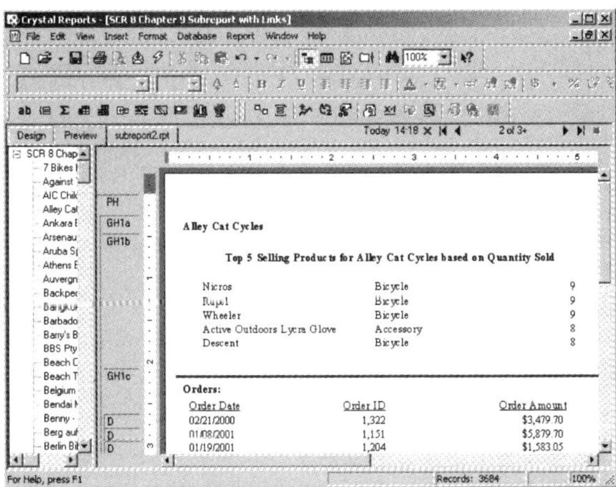

FIGURE 10-9 *Preview the report with the linked subreport. The subreport placed in the Group Footer section prints a subreport for each group, based on the linked field.*

The previous instructions for moving the subreport to the group header section include adding another Group Footer section to the report to hold the subreport. Adding a section to accommodate the subreport is almost always desirable for it provides much more consistent formatting control and is also necessary at times in order to ensure correct data. The section "Passing Data from a Subreport to the Main Report" explains this concept further.

Conditionally Format the Subreport to Print Only When a Condition is True

The report example previously discussed and shown in Figure 10-9 demonstrates how you can move a subreport into the group section of a report, and link the subreport to the main report. In this example, the subreport will print for every group, regardless of how many products were ordered by each customer. For many groups on this report, this subreport looks ridiculous with only one or two products ordered, and the title is incorrect, stating that the subreport is for the top five products when there might be only one product listed.

To "fix" this, write a conditional formula in the Section Expert (covered in Chapter 6) to suppress the entire Group Header section that contains the subreport if that group contains less than five products ordered. The formula, which would be placed in the Section Expert behind the suppress X+2 button for the Group Header #1b section, reads as follows:

```
count ({Product.Product Name},{Customer.Customer Name}) < 5
```

Check out this report, named Crystal 9 Chapter 10 Subreport With Links, on BridgeBuilder's Web site. The result of this formatting produces a subreport that only prints if there were five or more products ordered by that customer.

Linking a subreport to the main report allows you to control what data to include in the subreport. This allows you to have a subreport print for each group, which is how you can add specific or additional data to a report that enhances or "adds to" the information already there without making the report confusing by having too much data in the Details section.

Linking Subreports Using Date Fields

Many times, date fields are used in subreport linking. By linking the subreport to the main report via a date field, both the main report and subreport collect data for the same date range.

The reason for using a subreport in the first place determines your strategy when using date fields. Most reports are built to prompt the user of the report to enter the date range they want to run the report for each time they refresh the report. This is accomplished by building and using a parameter field, which is covered in Chapter 12.

Since many reports use prompts to determine the date range the main report runs for, it makes sense to link the subreport to the main report using this parameter field. The parameter field referred to here is *not* the parameter built by the subreport to actually link the main report and subreport; rather, this parameter is built by the report developer in the main report to prompt the user for a value to refresh the report for.

If you want a subreport to collect data for the same date range as the main report, and the main report contains a date parameter, you can use that parameter in the main report to link to the date field in the subreport (see Figure 10-10).

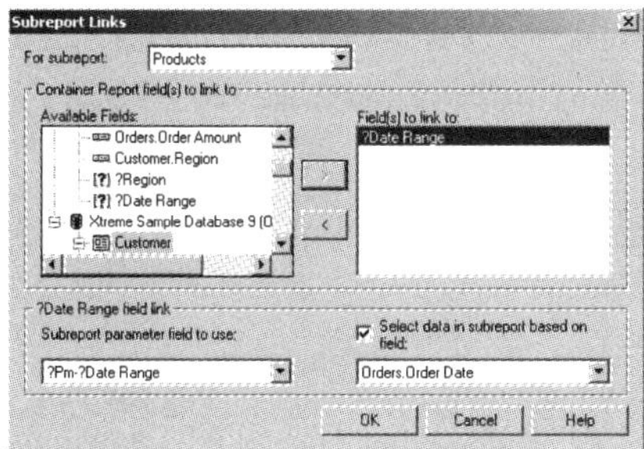

FIGURE 10-10 *Link a parameter field in the main report to a date field in the subreport.*

 **NOTE**

The format of the date field must be the same in both the main report and subreport to use date fields for subreport linking.

Linking Subreports Using More than One Field

Commonly, when linking subreports using date fields, you will need a second link field to collect the data needed. Figure 10-11 shows a subreport being linked using more than one field. In this example, the subreport will run for both the regions and the date range the main report runs for.

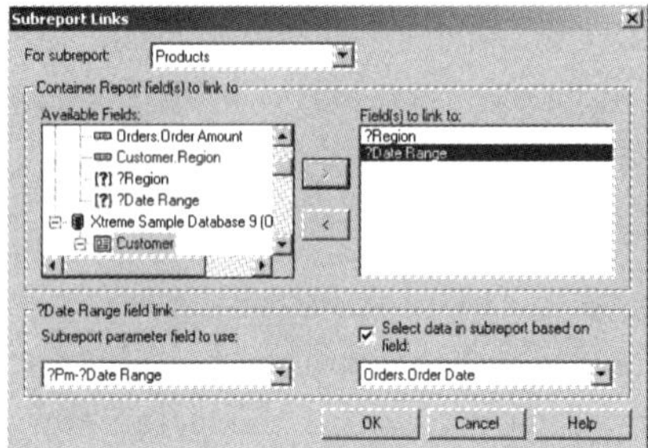

FIGURE 10-11 *Link subreports with several links if necessary to collect only the data wanted.*

Linking Subreports Using a Formula Field

If the field is a date type in the main report but a date time in the subreport, then you'll need to write a formula in the subreport to convert the date time to the date type and use that formula field for subreport linking (see Figure 10-12).

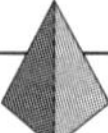

TIP

The fields used in linking subreports to main reports do not need to match name, they only need to have the same data type and format. Thus, linking from a database field in the main report to a formula field in a subreport, or vice versa, is acceptable.

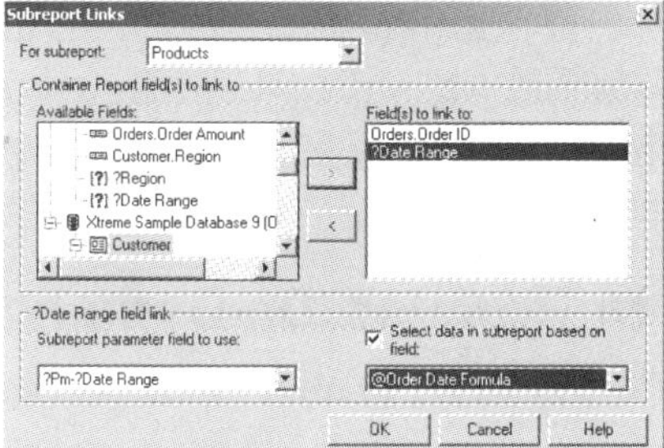

FIGURE 10-12 *Formulas can be used by either the main report or subreport for linking.*

On-Demand Subreports

On-demand subreports behave as their name implies—users call them up on demand, rather than having them appear automatically. You can designate a subreport to be an on-demand subreport when you add the subreport to the main report, or you can format the subreport after it has been inserted to be an on-demand subreport.

The on-demand feature of subreports allows you to process and preview the report without subreport data being retrieved from your database or printing on your report. This way, viewers of the report can request the subreport data only if they need or want to.

Why Use an On-Demand Subreport?

On-demand subreports are useful if report readers will not always need the data in the subreport. By not including the subreport data automatically, the main report will be smaller and process faster, as well as look cleaner and less jumbled with data. If readers need to see the subreport data, they can choose to generate the subreport.

On-demand subreports can be useful when inserting a subreport for each group (at any group level). Some users of the report may not need the subreport data because they do not need that much detail or extra information. On the other hand, another user of the same report may want to see some or all of the subreports.

The report and subreport linked in a previous section will serve as a good example here. We have a subreport that prints in each Group Header, providing information on the top five products ordered by each customer. Readers of the report may not need to see this information for every customer, but may want the ability to click a link to see that information if and when they want. Formatting the subreport to be "on-demand" provides this functionality.

How Do I Format a Subreport to Process On-Demand?

You have two ways to designate a subreport as an on-demand subreport:

◆ When you insert the subreport into the main report, you can select the On-demand subreport check box in the Insert Subreport dialog box (refer to Figure 10-4). This designates the subreport as on-demand from the start.

◆ Open the Format Subreport dialog box for an already inserted subreport, and select the On-demand subreport check box on the Subreport tab (refer to Figure 10-13).

To open the Format Subreport dialog box, right-click the subreport and choose Format Subreport from the shortcut menu. Or, with the subreport object selected in the main report's Design tab, choose Format, Format Subreport from the main menu.

The Subreport tab has a few additional formatting options specific to subreports, which the following sections describe more fully.

Other Subreport Formatting Options

The Subreport tab in the Format Expert is available for all subreports (see Figure 10-13). Use the following options on this tab to customize the subreport to look and behave they way you want:

◆ **Subreport Name.** Allows you to specify the name of the embedded subreport.

◆ **On-demand Subreport.** Allows you to toggle the on-demand functionality.

◆ **On-demand Subreport Caption.** Enables you to create text to display within the subreport object as it sits on the main report, such as "Click here to view subreport." To set up this feature, click the Conditional Formula (X+2) button next to this option to open the Formula Editor. Write a formula to print text, such as the sample shown in Figure 10-14.

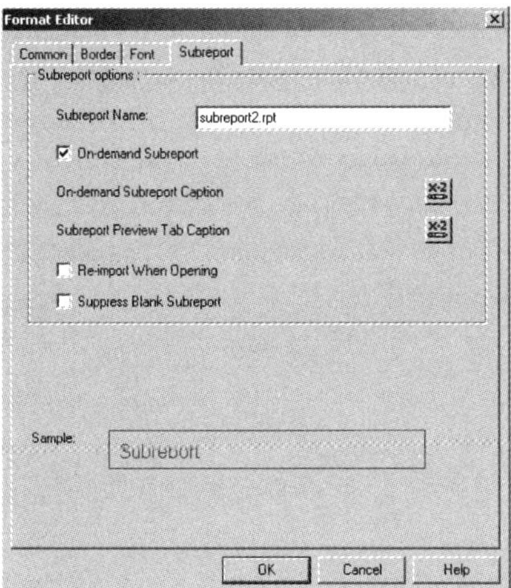

FIGURE 10-13 *Open the Subreport tab of the Format Editor for specific subreport formatting options.*

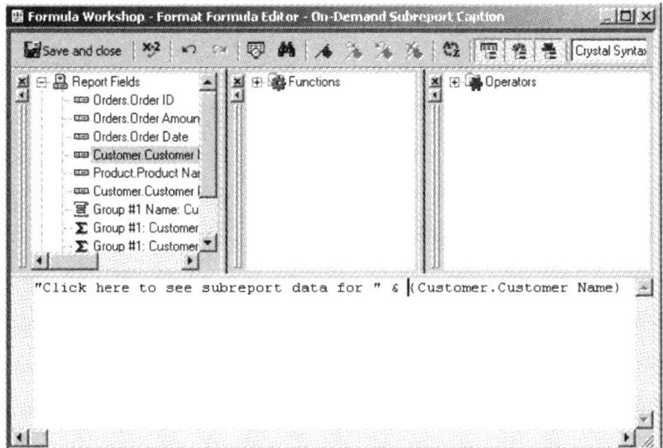

FIGURE 10-14 *Add a text formula so that the subreport label tells the report viewers what they might see if they click the subreport object.*

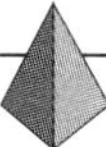

TIP

You can add database fields as well as text to on-demand subreport captions. For example, you could write the following formula: "Click here to see the sales for" + {Customer.Region}. If your report were grouped by region with the on-demand subreport in the region section, each on-demand subreport caption would say which region it is for.

◆ **Subreport Preview Tab Caption.** Enables you to customize the text that appears in the subreport's Preview tab label. Click the Conditional Formula button and write a formula containing the name to print on the Preview tab. Figure 10-15 shows an example.

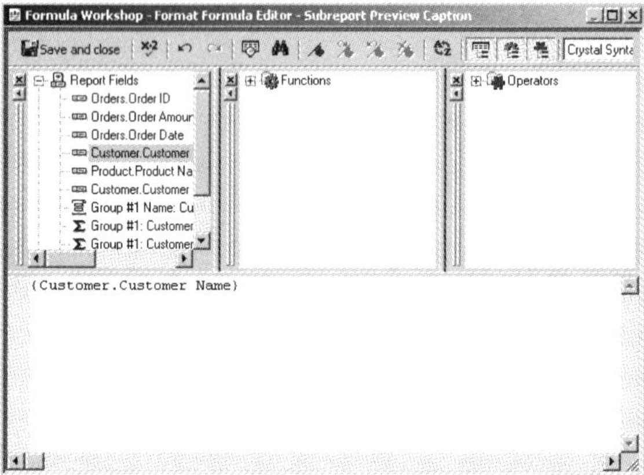

FIGURE 10-15 *Add a formula to customize the label for the subreport's Preview tab. You'll want to keep this text short!*

◆ **Re-import When Opening.** Applies only to subreports that originally existed as reports outside the main report. If you used the Choose a report option to import an existing report into the main report (refer to Figure 10-1), you can select this check box if you want to have the subreport reloaded from the original location into the main report.

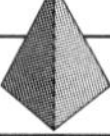

TIP

You may want to use the Re-import When Opening option if the subreport is used in multiple main reports and exists outside the main reports. This way, you have to make changes in only one place. You do not want to use this option if you have been making updates to a subreport within the main report, because you will overwrite those updates when you re-import!

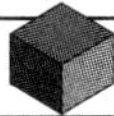

NOTE

You can also set a global option under File, Options to always have the subreport updated from the original report by selecting the check box on the New Report tab called Re-import Subreports When Loading Reports.

◆ **Suppress Blank Subreport.** This new option does exactly what its name implies—if the subreport contains no data, the subreport will not print at all. In the past, the subreport title and column headings would print with no data.

Using Subreports to Overcome Data Issues

Imagine that you have a report that contains contact information about your customers and that information is grouped by region. You decide that you want to include information for your suppliers in each region as well, on the same report. But the supplier data is located in a data file that cannot be linked to the main database table that contains all of your customer information.

Another scenario might be that you are building a report for your call center that collects details on the amount of time agents are on the phone, the number of calls taken, average call time, etc. You want to add information to that report that summarizes the number of customers each agent helped and the value of any transactions completed by each agent. The transactional system cannot be linked in any way to the call center, and all that is needed is numbers of customers and transaction values, not details on individual calls.

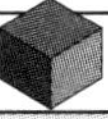

NOTE

A subreport does not need to be based on the same database as the main report. In fact, this is one of Crystal Reports' secret weapons—linking unlinkable data using a subreport.

You can use a subreport to overcome this problem of nonlinkable data. There are several scenarios in which you might not be able to link two tables together or improve report functionality using one or more subreports.

Linking Tables from Two Data Sources

Crystal Reports provides functionality allowing you to link two tables together from two different data sources. How well this works depends on many factors. You are no longer limited by data type. In previous versions of Crystal Reports you could use only string type fields to link between different data sources. Enhancements in version 9 allow you to use any field type for linking between data sources. You still may end up restricted because of ODBC incompatibilities, but subreports will still come to your rescue.

Link Field is Not Indexed

An issue arises when the fields needed for linking are not indexed. This can diminish report processing speed so much that the report will take days to process or not process at all. In either case, build a subreport to collect the data from the second source. The subreport link is much more forgiving, and by writing a formula, you can overcome data type differences for indexed fields, and use the formula to link the main report and subreport.

All Data Is within One Source, but Table Relationship Is Off

Believe it or not, sometimes tables in one database are difficult or impossible to link correctly. Even with linkable indexed fields, two tables when linked may not produce the desired results based on the way they were built. Or, they might work great for one report, but not for another report with a completely different purpose. Subreports come to the rescue again!

An example of this situation might be a system administrator's report regarding the monitoring of the activity in a CRM database. The administrator wants to run a report that lists all current users of the system and a count of how many activities each user scheduled in the past month. You'd think you could just link the Users table to a table containing activity information with a Left Outer join, to see all users with activities if they scheduled any. But in some cases, this doesn't work. In one particular situation encountered, the Left Outer join did not create the report I wanted—any user with zero activities scheduled was not included on the report, and I really needed all users listed with a zero if they scheduled zero activities. In this case, I used a subreport in the Details section to count the number of activities for each user from the other table and return a value.

Too Much Data Pulled into Report for Efficient Processing

Even if you can collect all the data needed in one report, the number of groups or calculations may become overwhelming. Also, the more data pulled into one report, and the more complicated the processing, the slower the report performance.

If you need extensively calculated values in a report at a group interval, and you are dealing with evaluating hundreds of thousands of records multiple times to do all the calculations, you may want to build subreports to pull subsets and do calculations and then pass only the values needed into the main report. This helps report performance because Crystal can process smaller subreports with more specific record selection quickly, and then pass the necessary values into the main report for further processing and analysis.

Combine Data from Unlinkable Sources

Some data sources are simply unwieldy. They were not built for reporting, and do not cooperate with ODBC. An example is Lotus Notes, which is not really a database, but rather a fabulous document handler. Lotus Notes "databases" can have many "forms," which contain data needed for reporting. I could go on and on about the intricacies of reporting from Notes, but instead will attempt to focus on one point—how well subreports work when reporting off Notes databases.

Lotus Notes in particular is not so cooperative when it comes to linking tables together with the ODBC drivers that Notes provides. And linking forms is impossible using the Notes native drivers, because Notes is not a relational database to begin with. Here you can unlock the potential of subreports! Separate subreports can be built to pull different parts of reports from separate Notes databases, and then put them together seamlessly into one report. Linking the main report and subreport by using fields, parameters, and formulas, in conjunction with date range parameters, allows you to pull all necessary data together in one report.

When building reports to overcome data issues, you most likely will be inserting the subreport into a Group Footer or even Details section to collect data for specific groups or records. Comprehensive formatting options allow you to format the subreport and main report to match exactly, as shown in Figure 10-16. When readers look at the report, they will have no idea that the supplier listing is actually a subreport.

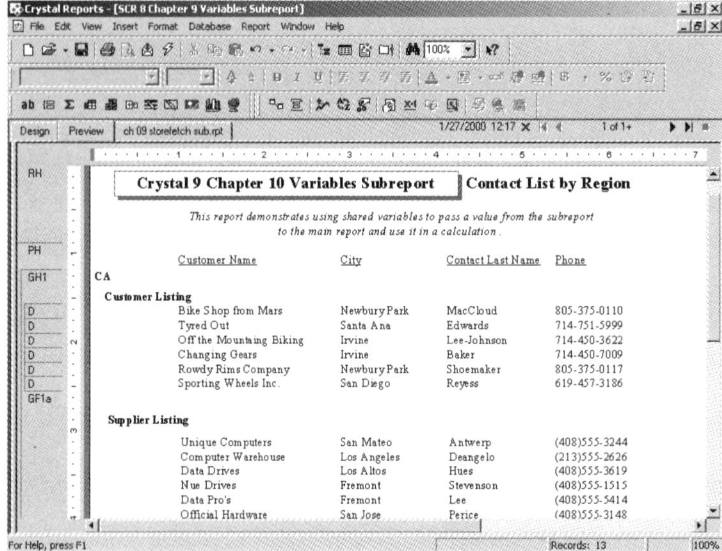

FIGURE 10-16 *This report has a subreport based on a different database than the main report, but you cannot tell because they are formatted to look the same.*

Use subreports to overcome other database shortcomings, as well. For example, if you have two tables linked for a report but the second table is not indexed, looking up values in that table may take a long time if Crystal has to do the work. If, instead, you design a subreport with effective selection criteria, the database server does the selection instead of Crystal, which speeds up the report processing time.

Passing Data from the Subreport to the Main Report

It is possible to store data in a variable in a subreport and then collect that same variable data in the main report. Chapter 7 covered formulas, variables, and variable scope, but here I want to specifically discuss the use of variables to pass data between a main report and a subreport.

To create a shared variable in a subreport, you write a formula declaring the variable scope and variable type, and set its value. Be sure to declare the variable's scope as Shared, indicating that this variable can and will be shared between the subreport and the main report.

As an example, I am using the report shown in Figure 10-16, which is a Customer Listing main report with a Supplier Listing subreport. I want to count the total number of contacts, from both customers and suppliers, for each region. To do this, I need the count of suppliers from the subreport to add to the count of customers in the main report. It takes a few steps to calculate a value for the variable in the subreport and then collect the value in the main report, but the steps involve just two formulas.

The subreport contains the formula that declares the variable. Open the subreport's Design tab and select Insert, Formula Field. Here, I need a formula to count the number of suppliers (for each region) and assign that number to a shared variable. The formula, which I've titled vrCountSupplier, appears in Figure 10-17.

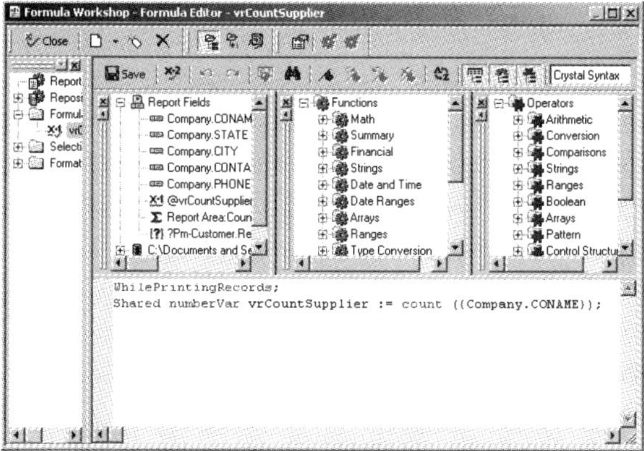

FIGURE 10-17 *Create a new variable formula to store the count of the suppliers in the subreport.*

This formula declares the scope as Shared. The variable type is numberVar and the variable name is vrCountSupplier. The variable value is equal to the count of the supplier names.

Next, I insert this formula on the subreport's Design tab, in the Report Footer section (as shown in Figure 10-18). The formula must go in the Report Footer because it calculates a total count of all suppliers on the report.

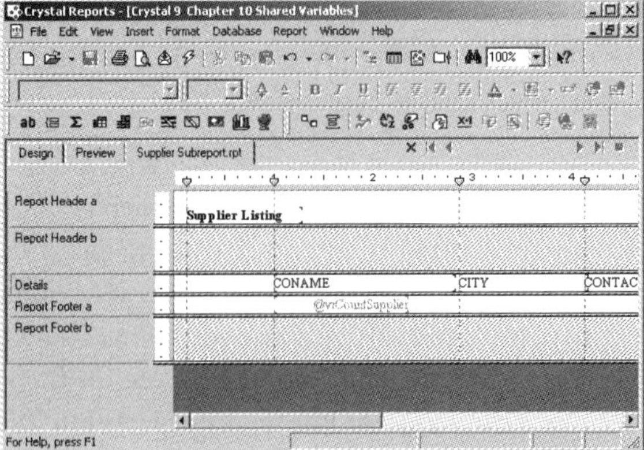

FIGURE 10-18 *Insert the vrCountSupplier formula in the Report Footer section of the subreport.*

Now that you have inserted the formula in the subreport, you will see it when you preview the main report. If you do not want it to print, go back to the subreport's Design tab and suppress the field. This way, it exists and the formula calculates the value for the variable, but it does not show on the Preview tab.

Let's collect that shared variable now, and add it to the count of customers in the main report. Open the Formula Editor from the main report's Design tab and create a new formula named vrTotalCust. Write a formula to count the customers and then add the stored variable vrCountSupplier to that count (see Figure 10-19).

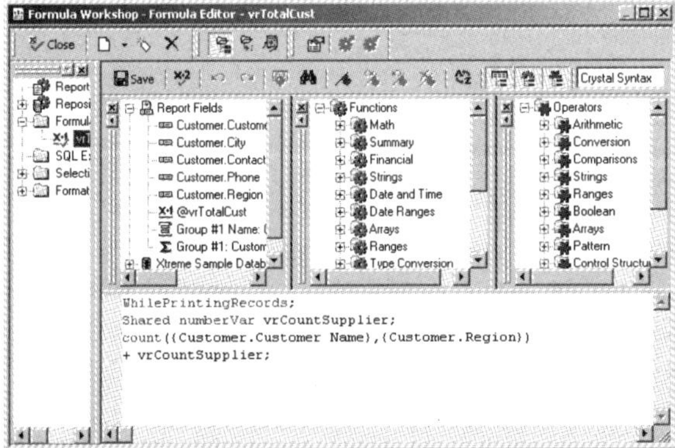

FIGURE 10-19 *Use the Formula Editor to use the variable in the subreport and add that value to the count of customers in the main report.*

This formula counts the customers per region and then adds the stored variable from the subreport to that number. This formula must occur after the section that contains the subreport, so first add a Group Footer #1b section and insert the formula there (see Figure 10-20).

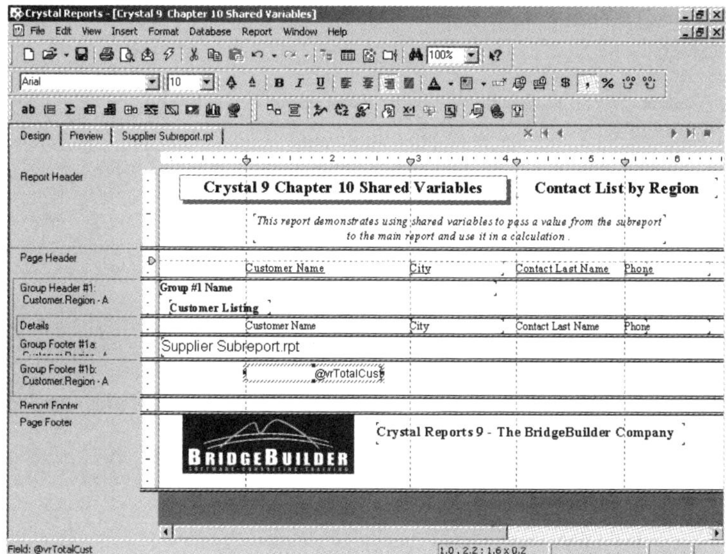

FIGURE 10-20 *Insert the vrTotalCust formula into the section below the section containing the subreport.*

Now when you preview the report, you will see that the number listed below the subreport is the total count of customers and suppliers for each region (as shown in Figure 10-21). For formatting, I added a text object, typed a label, and inserted the vrTotalCust formula field. I formatted the text object with a border and centered text. I also formatted the formula field to have no decimal places.

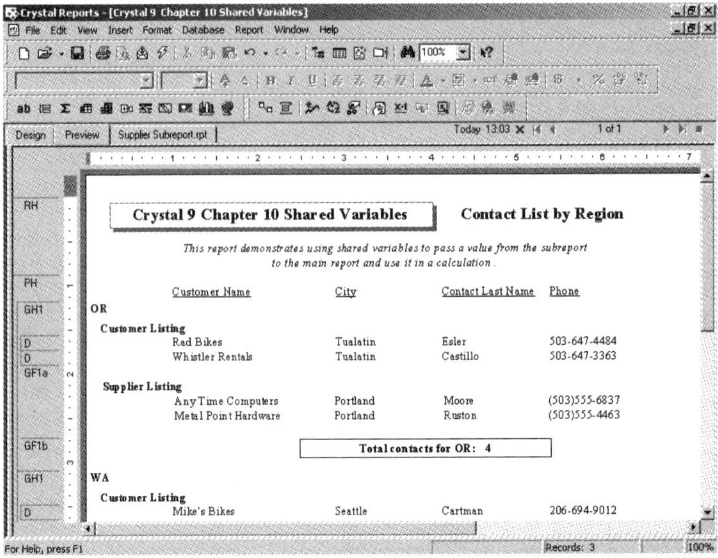

FIGURE 10-21 *Preview the report and see the value for vrTotalCust includes the count of both main and subreport customers.*

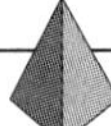

TIP

If you declare the shared variable in the main report, it can be accessed by multiple subreports. If you declare a shared variable in a subreport, it can be accessed by the main report, but not by any other subreports.

Summary

Subreports provide extensive flexibility for your reports and can help you overcome some fairly common database linking issues. By being able to have two separate reports formatted together into one, you are not limited in what information you can combine on one report. Keep in mind, though, that although there is no limit to the number of subreports you can have in one main report, a subreport cannot contain a subreport.

Chapter 11

Any Crystal Report you create can contain a cross-tab object. The cross-tab object can be in addition to the rest of the information on the report, to show a portion of the reports data in a grid-like format. A cross-tab can also be the sole representation of data in a report by either hiding or suppressing other report sections, or just not inserting detail line fields.

Identifying Potential Cross-Tab Data

Depending on the data you want a report to present, you may decide that a cross-tab is an effective representation, especially when you want to compare data or look at one field next to another. Cross-tabs display data in a row and column format, but unlike a basic spreadsheet format, the junction of each row and column can contain another database field or a summary field. Cross-tabs often display lists of data in a more concise format, so that you can view and analyze more data without having to page through a long report.

You insert a cross-tab into a report as an object. You can create a cross-tab in a subreport and then insert the subreport into the main report. Often, using a cross-tab enables you to display data in a more organized or concise fashion than would be possible if you were just listing the data on a report. Crystal Reports has many formatting options for cross-tabs that make them versatile tools. They do have limitations, but with some creative thinking and the tips in this chapter, you'll be able to put most any data into a cross-tab and make it look the way you want.

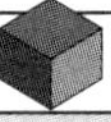

NOTE

Cross-tabs work great for displaying dates across columns, and using them is much easier than writing the dozens of formulas that would be necessary without the cross-tab.

Adding a Cross-Tab to a Report

You can add a cross-tab to an existing report to enhance it, by displaying the same or additional data in the summarized cross-tab format. You can also design a report that contains only a cross-tab, by inserting only the cross-tab object and not any database fields.

Any reports that you describe using the word "by" usually make good cross-tab candidates; for example, "Sales by Region," "Quantity of Products by Customer," and "Sales for Employee by Department." Figure 11-1 shows a sample report that contains data for bike sales by region. The report groups data by region and then by product name. This report shows the quantity of each different bike type ordered for each region.

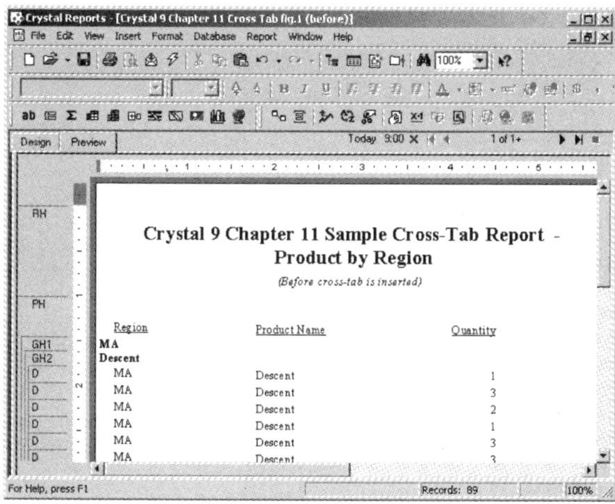

FIGURE 11-1 *This report is a good candidate for adding a cross-tab, which would display the summary data in a much more compact and easy-to-read format.*

You have two options for how to make this report's data shorter and easier to read. One option is to create a drill-down report by hiding the Details section. The report would then show the quantity of each bike model ordered in each region. This makes a nice report, but it's still possibly longer than you would like and does not give as much detail with one glance.

Inserting a cross-tab for this report creates a column-and-row display of the data (see Figure 11-2). Some find this type of display easiest to read and interpret.

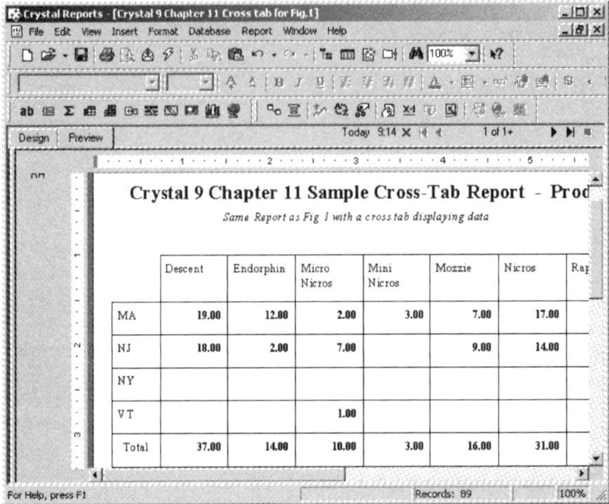

FIGURE 11-2 *Creating a cross-tab and inserting it into the report in Figure 11-1 shows much more data in the same amount of space, and may be easier to analyze.*

Creating the Cross-Tab

To begin creating a cross-tab for a report, click the Design tab and then open the Cross-Tab Expert dialog box. To do this, either select Insert, Cross-Tab or click the Cross-Tab button 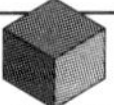.

With the Cross-Tab Expert dialog box open (see Figure 11-3), select fields from the Available Fields list for the Columns, Rows, and Summarized Fields areas. Selecting a field from the Available Fields list and then clicking the appropriate button on the right side of the dialog box moves the field to that list.

> **NOTE**
>
> You can drag and drop fields to put them in the appropriate boxes in addition to using the buttons on the Cross-Tab Expert.

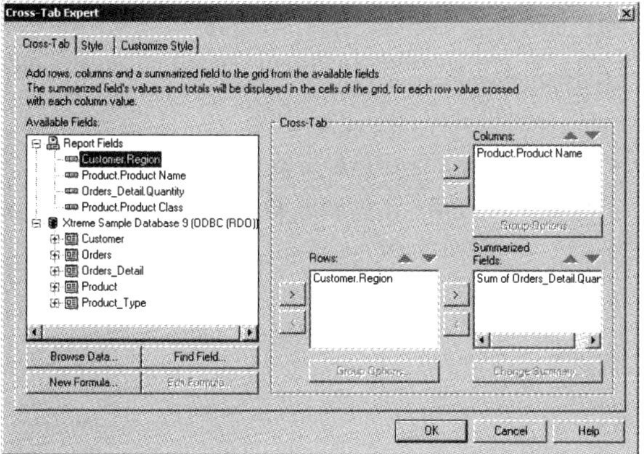

FIGURE 11-3 *Use the Cross-Tab tab of the Cross-Tab Expert dialog box to set the rows, columns, and summarized fields for your cross-tab object.*

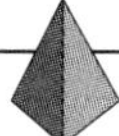

TIP

There is no limit to the number of fields you can have in the Rows, Columns, and Summarized Fields areas.

Inserting fields into cross-tab sections is straightforward. In addition to database fields being available to insert into a cross-tab, you can use formula fields already built in the report, or click the New Formula button to open the Formula Workshop and build a formula.

If a formula does not show up in the Available Fields list, this means that the formula processes after the cross-tab. To force that formula to process before the cross-tab and be available to use in the cross-tab, you must insert the formula onto the report in a section that processes before the cross-tab. For example, if the cross-tab is in the Group Footer, the formula would need to be in Details or above. Or, you could move the cross-tab to a Group Footer #1b and insert the formula into Group Footer #1a. Group Footer #1a could be suppressed so that you do not see the value printing on the report. Cross-tabs are now able to process either first or second pass, as described in Chapter 7. Due to the ability of a cross-tab to process during the second pass (WhilePrintingRecords) formulas that also process during that pass can be included in cross-tabs.

The next two sections discuss customizing a generic cross-tab.

Setting the Group Order and Sum Function

The column and row areas of the cross-tab are considered the groups. With either of these fields selected in the Cross-Tab Expert dialog box, the Group Options button becomes available. Click this button to open the Cross-Tab Group Options dialog box, shown in Figure 11-4, in which you can change the order in which the group data prints on the report and create a custom name, just as you learned in Chapter 5.

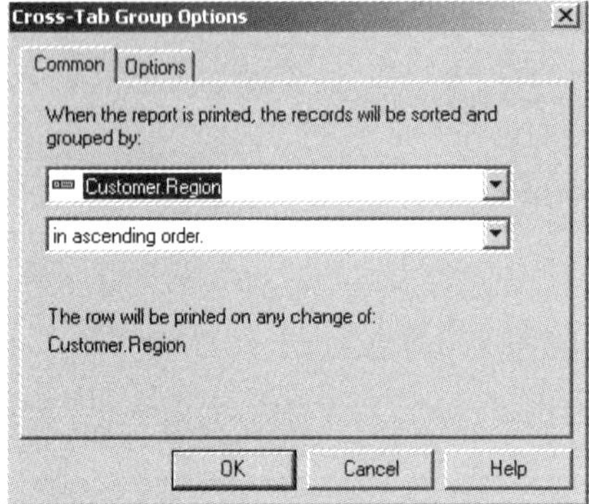

FIGURE 11-4 *Use the Cross-Tab Group Options dialog box to set the group order and a customized name.*

If you select a field in the Summarized Fields list of the Cross-Tab Expert, the Change Summary button becomes available. Clicking it opens the Edit Summary dialog box, which allows you to change the summary operation (see Figure 11-5). New functionality here allows you to show the summarized field as a percentage of a grand total or higher-level group.

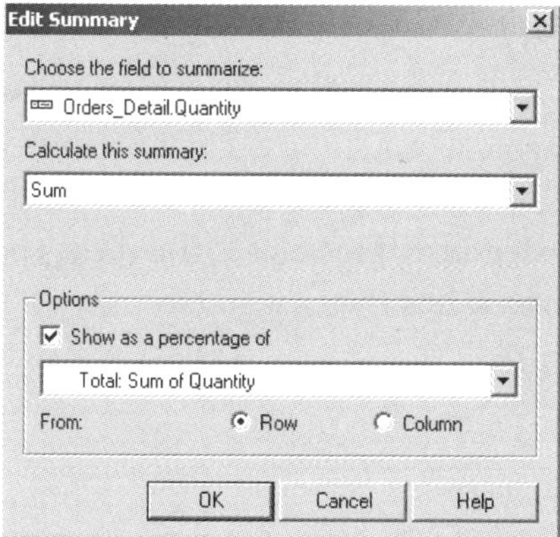

FIGURE 11-5 *Change the summary field, operation, or show as a percentage of another total using the Edit Summary dialog box.*

Cross-Tab Options

There are several options available in the Cross-Tab Expert depending on what field you have selected in the Available Fields or Cross-Tab area: a column, row, or summarized field.

- ◆ **Remove.** Select a field and click Remove to remove it from the cross-tab.

- ◆ **New Formula.** Click this button to launch the Formula Workshop and write a new formula. The formula is added to the Available Fields list and can be inserted into a cross-tab section as a row, column, or summarized field.

- ◆ **Edit Formula.** Select a formula from the Available Fields list and then click this button to open the Formula Workshop and edit the formula.

- ◆ **Browse Data.** Click this button to browse the field data for a field.

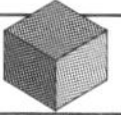 **NOTE**

Remember, as stated earlier, that if a formula is processed after the cross-tab (in the same section or below the cross-tab object), that formula might not be available to the cross-tab unless you insert it onto the report in a section above the cross-tab and refresh the report once to force it to process.

Insert Cross-Tab on the Report

After you have selected columns, rows, and summarized fields, the cross-tab is complete and you can insert it into the report. Formatting options are available on the Style and Customize Style tabs, covered in the next section. For now, click the OK button in the Format Cross-Tab dialog box. This closes the dialog box and attaches the cross-tab object to your pointer. Click the Design tab where you want to insert the cross-tab.

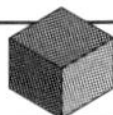

NOTE

You can only place a cross-tab in the Report Header/Footer or Group Header/Footer sections.

The cross-tab placeholder (which does not contain any data) is displayed on the Design tab where you inserted the object (see Figure 11-6). Click Preview to view your cross-tab with actual report data. When you preview the report, you will see the cross-tab in the section you placed it with all the corresponding data (see Figure 11-7).

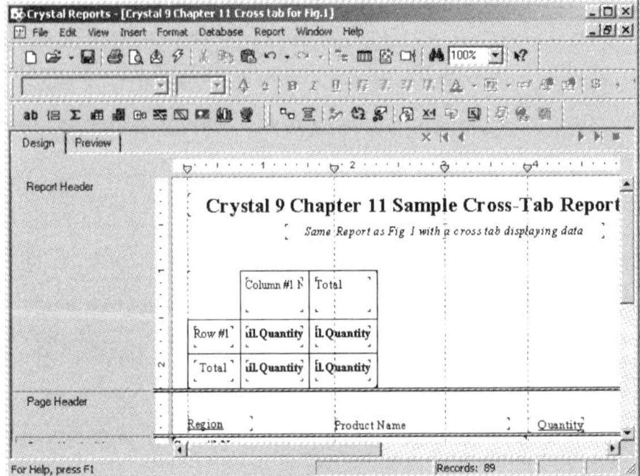

FIGURE 11-6 *Insert the cross-tab in the section you want it to print in.*

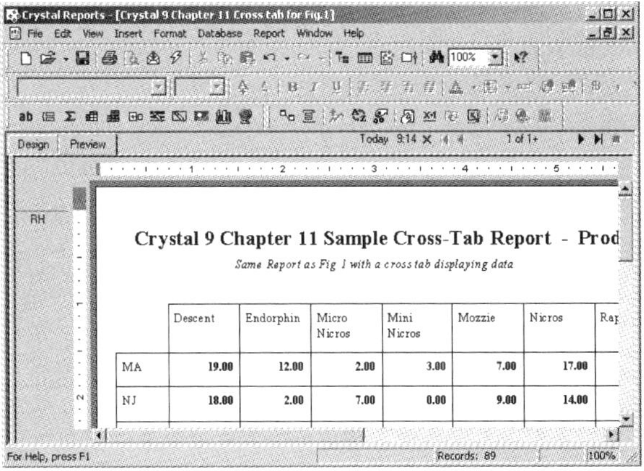

FIGURE 11-7 *The cross-tab object contains your data in rows and columns in the Preview tab.*

Once your cross-tab is on your report, you can move it into a different section. If you move the cross-tab from the Report Header to the Group Header, the cross-tab would contain only information for the group, and the report would have one cross-tab per group.

The cross-tab can be edited at any time to change fields displayed in the cross-tab or to manipulate formatting options. Select the cross-tab, right-click in the upper-left corner, and select Cross-Tab Expert.

Cross-Tab Formatting

You have many options for formatting your cross-tab to look just the way you want. Some options are conventional and listed in the Style and Customize Style tabs, whereas others are a bit less obvious.

Using the Style and Customize Style Tabs

You'll find the first set of options on the Style tab of the Cross-Tab Expert dialog box (as shown in Figure 11-8). Select a formatting option to see the preview of that formatting option in the right-hand panel. Most of these options involve cell borders and color to help separate your data from the totals and column headings.

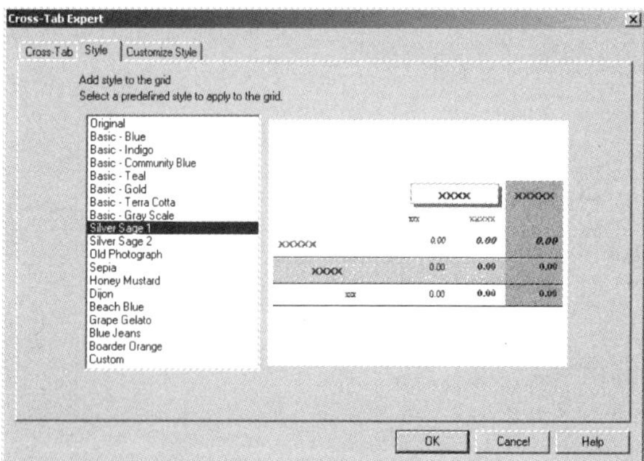

FIGURE 11-8 *Select a grid format and color scheme from the style choices, or customize your own by using the Custom choice.*

Regardless of which style you select, you can set many different formatting options on the Customize Style tab (see Figure 11-9):

◆ **Background Color.** Select a field and set the background color for each field.

◆ **Suppress Subtotal and Suppress Label (under Group Options).** Select a group in the Columns or Rows area for these options to become available. They suppress the subtotal for the group selected and suppress the group label, respectively.

◆ **Alias for Formulas.** Set an alias for a field used in formulas with the GridRowColumnValue function. (See the sidebar "Setting a Field Alias and Using the GridRowColumnValue Function," later in this chapter, for an explanation of this function.)

◆ **Show Cell Margins.** Uncheck this option to eliminate cell margins around each cell. This makes the cross-tab much smaller, with little or no space around each value in the cross-tab.

◆ **Indent Row Labels.** Check this option to indent the row label instead of using grid lines.

◆ **Repeat Row Labels.** Check this option to repeat the row labels on the next page if the cross-tab does not fit on one page and spills over to the following page.

◆ **Keep Columns Together.** Check this option to prevent a column being split over two pages. If a column does not fit on one page, the entire column is printed on the following page.

◆ **Column Totals on Top.** Check this option to list for each group the column totals on top of the columns rather than at the bottom.

◆ **Row Totals on Left.** Check this option to list the row totals on the left after the row names rather than on the far right.

◆ **Suppress Empty Rows.** Check this option to suppress any empty rows.

◆ **Suppress Empty Columns.** Check this option to suppress any empty columns.

◆ **Suppress Row Grand Totals.** Check this option to suppress the grand total for each row.

◆ **Suppress Column Grand Totals.** Check this option to suppress the grand total for each column.

◆ **Format Grid Lines.** Click this button to access options to format the grid lines on your cross-tab (see Figure 11-10).

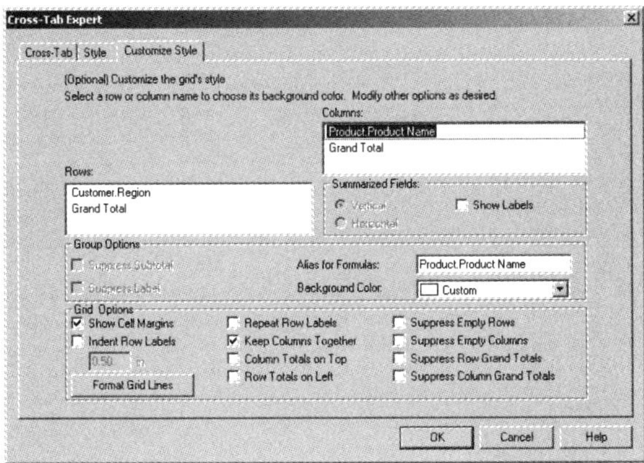

FIGURE 11-9 *More formatting options are available on the Customize Style tab of the Cross-Tab Expert dialog box.*

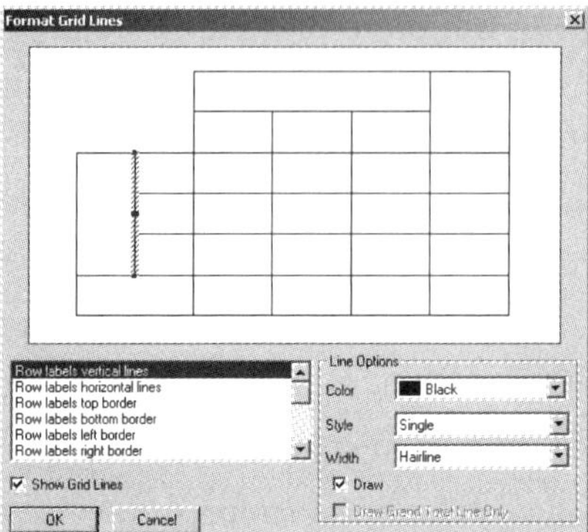

FIGURE 11-10 *Customize the grid for your cross-tab by selecting Custom on the Style tab and then clicking the Format Grid Lines button on the Customize Style tab.*

Format Editor and Options

To format the overall look and functionality of the cross-tab after it is on your report, right-click the cross-tab in its upper-left corner in either the Design or Preview tab. From the shortcut menu, choose Format Cross-Tab. This opens the Format Editor dialog box, in which you can make large-scale changes to the cross-tab (see Figure 11-11).

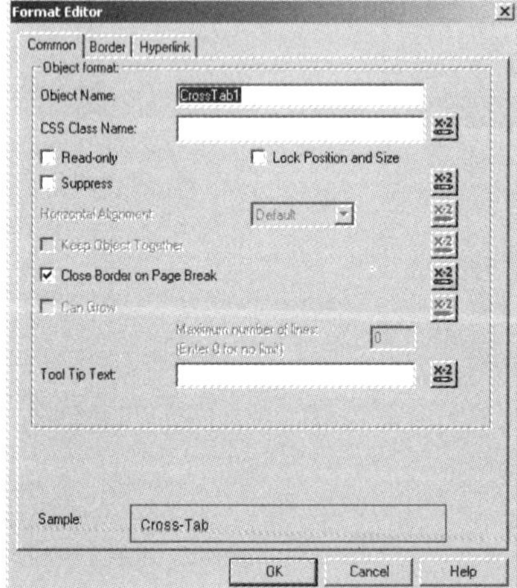

FIGURE 11-11 *Use the Format Editor to format the cross-tab.*

From the shortcut menu for the cross-tab, you have several more options for manipulating or adding to a cross-tab:

◆ Open the **Cross-Tab Expert.**

◆ **Format Cross-Tab.** Opens the Format Editor dialog box, in which you can change basic formatting options for the cross-tab object.

◆ **Group Sort Expert.** Opens this expert so that you can sort the groups based on summary values.

◆ Add a **Chart** or **Map** based on the cross-tab data.

◆ **Pivot Cross-Tab.** If the cross-tab does not fit well on the page, pivoting it will switch the rows and columns.

◆ **Move—Forward or To front.** If you have one object on top of another (overlapping), then you can designate which one is in front and which is in back.

◆ **Size and Position.** Enables you to manually set the exact size and position of the cross-tab object on the report.

Advanced Formatting Options and Hints

Cross-tabs provide an excellent format for displaying data on reports, but sometimes they appear to fall short on versatility or overall functionality. By using creativity and pushing Crystal Reports functionality to the maximum, some of the cross-tab reports I have created amaze me.

This section includes some simple ways to format fields of a cross-tab to behave the way you might want, edit column headings, and then get downright sneaky by combining functionality to make the object do exactly what you want.

Format Fields

Right-click any field in a cross-tab and then select Format Field in the shortcut menu to open the Format Editor for that field type. Format the field to your specifications, which includes writing any conditional formulas in the Format Editor. The Highlighting Expert is available for all within the cross-tab, providing some easy conditional formatting options.

Change the size of any field in the cross-tab by selecting the field and using the resizing handles. Resizing one object will resize all like objects the same. This applies to fields and column and row headings as well.

Customize Row or Column Names

There are two ways to customize row or column names in a cross-tab. The first is to write a formula using the Formula Workshop that displays the name desired for each value, using an If-Then-Else or Select Case type formula, and then base the row or column on this formula field rather than on the database field.

A new option is to write a conditional formula for the Display String option on the Common tab of the Format Editor for the field you want to edit. This new function allows you to write a formula to rename or add a display string value to the actual field value. Here are the steps to use this new option:

1. Open the Format Editor for the field that needs formatting.

2. On the Common tab, click the Conditional Formula button (X+2) for the Display String option, at the very bottom of the dialog box.

3. Write a formula to format the field. Figure 11-12 shows a generic If-Then-Else formula. Notice that you must use the CurrentFieldValue function, not the field name, in order for the formula to work correctly.

4. Click the Save and close button to close the Formula Workshop. Click OK on the Format Editor to see the change in the report.

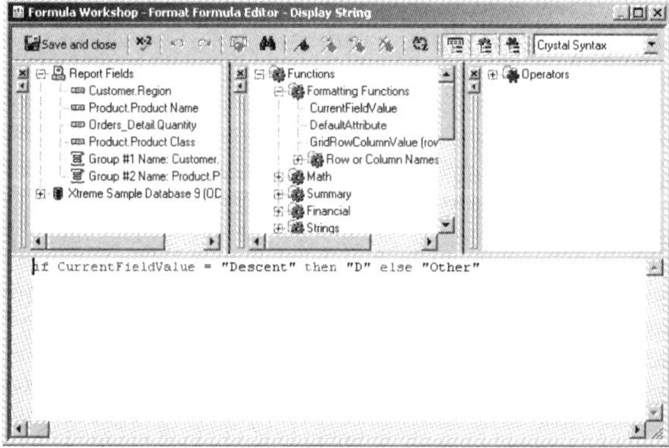

FIGURE 11-12 *Write a formula to format the current field value to read D if the value of the field is Descent.*

Suppress Zero Values

To get rid of zeros in the cross-tab cells, write a conditional formula for the Suppress option for the field. To do this, right-click the summarized field and then choose Format Field from the shortcut menu. On the Common tab, select the Conditional Formula button across from the Suppress check box. Write the following formula:

```
CurrentFieldValue = 0
```

If the value of the field equals zero, it will not print. This makes the cross-tab a bit easier to read (see Figure 11-13).

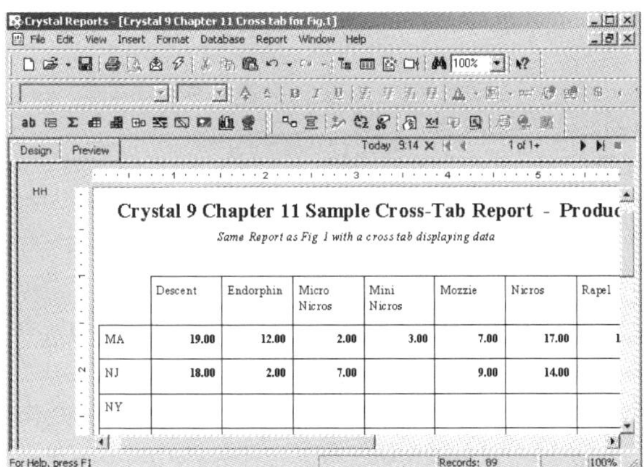

FIGURE 11-13 *By suppressing the zero values, the cross-tab becomes easier to read.*

Using the CurrentFieldValue Function

Use the CurrentFieldValue function in a formula to refer to the current field value of that field. For example, in the cross-tab sample report used in this chapter, the summarized field is Order Amount. When conditionally formatting this field, such as to print a green font color if the value is greater than 50,000, the conditional formula would read:

```
if currentfieldvalue > 50000 then crGreen else crBlack
```

SETTING A FIELD ALIAS AND USING THE GRIDROWCOLUMNVALUE FUNCTION

The Alias for Formulas list box on the Customize Style tab of the Format Cross-Tab dialog box allows you to name an alias for a row or column field so that you may write a conditional formula for the column name. Use the GridRowColumnValue function, which is only available when conditionally formatting fields in cross-tabs and OLAP reports, in a conditional formula. The following formula demonstrates this functionality. A sample report with this formula can be found at **www.bridge-builder.com**. This example uses "Alias Region" typed into the Alias for Formulas list box for the Customer.Region field. Then, conditionally format the font color (or other attribute) of the cross-tab with the following formula:

```
if GridRowColumnValue ("Alias Region") =
"AR" then crRed else crBlack
```

This formula will print the order amount in red if the column heading for the row is AR. By creating the alias and referring to it in the formula, Crystal is able to recognize the column name in order to format the Order Amount fields within that column.

Using the CurrentFieldValue function takes whatever the value is for the field and applies the condition. This function is only available when conditionally formatting fields, and must be used when conditionally formatting cross-tabs rather than the actual field name.

Forcing Formulas Available for Cross-Tabs

As already mentioned in this chapter, some formulas will not be available for use in a cross-tab unless they are processed in the report prior to when the cross-tab processes. This is due to the multipass processing Crystal Reports employs.

When the cross-tab processes is dependent on the actual formulas fields, if there are any, included in the cross-tab. A cross-tab with recurring and simple totaling formulas will process during the first pass or the evaluation time named WhileReadingRecords. Including any print time formulas in a cross-tab, or formulas that are processed during the WhilePrintingRecords evaluation time, will force that cross-tab object to process during the second WhilePrinting-Records pass. This allows the formula to be processed and then the cross-tab to be built using the formula value.

When building a cross-tab you may not see all formulas listed in the available fields list box. You can force formulas to be available to the cross-tab by inserting them into a section above the cross-tab object and refreshing the report. Now when you open the Cross-Tab Expert, the formula is available in the Available Fields list.

Add new sections to the report, such as extra Group Header, Footer, or Details sections for the necessary formula fields, and suppress the section so that it does not print and interfere with the look of the report.

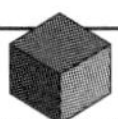

NOTE

Processing a cross-tab in the second pass is not new functionality, for I have built reports using version 8 with this functionality. You must remember to insert the print time formulas on the report in a section *above* the cross-tab object to force them to process before the cross-tab.

Adding Extra Labels

Depending on the structure of your report and/or cross-tab, you may want to add extra labels or headings within the cross-tab. This is not possible using the Cross-Tab Expert, but you can use basic text object functionality.

To "delete" labels or values that you cannot really delete, change the font color to white. To add text objects with the text you want, insert them "on top" of the cross-tab. This takes some patience to get the text object in just the right spot, and the cross-tab must be consistent in its data in order for this to work.

Other Cross-Tab Hints

The following section contains some specific hints for formatting a cross-tab creatively to produce specific, but fairly common, printed results.

- **Add a blank space to a cross-tab.** You may want to separate summarized values in a cross-tab with a space. Write a formula using the Formula Workshop where the value is blank. You might name the formula "blankspace":

```
//the result of this formula is a printed blank space
" "
```

    Add the formula to the Summarized Fields list and suppress it so that it does not print a default value.

- **A cross-tab is too large for one page.** It is possible to suppress grand totals in a cross-tab by selecting the Suppress Grand Totals options on the Customize Style tab of the Cross-Tab Expert. However, a problem might occur even if the grand totals are suppressed, because they still show in the Design tab, although shaded to show they will not print on the Preview tab. This could cause a problem if you are trying to fit a large cross-tab on one page. Select the grand total fields by clicking one of them once with your mouse, and then use the resizing handle to resize the field as short as possible. It does not matter that you can no longer read the text, because it is suppressed anyway. Now, hopefully, your cross-tab will fit on one page. Of course, you can also minimize the font size (I have found that a font size of 8 on legal-sized paper is acceptably legible).

◆ **Suppress sections with no data.** Sometimes a large cross-tab may have groups with no data for one month, and you do not want the cross-tab to print a section with column and row headings and all blank cells. Use a conditional formula in the Section Expert to suppress the section containing the cross-tab if the value you are printing is less than 1. Make sure if you use this type of conditional formatting that you also apply similar formatting to any labels for the group so that they do not print if the group is suppressed.

◆ **Use cross-tabs for reports needing date columns.** The easiest way to print data with date columns is by using a cross-tab object. You can create a "mock" cross-tab by writing formulas for each "cell" of a would-be cross-tab. Depending on the complexity of the calculations needed, sometimes this is the only option. With Crystal 9, you are now able to add Running Total summaries as summarized fields in a cross-tab, so this may alleviate some need for mock cross-tabs depending on the complexity of the running total and the number of records being evaluated.

Summary

Cross-tabs provide a different way to view and organize the data on a report. By using a row-and-column format, you can organize a large amount of data so that it can be viewed at a glance. You may find it easier to view comparison type data using a cross-tab object. A cross-tab can be placed in the Report Header, Group Header, or Group Footer section, or it can be placed in a subreport and then inserted into the main report.

Chapter 12

A parameter field prompts the user of the report for information that affects the report. Parameters can be used to affect the data contained in the report, or the title or formatting.

As an example, think of a sales report. The user of the report may want to view sales for only one region at a time. The report can be designed to collect and format the data desired with a parameter field to prompt users for the region for which they want to run the report. The user enters a region, FL for example, at the prompt. The report then collects only data for FL. That same parameter field can be used in the report title so that the title text reflects for which region the report has been run.

When and Where to Use Parameter Fields

Using parameter fields is usually a three-step process:

1. Create the parameter field.
2. Use that parameter field somewhere on a report.
3. Answer the prompt when running the report.

Parameter fields are often used in selection criteria to affect what data the report collects at the time it runs. They can also be used directly in your report, such as in the text object that contains the report title. Parameter fields can be used in formulas on a report, and they can be used in subreports.

Parameter fields can be created using all the standard data types: Boolean, currency, date, date/time, time, number, and string. When answering a prompt produced by a parameter field, the user must enter a value in the correct format for the field type. Providing pick lists helps users by giving them a set of choices, as well as examples of the correct format for the value they supply.

Creating a Parameter Field

Creating a parameter field is the first step regardless of how you plan to use it. This section covers the steps to create a parameter field. The following sections then describe how to use the parameter field in different places on a report.

To create a parameter, you must have a report open. It does not matter which tab you have open, the Design tab or the Preview tab, or how much of the report you've already designed.

To start creating a parameter field:

1. Open the Field Explorer by selecting View, Field Explorer or by clicking the Field Explorer icon in the toolbar.

2. Select the Parameter Fields option in the Field Explorer, and select the New button on the Field Explorer toolbar. This opens the Create Parameter Field dialog box, shown in Figure 12-1.

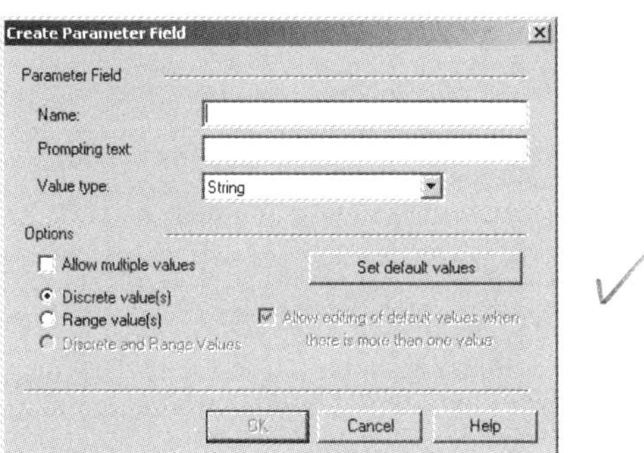

FIGURE 12-1 *Fill in the Create Parameter Field dialog box to create a parameter.*

Completing the Create Parameter Field Dialog Box

You use the Create Parameter Field dialog box to describe your parameter, as follows:

1. Enter a Name for the parameter. It can have any name, up to 65,534 characters.

2. Add a message in the Prompting text list box. This is the message users see when being prompted to enter a value for the parameter. This text can also be up to 65,534 characters.

3. Select the value type of the field from the Value type drop-down list. If the value entered for the parameter needs to work in conjunction with a database field, be sure to select the same value type as the database field's data type.

4. If you want users to be able to enter multiple values at the prompt, select the Allow multiple values check box. If you check this box, the Discrete value(s) and Range value(s) options become available (see Figure 12-2).

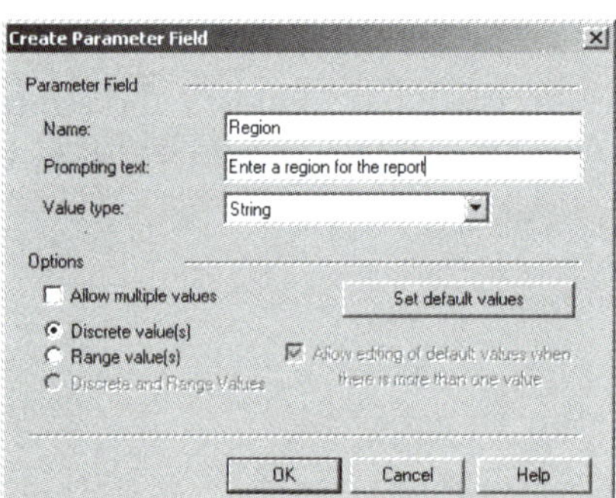

FIGURE 12-2 *Use the Options area to determine what kind of values users can enter for the parameter.*

5. Select Discrete value(s) if you want the prompt to accept only single values, not ranges. Select Range value(s) if you want the prompt to accept the start and end values of a range. Or, select both radio buttons if you want to allow users to enter both kinds of values.

6. Click the Set default values button if you want to set a default or specify a pick list of values. This opens the Set Default Values dialog box, shown in Figure 12-3.

NOTE

Selecting the Allow editing of default values when there is more than one value check box of the Create Parameter Field dialog box allows users to type their own value at the prompt rather than having to pick a value from the list. Clearing this check box forces users to select a value from the list.

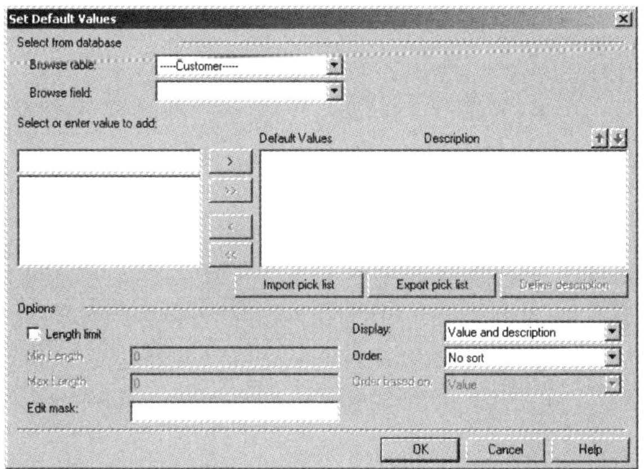

FIGURE 12-3 *Open the Set Default Values dialog box to create, import, or export a pick list for the parameter field.*

Creating a Pick List with the Set Default Values Dialog Box

The Set Default Values dialog box provides many options for creating a pick list, as well as controlling what users may enter as a response to a prompt. Use the following steps to select default values and create a pick list for the parameter.

1. Set the Browse table and Browse field drop-down list boxes by selecting the table and the field on which you want to base your parameter field. Once you select the table and field, the Select or enter value to add area fills with a list of the values found in the field from your database.

2. Use the arrow buttons to move individual or all values from the list to the Default Values list (see Figure 12-4). The items in this list appear in the prompt dialog box when users run the report.

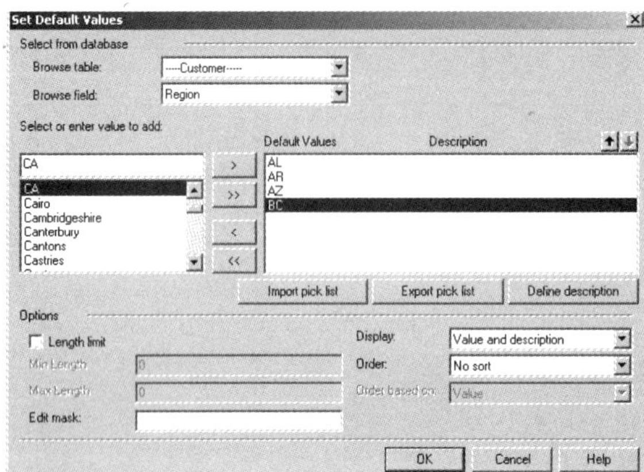

FIGURE 12-4 *Once you select a field in Browse field list, values from that field in your database appear in the Select or enter value to add list.*

3. Click the Import pick list button to import an existing pick list. Use the Export pick list button to export a pick list and save it for use elsewhere or in another parameter.

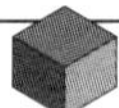

NOTE

To import a pick list, it must be in text file (TXT) format.

4. Clicking the Define Description button opens a Define Description dialog box, in which you can enter a description for each item in the Default Values list (see Figure 12-5).

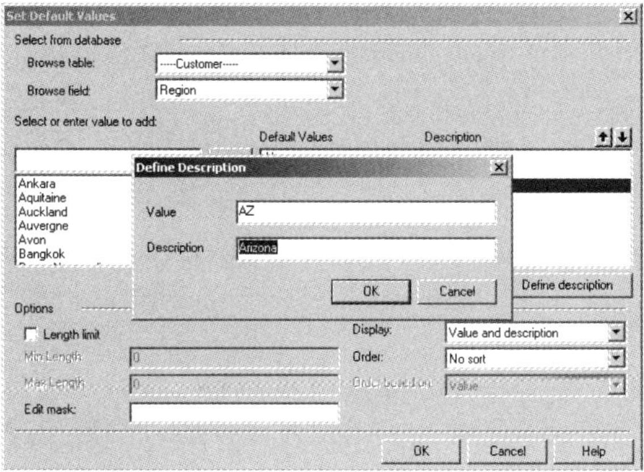

FIGURE 12-5 *Click the Import pick list button to open the Import Pick List dialog box where you can select an existing pick list to import.*

You'll find several more options at the bottom of the Set Default Values dialog box to help users enter values at the parameter prompt. The data type of your parameter field determines which options are available. The following list describes these options:

◆ **Length limit.** Set the minimum and/or maximum value length to be typed into the prompt area. For example, if you set the Min Length value to 5, users cannot enter the name Kyle at the prompt.

◆ **Edit mask.** Enter a string of edit mask characters to limit how users enter values for string parameter fields. See the following section, "Edit Mask Options," which covers the edit mask characters.

◆ **Display.** This option manipulates what users see in the pick list: both the value and description or just the description.

◆ **Order.** Adjusts the order of the values in the pick list. Select whether you want the sort to be ascending or descending for string, number, or dates.

◆ **Order based on.** Designate whether you want the sort based on the values or descriptions.

Edit Mask Options

You can enter any of the following mask characters, or any combination of them, in the Edit mask field of the Set Default Values dialog box. Only use edit mask characters when you are basing a parameter on a string field. Using an edit mask disables the Length limit options.

◆ **A.** Requires entry of an alphanumeric character in the parameter value.

◆ **a.** Allows but does not require entry of an alphanumeric character in the parameter value.

◆ **0.** Requires entry of a digit (0 to 9) in the parameter value.

◆ **9.** Allows but does not require a digit or a space in the parameter value.

◆ **#.** Allows but does not require entry of a digit, space, or plus or minus sign in the parameter value.

◆ **L.** Requires entry of a letter (A to Z) in the parameter value.

◆ **?.** Allows but does not require a letter to be entered in the parameter value.

◆ **&.** Requires entry of any character or space in the parameter value.

◆ **C.** Allows but does not require entry of any character or space in the parameter value.

◆ **. , : ; - /.** Act as literal or "hard-coded" separator characters. Separator characters contained in an edit mask appear in the value entry field of the prompting dialog box. Or, if you place the parameter field on the report, the separator characters appear in the field object, similar to this example: LLLL/0000. This example depicts an edit mask that requires four letters followed by four numbers.

◆ **<.** Converts subsequent characters to lowercase.

◆ **>.** Converts subsequent characters to uppercase.

- ◆ \. Displays the subsequent character as a literal. For example, entering \A in the edit mask would display a parameter value of A. If the edit mask is 00\A00, then a valid parameter value would consist of two digits, the letter *A*, and then two additional digits.

- ◆ **Password.** Allows you to create conditional formulas that require entry of a specific password in order to make certain report sections visible.

Create an edit mask that caters to your needs. To force users to enter a region as two letters, type LL in the edit mask. Add > before the mask (>LL) to convert whatever letters are entered into uppercase.

An edit mask of AAaa would require at least two alphanumeric values, and would accept three or four, but no more than four, values.

The edit mask 00099 requires three digits since the 0 requires the entry of a character. This mask can accommodate four or five digits, since the 9 does not require an entry but will accept one.

Taking Advantage of Displaying a Description

The Display option in the Set Default Values dialog box enables you to display just the value, both the value and description, or the description only for a default value. This can be useful to describe a value field that an end user of the report might not understand. For example, in a headcount report where the user is prompted for which status employees to count, the pick list might list F for full time, P for part time, R for retired, T for terminated, L for on leave, etc. If a user is not certain what these codes mean for the status field, they might not know which value to choose for their report. Adding a description to the Set Default Values dialog box (see Figure 12-6) helps the user to make the right choice. Open the Define Description dialog box by clicking the Define Description button on the Set Default Values dialog box with the field you want to define selected.

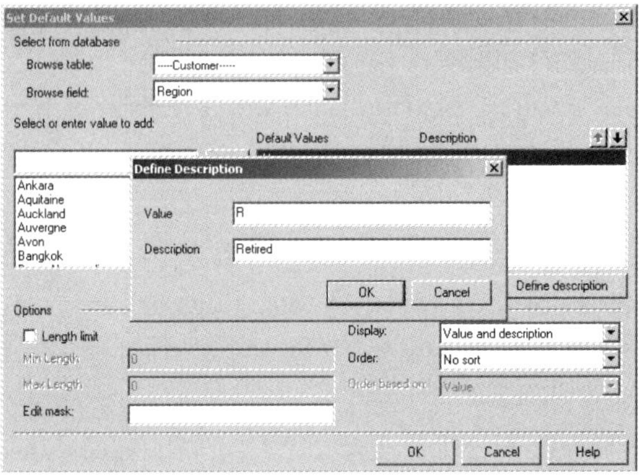

FIGURE 12-6 *Type a description for a prompting value and display both the value and description or just the description.*

Another example of using just the description option is if you are prompting for a percent where the value needed for the parameter is not what you want displayed in the prompting dialog box. Figure 12-7 shows a sales forecast prompt where the value needs to be 1.15, but the prompting value is 15% increase.

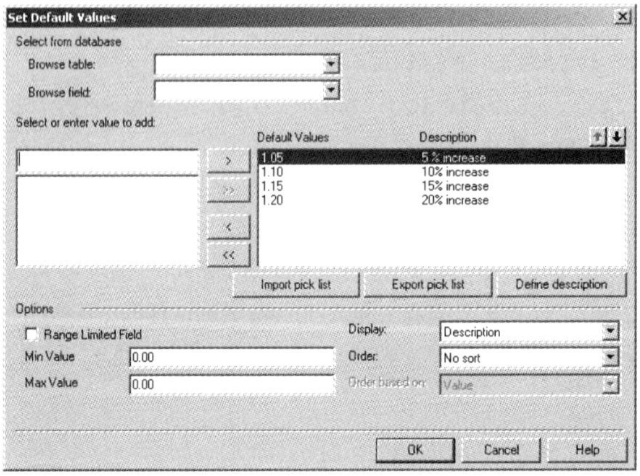

FIGURE 12-7 *Use the Description only option to display only the description for a pick list.*

Using Parameter Fields in a Report

Parameter fields can be used in several places on your reports. Any one parameter field can be used in just one or many different places—Crystal Reports places no limit on the number of times it can be used. Parameters are most commonly used in the selection criteria of a report, so that when the report is refreshed the user is prompted for what data they would like to see in the report. Dates are very useful, as are other fields, for so many reports are the same except for a different date range.

Beyond just being prompted for what data to include in a report, parameter fields are used in the report title and other objects so the report reflects the actual data included in the report. Parameters can also be used in more complex selection formulas to allow for multiple actions or scenarios to be accommodated in one report.

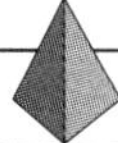

TIP

Parameter fields, like formulas, can be cut and pasted from one report to another. They cannot, however, be stored in the Crystal Repository.

Using Parameters in Selection Criteria

Possibly the most common use of a parameter field is in selection criteria. Using a parameter here allows users of the report to specify what data to include on the report when refreshing the report without having to go into the Select Expert itself.

Once you've created a parameter field, following the previous steps, the parameter appears in the Field Explorer under the Parameter Fields heading. To use a parameter in selection criteria, first open the Select Expert and then follow these steps:

1. Open the Select Expert by clicking the toolbar button or by selecting Report, Select Expert.

2. If no selection criteria have been previously defined for the database field related to the parameter, click the New button to open the Choose Field dialog box. Select the field the parameter is based on and click OK. If

the field already has associated selection criteria, select that field's tab in the Select Expert.

3. In the first drop-down list, select *is equal to*.

4. In the second drop-down list, select the parameter. It has curly braces around it and a question mark in front to designate it as a parameter field, as does the {?Region} parameter in Figure 12-8.

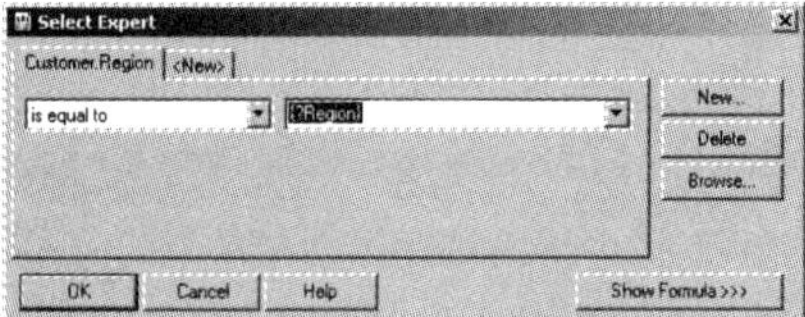

FIGURE 12-8 *Find the parameter field in the list. It may be first, last, or in the middle of the default values listed.*

5. Click OK to close the Select Expert.

Now preview your report. You first see the Enter Parameter Values dialog box. Enter a value to answer the prompt (as shown in Figure 12-9).

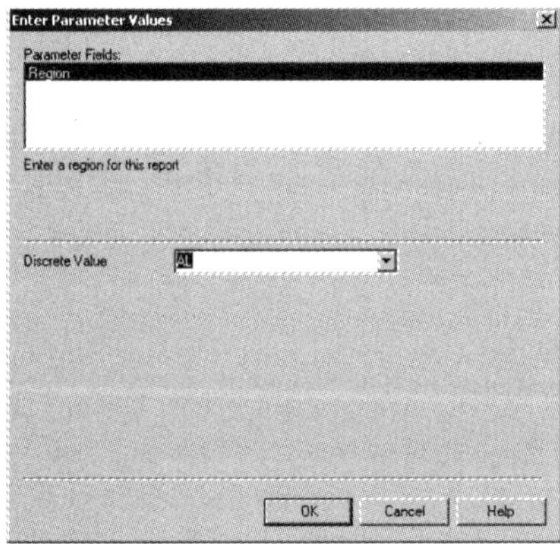

FIGURE 12-9 *Use the Enter Parameter Values dialog box to answer the prompting text and select a value for the report.*

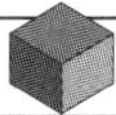

NOTE

The dialog box in Figure 12-9 allows users to enter only one region for the report. If it allowed more than one region, the dialog box would have an Add button so that users could add multiple choices from the list (see Figure 12-10).

Answer the prompt by selecting an item from the pick list. By default, the Allow editing of default values when there is more than one value check box is selected in the Create Parameter Field dialog box. Unless you cleared this check box, users can either select from the pick list or type their own response.

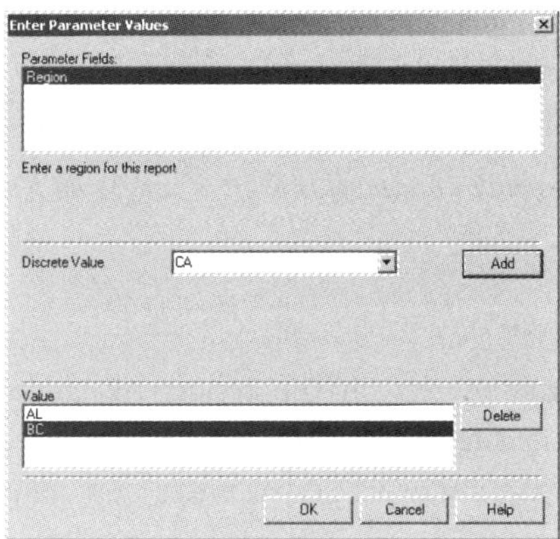

FIGURE 12-10 *When adding more than one value to the prompt, select a value and then click the Add button to move the value into the Value list*

If you selected the Range of value(s) radio button in the Create Parameter Field dialog box, Start of range and End of range drop-down list boxes are available in the Enter Parameter Values dialog box, as shown in Figure 12-11.

If you selected the Discrete value(s) and Range value(s) options in the Create Parameter Field dialog box, then the Enter Parameter Values dialog box has a combination of both prompts.

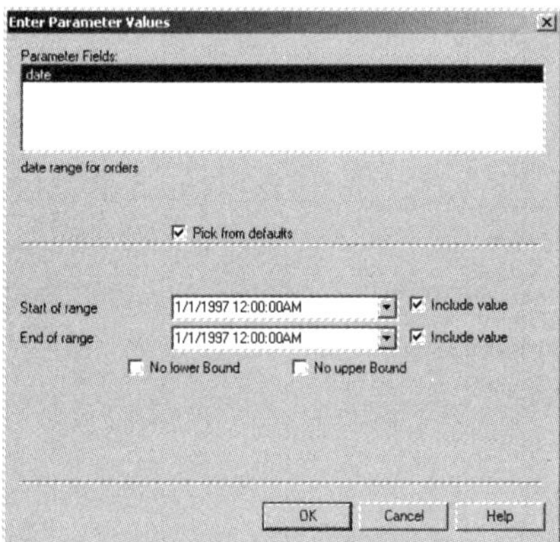

FIGURE 12-11 *Use the Enter Parameter Values dialog box to select Start of range and End of range values for the report.*

To enter different values for the parameter, refresh the report by clicking the Refresh button or pressing F5. This opens the Refresh Report Data dialog box, in which you can elect to use the current parameter values or enter new values (see Figure 12-12).

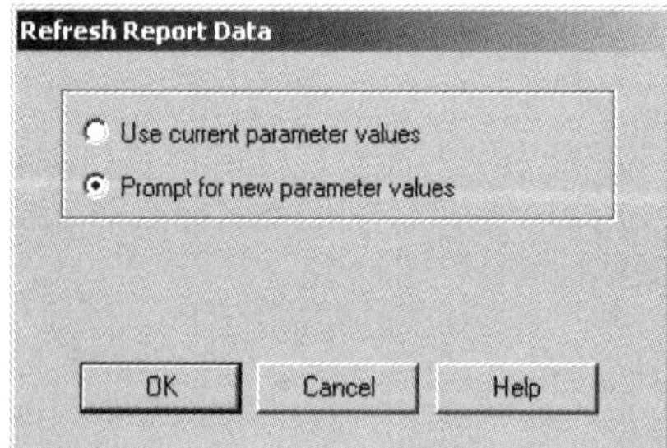

FIGURE 12-12 *Select Prompt for new parameter values to reopen the Enter Parameter Values dialog box.*

If you select Use current parameter values, the report refreshes but you will not be prompted for values. If you select Prompt for new parameter values, the Enter Parameter Values dialog box opens.

NOTE

If you use Crystal Enterprise, any parameters created within your reports will be accessible to users when viewing or scheduling reports. Thus, users viewing or scheduling the report have the ability to select the parameter values using the pick list or any other functionality that you take advantage of when designing the parameter field. Currently, Crystal Reports 9 is not compatible with Crystal Enterprise 8.5 however it will be compatible with Crystal Enterprise 9.

Using Parameters in Report Titles or Other Report Sections

Parameter fields can be inserted anywhere on your report that you might insert any other type of field. Commonly, you'll want the parameter field added to a report title, or to an area on the report that will alert the reader as to what data the report contains.

To add a parameter field to a report title, use a text object for the title and insert the parameter field into that object, as follows:

1. Be sure that the text object is in edit mode, and the blinking cursor is in the position where you want to insert the parameter field.

2. Open the Field Explorer and select the parameter field you want to insert into the title.

3. Click the Insert button or drag and drop the parameter field into the text object (see Figure 12-13). Be sure that you insert the parameter field into the text object and do not just drop it on top of the text object. (See Chapter 6 if you have questions about inserting a field into a text object.)

4. Format the parameter field to match the rest of the text if you want, or to stand out on a different line if you would rather. Preview your report to see the value you used at the prompt reflected in the title.

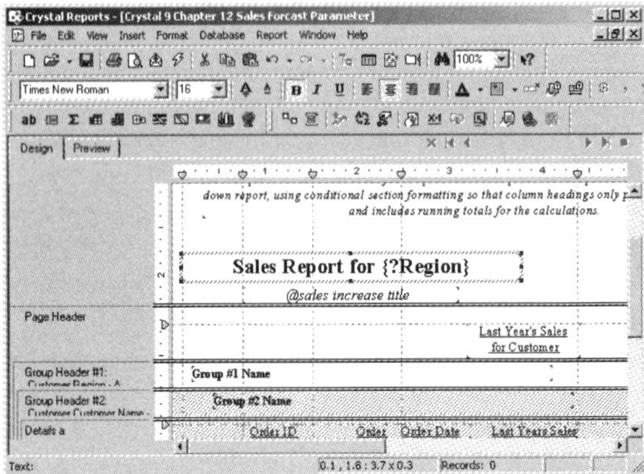

FIGURE 12-13 *The parameter field inserted into the title text object shows the entered value on the Design tab.*

 **NOTE**

Using the parameter field in a report title only works if you have a single value or two separate parameters for a start of range and end of range (such as a separate parameter for the start date and end date). If you have entered multiple values at the prompt, only the first will print. The next section provides a workaround for reports with multiple values entered.

In order to have all the values selected for the report print in the title, you need to write a separate formula to insert into the title or another area on your report, rather than just inserting the parameter field itself. You have many options for writing formulas that use parameter fields. See some samples below, and use your own creativity.

Using Parameters in Formulas

There are many places that you may want to use parameter fields in formulas. The most common is in the record selection formula. You also may want to build formulas to display a parameter value in a report title or other descriptive object.

Adding an "All" Option to the Pick List

As an example, imagine that you want to have an option in a pick list called All Regions because you want users to be able to run the report for all regions. The Select or enter value to add list doesn't contain an All Regions item. You must add this value by typing it in field box above the list and moving it to the Default Values list (see Figure 12-14). Save the parameter. Now you must write a custom selection formula to tell Crystal what to do when users select All Regions at the prompt (see Figure 12-15).

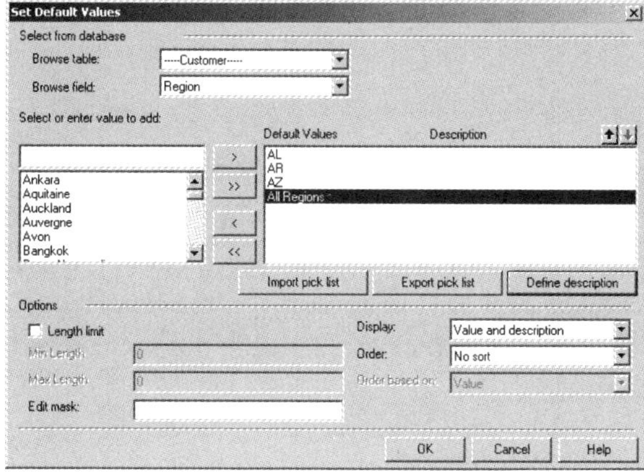

FIGURE 12-14 *Use the Set Default Values dialog box to create an item in the pick list called All Regions.*

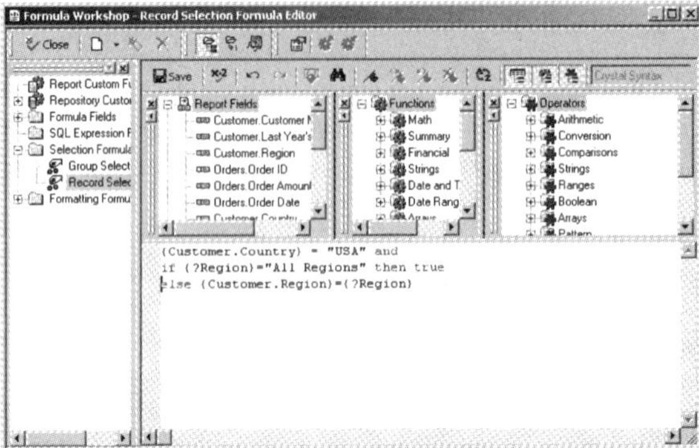

FIGURE 12-15 *Write a custom selection formula in the Formula Workshop to accommodate the All Regions option in the pick list.*

Forecasting Sales

Another example of using a parameter in a formula involves forecasting sales. A formula that forecasts different percentages in sales increases might read as follows:

```
{Customer.Last Year's Sales} * 1.20
```

To make a "what-if" type of report, you could replace the 20-percent (1.20) value with a parameter. This would allow users to input the forecast percentage. First create the parameter. In this example, I created a pick list including descriptions for each percent value (see Figure 12-16). The formula on the report would multiply the Last Year's Sales field by whatever percent value the user picked at the prompt.

```
{Customer.Last Year's Sales} * {?sales forecast}
```

To have this parameter print as part of a report subtitle, you could just insert the parameter field onto the report and format it. But this would print the actual default value of the parameter, not the description. So, for a 10-percent increase, the parameter would print 1.10. To make this print the way I want, which is to print 10% Sales Increase Forecast, I need another formula.

Using a Select Case statement, I set the Case to all the possible values that users might choose at the prompt (see Figure 12-17).

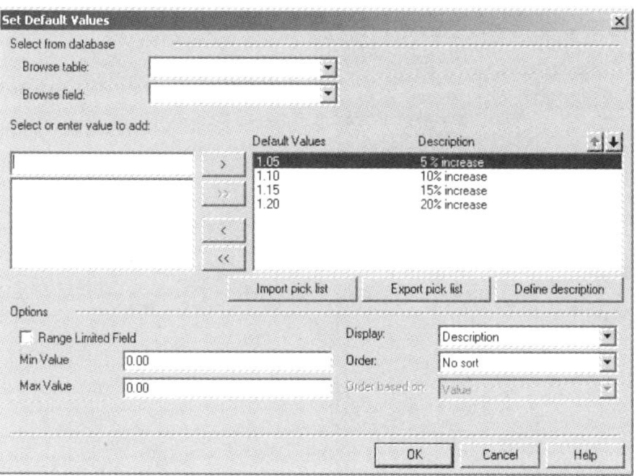

FIGURE 12-16 *Add a description and then set the Display option so that users only see the descriptions at the prompt, not the actual values.*

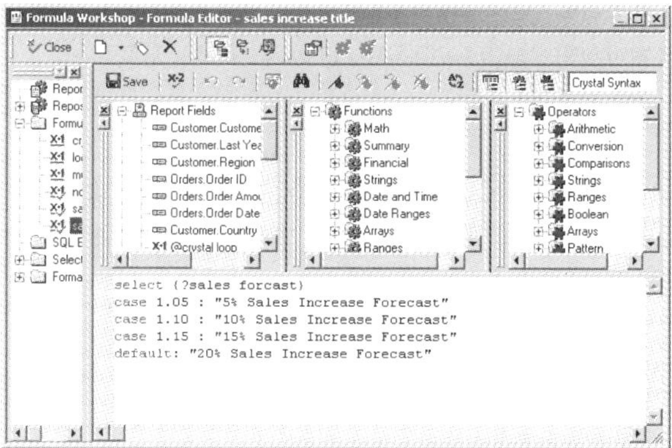

FIGURE 12-17 *Use a Select Case statement to name each value users might enter at the prompt. This will be more informative to print on the report.*

Multiple Prompt Values In a Title

If you want to allow users to select multiple values at a parameter prompt and you want to print all the selected values in the report title, you need to write a formula. To have all of the values print in the title, you could write a loop control structure formula.

Create a new formula in the Formula Editor, as shown in Figure 12-18.

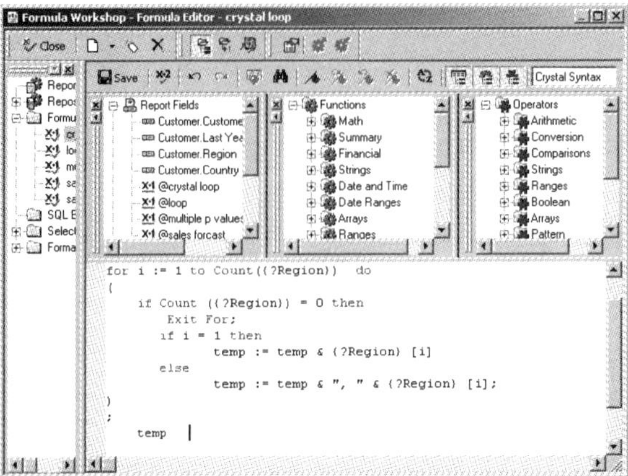

FIGURE 12-18 *Using the For loop, you can have multiple values print in the title of a report.*

As mentioned earlier in the book, you could also use the following formula to accomplish the same result as long as the parameter is a string type.

```
Join({?Region}, ", ")
```

Insert the formula shown in Figure 12-18 into the report title text object and format it to match the text. No matter how many regions users add at the prompt, they all print in the title (see Figure 12-19).

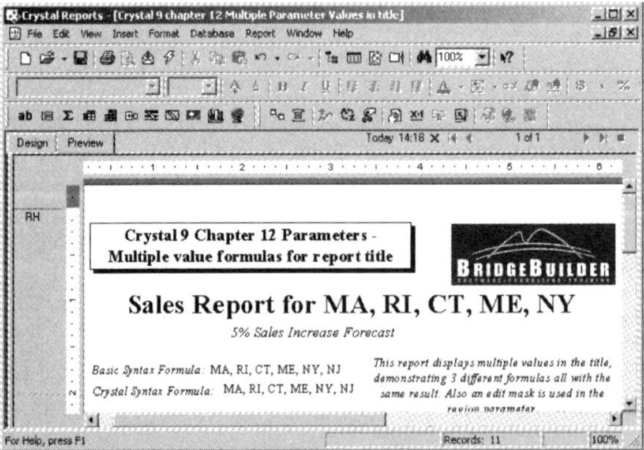

FIGURE 12-19 *The report title includes the formula in Figure 12-18, which prints as many regions as are added at the prompt.*

These are just a few examples of places you can use parameters in formulas in your reports. Be creative and experiment, since adding parameters to different areas can enhance the user-friendliness of your reports.

Use Parameters for Date Ranges

Parameter fields are useful when used with date fields. Reports become much more versatile when you are prompted for a date range for which to refresh a report.

Creating a Date Parameter

Creating a date parameter is similar to creating a string field parameter except that you must know a bit more about the field you wish to use. You need to check whether the field is a date or a datetime field, and if it is a datetime field, you must pay special attention to the time portion of the parameter in order to ensure you collect the intended data for the report. The following are the steps to create a date parameter:

1. Build a new parameter field by opening the Create Parameter Field dialog box from the Field Explorer.

2. Name the parameter appropriately (usually something like date range).

3. Type prompting text and select the field type. This is where you need to know whether the field is date or datetime.

4. Select the appropriate options for the prompt: it's okay for users to enter multiple values at the prompt (like multiple regions), and usually date parameters use a range.

5. Click the Set default values button to open the Set Default Values dialog box.

6. Add two prompting values. Select any value from the Select or enter value to add list, change the time value to 12:00:00 AM, and then add the value to the Default Values list. Select another value and edit this time field to read 11:59:59 PM. Add this field to the Default Values list.

7. Click OK to close the Set Default Values dialog box, and click OK again to close the Create Parameter Field dialog box. Now the parameter is ready to use on the report.

Use the parameter created above in the selection criteria for the appropriate date field on the report. When you refresh the report, you are prompted for the date range you want the report to collect data for as shown in Figure 12-20.

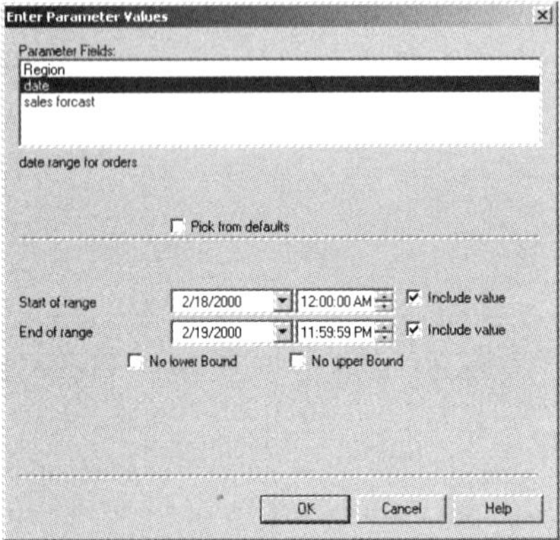

FIGURE 12-20 *Select a default datetime, then use the down arrow to see the calendar to pick actual dates.*

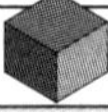

NOTE

The reason to add two default values for datetime fields, one with a 12:00:00 PM time and the other with a 11:59:59 PM time, is so that when selecting a date range, the user can select the first default value for the start date, possibly using the calendar to pick a date, but the default value listed automatically has the correct time. Then, the user needs to pick the second default value, which already has the correct end time, and then use the calendar to pick an exact end date.

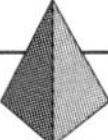

TIP

Uncheck the Pick from defaults option in the Enter Parameter Values dialog box so that the dates and times separate and you can use the calendars to choose dates.

Using the Date Parameter in One Report

Date parameters are used in selection criteria just like other types of parameters are used. Open the Select Expert, selecting the date field you wish to be prompted for. Make this field equal to the parameter value. Be sure that you use the *is equal to* option, not the *between* option. When you are prompted for values, the parameter will prompt you for a date range correctly.

When prompted for dates to run the report for, as long as the Allow editing of default values when there is more than one value check box is checked in the Create Parameter Field dialog box, you can use the down arrow on the date field to select a date from the calendar.

Select dates for both the Start of range and End of range fields. Be sure the Pick from defaults check box is clear, enabling you to use the calendars to select values.

Linking a Subreport via a Date Parameter

Using a date parameter field to link a subreport to a main report ensures that the subreport collects and prints data for the same date range as the main report.

First, build the main report with the appropriate parameter field prompting for a date range in which to run the report. Test the parameter and be sure the report is working as you intend.

Add the subreport to the main report (or build it on-the-fly using the Report Wizard) and use the Link tab to link the subreport to the main report. For the main report field that you are linking from, select the parameter field. In the subreport, select the date field that you wish the parameter to be applied to in the subreport (see Figure 12-21).

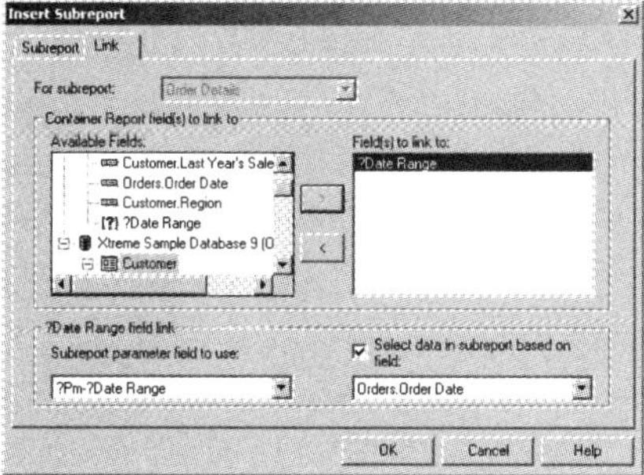

FIGURE 12-21 *Link a subreport to a main report via a parameter field.*

Printing Date Values Entered in the Report Title

Adding a date parameter directly to a report title will not print the dates correctly if there is a range of dates, or more than one date entered. To print the correct begin and end dates in a title or elsewhere on the report, you must write a formula for each the begin date and the end date, pulling those dates from the parameter field. This is actually a very easy solution for printing parameter date values on a report.

1. In the main report, open the Formula Workshop. Use the Formula Editor to build the following formula. Name the formula Begin Date.

   ```
   minimum({?dateparameterfield})
   ```

2. Save and close this formula, and write another, similar formula, and name it End Date:

   ```
   maximum({?dateparameterfield})
   ```

3. Use these two formula fields in text objects or labeled as the begin and end dates for the report.

Summary

Parameter fields lend flexibility to reports. They allow for user input before a report processes, and can then be referred to in other areas of the report through the use of the field itself or the field used in a formula. Parameters allow the user to interact with a report without knowing the intricacies of how that functionality is designed.

Chapter 13

Using charts and maps in your reports can help users understand data by providing a visual representation of the data. Crystal Reports offers 14 types of charts with countless formatting and customization options available such as pie charts, bar graphs, and line graphs. You can also add geographical maps to reports, which show how the report's data distributes across a region.

If your report compares the sales of different bike shops in a particular city, for example, it might be helpful to see in a visual representation which store generates the most sales. While a report showing only the numbers is no less accurate, a graph can have a stronger impact on the reader of the report.

In the same way, a map might add insight to a report if it shows the density of bike shops in cities across a region, or shows and compares sales in different regions. Like a chart, this map could be in addition to the details in the report, providing simply another way to look at the same data.

In this chapter, you will learn how to create charts and maps with the Chart Expert and Map Expert, and how to customize them using the various formatting options available.

Using the Chart Expert

The Chart Expert guides you through the process of creating a chart to be placed on your report. With the Chart Expert, you can add any of the types of charts listed in the Chart type list on the Type tab, shown in Figure 13-1.

Most of these chart types can be displayed in several ways. The chart type format buttons to the right of the list on the Chart Expert allow you to select the format for the chart type you choose. For example, Figure 13-1 shows the six chart type format buttons available for a bar chart. A description of each format appears in the text box below the buttons. Once you insert the chart into the report, there are many more formatting options available. This chapter covers these options a bit later, after you learn how to insert a chart into a report.

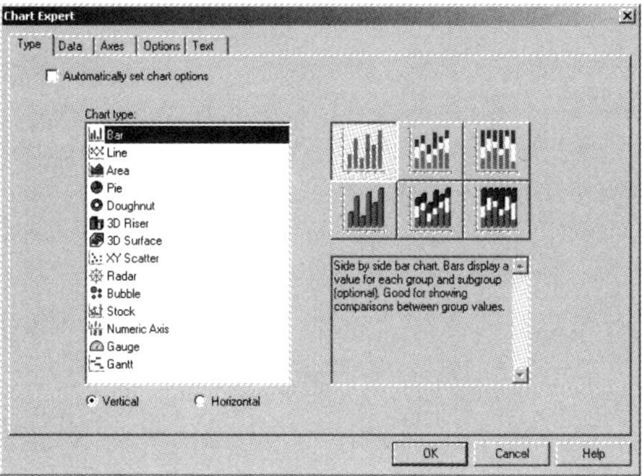

FIGURE 13-1 *The Type tab of the Chart Expert lists many types of charts from which to choose.*

The type of chart you select depends on the data to be analyzed and how many fields you want to compare. For example, if you want to see what percentage of the total number of bikes sold were of each bike type, you could use a pie chart. You could see how big a "pie slice" each bike type accounted for. Maybe 50 percent of the bikes sold were mountain bikes and only 8 percent were competition bikes. If you want to see how many of each type of bike were sold in each region, you might use a bar chart.

You may not know what type of chart to use when you begin, but the Chart Expert makes it easy to create a chart, preview it, and then change it if you want to see what a different chart type would look like with your data.

Inserting a Chart with the Chart Expert

To insert a chart on a report, you use the Chart Expert. This Expert has several tabs with prompts and instructions to follow that produce the chart. To open the Chart Expert and select a chart type:

1. Click the Insert Chart button ▦ on the toolbar or select Insert, Chart from the main menu. The Chart Expert appears with three tabs: Type, Data, and Text. Uncheck the Automatically set chart options checkbox to gain two more tabs, Axes and Options (refer to Figure 13-1).

2. On the Type tab, select in the Chart type list the type of chart or graph you want to insert into the report.

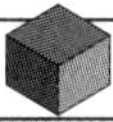

NOTE

Once you insert a chart into a report, you have many options available that allow you to customize the chart structure and work with formatting details such as legend, colors, labels, and more.

3. Most of the chart types have two or more basic format options from which to choose. As you highlight each chart type, the format options appear on buttons to the right of the Chart type list. Click the desired format type button, according to its description directly below the group of buttons. You can come back and easily change the chart type later, so do not hesitate to try a type even if you are not sure it will be the best way to chart your data.

Selecting Data Options on the Data Tab

The Data tab lets you select the placement of the graph within the report, the layout of the graph, and the data for the graph points (see Figure 13-2). You can choose from four available data options, by clicking a button in the Layout area:

- Advanced
- Group
- Cross-Tab
- OLAP

This chapter discusses the first three of these chart options. Chapter 15 covers adding a graph to an OLAP report. They all work essentially the same, with slight differences in this tab due to the different data types.

Using the Advanced layout

Use the Advanced layout for your chart if you want to chart detail data, or if you have not defined any groups on your report. You can have multiple chart values, and can use multiple dimensions to create a 3-D chart. Crystal Reports also allows you to base chart values on running total fields. Select the Advanced option on the Data tab to begin building a chart based on detail level data:

1. To plot points on detail data, click Advanced. The Data tab changes to display the appropriate options for creating this type of chart (see Figure 13-2).

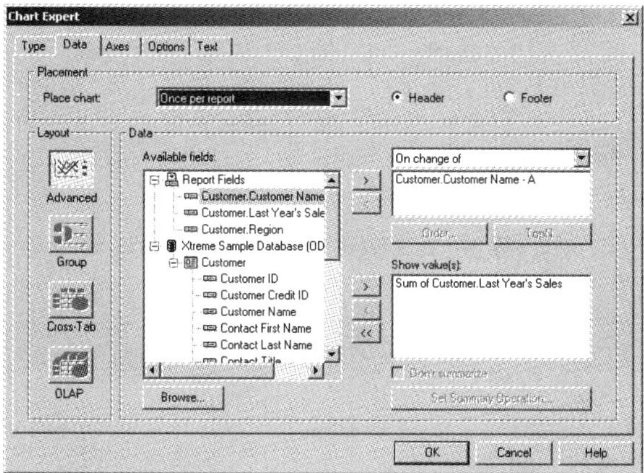

FIGURE 13-2 *The Advanced button on the Data tab lets you select the fields on which to base the chart.*

2. Indicate the field you want to use as a condition for plotting values by selecting a field from the Available fields list, and then clicking the forward arrow button between the field lists to move the selected field to the On change of list. The On change of list is actually a drop down list with other options, but On change of is the default. Once you move a field over, use the drop down list to select the appropriate option for your chart.

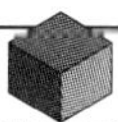

NOTE

Use the Advanced layout option if you want to create a detail chart for each group on a report. Select the For each *group name* option in the Place chart drop-down list so that the chart is inserted once for each group (see Figure 13-3). The field you move over to the On change of list is the field the group is based on, and you will have one chart for each occurrence of this group on the report.

3. Indicate the field values you want to plot in the chart by selecting a field from the Available fields list and using the arrow to move it over to the Show value(s) list. You can plot more than one value, but then you would need to select a chart type that accommodates multiple data points, like a line chart.

4. If your data allows and you want to have Crystal Reports automatically summarize the show value, be sure to clear the Don't summarize check box. Click Set Summary Operation to change the sum operation.

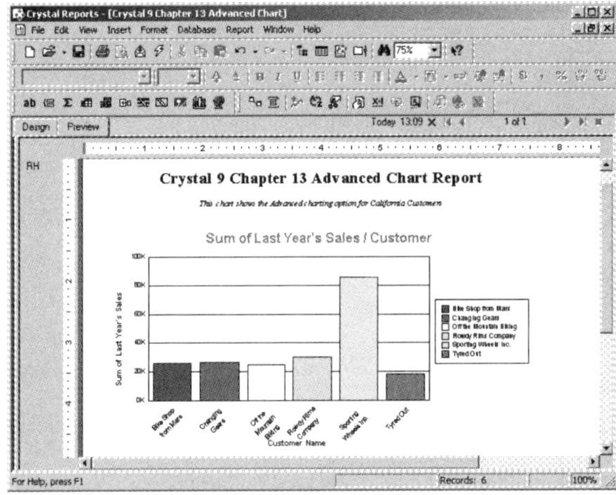

FIGURE 13-3 *This chart uses the Advanced option to chart detail data for California customers.*

Using the Group layout

Use the Group layout option when you have a group defined on your report. This option creates a chart in which each group represents one data point (such as one slice of the pie) with one chart printing for the entire report.

1. Click the Group button. Plotting based on group data means that each group is going to be a data point, a bar, or a slice of pie.

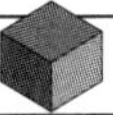

NOTE

If you do not have a summarized group on your report, the Group option is not available on the Data tab.

2. In the On change of drop-down list box, indicate the group field you want to use as the condition for plotting. If you have only one group on the report, you see only one group in the list.

3. In the Show drop-down list box, indicate the summary field value you want to plot in the graph. If you have more than one summary for the group, you can select which one you want to represent the size of the bar, piece of the pie, and so forth (see Figure 13-4).

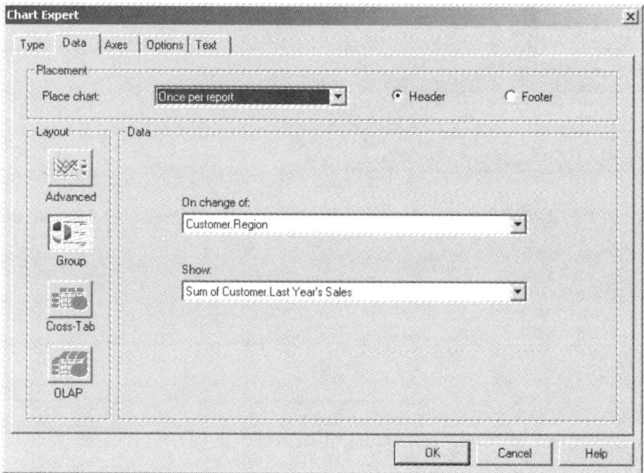

FIGURE 13-4 *The Group option on the Data tab lets you select the groups on which to base the chart.*

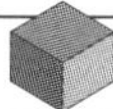

NOTE

If you have only one group on a report, then you can show charts based on that group only once per report. If you have more than one group, you can show charts based on the smaller group at the larger group level. For example, if you have grouped by Country and by Region, you would show a chart based on Country data for the entire report. You could then show a chart based on Region data for each country.

4. In the Placement area, select where you want the chart to appear on your report. Using the Group option, you only have two choices, which are to insert the chart once per report in either the Report Header or Report Footer section (see Figure 13-5).

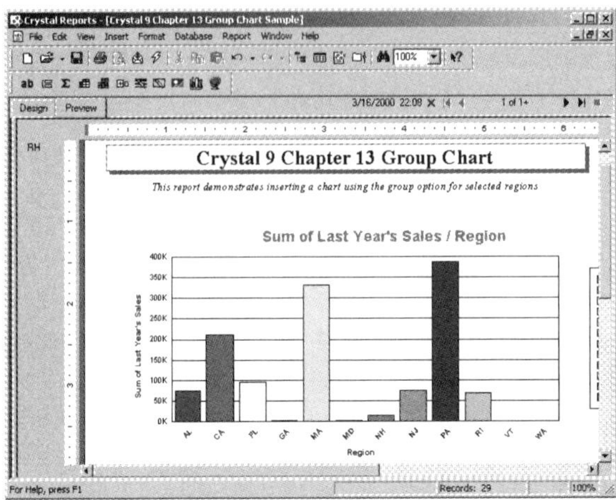

FIGURE 13-5 *Create a group chart to compare a value or summary of each group on one chart.*

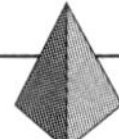

TIP

If you instead choose the Advanced layout, you can place your chart in the Report Header/Footer or Group Header/Footer sections.

Using the Cross-Tab layout

It is possible to create a chart based on cross-tab data on a report. Creating a chart based on a cross-tab uses only the cross-tab data.

1. If you have a cross-tab object selected in the report (in either the Design or Preview tab) the Cross-Tab option will be automatically selected in the Data tab. Otherwise, select the Cross-Tab Layout option.

2. In addition to the On change of and Show fields that appear when the Group layout is selected, a field called Subdivided By appears. This option provides a drop-down list of the rows and columns in your cross-tab, which you select from to appear on the chart (see Figure 13-6).

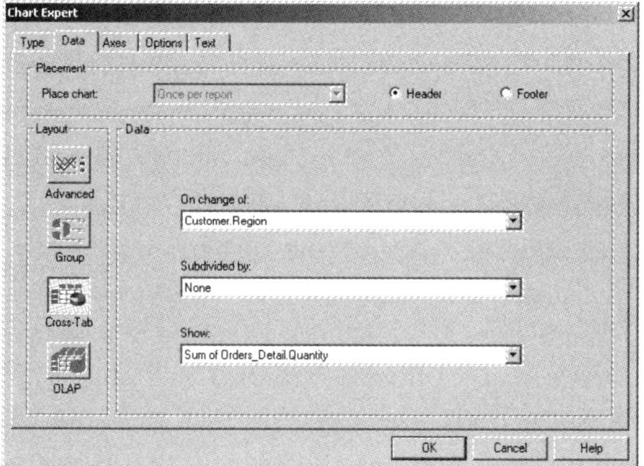

FIGURE 13-6 *The Subdivided by drop-down list contains the cross-tab rows and columns, which you can choose from for your graph.*

Selecting Axis Options on the Axes Tab

The Axes tab lets you select options affecting the chart's axes. You can set options for the gridlines, data values, and number of divisions. The options on the Axes tab apply only to those chart types that have X and Y coordinates, such as bar charts, line charts, and area charts (see Figure 13-7). Pie and doughnut charts do not use the Axes tab.

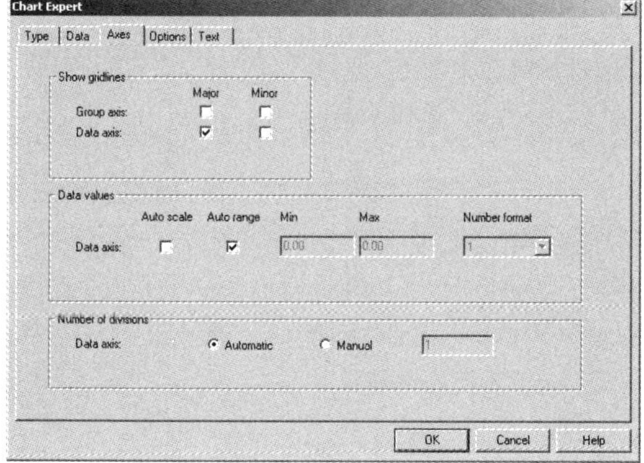

FIGURE 13-7 *Use the Axes tab on the Chart Expert to set options if your chart type has axes.*

To set axes options, follow these steps:

1. In the Show gridlines area, indicate which, if any, gridlines you want to display in the graph. You can display the major and/or minor guidelines for the X axis (group values) and the Y axis (data values). You can also set the Y2 axis (data2 values) for cross-tab or OLAP charts.

2. In the Data values area, indicate whether you want to include only certain data ranges as minimums and maximums. With Auto range selected, the default ranges are used. Uncheck Auto range to set your own range and number format for the axis values. The Number format option allows you to choose from format options such as 1, 1.0, 1K, 1M, $1, $1K, 1%, and more. Check Auto scale to have Crystal Reports set the scale based on what the program thinks will display the data best.

3. In the Number of divisions area, indicate whether you want Crystal Reports to set the number of divisions for the chart, or whether you want to set the number manually. The divisions represent the number of X-axis lines between the lowest value on the chart and the highest. If you choose the Manual option, indicate the number of divisions to set.

Selecting General Options on the Options Tab

On the Options tab, you can select general chart options such as color or black and white, legend options, and labels for the data points (see Figure 13-8).

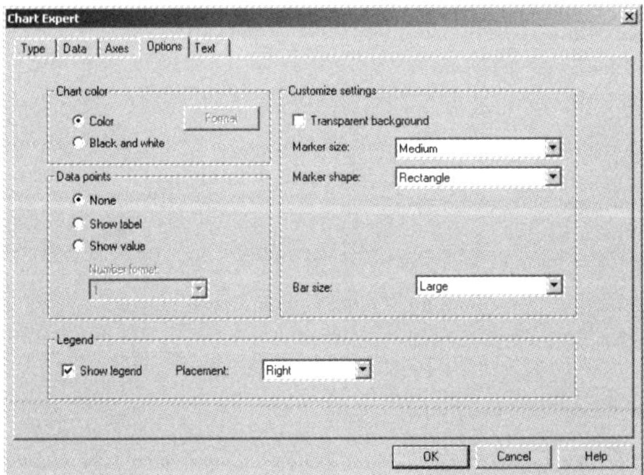

FIGURE 13-8 *The Options tab lets you set options for the general appearance of the chart. This figure shows options for a bar chart.*

To select general options for a chart:

1. In the Chart color area, indicate whether you want the chart to appear in color or in black and white.

2. In the Data points area, indicate whether you would like no label to appear for each data point, the field name as the label, or the value as the label. If you select Show value, you have the option of formatting it by choosing the desired format style in the Number format list.

3. In the Customize settings area, select from the following options (the options available depend on which type of chart you are creating):

   ◆ **Transparent background.** Creates a transparent background so that objects behind the chart can be seen through it.

   ◆ **Pie size (for pie charts).** Determines the size of the pie chart. Choices include: minimum, small, average, large, and maximum.

   ◆ **Detach pie slice (for pie charts).** If you want the largest or smallest pie slice detached from the rest of the pie, select this option.

   ◆ **Bar size (for bar charts).** Determines the width of bars on a bar chart. Choices include: minimum, small, average, large, and maximum.

   ◆ **Marker size (namely for line charts).** Determines the size of markers on a line chart. The option also appears on other types of charts, but the marker size is most apparent on line charts where you see the markers more clearly.

   ◆ **Marker shape (for line and bar charts).** Determines the shape of the marker in the chart. Available shapes include rectangle, circle, diamond, and triangle. For other chart types, the marker shape determines the shape of the markers in the legend.

4. In the Legend area, indicate whether you want a legend for the chart, and where in relation to the chart itself. Choices include upper-right corner, bottom center, top center, right, and left.

 **NOTE**

If your chart is a custom chart, the legend may have a custom placement and layout for the legend. If you are creating a pie or doughnut type chart, it is possible to display percentage and amounts on the chart legend.

Selecting Text Options on the Text Tab

On the Text tab, you enter the text that will appear on the chart itself. You can include a title and subtitle, labels for the group and data axes, and footnotes. You can also set font attributes for each of these items (see Figure 13-9). Crystal Reports enters suggested titles for you based on your chart, which you can change if you want.

1. For each type of text in the Titles area, accept Crystal Reports' autotext; or, clear the Auto-Text check box and either leave the field blank for no text or enter your own custom label.

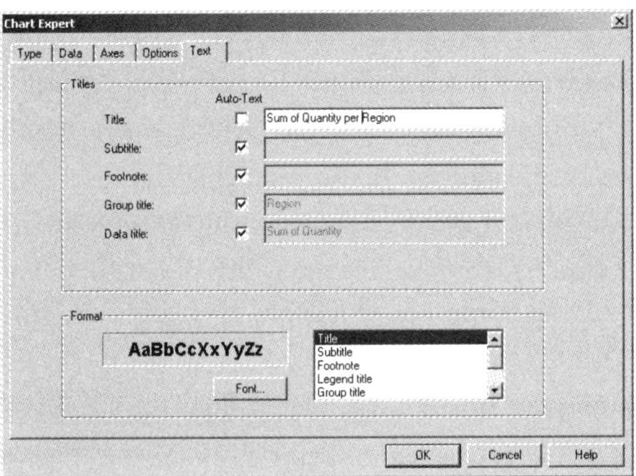

FIGURE 13-9 *The Text tab lets you define the titles, subtitles, and other text that appears on the chart.*

2. In the Format area, select the desired font attributes for each of the items listed in the Titles area.

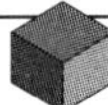

NOTE

Use the Staggered Text check box to stagger the text in your labels. This check box is only active when you have Group labels, Data labels, or Series labels selected in the Format list.

When you finish with the Text tab and all previous tabs, click the OK button on the Chart Expert. Crystal Reports draws the chart and places it in the section you selected in the report. If you select the Design tab, Crystal Reports shows a generic chart of the type you created. To view the real data in the chart, click the report's Preview tab.

You will likely need to adjust the location of the chart. Crystal Reports inserts the chart into the upper-left corner of the section. This placement may put it on top of other information. The chart behaves the same as any other object on a report, so just use your pointer to pick it up and move it or resize it.

Drilling Down on a Chart

Charts have drill-down capability. If you have a chart in which the data represented is a summary or group of any sort, then when hovering the mouse cursor over the desired value in the chart, the drill-down cursor appears. Thus, if you have a bar chart in which the height of the bar is dependent on that region's sales, you could drill down on the bar to see the data that makes up the bar. If your chart contains the detail data, then there is nothing more to see and thus drill down is not possible.

In addition to drilling down on the chart itself, you can drill down on the chart's legend. Hover the mouse cursor over the legend label you want to drill down on and double-click to activate the drill-down tab.

Changing an Existing Chart

Once you create a chart and insert it into your report, you may decide that you want to adjust something small, try a new chart type, or change a field. All chart options are available from either the Design or Preview tabs by simply selecting the chart object, right clicking, and selecting an option from the shortcut menu. If you prefer, you can also get back to the Chart Expert to make changes to the chart by selecting Chart Expert from the shortcut menu.

Formatting the chart object in place, right in either the Design or Preview tab, offers countless formatting options and features in addition to the Chart Expert.

Customizing with Chart Options

Crystal Reports provides countless options for editing and formatting a chart object once it is on a report. All changes to a chart can be made from either the Design or Preview tabs by selecting the chart object you want to edit, right-clicking, and choosing Chart Options. Selecting Chart Options opens a second list of categories of options, each representing a dialog box full of options for changing the chart. The specific Chart Options categories are Template, General, Titles, Grid, and Selected Item.

Formatting Options

Both the Design and Preview tabs have many options available for editing and formatting a chart. Select the chart object and right-click to view the shortcut menu of options. The expandable options are listed and described in the following sections.

- ◆ **Chart Expert.** This opens the Chart Expert in which you can select different data for your chart or change any options in the tabs.

- ◆ **Format Chart.** This opens the Format Editor with Common, Border, and Hyperlink tabs to format the overall cross-tab object.

- ◆ **Chart Options.** Select this option and a submenu opens with an expanded list of chart formatting options. Choose an option from the list to open a dialog box with tabs that is specific to the actual option selected.

- ◆ **Auto-Arrange Chart.** Lets Crystal Reports consider your chart and auto-arrange it as best as it can, based on the type and data in the chart.

- ◆ **Move.** Moves the chart backward or to the back if it is in front, and moves it forward or to the front if it is in back (of other objects on the report).

- ◆ **Size and Position.** Opens the Object Size and Position dialog where you can set the exact location of the chart object on the report.

- ◆ **Select Mode.** The mouse cursor selects any object you click with your mouse. This option is on by default.

- ◆ **Zoom In.** Zooms in to give you a closer look at a portion of a chart. Click on the chart where you want to zoom in by dragging the mouse cursor to select an area to zoom in. A Zoom Out option also becomes available, allowing you to reverse the magnification. Save the data with the report in order to save the chart instance that has been zoomed in or out.

◆ **Save As Template.** Saves the changes made as a user-defined template. You can later base other charts on this template.

◆ **Copy Smart Tag.** Copies the selected chart as a smart tag object for pasting into Windows XP applications.

Select Chart Options from the shortcut menu and a submenu options listing specific options. Each of these options are described in the following sections.

Template

This command opens the Choose a Chart type dialog box, in which you can select a new chart type from the Gallery tab or a custom type from the Custom tab. To have custom charts listed, you must have saved a chart as a template previously.

1. In the Design or Preview tab, select the chart you want to edit. Right-click and select Chart Options from the shortcut menu. The Choose a Chart type dialog box opens, as shown in Figure 13-10.

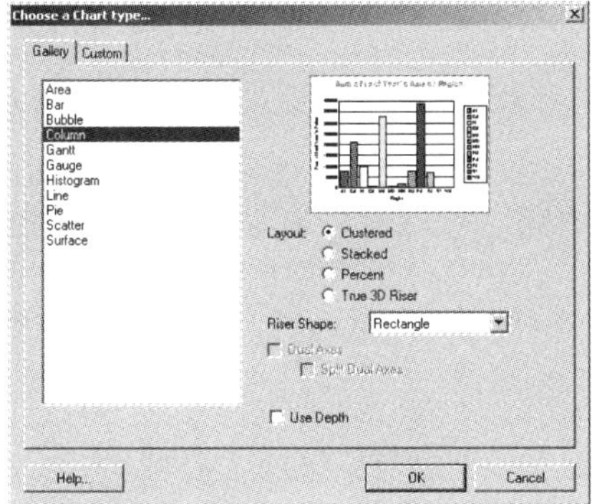

FIGURE 13-10 *The Gallery tab of the Choose a Chart type dialog box provides options for each available chart template.*

2. Use the options on the Gallery tab to customize the chart type selected.

3. Use the Custom tab to select from more options for accommodating black and white charts, large datasets, and more.

4. Once you have made any changes to the chart, just click OK to close the dialog box. Any changes you made automatically apply to the Preview tab.

General

The General command opens the Chart Options dialog box with the following tabs (see Figure 13-11): General, Layout, Data Labels, Numbers, Data2 Options, Look, and Display Status. Each tab has several formatting options, many of which are also available in the Chart Expert.

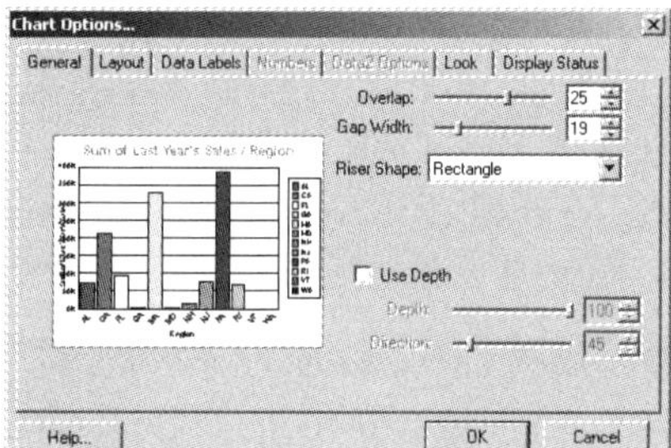

FIGURE 13-11 *Use the tabs to select general chart options based on the type of chart already selected.*

Titles

The Titles command opens the Titles dialog box, shown in Figure 13-12, which looks similar to the Text tab of the Chart Expert. Here, you can change the titles for the chart.

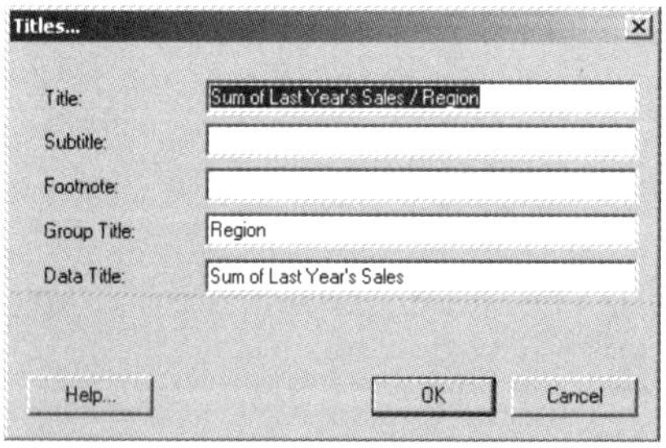

FIGURE 13-12 *Change the titles for your chart.*

Grid

The Grid command opens the Numeric Axis Grids & Scales dialog box with the following tabs (see Figure 13-13): General, Scales, Labels, Numbers, and Grids. Many of these options are available in the Chart Expert, and are laid out again here with more options and functionality.

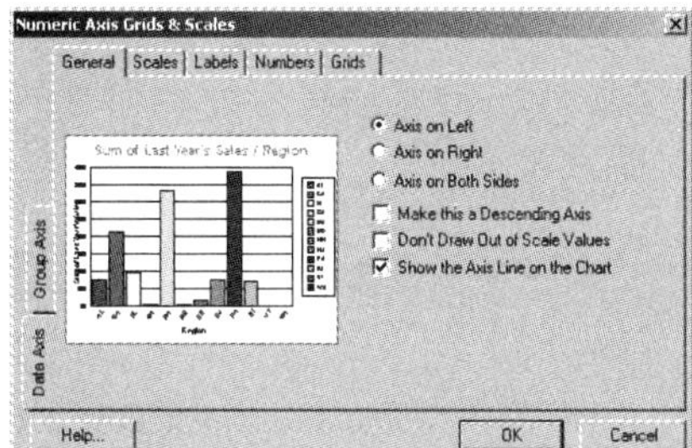

FIGURE 13-13 *Format how the numbers on the chart grid look using the Numbers tab.*

Selected Item

The Selected Item command opens the Formatting dialog box with Font, Line, and Fill tabs, as shown in Figure 13-14. What you had selected when you clicked this option determines what tabs are available. This is where you change the font and color of a title, or a bar, line, or pie slice on a chart.

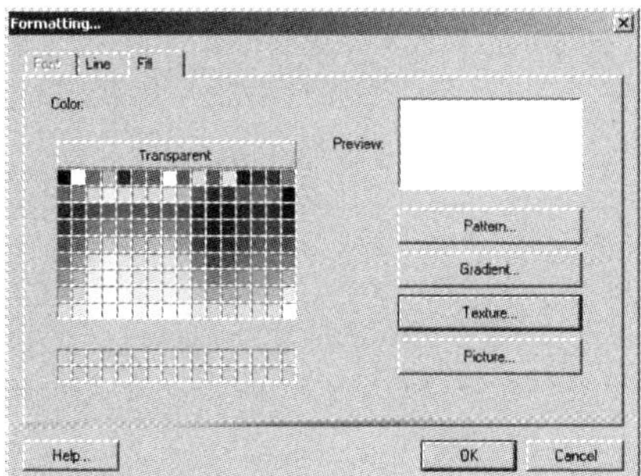

FIGURE 13-14 *Select formatting options for the item selected.*

The Chart Expert provides basic options for creating a chart to add to a report. Once you have added the chart to the report, the Chart Options and Format

Chart provide many editing, formatting, and style options. You can go back to the Chart Expert at any time to make changes to the data included in the chart.

Using the Map Expert

Maps help you analyze report data and identify trends based on geographical data. Once you create a map, you can drill down on the map regions, analyze the data, and format the appearance of the map. You can zoom in or out on an area of the map to see how the data is distributed over a smaller or larger area.

Maps are really only useful if you have geographical data in your report, such as countries, states, provinces, counties, or cities. Just identify the geographical field and the Map Expert draws the map and shows you how the data is distributed within a region or across many regions.

When you installed Crystal Reports, if you selected the default options, you may not have installed all the mapping options. If you encounter a dialog box with a message that you do not have mapping DLLs available (as in Figure 13-15), insert your CD and click OK to install the missing files.

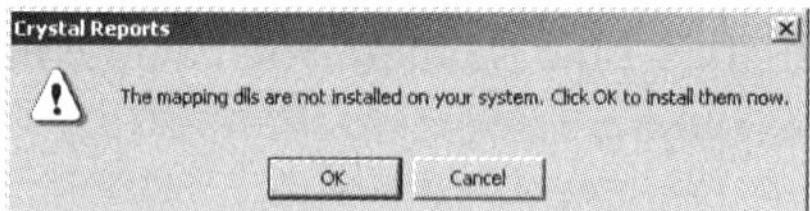

FIGURE 13-15 *Insert your CD and click OK to install all files needed for mapping.*

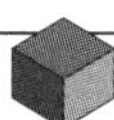

NOTE

If you group on more than one geographical field, it is important that you select them in order from largest (country, at the top of the sort list) to smallest (city, at the bottom of the sort list).

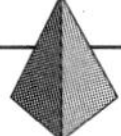

TIP

When creating a group-based map, the report must have a summarized group. The Advanced layout is available to create maps for reports that do not contain any groups.

Layouts and Types of Maps

You can choose from several layouts and types of maps, depending on your data and what you want the map to show. Some map types work much better than others for different types of data. The following sections explain the four map layouts and five map types.

Choosing a Map Layout

Crystal Reports provides four map layouts to choose from, depending on your data:

- **Advanced.** This type of map works well for reports with no groups, or where you do not want to map by the group values.
- **Group.** This map type formats a map based on summary information for a group. The group needs to be based on a geographical field (such as country, region, state, or city).
- **Cross-Tab.** Use this option when creating a map based on a cross-tab object in a report. This type of map, like the Advanced map type, does not require groups or summarized fields.
- **OLAP.** Use this option to base a map on an OLAP grid. This option does not require groups or summary fields.

Map Types

Once you have selected a map layout, you need to select a map type. You can choose from five main map types. Use a ranged, dot density, or graduated map if you want one data item for each geographical area. If you want to show more than one data value for each geographical division, then either the pie or bar chart map option is better.

Ranged map type

This type of map breaks the data down into color-coded ranges based on whatever geographical breakdown you specify. An example of a ranged map might show the United States, mapping the states in different colors according to their last year's sales values (as shown in Figure 13-16). Crystal Reports creates the range for you based on which of the following distribution methods you select:

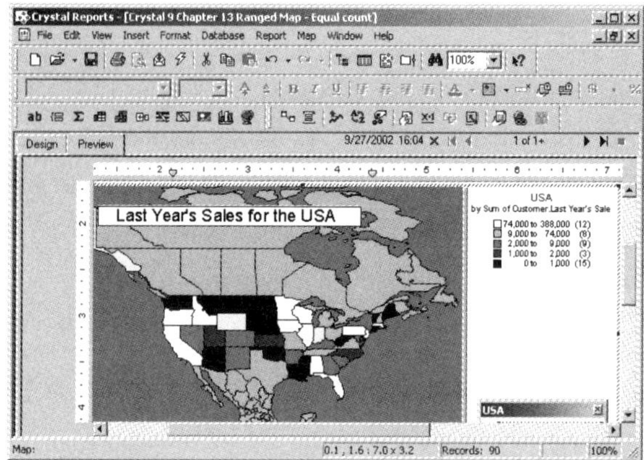

FIGURE 13-16 *Each state is color-coded according to its last year's sales value. The Map Expert made the legend using the Equal Count distribution method.*

◆ **Equal Count.** Assigns the same, or as close to the same as possible, number of geographical regions to each range, regardless of data values (shown in Figure 13-16).

◆ **Equal Ranges.** Assigns intervals so that the *sum of the values* in each interval is equal.

◆ **Natural Break.** Assigns intervals based on an algorithm that tries to make range breaks that minimize the difference between the summary values and the average of the summary values for the interval (shown in Figure 13-17).

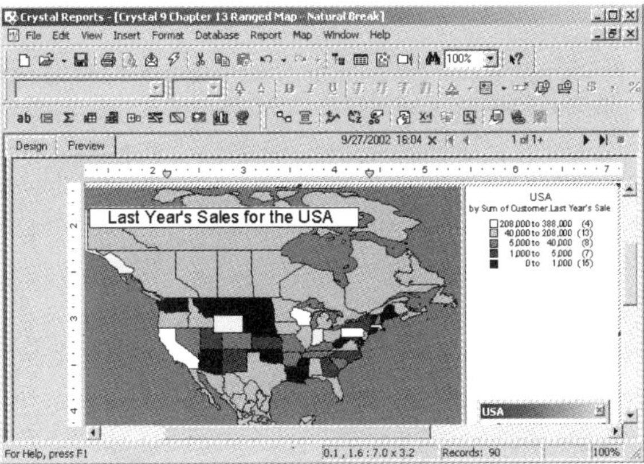

FIGURE 13-17 *Using the same ranged map, this example shows the Natural Break distribution. Compare the legend to the one in Figure 13-16 and it's easy to see the differences.*

◆ **Standard Deviation.** Assigns intervals so that the middle interval is at the mean (average) of all the data values, and the surrounding intervals are one standard deviation above or below the mean.

Dot density map type

This map type displays a dot for each data value, showing an overall view of the distribution of the data points (as illustrated in Figure 13-18).

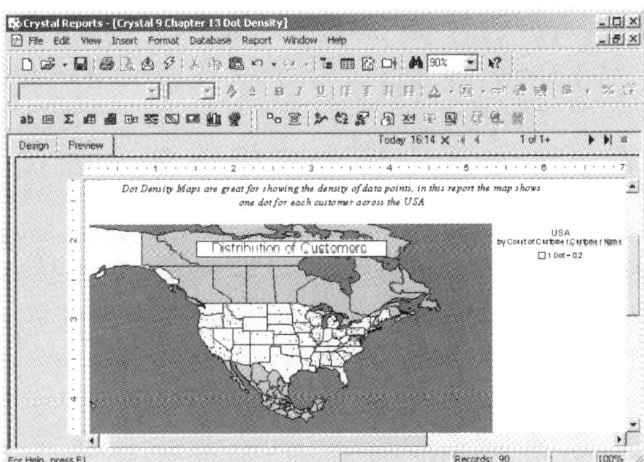

FIGURE 13-18 *A dot density map shows the density of data points (customers, in this case) geographically.*

Graduated map type

A graduated map shows one symbol per data item (see Figure 13-19). You can select which symbol you want to use (a circle is the default). Each symbol is proportional in size to the data value it describes within a range of three sizes.

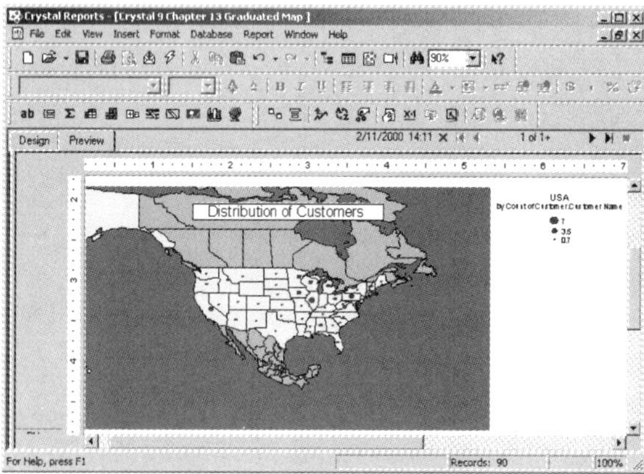

FIGURE 13-19 *A graduated map has symbols for each region. The symbol size is determined by the data value specified.*

Pie chart map type

This type of map displays a pie chart over each geographical area. Each pie slice represents an individual data item as a percentage of the whole for that geographical area. This type of map works best if the data item makes up a whole, or 100 percent. For example, you might want to show a pie over each region showing the percentage of each bike type that was purchased. Maybe 75 percent of the bikes bought in California were mountain bikes, whereas 65 percent of the bikes sold in Florida were competition bikes.

Bar chart map type

A bar chart map shows bar charts over each geographical region. This option works like the pie chart, but is better suited for data values that do not equal 100 percent.

Inserting a Map with the Map Expert

The Map Expert guides you through creating a map for your report. To use the
Map Expert:

1. Click the Insert Map button 🌐 on the toolbar or select Insert, Map
   from the main menu. The Map Expert opens (see Figure 13-20).

2. On the Data tab, indicate whether you want the map to appear in the
   Report Header or in the Report Footer. In the Layout area, select the
   layout of the map. If you have groups in your report, choose the Group
   layout. If you don't have groups, or if you want to map on multiple values, select Advanced. If you are mapping cross-tab or OLAP data, select
   the appropriate option. In the Data area, select the data to illustrate in
   the map.

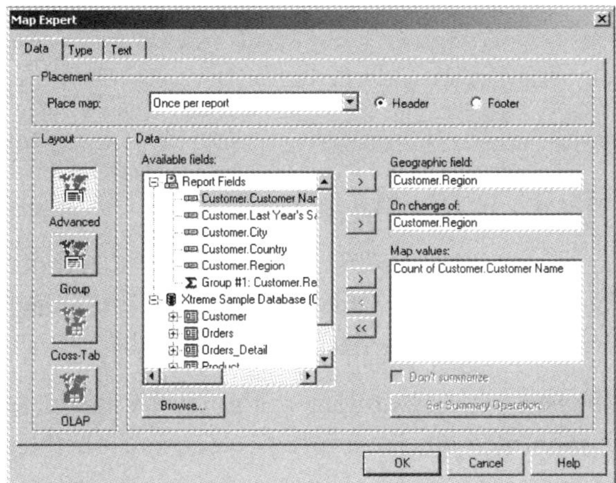

FIGURE 13-20 *The Map Expert Data tab lets you select the layout information and which data
you want to use for the map.*

3. For Group layouts, select the group on which to base the mapped data in
   the On change of drop-down list. Select the summary field to map from
   the Available Fields list (refer to Figure 13-20).

4. For Advanced layouts, from the Available fields list, select the field on
   which to break down the data geographically and click the right arrow
   button beside the Geographic field box. This moves the selected field
   into both the Geographic field and On change of boxes.

5. If you want a different field as the On change of field, select the field from the Available fields list and click the right arrow button to move it into the On change of field. It replaces the field listed there by default from the previous step.

6. Select the fields on which to map and click the right arrow button beside the Map values box.

NOTE

Select the value you added to the Map values list in order for the Don't summarize check box and Set Summary Operation button to be available. These options work the same here as for charting.

7. When you finish selecting the data elements for the map, click the Type tab.

Selecting the Map Type on the Type Tab

The Type tab lets you select the map type with the options listed and described next (see Figure 13-21). This determines how the data appears on the map. Each map type has options specific to that type, as described previously.

◆ **Ranged.** The Map Expert presents options to format the number of intervals, the distribution method, the interval colors, and whether or not to allow empty intervals.

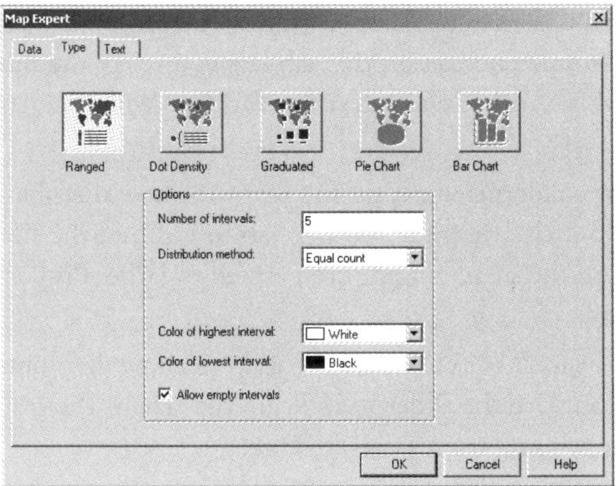

FIGURE 13-21 *The Type tab for a ranged map with Equal count selected in the Distribution method drop-down list.*

◆ **Dot Density.** Shows points on the map to indicate the data distribution. Choose whether you want the dots to appear small or large (see Figure 13-22).

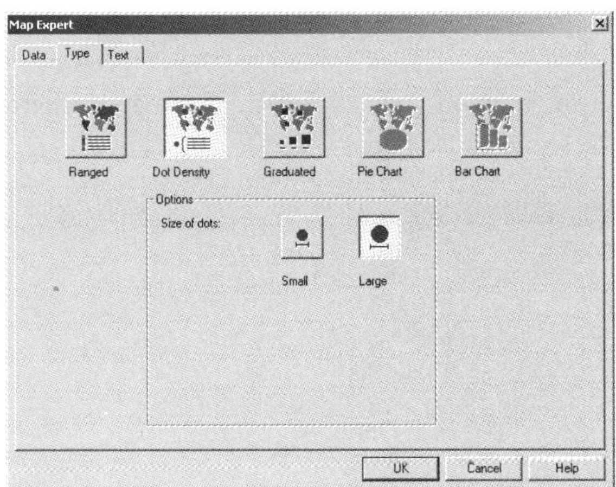

FIGURE 13-22 *If you choose the Dot Density map type option, you have only one option to set.*

◆ **Graduated.** Shows a designated symbol in various sizes to indicate data distribution. A Customize button on this tab lets you select the font style for the symbol, and other characteristics for displaying the desired symbol.

◆ **Pie Chart.** Displays small pie charts on the maps to show distribution of data across the region. Use the slider on this tab to indicate the size of the pies to display on the map, ranging from small to large. Proportional sizing is also available.

◆ **Bar Chart.** Displays small bar charts on the map to show distribution of data across the region. Use the slider to indicate the size of the bars to display on the map, ranging from small to large.

Selecting Text Options on the Text Tab

The Text tab lets you enter a title for the map and select legend options, as shown in Figure 13-23. To select the text options:

1. Type the desired title in the Map title text box.

2. In the Legend area, indicate whether you want a full legend, compact legend, or no legend. If you select Full legend, you can select the legend title and subtitle options.

3. When you finish setting map options, click OK. The map is inserted into the report in the section specified.

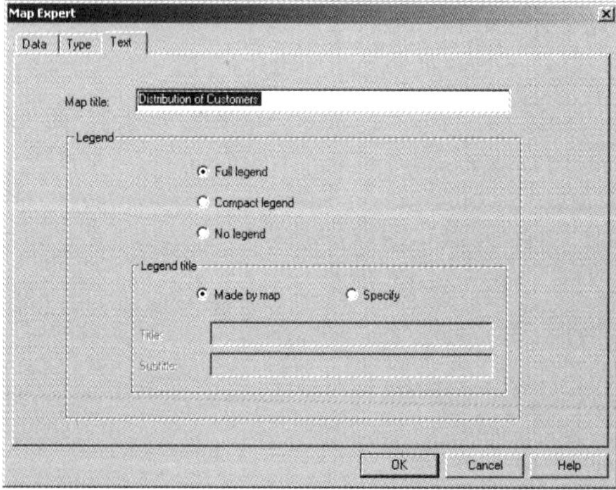

FIGURE 13-23 *Use the Text tab to specify a title and legend options for your map.*

Drilling Down on Maps

Maps provide the drill-down cursor when you hover the mouse cursor over an area of the map that has detail data contained in the report. Just like drilling down on charts, there must be detail data being summarized in some way by the area on the map in order to drill down to see the details. For example, on a ranged map of the United States, where the color of each state is dependent on that state's sales, you could drill down on any state to see a tab listing the details of the customers and sales values that make the total sales value for that state.

Working with Map Options

Options for working with a map are located right on the shortcut menu. You must be in the Preview tab to get all the map options. Similar to the options for editing and formatting charts, in general you can do all of the changing and formatting "in place" on the Preview tab. If you want to change the data that is included in the map then you'll need to go back into the Map Expert.

Using Map Options

You have many options beyond those you worked with in the Map Expert when you initially created the map. When a map appears in the Preview tab, you can right-click the map to view the shortcut menu of available options, shown in Figure 13-24 and described next.

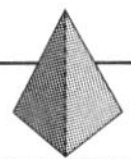

TIP

That miniversion of the map you see in the lower-right corner of the map when selected is the Map Navigator. The superimposed box on the navigator shows you how much of the actual map is going to print on your report. Move the box border with your mouse to control how much of the map prints on your report.

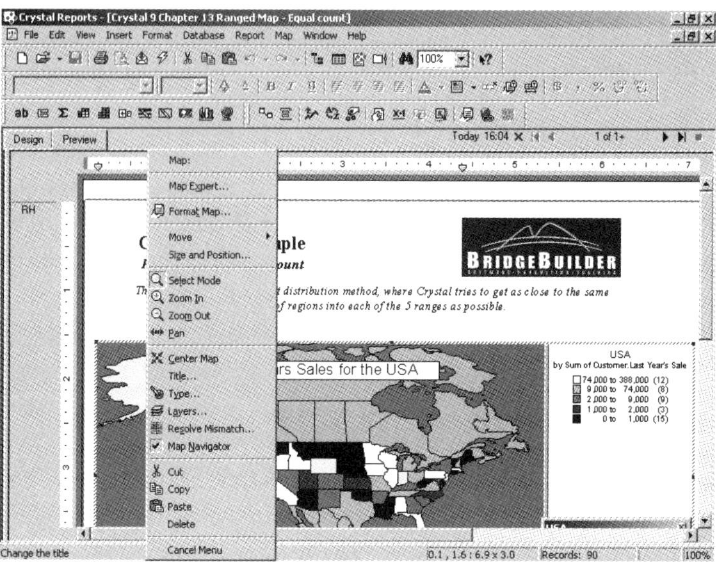

FIGURE 13-24 *Use the Map options on the shortcut menu to customize your map.*

◆ **Map Expert.** Opens the Map Expert where you can change the Data, Type, or Text tabs for the map.

◆ **Format Map.** Opens Format Editor tabs to format the whole map.

◆ **Move.** Moves the map backward or to the back, or forward or to the front.

◆ **Size and Position.** Opens the Object Size and Position dialog where you can set the exact location of the map object on the report.

◆ **Select Mode.** The mouse cursor selects any object you click with your mouse. This option is on by default.

◆ **Zoom In and Zoom Out.** Click Zoom In and your pointer changes. Drag your pointer to create a box shape on the part of the map you want to zoom into. Move the colored box around in the Map Navigator to see different areas of the map zoomed in. Click Zoom Out and then click anywhere on the map to zoom out. Successive clicks continue to zoom out until you reach the desired level. The Map Navigator shows all of these changes so you can monitor where and how much of the map you are viewing and will print on your report.

◆ **Pan.** Click Pan and drag your pointer across the map. The map moves in a manner similar to when you use your hand to slide a piece of paper across your desk.

◆ **Center Map.** Centers the selected area of the map within the map object.

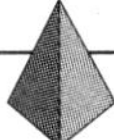

TIP

Be sure that once you finish zooming or panning, you click the Select Mode command from the shortcut menu. Otherwise, every click will zoom or pan, and your map will misbehave!

◆ **Title.** Opens a small dialog box in which you can retype a title for your map.

◆ **Type.** Opens a dialog box with the same options as the Type tab on the Map Expert. It just looks a little different.

◆ **Layers.** Allows you to determine the level of detail in your map (see Figure 13-25).

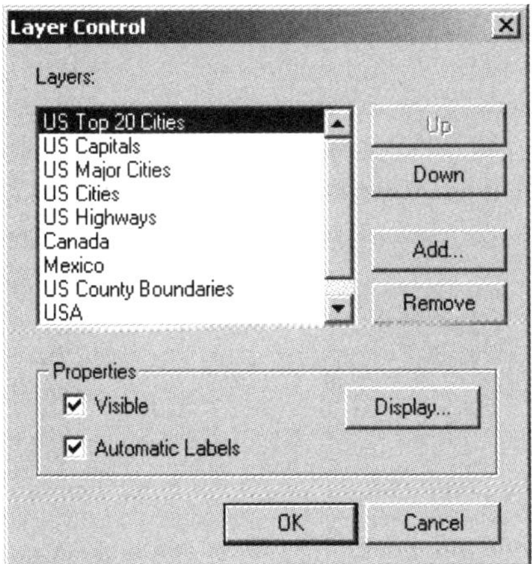

FIGURE 13-25 *Choosing Layers allows you to select the levels at which you zoom in to during preview.*

◆ **Resolve Mismatch.** Change the map being used or resolve a data mismatch using this option (details are outlined in the next section).

◆ **Map Navigator.** Choose this command to view or hide the Map Navigator. Once hidden, the option has no check mark next to it. Click this to get the Map Navigator back.

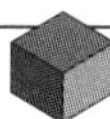

NOTE

Map layers are found in the MapInfo MapX folder. You may also purchase additional map layers from Map Info. Visit its Web site at **www.mapinfo.com**.

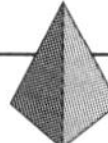

TIP

When you create a map, Crystal Reports automatically constructs map layers, each of which shows the map regions at a particular detail level. You can change the order of the layers so that as you zoom in on the preview, you zoom to the next layer. Click a layer name, and then use the Up and Down buttons to move the layers up or down in the hierarchy shown in the Layers list. In the Properties area, select the Visible check box to indicate whether the selected layer displays. Each layer's visibility property can be turned on or off independently by selecting it in turn and selecting or clearing the Visible check box.

Resolving Mismatched Data

Sometimes Map Info maps used by Crystal do not match your data. For example, you may list England as a country in your database, where Map Info calls that same country Great Britain. Or, you may wish to select a different map to display your data from the one that Crystal chose for you. Use the Resolve Mismatch option to correct this problem or choose a new map.

To change maps or match up mismatched data, select the Map in the Preview tab and choose Resolve Mismatch from the shortcut menu (see Figure 13-26).

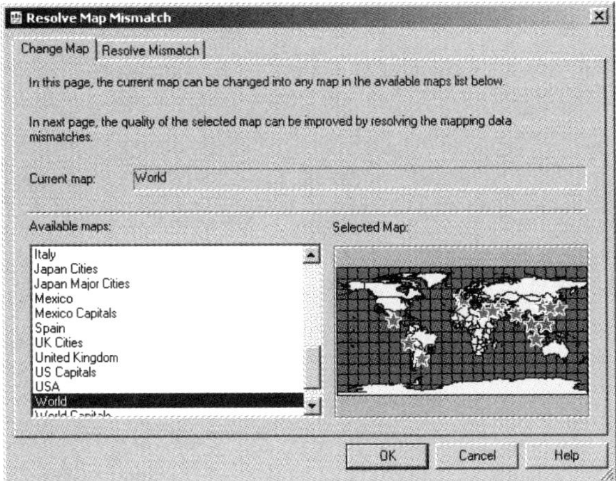

FIGURE 13-26 *Select Resolve Mismatch to open the Resolve Map Mismatch dialog box.*

Use the Change Map tab to change the map the current report is using to display your data. More maps can be added from Map Info if the ones listed do not meet your needs.

Select the Resolve Mismatch tab to match up field names in the report with map names (see Figure 13-27). Click the Match or Unmatch buttons to perform those actions. Results are listed below in the Matched results list. Click OK, and the map reflects the data that it was missing before because it did not recognize the data match on the map.

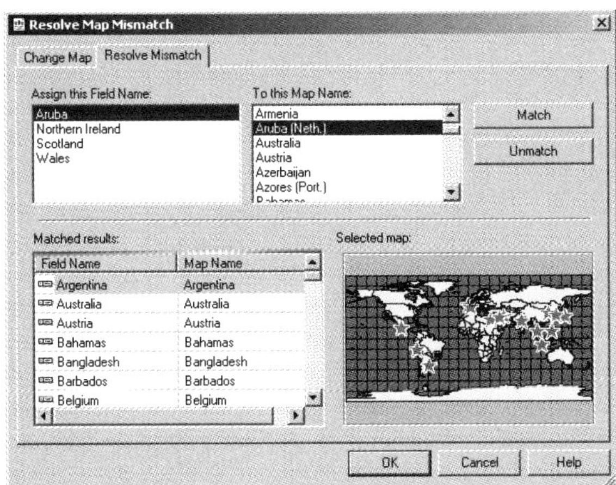

FIGURE 13-27 *Use the Resolve Mismatch tab to assign a heading to a keyword on the map.*

Summary

In this chapter, you learned how to use the Chart and Map Experts along with many available formatting options not only to create charts and maps, but also to fine-tune them. Though many details were given in this chapter on where to find options for both charts and maps, your best approach is to experiment.

Chapter 14

Leveraging SQL
Commands for
Efficient
Reporting

For anyone who is not new to Crystal Reports but is upgrading, there are significant improvements to how Crystal Reports uses SQL in Crystal Reports 9. Possibly the most exciting enhancement to Crystal Reports 9 is the ability to build completely customizable SQL Select statements within Crystal Reports. Crystal Reports and SQL are finally friends!

In the past, parts of the SQL Query that Crystal Reports wrote for you were editable, with mixed results and no support from Crystal Decisions. SQL Commands (also referred to throughout the chapter as just commands) are a new feature of Crystal Reports 9 within the Database Expert that provide a place to write your own SQL Query on which to base a report right from within Crystal Reports.

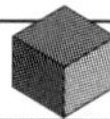

NOTE

The SQL Query within Crystal Reports under Database/Show SQL Query is no longer editable. You must use the Database Expert and write your own SQL Query.

SQL Commands add tremendous functionality and flexibility to Crystal Reports.

- ◆ SQL Commands can be written from scratch by typing SQL into the dialog box, using any and all SQL functions supported by the particular database to which you are connected.

- ◆ Use another SQL tool to build a SQL Command (such as your proprietary database tool) and then cut and paste the Select statement into the command window.

- ◆ Save SQL Commands to the Repository for sharing among users or for use by more than one report.

- ◆ A database developer can build a SQL Command and save it to the Repository, and a report developer can use the command to call up data for use in a report. In this way, the report developer does not have to be a SQL expert in order to take advantage of the functionality.

◆ Integrating database-specific functions in the SQL Command to process selection criteria on the database server helps reports process faster and more efficiently.

Before I get too excited about this new functionality, the following section gives some background on SQL and ODBC to help you understand why processing a Select statement on your database server using a SQL Command is sometimes more efficient than connecting to your database directly.

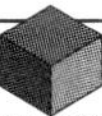

NOTE

Though this chapter discusses writing and using SQL Commands and basing reports on commands rather than directly from your database, each method has its merits. Sometimes one method is better than the other, and sometimes it really does not matter. In this chapter, I will try to clarify when it is best to use a SQL Command, and when Crystal Reports is doing just fine on its own and does not change much if you use a SQL Command.

Crystal Reports and SQL Interact

You can create reports with Crystal Reports without knowing a thing about Structured Query Language (SQL). However, most report designers find that some basic SQL knowledge comes in handy when creating record or group selection formulas and verifying that Crystal Reports created the SQL Query as you intended. This section introduces you to a few of the mainstay concepts in the SQL language.

SQL is a script language used to access data from databases. The American National Standards Institute (ANSI) standard for SQL includes a set of commands supported by all major databases. Many database manufacturers include their own version of SQL that supports the ANSI commands, as well as proprietary commands and functions.

SQL consists of a set of reserved words; many of them are directions or function names that perform a certain task. You cannot use these reserved words to name a table, variable, or stored procedure; doing so would generate an error. Many of the reserved words are specific to creating and managing the database itself and would never be used in writing queries for reporting anyway.

Options for Connecting to a Database

Before covering SQL Commands, let's first review how Crystal Reports connects to your database. There are two types of connections to a database: native and ODBC. A specific driver written to connect Crystal Reports to a database handles the native connection. Crystal Decisions includes native drivers for most of the popular databases.

However, not all databases are "popular," or some "popular" databases are proprietary. It's not realistic to think that Crystal Decisions could write specific drivers for each and every type of proprietary or less mainstream database. There is a solution: ODBC.

ODBC stands for Open Database Connectivity and means that any database that conforms to this standard can communicate with other applications that also conform to the ODBC standard. This allows Crystal Reports to access databases that don't have native drivers.

Most database vendors offer an ODBC driver with their software. Sometimes companies who use Crystal Reports choose to work with ODBC even though native drivers exist for their database. One method of connecting to the database is not necessarily better than the other, but both offer different options. To explore these options, we need to focus on the advantages and disadvantages that each offers.

Advantages and Disadvantages of Native Drivers

Crystal Reports connects natively to two types of databases: PC databases (data files) and SQL. Examples of PC databases include Microsoft Access, Dbase, Paradox, and Btrieve. Examples of SQL databases include Oracle, Microsoft SQL Server, Sybase, Informix, and IBM DB2.

> **NOTE**
>
> Microsoft Access is a rare example of a database that fits into both categories. Generally, PC-type databases are composed of one file and reside on a PC, not a dedicated server. MS Access behaves more like a larger client server database, but it can easily reside on a PC workstation or home computer. MS Access has all the options of both connection types.

The main advantage of a native driver rather than an ODBC driver is fewer layers of software between Crystal Reports and the database. In theory, this increases the speed and performance of communication between Crystal Reports and the database.

Another advantage of the native driver is that specific features of a database can be utilized in the query. Because the driver is designed to connect Crystal Reports to the specific database, programmers of the native driver can take advantage of features in the database that ODBC cannot. Again, this improves speed and performance.

The main disadvantage to using some native drivers, particularly with PC-type databases, is that you cannot change the join type when linking tables together. Crystal Reports limits the join type to Left Outer only. This is a disadvantage, because not all reports will pull the data you want or need correctly if limited to a Left Outer join type. Chapter 3 discusses SQL join types and when and why this becomes an issue.

Advantages and Disadvantages of ODBC

ODBC is a more generic form of connecting two applications or databases but provides much more desirable flexibility. Sometimes you think that the tool made especially for the job is best, such as a native driver, but in reporting, that is not always true. ODBC may provide more flexibility and desirable options. Every database is different and there are exceptions to every rule, so consider your specific situation and database when choosing a connection type.

To make things more confusing, some databases build native drivers that use SQL to communicate between the driver and the database. This can be the best of both worlds: the speed of a native connection and the flexibility of SQL. Look for this with some of the larger databases, such as Oracle, SQL Server, and DB2. Refer to your database administrator, network administrator, or vendor for suggestions on which method to use if the choice is not obvious.

NOTE

To stick my neck out on this topic, it seems that many more people use ODBC than native drivers, and their reports work just great.

The main advantage of ODBC is that it is fairly universal across databases and applications. This allows Crystal Reports to work with many different databases that do not have native drivers available and to be more flexible with those databases.

Another key advantage of using ODBC to connect to your database is that you can choose which join type to use to link tables for a report. Using a native driver, you are usually limited to a Left Outer join type, only without the ability to change the type. The ability to change join type is critical to correcting data in many reports.

Using ODBC also makes it easier to change the data source from which a report pulls data. This can be useful when upgrading to a newer version of the same server type or if changing server type. ODBC and Crystal Reports can usually accommodate the driver change; in a few simple steps, the report is pointed to the new database with a new driver.

Yet another advantage of using ODBC, which is really the topic of this whole chapter, is that by using ODBC, you can edit the SQL Query that calls data from the database for the report.

The main disadvantage of using ODBC is that drivers must be set up to connect your PC to a data source via ODBC. Native drivers require very little setup and tweaking compared to the setup of ODBC. However, once the process of setting up ODBC is documented, this is not a major issue at most companies.

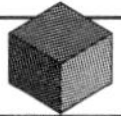

> **NOTE**
>
> Setting up ODBC data sources is not difficult, and many times it has already been done before you even have Crystal Reports installed on your PC by a system administrator. ODBC configurations can sometimes be tricky, but they are usually simple to set up and maintain.

Overall, most companies and report developers prefer ODBC to native drivers because of the added flexibility when choosing join types and the ability to change database locations and types.

Sending Data from Your Database to Crystal Reports

Now that we've discussed native drivers and ODBC, let's take a closer look at the way data is returned to Crystal Reports. This section will give you a better understanding of why it's helpful to understand the basics of SQL.

Let's assume that you can connect to a database through either ODBC or a native SQL driver. In both cases, you have the opportunity to review the query that Crystal Reports generates for you based on the information in the design tab. To see the query, select Database, Show SQL Query (see Figure 14-1).

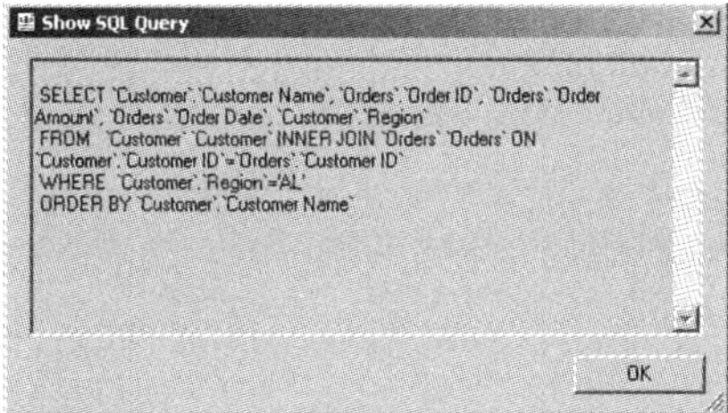

FIGURE 14-1 *The Show SQL Query dialog box is available for viewing when reporting with an ODBC or a SQL connection to your data.*

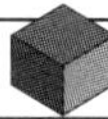

NOTE

A previous section distinguished between the differences in how native and ODBC drivers connect to the database. Yet in the last section, ODBC and native SQL drivers are mentioned as if they connect to the database in a similar way. Some databases have native drivers that use SQL to communicate; these drivers are in the middle between fully native drivers and fully ODBC drivers. Regardless of driver, what is important is whether the database you are using is SQL based or not. If the database is SQL based, then you can use commands and change the SQL to pull a tighter dataset from the database for Crystal to base the report on.

The SQL Query you see is the set of instructions sent to the database requesting data for the report. The most efficient process is for the database to send back only the data that's absolutely required, so Crystal Reports has less work to do filtering out unwanted records. This query is not editable, only viewable. The most important part of this query is the WHERE clause, which instructs the query as to which records to include and send back to the report. If there is no WHERE clause, you want to write a SQL Command so that you can add a WHERE clause to the query. If you see the complete WHERE clause, including all the criteria you set in the Select Expert, a SQL Command will probably not improve the speed of your report significantly and you may decide not to bother using one.

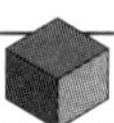

NOTE

A section later in this chapter describes the different parts of the SQL Query in detail, including the WHERE clause.

Crystal Reports Builds a SQL Query

Crystal Reports does its best using your Design tab instructions to create an ANSI standard SQL statement (or SQL Query) to bring back the data necessary to build the report. However, this statement is often generic and brings back too much data if anything but the most standard selection criteria are used. This causes the report to take longer to process, the database server to run longer, network traffic to increase while transferring records, and the person running the report to wait. Understanding how and why data is brought back to Crystal Reports can reduce all of these.

To make a report run efficiently, most of the data crunching needs to occur on the database server. Generally, a server class machine (with more memory and a faster processor than a typical desktop machine) hosts the database. Including more specific requirements to the database server offloads some of the processing work to the database server machine, which means that only the smallest amount of required data transfers to the workstation running Crystal Reports.

Many queries that are automatically generated by Crystal Reports can be improved upon. Crystal Reports does a mediocre job building the SQL Queries itself partly because it must use only the most generic ANSI standard SQL functions in order to be certain that any and all ODBC data sources are able to understand the SQL statement. This leaves each of us a little high and dry if we employ more complex selection criteria or use formulas in selection, because Crystal Reports cannot reliably translate the customized selection criteria into ANSI-standard SQL.

What Options Do I Have?

Do not despair, for we do have options! The new option in version 9 is to write a SQL Command in the Database Expert on which to base the report. Other options (which are not new) that force data collection work to the server include building database views and stored procedures.

SQL Commands

Building SQL Commands is covered in detail in the next sections. Essentially, you write your own SQL statement using any specific SQL functions for your particular database and save this command either in the Database Explorer for the specific report or to the Crystal Repository for sharing or future use.

Using database views

A *database view* is a virtual table that can include fields from many tables. The linking (including join types) is taken care of when the view is built. This leaves one table to use in the report and makes building reports easier and faster, because the linking occurs on the database server. Views are often built by database

administrators or developers who have a good understanding of the database structure and data and have developer rights on the database server. Views are built on the database server, not within Crystal Reports.

Calling stored procedures

A *stored procedure* is a type of predefined query that executes on demand (and can be called from a Crystal Report). This predefined script collects the desired data for the report when it is called, can contain data manipulation instructions and complex selection statements, and has parameters passed out to Crystal Reports. A stored procedure is processed on the database server, sending back only required records to the report. Again, the report writer sees the resulting table and fields, so report writing is easier and much faster with Crystal Reports doing less of the work. This option requires a database administrator or developer or someone with database developer rights on the database server to build and save the stored procedure. You cannot build stored procedures from within Crystal Reports.

Though all options require a comfort level with writing SQL, stored procedures offer the best methods for improving the performance of a report.

Using SQL Commands in Crystal Reports

SQL Commands are used in the Database Expert in Crystal Reports. There are several ways to get a SQL Command for a report or to build your own.

◆ Build your own SQL Command from scratch by typing SQL syntax directly into the Command window.

◆ Select a prewritten SQL Command from the Crystal Repository to use or edit for the report. You, or someone in your organization, would have needed to save a SQL Command in the Repository in order for it to be listed and available for use.

◆ Build a SQL Query using the Crystal Decisions query-building tool called the Crystal SQL Designer. This tool is not shipped with Crystal Reports anymore, but you can download it from the Web site with the following address: **www.support.crystaldecisions.com/communityCS/ FilesAndUpdates/cr9_data_tools.zip.asp.**

◆ Build a SQL Query using some other query-building tool. Most databases include their own tool specific for their database, and there are several available for free on the Web, such as TOAD (which is an Oracle tool, but a trial version is downloadable for free).

Building a SQL Command in the Database Expert

Discussed below are several ways to acquire a SQL Statement to enter into the Command window in the Database Expert. When you use a SQL Command to collect data from a data source, you do not select tables or link tables using the Database Expert—these functions are carried out by the SQL Statement itself.

Writing a Custom Command

Commands are written in the Database Expert. When you begin a new report, the Database Expert opens, allowing you to select which data source you want to report from. Navigate to the data source you wish to use, either in the Favorites folder or another folder (see Figure 14-2). Each data source has a Command node.

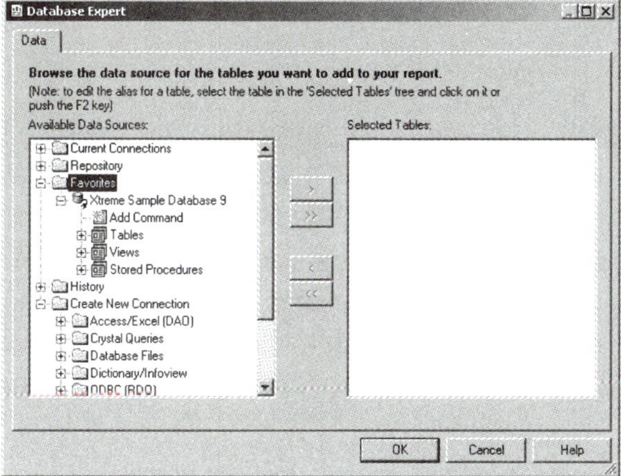

FIGURE 14-2 *Navigate in the Database Expert to the data source for the current report.*

1. Create a new blank report. With the Database Expert open and the data source you wish to report from expanded, double-click the Add Command node under the data source name, or select the Add Command node and click the forward arrow button.

2. The Add Command to Report dialog box opens. Type the SQL Statement you wish to use to collect data from the data source for your report in the Command window (see Figure 14-3).

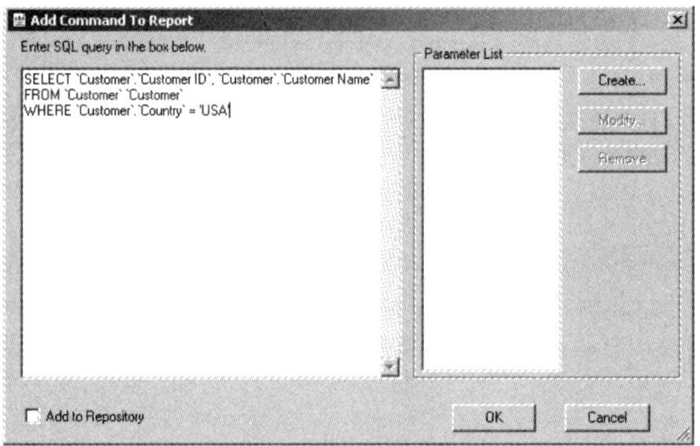

FIGURE 14-3 *Type a SQL Command that Crystal Reports will use to pull data from your data source into Crystal Reports for manipulation and formatting.*

3. Once you have typed a command, click OK on the Add Command to Report dialog box. I suggest ignoring the other options on the dialog box until you are sure that your command is correct.

4. If the command contains correct syntax, it is run and you are returned to the Database Expert. You'll see the command listed under the data source name in the Selected Tables window. Click OK, and the Design window opens, ready for you to begin designing a report with the dataset you collected with the command.

5. If the command has any errors, an error dialog box opens (see Figure 14-4). Click OK to return to the Add Command to Report dialog box. Edit the command and try again.

NOTE

There is no check button, but by clicking OK, Crystal Reports will attempt to run your command to pull data from the data source. If there is an error, you may see a message similar to that in Figure 14-4, depending on the actual syntax error.

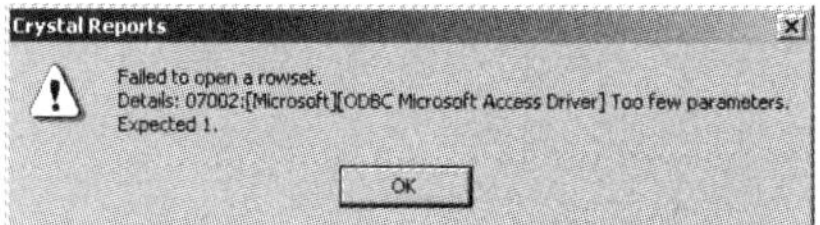

FIGURE 14-4 *An error dialog box will open if there is an error in your Command.*

Adding a Parameter to a Command

If you want to have the command affected by an input parameter when the report is run, you can edit the command to include a parameter. Open the Database Expert, right-click the command you want to add a parameter to, and select Edit Command.

This opens the Modify Command dialog box, where you can add a parameter and then refer to the parameter field in the query.

1. Click the Create button to the right of the Parameter window to open the Command Parameter dialog box. Create the parameter (see Figure 14-5) and click OK. This closes the Command Parameter dialog box and adds the parameter to the Parameter list.

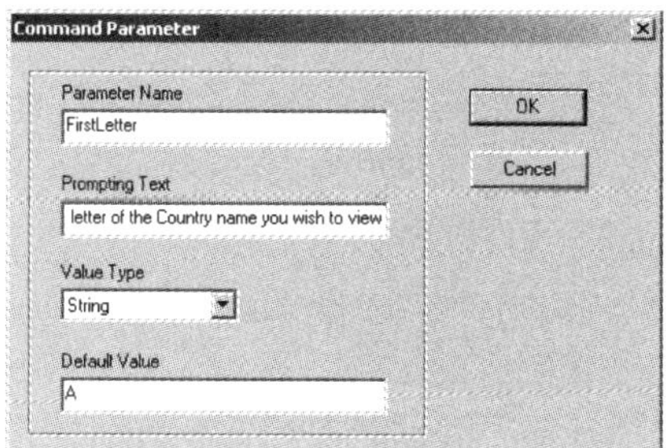

FIGURE 14-5 *Create a parameter for inclusion in the SQL query.*

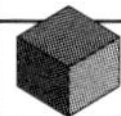

NOTE

Refer to Chapter 12 for details on creating parameter fields.

2. Edit the SQL query in the Command window to use the parameter (see Figure 14-6).

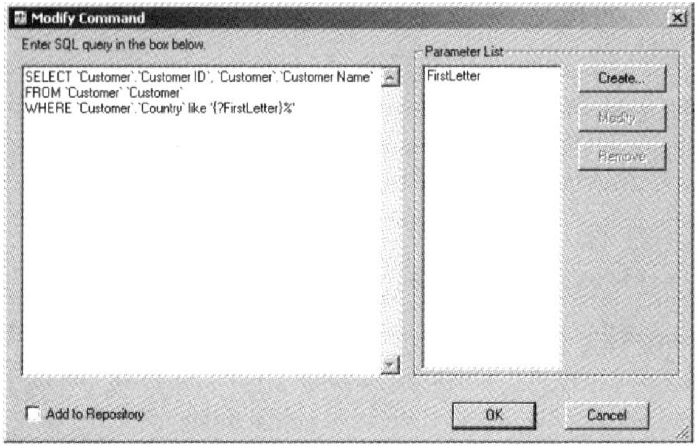

FIGURE 14-6 *Edit the SQL query to include the parameter field.*

3. Click the OK button on the Modify Command dialog box to see if the command runs correctly. You will be prompted to enter a value for the parameter before the command runs (see Figure 14-7).

4. You are back at the Database Expert, with the command listed in the Selected Tables window. Click OK to close the Database Expert and open the Report Design Window.

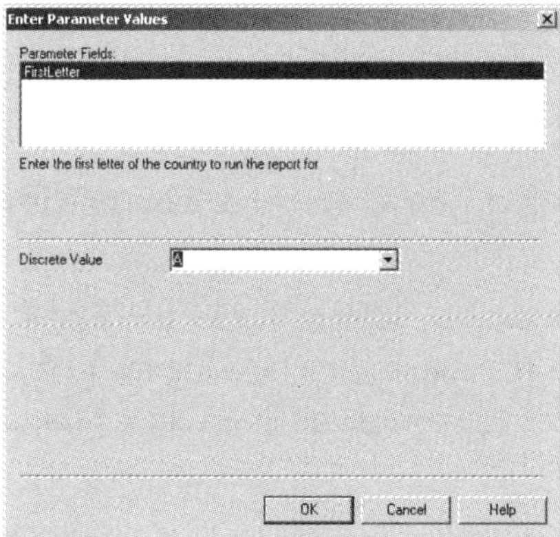

FIGURE 14-7 *Enter a value for the parameter at the prompt.*

You are ready to build a report based on the data collected from your database in the SQL Command. You'll notice that only the fields you specified are listed in the Database Fields folder of the Field Expert. You can edit the SQL Command at any time to add fields or make changes.

Selecting a Repository Object

This idea of using custom commands may sound nice to you, but what if you are not ready to build your own SQL Commands from scratch? Or what if you want to leverage the excellent knowledge and speed of your database development team to assist you?

The Repository can store commands. On the Add Command to Report dialog box, you may have noticed a check box at the bottom named Add to Repository. SQL Commands can be saved to your Repository for future use or sharing. This means that you can get assistance building a command; a developer can build, test, and save the command into the Repository, and then you can pull the command when ready to use it for a report.

Saving a Command to the Repository

1. Open the Database Expert and select the command you wish to save to the Repository in the Selected Tables window.

2. Right-click the command and select Edit Command. This opens the Modify Command dialog box.

3. Click the Save to Repository dialog box. This launches the Add Item dialog box for adding an item to the Repository (see Figure 14-8). Enter the appropriate information about the command and select a folder to save it in.

4. Click OK. If the command uses a parameter, you may be prompted to answer the prompt before the command is saved. The command is now listed in the Repository in the folder specified.

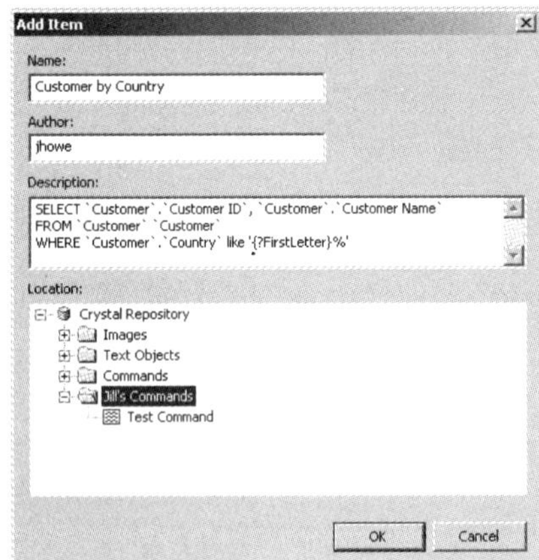

FIGURE 14-8 *Fill in the Add Item dialog box to add a command to the Repository.*

Using a Command from the Repository

To use a command from the Repository in a new report, begin a new report, and in the Database Explorer, expand the Repository folder.

1. Find and select the command you wish to use in the report. The command is actually listed under the folder with its name.

2. Click the forward arrow button or double-click the command to move it to the Selected Tables window (see Figure 14-9).

3. Click OK to close the Database Expert. The command will run, and the Design window will open, ready for you to begin building a report.

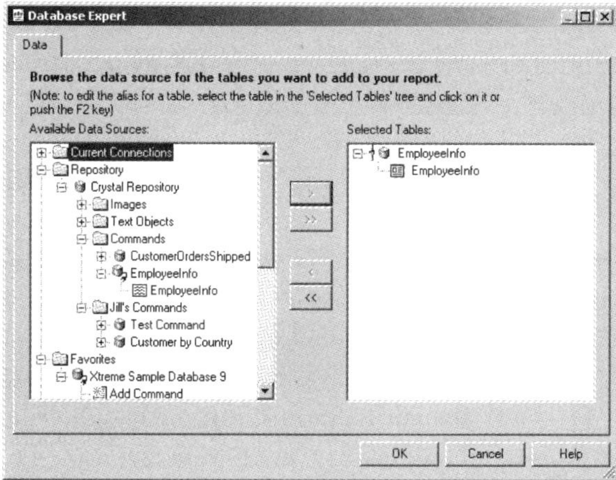

FIGURE 14-9 *Select a command from the Repository to use for a report.*

The Repository provides an excellent common place to store command objects for use in many reports by many users. If you want to use a command that is stored in the Repository, you must have the correct ODBC DSN configured on your machine. This DSN must have the same name and point to the same type of database as the DSN which was used to create the command.

Copy and Paste SQL Syntax from Another Tool

Along with being able to write your own SQL Command syntax on the fly as you build a report, you can write a SQL Statement in another tool and paste it into the Command window.

Many databases provide a Query-writing tool of some sort with their database tools. Many of these tools are quite good and contain information on all the specific SQL functions that the particular database supports. You may or may not have access to one for your specific database, but you can download Crystal's SQL tool to add the functionality to your Crystal Reports 9 installation.

Why Write a Query in Another Tool?

You may want to write and test your SQL Statement in another tool to easily test the query before pasting it into the Command window. Many SQL tools provide troubleshooting tips and utilities to view the dataset returned, which can be helpful to be sure you are collecting the dataset you intend to.

Why Use the Crystal SQL Designer?

Using Crystal's SQL Designer is a great way to get your feet wet with SQL. The SQL Designer is not shipped with Crystal Reports 9 for the first time, but you can download it from the Web site at the following URL: www.support.crystal-decisions.com/communityCS/FilesAnd-Updates/cr9_data_tools.zip.asp. This is a 21.6MB file and contains both the Crystal SQL Designer and the Crystal Dictionary tools.

Once you download the file, there is a Word document with simple instructions and version numbers for the tools installed. The installation is very easy: just double-click on the executable program, and the install wizard takes care of the rest. Once installed, the tools show up in your Start menu under Programs, Crystal Data Compatibility Tools.

If you are new to SQL, the Crystal SQL Designer might be a good learning tool. The Crystal SQL Designer includes a Design Expert that walks you through building a SQL Query step by step, relating the parts of the SQL statement to parts of the Design tab that you are familiar with. This helps you understand which parts of a

---

WHY USE THE CRYSTAL SQL DESIGNER?

The Crystal SQL Designer is good for people less familiar with SQL syntax. The Design Expert provides prompting dialog boxes, similar to those found in the Report Wizards, which help new SQL writers learn which part of their report data is affected by each clause in the SQL Statement.

SQL queries written in the Crystal SQL Designer can be cut and pasted from the SQL tab into the Command window in the Database Expert and saved in the report or to the Repository.

The Expert with this Designer uses only ANSI-standard SQL, and contains its share of quirks. You will quickly outgrow the tool and want to use more specific SQL functions useful for your particular database. But this SQL tool is a great starter for those with no SQL background looking to familiarize themselves with SQL and how it relates to their data and Crystal Reports before trying to use less intuitive and more powerful tools.

NOTE

Both the Crystal SQL Designer and Crystal Dictionary Designer are being phased out of Crystal Reports. Both tools are available for download to support backwards compatibility only. SQL Commands replace the functionality of the SQL Designer making using the tool unnecessary. Crystal Decisions is also developing a yet to be released replacement for Crystal Dictionaries. Many companies make their specific database's SQL tool available to report designers, in which case you may choose to use that tool rather than Crystal's tool, because it will be more specific to your particular database.

report's data relate to which part of a SQL Statement. Once you get familiar with the parts of the SQL Statement, it is advisable to use a more advanced less quirky tool, such as one provided by your database vendor.

Using the Crystal SQL Designer

The Crystal SQL Designer is an application available from Crystal Decisions that helps you build a SQL query outside of the Database Expert. When you build a query independently of a report, you can test it for errors and see the data set returned which you may find easier outside of the Database Expert itself. Once you build a successful query, you paste the contents of the SQL tab into the Database Expert as a command. Once a SQL query is saved as a command, it can be added to the Repository and then used for multiple reports, such as in detail-level and summary-level reports needing similar data.

If you are familiar with SQL, you will be better off using a more robust SQL tool than the Crystal SQL Designer. The usefulness of this tool is to help teach people completely new to SQL concepts how the parts of a SQL statement relate to design functionality in a report.

Start the Crystal SQL Designer by choosing Start, Programs, Crystal Data Compatibility Tools, Crystal SQL Designer. The Crystal SQL Designer window opens. The standard toolbar in the Crystal SQL Designer offers a quick way to execute the following menu functions:

◆ Start a New Query

◆ Open a Query

- Save a Query
- Edit a Query
- Execute a Query

To create a new query, click the New Query button on the toolbar, or select File, New from the main menu. This opens the New Query dialog box, which allows you to choose how to create your query (see Figure 14-10).

- If you want to use the SQL Expert, see the section "Using the SQL Expert."
- If you want to enter a SQL statement directly, see the section "Entering a SQL Statement Directly."
- If you want to start from an existing query, see the section "Starting from Existing Query."

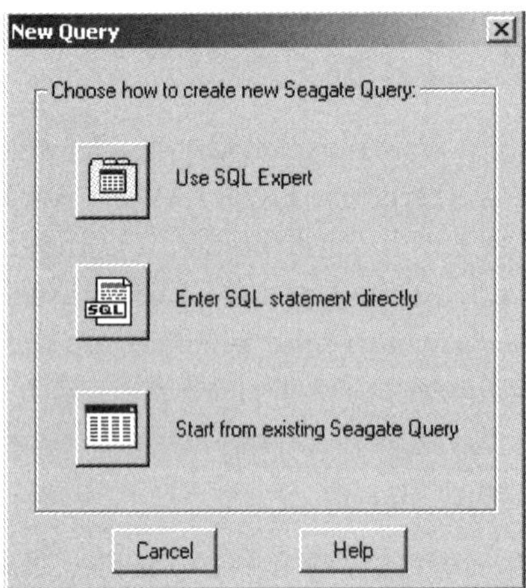

FIGURE 14-10 *The New Query dialog box lets you specify how to create a new query.*

Using the SQL Expert

The SQL Expert is a simple tool that uses a tabbed dialog box similar to the Report Wizards. After clicking the Use SQL Expert button on the New Query dialog box, the Create SQL Expert opens.

Tables Tab: Selecting the Data Source and Tables

The Tables tab lets you specify the name of your query and choose the data source and tables for your report (see Figure 14-11).

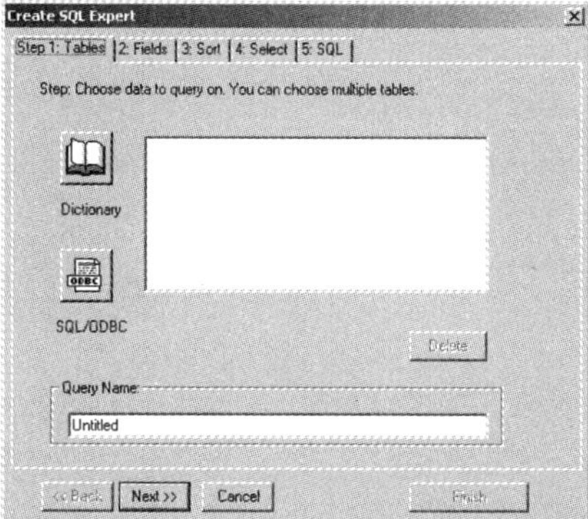

FIGURE 14-11 *The Tables tab on the Create SQL Expert allows you to specify the tables to include in the report.*

To select the data source and tables to use in the query:

1. Type the name for your query in the Query Name box.
2. Choose the source for the data. Select a SQL or ODBC data source by clicking the SQL/ODBC button.

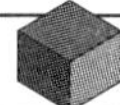 **NOTE**

The Crystal Dictionary tool is being phased out and is included for backwards compatibility only. I highly recommended that you not use it as a data source for a query or report.

3. In the Log On Server dialog box (see Figure 14-12), select the name of the SQL or ODBC server you want to log on to and click OK. If the logon is successful, the Choose SQL Table dialog box appears (see Figure 14-13).

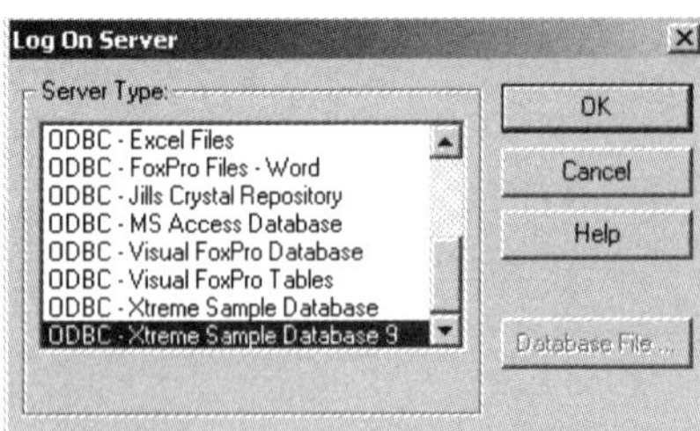

FIGURE 14-12 *The Choose SQL Table dialog box lets you select the tables to include in your query.*

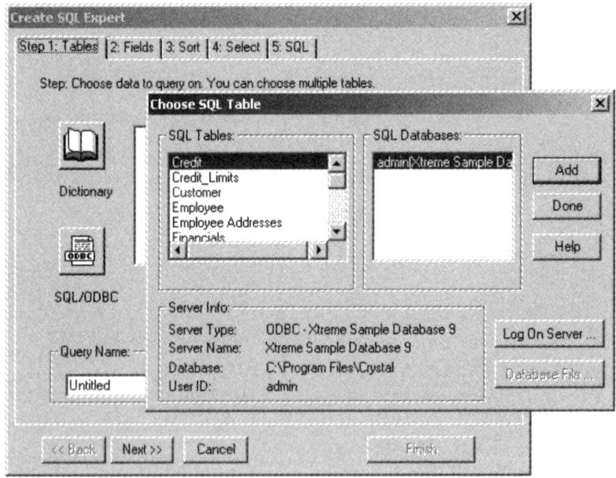

FIGURE 14-13 *The New Query dialog box lets you specify how to create a new query.*

4. Select the tables you want to include in the query. Click the Add button to add each one to the list on the Create SQL Expert.

NOTE

If you need to log on to another server to access additional tables, click the Log On Server button.

5. When you finish selecting tables, click Done. The Links tab appears automatically if you've selected multiple tables. If you selected only one table, click the Fields tab and skip to the section "Fields Tab: Selecting Fields."

Links Tab: Linking Tables

On the Links tab, you specify the relationships between the tables (see Figure 14-14). Its use is very similar to the Links tab on the Database Expert in Crystal Reports.

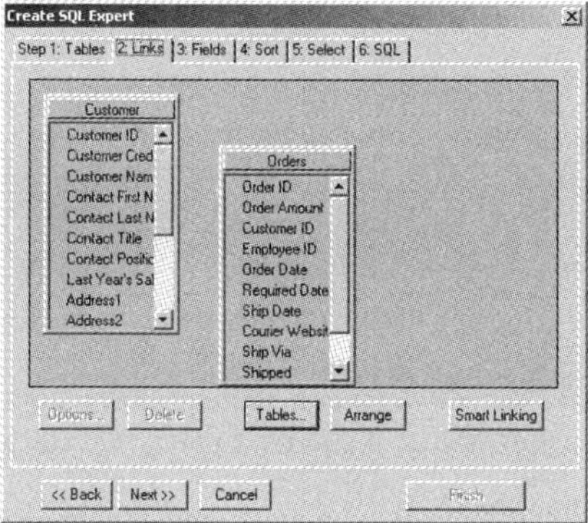

FIGURE 14-14 *The Links tab on the Create SQL Expert allows you to specify the relationship between the tables.*

To indicate relationships between tables:

1. Click the field you wish to link from on one table, then drag your cursor to the corresponding field in another table and release the cursor. This establishes a link.

2. If you want to set the link options to specify a join type or take advantage of an index for the tables being linked, click the Options button. The Link Options dialog box appears (see Figure 14-15). Use the Index In Use field to specify an index to use other than the primary key. Next, enter the field you want to link on. To specify a join type other than the default, select the desired join type from the SQL Join Type area. Click OK to return to the Links tab.

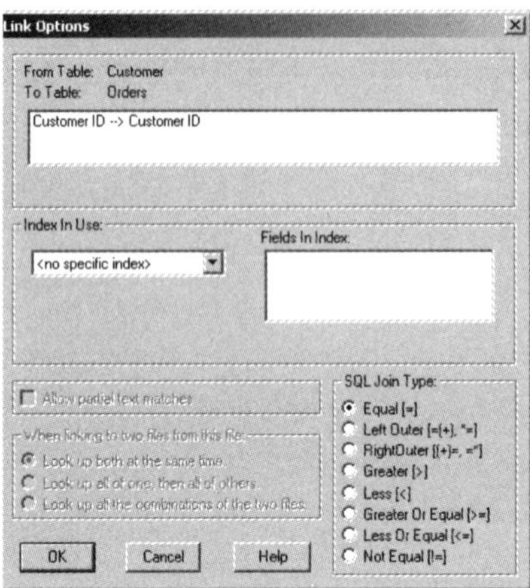

FIGURE 14-15 *The Link Options dialog box lets you configure how to link fields between tables.*

3. To delete a link created in error, click the line that identifies the link and press the Del key or click the Delete button.

4. Click the Tables button to view a description of the tables selected.

5. Click Arrange to arrange the tables so that their links are easier to follow.

6. Click Smart Linking to have Crystal Reports' Auto Link tool "guess" the links between tables.

7. Continue creating links until you've identified all of the table relationships.

8. Click the Next button, or click the Fields tab.

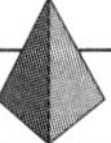

TIP

Auto Link is improved in Crystal Reports 9 to use indexed fields when linking. This tool was not updated with this functionality so the Auto Link links by name and type only, thus is not as effective.

Fields Tab: Selecting Fields

The Fields tab lets you indicate the fields to include in the query. You can place table fields or SQL Expressions in the query using the Fields tab options (see Figure 14-16). You'll find more information on SQL Expression fields later in this chapter.

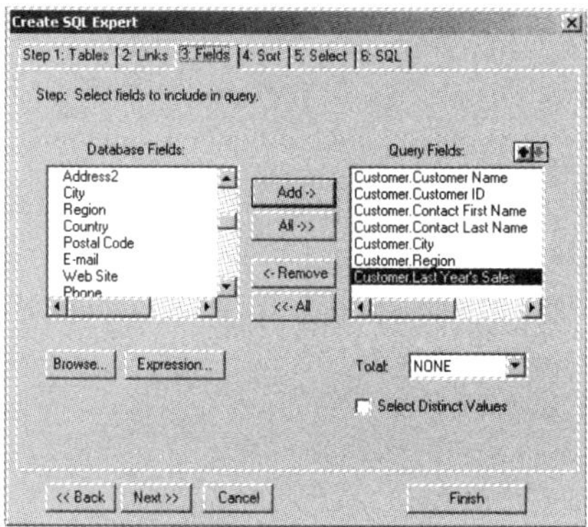

FIGURE 14-16 *The Fields tab on the Create SQL Expert allows you to specify the fields you want to include in your query.*

To choose the fields to include in the query:

1. Select the fields to appear in the query's data set from the Database Fields list and click the Add button to add them to the Query Fields list.

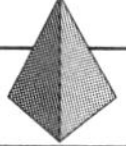

TIP

You can move the field names up and down in the list by clicking the up and down arrow buttons just above the Query Fields list. This is the equivalent of changing their order in the SELECT statement and only serves to change the order in which they appear in the query results.

2. To browse through the data in the table for a particular field, select a field in the Database Fields list and then click the Browse button.

3. To use a SQL Expression, select a field in the Database Fields list and click the Expression button. Enter a name for the expression. Type a new name to create a new SQL expression, or type an existing name to edit an expression. The SQL Expression dialog box appears (see Figure 14-17). You can double-click the field name in the Fields list to use it in your SQL statement.

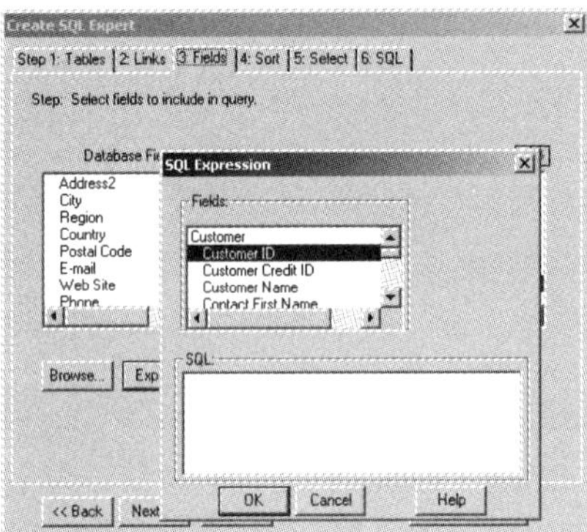

FIGURE 14-17 *The SQL Expression dialog box lets you specify a SQL Expression to include in the query.*

4. To create a summary field, select a field in the Query Fields list and then select the desired aggregate function in the Total list. The aggregate types are SUM, COUNT, AVG, MIN, and MAX. These functions are performed for the entire group of records in the report.

5. Select the Select Distinct Values check box to construct the query to show only distinct values for *all* of the fields.

6. Click the Next button, or click the Sort tab at the top of the Create SQL Expert dialog box.

Sort Tab: Sorting and Grouping

The Sort tab lets you define groups for the query (see Figure 14-18). The fields you select here will be written to the query's GROUP BY clause. This can make the data more meaningful by providing groupings such as by date, by location, and so on.

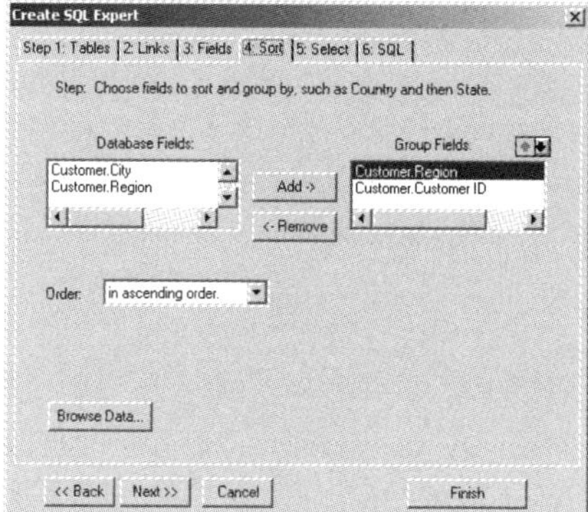

FIGURE 14-18 *The Sort tab on the Create SQL Expert allows you to sort and group data.*

To indicate the fields on which you would like the query results grouped and sorted:

1. Select a field name in the Database Fields list and click Add to display the field name in the Group Fields list.

2. To specify the order for the data, select the desired choice from the Order list.

3. Click Next or the Select tab.

Select Tab: Indicating the Select Conditions

The Select tab lets you narrow down the conditions for the data set (see Figure 14-19). The field conditions you specify here will be written to the query's WHERE clause. This tab is very similar to the Select tab on the Standard Report Wizard. Refer to Chapter 2 for detailed instructions on using this tab.

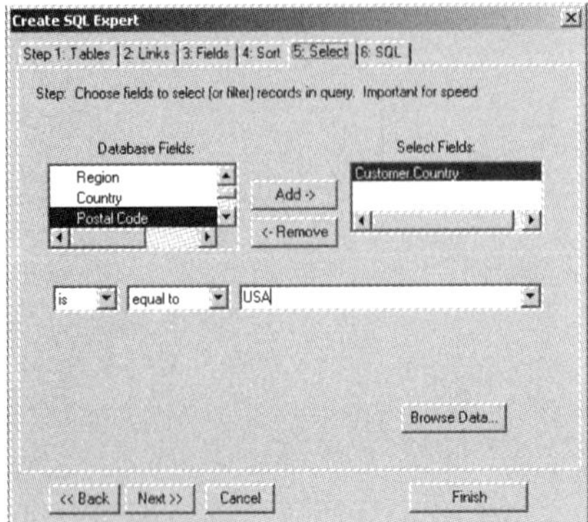

FIGURE 14-19 *The Select tab on the Create SQL Expert allows you to create a WHERE clause.*

To filter data on a particular field:

1. Select the field in the Database Fields list and click Add to display the field name in the Select Fields list.

2. Below the field name list boxes, select the operators and values to complete the filter. Refer to Chapter 2 for details on these operators and how they are used.

3. To see the data in the tables for the field selected, click Browse Data to open a dialog box listing all the values in that field.

4. Click the Next button or the SQL tab.

SQL Tab: Viewing the SQL Statement

The last tab on the Create SQL Expert lets you view the SQL query that the Expert created for you (see Figure 14-20).

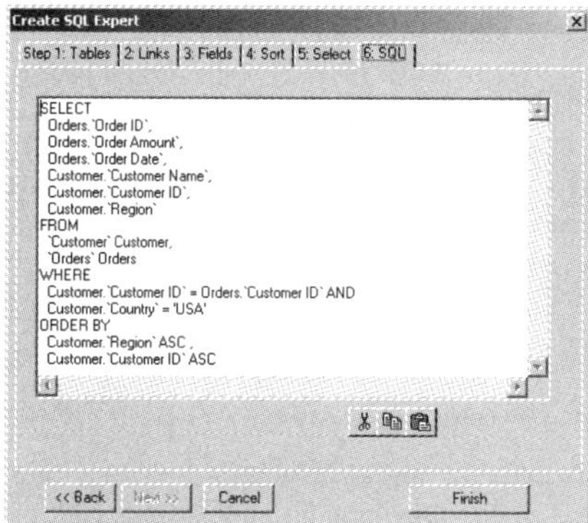

FIGURE 14-20 *The SQL tab on the Create SQL Expert shows you the SQL statement the Expert created.*

To view and run the SQL statement:

1. Make any necessary adjustments to the SQL statement as desired by going back into the tabs. Click Finish to execute the query. A dialog box appears, asking if you want to process the query now.

2. To save the query and its data set, select File, Save As and provide a path and file name.

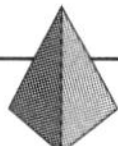

TIP

The Save Data with Query command on the File menu is selected by default. This option allows you to edit and work with your query in the SQL Designer without having to wait for the database to return a dataset. For large datasets, this option saves time during query design and edit.

Editing a SQL Statement Built with the Expert

You can take the Select Statement the Expert wrote for you one step further and customize it, for example, in order to use a select distinct function or employ a function specific to your database. Once you make any manual change to the SQL tab, all the other tabs will disappear, never to return.

Because of inconsistent results when manually editing the query from this SQL dialog (refer back to Figure 14-20), it is suggested that if you want to edit this query further, copy and paste it into a new query. You can still use the Crystal SQL Designer: just copy the query from the SQL tab in the Expert, open a new query by clicking New, and rather than using the Expert, select the option Enter SQL Statement Directly. This opens a dialog box where you can paste the SQL you cut from the Expert and edit all you want with consistent results.

Once you get a query collecting the data you want, you can copy and paste the Select Statement into the Command window of the Database Expert.

Entering a SQL Statement Directly

The Crystal SQL Designer also gives you the option of entering a SQL statement directly, as mentioned in the last section. If you are comfortable enough to write your own SQL statement, using the Crystal SQL Designer is not necessary and you may want to consider typing the SQL Statement right into the Command window.

Starting from an Existing Query

If you have already written a query that is useful for one report but needs only a few changes in order to make it useful for another report, you can use that query to write another. This eliminates the need to rewrite the portion of the query that is useful in your new report.

When you start from an existing query, you use the same dialog box and tabs you used when you initially created that query. The steps that follow call attention to only those items that you may need to use differently.

To base a new query on an existing query:

1. Click the Start from Existing Seagate Query button on the New Query dialog box. The File Open dialog box appears, listing existing queries in the default query path. Surf through your network to the folder where the query you wish to use as a template is saved.

2. Select the query file you want to use and click OK. The query opens in the SQL Designer window.

3. Click the Edit Query toolbar button, or select the Edit, Query menu command. The Create SQL Expert appears.

4. Enter a name for the new query in the Query name text box.

5. Edit the query text as required. Click OK when you finish.

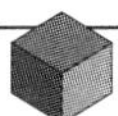

NOTE

If you've previously saved data with a query and you execute the revised query by clicking the Execute Query button or by selecting Edit, Refresh Data, the SQL Designer discards the saved data and runs the query against the database again.

The Crystal SQL Designer is a functional tool, especially good for people new to SQL syntax. More seasoned SQL users will want to use whatever tool they already use to generate SQL queries from their database.

SQL Basics

SQL is a relatively easy language to pick up once you understand how it relates to reports. The following commands make up the basic building blocks of the language:

- SELECT
- FROM
- WHERE
- ORDER BY
- GROUP BY
- HAVING

We will examine each of the clauses and how they relate to the SQL Query built automatically by Crystal Reports. All clauses are not included in every query; which are included depends on the instructions and needs of each individual query.

Many experienced SQL designers use a SQL tool provided by their specific database vendor or a word processor (such as Notepad) to write their SQL statements.

This makes it easy to copy and paste the query into whatever tool you are running it in and also easy to read and edit on the fly. You can copy and paste to and from the Command window easily. You can also keep different versions of the same statement for testing depending on the functionality of your tool. Most other tools are easier to maneuver in than the small window of the SQL Designer!

The SELECT and FROM Statements

The SELECT statement brings back specific fields (or columns) from the database. All SQL queries require the first two statements, SELECT and FROM. The FROM statement tells the database which table the selected fields come from.

Crystal Reports generates the SELECT statement according to which fields the report calls for. This includes all fields on the report: those printed, used in formulas, and so on. The FROM statement lists all tables added to the report.

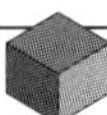

NOTE

The use of uppercase for SQL commands is a common practice among database administrators and programmers. The SQL query language is not case-sensitive. The command "SELECT * FROM customers" gives the same results as "select * from customers".

Adding a WHERE Clause

More often than not, you'll want data to match a particular set of criteria, such as transactions within a date range, products of a particular type, or names of customers in a single city or state. The WHERE clause provides a way for you to specify selection conditions. Think of the WHERE clause in SQL as the equivalent of the Select Expert in Crystal Reports. The SELECT statement with a WHERE clause follows this syntax:

```
SELECT fieldname(s)
FROM tablename(s)
[WHERE <clause>]
```

The *<clause>* after the WHERE keyword specifies the relationship between fields or the condition that you want the data to meet. Usually, the WHERE clause involves a comparison operator that designates how the data should relate to the statement. Make sure you enclose strings and dates used in the WHERE clause in single or double quotes. The ANSI standard operators permitted in the WHERE clause include:

- ◆ = (Equal)
- ◆ > (Greater than)
- ◆ < (Less than)
- ◆ >= (Greater than or equal to)
- ◆ <= (Less than or equal to)
- ◆ <> (Not equal)

As an example, the following statement selects the first and last names from the customers table for users who live in Georgia.

```
SELECT first, last
FROM customers
WHERE state = 'GA'
```

The fields in the WHERE clause don't need to be included in the SELECT clause. The fields in the WHERE clause are most likely going to affect and improve processing speed because the WHERE clause determines which fields are brought from the database into Crystal Reports for more processing or formatting.

Logical Operators in the WHERE Clause

To create more complex statements, SQL allows multiple clauses to be strung together in the WHERE clause. This is accomplished by using the AND, OR, and NOT operators.

The AND operator allows you to require that the data brought back meets more than one restriction. For example, in the last section, you asked the database for users in the customers table who live in GA. Let's say that now you only want to bring back your best customers. You define your best customers as people who generated at least $500,000 in sales. The SQL statement for this request would look like the following.

```
SELECT first, last
FROM customers
WHERE state = 'GA'
AND sales >= 500000
```

You can also use the OR operator. This is a bit different in that you generally get back a larger data set than you would using the AND statement. For example, let's say that you just changed the word AND to OR in the statement above. It would look like this.

```
SELECT first, last
FROM customers
WHERE state = 'GA'
OR sales >= 500000
```

This would bring back everyone in Georgia and also everyone who had sales greater than or equal to $500,000 anywhere in the world (not just Georgia). The OR operator says that if *either* condition is met, bring back the record. In this case, everyone from Georgia (regardless of sales) comes back and everyone who has sales greater than or equal to $500,000 (regardless of location) is included in the data set.

The NOT operator is useful because sometimes it's easier to say what you don't want to include in the data set. For example, let's say you want to see people that live in Georgia but don't have sales of at least $500,000.

```
SELECT first, last
FROM customers
WHERE state = 'GA'
AND NOT sales >= 500000
```

Also be aware that you can use parentheses to differentiate parts of a SQL statement within the WHERE clause. For example, let's say that you want to have only people in Georgia but you want to restrict who comes back further by either sales greater than or equal to $500,000 or customers who purchase more than 1000 items in a year. In this case, you only want Georgia customers, but you need to use the OR operator to help with the last part of the WHERE clause.

```
SELECT first, last
FROM customers
WHERE state = 'GA'
AND (sales >= 500000
OR items>=1000)
```

By using the parentheses around the last two qualifiers, you tell the database that you want only customers in Georgia that have either sales greater than or equal to $500,000 or have purchased at least 1000 items. You can use multiple sets of parentheses in a statement but they all must match up. (By this I mean that if you open a parenthesis, you must have one that matches and closes it.)

Remember, the WHERE clause is the same as the Select Expert in the Designer. If the WHERE clause includes all selection criteria set in the Select Expert, you are assured that the report will process as efficiently as possible. If all the criteria in the Select Expert are not included in the WHERE clause, you may want to consider building a Command for the report with a WHERE clause including as many criteria as possible to improve processing time.

The ORDER BY Clause

The ORDER BY clause allows you to change the order of the data on the report. By default, the data appears in the same order as it appears in the database. By asking the database server to organize it further, it saves Crystal from time-consuming processing.

The two most popular choices for sorting data are in ascending or descending order. By default, SQL sorts in ascending order if no sequence is specified.

The following statement brings back customers in Georgia who either have at least $500,000 in sales or purchased at least 1000 items, and then it sorts records based on last name (from *A* to *Z*).

```
SELECT first, last
FROM customers
WHERE state = 'GA' AND (sales >= 500000 OR items>=1000)
ORDER BY last asc
```

The ORDER BY clause relates most closely to the Sort Records command in Crystal. You can modify this clause in the SQL statement.

The GROUP BY and HAVING Clauses

The GROUP BY clause organizes data into groups. Crystal Reports builds this clause and passes it to the server if you have enabled Perform Grouping On Server on the Database menu and several other report design considerations are met. If this clause does not show up in the Show SQL Query window, you'll need to check the report or global options to make sure Perform Grouping On Server is selected and that the other required conditions are met. Refer to the section "Benefits of Server Side Processing" later in this Chapter for the list of conditions for server side processing.

The GROUP BY function can be used to form aggregates such as SUM, MIN, MAX, and COUNT. The aggregates perform the function on the database server and return the result only (no individual records).

Let's modify the example SQL statement and group the data set by city within the state of Georgia.

```
SELECT first, last
FROM customers
WHERE state = 'GA' AND (sales >= 500000 OR items>=1000)
ORDER BY last asc
GROUP BY city
```

The HAVING clause is used less often. The HAVING clause specifies conditions for group selection. Crystal Reports will not generate a HAVING clause in its own SQL Query under Database/Show SQL Query, but SQL Commands used in the Database Expert will accept a HAVING clause.

In order to use the HAVING clause, you must also use the GROUP BY clause. Also, unlike WHERE clauses, HAVING can include aggregate functions. For example, if you want to select only groups of cities in Georgia that had more than ten customers, you would add the following to the SQL statement:

```
SELECT first, last
FROM customers
WHERE state = 'GA' AND (sales >= 500000 OR items>=1000)
ORDER BY last asc
GROUP BY city
HAVING count(city)>=10
```

This returns only groups where the count of customers in the city exceeds or equals ten.

This section covers only the most basic functionality of the Select Statement. The real power of the syntax comes from the functions within each database's specific "version" of SQL that allows you to manipulate or collect just the specific data you need for a report.

Benefits of Server-Side Processing

Server-side processing refers to those report-processing functions performed on the database server. Mostly, those functions have to do with gathering the data based on the instructions in the SQL Query for use in the report. The benefits of server-side processing include:

◆ Less time connected to the server

◆ Less memory required by the client computer to process the report

◆ Less time to transfer data from the server to the client

When you turn server-side processing on, the client computer sends the SQL statements to the database server through ODBC, which then processes and returns the data set. Crystal Reports relies on the server to process the SQL request, sort the data and return it so that the client computer can perform other duties. Keep in mind a couple of rules when considering whether to use server-side processing:

◆ **You must sort and group your reports in order to use server-side processing.** For simple lists and other types of reports that you don't sort or group, the server has very little processing to do, other than simply returning the data set.

◆ **You must choose a data source that supports SQL.** Reports based on a non-SQL data source such as a query or data dictionary cannot use server-side processing.

To perform the sorting and grouping on the server, your report must follow these guidelines:

◆ The Perform Grouping On Server option must be turned on.

◆ Some form of grouping needs to be used.

◆ The Details section must be hidden. The server processes only hidden sections.

◆ Grouping must be on a database field. Formula fields are processed only on the client.

◆ All running totals need to be based on summary fields.

◆ It must not contain Average or Distinct Count summaries.

◆ It must not contain Top N values. Use the Sort All option.

◆ It must not contain specified order grouping.

If a report contains Date and Time fields, server-side processing works if you group on days or on seconds. Server-side processing does not work if you group on month, year, minutes, or hours.

When you drill down on a hidden section of a report that has server-side processing turned on, Crystal Reports automatically initiates a connection to the server. If the client cannot connect to the server, drilling down on data generates an error.

To turn on server-side processing, choose File, Options from the main menu, and then select the Perform Grouping On Server check box on the Database tab. You can also select Perform Grouping On Server from the Database menu.

Using SQL Expressions

SQL Expressions are special SQL statements that take advantage of some of the more powerful functions provided with your database, such as aggregate functions, date/time functions, or other database-specific functions. A SQL Expression is very similar in function to a Crystal formula. Once you create the SQL Expression, you can include it as a field on your report, reference it in formulas, and sort or group data based on the results of the SQL Expression. The benefit of SQL Expressions is that they are evaluated on the database server, making them fast and efficient.

Many databases provide special functions called *aggregates* that perform summary calculations on database fields. Examples of aggregate functions are SUM, COUNT, MIN, MAX, and AVG. How you use these functions depends on the specific database; refer to your database documentation for instructions on using these and other functions.

You can also use SQL Expressions to perform arithmetic expressions on database fields, such as adding, subtracting, multiplying, and dividing fields of the same data type.

The following examples of functions and arithmetic operators work for Microsoft SQL Server databases.

```
SUM(sales.amount)
DATEPART(MM,titles.pubdate)
(sales.qty) * (titles.price)
```

The SQL Expression Editor is quite similar to the Formula Editor. To use the SQL Expression Editor:

1. Open the Field Explorer and select SQL Expression Field from the list. Click the New icon on the Field Explorer toolbar or right-click SQL Expression Fiend and select New to open the SQL Expression Name dialog box.

2. Once a name is typed in the SQL Expression Name dialog box for the new expression, click OK, and the Expression Editor opens in the Formula Workshop.

3. You can also open the Formula Workshop and either select the SQL Expressions folder and click the New button, or click the down arrow on the New button and select SQL Expression (see Figure 14-21). Either method opens the SQL Expression Editor in the Formula Workshop.

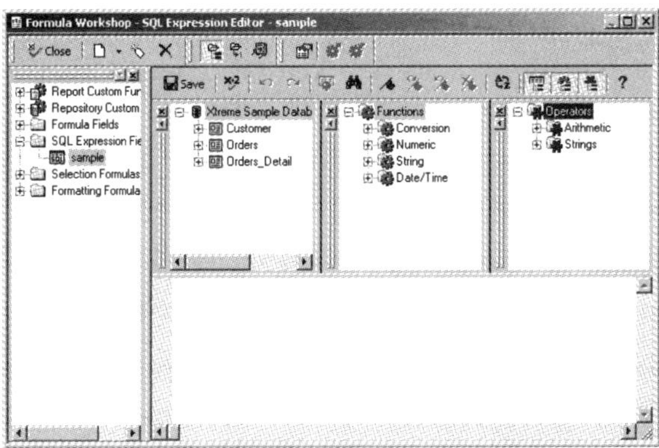

FIGURE 14-21 *You can use SQL Expressions to access specific database functions.*

4. Type the SQL expression into the Editor, using the Field, Function, and Operator trees to add components to the expression.

5. Save the SQL Expression. Crystal provides messages if it finds any errors.

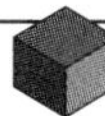

NOTE

The functions in the SQL functions listed are based on the database driver being used to connect to your database. Any database specific functions that the database driver allows will be available in the Function tree.

Creating Reports from Stored Procedures

For very complex queries, it may be beneficial to have the query run on the database server rather than on the client workstation, then port the data into the report. Doing so can speed up the time it takes to generate the data.

A *stored procedure* is a SQL query or series of queries executed upon a call to the stored procedure name with the SQL EXEC command. The main differences between SQL statements in a saved file and a stored procedure is that a stored procedure can take parameters (values you can pass into the procedure), use variables, and access database system functions. Stored Procedures are also stored on the database server, not a client machine, so maintenance is easier.

The main advantage to using a stored procedure over a query is that the dataset is processed on the database server, which speeds up the run time of the query.

To base a report on a stored procedure, first write the stored procedure and save it on the database server. Your stored procedure can use parameters, if you like. You can specify the values to pass in later.

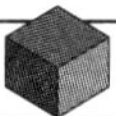

NOTE

Not all SQL database types support stored procedures. Check the documentation for your database to determine whether this is an option for you. Stored procedures are created within the database, not within Crystal Reports or the Crystal SQL Designer.

To create a new report based on a stored procedure:

1. Select the Database tab in the File, Options menu. Make sure the Stored Procedure box is checked (see Figure 14-22). This allows reporting on stored procedures in the database.

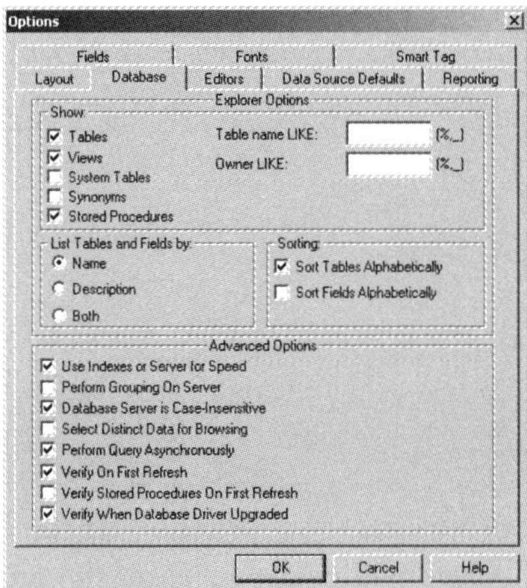

FIGURE 14-22 *The Database tab lets you select the types of data objects upon which you can base your reports.*

2. Start a new report. Select the data source you want to report from in the Database Expert.

3. Expand the list of Stored Procedures for that data source. The folder structure for Tables, Views, and Stored Procedures (as seen in Figure 14-23) is built into the Database Expert. If your data source does not have any stored procedures, the folder name will not be listed.

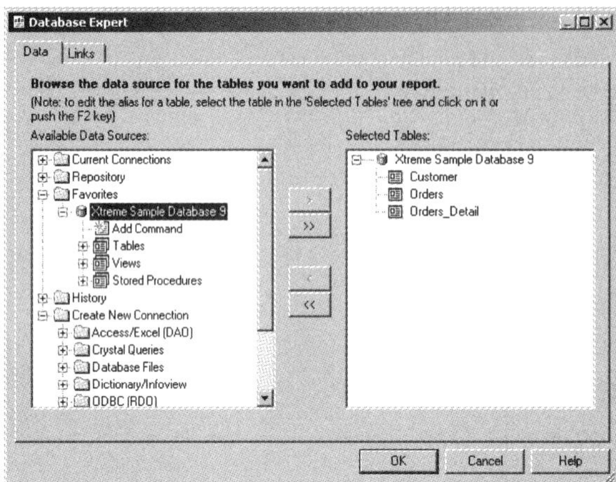

FIGURE 14-23 *The sample database includes all three categories of object types.*

4. Select the stored procedure you wish to use for your report. If the stored procedure contains any parameters, you will need to answer the prompt when you connect to the procedure. The prompt will also automatically show up in the Parameter Fields list in the Field Explorer. You may want to edit the parameter and add prompting text.

5. Continue building the report as described in Chapter 2.

When you click the Preview tab, Crystal Reports collects data for the report. Each time you refresh the report data by clicking the Refresh button, Crystal Reports executes the stored procedure on the database server and returns data as you identified in the stored procedure's SELECT statement. If your stored procedure requires parameters, the Stored Procedure Input Parameters dialog box appears, enabling you to enter values for each parameter.

Final Suggestions for Working with Your Data

When working with any database, often the location or the structure is modified after you first create the report. Crystal Reports has several features that allow you to verify the database structure, to change the location of the data used in the report, and to change the database driver completely.

Verifying a Database

If a table, query, or stored procedure changes after designing a report, it is a good idea to have Crystal Reports communicate with the database to update its own internal references. For example, if a field in the database was changed from a varchar data type to a char data type, you may get an error when you try to run a report using that field. By running the Verify Database utility, however, you can put the report in sync with the updated database.

1. With the affected report open in Crystal Reports, choose Database, Verify Database.

2. If the table, query, or stored procedure has been changed since the report was created or the last Verify Database operation, Crystal Reports asks whether you want to update the report. If the report has the current data, a message box lets you know that the database is up-to-date.

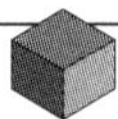

NOTE

It is possible to set some automatic Verify Database options. Under File, Options, the Database tab provides several alternatives.

Changing the Location of a Database

From time to time, you might need to connect to a database on a server other than the one you used when you created the report. This might happen if you develop the report on a test database and move the report to a production database later. To specify the location of a different database, use the Set Datasource Location command. If the database is different, Crystal Reports automatically detects this and brings up a Map Fields dialog box.

The purpose of the Map Fields dialog box is to allow you to specify fields that may be the same in both databases, but named differently. In past versions of Crystal Reports, this would cause an error, and you would have to reinsert all of the fields that didn't have an exact name match. The Map Fields feature allows you the option of mapping fields from one database to another on your report.

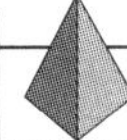

TIP

The Map Fields dialog box only appears once, so make sure you are careful to map all of your fields from one database to the other.

1. With the report open, select Database, Set Datasource Location. If your report is based on a database, the Set Datasource Location dialog box opens (see Figure 14-24). Continue with step 2. If your report is based on a dictionary, the Choose New Location dialog box appears, showing the current path and file name for the data file selected. Set the new path and file name as desired, then click Open. Crystal asks if you want to set (propagate) the path for all the tables in the database to the newly selected path.

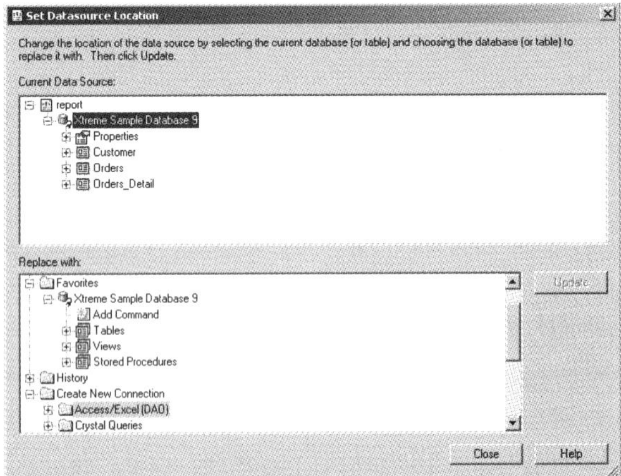

FIGURE 14-24 *Use the Set Datasource Location dialog box to change the location of the report tables.*

2. Select the table name for which you need to change the location from the Current Data Source list.

3. Click the appropriate new or other table name in the Replace With list.

4. If the table contains fields that are named differently or have changed type, you will be presented with the Map Fields dialog box (see Figure

14-25). Simply select the unmapped fields in the upper left window and match them to the new name or type field on the upper right window. When they match, click on the Map button. Continue with all of the other unmapped fields on the report.

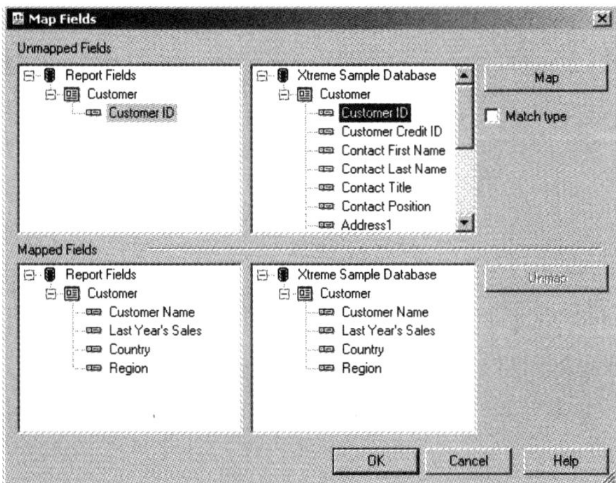

FIGURE 14-25 *Match unmapped fields from one database to the new name in the target database so the report will work correctly.*

NOTE

If you use a SQL/ODBC data source, you may want to remove the server name from the location. This way, the report can be copied to multiple servers and databases without having to set the location each time it is copied. To do this, simply remove the server name from the table's location in the Table text box. For example, rather than having the authors table displayed as "pubs.dbo.authors", it appears as "dbo.authors".

5. When you finish setting the location for all the tables, click the Done button.

Changing the Database Driver

Sometimes a situation arises in which you need to change the driver with which you connect to a particular database, such as when moving from an ODBC driver to a native driver or when the ODBC driver is updated. Use the Set Datasource Location dialog box to convert to a different database driver:

1. Select Database, Set Datasource Location from the main menu. The Set Datasource Location dialog box opens.

2. Select the current data source from the Current Datasource list.

3. Click the data source name that you want to use to replace the old data source in the Replace With list. This can be the same data source with a new driver associated with it.

4. Click Update. Crystal updates the data source in the report with the data source you selected, including the driver.

5. Click Close.

Summary

You can retrieve data from a database to use in a report in several ways:

- Let Crystal Reports build a SQL query for the report.
- Write a SQL Command or use a SQL Command from the Repository.
- Use the Crystal SQL Designer or another SQL tool to build your own SQL statements for use as a Command.
- Base reports on stored procedures or database views

Once you define a report, you can also use SQL Expressions directly in the report as though they were a field in the database tables. Crystal evaluates these SQL Expressions on the server, which speeds up their performance.

Through the Verify Database feature, you can query the database to update the fields in the report based on changes to tables or stored procedures. If you need to change the location of a database or table, you can use the Set Datasource Location option to designate a different database or server upon which to base the report.

Chapter 15

This chapter introduces you to OLAP concepts and focuses on designing reports from an OLAP data source using the OLAP Report Creation Wizard in Crystal Reports. You must have knowledge of your specific OLAP data source in order to design reports for it. Building OLAP reports is usually more difficult than building reports from relational data sources because the data itself is more complex.

NOTE

An OLAP report looks similar to the cross-tab type report you have already seen. In some ways, OLAP describes the data source being used more than the style of the report.

What Is OLAP?

OLAP, short for Online Analytical Processing, is a technology for creating multidimensional structures for use in data analysis. The term *cubes*, or *hypercubes*, refers to these structures. They are referred to as *cubes* throughout this chapter.

OLAP technology allows people to design cubes of data; Crystal Reports is the tool for designing reports using those cubes as the data source. This multidimensional concept (OLAP) allows for more sophisticated and compounded analysis of data. Multi-dimensional data (MDD) sources (cubes) have become more popular because of the analysis power of reviewing data in three or more dimensions rather than in only two.

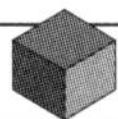

NOTE

The only difference between a cube and a hypercube is that a hypercube has more than three dimensions. The OLAP industry uses both terms to generically describe OLAP structures. You can use Crystal Reports to design reports from both cubes and hypercubes. As mentioned earlier, both structures are referred to simply as *cubes* throughout this chapter.

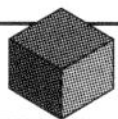

NOTE

Crystal Analysis Professional is a cube analyzing tool, providing advanced OLAP functionality from a dashboard-like interface. This tool integrates with Crystal Enterprise, just as Crystal Reports does, to create an impressive suite of tools. Learn more from the Crystal Decisions Web site at **www.crystaldecisions.com**, or call Bridge-Builder at 1-888-274-3432 with questions or for more information.

Crystal Reports helps you design reports based on existing cubes. These reports take advantage of the dimensional and hierarchical structure of cubes. Think of OLAP reports as a smaller, more manageable subset of the cube data.

Finance, marketing, and modeling research and analysis companies (or areas of companies) commonly use cubes and OLAP because of the powerful analysis capabilities they offer. Cubes provide a large amount of data all at once, all in relation to other data, allowing deeper analysis.

How OLAP Differs from Relational Databases

Relational databases are two-dimensional, and tables are linked to have all of the fields from each table available for a report. OLAP uses a different structure. OLAP defines a data set in terms of *dimensions* and *hierarchies*. These dimensions and hierarchies display in a three-dimensional or more grid structure. Picture something like a Rubik's Cube (see Figure 15-1). The major entities, factors, or components of a data set represent the dimensions. If you typically work with key fields in relational databases, you can think of dimensions as being like a key field.

Each dimension contains data organized in hierarchies. Hierarchies have multiple levels representing the different levels of data in a dimension. A date dimension might have hierarchical levels such as year, quarter, and month. Each level of the hierarchy is referred to   in this case, year, quarter, and month—as *members* of the date dimension.

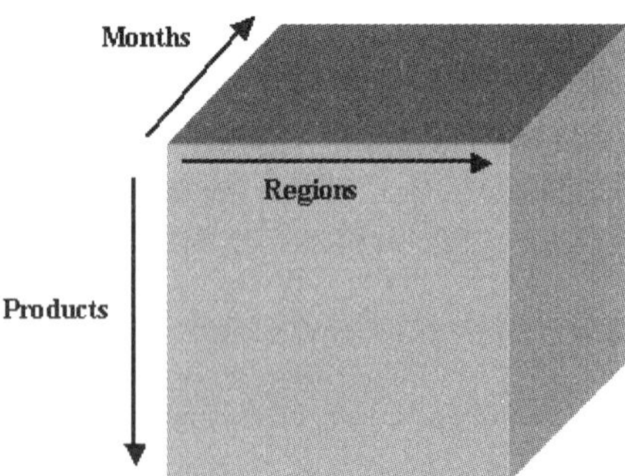

FIGURE 15-1 *You can think of an OLAP cube like a Rubik's Cube, where each side represents a different dimension of the data.*

The relationships between levels can have many different names. Each OLAP tool uses specific names for the relationship among hierarchical levels. Some common names include *levels*, *children*, *parents*, or *descendants*. Generally, a downward connection from a parent to children is a one-to-many relationship, whereas an upward connection from children to parent is a many-to-one relationship.

To better understand the relationships within a dimension, look at the sample dimension in Figure 15-2. This region dimension is from a Crystal Holos cube. Think of a cube relationship like the parts of a tree. The following bullets explain the relationships in the region dimension:

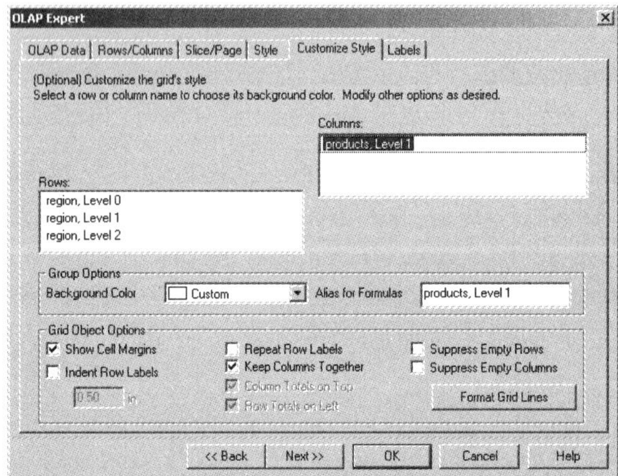

FIGURE 15-2 *The region dimension has a hierarchical structure. Crystal Holos uses the word* Level *to describe the different hierarchical levels of data in the region dimension.*

◆ Any value in the dimension is called a member. For example, World, Region, and Country (levels 0, 1, and 2) would all be members of the Region dimension. In Figure 15-2, region has Level 0 (world), Level 1 (regions), and Level 2 (country) dimensions.

◆ Generally, a member can have only one parent. Here, world, Level 0 is the parent of region, Level 1; region has no other parent.

◆ A member with no parent is the root member. World, Level 0 would be the root member—it has no parent.

◆ A member with no children is a leaf, leaf node, or outermost branch member. Country, Level 2 is an outermost branch member. It has no children.

◆ All children of a parent are sometimes called descendants. Thus, all levels below region, Level 0 would be considered descendants.

In the region dimension shown in Figure 15-2, notice that Crystal Holos refers to the hierarchical levels of data as Level 0, Level 1, and so on. As mentioned earlier, you must know your OLAP data source or at least the particulars of the cube you use for a report. This now becomes evident because to use this cube, you need to know that Level 0 represents world, Level 1 represents regions, and Level 2 represents country.

You do not need to know how to design cubes (assuming you can access cubes built by others), but you do need to understand their structure and the relationship between dimensions and hierarchies to design meaningful reports. If you feel comfortable designing reports based on relational databases, you can become accustomed to designing reports based on OLAP cubes.

OLAP Data Sources

You can use Crystal Reports to design a report from any of the following OLAP data sources:

◆ Hyperion Essbase
◆ IBM DB2 OLAP Server
◆ Crystal Holos HDC cube
◆ Microsoft OLE DB Provider for OLAP Services

If your company currently uses any of the OLAP data sources listed above, you can design a Crystal Report from that source. The OLAP Report Creation Wizard employs a grid object method to build a report. A grid object resembles a cross-tab object, plotting data across rows and columns and organizing hierarchies that you specify into bands. Three or more dimensions can be included in a single grid object, and that object can be formatted and pivoted to meet your analysis needs. Crystal's OLAP Report Creation Wizard uses this method.

Creating OLAP Reports

The next section guides you through using the OLAP Report Creation Wizard. The steps are fairly generic because each data source differs slightly. Once you have an OLAP report or two designed based on your particular OLAP source, you will become familiar with the language and details of your specific data source and find these reports to be exceptionally useful.

NOTE

To use the OLAP Report Creation Wizard, you need to have an OLAP data source. The screen shots in this section use a sample cube built by Crystal Holos. A sample Crystal Holos cube can be found in the Crystal Decisions\Crystal Reports\Samples\ Databases\OLAP Data directory.

Using the OLAP Report Creation Wizard

You must start the OLAP Report Creation Wizard by choosing New Report from the File menu. The wizard walks you though designing a report step by step, just like the other Report Wizards described in Chapter 2.

In Crystal Reports, select File, New or click the New button to open the Crystal Reports Gallery. Click the OLAP option to open the OLAP Report Creation Wizard with the OLAP Data screen displayed (see Figure 15-3).

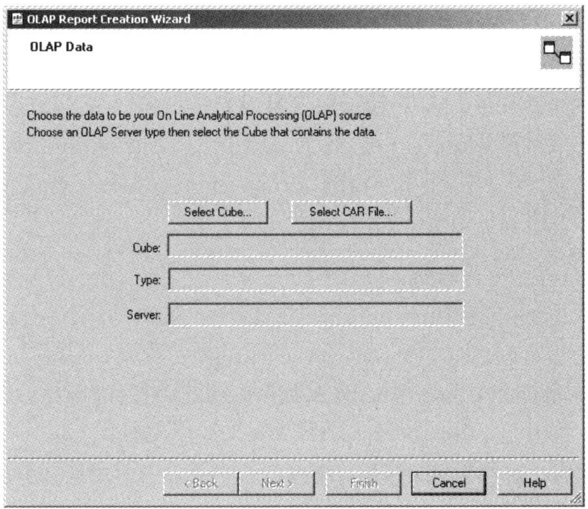

FIGURE 15-3 *Start with the OLAP Data screen in the OLAP Report Creation Wizard.*

The OLAP Report Creation Wizard is updated in version 9 from previous versions of Crystal Reports. The windows are redesigned to match the changes to the other Report Wizards. The first time through the wizard you will use the same page functionality as the other wizards. Once you have a report built, you can reopen the OLAP Expert and scroll through the tabs listed below. For now, you must complete each page in the order it is presented to build the initial report. The tabs you'll see in the OLAP Expert include:

◆ OLAP Data

◆ Rows/Columns

◆ Slice/Page

◆ Style

◆ Chart

◆ Customize Style

◆ Labels

You can choose what data shows on the report and up to 20 different ways of displaying the resulting data. Conditional formatting using formulas or the Highlighting Expert is supported, along with Report Parts functionality to make critical report data available for limited-size PDA viewers.

Selecting Your Data Source on the Data Page

Building a new OLAP report walks you through the wizard page by page. You must address each page sequentially to build the OLAP report. Once the report is built, you can use the OLAP Expert, which is similar in functionality to the OLAP Report Creation Wizard, which has tabs across the top for easy navigation to the element of the report that you want to edit.

The Data page contains blank areas when you first open it. You specify your data source here, but unlike selecting a button on the Data page of the Standard Report Creation Wizard, you need to maneuver through a few dialog boxes to select your data source. To select a data source for your OLAP report, you must first choose between selecting a cube or a CAR file. A CAR file is a Crystal Analysis report. The following steps describe connecting to an OLAP data source using the Select Cube option:

1. With the Data screen open in the OLAP Report Creation Wizard, click the Select Cube button. This opens the Crystal OLAP Connection Browser dialog box. Expand any nodes in this dialog box to see whether the cube you wish to report from has already been added.

2. If the cube you wish to use is listed, select it and click OK. If it is not listed, click the Add Server button on the Crystal OLAP Connection Browser to open the New Server dialog box. Select a server type from the list, using the down arrow. The options listed here may vary from network to network, depending on the data sources available to you. In most cases, you will see at least four choices: Microsoft OLE DB Provider for OLAP Services, IBM DB2 OLAP Server, Hyperion Essbase server, and Holos HDC cubes.

3. In the New Server dialog box, choose the type of OLAP data source you want to use. For this example, Holos HDC cube is chosen.

4. Enter a path or click the Browse button and specify the path to your data source. You must also enter a caption or a cube name to the text box before the OK button becomes available. Choose your cube as shown in Figure 15-4 and click OK. Doing so brings you back to the Data tab with the appropriate fields filled in, as shown in Figure 15-5.

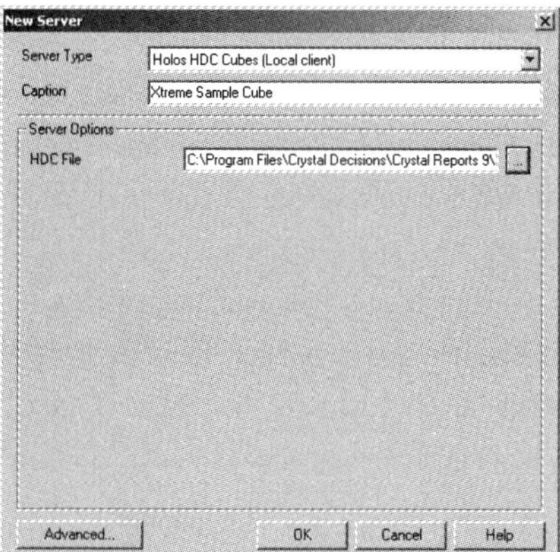

FIGURE 15-4 *Select the Holos HDC cubes Server type, and then browse to the HDC file you want to use as a data source.*

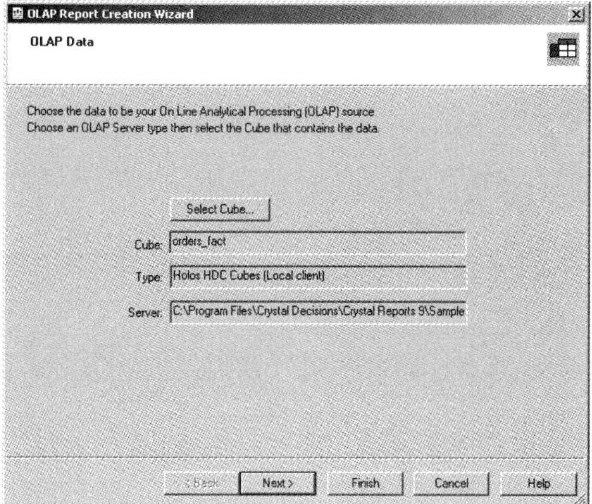

FIGURE 15-5 *After setting the path to your data source, Crystal Reports fills in the appropriate fields on the OLAP Data tab.*

Crystal Reports 9 includes a sample HDC data source for your use and experimentation. This data source is found under C:\Program Files\Crystal Decisions\Crystal Reports 9\Samples\En\Databases\Olap Data\Xtreme.hdc.

Adding Rows and Columns

The Rows/Columns page lists all the dimensions of your cube in the Dimensions list. This tab allows you to select which dimensions you want to use for your report. Add the dimensions that you want for the rows and columns in your report by selecting the name of the dimension from the Dimension list and clicking the forward or backward buttons (see Figure 15-6). Once you add the dimensions you want on your report, notice that you can click on the Select Row Members button to specify values within the dimension to include on the report (see Figure 15-7).

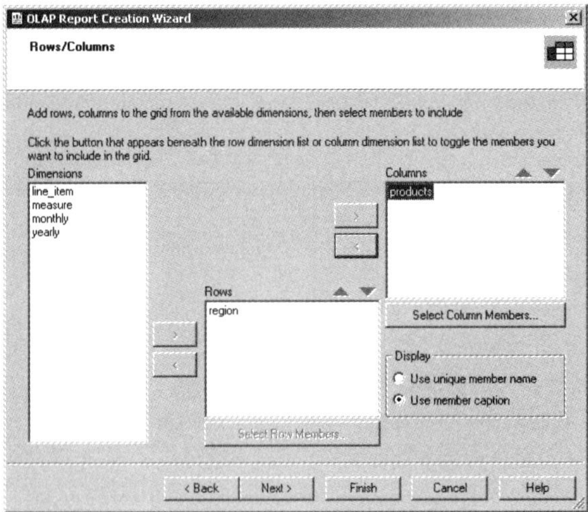

FIGURE 15-6 *Select the row and column dimensions for your report from the Dimensions list.*

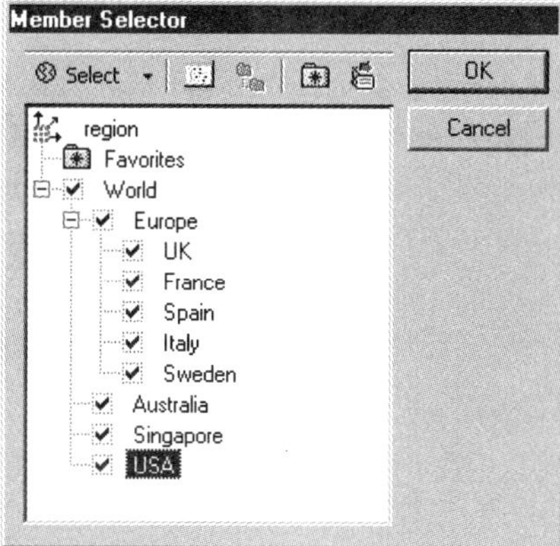

FIGURE 15-7 *Select the hierarchy of values to show in the columns and rows using the Member Selector dialog box.*

NOTE

Figure 15-6 looks and acts similar to the Cross-Tab Expert described in Chapter 11. Similarly, the report created using this wizard has a cross-tab feel.

To add the dimensions to the report:

1. Highlight the Region dimension and click the forward button to the left of the Rows list. Highlight the Products dimension and click the forward button next to the Columns list.

2. If you click the Select Row Member button with Products selected, you'll see the Member Selector window for products. If you click a plus sign, you'll see all of the product categories. You can select the products that you wish to see on the report.

3. Do the same thing with the Region dimension Select Row Members button. Choose the regions to include in the report (see Figure 15-7). Click OK to close the dialog box.

4. Click on the Next button to continue to the next page.

Working with the Slice/Page Page

This page allows you to limit the number of records that are returned (similar to the Report Selection Expert). Also, you can specify the number of grids that will be displayed (see Figure 15-8). The Page area allows you to specify which levels of the OLAP data source to use in the report. For each level you bring back, you create an additional grid.

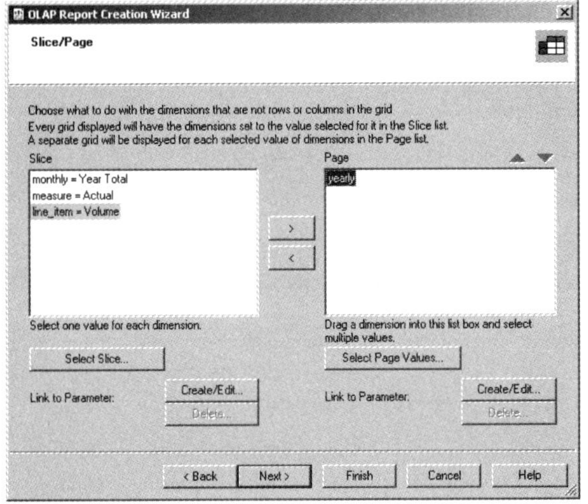

FIGURE 15-8 *The Slice/Page page allows you to control how the dimensions on your report display.*

To modify other dimensions using the Slice/Page page:

1. Select a dimension name from the Slice list. Click the Select Slice button to open the Member Selector dialog box. Select the values you want to see in the report by checking and/or clearing boxes next to the options for that field.

2. Click OK to close the Member Selector dialog box.

3. Click the forward button to add the slice to the Page area.

4. Click on the Select Page Values button and you'll see the same list of members selected in the Member Selector for that page. Remember, the number of fields you pick here determines the number of OLAP grids on your report.

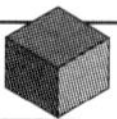

NOTE

Using the Member Selector, you can select members of a dimension to be included in the grid using the checkboxes next to an item name, or by clicking the Select button down arrow to expand a list of options for selecting some or all members of that dimension.

Formatting Your Report with the Style Page

The Style page gives you some options for formatting your report (see Figure 15-9). OLAP reports look similar to cross-tab reports, and you have 20 different report styles to choose from.

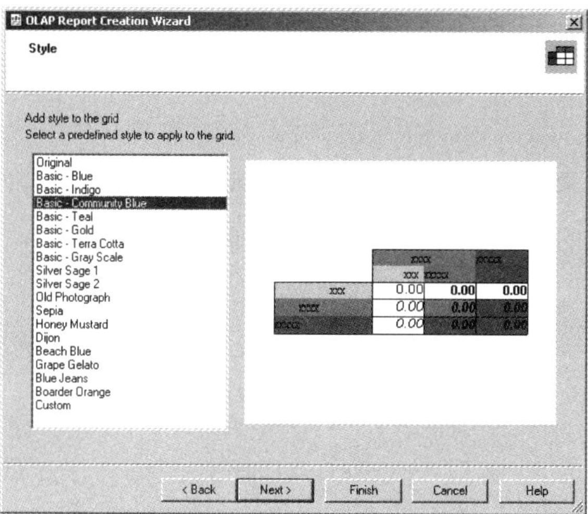

FIGURE 15-9 *Format your grid using the Style tab options.*

Using colors or shading helps with viewing the data in your grid. Experimenting with the options on this tab will help you determine the format that works best with your data, depending on what you want the report to focus on.

Showing Data Pictorially Using the Chart Page

You can create a chart for each grid based on the data within it. The Chart tab works similarly to the Standard Report Creation Wizard or inserting a chart within Crystal Reports (see Figure 15-10). Refer to Chapter 13 for more information on using the charting functions in Crystal Reports.

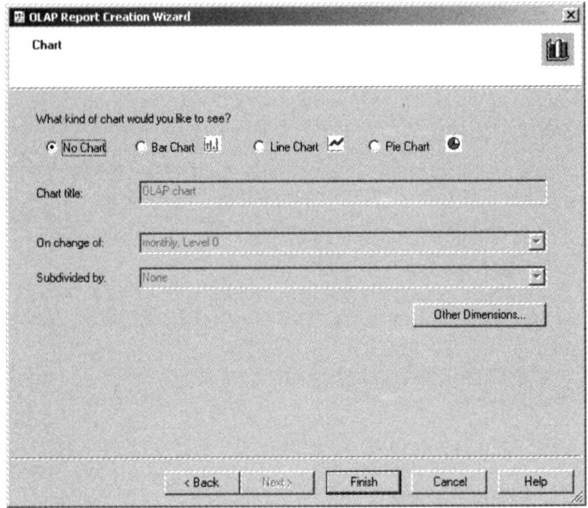

FIGURE 15-10 *Add a chart based on OLAP grid data to the report.*

Click Finish to exit the wizard and insert the OLAP grid on the report. The grid is in the report header section or Group Header section, depending on how many members you selected for the Page dimension. By default the OLAP report opens on the Preview tab. You can toggle between Design and Preview like any other type of report to format the report. There are many more formatting options available now that you have your basic grid layout determined.

Once an OLAP grid object is on the report, you can open the OLAP Expert to edit the grid. Select the OLAP grid object in the Design or Preview tab, right-click in the upper left corner, and from the shortcut menu select OLAP Expert. This opens a dialog box with tabs which allow you to edit the OLAP grid on the report.

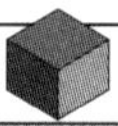

NOTE

If you right-click on the grid object in the Design tab, the options available in the shortcut menu will be slightly different than if you were on the Preview tab. Both menus are covered in the following sections of this chapter.

Looking at the OLAP Grid

The result of the OLAP Report Creation Wizard displays a report containing a grid object that looks very similar to a cross-tab. Grid objects have some similarities with cross-tab objects when it comes to formatting, but also contain many additional functions which take advantage of OLAP data. Both the formatting options and the functional options are discussed in the following sections.

Let's look at the grid object in Figure 15-11 carefully. The values you see listed across the top of the grid object are the slices of each dimension that the OLAP grid is displaying. For example, the data in the grid is showing the actual volume for the world for last year. This information comes from the label fields listed right above the grid object. These are the options selected on the Slice/Page page of the Expert or Wizard.

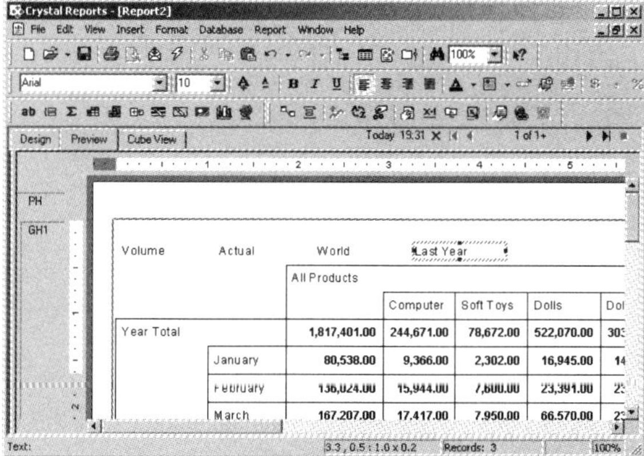

FIGURE 15-11 *OLAP grids look similar to cross-tabs, but actually contain much more data due to the OLAP data source for the grid.*

Manipulating the OLAP Grid

Once you have an OLAP grid on the report, you have many options to change the data displayed in the grid and the formatting for both individual fields within the grid, and the overall grid itself.

To format the grid object as a whole, follow these steps:

1. Select the grid object by clicking the blank white space in the upper left corner of the grid object on either the Design or Preview tabs. Be sure you are clicking the object, not a particular field within the object.

2. Right-click, and select Format OLAP Grid from the shortcut menu.

3. The Format Editor opens for the OLAP grid object with formatting tabs available for use in formatting the grid as a whole.

4. Set any formatting options then click OK to close the Format Editor.

Drilling Down on the Grid Object

Depending on the depth of the data in the OLAP data source used by the report, you may be able to drill down on levels of the grid object to see child member data. For example, if the grid object currently displays regional data (see Figure 15-12), you could double click on that level name in the grid to expand the grid to see the child data to that regional level (see Figure 15-13). If there is no child data for a row or column, then drilling down has no effect on the grid object.

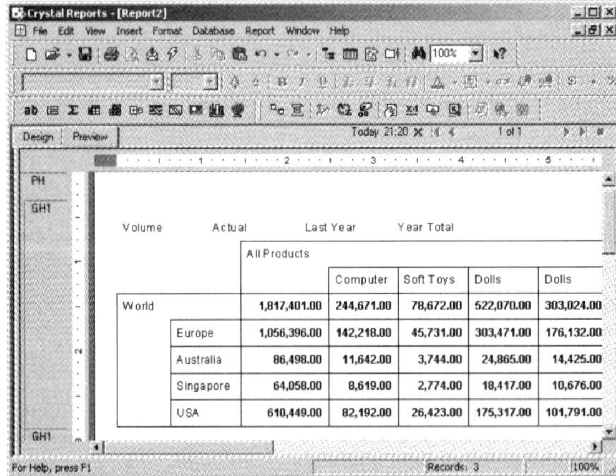

FIGURE 15-12 *This report shows two members of the Region row on the grid, World and Regions (Europe, Australia, Singapore, and USA).*

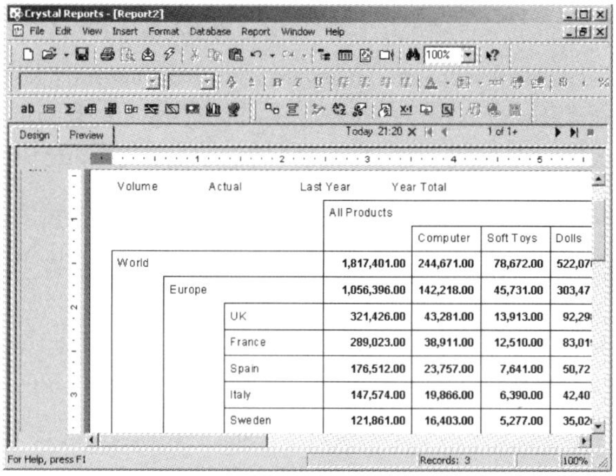

FIGURE 15-13 *Double-click Europe on the grid object to drill down to child data for Europe.*

Resize any of the cells on the grid object by selecting the cell you want to resize and using the resizing handles to adjust the cell. You'll notice that just like cross-tabs, the cell you select will select all cells of that same level. For example, if you select the cell at the junction of UK and All Products shown in Figure 15-13, you will select all values in the All Products column, for every region within Europe (at products, level 2). If you select the value at the junction of UK and Computer (see Figure 15-14) you will select all values for products, level 2 for all toys.

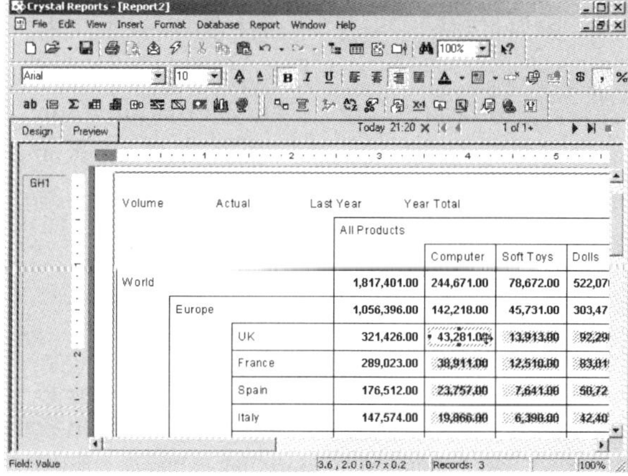

FIGURE 15-14 *Select the cell at the junction of UK and Computer to select all cells at that level.*

Options for Adding to or Changing the Grid Object

Once you right-click on the grid object, the shortcut menu that opens has many options for manipulating and changing the grid object listed below. If you are on the Details tab when you right-click, the Launch Analyzer option is not listed.

- ◆ **OLAP Expert.** This option opens the OLAP Expert where you can change most elements of the grid object. This option is covered in detail in this chapter.

- ◆ **Format OLAP Grid.** This option opens the Format Editor for the OLAP grid object and allows formatting of the object as a whole.

- ◆ **Insert Chart.** This option opens the Chart Expert with appropriate tabs for OLAP data to insert a chart onto the report.

- ◆ **Insert Map.** This option opens the Map Expert with the OLAP type map selected. Use the Map Expert to build a map based on the geographical data in your OLAP grid.

- ◆ **Launch Analyzer.** This option opens the Cube View tab which is an OLAP Analyzer with its own full set of functionality for manipulating the OLAP grid in a worksheet style environment rather than the grid. Any changes you make using the Analyzer will be applied to the Design and Preview tabs of the report.

- ◆ **Pivot OLAP Grid.** This option pivots the OLAP grid's rows and columns.

- ◆ **Set OLAP Cube Location.** This option allows you to point the OLAP report to a new OLAP data source location. This option cannot be undone.

- ◆ **Size and Position.** This option opens the Size and Position dialog box providing the ability to set the exact size and position of the X and Y axis of the OLAP grid object on the report.

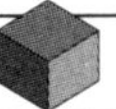 **NOTE**

If you select an individual field on the grid object then right-click, you will see different options on the shortcut menu which are described later in this chapter.

Using the OLAP Expert

The OLAP Expert contains many options already seen in the OLAP Report Creation Wizard. Once you have an OLAP grid object on the report, you can use the OLAP Expert functionality to manipulate most elements of the grid object.

As an example of what you would manipulate and why, take the report in Figure 15-11. This report shows information for last year. Maybe you want to change the report to see data for this year, or you want to see budget rather than actual. This is easily changed using the OLAP Expert.

The following list explains the tabs available on the OLAP Expert.

◆ **OLAP Data.** You are not able to edit this tab.

◆ **Rows/Columns.** Manipulate the rows or columns to include in the grid object. You can also change the row members to include in the grid object.

◆ **Slice/Page.** Change the slice value being viewed in the grid object. This is where you can change actual to budget to see an entire new dataset in the grid. You cannot change the Page dimension using the OLAP Expert, rather you must re-open the OLAP Report Creation Wizard by Selecting Report, OLAP Report Settings. (How to do this is covered later in this chapter.)

◆ **Style.** Select a different style for the grid object.

◆ **Customize Style.** Refine the grid object using the style options on this tab. Use the Alias for formulas option, which allows for creating an alias of a row or column so that you can refer to it in the Formula Editor. See the "Conditionally Formatting the Grid Object" section in this chapter for an explanation of this option.

◆ **Labels.** Manipulate the order, position, and spacing of the labels on the grid object. The labels listed here refer to the labels listed across the top of the grid object identifying which slice of data the grid is currently showing.

To change the slices of the grid on the report, follow these steps:

1. Right-click on the grid object and from the shortcut menu select OLAP Expert. Be sure you are not clicking on a value in the grid, but in the white space in the upper left corner.

2. Go to the Slice/Page page in the OLAP Expert.

3. Select measure = Actual in the Slice list (see Figure 15-15). Click Select Slice to open the Member Selector dialog box. Select Budget and click OK. Now measure = Budget appears in the Slice list.

4. Click OK to close the OLAP Expert. The changes you just made are applied to the grid object immediately. The numbers in the cells are now budget, not actual.

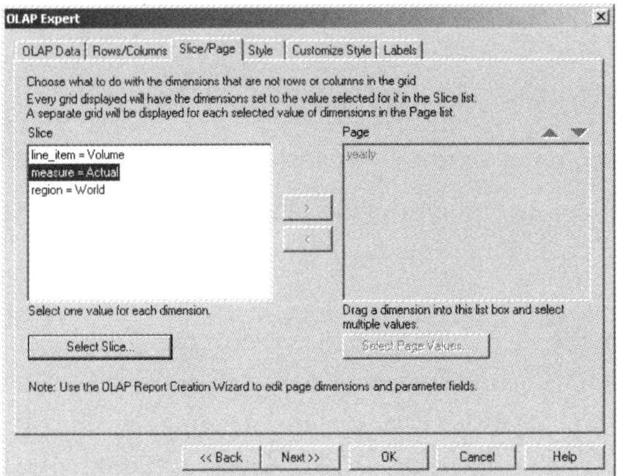

FIGURE 15-15 *Click the Select Slice button to open the Member Selector dialog box to change the member that represents the slice on the grid object.*

Formatting Grid Values

Once you have an OLAP grid object on a report, you can format the values in the grid. Select any row or column name or value in the grid, right-click, and a short-cut menu opens with options. The Design tab provides basic options for all fields, including Format Field, Highlighting Expert, and Size and Position. If you are in the Preview tab you will see the same options for cell values, but many more options are available for the row and column names (see Figure 15-16).

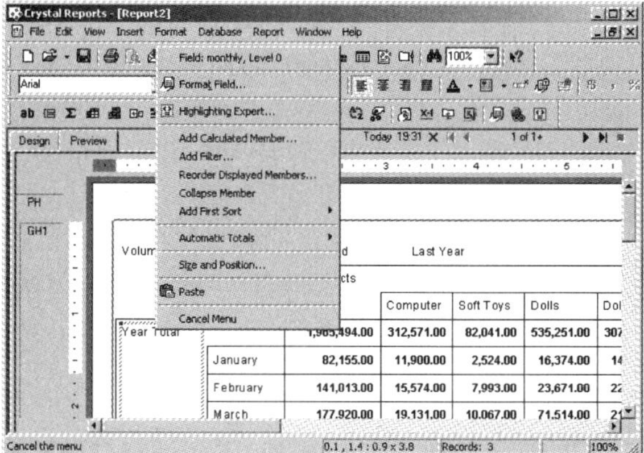

FIGURE 15-16 *Many options are available for manipulating the rows and columns of the grid.*

NOTE

You must be on the Preview tab to see all the options in Figure 15-16, which are described below.

Additional options on the shortcut menu for rows and columns include:

◆ **Add Calculated Member.** This option opens the Calculated Member dialog box where you can create additional calculated fields to add to the grid object.

◆ **Add Filter.** This opens the Define Filter dialog box where you can define an actual value filter or a top/bottom N filter for the selected row.

◆ **Reorder Displayed Members.** This opens the Reorder Displayed Members dialog where you can set the exact order in which you want the members of that row or column to be listed.

◆ **Collapse or Expand Member.** This option either collapses or expands the member selected. Essentially this drills down to the next level of data in the data source, or collapses back up to the next higher level.

CONDITIONALLY FORMATTING GRID CELLS USING FORMULAS

The Alias for Formulas option allows for creating an alias of a row or column so that you can refer to it in the Formula Editor. The function used in the Formula Editor is GridRowColumnValue.

Here's an example of how to work with the conditional formatting.

1. First, you need to create an alias name in the Customize Style tab of the OLAP Expert for the row name you want to conditionally format. For this example, I selected products, level 1.

2. In the Alias for Formulas box, type an alias you will refer to in the formula, such as the word products. Close the OLAP Expert.

3. Open the Format Editor for the products, level 1 row, go to the Font tab, and select the X+2 button across from Color. Enter the following formula:

```
If GridRowColumnValue("Product") =
"Computer Games" then crRed else
crBlack
```

4. Close and Save the formula, then click OK to close the Format Editor.

5. Preview the report to see the Computer Games row name in red.

This formula, applied to the products, level 1 row would cause the Computer Games row name to print red. Apply this formula to the font color of a value in the grid object, and if that value were in the Computer Games row it would print red.

◆ **Add First Sort.** This option opens a submenu with sorting options. Once you change the sort, you may see additional items in the shortcut menu regarding sorting.

◆ **Automatic Totals.** This option opens a submenu with choices for adding or removing the automatic totals from the grid object.

Conditionally Formatting the Grid Object

There are two different ways to conditionally format grid object values: using the Highlighting Expert or writing formulas using the Formula Workshop. Using the Highlighting Expert is much easier than writing out formulas. The highlighting Expert is covered in detail in Chapter 6, and formulas are discussed in Chapter 7.

Launching the Analyzer

Launching the Analyzer opens a new Cube View tab on top of the Preview tab that looks and functions much like an OLAP worksheet (see Figure 15-17). If you are familiar with previous members of the Crystal family of products, you may notice that this tool looks and functions very much like the Info Worksheet (that was included with Crystal Info) and Crystal Analysis Professional. This tab provides a different interface for manipulating what information prints in the grid.

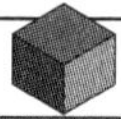

NOTE

The Alias for Formula option on the Customize Style tab is still necessary if writing out formulas using the Formula Workshop for conditionally formatting OLAP grid fields. I would suggest using the Highlighting Expert rather that writing formulas. See the sidebar in this chapter for information on using the Alias for Formulas option and the special functions available for conditionally formatting grid object and cross-tab fields if you find this necessary.

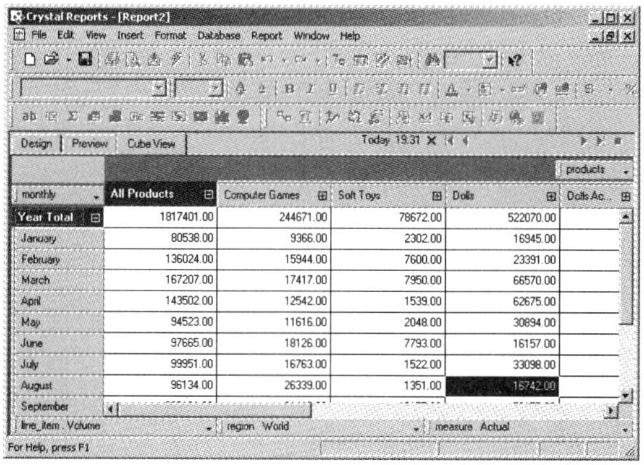

FIGURE 15-17 *Use the Cube View tab to manipulate which data prints in the grid object on the Preview tab.*

The Cube View tab has all of the functionality found in the Preview tab of the OLAP Report through the shortcut menu options. It also allows you to change the "slice" and "members" without opening the OLAP Expert—you drag and drop or use shortcut menus.

The Cube Tab provides another interface for manipulating the items viewed in the grid object. You may find this analyzer easier or more intuitive than the OLAP Expert; the option is yours.

Modifying the Report by Changing the Grid Dimensions

By using an OLAP cube as a data source, you can change the grid dimensions of an existing report and create an entirely new report with just a few clicks of your mouse. As you'll see, the grid dimension can be changed and a new report generated easily and quickly.

You are unable to change the dimension of the grid object using any of the formatting or editing options discussed thus far. The dimension referred to here that you may want to change is the Page option in the Slice/Page page of the OLAP Expert. The only way to change the dimension is by going back into the OLAP Report Creation Wizard, which has some disadvantages you'll want to be aware of.

1. From Crystal Reports and with your OLAP report open, select Report, OLAP Report Settings to go back to the OLAP Report Creation Wizard.

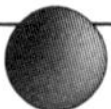

CAUTION

A warning message appears, reminding you that any formatting changes you made directly on the Design or Preview tabs are overwritten when you exit the wizard and apply the style you selected on the Style tab.

2. Using the Slice/Page tab, change or remove the present dimension from the Page list, and add another dimension from the Slice list (see Figure 15-18). This becomes the new page dimension for the report. Or, you may just want to change the members of the existing page to include more or different data on the report.

3. Click Preview Report (see Figure 15-19). Crystal Reports displays the report using the new page dimension you specified. In this example, I changed the Page dimension from only Last Year to include all members. The Grid Object has automatically been moved to the Group Header section and there is one grid for each dimension.

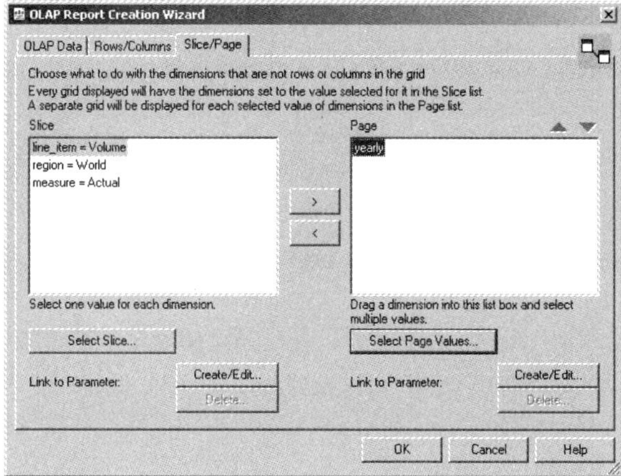

FIGURE 15-18 *Use the Slice/Page tab to change the Page dimension of your report.*

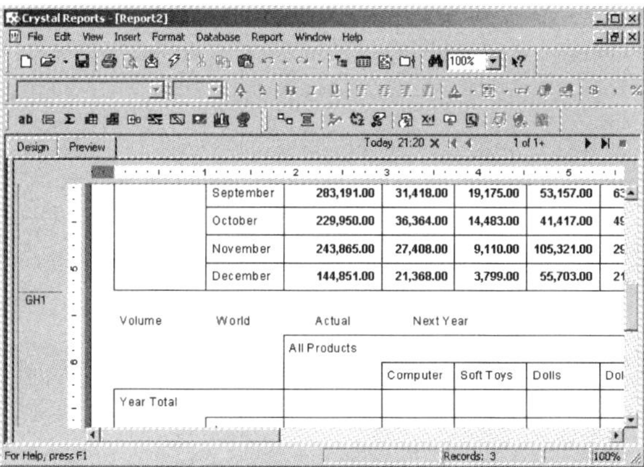

FIGURE 15-19 *Changing the Page dimension creates a grid for each year dimension.*

Changing the Location of the OLAP Cube

Data isn't static, so your reports based on OLAP data need to change when the data changes. When a new cube is generated, you need to reset the current report to the new cube location. This allows the data on the OLAP grid to update.

To change the location of an OLAP data source:

1. From the Database menu, select Database, Set OLAP Cube Location.

2. Click OK to the Confirm Command window and then click Select. When the OLAP Type dialog box appears, select the correct OLAP type. Click OK.

3. Enter the OLAP server name, user ID, and password. (Note: These fields can differ based on the type of OLAP you're connecting to.) Click Connect to confirm and select the cube. Click OK to allow Crystal Reports to update the location of all of the other OLAP grids in the report.

NOTE

You can also select Report, OLAP Report Settings to open the OLAP Report Creation Wizard. If you open the wizard, use the OLAP Data tab to select the new data source.

This process is similar to the Set Datasource Location process used for relational data sources covered in Chapter 3.

Summary

Reports designed and generated from an OLAP data source allow you to create and manipulate OLAP data. Reporting from large OLAP sources allows you to separate and manipulate manageable pieces of a large cube structure for analysis. One OLAP structure provides the opportunity for many reports to be generated.

Like relational reports, you can easily update the location of a refreshed OLAP source. You can point your report to a refreshed copy of the OLAP cube or structure at any time. You can also use a shortcut menu by right-clicking the cube placeholder on the Design tab of your report for many formatting and object manipulation options.

PART IV

Managing Your Data and Reports

Chapter 16

In this chapter, you'll learn how to export reports to other formats and about designating Report Parts for distributing critical report information to wireless devices. This chapter also discusses using the Microsoft Excel and Access add-ins, which enable on-the-fly report creation from within Excel or Access. Chapter 17 discusses Web distribution options in detail.

Crystal Reports is a developer-friendly software program. The Crystal Reports print engine can be integrated into applications built with .NET development applications and other programming languages. The ability to integrate the reporting power of Crystal Reports into custom applications is far-reaching. Several options are available for integrating and designing reports and making them behave in a custom application. These developer topics are beyond the scope of this book, but there is excellent help available on the Crystal Decisions Web site specifically for developers. A Developer's Guide comes with the Developer and Advanced versions of Crystal Reports 9. This manual is shipped with the software and can also be found in .PDF format on the installation CD in the "/docs" directory.

Exporting Reports

Crystal Report files export well to many other file types for broad distribution. Once you've designed and run a report in Crystal, it can be exported to another format or directly to another application. This makes the reports that you create in Crystal Reports available electronically to people who do not have Crystal Reports. It also makes the data available in other formats if you choose to manipulate it in an application other than Crystal Reports.

Crystal Report files can be exported directly to .PDF, Excel, and HTML, among many other file formats. Additionally, you can export directly to an application, a disk file, an Exchange folder, a Lotus Notes database, or a Microsoft Mail (MAPI) destination. The following sections describe some of these export options.

Exporting to Other Applications and File Types

Once you have a report designed and saved, it can be exported into another format. To export a report, complete the following steps:

1. Have the report that you want to export open in Crystal Reports.

2. Select File, Export or click the Export toolbar button ⬛. This opens the Export dialog box, as shown in Figure 16-1.

3. Choose the export format from the upper drop-down list and a destination from the lower drop-down list. Click OK (see Figures 16-1 and 16-2). Your report now exports to the chosen format and destination.

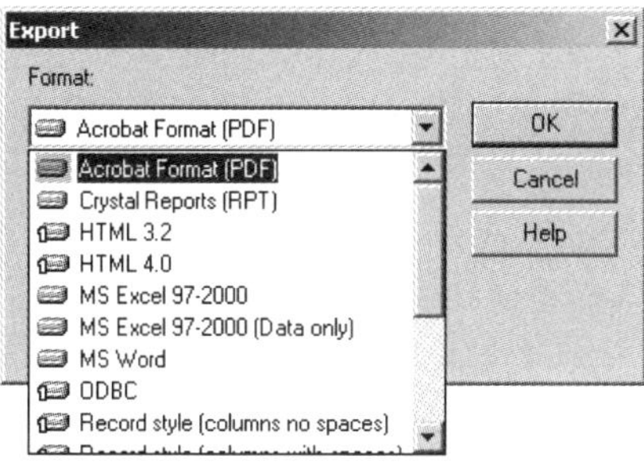

FIGURE 16-1 *You can export to many formats from Crystal Reports. Scroll down the list to see all your options.*

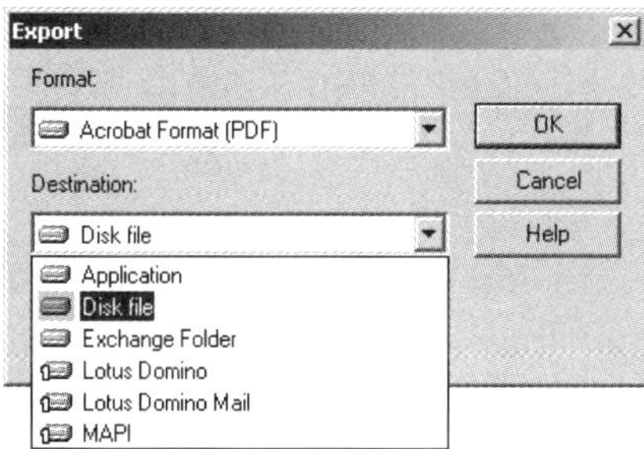

FIGURE 16-2 *Choose from many destinations when exporting a report.*

EXPORT OPTIONS

The following is a list of available export formats. You may have even more, depending on other DLLs installed on your computer.

- Acrobat Format (PDF)
- Crystal Reports (RPT)
- HTML 3.2
- HTML 4.0
- MS Excel 97-2000
- MS Excel 97-2000 (Data only)
- MS Word
- ODBC
- Record style (columns no spaces)
- Record style (columns with spaces)
- Report Definition
- Rich Text Format
- Separated values (CSV)
- Tab-separated text
- Text
- XML

As you see in the list in the sidebar, there are many export options to choose from. Many of the options do not support all of the features in Crystal Reports. There is an excellent document on the Crystal Decisions support Web site that lists every export option and what functions are and are not supported. Go to the following URL: **http://support.crystaldecisions.com/communityCS/TechnicalPapers/cr9_exportlimitations.pdf.asp**.

Since the Web site changes so frequently, you can also search for this document by going to the Crystal Decisions Home Page, selecting the Support option, and then selecting Search technical briefs in the first drop-down list. On the page that appears, select Crystal Reports, version 9, English, Technical Briefs, and Exporting.

Exporting to MS Excel

Two options for exporting to Microsoft Excel are available. If you intend to export the entire report with all its formatting, use the MS Excel 97-2000 option. If you wish to export only the data in the report for further manipulation in Excel, use the MS Excel 97-2000 (Data only) option.

If you choose either option, an Excel Format Options dialog box opens, providing basic formatting options for each specific format. Figure 16-3 shows the dialog box for the MS Excel 97-2000 option.

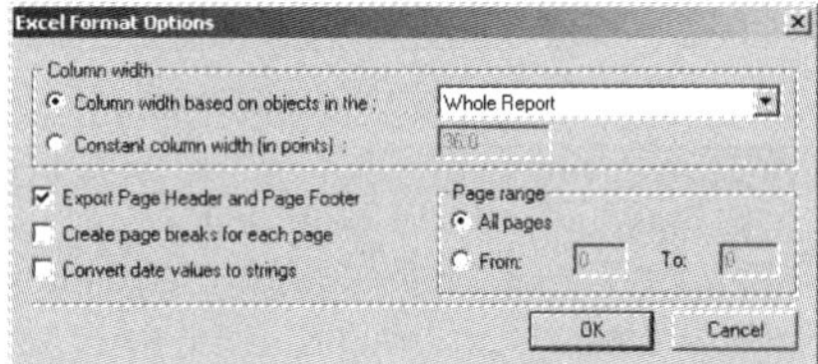

FIGURE 16-3 *Select formatting options for the report being exported.*

If you choose an application as your destination, the application you picked automatically opens with your new document displayed. If you choose a disk file, Crystal Reports prompts you to choose where to save your exported file from the Choose Export File dialog box.

Exporting to HTML

Reports export very well into the HTML format. When exporting to HTML you can select an application from the Destination list, but you will be prompted to choose a directory in which to save the file. When you export to HTML, more than one file may be created; therefore, you need to choose a directory or create a new one to put the files into (see Figure 16-4). Once you click OK after selecting a directory, the export proceeds, and the report is exported and launched in your default browser application. Exporting to HTML 4.0 uses DHTML format and has advantages. This format creates a paginated report, more like the Crystal Report file, and images are clearer and as close to WYSIWYG as you can get with exporting.

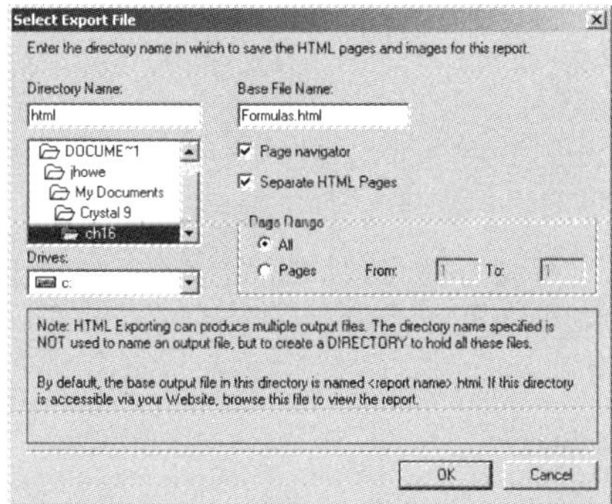

FIGURE 16-4 *When exporting to HTML, you must designate a file directory in which to save the exported files.*

NOTE

When you save a file in the HTML format, it is saved as ReportName.HTM to the directory you specify. You can choose a directory on your Web server or a regular network destination. To view a report in HTML format, open the file using your Web browser.

Exporting the Report Definition

Crystal Reports supports the export of a report definition. This is a text file that explains the definitions of the report, including the tables used, record and group selection criteria, formulas used, and the definition of each section and all fields within those sections, including their formatting specifications. This file can be opened in any application supporting .TXT files.

When exporting a report definition file, most of the pertinent information is in the beginning. There is excessive formatting information for every field on the report, which is of limited usefulness. When saving a report definition file, you may want to delete the information regarding formatting. Be careful when deleting that you do not delete the definition for any subreports in the report, as their definition is included in the main report definition.

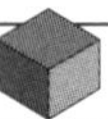

NOTE

The report definition file only defines fields that are printing on the report. Thus, a formula field that is built and used only in the selection criteria is not included on the report. Also, a summary formula field that is embedded into a text object is also not included in the report definition. To add these fields to the definition, add the fields to an empty report footer section, export the report definition, and then delete the fields back out before you save the report. Parameter fields are not included in the report definition.

Exporting Your Reports to E-mail

Crystal offers several ways to export reports to e-mail. You can export directly to an e-mail destination using Microsoft MAPI. Another option is to export your report to an Exchange Folder on your Exchange Server. You could also export your report to one of your Microsoft Outlook folders by means of the Exchange Folder destination. And lastly, if your particular e-mail program is not capable of direct export, you can attach any report file to an e-mail message using whichever e-mail client you currently use. Just create your message as usual, and attach the report file as an attachment.

Search the Crystal Reports help files, or go online and search the knowledge base or technical briefs areas of the Crystal Decisions Web site for specific documentation on your particular e-mail and network configuration.

Exporting Considerations

When designing reports in Crystal Reports, keep in mind how you plan to distribute reports throughout your organization. A few questions to ask yourself include:

- Who will I need to send the reports to? Will I be sending hard copies or electronic copies? Will the receiver have Crystal Reports?
- How often will I be distributing a certain report? Daily, weekly, monthly?
- What will the report be used for? Daily or weekly business decisions? Tracking information? Will the report be used for invoicing?
- Will a certain report be used on the Web, for example, by salespeople or at a major project presentation being given at a conference?

The above list gives a sampling of potential uses for reports that you design in Crystal Reports. How you export or distribute them depends on to whom they need to go and how to achieve the best presentation quality report within the constraints of your business.

Choosing an Export Format

If you run weekly reports that keep track of the movement of inventory, a basic report with little complicated formatting might be best. But if you want to compare the movement of inventory over months or among products, you need a more sophisticated report. If you need to export the report to coworkers who do not have Crystal Reports and you plan to export to Word, you may want to use less conditional formatting, such as conditionally changing the font colors, because formatting does not export as well. If you need the exported file to look as true to the original report file as possible, you may want to export to the HTML 4.0 format and instruct your coworkers to view the report using their Web browsers. If you need to export your report for download into another data source for future manipulation in a spreadsheet, Excel would be a good option.

Experiment with exporting your reports to different formats. Much of how your exported reports look depends on the print driver itself. If the print driver on one machine differs from the machine where the report was designed—or it's an older version—your report might not look right when printed. Some fields might not align correctly or might be missing altogether. To fix this problem, install the most recently updated drivers for your printer. If fields get cut off even after installing the updated printer drivers, increase the size of the fields on your report by expanding the objects. This way, they are more apt to print fully, even if one printer driver uses a wider font size than the driver on the designer's machine.

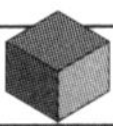

NOTE

Some of the best documentation you will find regarding the particulars of printing issues and printing dependencies is found at **http://support.crystaldecisions.com**. Look under the Support head and select Search Technical Briefs from the drop down list for documentation. Select Crystal Reports, All versions, English, Technical briefs, Printing issues. Several excellent documents outline particular issues and basic information that is not specific only to Crystal Reports 9 but to earlier versions, as well. New articles are added regularly, so check often for the most up-to-date information. If you search as above under Crystal Reports, Technical briefs, Report Design, a document regarding formatting guidelines for consistent reports may prove to be helpful.

Pagination Consistency

If you have problems with pagination or how your report looks and fits on the page, here are a few hints:

◆ Set your own margins when designing a report. If you use the default, and then the machine you print from has a different default setting, you may cut off information or your report may not be properly formatted.

◆ Printed reports most closely match previewed reports when you set your video driver resolution to 640×480 pixels. If you design a report using 800×600 resolution, you may encounter formatting changes that you did not anticipate.

◆ Always leave Free Form Placement turned on. This helps ensure that your formatting stays true to whatever machine you open your report on.

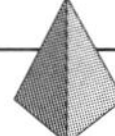

TIP

Free Form Placement is on by default. Change this option globally on the Layout tab of the Options dialog box (click File, Options). Or change this option per section of a report using the Section Expert.

Using the MS Excel and MS Access Add-Ins

In this section, you'll learn how to use the Microsoft Excel and Microsoft Access add-ins. These are Crystal Report wizards that you can "add in" to your Excel or Access application to create reports right from within the application.

Using the Excel Add-In

Using an add-in, you can create a report using a Crystal Report 9 Wizard. The report saves in the RPT format. This means that you can design the report using the add-in and then later open it in Crystal Reports to add formatting or options not offered with the add-in. This is much easier than setting up new data sources through the Data Explorer each time you want to design a new report for an Excel spreadsheet.

Installing the Excel Add-In

If you already have MS Excel 97 or 2000 installed on your computer and then you install Crystal Reports 9, the Excel add-in automatically installs and you do not need to do anything except use it. If you installed Excel *after* you installed Crystal Reports 9, then you need to install the add-in.

To check whether the Excel add-in is in fact installed, open Excel and look for the Crystal Report 9 Wizard button in the upper right-hand corner of the toolbar ⊞. Since you may not have the toolbar in view, you can also look under Tools for the Crystal Report 9 Wizard. If you do not see the icon, you need to install the add-in using the instructions below.

To install the Excel add-in, you must have a spreadsheet open in Excel.

1. Select Tools, Add-Ins from the main menu in Excel. This opens the Add-Ins dialog box.

2. If Crystal Report 9 Wizard is not listed in the box, you'll need to click Browse and search the Open dialog box for the file named crexcel9, which you should find in the \\Program Files\Crystal Decisions\Report Designer Component directory (see Figure 16-5).

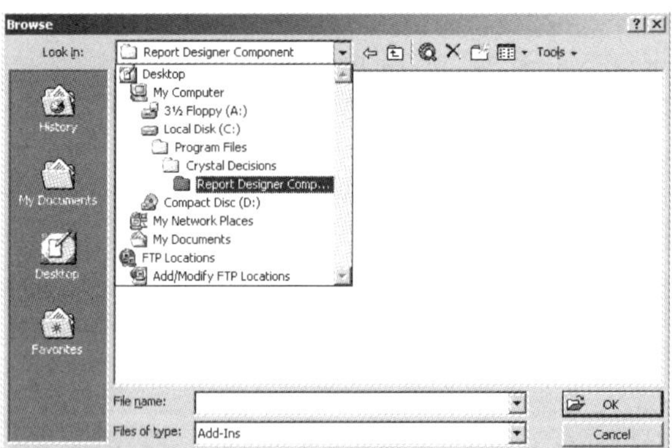

FIGURE 16-5 *Browse to find the file crexcel9, the Excel add-in.*

3. Select crexcel9 and click OK. This returns you to the Add-Ins dialog box, where the Crystal Report 9 Wizard now appears selected in the list of add-ins (as shown in Figure 16-6).

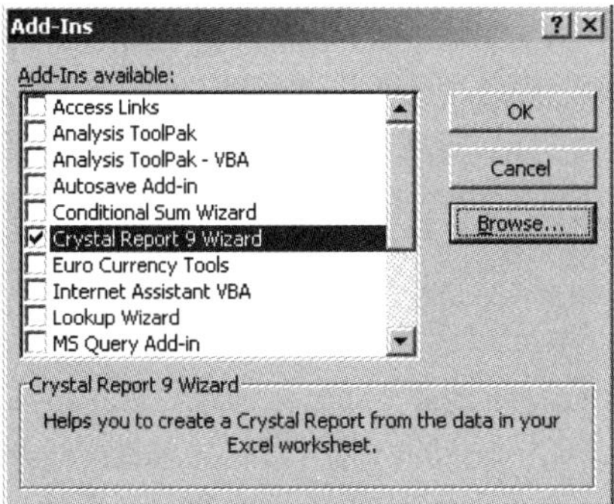

FIGURE 16-6 *Click OK once the Crystal Report 9 Wizard appears selected in the add-ins list.*

4. Click OK to close the Add-Ins dialog box. Now the Crystal Report 9 Wizard adds on its own little toolbar and is listed as a command on the Tools menu.

Designing a Crystal Report in Excel

With the Excel file for which you want to create a report open, you are ready to start the Crystal Report 9 Wizard and design a report. If you do not have your own Excel file handy, you can find a sample file to use at C:\Program Files\Crystal Decisions\Crystal Reports 9\Samples\En\Databases\xtreme.xls.

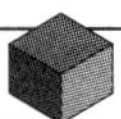

NOTE

If you have not saved the spreadsheet, Excel prompts you to save the file before you proceed.

1. Open the wizard by selecting Tools, Crystal Report 9 Wizard, or use the toolbar button. This opens the Crystal Report 9 Wizard.

2. Drag your mouse cursor on the Excel sheet to select a range of data to include in your report (see Figure 16-7). Once you click the mouse button to start selecting, a small dialog box opens near the top of your screen indicating the data range you are selecting.

3. Though you can type a range into the dialog box, I recommend that you select the range directly in the spreadsheet (notice that the pointer becomes a thick plus sign). After selecting a range, the Crystal Report 9 Wizard dialog box reappears with the selected range listed.

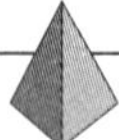

TIP

When selecting a range of data to base a report on, the first value in each column becomes the field name.

FIGURE 16-7 *The small dialog box appears when you click the button to select a range.*

4. The range you selected now appears in the Crystal Report 9 Wizard, as shown in Figure 16-8. Click the Expand the selected range automatically button if you want to expand the range to include all cells in the spreadsheet.

5. Click the Create Crystal Report button to begin designing your report.

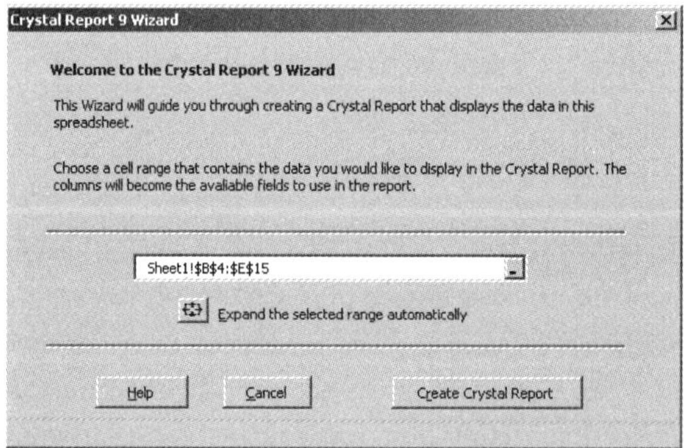

FIGURE 16-8 *The Crystal Report 9 Wizard dialog box lists the range selected.*

6. To choose the information to display on the report, move fields from the Available Fields list to the Fields to Display list using the arrow buttons (see Figure 16-9). Use the up and down arrows on the right side of the wizard to adjust the order of the fields. Click Next to move to the next step.

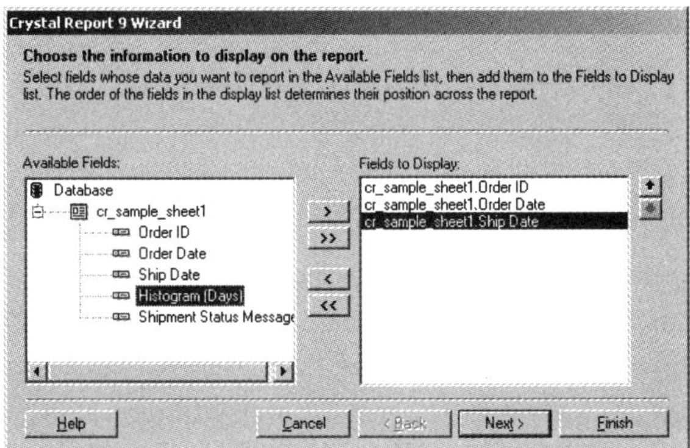

FIGURE 16-9 *Move fields from the Available Fields list to the Fields to Display list.*

 **NOTE**

If you forget to include the entire range that you need or need to increase the size of the range of selected cells, you need to exit the wizard and start over. You cannot go back and select a larger range once you have clicked the Create Report Wizard button.

7. To group the information on the report, move any fields that you want to group by to the Group By list (as shown Figure 16-10). Use the Sort Order list to adjust the group sort order. Click the Next button.

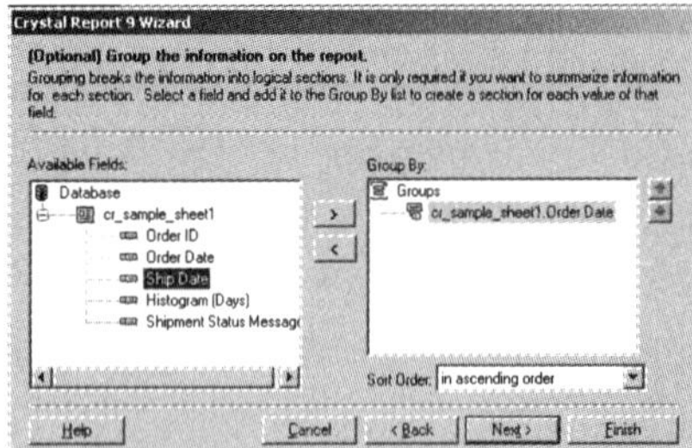

FIGURE 16-10 *Move fields you want to group by to the Group By list.*

8. Next, you can add summary information to the report. The group or groups you just created appear in the For the Group list. Select a group, then move the field you want to summarize from the Available Fields list to the Summarized Fields list. Select a summary function and indicate whether you want to Add Grand Totals (see Figure 16-11). Click Next to move to the next step.

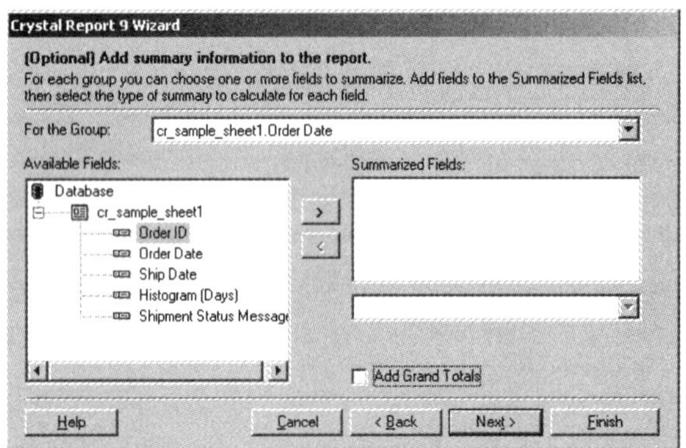

FIGURE 16-11 *Select the fields that you want to summarize and designate a summary operation.*

9. The next step works like the Sort Group Expert in Crystal Reports. Sort groups based on a summarized value on your report or create a Top N or Bottom N sort (see Figure 16-12). Click Next.

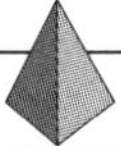

TIP

Even though this page states that it is optional, I have not been able to create a report using this wizard without a group sort based on a summarized field. You can remove this sort if you open the report in Crystal Reports.

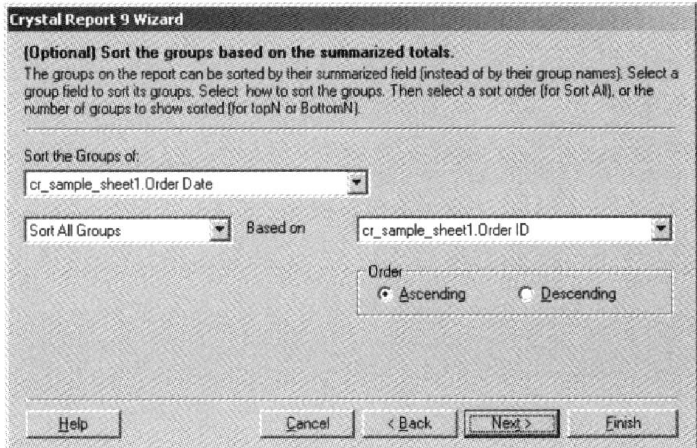

FIGURE 16-12 *Sort all groups by a summary field or include only the Top N or Bottom N groups on your report.*

10. The next step is to filter the information that prints on your report (see Figure 16-13). Click Next.

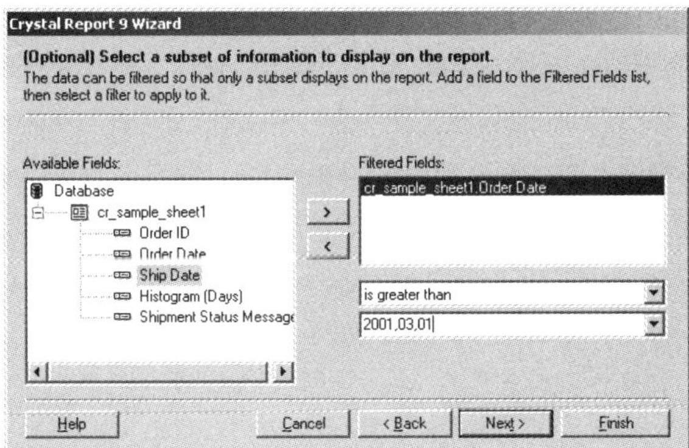

FIGURE 16-13 *Select which fields to include in your report, just like the Select Expert in Crystal Reports.*

11. You must select a style for your report from the list of options. You can also type a title into the Report Title field (as seen in Figure 16-14). Click Next.

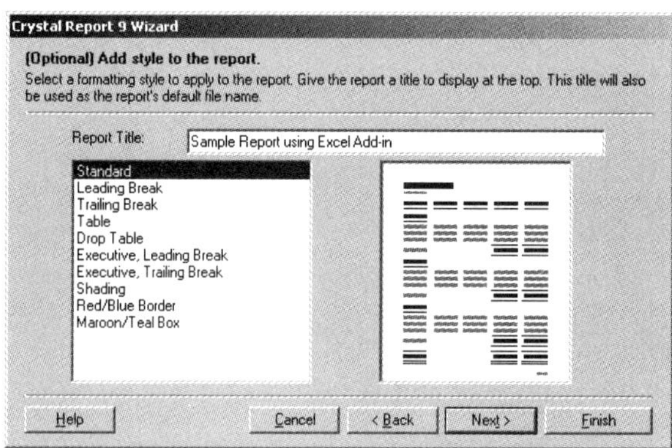

FIGURE 16-14 *Select a style for your report and add a title.*

12. In the last step, you designate where to save the report created with this wizard and how you want to view it (see Figure 16-15). You have several choices for viewing the report.

   ◆ **Preview (read only).** Opens the report in an Active X viewer where you can print and refresh the report.

   ◆ **Edit with Crystal Report Designer.** Opens the report in Crystal Reports 9, which provides full functionality to view and edit the report.

   ◆ **View Later.** Saves the report with the name you gave it, but doesn't open any other applications. You can view the report later.

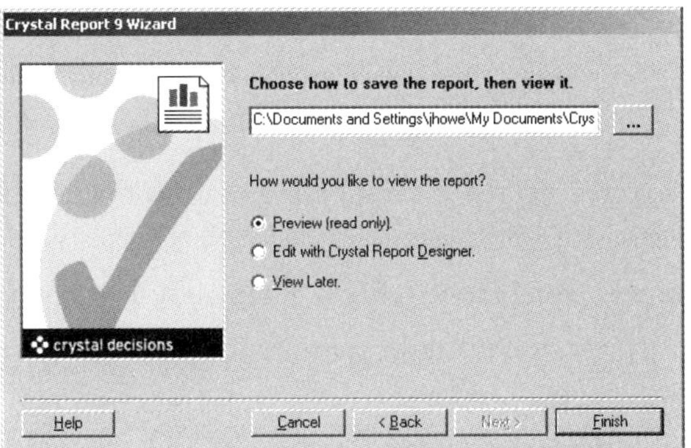

FIGURE 16-15 *Set the path where you want to save the report and select how you want to view it from the choices listed.*

13. Selecting the Preview option opens the report in a preview viewer with simple analyzer functionality, including printing, refreshing, zooming, page controls, and search (see Figure 16-16).

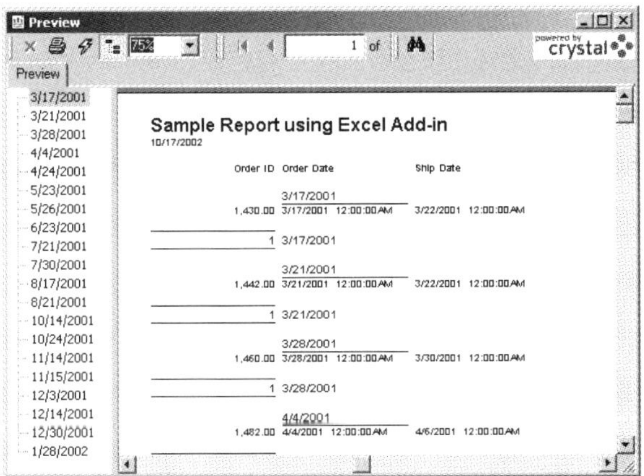

FIGURE 16-16 *Choosing Preview opens the report in a simple viewer with analyzer functionality only.*

Troubleshooting in Excel

If you make changes to the Excel spreadsheet that a report is based on, the report reflects those changes upon refreshing, according to the following guidelines:

◆ Adding a row to a selected range (but not before or after the range) includes the row in your refreshed report.

◆ Deleting a row from a selected range reflects in the refreshed report.

◆ If you change the cell type (for example, number to string), the change may not reflect in your report.

◆ You may *not* add a column to a selected range.

◆ Any modification, addition, or deletion outside the selected range does not affect the report in any way.

Using the Access Add-In

The Microsoft Access add-in allows you to open a Crystal Report 9 Wizard from within Access, from which you can design a Crystal Report.

Do I Need to Install It?

If you already have MS Access 97 or 2000 installed on your computer and you then install Crystal 9, the Access add-in is automatically installed and you do not need to do anything except use it.

If you installed Access after you installed Crystal Reports 9, then you will need to install the add-in. To check whether the Access add-in is installed, open a database in Access and open Tools, Add-Ins. If Crystal Report 9 Wizard appears in the submenu, you already have it installed. If not, follow the instructions below.

Installing the Access Add-In

You must have Access open with a database in order to install the Access add-in.

1. With a database open in Access, select Tools, Add-Ins, Add-In Manager. Click Add New in the Add-In Manager dialog box.

2. In the Open dialog box, search for the appropriate file, depending on which version of Access you have installed. In the directory \\Program Files\Crystal Decisions\Report Designer Component, select craccess97wz if you use Access 97 and craccess2kwz for Access 2000.

3. With the appropriate file selected, click Open. The Crystal Report 9 Wizard now appears in the Add-In Manager dialog box.

4. Click Close. The add-in now appears in the Tools, Add-Ins submenu.

Designing a Crystal Report in Access

There are two ways to open the Crystal Report 9 Wizard from within Access. In general, this wizard is exactly the same as the Excel wizard. The differences are in the first steps connecting to the database. The following list explains your options. Be sure that you have saved your Access database before starting to create a report.

When opening the Crystal Report 9 Wizard in Access, you have a few options.

◆ With Access open and a table selected, select Tools, Add-Ins, Crystal Report 9 Wizard. This opens the Crystal Report 9 Wizard. Follow the steps listed for Excel to work through the wizard.

◆ If you do not have a table selected and you select Tools, Add-Ins, Crystal Report 9 Wizard, the Choose a Table or Query dialog box opens. In this dialog box, you can select a table or query to base your report on (see Figure 16-17). After selecting a table or query, click OK. The Crystal Report 9 Wizard opens, ready for you to design your report.

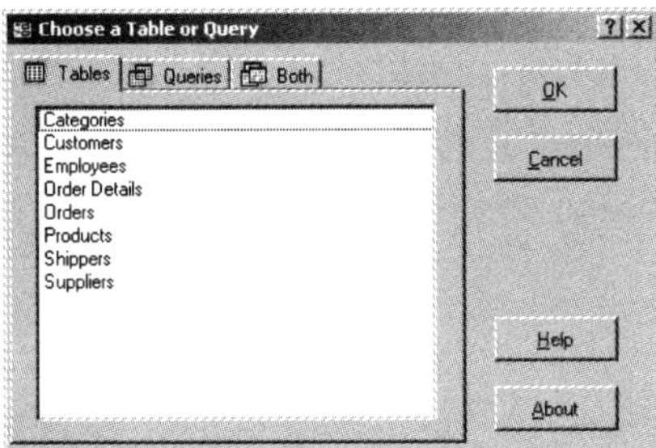

FIGURE 16-17 *Select the table or query on which you want to base your report.*

◆ From within the Reports page in Access, click New. The New Report dialog box opens, where you can select the Crystal Report 9 Wizard and a table for the report (see Figure 16-18).

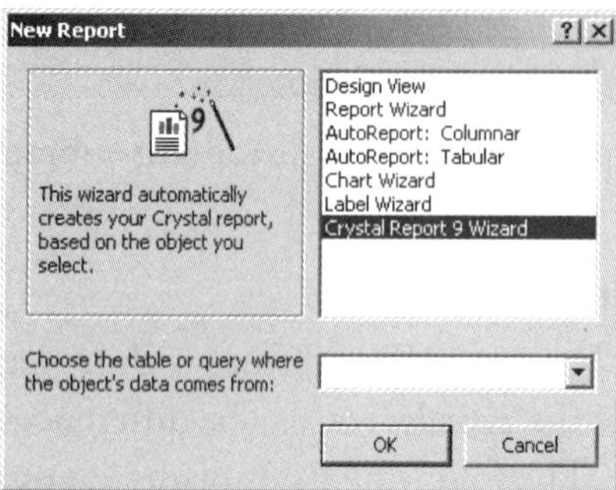

FIGURE 16-18 *Select the table from which to create the report using the drop-down list.*

The Access Crystal Report 9 Wizard functions exactly the same way as explained previously for Excel. Follow the steps for Excel, beginning with step 5. Once you complete the report, the viewing options are also the same as those outlined for Excel.

Designating Report Parts

Report Parts are report objects displayed in a viewer without the rest of the report. Precisely, Crystal Decisions defines Report Parts as hyperlink definitions that point from a home report object to a destination object.

Report Parts work with the DHTML viewers and can hyperlink from object to object within the same report or between separate reports to create a string or path of information.

Viewing Report Information Using a Report Part Viewer

The Report Part Viewer is a new viewer that displays Report Parts (rather than the whole report). This viewer can be integrated into Web applications so that only specific report objects (Report Parts) are displayed.

Report Part hyperlinks are set up in the Report Designer, and you take advantage of their functionality in the report viewers.

Setting Up Report Parts

Report Parts are set up in a two-step process. First, the report options must be set with a destination Report Part to start the process, then other objects can be hyperlinked to the initial part for a chain of viewable objects.

Initial Report Part Settings

First, you must designate a Default Home Object. This is the first object (or Report Part) shown when the report is viewed through a Report Part Viewer.

1. Open the report in which you want to designate a Report Part. You'll find it helpful to open the Report Explorer so that you can refer to the object's field name when filling in the dialog box.

2. Select the object in the report that you want to serve as the Default Home Object (see Figure 16-19). This will also highlight that object's name in the Report Explorer.

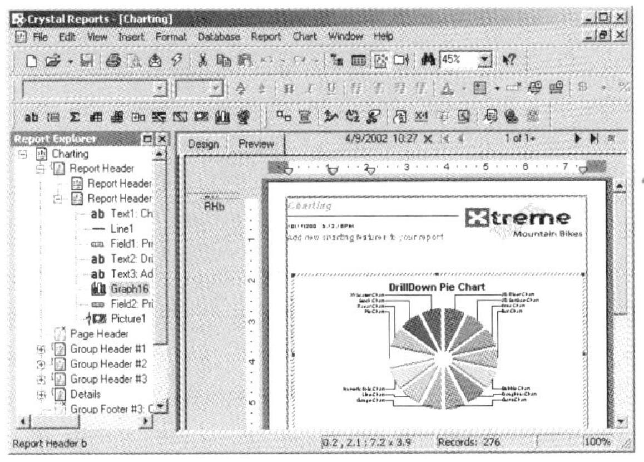

FIGURE 16-19 *Select the object you want as the Default Home Object on the Design tab, and that object is automatically selected in the Report Explorer for easy identification.*

3. Click File, Report Options to open the Report Options dialog box. Enter the selected object's name in the Object Name section of the Initial Report Part Settings area of the Report Options dialog box (see Figure 16-20).

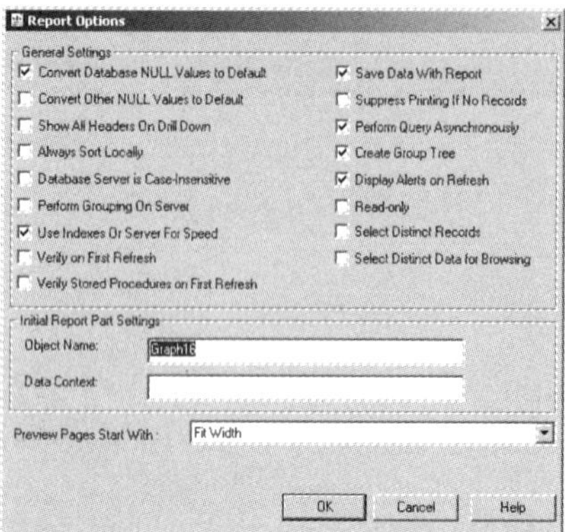

FIGURE 16-20 *Enter the object name into the Object Name area of the Report Options dialog box.*

4. Now when you view this report in a Report Part Viewer, you will see the report object named in the Initial Report Part Settings area.

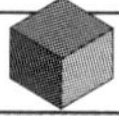

NOTE

You can designate more than one object as the Object Name in the Initial Report Part Settings area of the Report Options dialog. All objects will print as the Default Home Object.

With a Default Home Object designated, hyperlinks can be created to link to other report objects from this home object. You can drill down from the home object to one or several objects within the same report section. In this way, you can add hyperlinks from object to object. A path or chain of data is created; each time you drill down you are using a hyperlink to view the next predefined Report Part.

Setting Up a Report Part Data Path

Once an object in a report is designated as the Default Home Object, hyperlinks can be added to that object to link to other report part objects within that same report.

1. Select the object in a report that has been designated as the Default Home Object. (Follow the steps in the previous section to designate the Default Home Object.)

2. Right-click the object and select Format Field; select Format, Format Field from the main menu; or use the Report Explorer to open the Format Editor for the default field.

3. On the Hyperlink tab, select Report Part Drilldown in the Hyperlink information area to designate the report part that you want to be able to drill down and view.

4. Use the drop-down list and select an object name. Using the Report Explorer makes it much easier to learn the object name for each object on the report (see Figure 16-21).

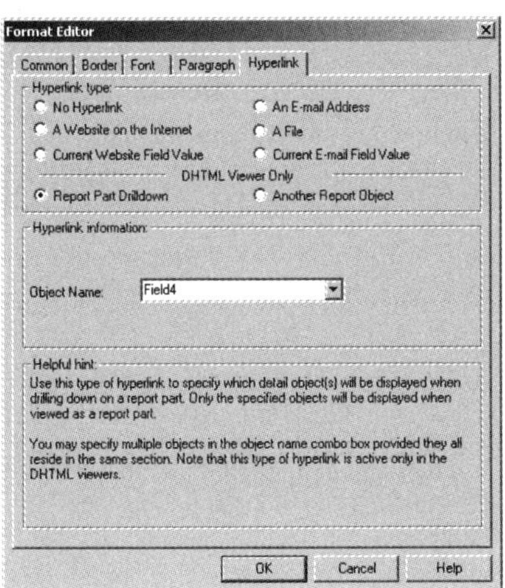

FIGURE 16-21 *Enter the name of the object or objects you want to hyperlink to in the Hyperlink information area of the Format Editor*

NOTE

Add more than one object name in the Object Name drop-down list by adding a semicolon and space, then the next object name.

Drilling Down to a Report Part in Another Report

If you want to create a hyperlink to information in another report, select the Another Report Object option on the Hyperlink tab of the Format Editor for the Default Home Object. Selecting this option changes the Hyperlink information area to accommodate linking to another report.

In order to link to another report, both the report with the Default Home Object and the report with the hyperlink object must be open.

1. Format a Default Home Object in the first report.

2. Open the second report, which contains the report part object to which you want to hyperlink from the Default Home Object.

3. Select the object in the second report that you want to designate as a Report Part. Right-click on this object and select Copy from the shortcut menu. This will copy the object name and location.

4. Go back to the first report by clicking Window in the main menu and selecting the first report's name in the drop-down menu.

5. Right-click the Default Home Object in the first report and select Format Field.

6. On the Hyperlink tab, select the Another Report Object from the Hyperlink information area.

7. Right-click in the Select From box, and select Paste from the shortcut menu. This will populate all three boxes with the field name and path from the second report (see Figure 16-22).

8. Click OK to close the Format Editor.

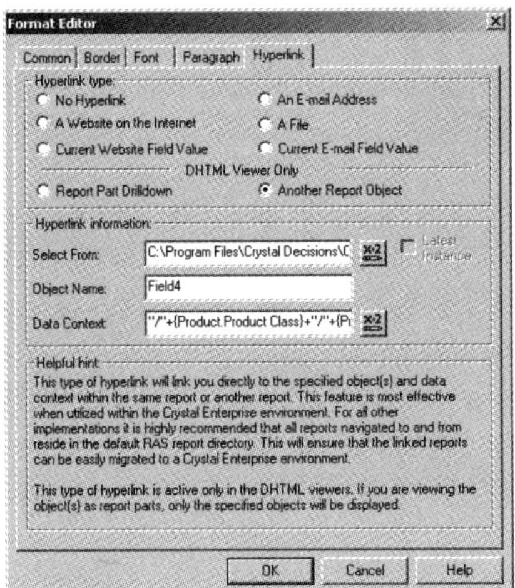

FIGURE 16-22 *Paste the information about the Report Part object in the second report into the Format Editor of the Default Home Object.*

Now that the first report has a designated Default Home Object, if this report is opened using a Report Part Viewer, only the Default Home Object report part will be viewed. If that object is double-clicked (drilled down), the report parts that were hyperlinked to that default object will appear. If the default object was hyperlinked to Report Parts in another report, those objects will appear when drilling down.

To view a report object containing Report Parts you must have the Report Application Server (RAS) installed. The RAS includes the Report Part Viewer that is necessary for viewing Report Parts. Chapter 17 covers setting up and using RAS.

To view Report Parts you must set your preferences in ePortfolio Lite to view your reports using the Report Parts Viewer.

1. Open ePortfolio Lite from the Report Application Server Launchpad. If your RAS has been customized you may just go to a Web address to access ePortfolio Lite.

2. Click the Preferences button on the toolbar to open the User Preferences Explorer window.

3. Select the option Report Parts Viewer from the View my reports using the... section of the window (see Figure 16-23).

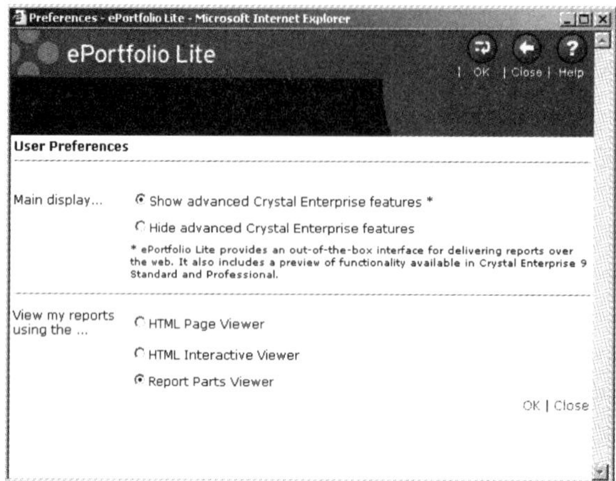

FIGURE 16-23 *Change your User Preferences to view reports using the Report Parts Viewer.*

4. Click OK to close the User Preferences Explorer window.

5. Double-click a sample report and the report will open in the Report Parts Viewer displaying on the objects in the report which have been designated as Report Parts (see Figure 16-24).

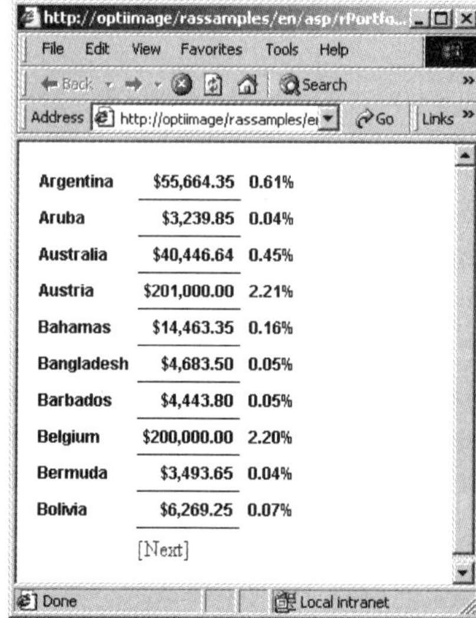

FIGURE 16-24 *You will only see objects designated as Report Parts after setting your preferred viewer to the Report Parts Viewer.*

Custom Web applications can be developed for use with the Report Part Viewer. Report Parts can be viewed through a corporate portal or via WML cellular phones, RIM devices, or iPAQs.

Making Use of Smart Tags within MS Office XP

A *Smart Tag* is a label that identifies a piece of information in a document as a certain type and assigns potential functionality to that type. For example, the name "Joe Smith" in a document can be recognized with a Smart Tag as a "person's name." That particular Smart Tag can have potential actions associated with it, such as Add to Contacts, Add to Address Book, Open Contact, or Schedule Meeting.

Crystal Reports takes advantage of Microsoft XP's Smart Tag technology. Three object types are supported by Smart Tags:

- Charts
- Text objects
- Field objects

Several actions must occur in order for Crystal Reports Smart Tags to work:

- Web server options must be configured on the Smart Tag tab of the File, Options dialog box in Crystal Reports.
- An .ASP or .JSP Web page must be built for viewing report details.
- The reports referred to in the Smart Tags must exist on the Web server named in the Options dialog box in a directory that mirrors their real location, or the Web server must be configured to accept a UNC path.

Smart tags can be added to Microsoft Word 2002, Excel 2002, and Outlook 2002. To add a report object to one of these Office XP applications, open the report containing the object and set the Web server, virtual directory, and viewing page in the Options dialog box (see Figure 16-25).

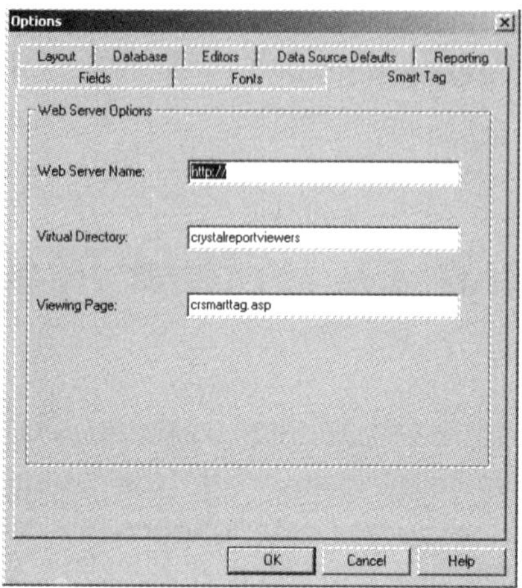

FIGURE 16-25 *Set Smart Tag options on the Smart Tag tab of the Options dialog box.*

1. Open the Preview tab of the report and select the object you want to add to the XP application. Right-click the object and select Copy Smart Tag from the shortcut menu.

2. Open the XP application and paste the report object into the document.

3. Choose the appropriate Smart Tag from the options in the XP application for the pasted report object.

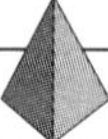

TIP

Go to Crystal Decisions Web site and download the following file for more information. This white paper contains good information on smart tags: **http://www.crystal-decisions.com/products/crystalreports/downloads/cr9_mstags.pdf**

Summary

A Crystal Report file can be exported into many different formats to meet your needs. Experiment with exporting to find which formats work best for you and your company, considering viewing preferences and whether data manipulation is desired in Excel.

The Access and Excel add-ins provide an easy way to create a quick report from a selected data set. Using the Crystal Report 9 Wizard, you are able to design a report from within either of these Microsoft applications. Depending on your needs, you can design reports using the add-ins or by connecting directly to either an MS Access database or an Excel spreadsheet in the Report Designer.

Depending on your corporate needs, you may find using Report Parts for custom web or wireless distribution an effective way to leverage Crystal Reports's cutting-edge technologies and integration with other tools. Crystal Reports's continued compatibility with Microsoft products is exemplified with its ability to use Smart Tags for some report object types.

Chapter 17

Publishing Crystal Reports to the Web: Report Application Server vs. Crystal Enterprise

One of the biggest issues associated with reporting is report distribution. Once you have created a report that you would like to share with others, what is the best distribution method to allow others to view your report? Many solutions are offered by Crystal Decisions to solve this problem. The two most popular ways of sharing reports are exporting using Crystal Reports and distributing reports via Web reporting. This chapter will discuss the broad topic of Web reporting as well as the different options available to implement Web reporting, including an in depth discussion of RAS. For information regarding exporting options, refer to Chapter 16.

What Is Web Reporting?

Web reporting is a fancy way to describe viewing reports built using Crystal Reports via a Web browser. Reports are run on a server, and the finished report is displayed in the user's Web browser. Unlike running reports "by hand" on a client machine (your computer), configuring and using Report Application Server (RAS) allows you to save your reports to a common environment and view reports on demand via a Web browser rather than opening the report in Crystal Reports and then refreshing. Refer to Figure 17-1 to see what a Crystal Report looks like when opened in a Web browser.

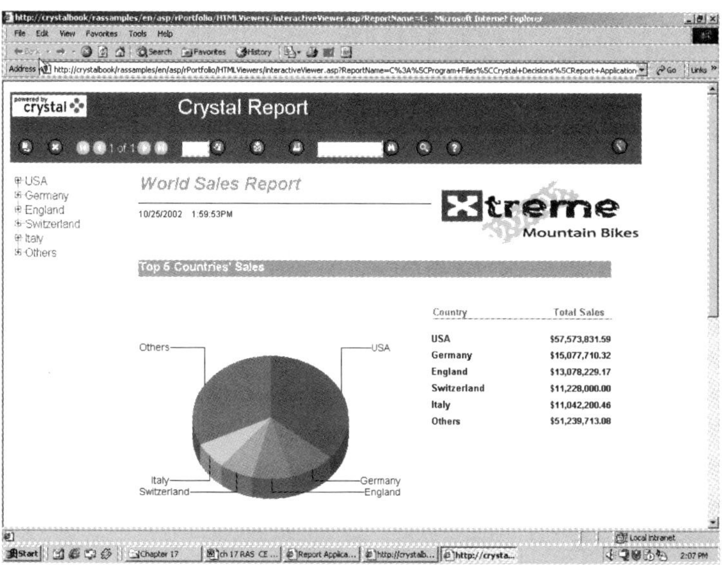

FIGURE 17-1 *Reports viewed using your browser from the RAS Web server maintain Crystal functionality, like drill-down capability, because they are not exported into another format.*

Benefits of Web Reporting over Paper Reporting or Exporting

Processing and distributing reports via your company's intranet or extranet can be more efficient and easier to maintain than printing all of your reports, requiring users to have a Crystal Reports license, or exporting into viewable formats. There are many reasons to consider using a Web server:

◆ Reduces administrative overhead

◆ No software needed on the client machine

◆ Saves company resources (paper, ink, printing hardware, etc.)

◆ Maintains a report's functionality (drill-down, on-demand subreports, hyperlinks, vivid colors)

◆ Allows reports to be shared worldwide

◆ Allows for report scheduling

◆ Allows for report security

◆ Allows for report management and organization

◆ Allows for robust report customization

Web Publishing Options

Two options are available when considering publishing and distributing reports via the Web. The first option is to use Crystal Reports Report Application Server (RAS) to share your reports over the Web. This option comes packaged with Crystal Reports 9 Professional, Developer, and Advanced editions. The edition of Crystal Reports that you purchase determines the amount of functionality you get with RAS. The second option is to upgrade to Crystal Enterprise 9 (CE), Standard, Professional, or Premium edition.

Using the Report Application Server

RAS is a new component available in Crystal Reports Professional, Developer, and Advanced editions that provides server-based report services. These services include report viewing via the Web, report processing, and report runtime modification. From this point forward, RAS refers to the version that is bundled with the Advanced edition of Crystal Reports. Depending on the edition of Crystal Reports 9 you purchase, some of the features being discussed may not be available.

Benefits of Using Crystal Enterprise 9

Crystal Enterprise comes in three editions: Standard, Professional, and Premium. CE is a tool that expands the Web reporting features offered with RAS by allowing reports to be organized, secured, and scheduled via the Web.

CE allows your organization to create a folder structure for storing your reports in a centralized repository. You can then set security rules on these reports and folders based on users and groups that you add to the CE environment. Users are then only able to access the reports and folders to which they have been granted rights based on your security model.

Another advantage of upgrading to CE is the ability to schedule your reports. CE offers a wide range of recurring scheduling options and also allows your reports to be output to a variety of destinations and formats. Some of the destinations available are an unmanaged disk (a location on your hard drive or a shared network location), printer, FTP site, or e-mail. A few of the formats available for scheduling are Adobe Acrobat (.pdf), Microsoft Excel, Microsoft Word, Rich Text Format (.rtf), and character separated values (.csv).

RAS is a stand-alone edition of Crystal Enterprise 9 (CE) that incorporates basic Crystal Enterprise functionality and is mainly used as a method for viewing reports on the Web. However, RAS also includes other server-based features not found in all editions of CE and can be considered an add-on product. The main feature RAS adds is the ability to perform ad-hoc reporting over the Web. This feature enables end users to modify the structure of an existing report or to create a new report, all of this being done over the Web. The major advantage of this feature is that it allows your end users to create new reports or edit existing reports without ever having to install a report creation application onto their computer.

RAS also allows developers to integrate Web reporting into applications and includes software development kits (SDKs) for Java, .NET, and COM. Because RAS is a Web-based interface, it can be completely customized to the look and feel of your organization by using the SDKs supplied with the software. By using RAS and Report Parts (a new feature in Crystal Reports 9), developers can share reports on portable business devices such as mobile phones and PDAs. For more information regarding Report Parts, refer to Chapter 16.

> **WHAT EDITION OF CRYSTAL REPORTS DO YOU HAVE?**
>
> Crystal Reports 9 is released in the following editions. The edition you purchased determines the amount of functionality and which additional tools are included.
>
> ◆ **Standard.** This edition has all Report Designer functionality, but has a more limited set of data connectivity options, no Repository, and no Web reporting.
>
> ◆ **Professional.** This edition adds more data connectivity methods, limited development options, and limited RAS.
>
> ◆ **Developer.** This edition adds greater development functionality and greater RAS functionality.
>
> ◆ **Advanced.** This edition adds full RAS functionality.

Configuring and Using RAS for Web Reporting

As mentioned earlier, RAS is a tool used to publish your Crystal reports over the Web. This section walks you through the installation procedure for RAS as well as how to configure and use RAS after installation.

What RAS Can Do

RAS has the most basic level of Crystal Enterprise functionality of all editions of CE. Although it is limited in this aspect, RAS still enables you to perform many of the crucial tasks related to Web reporting:

◆ Run reports on demand and requires no client-side software

◆ Modify reports over the Web

◆ Create new reports over the Web

What RAS Can't Do

Though RAS has excellent functionality in many areas, it is missing some key components that are included in the other editions of CE. RAS does not include the following features:

◆ The ability to schedule reports

◆ Built-in security functionality

◆ Tools for organizing reports

RAS includes ePortfolio Lite, which is similar to the ePortfolio application in CE Standard and Professional. Depending on the needs of your organization, the features found in RAS may be a good fit and thus RAS may be the correct choice for you.

 **NOTE**

The differences between the editions of Crystal Enterprise are discussed in Chapter 18.

Installing RAS

RAS can be installed either as a stand-alone tool used to publish your reports to the Web or as an add-on tool to Crystal Enterprise to allow for ad-hoc reporting over the Web. The following information refers to installing RAS as a stand-alone tool.

The machine must meet the following minimum software and hardware requirements for the installation to be successful. For more detailed installation instructions, view the Crystal Reports 9 release notes.

- ◆ Operating system requirements:
  - ◆ Windows NT 4 Workstation (SP6a)
  - ◆ Windows NT 4 Server (SP6a)
  - ◆ Windows 2000 Professional (SP2)
  - ◆ Windows 2000 Server (SP2)
  - ◆ Windows 2000 Advanced Server
  - ◆ Windows XP Professional
- ◆ Microsoft Internet Information Server (IIS) 4
- ◆ 128MB RAM
- ◆ 100MB free disk space

Once you have a machine that meets these minimum requirements, you may begin the installation of the RAS installation CD-ROM. For detailed installation instructions, view the product documentation help file RAS_User.chm in the Docs folder on the installation CD-ROM.

Configuring RAS

Configuration of RAS can be broken into two areas. One area deals with setting the properties of RAS itself. This configuration is done using RAS Configuration Manager. The second area deals with setting the preferences for ePortfolio Lite (the end user tool for viewing reports). This configuration is done in the Preferences area of the ePortfolio Lite tool.

Using RAS Configuration Manager

RAS Configuration Manager is the Windows-based administrative tool that is installed with RAS (see Figure 17-2). Because it is a Windows installed component, you must run this tool from the actual machine where RAS is installed. You can access it by selecting Start, Programs, Crystal Enterprise 9, Tools, RAS Configuration Manager. You can manipulate the following settings using RAS Configuration Manager:

◆ **Max Number of Records.** Unlimited (default) or Records limited to x. Use this setting to limit the number of records that are returned from the database.

◆ **Batch Size.** Number of records per batch x (default 100). When records are returned from the database, they are sent to the RAS server in batches. This option allows you to specify the number of records that are contained in each batch.

◆ **Browse Data Size.** Number of records to browse (default 100). This option allows you to specify the number of distinct records that are returned from the database when a user browses a field's data.

◆ **SQL Options.** The first option, Perform "GROUP BY" on server allows most of the report processing to be performed on the database server. Using this option will cause the details of each group on the report to be hidden until the user manually drills down on a group. The second option, Select Distinct Records, forces only unique records to be returned from the database. This option is only applied when a new document is created.

◆ **Report Directory.** This is the directory in which you place all of your reports that you would like RAS to manage. To use a report with RAS, simply copy it to this directory.

◆ **Temp Directory.** Path (default is blank). This option will allow you to set the default directory for temporary files created by RAS.

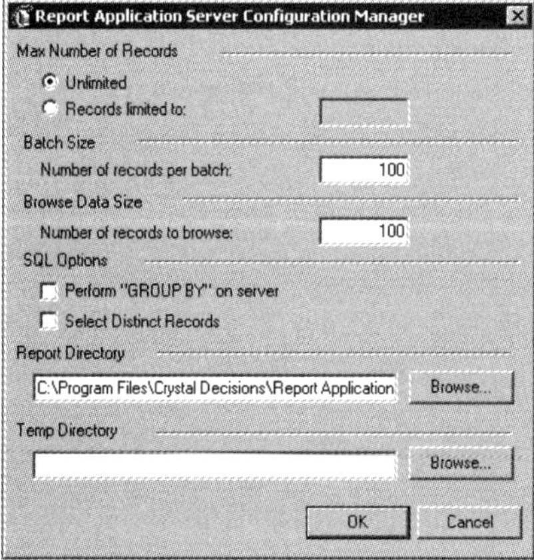

FIGURE 17-2 *RAS Configuration Manager provides configuration options for your RAS server.*

ePortfolio Lite Preferences

Clicking the Preferences button on the main ePortfolio Lite window allows users to set basic display and viewer preferences. To configure these settings, open ePortfolio Lite and click the Preferences button in the top-right corner of the Web page. The following settings can be manipulated in the User Preferences area (see Figure 17-3):

◆ **Main display.** Allows you to show or hide the areas that only apply to other editions of CE.

◆ **View my reports using the….** Allows you to set the type of report viewer ePortfolio Lite will use to display reports.

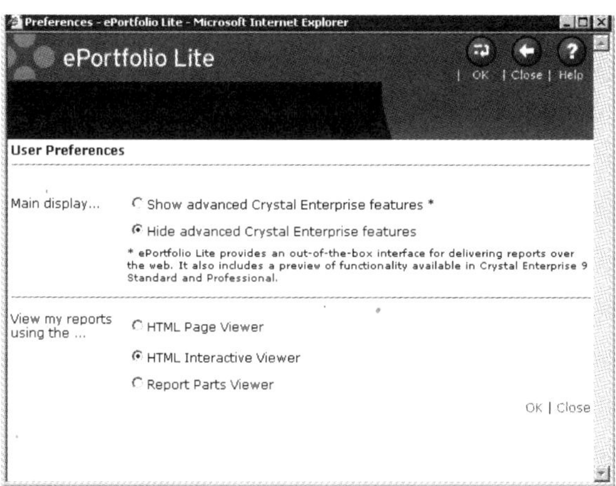

FIGURE 17-3 *ePortfolio Lite User Preferences page.*

Client Tools of RAS

Now that RAS is installed and configured, your end users need to know what it can do for them and how they can use the system. All the client tools used with RAS are Web-based tools and therefore are accessed via a Web browser. The RAS Launchpad, shown in Figure 17-4, is a centralized location that displays links to all the client tools of RAS. The RAS Launchpad page can be customized to the look and feel of your organization. To access the RAS Launchpad, type the following URL into your Web browser: http://*ServerName*/rassamples/en (where *ServerName* is the name of your Web server).

The RAS Launchpad can also be accessed on the server where RAS is installed by selecting Start, Programs, Crystal Enterprise 9, Report Application Server Launchpad.

The two Web client tools included with RAS are ePortfolio Lite and the Web Report Design Wizard. ePortfolio Lite is the tool that your end users utilize to view reports on demand over the Web. The Web Report Design Wizard is the ad-hoc reporting tool that allows you to modify existing reports over the Web as well as use an existing report as the source for a new report.

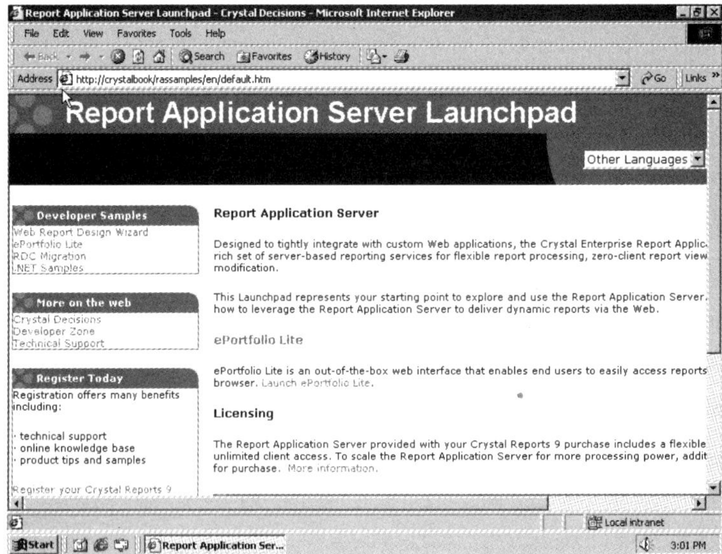

FIGURE 17-4 *RAS Launchpad provides a starting point for accessing client tools.*

ePortfolio Lite

The major functionality of RAS is the ability to view your Crystal Reports over the Web. To do this, you need a Web-based application that allows you access to the RAS Web server. This is exactly what ePortfolio Lite is—an easy-to-use end-user Web application that allows your reports to be run on demand over the Web.

This Web application can be accessed either from the RAS Launchpad or directly by using its URL. To access ePortfolio Lite from the Launchpad, simply open the

Launchpad using one of the methods previously described and click the ePortfo-lio Lite Link in the middle of the page.

To access ePortfolio Lite directly by using its URL, type the following address into your Web browser: http://*ServerName*/rassamples/en/asp/rPortfolio (where *ServerName* is the name of your Web server).

Once ePortfolio Lite opens, simply navigate to the report you wish to view and click the View link (see Figure 17-5). The look of your application may differ from the figures in this book based on your settings in the User Preferences area, discussed earlier.

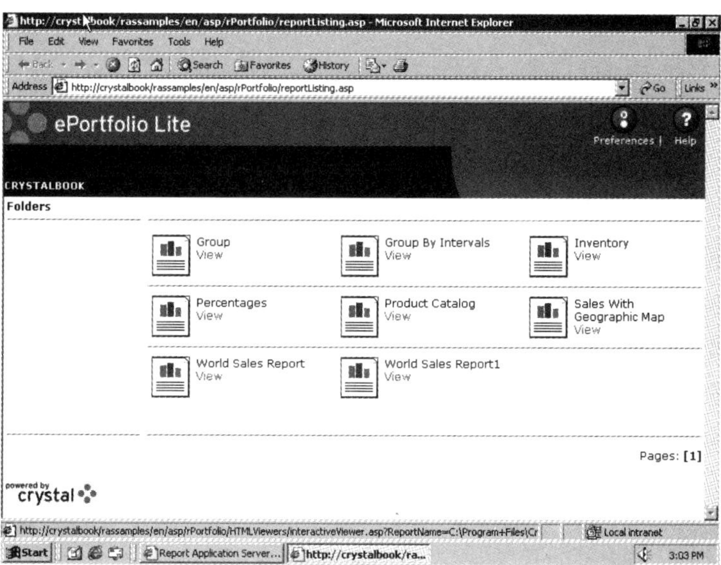

FIGURE 17-5 *The ePortfolio Lite main view provides a starting point for viewing reports.*

Web Design Report Wizard

The Web Design Report Wizard is the Web-based tool that allows your users to modify Crystal Reports over the Web as well as create new reports over the Web by using an existing report as its source. The wizard's Welcome page is shown in Figure 17-6.

Much like ePortfolio Lite, the Web Design Report Wizard can be accessed either from the RAS Launchpad or directly by its URL. To access the Web Design

Report Wizard from the Launchpad, simply open the Launchpad using one of the methods previously described and click the Web Design Report Wizard link in the Developer Samples area.

To access the Web Design Report Wizard directly by using its URL, type http://*ServerName*/rassamples/en/asp/WebDesignReportWizard/index.htm into your Web browser (where *ServerName* is the name of your Web server).

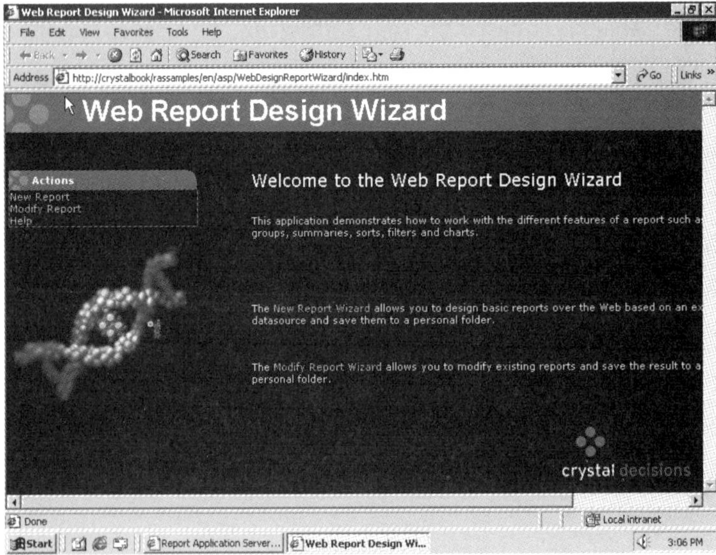

FIGURE 17-6 *Web Report Design Wizard main view.*

The Web Report Design Wizard has two options: New Report Wizard and Modify Report Wizard. An important note is that the Modify Report Wizard uses the format of an existing report as the source, but not the actual report data contained in the target report. Any fields that reside in the tables that are in the original report's data source are available for use in the new report you are building.

The screens in the wizards are very similar to those found in the Standard Report Wizard. These screens include the following: Choose your data, Choose the information to display, Group the information, Summarize the information, Sort the information, Filter the information, Add a chart, Apply a style, and Save. The following screenshots were taken using the New Report Wizard.

When you select the New Report option on the Welcome page, the first New Report Wizard page is labeled Choose your data, shown in Figure 17-7. Select which report is to serve as the source for the new report you are building. The only directory that you can pull reports from is the RAS report directory (set using RAS Configuration Manager, discussed earlier). After you have selected your data source, click Next.

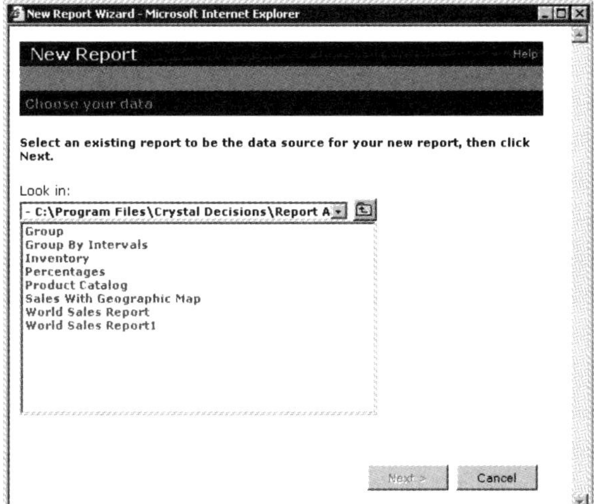

FIGURE 17-7 *The Choose your data page allows you to select a report to use as your data source.*

The next New Report Wizard page, shown in Figure 17-8, is labeled Choose the information to display. This page allows you to select fields for the new report, although the fields that you can select are limited to the fields that already exist on the data source target report. After you have selected the fields to display in your report by moving them into the Fields to Display box, click Next.

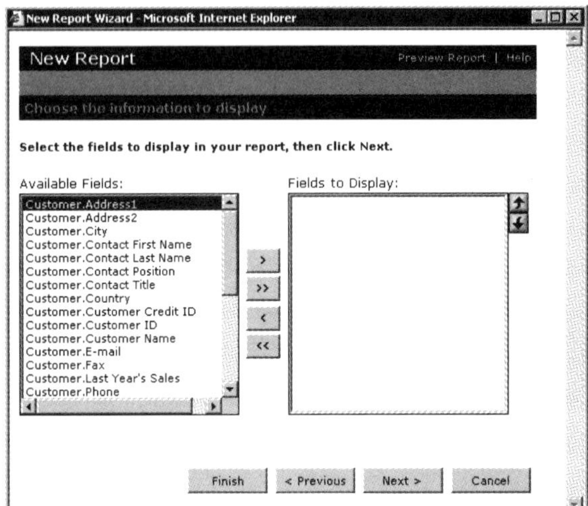

FIGURE 17-8 *The Choose the information to display page allows you to select the fields you would like to display as report detail.*

The New Report Wizard's Group the information page, shown in Figure 17-9, enables you to select the fields you would like to have your new report grouped by. After you select those fields by moving them into the Group By box, click Next.

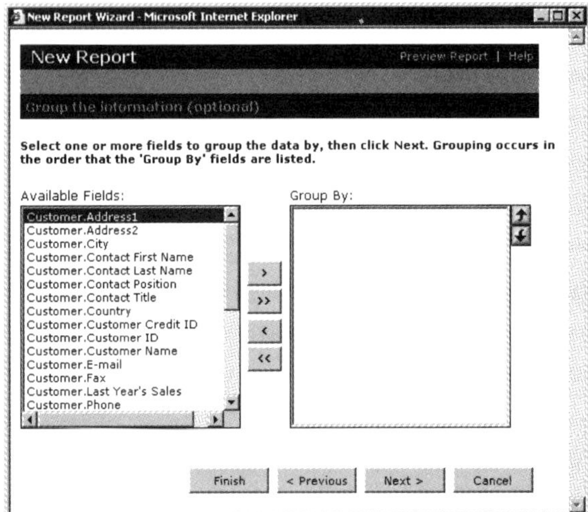

FIGURE 17-9 *The Group the information page allows you to set report groupings.*

In the Summarize the information page, shown in Figure 17-10, you can create any summaries or totals for either groups or the grand total. Notice that the wizard automatically provides the correct choices in the Summary Type drop-down list box based on which type of field you select in the Summary Of drop-down list box. After you have selected the type of summary you want for each field, click Next.

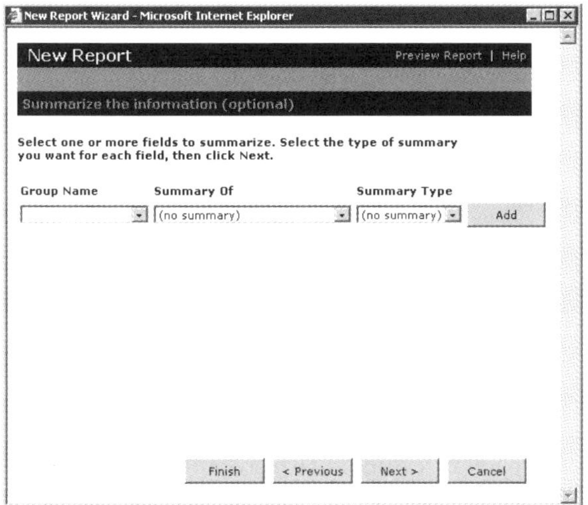

FIGURE 17-10 *The Summarize the information page allows you to create basic summaries.*

On the Sort the information page, shown in Figure 17-11, you can select any sort (within a group or for the entire report if no group was created). Notice that you can select either ascending or descending order for the type of sort. After you select the type of sorting you want for each field, click Next.

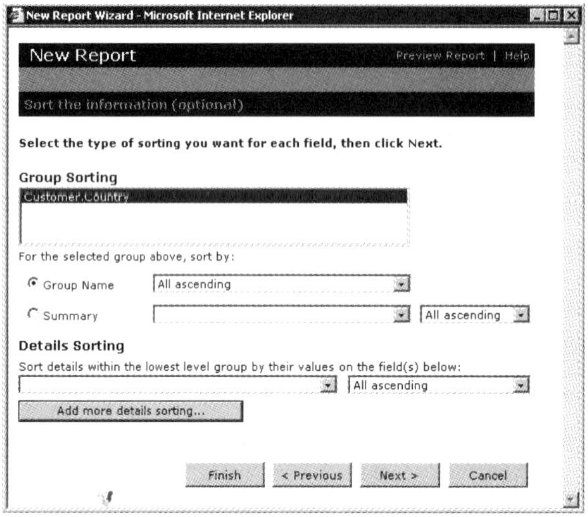

FIGURE 17-11   *The Sort the information page allows you to set the sort order of the report.*

The Filter the information New Report Wizard page, shown in Figure 17-12, is similar to the Record Selection page in a Report Wizard, the exception being that the Filter Type options in the New Report Wizard are somewhat limited to basic choices such as equal to, not equal to, less than, greater than, etc. You're not allowed to use the One Of, Like, Starts With, In the Period, or Formula options.

The Filter the information page enables you to add one or more filters so that only relevant data will be displayed in your report. After you add filters, click Next.

If you would like to add a chart to the report, use the New Report Wizard's Add a chart page, shown in Figure 17-13, to create a bar chart, line chart, or pie chart. You must have created a summary in the Summarize the information page that the chart can be based on. After you choose the type of chart and the data to display, click Next.

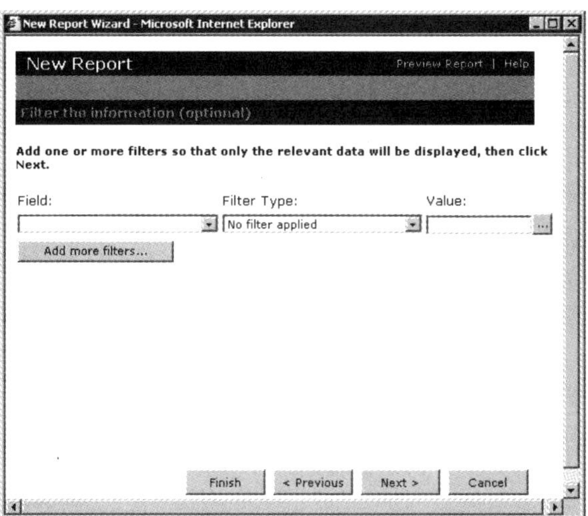

FIGURE 17-12 *The Filter the information page allows you to filter the report's data. This step creates the report's Record Selection Formula.*

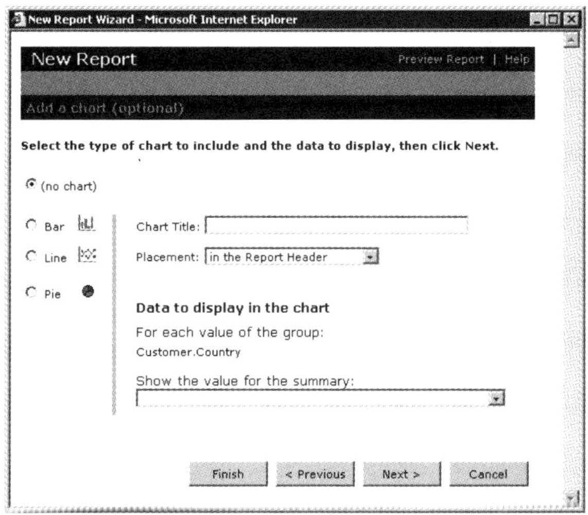

FIGURE 17-13 *The Add a chart page allows you to create a chart for the report.*

On the Apply a style page, shown in Figure 17-14, you can choose one of four basic styles to apply to your report or choose to apply a template from your RAS system. After you select a style, click Next.

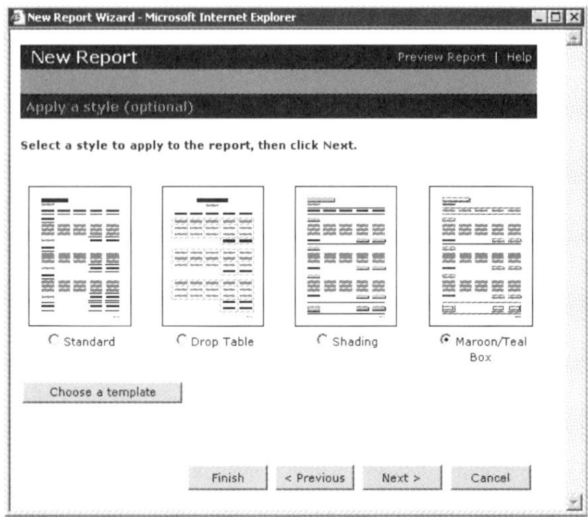

FIGURE 17-14 *The Apply a style page allows you to format the report with a predefined style.*

The final wizard screen, Save (see Figure 17-15), asks you to name the new report and allows you to choose where to save the report. The default directory is the RAS default setting.

Overall, the Web Report Design Wizard is very similar to the Report Wizard in Crystal Reports. There are some differences in the options displayed, but it provides powerful new capabilities to RAS power users.

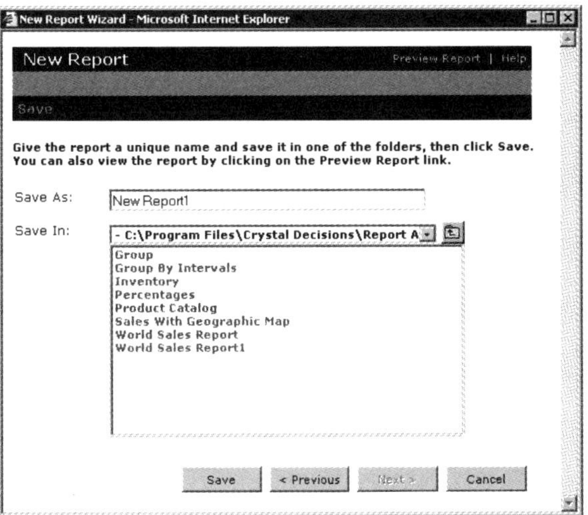

FIGURE 17-15 *The Save page allows you to save your report.*

Summary

The decision to move into Web reporting is an extremely important business decision. The biggest determination that you need to make is the level of Web reporting technology your organization needs. For many organizations, the RAS server is the correct choice, offering the ability to view on-demand reports as well as perform ad-hoc reporting. Other organizations are better suited to upgrade to Crystal Enterprise to incorporate report scheduling, organization, and security. Chapter 18 provides a more in-depth look at Crystal Enterprise.

Chapter 18

Crystal Enterprise (CE) is a server-based software package that is used to greatly improve your organization's Web-reporting capabilities. Crystal Enterprise comes in three editions: Standard, Professional, and Premium. Not to be confused with Crystal Enterprise is the RAS that is included with Crystal Reports 9 (refer to Chapter 17). Report Application Server (RAS) exposes basic CE functionality. Very simply stated, RAS allows users to view reports on demand over the Web. Various versions of RAS are available depending on the edition of Crystal Reports 9 you have purchased. These versions of RAS allow users to perform ad-hoc reporting over the Web, which enables them to create new reports over the Web as well as modify existing reports without the need for additional software on their desktops. Crystal Enterprise expands the Web-reporting features offered with RAS by allowing reports to be organized, secured using users and groups, and scheduled via the Web. Crystal Reports 9 is only compatible with Crystal Enterprise 9 and will not function correctly with other versions of CE.

NOTE

From this point on, references to CE or Crystal Enterprise refer to the Premium Edition of Crystal Enterprise 9. Depending on the edition of Crystal Enterprise 9 you purchase, some of the features being discussed may not be available. Screenshots included were captured using Crystal Enterprise 8.5 Professional due to the lack of availability of non-beta Crystal Enterprise 9 software at the time of publication.

CE allows you to create a folder structure for organizing your reports, which are stored in a centralized repository. You can then set security rules on these reports and folders based on users and groups that are created or mapped into the CE environment. Users are then only able to see the reports and folders that they have access to based on your security model. CE also allows for row-level security on your reports. This feature is an advanced topic and is discussed in more detail later in this chapter.

Another advantage of upgrading to CE is the ability to schedule your reports. CE offers a wide range of recurring scheduling options and also allows your reports to be output to a variety of destinations and formats. Some of the destinations available are an unmanaged disk (a location on your hard drive or a shared network location), printer, FTP site, or e-mail. A few of the formats available for scheduling are to Adobe Acrobat (.pdf), Microsoft Excel, Microsoft Word, Rich Text Format (.rtf), and character separated values (.csv). Each of these scheduling features is made even more powerful by using event-based scheduling. CE is able to monitor multiple types of events and allows you to base the scheduling of your reports on the status of these events.

Some Benefits of Using Crystal Enterprise

Crystal Enterprise brings many powerful features to your reporting environment as a whole. Rather than having your reports scattered all over your organization, processed on individual workstations, and then manually distributed, CE provides one enterprise-wide Web reporting system for managing, processing, and distributing all reports.

Server-Based Processing

Server-based processing (or server-side processing) means that all the work associated with the processing of a report is performed on the CE server(s). When a user makes a request for a report, the report is processed on the server and the result is sent to the user's Web browser and displayed in a report viewer.

Server-based processing has many benefits. One major benefit is that the end user's machine is not responsible for performing processor-intensive tasks, such as querying the database or formatting the report. A second benefit is that the server is the primary machine on the network that is making queries to the database. This reduction in the number of computers that are performing database queries can have a very positive effect on the overall performance of your network.

Web-Based Administrative and Client Tools

Crystal Enterprise is a Web-based system. This means that report viewing and system administration can be done remotely over the Web. The following are a few of the benefits of Web-based administration and zero-client report viewing:

◆ **No client-side software needed.** Because many of the administrative and client tools are Web-based, no software has to be installed on the end users' machines. The only installed component is an optional Web viewer, which is a very small add-in to the Web browser (the size depends on which viewer you implement).

◆ **Easily customizable Web interfaces.** The Web applications are based on Crystal Server Pages (CSP), which are similar to Active Server Pages (ASP). Because of this, you can customize or rewrite all the CSP pages that are used in the Web applications to give the application the look and feel of your choice.

◆ **Easily integrated into a custom Web application.** Because of the open architecture of the Crystal Enterprise system, the functionality, and the ease of use of the SDK, CE can be easily integrated into other Web applications.

On-Demand and Scheduled Reporting

One advantage of the CE system is that it separates the processing of your reports into two broad areas: on-demand reports and scheduled reports.

On-demand reports are processed as soon as the request to view the report is made by a user. In other words, the report is run the moment a user requests it and contains the newest data available from the database.

The opposite of an on-demand report is a scheduled report. To schedule a report, a user inputs certain information into the system, such as parameters to use when the report is run, the database logon to use, the schedule time, the destination, and the file format to output. After the user inputs the information required, the report is scheduled to the enterprise system. At the specified scheduled time, CE processes the report and stores the finished product as a report *instance*. This instance is then available for viewing by users with the proper security level.

The following are the benefits of on-demand reports:

- Data contained in the report is live
- No storage space on the server is needed because no report instance is created or saved.

By comparison, the following are the benefits of scheduled reports:

- Reports can be placed on a recurring schedule
- Reports can be sent to multiple destinations
- CE is able to output the report in multiple file formats
- Scheduling can be event-driven
- Reports can be processed off-hours thus reducing network activity during business hours
- Large reports that take longer to process can be run ahead of time and can be available immediately when users need to view them
- Reports containing data that does not change often can be scheduled to process on a regular basis thus reducing the number of requests made to the database server

Ad-Hoc Reporting

Report Application Server (RAS), also referred to as Smart Reporting, enables you to perform ad-hoc reporting on your Crystal Reports that are published to the Crystal Enterprise system. Ad-hoc reporting refers to the ability to either create new reports or modify existing reports over the Web. This feature is a huge benefit to companies that have users who need to be able to create and modify reports but do not need the full functionality offered by Crystal Reports. By using a combination of Crystal Reports and Smart Reporting, report designers can create the majority of your reports, and then you can give power users the ability to modify these reports via the Web.

Multiple Authentication Methods

One of the biggest advantages of using Crystal Enterprise is that it enables you to set security on your folders and reports to restrict access to those objects. To do this, individual users that are accessing CE resources must be authenticated as valid users. A number of methods can be used to authenticate your users, including the following:

- **Enterprise Authentication.** Enterprise Authentication is used to validate any user accounts that are created through the administrative tools of CE.

- **NT Authentication.** One feature of CE is the ability to "map" Windows NT users and groups into the system. By using Windows NT account mapping, you can drastically reduce the duplication of user accounts and the administrative time that it takes to set up these users. NT Authentication allows Windows NT users to access Crystal Enterprise by authenticating them through your Windows NT domain.

- **LDAP Authentication.** LDAP Authentication uses the same concept as NT Authentication. It allows LDAP users to access Crystal Enterprise by authenticating them through your LDAP server.

Row-level Security Using Processing Extensions

Setting security on report objects can be one of the most taxing jobs when administering a reporting system. Row-level security can make this job easier. By using row-level security, the data being displayed on a report is filtered when being viewed based on a set of business rules or logic.

For example, suppose your organization has a sales report that is grouped by sales department. You want every sales department to be able to use this report, but you do not want them to be able to view each other's data on the report. This is a perfect time to use row-level security. By implementing your business logic, you can filter the data that is displayed on the report based on the sales group that the person viewing the report belongs to in Crystal Enterprise.

CE is able to filter a report's data by using a technology called Processing Extensions. By using custom programming, Processing Extension DLL files are created that affect the data being displayed on a report based on business logic being stored in a third-party database (such as Microsoft Access). More information about advanced features such as Processing Extensions is available on the Crystal Decisions Web site at **www.crystaldecisions.com**.

Publishing and Organizing Your Reports

Another benefit of Crystal Enterprise is that is enables you to create a folder structure within the system to organize your reports. By creating sets of folders with embedded subfolders, organizing your reports becomes a simple task.

Once you create a folder structure, the next step is to populate those folders with reports. Reports are brought into CE through a method called *publishing*. Any report that you would like CE to manage needs to be published to the CE environment. CE offers a number of methods for publishing your Crystal Reports to Crystal Enterprise, including both Web-based and PC-based methods.

Flexible Folder Structure

A well-planned folder structure can be the key to a successful CE implementation, because users will navigate through these folders to find the reports that they would like to view. If the folder structure is too difficult to navigate, users will find the system less useful. Security is another reason to have a well-planned folder structure. Enterprise security is based on setting user and group access permissions to reports and folders in the system. Therefore, if your folder structure is too complex, creating your security model will be much more difficult. Folders are created using the Crystal Management Console (discussed later in this chapter).

Methods of Publishing Your Reports

To allow Crystal Enterprise to control your report files, the reports must first be published to the Crystal Enterprise System. There are multiple methods available to publish your reports including using Crystal Reports 9, the Publishing Wizard, or the Crystal Management Console.

Using Crystal Reports 9

This method allows report designers to save reports directly to CE. It is a good idea to use this option when you have access to the report designer and are in the process of creating new reports for CE or editing existing reports in CE. The drawback of using this method is that only one report can be published at a time.

Using the Crystal Publishing Wizard

The Crystal Publishing Wizard, shown in Figure 18-1, is the most powerful method of publishing reports. It is a PC-based client tool that can be installed as a separate component from the Crystal Enterprise installation CD-ROM. The Publishing Wizard allows you to publish an individual report or multiple reports in one step. It also allows you to modify certain report properties at publication time, such as the report title and description, default parameter values, and default database logon information.

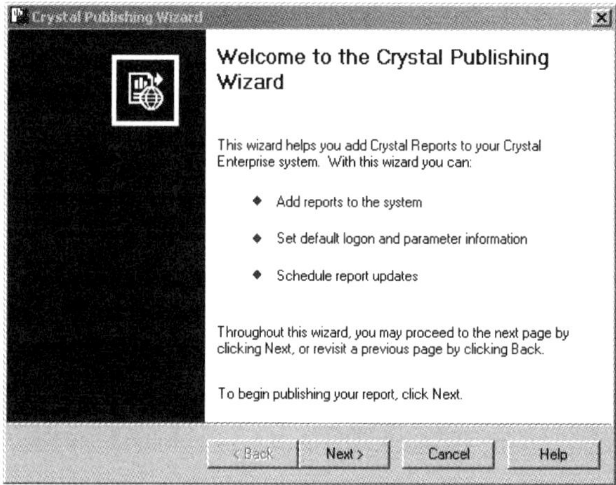

FIGURE 18-1 *Use the Crystal Publishing Wizard for the most powerful and flexible report publishing to CE.*

Using the Crystal Management Console

The Crystal Management Console (CMC) is the Web-based administrative tool of CE (see Figure 18-2). One major benefit of publishing your reports using the CMC is that you can use it remotely. As long as you have access to your organization's CE Web site, you can use the CMC to publish. The CMC is a good method to use to publish when you are already performing administrative tasks using the CMC or need to publish remotely.

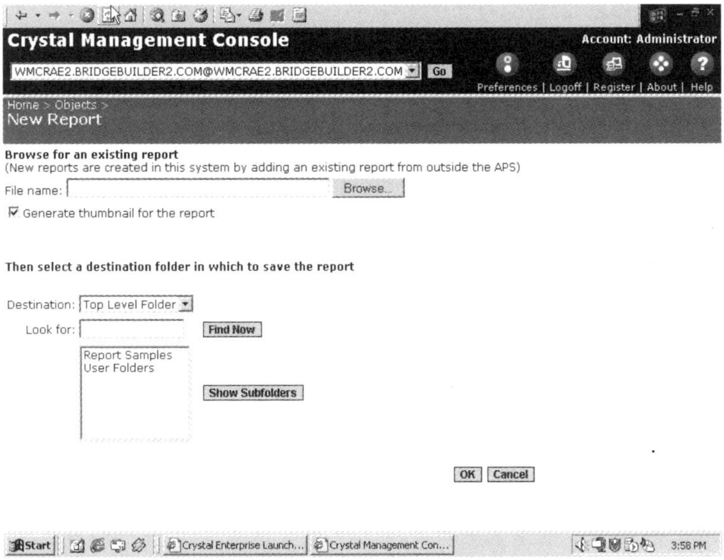

FIGURE 18-2 *Use the CMC to publish reports to CE remotely.*

How Crystal Enterprise Works

Crystal Enterprise is a server-side system whose purpose is to aid in the enterprise-wide distribution of your reports over the Web. This means that the software that performs the key tasks of CE will be installed on a single server or multiple servers that make up one enterprise system.

CE is broken up into a number of services that run simultaneously. Each service is responsible for a specific piece of CE functionality. All of these services communicate with one another through the Crystal eBusiness Framework. All of the services, as well as the eBusiness Framework, are discussed in the next section.

One large benefit of CE's architecture is that it is scalable. Because the different components of the system are broken up into individual services, most of these components can be redundant in the system. For example, if you know that the reports your users will be processing are going to be mostly on-demand reports, you may choose to add a second Page Server service to your architecture to increase the performance of your system.

Server Architecture

Crystal Enterprise has a flexible and scalable server architecture that is completely customizable to how you use the system and which components you decide to implement. The architecture is made up of a number of servers that communicate to each other over an eBusiness Framework. The following sections break up each server and describe its purpose in the architecture. For a graphical representation of the CE architecture, refer to Figure 18-3.

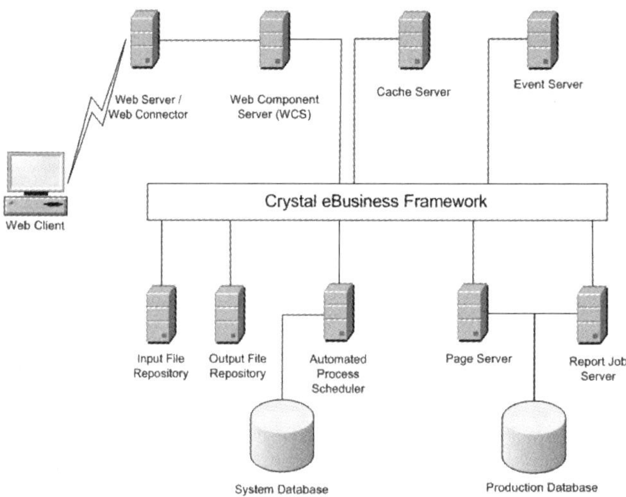

FIGURE 18-3 *Crystal Enterprise has a flexible and extensive architecture.*

Crystal eBusiness Framework

The Crystal eBusiness Framework is the method that all Crystal Enterprise Services use to communicate with one another. The framework uses a CORBA convention that uses TCP/IP for network communication. This is the reason CE is restricted to a TCP/IP-based network.

Web Connector

The Web Connector is the only component of the CE system that has a restrictive install location. The Web Connector must be installed on a Web server. Many Web server platforms are supported, including Web servers that are compliant with ISAPI, NSAPI, DSAPI, ASAPI, or CGI. The purpose of the Web Connector is to monitor file extensions that are being passed to the Web server. If a file extension matches one of the file types associated with the CE, the request is forwarded to the Web Component Server for processing. The appropriate Web Connector is installed automatically during the CE install process.

Web Component Server (WCS)

The job of the WCS is to decipher the requests that are forwarded into the system from the Web connector. The WCS is the only service in the CE architecture that communicates to the Web connector.

Automated Process Scheduler (APS)

The main functionality of the APS stems from its ability to read from and write to the CE system database (discussed next). The APS manages security and user authentication by keeping a listing of users and their assigned system rights in the system database. The APS also keeps track of the location of objects (reports and folder hierarchy) in the system by writing to the system database.

Another job of the APS is to communicate scheduling information with the Report Job Server. By communicating with the Report Job Server, the APS acts as a "manager" over the system and tells the Report Job Server all the information that it needs to know to process the scheduled job.

A final job of the APS is to keep track of all servers registered with the system. The APS can then act as a directory for a server when that server needs to communicate with other servers in the system. Because the APS is such a crucial component of the CE architecture, multiple APS services can be joined together to form a "cluster." This improves performance and also provides failover support.

System Database

The system database is responsible for storing all information dealing with CE, such as usernames, passwords, object names and locations, and the services that are registered with the APS machine. By default, the system database is created as a Microsoft Data Engine (MSDE) database, but it can be migrated to a number of other database platforms. The APS is the only service that ever interacts directly with the system database.

Input File Repository

The Input File Repository is responsible for storing all report files that are published to CE. These report files are stripped of any saved data at the time they are published to the system to minimize the size of the file. There can only be one Input File Repository in a CE implementation.

Output File Repository

The Output File Repository is responsible for storing any *report instances*. After a scheduled report has run successfully, the report is saved with the data that was used to process that report as a report instance in the Output File Repository. There can only be one Output File Repository in a CE implementation.

Page Server and Report Job Server

The Page Server and the Report Job Server are the "workhorses" of the CE system. These are the two servers that are responsible for the processing of your reports. The Page Server is responsible for processing on-demand report requests. When the Page Server processes a request for an on-demand report, it creates an Encapsulated Page Format (.epf) file for each page of the report that is viewed. This is done to minimize traffic over the network. Instead of sending an entire report to a user, only the pages that they request are processed and delivered to them over the Web. These EPF pages are then stored by the cache server to allow for sharing of the files between user requests.

The Report Job Server is responsible for processing scheduled reports. The APS keeps track of all scheduling information and then communicates this information to the Report Job Server at the scheduled time. The Report Job Server then processes the report and saves the completed instance in the Output File Repository and updates the APS to the status of the job.

These are the only two services in the out-of-the-box CE system that will query your production database. Keep in mind that any method you use in your reports to connect to the report's data source must also reside on both the Page Server and Report Job Server (ODBC connections, native drivers, etc.).

Cache Server

The Cache Server is responsible for storing EPF pages that are created by the Page Server. Other cache files are also stored in order to enhance the speed of the caching and reporting processes. All initial requests to view a report are forwarded from the WCS to the Cache Server. The purpose of this is to check to see if the page being requested already has an EPF page stored in the Cache Server that can be shared and sent to the user. Having sharable EPF pages reduces the time it takes to serve a page to the user, the workload of the page server, and the number of hits to the database.

Event Server

The Event Server is responsible for monitoring file-based events that are registered with CE. The Event Server monitors a specified directory for the existence of a specific file. If the file exists, the event is triggered. When an event is triggered, the Event Server is responsible for letting the APS know that any reports based on the event can now be processed.

Report Application Server

The Report Application Server (RAS), which is optional, is responsible for performing functions related to ad-hoc reporting. It gives your users the ability to modify existing reports or use an existing report as the source for a new report, all being done over the Web.

How Do I Use Crystal Enterprise?

Crystal Enterprise is a server-centric Web-based software package. Therefore, most of the client tools used to interact with the system are Web-applications. The two major client tools used to interact with the system are ePortfolio and the Crystal Management Console (CMC). ePortfolio is used for end-user interaction with the system, such as viewing and scheduling reports. The CMC is used to perform administrative tasks, such as creating users, groups, and folders, setting report properties, and applying security. If your Web services are not available and you need to perform administrative tasks, a third application is available, the Crystal Configuration Manager (CCM), a Windows-installed administrative component. With this tool, administrators can start, stop, and restart services, add and delete services, and modify service properties.

Client Application (ePortfolio or Customized Application)

The report-viewing application that comes with CE is ePortfolio, which is a more advanced reporting tool than ePortfolio Lite discussed in Chapter 17. ePortfolio Lite, used with RAS, is a basic tool used to view reports on demand over the Web while ePortfolio, included with CE, is an advanced reporting that adds the functionality of scheduling, organizing reports and folders, alerting, and is controlled by your CE security model. This tool is used by end users to perform all tasks related to viewing reports on demand, scheduling reports, and viewing report instances. If ePortfolio doesn't fit all of your reporting needs, you can create a custom end-user application by using the Crystal Enterprise SDK.

Logging in to ePortfolio

You can access ePortfolio by clicking its link on the Crystal Launchpad or directly by its URL. To access ePortfolio by using its URL, type the following address into your Web browser: http://*ServerName*/crystal/enterprise/eportfolio (where *ServerName* is the name of your Web server). To log in to ePortfolio, type your username and password and select an authentication type from the drop-down list (see Figure 18-4).

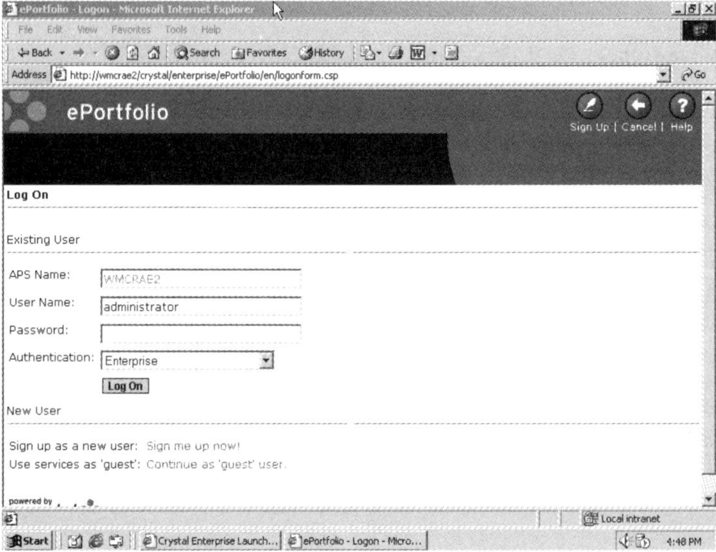

FIGURE 18-4 *You must log in to ePortfolio to use the tool.*

Navigating ePortfolio

Begin navigating ePortfolio by selecting your starting point (either Favorites or Public). Any folders that you have access to will be under the Folders heading. Drill down through the folder structure by clicking on the name of the desired folder until you find the desired report (see Figure 18-5). Any reports that exist in the folder you drilled into and that you have access to will automatically be displayed in the main window.

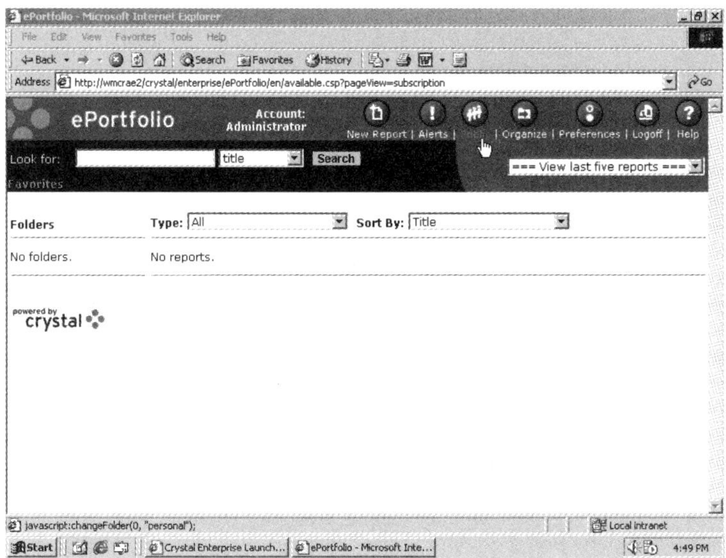

FIGURE 18-5 *Drill down through the folder structure to find the report you want.*

Viewing Reports On Demand

To view a report on demand, click the desired report name and then click the View link that appears (see Figure 18-6). The report is displayed in a report viewer. If the View option doesn't appear, you do not have sufficient security rights to view on demand.

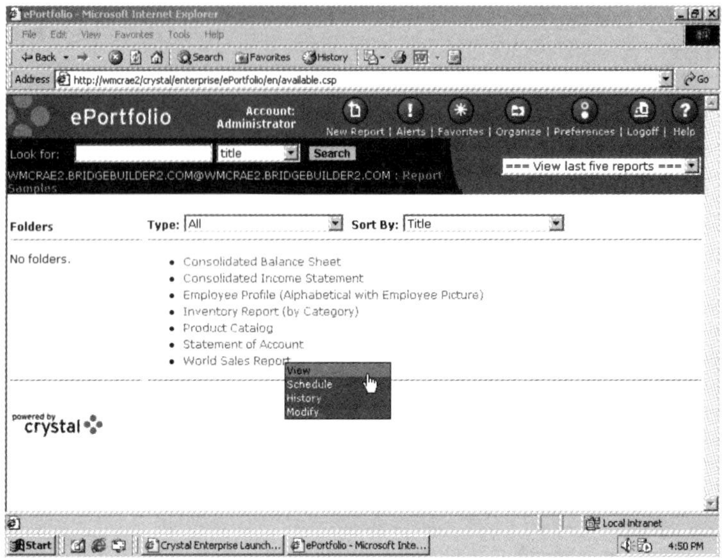

FIGURE 18-6 *Click the View link in order to view a report on demand in ePortfolio.*

Scheduling Report Objects

To schedule a report, click the desired report name and then click the Schedule link (see Figure 18-7). If the Schedule option doesn't appear, you do not have sufficient security rights to schedule the report. Next, enter the required scheduling information and click the Schedule button in the top-right corner.

Viewing Report Instances

To view a report instance, click the desired report name and then click the History link (see Figure 18-8). On the History screen, click the link for the instance you want to view. The instance is displayed in a report viewer.

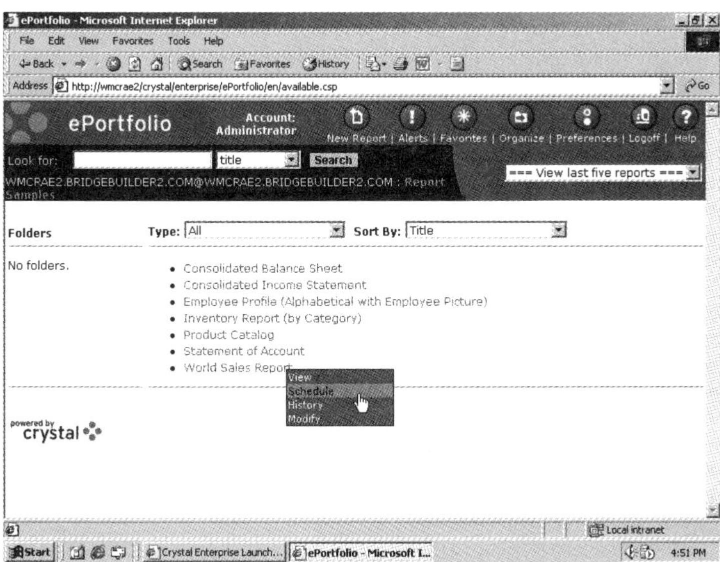

FIGURE 18-7 *Schedule a report in ePortfolio by clicking the Schedule link.*

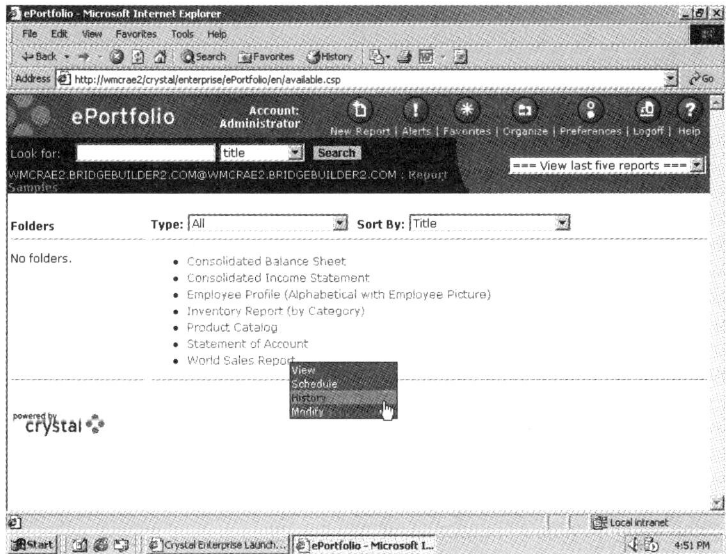

FIGURE 18-8 *Access the historical instances of a report by clicking the History link.*

Customizing User Settings

To modify ePortfolio preferences, click the Preferences button at the top of the ePortfolio window. The settings in the User Preferences screen, shown in Figure 18-9, are user specific, not global to all users.

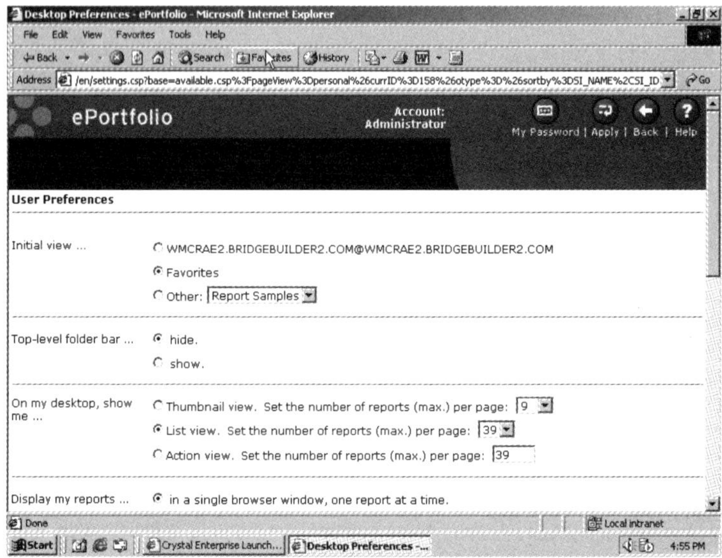

FIGURE 18-9 *Customize ePortfolio settings by clicking the preferences button at the top of the ePortfolio window.*

Administrative Tools

Crystal Enterprise has two administrative tools to help you set up and maintain your system. To administer the system, you will need to understand when and how to use each of these tools. The Crystal Management Console is a Web-based administrative tool while the Crystal Configuration Manager is a PC-based tool.

Crystal Management Console

The CMC is the Web-based administrative tool of CE. By using it, you can perform almost any administrative task. However, some tasks, such as adding a new service, must be done through the PC-based administrative tool, the Crystal Configuration Manager.

Logging in to the CMC

You can access the CMC by clicking its link on the Crystal Launchpad or directly by its URL. To access the CMC by using its URL, type the following address into your Web browser: http://*ServerName*/crystal/enterprise/admin (where *ServerName* is the name of your Web server). To log in to the CMC, type your username and password and select an authentication type from the drop-down list (see Figure 18-10).

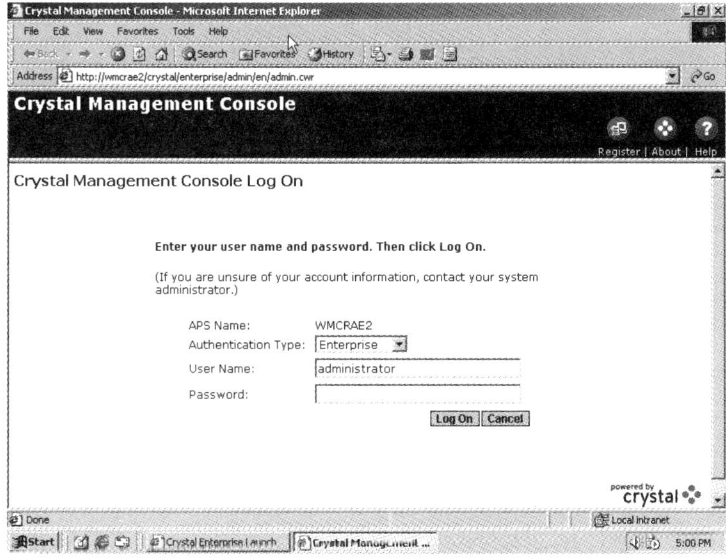

FIGURE 18-10 *You must log in to the CMC to administer Crystal Enterprise over the Web.*

Managing Users

To manage your users, either click the Manage Users button on the main page of the CMC or select Users from the drop-down list box on the top toolbar. Use the Users screen, shown in Figure 18-11, to create new enterprise users or to modify individual user settings. By default you should have three users: Guest, Administrator, and an account that was created for the user that was logged into the machine at the time of the software install. If the local or domain Administrator account was used to install Crystal Enterprise, the install process will automatically alias the Crystal Enterprise Administrator account to the local or domain Administrator account. In this instance, only two users (Guest and Administrator) will be displayed in Crystal Enterprise.

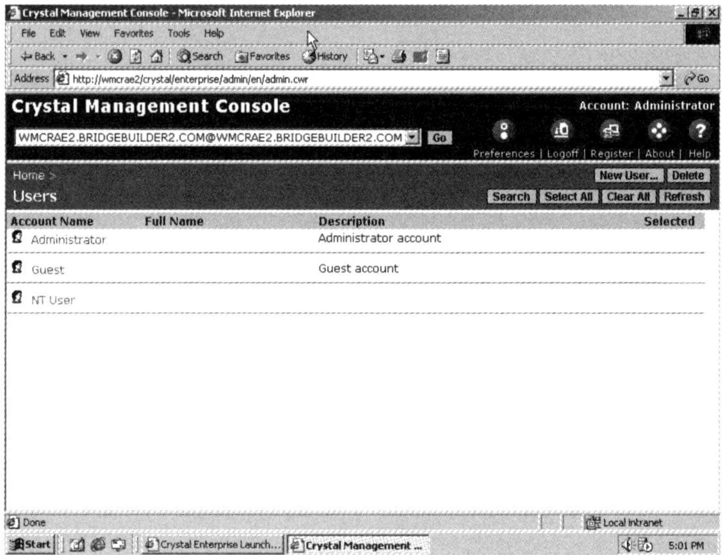

FIGURE 18-11 *The Users screen of the CMC is used to add new users and to delete existing users.*

Managing Groups

To manage your groups, either click the Manage Groups button on the main page of the CMC or select Groups from the drop-down list box on the top toolbar. Use the Groups screen, shown in Figure 18-12, to create new groups or to modify existing group properties. By default, you will have four groups: Administrators, New Sign-up Accounts, Crystal NT Users, and Everyone.

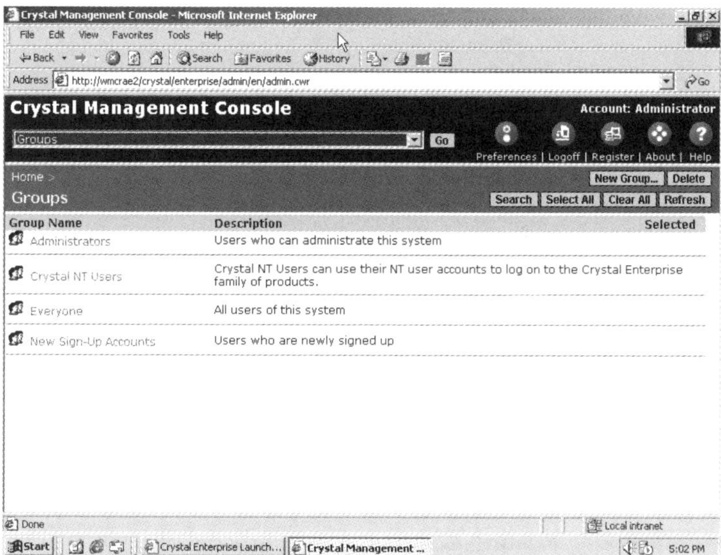

FIGURE 18-12 *Use the Groups screen of the CMC to add new groups and to delete existing groups.*

Managing Objects

To manage your objects, either click the Manage Objects button on the main page of the CMC or select Objects from the drop-down list box on the top toolbar. Use the Objects screen, shown in Figure 18-13, to publish new reports to the system, copy or move existing reports, or modify existing report properties.

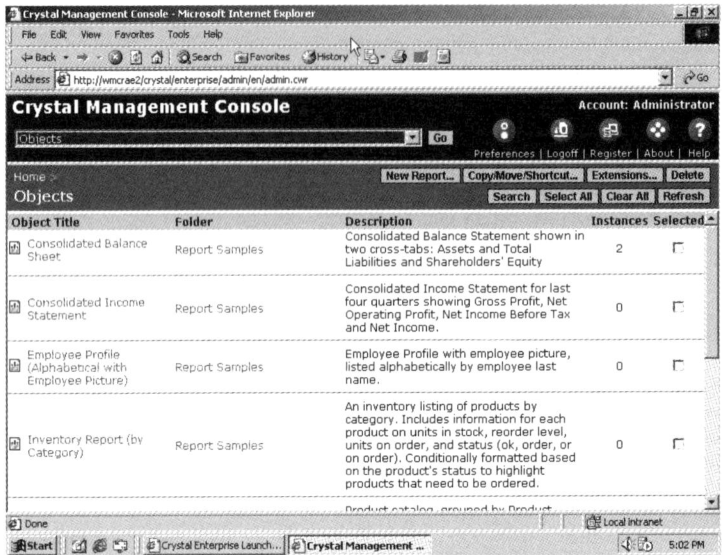

FIGURE 18-13 *Use the Objects screen of the CMC to publish reports, delete existing reports, and reorganize your reports.*

Managing Folders

To manage your folders, either click the Manage Folders button on the main page of the CMC or select Folders from the drop-down list box on the top toolbar. Use the Folders screen, shown in Figure 18-14, to create new folders, copy or move existing folders, or modify existing folder properties. By default, you will have two top-level folders, Sample Reports and User Folders. A folder with a user's name will be created automatically as a subfolder in the User Folder for every user added to Crystal Enterprise.

Managing Events

To manage your events, either click the Manage Events button on the main page of the CMC or select Events from the drop-down list box on the top toolbar. Use the Events screen, shown in Figure 18-15, to create new file-based, schedule-based, or custom events.

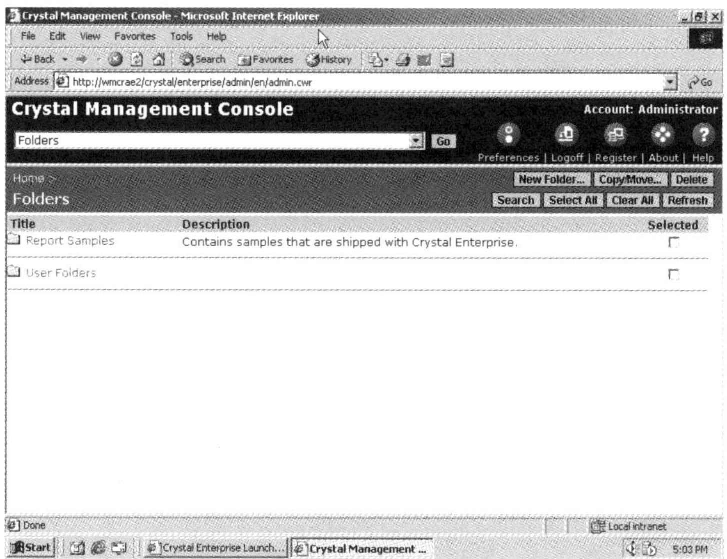

FIGURE 18-14 *By using the Folders screen of the CMC you can create new top-level folders, reorganize your folder structure, and delete existing folders.*

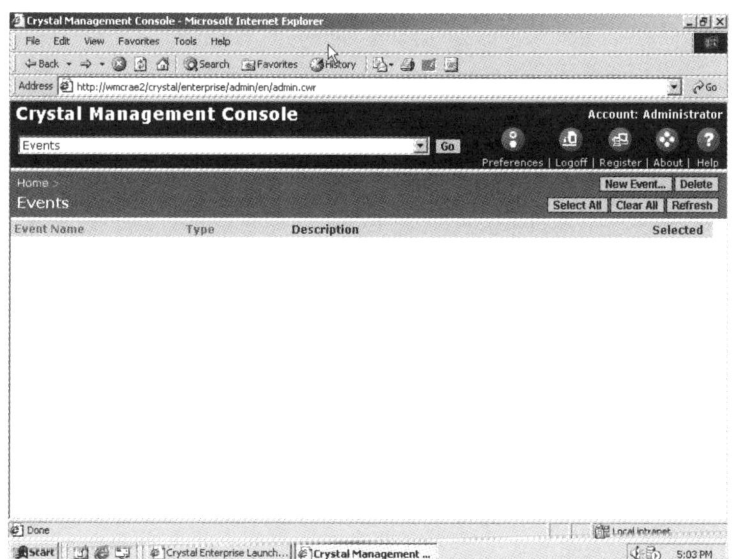

FIGURE 18-15 *The Events screen of the CMC is used to create new events.*

Managing Servers

To manage your servers, either click the Manage Servers button on the main page of the CMC or select Servers from the drop-down list box on the top toolbar. Use the Servers screen, shown in Figure 18-16, to perform tasks such as starting, stopping, or restarting a service. You will also use this screen to set very important service properties.

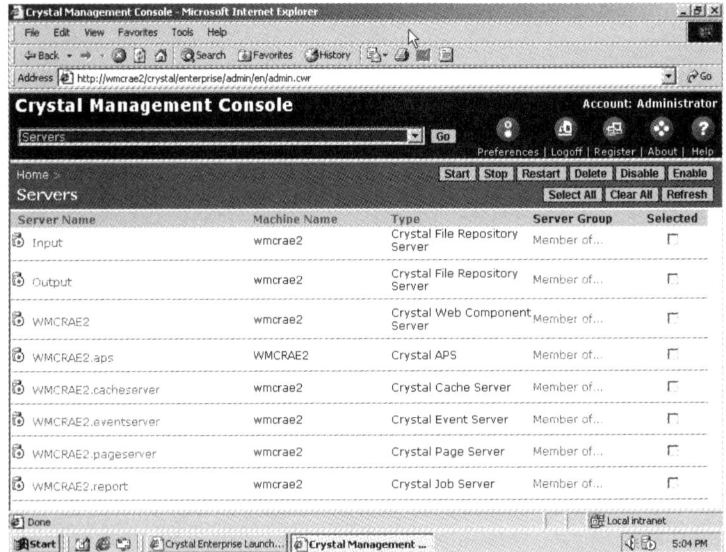

FIGURE 18-16 *The Servers screen of the CMC is used to perform administrative tasks over the Web.*

Managing Server Groups

To manage your server groups, either click the Manage Server Groups button on the main page of the CMC or select Server Groups from the drop-down list box on the top toolbar to open the Server Groups screen, shown in Figure 18-17.

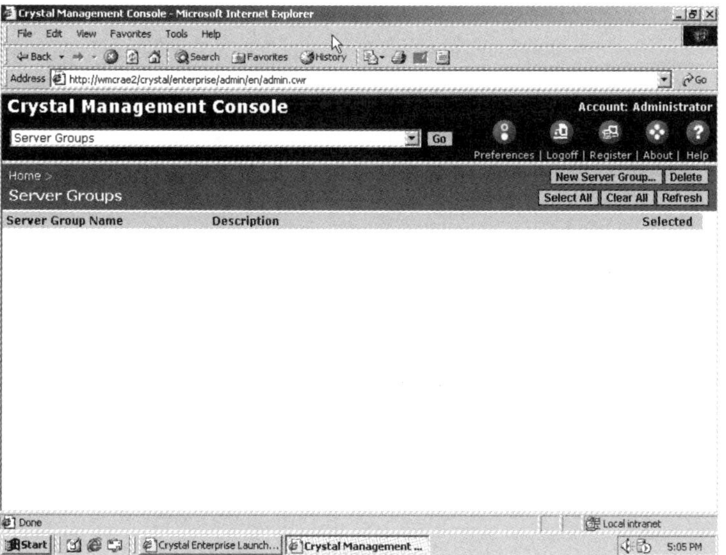

FIGURE 18-17 *Using the Server Groups screen of the CMC, you can organize your Crystal Enterprise servers into meaningful groups.*

Managing Global Settings

To manage your global settings, either click the Manage Settings button on the main page of the CMC or select Settings from the drop-down list box on the top toolbar. Use the Settings screen, shown in Figure 18-18, to set global properties, add licensing, and view global metrics.

Managing Authorization

To manage your authorization settings, either click the Manage Authorization button on the main page of the CMC or select Authorization from the drop-down list box on the top toolbar. Use the Authorization screen, shown in Figure 18-19, to set Enterprise Authentication password settings, map Windows NT Groups, and add LDAP servers to the CE environment.

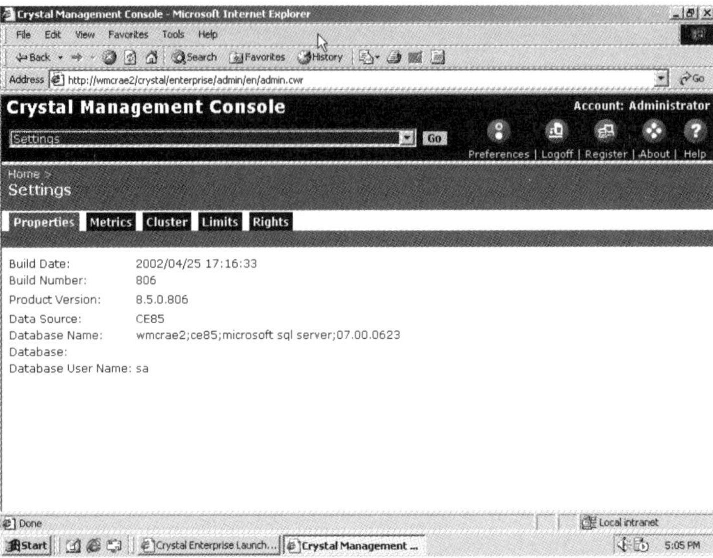

FIGURE 18-18 *The Settings screen of the CMC is used to set system preferences for Limits and Rights and is also used to view Cluster information, system properties, and global metrics.*

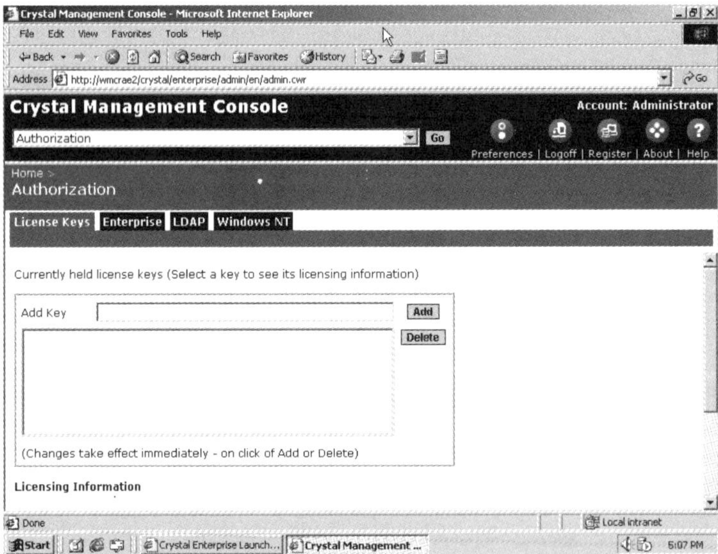

FIGURE 18-19 *The Authorization screen is used for adding licenses, setting password rules, and for setting authorization preferences.*

Crystal Configuration Manager

The Crystal Configuration Manager (CCM) is the Windows-based administrative tool used in CE (see Figure 18-20). The CCM is an extremely important tool to use in situations where you cannot access your Web administrative tool. Also, certain tasks can only be done using this tool, such as adding additional services to the system, configuring the system database, and configuring the Web connector.

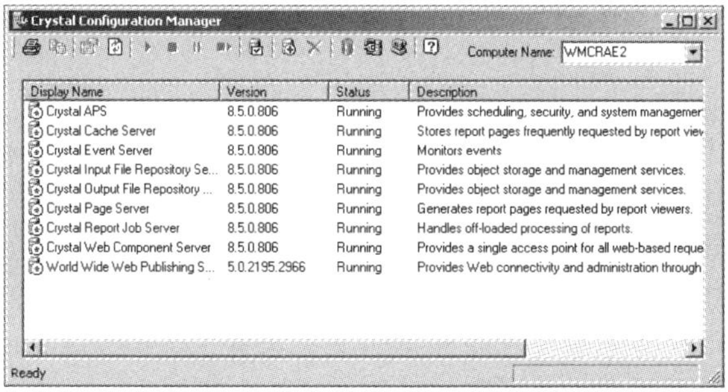

FIGURE 18-20 *Use the CCM to perform many administrative tasks on the CE server(s).*

Editions of CE 9

CE is available in three editions: Standard, Professional, and Premium. Each edition offers a certain level of functionality to meet your reporting needs. The most basic edition is Standard, allowing the smallest subset of CE functionality. The Standard edition allows you to view reports on demand, schedule reports, and organize reports in a folder structure. The major limitations of this edition are that you do not have the ability to add users and groups and that you are limited to installing all CE servers on a single machine. The Standard edition is best suited for organizations that are not interested in securing their reports using the built-in security features of CE and would like to use CE as a method of viewing and scheduling reports over the Web.

The Professional edition offers the second tier of CE functionality. CE Professional includes all the functionality of Standard and adds many features such as security, named user licensing, multiple authentication methods, fail over support and redundancy, and support of a multi-server deployment.

The third edition, Premium, expands on the functionality of the Professional edition by including RAS (discussed in Chapter 17), Crystal Analysis Professional, and the pre-built ad hoc reporting tool. While RAS and Crystal Analysis Professional can be purchased as add-on components to the Professional edition, the pre-built ad hoc tool can only be obtained by purchasing the Premium edition. For more information on these editions or other Crystal Decisions products, please refer to the Crystal Decisions Web site at **www.crystaldecisions.com/products**.

Summary

Sharing information through reporting is an extremely important business need. Depending on the reporting requirements of your organization, Crystal Enterprise can be an extremely beneficial addition to your existing set of enterprise-wide software solutions. Through on-demand reporting, powerful scheduling, and advanced security features, Crystal Enterprise can boost your organization's report usage and maximize the value of your data.

Chapter 19

Tips for Report Development Projects

This chapter provides tips for getting started in planning report projects and writing reports. People generally ask, "Where do I start?" My recommended approach begins with placing the simple items first and then progressing to the more advanced items on the report. This philosophy builds confidence because it's result-oriented.

You'll also find a list of tips for changing the preferences in Crystal Reports in this chapter. This listing results from years of training and troubleshooting with clients who are new to Crystal Reports. I believe you'll find these tips valuable and that they will make your experience in Crystal Reports much friendlier.

Planning a Report

It is very important to plan your project before you start writing reports. Before you even open the software, you should complete a number of actions, as described in the following sections.

Becoming Familiar with Your Data

You build your reports from data, so it makes sense to be familiar with the structure, fields, relationships, and location of that data. First, find out who the database administrator (DBA) is and whether he or she is available to help with questions during your project. For example, you can ask the DBA where to locate the tables and fields for the report. Often, the DBA can help with linking tables or creating views in the database.

Views are a collection of tables and fields that the DBA turns into a virtual table so that the report writer needs only one view to complete the report. Like dictionaries, views can simplify report writing by handling all the table linking, freeing the report writer from having to do so.

The DBA can also provide you with a printed data model or relationship diagram to help with the report writing process. It's helpful to see your data represented visually when linking tables.

If you do not have access to a DBA or a data model of your database, you need to build your own model. Refer to your database's documentation about the relationships between the tables and fields. This provides a starting point to work from.

The type of information you need to understand about your database includes:

- Keys (or indexed fields)
- Field names
- Field types (string, numeric, currency, and so on)
- Field lengths

These pieces of information about your database dictate how to link the tables (which is one of the most important steps in writing a report). If you create incorrect links, you are likely to get bad data returned on the report.

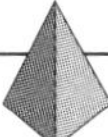

TIP

Make sure that you understand your database relationships before attempting to create the report.

Interviewing Your Customer

The next step to building a report is understanding how the data needs to appear on the report. Generally, the fastest way to gather this important information is to interview your customer. I define the *customer* as the person or group who will ultimately use the report.

Ask them to provide you with copies of existing reports that need to be converted to Crystal. In addition to seeing what fields a report should include, an advantage to having an older report is that you can see how the formulas have been structured. You should also review other reports that the organization uses to see how the reports use logos, colors, and other graphics.

Even if old reports exist to use as a reference, it is extremely helpful to build *mock* reports. Mock reports let you and your customer plan the layout of the report you need to build. I suggest using a spreadsheet or a simple piece of notebook paper for sketching the basic layout of the report. I cannot emphasize enough how important it is to know how your customer envisions the report *appearing*.

Understand how the report will be deployed and to whom. Distribution can definitely impact how the report is built—will it be viewed on the Web, on paper copies only, or will it exported to .PDF or Excel? Or is the report really just a data pull for another group to use and manipulate? It is a waste to spend time formatting a report when the data is needed only in Excel.

Look for the key items to include on the report, such as:

◆ Fields

◆ Formulas or calculations

◆ Groups

◆ Sorts

◆ Charts

◆ Subtotals

◆ Record selection

◆ Parameters

The goal of this step is to provide yourself with a target that you and the customer agree on before the report development begins in Crystal Reports.

Understanding the Chain of Command

If you need to make a change to the design of an existing report, whom do you need to ask? It's helpful to understand who approves changes or new ideas for the reports. Sometimes one person can answer a question about data included on a report; other times a committee exists to approve or disapprove the different types of reports that are implemented. Finding out how reports are approved helps with forecasting the length of the project.

Checking the Printer Drivers and Fonts

One key rule to keep in mind is that Crystal uses the current printer driver on the client machine to create the output on the screen or printer. In other words, Crystal uses your default printer to "draw" the report. This means that your report output *can* and *will change* depending on the printer driver selected on the machine used for viewing the report. Find out the types of printers used in the organization and test them before you publish the reports. Otherwise, you might find that your fields have moved (or overlapped) when the printer drivers change.

I recommend that you use common Windows fonts, such as Arial and Times New Roman, to avoid font substitution. If a font doesn't exist on the client machine, Windows substitutes another font in its place. This can change the formatting and look of the report dramatically.

Determining How Reports Will Be Viewed

Crystal Reports is very flexible when it comes to different ways to viewing reports. A good question to ask is, "How will the reports we create be viewed—on the screen, printed, or on the Web?"

If the reports will print to a black-and-white printer, you might want to try the pattern fills instead of colors for charts and maps. The colors might look great when you preview the report on-screen, but might print too faintly to read easily on paper.

If the reports are to go to the Web, you'll use the Viewers within ePortfolio Lite (see more about this in Chapter 17). These viewers retain the Crystal Report format and eliminate export issues commonly found when converting to HTML.

Creating a Template with Common Elements

After the interview process, create a template with the common elements for the reports. Include items such as logos, colors, boxes and lines, shading, and so on. Keep it simple so that you don't need to delete many items before building each report.

Consider including information about you (the report writer), your company, and the report itself in the Summary Info window. You open Summary Info by selecting it from the File menu. On the Summary tab, you can enter your name, your company, the title of the report, a description of the report, keywords, and a subject, which helps when searching for a report. You can also review some interesting statistics about your report on the Statistics tab, such as creation date and amount of editing time.

You might also have the template include special fields such as Print Date/Time, Data Date/Time, File Path/Name, or Page Number in the Page Header or Page Footer sections. Use a small font size to keep this helpful, but not critical, information out of the spotlight. When looking at a printed document, these fields can show information such as when the report ran, the age of the report data, and where to find the report.

If you're working with a team of report developers, you might want to investigate using a version control product (such as Microsoft Visual SourceSafe) to allow only one developer at a time to check out and work on a report. In any case, make sure that you save your report with different file names from time to time so that you can go back to an older version if you accidentally "break" your report.

Also, report files sometimes get corrupted for unknown reasons. It's a relief to have copies in case a particular file won't open or work. Please note that Crystal Reports has an Autosave feature, so you'll want to make sure that this setting is on. In any event, I recommend that you always have a backup just in case.

Almost Ready to Begin the Report

As you can see, a lot of questions need answering before you can start. Overall, you want to have a good idea of what tables and fields you need and how to get help with the database if you need it. Generally, a database expert will be available to you. If you don't know where the data needs to come from, ask someone for help. You might not know that you've incorrectly linked tables, and then you will have trouble figuring out the problem if your report does not look right or contain the right data.

Building a Report Step-by-Step

Now that you have a template to work with, you can start building an individual report. Complete the basics of the report first and then add more advanced options, such as formulas, parameters, subreports, cross-tabs, graphs, and maps. Using this method, you can see results as you go.

1. Add tables to the report and link. If you use a view, query, or dictionary, linking becomes less of an issue.

2. Add fields to the report. Use the information from the interview and mock report to add the columns and data to the report.

3. Define the record selection to limit the number of records to be returned. Add parameters for record selection, if necessary. Sometimes these steps are difficult, however, so feel free to skip them now and add them later. But including some record selection criteria early limits the amount of work your machine does when processing the report in the next step.

4. Preview the report to see what it looks like at this point. At this time, resize and rearrange fields as necessary. Make sure that the column headings read the way you want. You should probably wait a few more steps before doing further formatting. But make sure you save your report frequently!

5. Set up groups defined in the interview and on the mock report. Check the sorting on the groups (Ascending, Descending, Original, or Specified Order). Make sure to check for second and third level sorts. At this point, your report should really begin taking shape. If your report does not look like the mock report, recheck the groups and record selection and fields on the report. This is an important checkpoint, because grouping is critical to making the report look correct.

6. Add summaries and subtotals to all groups that need them. Also, add text to explain what the numbers indicate.

7. Format objects (such as fields) so that they display data in the format needed for the report (such as currency or date). Make modifications to fonts, colors, borders, and other format options in order to call attention to an important field. Save your report.

8. Look at the report on the Preview tab and take a few minutes to be sure that your report is taking the shape you want. You might want to offset the groups, format all the column headings the same way, get rid of decimals, and so on. At this point, you might want to add conditional formatting to use on fields on the report.

9. Add formulas to build calculated fields. Formulas often stump report developers—even experienced report developers. Don't stop the report development process to work on a tough formula. You can use double slashes (//) to comment out sections in a formula or add comments to document your formula. This is useful when troubleshooting a formula (to test specific sections or lines). If you encounter a tough formula and get stumped, comment out the entire formula and leave it on the report.

The Formula Editor ignores anything to the right of the double slashes. This enables you to keep the formula on the report and still allow the report to process (without getting errors). Save your report.

10. Add other advanced items such as parameters, subreports, cross-tabs, graphs, and maps. This, of course, depends on your specific report.

11. Do any section formatting or section conditional formatting. You might need or want to manipulate the sections containing a graph or spend some time with a subreport.

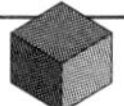

NOTE

You will find that previewing your report often helps you format it the way you like.

12. Test data for correct results. Verify your formulas, record selection, groups, and summaries against a legacy report or the database itself. Though often time-consuming, this step is important for ensuring the accuracy of the data on your report.

13. Clean up the report and get the formatting perfect. If you plan to export to another program, experiment with the export. You might want to try other export formats to see whether the results change. Try both Excel options, or try both .PDF and HTML, to see how those options format the report. You can also try exporting to Lotus 1-2-3 and importing into Excel. All of these formats are compatible with Excel, but they give differing results. Save your report.

14. Publish the report.

By step 7, the report generally really starts taking shape. Do as much without formulas or conditional formatting as possible, because formulas can be complicated. It's important to get the look of the report early on so that you have the structure in place before you start adding specific special items.

It's easiest to work on the formulas toward the end of the report development process for two reasons. First, formulas can sometimes be frustrating if you are trying something totally new. Don't hold up your report design because you cannot get one formula. Second, formulas usually don't add much to the structure of the report. Thus, if you get the basic structure and format set, you can focus on just the formula problem later—and relax about not having accomplished anything yet.

Formulas, parameters, subreports, graphs, and maps are usually important to the report itself, but not to the structure of the data in the report. Get some success before taking on the more difficult portions of the report! You often use the Formula Editor in formatting as well, but wait until you have the structure of the report intact before creating conditional formulas. Formulas often manipulate or possibly replace database fields. With the format of your report set, you can easily replace database fields with formula fields.

When adding subreports, cross-tabs, graphs, and maps to reports, simply add the extra sections needed and format accordingly. Of course, you can modify existing sections in order to accommodate insertion of a graph or other large object, but it is easier if you have the basic format set before inserting additional large objects.

NOTE

When adding subreports to a report, you might find it easier to complete only basic formatting before you insert the subreport. This way, you can format both the main report and subreport at the same time so that they match.

Recommended Settings and Tips

The rest of this chapter is geared toward sharing tips and suggestions. Some are strategies and some are settings. Use the suggestions that apply, and feel free to refer to the BridgeBuilder Web site (**www.bridgebuilder.com**) to find new tips for future versions.

Editing SQL Statements in Crystal

If you're used to being able to modify the SQL statement Crystal sends to the database server, you may be upset to learn that this is no longer possible. However, you are able to build fully functional SQL Commands in the Database Expert to collect data from your data source. Rather than juggle between real

SQL and Crystal SQL and what you can edit and what you cannot, SQL Commands solve the whole issue.

Modifying the SQL statement can have dramatic impacts on the speed at which data returns from the server. The SQL statement that Crystal generates is ANSI standard and not specific to any database. Thus, Crystal attempts to do more of the work on your local machine versus doing the work on the SQL server (which is more efficient). If you're comfortable with writing SQL directly, please do so. You'll find that expressions can be added and your machine does less work. Using the Repository, you can hopefully leverage the help of accomplished SQL developers to build more complex commands for you, and ask that the developer just save the object in the Commands folder of the Repository for you to use.

Using Database Views and Stored Procedures

This tip is similar to the last in that it helps you use the database server efficiently. When feasible, consider using views or stored procedures to force record selection to take place on the server instead of bringing a larger set of data back to your machine and then applying record selection. Views and stored procedures exist on the database server and always process there. Generally, someone familiar with the database designs these views and stored procedures and writes the SQL manually.

Controlling Fields with a Smaller Grid

To maximize control over moving objects on your report, change the grid size to 0.011 on the Layout tab of the File, Options dialog box (see Figure 19-1). By default, Crystal sets the grid size to 0.83.

The grid is similar to graph paper in that Crystal views the report as small intersections of the grid. By making the grid smaller, you create more intersections. This allows you to control better where objects line up on the report. Once you make this change, you will not want to view the grid; because you've made the grid so small, the screen will appear black and you won't be able to see the report!

FIGURE 19-1 *Settings found on the Layout tab of the Options dialog box enhance control over object placement.*

Using the Total Page Count Special Field

Although this version of Crystal brings better performance, I recommend that you wait to put the Total Page Count special field on the report until one of the last stages of the design. This special field forces Crystal to calculate the entire report instead of just up to the page you're currently on. This can create delays in returning control back to you as the designer.

Because most reports do have the need for a Total Page Count, I recommend putting it on once the rest of the report is developed and tested. This gives maximum control back to you.

Handling Null Values

Crystal Reports has a built-in method for converting null values to a default value in your reports. This option is found under File, Options on the Reporting tab. Instead of trying to handle null values through formulas, you can convert null values to a default and handle them normally by comparing them to spaces or zeros.

Creating Documentation

Crystal Reports has a Report Definition export that allows you to document your report quickly. This format creates a text file that documents your fields, formatting, record selection, formulas, groups, and other items on the report. By having the definition of your report documented separately from the report itself, you can print this document and save it in a binder for reference. For example, if you need to troubleshoot a report built by someone else, a report document will be helpful to learn what formulas the report contains, and whether there are subreports, before you start trying to fix it. Unfortunately, the report definition only includes formulas that are on the report, not formulas that are used either in other formulas or as part of text objects. Learn more about the Report Definition and how to overcome some if its quirks in Chapter 16.

Summary

Although there is no right or wrong way to design a report, a list of steps helps when faced with designing a report. In this chapter, you learned one approach that is helpful in making quick, measurable progress toward the final report.

Remember to save your report frequently and under different file names so that you'll have "old" versions to refer to if you introduce a change when fixing another problem. As you keep writing reports, you'll continually learn more about the process.

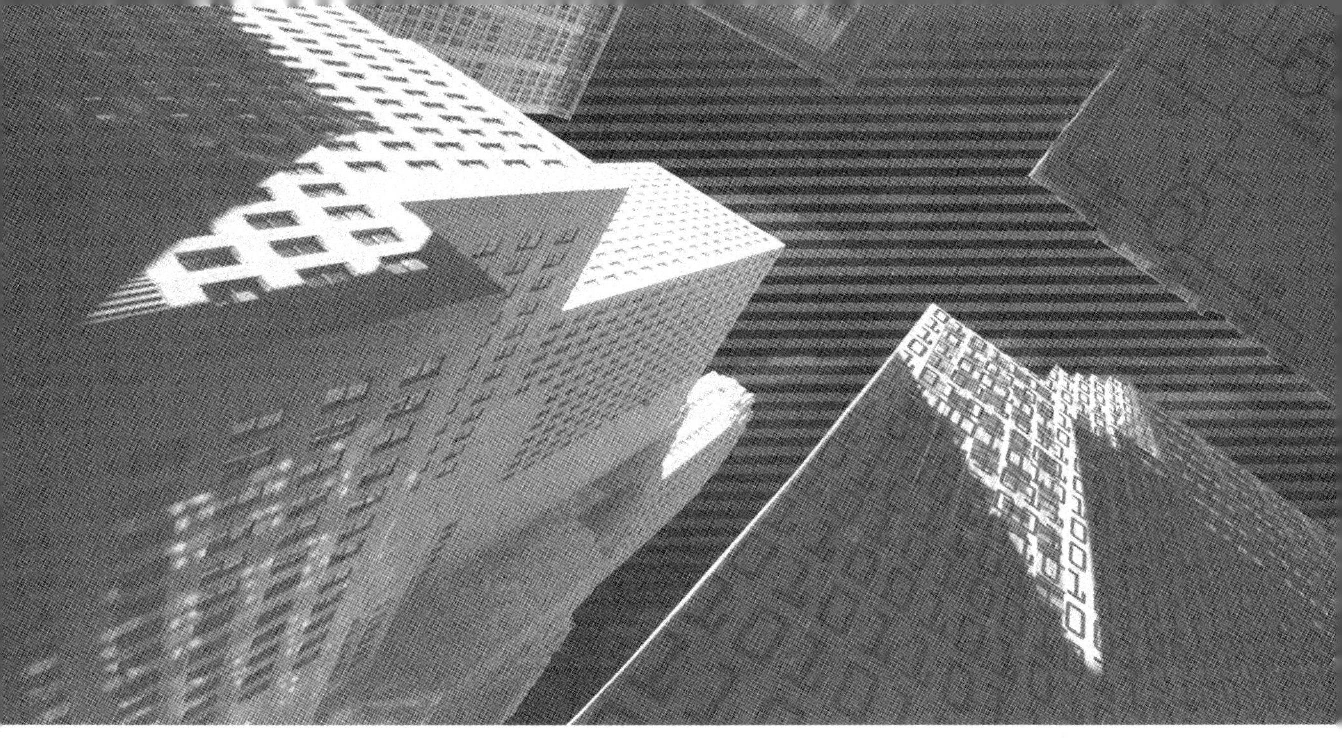

PART V

Appendixes

Appendix A

Common problems that report writers face are that of data quality and data integrity. Although a Crystal Report is built correctly, poor data quality can create new problems that are difficult to resolve inside your report. Examples of poor data quality include duplicates, nonstandard field values, and missing data.

Another important topic in today's computing environment is the integration of multiple data sources to provide accurate data. Instead of different corporate departments entering the same data in different databases, integrating them together allows data to be entered into one system and flow into others. Examples include integrating accounting, sales, and manufacturing data together to create more accurate systems. Of course, every field in each database is usually not integrated. In most cases, only information that is common between each database is shared between the integrated systems.

Unfortunately, maintaining high data quality is an ongoing effort. Crystal Reports are very useful for monitoring your data from period to period. There are also other tools that assist in maintaining high data quality. We'll outline several tools in this appendix to help you in this ongoing effort.

Measures of Data Quality

Data is considered quality data if it is accurate, clean, and has high integrity. A report simply collects, manipulates, and displays data. If the quality of the data collected is poor, there is little that a report can do to fix it.

Ensuring that your data is quality data is extremely important *before* you build a report based on that data. As previously stated, quality data is accurate, has high integrity, and is clean.

- ◆ Accurate data
- ◆ Data integrity
- ◆ Clean data

Let's examine these concepts in more detail by defining them and looking at some examples.

Accurate Data

To ensure that data is accurate, it must be continuously reviewed and frequently maintained. For example, Crystal Reports that run each week to verify that data entered into the company's CRM (Customer Relationship Management) system was entered properly. Such a report might show records that are incomplete (data missing from a key field) or duplicate data that is found.

Data Integrity

Good data integrity is ensured when measures are taken to allow only those individuals who are qualified and held accountable to edit the data. Data integrity can also be implemented through the use of field types and rules that are set up on database fields. For example, the CRM system may allow users to modify only their own records (contacts, accounts) and not the records of others. This system may also require that any new record added must include a company name or other required contact information before the record will be accepted in the database.

Clean Data

There are many questions to ask when researching whether or not your data is clean. Three questions to ask when examining the cleanliness of your data are:

- Is my data standardized?
- Do I have duplicate values in my database?
- Is my data consistent?

Is My Data Standardized?

Data standardization pertains to the actual format in which the data exists in your system. Crystal Reports are more legible and professional looking when all values are formatted the same way. For example:

- **Proper case.** Convert data such as "SMITH" or "smith" to "Smith"
- **Phone numbers.** Convert data such as 7045551212 to 704-555-1212
- **Uppercase.** Convert data such as "nc" to "NC"

Do I Have Duplicate Values in My Database?

Duplicate values are identical or highly similar data existing in your database. Duplicate data creates confusion in reports such as incorrect groups, incorrect totals, and incorrect record selection. Crystal Reports are useful for finding this type of problem, but ultimately the correction needs to take place in the raw data itself.

Is My Data Consistent?

Data is consistent when information appears the same inside the database field. Inconsistent data is a very common issue when the database or software application does not limit how data can be entered. For example, a user could enter IBM's name into a database in the following ways:

- IBM
- I.B.M.
- International Business Machines
- Intl Bus Machines

When a Crystal Report runs against this data, these variations of the company name are viewed as different and distinct. This will cause Crystal Reports to create new groups (if a group is built on the company name), and format the report in ways that were not intended by the designer. By keeping data consistent, reports are much more useful, and correct.

Another benefit is that there is no confusion as to which record is the correct record. For example, if you needed to update a phone number for the record at IBM but had four different records, how would you know which one of the four records is the most current? By maintaining the data, you help to ensure that people will continue to use the database, and you may solve future problems that others may encounter.

DataFlux—Recommended Tool to Maintain High Data Quality

Maintaining data quality is a time-consuming and never-ending task. Fortunately, there are tool sets available on the market that are designed to aid database administrators with this battle.

BridgeBuilder recommends and regularly uses DataFlux software (**www.dataflux.com**) in consulting projects. DataFlux is a data cleansing tool that can connect to any database through ODBC and allows changes to be made directly to the data itself. DataFlux helps solve many issues including:

- **Standardization.** Using Fuzzy logic, DataFlux is able to identify and correct inconsistencies in your corporate data. This fuzzy logic allows the program to make associations between data that needs to be standardized that are not apparent when viewing a report or table. For example, DataFlux can make the association between 1st Union and First Union, and can identify William Henry and Bill Henry as being the same person. After identifying these permutations of data, you can create a scheme to go back and change each variation to the correct value. It is also possible to standardize fields that have mixed cases (upper, lower, or proper).

- **Duplicate elimination.** DataFlux can also use fuzzy logic to identify duplicate information within your database. After duplicates are identified, you can create rules to automatically remove duplicate records based on a number of attributes.

- **Address verification.** This feature helps maintain data integrity and accuracy by assuring that the addresses are accurate. DataFlux is able to authenticate addresses in your database by comparing them with the nationwide United States Postal Service address list. This helps ensure that all addresses found in your database and reports are accurate. It is also possible to perform the same operation on Canadian addresses.

- **Custom programming.** You can create custom business rules, filters, and routines. Custom scripts can be applied and used many times to continuously review and clean data.

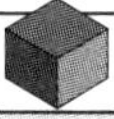 **NOTE**

To learn more about DataFlux, visit BridgeBuilder's Web site at **www.bridgebuilder.com** and click the DataFlux link.

Data Integration

Data integration is the process of creating a connection between two or more data sources to allow information sharing between the databases. For example, data integration could exist between a CRM system and an accounting system. This integration allows for all contact and account information to actually be added, removed, and edited in the CRM tool. Any address or contact information that is updated is automatically passed into the accounting system (database) and updated.

You can also send data from the accounting system back to the CRM system. For example, salespeople often benefit from knowing if an account has a past due balance and how much it is. The integration can take any outstanding invoices and place the total in the CRM system (database) so that it displays when the account is viewed. Now when a salesperson speaks with the account, they can reference the updated accounting data and help accounting resolve the past due collection.

Database integration is a popular need in today's data-intensive world. Companies who integrate data realize immediate return because the various departments can now work together with the same data. This is a powerful competitive advantage and one that many companies desire.

Crystal Reports and Active Server Page (Hosted) Data

Crystal Reports is a robust tool that can connect to almost any database through either native drivers or ODBC. However, due to the tremendous success of the Internet, and the global advantage of having databases online, the IT industry is beginning to see many different flavors and renditions of Active Server Page (ASP)-based systems today.

Benefits of an ASP model include:

◆ Strain on internal IT resources is reduced.

◆ No software other than an Internet browser has to be installed.

◆ Data is continuously backed up and kept secure at the ASP vendor's site.

◆ Data is accessible anywhere (worldwide) wherever Internet access is available.

◆ Data is "live" and any new information appears immediately regardless of the data entry location.

◆ Customizations to hosted software systems are generally easy and wizard-driven.

However, users must deal with some tradeoffs when utilizing ASP systems. Since data is not stored locally on a client site, Crystal Reports generally cannot connect directly to the ASP system's database. Since the benefits of using Crystal Reports on ASP systems are apparent, data integration strategies serve as a great solution to this problem.

Using data integration software, data from these online databases can be automatically retrieved or updated numerous times a day into a local onsite database. Crystal Reports or other applications can then access this local database for reporting and other data services. In a scenario such as this, the corporation has the advantages of an ASP model system as well as many advantages of the in-house model.

Data Junction—Recommended Database Integration Tool

Data Junction is a data integration tool that has over 100 spokes (data type connectors), allowing data to be appended, deleted, or updated between almost any data source that exists to this date. This tool is quite powerful. You can schedule maps for integration purposes, parse data, concatenate fields, perform calculations, and accomplish many others tasks. This tool offers a solution to integrating and migrating data between a large number of systems without having to create and maintain complex programs or coding to perform the same job. The following tools are found within Data Junction:

Map Designer

Map Designer is an intuitive GUI for visually mapping data from source databases to target databases. Data can also be manipulated in many ways through the use of various formulas and functions. Map Designer also allows map verification, which guards against creating incorrect maps, functions, and formulas.

Process Designer

Process Designer allows a designer to create a process in which the steps can be dragged and dropped and interconnected. It employs simple flow-chart symbols to link transformation objects together into an automated project. For instance, this tool enables you to automate the execution of maps that are created in Map Designer. You then can use logic to execute one map based on specific criteria or another map based on other criteria.

Integration Engine and Other Features

Integration Engine is used to schedule the processes and maps that are created to manipulate your databases. Data Junction software has other features that are not listed here. For more information on Data Junction, visit BridgeBuilder's Web site at **www.bridgebuilder.com** and click the Data Junction link.

Summary

Data quality and integration are issues that affect reporting. By maintaining data and integrating data sources together, Crystal Reports can be leveraged for more accurate and timely information presentation.

Appendix B

Setting Up an
ODBC Data Source

Chapter 3 introduced ODBC and discussed creating a report from an ODBC data source using the Database Expert. This appendix examines how to set up this data connection using the Windows ODBC Administrator and what to look for if you have problems.

What Is ODBC?

ODBC stands for Open Database Connectivity. According to Microsoft Corporation, ODBC is "...a programming interface that enables applications to access data in database management systems that use Structured Query Language (SQL) as a data access standard." ODBC allows programs to send data back and forth to many different types of databases, without having specific drivers written to form a bridge. With ODBC, a single application can work on a variety of database platforms.

So why doesn't everyone use ODBC? Perhaps because using ODBC is sometimes rather complex to set up and slow in performance. Software vendors write native drivers specifically for connecting to a particular database, usually requiring no special setup instructions. Because native drivers specifically connect the application and database, they usually perform faster and take advantage of specific "bells and whistles" offered by the database.

Unfortunately, native drivers exist for only the most popular software packages and database standards on the market—that's a majority of the marketplace, but not the entire marketplace. Thus, many companies use the universal standard of ODBC.

Creating an ODBC Data Source

Since a lot of different programs use ODBC, many packages include it in their setup process. Crystal Reports automatically installs ODBC version 3.5 on your system. Version 3.5, in addition to the ODBC Administrator application, includes many of the more common ODBC drivers for Excel, dBase, Access, Text, Oracle, Sybase, SQL Server, Informix, and DB2.

NOTE

This discussion focuses on the 32-bit version of ODBC rather than the 16-bit (Windows 3.x) version.

Checking for or Installing a Driver

If you want to connect to your company database but do not see a data source name (DSN) in the Database Expert that is right for your database, you must go to the ODBC Administrator to set up a new ODBC DSN.

The first step in the process of creating an ODBC data source involves installing the ODBC driver provided by the software manufacturer. The setup for each driver differs, and no universal "how to" guide exists. Before you decide to add a driver, however, check to be sure it has not already been installed on your computer:

1. Open the ODBC Administrator by clicking the ODBC icon in the Control Panel. If you're using Windows 2000, select Administrative Tools and then find the ODBC option.

2. Click the Drivers tab. This tab displays information about each installed driver, including the version, company who wrote the driver, file name, and file date (see Figure B-1).

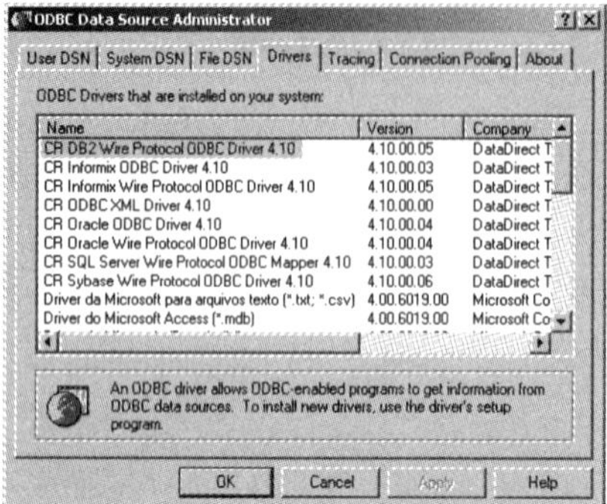

FIGURE B-1 *Look at the Drivers tab to see which drivers have already been installed on your system.*

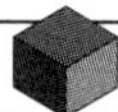

> **NOTE**
>
> Checking first for a driver on the Drivers tab can save you unnecessary work, as well as prevent unintentional changes to your system.

If the ODBC driver you require does not appear on the ODBC Drivers tab, you need to install it. Refer to the driver's documentation for installation instructions. You may want to seek assistance from your IT department or a database administrator.

Adding a DSN

Now that you know the right driver is available, you can build a DSN (Data Source Name). As described in detail in Chapter 3, a DSN is a set of instructions that contains the database driver and other information about the connection that will be made using the DSN. The ODBC Administrator lets you set up three types of DSNs: User, System, and File. The User DSN is available only to the current user. A System DSN is available to all users on a machine (different profiles or logon names), including NT services. A File DSN is a file-based data source that can be shared by people with the same drivers. System DSNs are especially useful because they can be used by others and by your system automatically (see Figure B-2).

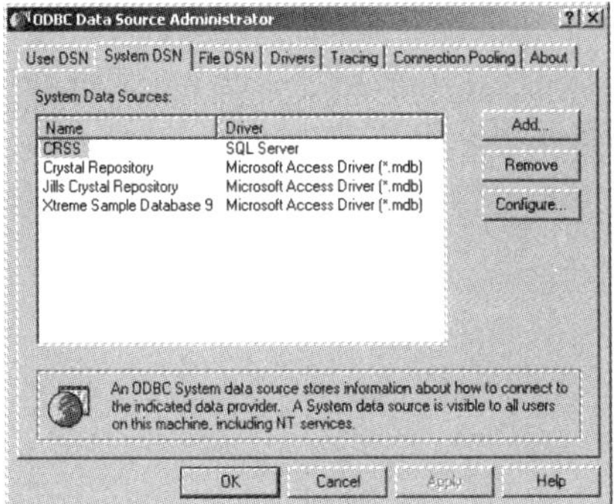

FIGURE B-2 *Click the Add button on the System DSN tab to set up a new ODBC connection to your database.*

Generally, you need to configure an ODBC connection with information such as a username, password, server, and file location. The format of the dialog boxes varies depending on the driver, but the following steps cover the basic things that must be set up for the ODBC connection to work:

1. Choose ODBC Administrator from the Control Panel or Administrative Tools.

2. Click the System DSN tab, and then click Add. The Create New Data Source dialog box opens (see Figure B-3).

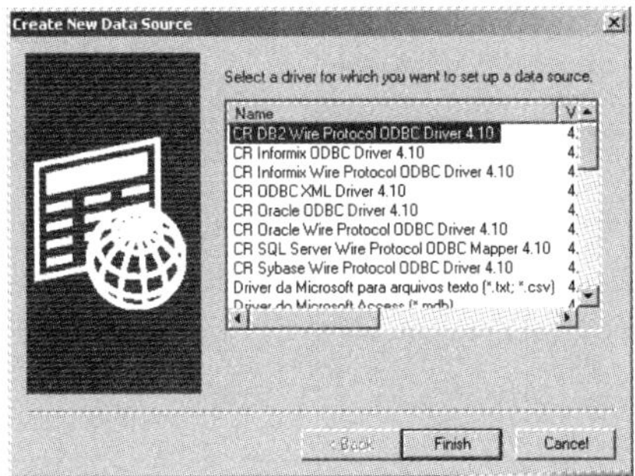

FIGURE B-3 *When setting up a new ODBC DSN, the setup wizard shows all the drivers available to create the DSN.*

3. Select the driver required to connect to your database, and then click Finish.

4. Most drivers now open a dialog box or a wizard (a series of dialog boxes) that prompts you to provide information such as server name, username, password, and file location (see Figure B-4). You may need to refer to the instructions in the driver's documentation to complete the dialog box or wizard.

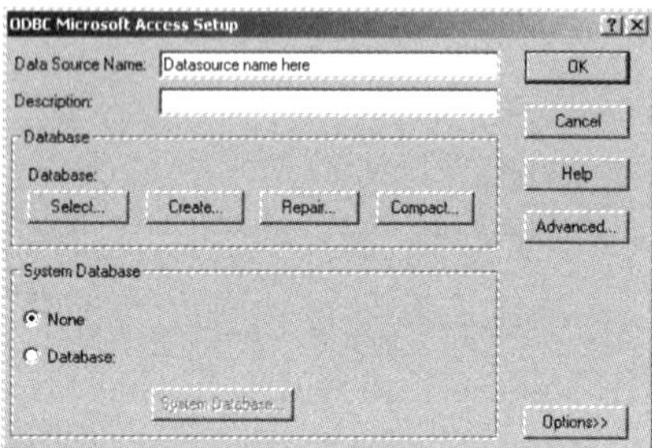

FIGURE B-4 *Use the Setup dialog box for your specific server choice to create the new ODBC connection.*

5. Save the connection and then test it by trying to log on to your database through Crystal Reports or a data connection utility like SQLCon that may be included with the driver.

NOTE

You can download information on SQLCon from Crystal Decisions Web site at **http://support.crystaldecisions.com/library/kbase/articles/c2007753.asp**, which will also direct you to downloading the tool.

Troubleshooting Suggestions

One of the first steps in troubleshooting an ODBC error is to check the versions of ODBC files on your computer. To do this, open the About tab in the ODBC Administrator (see Figure B-5). The files listed here should all have matching version numbers. If the version numbers do not match, you may need to reinstall ODBC.

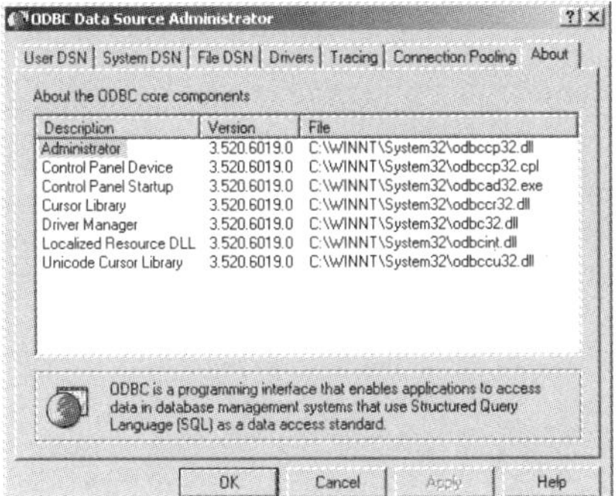

FIGURE B-5 *Check the version number of your ODBC files in the About tab of the ODBC Administrator.*

Crystal has a very good document on troubleshooting ODBC problems. You can find it in the Knowledge Base on its Web site. The name of the article is "How to Fix ODBC 3.0 Problems—Summary." Search for article number C2001040. Even though this version of Crystal uses ODBC 3.5, this document contains good generic information that is not version-specific.

You will notice that there are many DSNs set up in the Database Expert by default. These are read from your system, from the information here in the ODBC Administrator. These DSNs may not contain the most up-to-date instructions and drivers for connecting to your database. When using the existing DSNs, check that they contain the correct and most up-to-date driver for communicating with your database.

Summary

The ODBC Administrator provides a method for creating new data source DSNs and is a good tool for updating database drivers to assure that you have the best one for your particular database, and the most up-to-date version. For more infor mation, refer to Chapter 3, which covers DSNs and using data sources in detail, as well as Chapter 14, which contains useful database and ODBC information that is not specific to just SQL.

Appendix C

This appendix outlines the best ways to find help with your questions about Crystal Reports. You can get help from several different sources, including online help on your computer, the Crystal Decisions Web site, technical support by telephone, and from certified trainers and consultants.

Online Help

The easiest way to get assistance is to check out the online help on your own machine. The main Crystal Reports help file serves as a gateway to other online documentation installed with Crystal Reports.

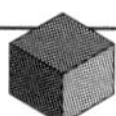

NOTE

When you choose Crystal Reports Help from the Help menu in the Crystal Report Designer, you open the main help file for report design.

A little-known fact is that Crystal Reports actually comes with many additional help files and several online documents. The main help file for the Crystal Report Designer is CRW.HLP. You can open this help file easily at any time by selecting Help, Crystal Reports Help or by pressing the F1 key (see Figure C-1).

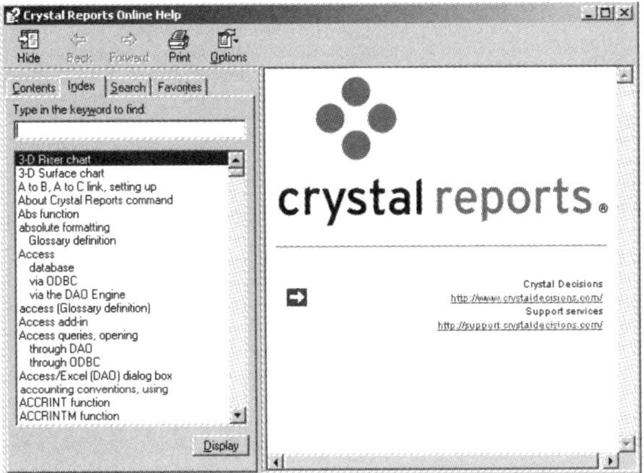

FIGURE C-1 *The online help file has in-depth information on all basic Crystal Reports functionality.*

This online help file has comprehensive information on all the basic functionality of Crystal Reports. My personal favorite method is to jump right to the Search tab and type in some keywords to look up in the help file. If you are looking for developer help or Web server help, Crystal provides other, more comprehensive help files for you to use. So, if you search for a topic and do not find it in the main help file, do not think that help does not exist! All the information for designing reports, including all the advanced functionality, can be found in this one main help file. Other information can be found in the other help files, which the next section outlines and shows you how to find and open.

The easiest way to find and open another help file, such as the help file for developers or the help file for the Report Design Component add-ins, is to use the Find feature in Windows Explorer and search for all *.CHM and *.HLP files in the Crystal Decisions folder. If you used the suggested default path when you installed Crystal Reports, use the Browse button to select C:\Program Files\Crystal Decisions as the path for the Look in field (see Figure C-2).

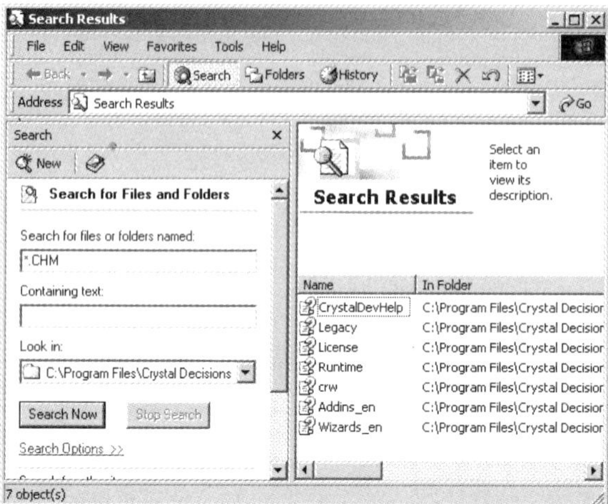

FIGURE C-2 *Use Find to locate all the help files available to you.*

Depending on the components installed on your machine, you may not have all of these help files, or you may have help files in addition to the ones listed here.

There are also several large technical reference documents on your software CD that you can install on your PC, run off the CD-ROM, or even print out. In Windows Explorer, select your CD-ROM drive (with the Crystal CD inserted). Navigate to the Docs folder, which includes several documents, including the User's Guide, a Web Reporting Guide, a Developers Guide, and Technical Reference Guides. Crystal Reports has provided these documents in PDF format.

These documents all have good tables of contents in the beginning, and even though the page numbers are off a bit (due to unavoidable format conversion), I have found that these documents provide good information and are easy to use. Unfortunately, they are not as complete as I would like, containing many sections that are severely lacking in detail, but this just gave me more reason to write this book!

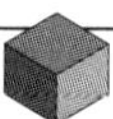

NOTE

Most information contained in the User's Guide is also included in the online help files mentioned previously.

Using System Information

If you experience unusual problems when working with Crystal Reports, built-in utilities help you see what is going on with your computer. Click the Help menu and choose About Crystal Reports.

The About dialog box displays your version of Crystal Reports along with your registration number (which is very important for technical support). You also see helpful information on how to contact Crystal Decisions via their Web site, e-mail, fax, and telephone. At the bottom of the dialog box you'll see two buttons: More Info and System Info. These are the utilities you're looking for.

Click More Info to show files currently loaded into your computer's memory (see Figure C-3). This information helps when searching for the cause of a problem. If you call in for technical support, you may be asked to look here to help the technician identify the source of the problem.

Loaded Modules

Name	Version	Path
ADVAPI32.DLL	5.0.2195.2867	C:\WINNT\system32
CLBCATQ.DLL	2000.2.3471.1	C:\WINNT\System32
COMCTL32.DLL	5.81.3103.1000	C:\WINNT\system32
COMDLG32.DLL	5.0.3103.1000	C:\WINNT\system32
CRABOUT.DLL	9.2.0.9	C:\Program Files\Crystal Decisions\Crystal Reports 9
CRHEAPALLOC....	9.2.0.2	C:\Program Files\Common Files\Crystal Decisions\2.0
CRTOWORDS_E...	9.2.0.14	C:\Program Files\Common Files\Crystal Decisions\2.0
CRW32.EXE	9.2.0.448	C:\Program Files\Crystal Decisions\Crystal Reports 9
CSCDLL.DLL	5.0.2195.2401	C:\WINNT\System32
CSCUI.DLL	5.0.2195.2959	C:\WINNT\System32
DBGHELP.DLL	5.0.2195.2104	C:\WINNT\System32
ENTERPRISEAP...	9.0.0.147	C:\Program Files\Common Files\Crystal Decisions\2.0
GDI32.DLL	5.0.2195.2778	C:\WINNT\system32
HHCTRL.OCX	4.74.8793.0	C:\WINNT\System32
IMM32.DLL	5.0.2195.2821	C:\WINNT\System32
ITSS.DLL	4.72.8085.0	C:\WINNT\System32
JSCRIPT.DLL	5.1.0.5907	C:\WINNT\System32
JVMMANAGER.D...	9.2.0.7	C:\Program Files\Common Files\Crystal Decisions\2.0

FIGURE C-3 *Use the Loaded Modules dialog box to find different files loaded on your system.*

The dialog box in Figure C-3 lists the following file types:

- Dynamic Link Libraries (DLL)
- Drivers (DRV)
- Executables (EXE)
- Fonts (FON)
- Others

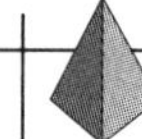

TIP

The Loaded Modules dialog box enables you to look at the file's path (location on hard drive), version number, and creation date.

Click System Info to display information about your computer, such as its operating system, amount of free memory, video driver, printer driver, and network. Again, this information may be helpful to the technician for technical support depending on the problem your system is experiencing.

Getting Help at the Crystal Decisions Web Site

Crystal Decisions has a Web site at **support.crystaldecisions.com** that provides product information, technical support, access to the Knowledge Base of past technical support incidents, white papers, downloadable files and updates, and technical newsletters (see Figure C-4). You can access this site by selecting Help, Visit Crystal Decisions on the World Wide Web. This launches your browser and connects you right to the Crystal Decisions home page, making all kinds of information available at your fingertips. Click the word Support to get to the support page, where all the support information is found.

FIGURE C-4 *Crystal Decisions has a good Web site with useful information, including comprehensive support areas.*

The white papers provide a very rich source of common questions and answers, as well as how-to guides on many subjects. Papers on new support incidents are continually being added to this area, so it is worthwhile to search it from time to time for any issues or questions, for a new paper could be out there. From the home page, select Support to get to the Support home page. From there, click Documentation and then use the drop-down lists to select what category of documentation you are looking for. You will find technical briefs on printing issues, report design, exporting considerations, formatting guidelines, and many other topics. New information is added to this and other areas of the site almost daily, so check it out often for the most up-to-date information and tips.

The Knowledge Base is a Web-based method to search existing specific technical support questions and answers. The search engine takes some getting used to, because it has several ways to search using keywords, but with patience, it can be a great tool for getting help on a variety of subjects. These documents come from solved technical support incidents that tech support representatives have written up and made available to everyone. It is likely that someone has had the same or a similar question or problem that you have, so searching the Knowledge Base is a good start to solving reporting problems and issues.

Crystal Decisions provides Technical Newsletters, which are automated news bulletins and hints that can be sent to you each month via e-mail. They include information on product updates, current events, and new product releases, along with marketing and technical information. You can subscribe to this free service (or later unsubscribe) at **www.crystaldecisions.com/myprofile/subscribe.asp**.

Requesting Technical Support by E-mail

In addition to getting help at the Crystal Decisions Web site, you can submit a support request directly. The turnaround for an average response is 24 to 48 hours. Although not as fast as a telephone call, e-mail support offers an easy and painless way to get help for questions that aren't critical today. You do need a valid registration number to receive e-mail support.

Using the Telephone for Technical Support

You can choose from several types of available telephone support: free and pre-paid. Crystal Decisions offers free support to anyone with a registered product for the first 60 days. The only cost is for long-distance charges (to Vancouver, B.C., Canada). The technical support phone number is 604-669-8379.

The second type of support is Priority Support, which has an annual fee. There are three major advantages to using the Priority Support plan:

- ◆ When you call technical support, you are moved to the front of the line (but still behind other Priority Support callers ahead of you), thereby reducing your wait times.

- ◆ You get an 800 toll-free number to use (no long-distance charges), so you can call as often as necessary.

- ◆ Priority Support members get extended hours to call (hours vary by the plan purchased). If you are responsible for supporting Crystal Reports in your organization, the conveniences of Priority Support are highly recommended. For more information about Priority Support, contact Crystal Decisions at 800-877-2340.

A third type of technical support is on an incident by incident basis, sold in packs of 5 incidents. Contact Crystal Decisions via phone or the Web for more information on these types of support packages.

When you call for technical support, regardless of whether or not you have Priority Support, you *must* have a registration number. You can find this number under Help, About Crystal Reports in the main menu. Your support technician will also ask for your product name and version, which is found under Help, About, and what operating system you are using. If your questions concern your connection to your database, you will need information about that as well, such as the type and version. Be in front of your computer when you call tech support, ready to discuss your questions and re-create the problem you are experiencing. They may ask you to do certain things while on the phone as they try to fix your problem or help with your report development.

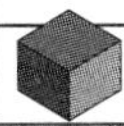

NOTE

There is a link on the Crystal Decisions Support page (see Figure C-4) to download a document "Customer Guide to Technical Support."

Making the Most of Certified Trainers and Consultants

The Professional Services Organization at Crystal Decisions launched a Certified Training program in 1995 and a Certified Consultants program in 1998. Certification currently requires prescreening, classroom training, and a difficult exam (which usually takes at least 30 hours to complete) that requires a score of at least 85 percent to pass. Certified Trainers and Certified Consultants have differing backgrounds and experience and can help you with your Crystal Reports or Crystal Enterprise questions and projects.

It is important that you ask for a Certified Trainer or a Certified Consultant, because uncertified trainers or consultants often charge the same prices for a vastly different service. To get the most for your money, make sure that you're getting a Certified Trainer or Certified Consultant who has proven themselves to Crystal Decisions and is authorized to use official materials. The following is a list of the different types of Certified Training available:

- Onsite (or private) training
- Public training conducted at a Certified Training center and offered throughout the world every week
- Computer Based Training (CBT)
- Custom Computer Based Training specific to your company and needs
- Custom Courseware and Training from a Certified Trainer

For more information on training or consulting, contact Crystal Decisions at 800-877-2340, or contact The BridgeBuilder Company at 888-274-3432. You can also visit **www.bridgebuilder.com** for additional information on custom courseware, training, report development services and Crystal Enterprise installation.

Appendix D

This chapter serves as a resource to the top tech support issues, based on support calls to the call center and visits to Knowledge Base articles on Crystal Decisions' Web site. A list of top article visits was supplied by the Crystal Decisions Technical Support Team for use in this book.

Appendix C suggests places to look for extra help with regard to using Crystal Reports. One of the main sources of specific technical information is the Knowledge Base (Kbase) on Crystal Decisions' Web site.

The Kbase changes daily, with new articles being added based on technical support questions that are called in. The technical support teams work diligently to write articles to answer frequently asked questions of callers.

Though the Kbase has fewer basic report design articles, it is rich with articles on specific error messages or issues people encounter when using all of the Crystal tools.

Accessing the Kbase

Crystal Decisions seems to change the organization of its Web site more than some other sites I have visited, but that will not negatively affect your ability to find it and search it when you need it.

I have found the easiest route to the Kbase is always from the home page. This way, when things change, you can always start with home and go to support.

1. Go to Crystal Decisions' Web site at **www.crystaldecisions.com** (see Figure D-1).

2. Select the Support option. This is usually one of the options listed across the top under Crystal Decisions' logos.

3. The Support page has a main drop-down list asking where you want to go (see Figure D-2).

4. Select the option that includes Kbase, Knowledge Base, or Kbase Articles (this title has been known to change from time to time).

5. A page opens asking if you know the article number, or want to search by product, category, or subject (see Figure D-3). I highly recommend that you try to narrow your search as much as possible, to avoid the return of an overwhelming number of articles.

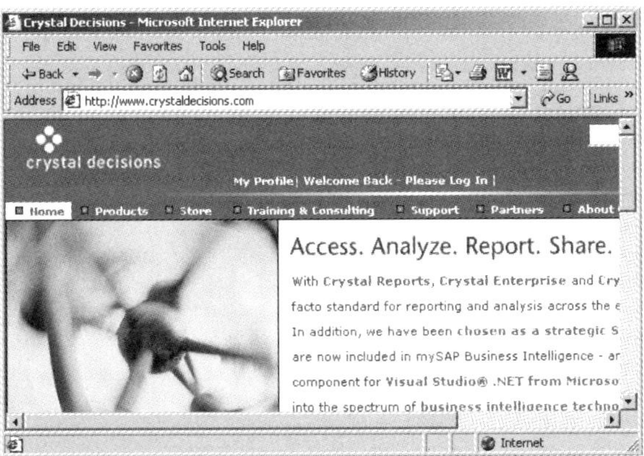

FIGURE D-1 *Go to the Crystal Decisions home page to start your search.*

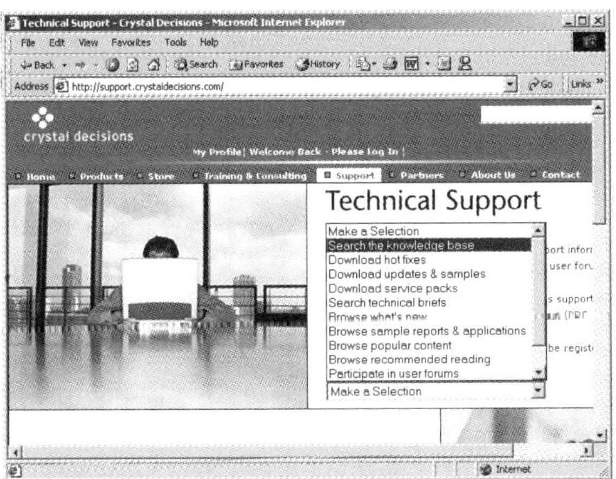

FIGURE D-2 *Go to the Support page and select from the drop-down list of support options.*

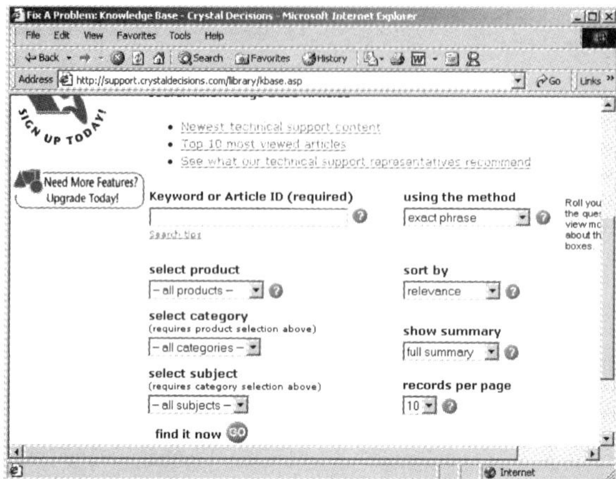

FIGURE D-3 *On the Search the Kbase page, narrow your search by using the drop-down lists or by typing an article number in the Keyword or Article ID box.*

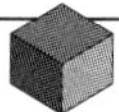

NOTE

If you do not find what you need when searching, change to another tool (such as the Web rather than Crystal Reports) or change to another category.

When you run into any issues in Crystal Reports, check out the Kbase first. It is a wealth of information. Though some complain that information is hard to find, the search engine is really quite good and there are so many helpful articles out there. Be patient and try your search from more than one angle if at first you are not finding anything on your topic of interest.

To get you started working with the Kbase, the following sections list the top 20 downloaded Kbase articles from Crystal Decisions' Web site over the month of September 2002. Though this is already out of date, peruse the article titles to get a feel for what types of information is found in these articles. Though you may never need any of these specifically, hopefully this list will peak your interest enough to get you out there. At this time, there are fewer articles specific to version 9 of Crystal Reports, because many questions are going to apply not only to version 9 of Crystal but previous versions as well. So, as long as you are not searching on a new feature in version 9, I suggest not narrowing your search to only version 9 articles.

Database Connectivity

The following table contains the Top 20 downloaded Kbase white papers on database connectivity issues for September 2002.

Top 20 Database Connectivity Kbase Articles

Article Number	Article Title
c2007974	What SQL Syntax is used for a Left Outer Join?
c2006831	Error: "Physical database not found" in Crystal Reports 8
c2008838	Connecting to Multiple Data Sources in a Report
c2011370	Database object name does not change after setting location
c2003961	Connecting to Access 2000 Natively
c2008882	How to access an XML file through a URL in Crystal Reports 8.5 and later
c2008883	Reporting off Data Sources of XML Data Island and ADO Persisted XML Files
c2007753	How to use SQLCON to test an ODBC Driver and Database Connectivity
c2000028	Seagate Crystal Reports and Integrated Security Connections for SQL Server
c2005611	How to 'Set Location' to a new data source in the Crystal Reports Designer
c2009954	Why is a field not available for sorting?
c2001157	Using Oracle Stored Procedures
c2007340	Database field containing JPRGS appears blank in report
c2000282	How to Convert database Drivers in Crystal Reports (CR)
c2011331	How to avoid database login prompts when refreshing reports in Crystal Reports
c2002997	"Server has not yet been opened" Error when converting P2SOLEDB.DLL
c2005680	Create temporary tables within MS SQL Server stored procedures

(continues)

Top 20 Database Connectivity Kbase Articles, continued

Article Number	Article Title
c2002377	Performance differences between stored procedures and views
c2005338	Troubleshooting 1157 and 126 ODBC Errors
c2000335	Can a subquery be included in a SQL Statement?

Report Design

The following table lists the top 20 downloaded Kbase articles in the report design category.

Top 20 Report Design Kbase Articles

Article Number	Article Title
c2006248	Exporting to PDF or RTF in Crystal Reports
c2007600	How to Share subreport Data with the Main Report
c2011366	Exporting to PDF and XLS improved in Crystal Reports 9
c2000055	Suppressing a blank subreport from displaying on the main report
c2000454	Export Row Limits for Microsoft Excel and Lotus 123 (Spreadsheet formats)
c2005853	Suppress a section that contains a blank subreport
c2010175	Creating a custom paper size form to use in Crystal Reports
c2010715	How Different 'Keep Together' Options Affect the Report
c2007015	Unable to insert summaries or subtotals on certain formulas
c2010914	How to evaluate null field values in formulas or record selection criteria
c2002084	Linking a main report to a subreport based off a stored procedure
c2011207	Dbexdrvr.zip did not update Exportmodeller.dll & Crtslv.dll in \Shared directory
c2006244	Exporting to Excel results in shifting columns and extra blank rows

(continues)

Top 20 Report Design Kbase Articles, continued

Article Number	Article Title
c2002270	Displaying a Range Parameter on a Report
c2005464	Using parameters to select one, some or all values in a record selection formula
c2000534	How to Display a Date Range Parameter on a Report
c2008983	Preventing Widowed Group Headers and Footers on a Report
c2011784	Error when installing Crystal Reports 9 from the installation CD
c2006365	Create a manual running total in Crystal Reports using variables in Basic syntax
c2000056	Distributed reports not printing correctly

Top 20 Web-Related Kbase Articles

The following table lists the top 20 downloaded Web-related Kbase articles from Crystal Decisions' Web site for the month of September 2002. This is a small sampling of the articles available to help you with your technical questions on Web reporting.

Top 20 Web Kbase Articles

Article Number	Article Title
c2004405	Troubleshooting the Installation of the Report Viewer for ActiveX
c2007701	Err Msg: "An Error Has Occurred on the Server...Server Has Not Yet Been Opened"
c2006825	Err Msg: "Data Source Name not Found" calling a report through ASP
c2008233	How can I resolve the message, "Error Detected by Database DLL" over the Web?
c2007895	How to create a report dynamically through an Active Server Pages application

(*continues*)

Top 20 Web Kbase Articles, continued

Article Number	Article Title
c2007877	Displaying Reports Based on Crystal Query (.qry) Files Through the WCS
c2004178	Err Msg: "Error 20599 Cannot Open SQL Server" running a report through ASP
c2006178	Converting Active Server Pages Applications from Version 7 to Version 8
c2008005	Why isn't the data in my web report being updated?
c2011586	ActiveX Viewer enhancements for Crystal Reports version 9
c2010602	Err Msg: "CRAXDRT Error occurred on Server −2147190908: Failed to export..."
c2006386	Err Msg: "Failed to Export the Report" via the Crystal Reports Web Components
c2009021	How can Craxdrt.dll be run in a Microsoft Transaction Server package?
c2009015	"There are not enough Concurrent Access Licenses to log you on." through ASP
c2003059	Error Message: "Missing or Out of Date Export Dll's" when Exporting through ASP
c2007866	How do I export subreports and drill down views from web viewers?
c2008208	Troubleshooting Active Server Pages (ASP) and Active Data Objects (ADO)
c2008089	Export Formats available through the Crystal Reports Web Components
c2010422	How do I upgrade my ASP Code from Crystal Reports 8.0 to Crystal Reports 8.5?
c2011509	Recommended version of Internet Explorer when viewing web reports in CR 9

Index

A

absolute formatting, 172–178

Access. *See also* databases
- add-ins, 532–534
- designing reports, 533–534

access
- CMC (Crystal Management Console), 583
- ePortfolio, 578

actions, repeating. *See* loops

adding
- boxes, 195–196
- bubble text, 162
- charts, 31–32, 411–412
- columns (OLAP), 496–497
- commands, 301–302
- cross-tab reports, 369–375
- custom functions, 326–327, 300–301
- databases, 88–89
- fields, 26–27, 45–48
- folders, 297–298
- graphics, 193–196
- Group Headers, 183
- groups, 27–28, 122–128
- indexes, 117
- labels
    - cross-tab reports, 383
    - ToText function, 231–234
- lines, 195–196
- maps, 431–432
- multiple groups, 129
- objects
    - bitmap images, 303
    - Crystal Repository, 298–302
    - text, 303
- parameters to commands, 453–455
- rows (OLAP), 496–497
- sections, 182
- selection criteria, 95–99
- shapes, 195–196
- special fields, 52–55
- subreports, 340–355
- summaries, 28–30, 51–52
- tables, 42, 88–89

titles, 52–55

totals, 139–144

add-ins
- Access, 532–534
- Excel, 523–532

Add-Ins dialog box, 524

ad-hoc reporting, 569

administrative tools, 582–591

Advanced layout (charts), 412–414

All Regions pick list, 401–402

Analyzer, launching, 508–509

AND clause, 104–105

applications
- DataFlux, 610–611
- exporting, 517–521
- RAS (Report Application Server), 14

applying
- commands from Repository, 456–457
- Crystal Repository, 294–296
- Crystal SQL Designer, 458
- custom functions, 310–311
- objects, 302–304
- on-demand subreports, 355–356
- Report Wizards, 7–8
- Slice/Page page (OLAP), 498–499
- SQL commands, 450–459
- templates, 34–36

APS (Automated Process Scheduler), 575

architecture, Crystal Enterprise, 573–574

arguments, custom functions, 322–329

arrays, 269–270, 280–281

articles, Kbase Web site, 639–640

authentication, 569–580

authorization management, 589–590

Auto Link, 82–83

Automated Process Scheduler (APS), 575

Avery labels, 38. *See also* labels

Axis tab (Chart Expert), 417–418

B

backgrounds, 186

bar chart maps, 430

fast&easy web development

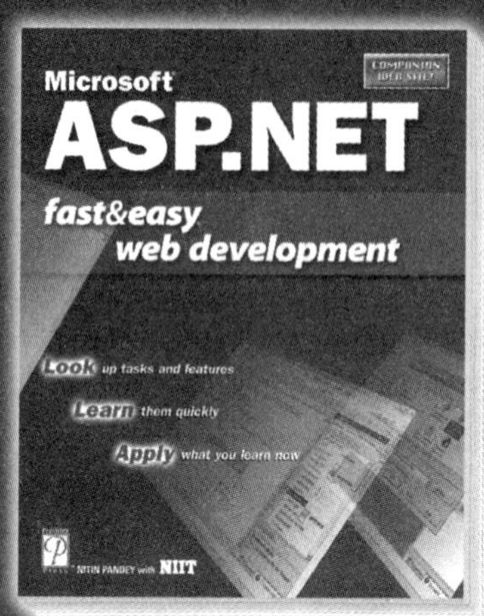

Less Time. Less Effort. More Development.

Don't spend your time leafing through lengthy manuals looking for the information you need. Spend it doing what you do best—Web development. The Premier Press *fast & easy* web development series leads the way with step-by-step instructions and real screen shots to help you grasp concepts and master skills quickly and easily.

Microsoft® ASP.NET
Fast & Easy®
Web Development
1-931841-46-2 • Companion Web Site

Adobe® LiveMotion™
Fast & Easy®
Web Development
0-7615-3254-4 • CD Included

ASP 3 *Fast & Easy®*
Web Development
0-7615-2854-7 • CD Included

CGI *Fast & Easy®*
Web Development
0-7615-2938-1 • CD Included

Java™ 2 *Fast & Easy®*
Web Development
0-7615-3056-8 • CD Included

JavaServer Pages™
Fast & Easy®
Web Development
0-7615-3428-8 • CD Included

Macromedia®
Director® 8 and Lingo™
Fast & Easy®
Web Development
0-7615-3049-5 • CD Included

Macromedia®
Dreamweaver® MX
Fast & Easy®
Web Development
1-931841-88-8 • Companion Web Site

Macromedia®
Dreamweaver® UltraDev™ 4
Fast & Easy®
Web Development
0-7615-3517-9 • CD Included

Macromedia®
Fireworks® MX *Fast & Easy®*
Web Development
1-59200-031-2 • Companion Web Site

Macromedia®
Flash™ 5 *Fast & Easy®*
Web Development
0-7615-2930-6 • CD Included

Microsoft® C# *Fast & Easy®*
Web Development
1-931841-05-5 • Companion Web Site

Perl *Fast & Easy®*
Web Development
1-931841-17-9 • Companion Web Site

PHP *Fast & Easy®*
Web Development,
2nd Edition
1-931841-87-X • Companion Web Site

Premier Press
A Division of Course Technology
www.premierpressbooks.com

Call now to order!
1.800.842.3636